Intelligent Data Analysis for Real–Life Applications:

Theory and Practice

Rafael Magdalena-Benedito
University of Valencia, Spain

Marcelino Martínez-Sober
University of Valencia, Spain

José María Martínez-Martínez
University of Valencia, Spain

Pablo Escandell-Montero
University of Valencia, Spain

Joan Vila-Francés
University of Valencia, Spain

Managing Director:	Lindsay Johnston
Senior Editorial Director:	Heather A. Probst
Book Production Manager:	Sean Woznicki
Development Manager:	Joel Gamon
Assistant Acquisitions Editor:	Kayla Wolfe
Cover Design:	Nick Newcomer

Published in the United States of America by
Information Science Reference (an imprint of IGI Global)
701 E. Chocolate Avenue
Hershey PA 17033
Tel: 717-533-8845
Fax: 717-533-8661
E-mail: cust@igi-global.com
Web site: http://www.igi-global.com

Library of Congress Cataloging-in-Publication Data

Intelligent data analysis for real-life applications: theory and practice / Rafael Magdalena-Benedito ... [et al.], editors.
    p. cm.
  Includes bibliographical references and index.
  ISBN 978-1-4666-1806-0 (hardcover) -- ISBN 978-1-4666-1807-7 (ebook) -- ISBN 978-1-4666-1808-4 (print & perpetual access) 1. Data mining. 2. Computer algorithms. 3. Machine learning. I. Magdalena Benedito, Rafael, 1968-
  QA76.9.D343I5743 2012
  006.3'12--dc23
                        2012002867

British Cataloguing in Publication Data
A Cataloguing in Publication record for this book is available from the British Library.

All work contributed to this book is new, previously-unpublished material. The views expressed in this book are those of the authors, but not necessarily of the publisher.

Table of Contents

Section 1
Machine Learning Methods Applied to Real-World Problems

Section 2
Machine Learning Applications in Computer Vision

Section 3
Other Machine Learning Applications

Detailed Table of Contents

Section 1
Machine Learning Methods Applied to Real-World Problems

Shigeaki Sakurai, Tokyo Institute of Technology, Japan

This chapter introduces a discovery method of attractive rules from the tabular structured data. The data is a set of examples composed of attributes and their attribute values. The method is included in the research field discovering frequent patterns from transactions composed of items. Here, the transaction and the item are a receipt and a sales item in the case of the retail business. The method focuses on relationships between the attributes and the attribute values in order to efficiently discover patterns based on their frequencies from the tabular structured data. Also, the method needs to deal with missing values. This is because parts of attribute values are missing due to the problems of data collection and data storage. Thus, this chapter introduces a method dealing with the missing values. The method defines two evaluation criteria related to the patterns and introduces a method that discovers the patterns based on the two-stepwise evaluation method. In addition, this chapter introduces evaluation criteria of the attractive rules in order to discover the rules from the patterns.

Fernando Benites, University of Konstanz, Germany
Elena Sapozhnikova, University of Konstanz, Germany

Methods for the automatic extraction of taxonomies and concept hierarchies from data have recently emerged as essential assistance for humans in ontology construction. The objective of this chapter is to show how the extraction of concept hierarchies and finding relations between them can be effectively coupled with a multi-label classification task. The authors introduce a data mining system which performs classification and addresses both issues by means of association rule mining. The proposed system has been tested on two real-world datasets with the class labels of each dataset coming from two different class hierarchies. Several experiments on hierarchy extraction and concept relation were conducted in order to evaluate the system and three different interestingness measures were applied, to select the most important relations between concepts. One of the measures was developed by the authors. The experimental results showed that the system is able to infer quite accurate concept hierarchies and associations among the concepts. It is therefore well suited for classification-based reasoning.

Darko Pevec, University of Ljubljana, Slovenia
Zoran Bosnić, University of Ljubljana, Slovenia
Igor Kononenko, University of Ljubljana, Slovenia

Current machine learning algorithms perform well in many problem domains, but in risk-sensitive decision making – for example, in medicine and finance – experts do not rely on common evaluation methods that provide overall assessments of models because such techniques do not provide any information about single predictions. This chapter summarizes the research areas that have motivated the development of various approaches to individual prediction reliability. Based on these motivations, the authors describe six approaches to reliability estimation: inverse transduction, local sensitivity analysis, bagging variance, local cross-validation, local error modelling, and density-based estimation. Empirical evaluation of the benchmark datasets provides promising results, especially for use with decision and regression trees. The testing results also reveal that the reliability estimators exhibit different performance levels when used with different models and in different domains. The authors show the usefulness of individual prediction reliability estimates in attempts to predict breast cancer recurrence. In this context, estimating prediction reliability for individual predictions is of crucial importance for physicians seeking to validate predictions derived using classification and regression models.

Pahal Dalal, University of South Carolina, USA
Song Wang, University of South Carolina, USA

Shape correspondence, which aims at accurately identifying corresponding landmarks from a given population of shape instances, is a very challenging step in constructing a statistical shape model such as the Point Distribution Model. Many shape correspondence methods are primarily focused on closed-surface shape correspondence. The authors of this chapter discuss the 3D Landmark Sliding method of shape correspondence, which is able to identify accurately corresponding landmarks on 3D closed-surfaces and open-surfaces. In particular, they introduce a shape correspondence measure based on Thin-plate splines and the concept of explicit topology consistency on the identified landmarks to ensure that they form a simple, consistent triangle mesh to more accurately model the correspondence of the underlying continuous shape instances. The authors also discuss issues such as correspondence of boundary landmarks for open-surface shapes and different strategies to obtain an initial estimate of correspondence before performing landmark sliding.

Bayesian Network classifiers (BNCs) are Bayesian Network (BN) models specifically tailored for classification tasks. There is a wide range of existing models that vary in complexity and efficiency. All of them have in common the ability to deal with uncertainty in a very natural way, at the same time providing a descriptive environment. In this chapter, the authors focus on the family of semi-naïve Bayesian classifiers (naïve Bayes, AODE, TAN, kDB, etc.), motivated by the good trade-off between efficiency and performance they provide. The domain of the BNs is generally of discrete nature, but since the presence of continuous variables is very common, the chapter discusses more classical and novel approaches to handling numeric data. In this chapter the authors also discuss more recent techniques such as multi-dimensional and dynamic models. Last but not least, they focus on applications and recent developments, including some of the BNCs approaches to the multi-class problem together with other traditionally successful and cutting edge cases regarding real-world applications.

Section 2
Machine Learning Applications in Computer Vision

The citrus industry is nowadays an important part of the Spanish agricultural sector. One of the main problems present in the citrus industry is decay caused by Penicillium digitatum and Penicillium italicum fungi. Early detection of decay produced by fungi in citrus is especially important for the citrus industry of distribution. This chapter presents a hyperspectral computer vision system and a set of machine learning techniques in order to detect decay caused by Penicillium digitatum and Penicillium italicum fungi that produce more economic losses to the sector. More specifically, the authors employ a hyperspectral system and artificial neural networks. Nowadays, inspection and removal of damaged citrus is done manually by workers using dangerous ultraviolet light. The proposed system constitutes a feasible and implementable solution for the citrus industry; this has been proven by the fact that several machinery enterprises have shown their interest in the implementation and patent of the system.

Chapter 7

J. Blasco, Instituto Valenciano de Investigaciones Agrarias, Spain

N. Aleixos, Instituto en Bioingeniería y Tecnología Orientada al Ser Humano, Universitat Politècnica de València, Spain

S. Cubero, Instituto Valenciano de Investigaciones Agrarias, Spain

F. Albert, Instituto en Bioingeniería y Tecnología Orientada al Ser Humano, Universitat Politècnica de València, Spain

D. Lorente, Instituto Valenciano de Investigaciones Agrarias, Spain

J. Gómez-Sanchis, Intelligent Data Analysis Laboratory, Universitat de València, Spain

Nowadays, there is a growing demand for quality fruits and vegetables that are simple to prepare and consume, like minimally processed fruits. These products have to accomplish some particular characteristics to make them more attractive to the consumers, like a similar appearance and the total absence of external defects. Although recent advances in machine vision have allowed for the automatic inspection of fresh fruit and vegetables, there are no commercially available equipments for sorting of minority processed fruits, like arils of pomegranate (Punica granatum L) or segments of Satsuma mandarin (Citrus unshiu) ready to eat. This work describes a complete solution based on machine vision for the automatic inspection and classification of these fruits based on their estimated quality. The classification is based on morphological and colour features estimated from images taken in-line, and their analysis using statistical methods in order to grade the fruit into commercial categories.

Chapter 8

T. F. Stepinski, University of Cincinnati, USA

Wei Ding, University of Massachusetts Boston, USA

R. Vilalta, University of Houston, USA

Prompted by crater counts as the only available tool for measuring remotely the relative ages of geologic formations on planets, advances in remote sensing have produced a very large database of high resolution planetary images, opening up an opportunity to survey much more numerous small craters improving the spatial and temporal resolution of stratigraphy. Automating the process of crater detection is key to generate comprehensive surveys of smaller craters. Here, the authors discuss two supervised machine learning techniques for crater detection algorithms (CDA): identification of craters from digital elevation models (also known as range images), and identification of craters from panchromatic images. They present applications of both techniques and demonstrate how such automated analysis has produced new knowledge about planet Mars.

Chapter 9

Gennady K. Khakhalin, Freelancer, Russia

Sergey S. Kurbatov, Research Centre of Electronic Computing Engineering (RCECE), Russia

Xenia A. Naidenova, Research Centre of Military Medical Academy (RCMMA), Russia

Alex P. Lobzin, Research Centre of Electronic Computing Engineering (RCECE), Russia

A complex combining multimodal intelligent systems is described. The complex consists of the following systems: image analyzer, image synthesizer, linguistic analyzer of NL-text, and synthesizer of NL-text and applied ontology. The ontology describes the knowledge common for these systems. The analyzers use the applied ontology language for describing the results of their work, and this language is input for the synthesizers. The language of semantic hypergraphs has been selected for ontological knowledge representation. It is an extension of semantic networks. Plane geometry (planimetry) has been selected as an applied domain of the complex. The complex's systems and their interaction are described.

Section 3
Other Machine Learning Applications

Chapter 10

Sunan Huang, National University of Singapore, Singapore

Kok Kiong Tan, National University of Singapore, Singapore

Tong Heng Lee, National University of Singapore, Singapore

Due to harsh working environment, control systems may degrade to an unacceptable level, causing more regular fault occurrences. In this case, it is necessary to provide the fault-tolerant control for operating the system continuously. The existing control techniques have given some ways to solve this problem, but if the system behaves in an unanticipated manner, then the control system may need to be modified, so that it handles the modified system. In this chapter, the authors are concerned with how this control system can be done automatically, and when it can be done successfully. They aimed in this work at handling unanticipated failure modes, for which solutions have not been solved completely. The model-based fault-tolerant controller with a self-detecting algorithm is proposed. Here, the radial basis function neural network is used in the controller to estimate the unknown failures. Once the failure is detected, the re-configured control is activated and then maintains the system continously. The fault-tolerant control is illustrated in two cases. It is shown that the proposed method can cope with different failure modes which are unknown a priori. The result indicates that the solution is suitable for a class of mechanical systems whose dynamics are subject to sudden changes resulting from component failures when working in a harsh environment.

Chapter 11

Ignacio Díaz, Universidad de Oviedo, Spain

Abel A. Cuadrado, Universidad de Oviedo, Spain

Alberto B. Diez, Universidad de Oviedo, Spain

Manuel Domínguez, Instituto de Automática y Fabricación, Universidad de León, Spain

Juan J. Fuertes, Instituto de Automática y Fabricación, Universidad de León, Spain

Miguel A. Prada, Instituto de Automática y Fabricación, Universidad de León, Spain

The objective of this chapter is to present, in a comprehensive and unified way, a corpus of data and knowledge visualization techniques based on the Self-Organizing Map (SOM). These techniques allow exploring the behavior of the process in a visual and intuitive way through the integration of existing process-related knowledge with information extracted from data, providing new ways for knowledge discovery. With a special focus on the application to process supervision and modeling, the chapter reviews well known techniques –such as component planes, u-matrix, and projection of the process state– but also presents recent developments for visualizing process-related knowledge, such as fuzzy maps, local correlation maps, and model maps. It also introduces the maps of dynamics, which allow users to visualize the dynamical behavior of the process on a local model basis, in a seamless integration with the former visualizations, making it possible to confront all them for discovery of new knowledge.

The authors employed traditional and novel machine learning to improve insight into the connections between the quality of an organization of enterprises as a type of formal social units and the results of enterprises' performance in this chapter. The analyzed data set contains 72 Slovenian enterprises' economic results across four years and indicators of their organizational quality. The authors hypothesize that a causal relationship exists between the latter and the former. In the first part of a two-part process, they use several classification algorithms to study these relationships and to evaluate how accurately they predict the target economic results. However, the most successful models were often very complex and difficult to interpret, especially for non-technical users. Therefore, in the second part, the authors take advantage of a novel general explanation method that can be used to explain the influence of individual features on the model's prediction. Results show that traditional machine-learning approaches are successful at modeling the dependency relationship. Furthermore, the explanation of the influence of the input features on the predicted economic results provides insights that have a meaningful economic interpretation.

Chapter 13

Automatic text classification is a process that applies information retrieval technology and machine learning algorithms to build models from pre-labeled training samples and then deploys the models to previously unseen documents for classification. Text classification has been widely applied in many fields ranging from Web page indexing, document filtering, and information security, to business intelligence mining. This chapter presents a semi-supervised text classification framework that is based on the radial basis function (RBF) neural networks. The framework integrates an Expectation Maximization (EM) process into a RBF network and can learn for classification effectively from a very small quantity of labeled training samples and a large pool of additional unlabeled documents. The effectiveness of the framework is demonstrated and confirmed by some experiments of the framework on two popular text classification corpora.

Chapter 14

Currently, important advances are being carried out in CAD (Computer Aided Design) applications; however, these advances have not yet taken place for CAS (Computer Aided Sketching) applications. These applications are intended to replace complex menus with natural interfaces that support sketching for commands and drawing, but the recognition process is very complex and doesn't allow its application yet. So, although natural interfaces for CAD applications have not yet been solved, works based on sketching devices have been explored to some extent. In this work, the authors propose a solution for the problem of recognition of sketches using an agent-based architecture, which distributes the agents hierarchically to achieve the best decision possible and to avoid reliance on of the drawing sequence.

Chapter 15

Guoliang Fan, Oklahoma State University, USA
Xin Zhang, South China University of Technology, P. R. China

This chapter studies the human walking motion that is unique for every individual and could be used for many medical and biometric applications. The authors' goal is to develop a general low-dimensional (LD) model from of a set of high-dimensional (HD) motion capture (MoCap) data acquired from different individuals, where there are two main factors involved, i.e., pose (a specific posture in a walking cycle) and gait (a specific walking style). Many Gaussian process (GP)-based manifold learning methods have been proposed to explore a compact LD manifold embedding for motion representation where only one factor (i.e., pose) is normally revealed explicitly with the other factor (i.e., gait) implicitly or independently treated. The authors recently proposed a new GP-based joint gait-pose manifold (JGPM) that unifies these two variables into one manifold structure to capture the coupling effect between them. As the result, JGPM is able to capture the motion variability both across different poses and among multiple gaits (i.e., individuals) simultaneously. In order to show advantages of joint modeling of combining the two factors in one manifold, they develop a validation technique to compare JGPM with recent GP-based methods in terms of their capability of motion interpolation, extrapolation, denoising, and recognition. The experimental results further demonstrate advantages of the proposed JGPM for human motion modeling.

Chapter 16

Guoliang Fan, Oklahoma State University, USA
Yi Ding, Oklahoma State University, USA

Semantic analysis is an active and interesting research topic in the field of sports video mining. In this chapter, the authors present a multi-level video semantic analysis framework that is featured by hybrid generative-discriminative probabilistic graphical models. A three-layer semantic space is proposed, by which the semantic video analysis is cast into two inter-related inference problems defined at different semantic levels. In the first stage, a multi-channel segmental hidden Markov model (MCSHMM) is developed to jointly detect multiple co-existent mid-level keywords from low-level visual features, which can serve as building blocks for high-level semantics. In the second stage, authors propose the auxiliary segmentation conditional random fields (ASCRFs) to discover the game flow from multi-channel keywords, which provides a unified semantic representation for both event and structure analysis. The use of hybrid generative-discriminative approaches in two different stages is proved to be effective and appropriate for multi-level semantic analysis in sports video. The experimental results from a set of American football video data demonstrate that the proposed framework offers superior results compared with other traditional machine learning-based video mining approaches.

In recent years there has been an increasing interest in the application of robot teams to solve some kind of problems. Although there are several environments and tasks where a team of robots can deliver better results than a single robot, one of the most active attention focus is concerned with solving coverage problems, either static or dynamic, mainly in unknown environments. The authors propose a method in this work to solve these problems in simulation by means of grammatical evolution of high-level controllers. Evolutionary algorithms have been successfully applied in many applications, but better results can be achieved when evolution and learning are combined in some way. This work uses one of this hybrid algorithms called Grammatical Evolution guided by Reinforcement but the authors enhance it by adding semantic rules in the grammatical production rules. This way, they can build automatic high-level controllers in fewer generations and the solutions found are more readable as well. Additionally, a study about the influence of the number of members implied in the evolutionary process is addressed.

Chapter 18

Controlling Graphical avatars intelligently in real-time applications such as 3D computer simulating environment has become important as the storage and computational power of computers has increased. Such avatars are usually controlled by Finite State Machines (FSM), in which each individual state represents the status of the avatars. The FSMs are usually manually designed, and the number of states and transitions are therefore limited. A more complex approach is needed for the avatar's actions, which are automatically generated to adapt to different situation. The levels of the missions and algorithms for the control are the essential elements to achieve the requirements, respectively. Reinforcement Learning can be used to control the avatar intelligently in the 3D environment. When simulating the interactions between avatars and changeable environments, the problem becomes more difficult than working in a certain unchanged situation. Specific Framework and methods should be created for controlling the behaviors of avatars, such as using hierarchical structure to describe these actions. The approach has many problems to solve such as where the levels of the missions will be defined and how the learning algorithm will be used to control the avatars, et cetera. In this chapter, these problems will be discussed.

Foreword

Transition of promising technologies from the research / experimental phase into the mainstream is always accelerated by successful applications in multiple domains. Nowhere has this principle been more true than in the area of personal computing, one of the most important inventions of the last century. Thanks to the Silicon Revolution and the on-going quest for miniaturization in hardware, computers surround us and can provide assistance not only in highly-specialized tasks they were originally designed for, but also in our regular daily activities and including entertainment. The new trend in personal computing is to equip "electronic brain"-based devices with more intelligence to allow them to collaborate with humans instead of simply performing pre-programmed tasks. Intelligent Data Analysis and Machine Learning play the key role in this endeavour.

Machine Learning is a discipline of science that has garnered interest in the second half of the twentieth century in concert with the development of computers. It focuses on the design of algorithms, broadly speaking, capable of learning behaviors from observed data and examples in a similar vein that humans do. Modern Machine Learning and Intelligent Data Analysis methods include a number of such algorithms: Artificial Neural Networks, Approximate Reasoning, Evolutionary Programming, Reinforcement Learning, Bayesian Networks, or Self-Organizing Maps, to mention a few. For a long period of time Machine Learning techniques have been considered primarily experimental. The present need for "smart" computers opens up new application avenues and brings out these techniques to the mainstream.

This handbook provides a state-of-the-art overview of Intelligent Data Analysis methods and a wide range of application domains. The Machine Learning methods presented comprehensively cover the spectrum of approaches from Supervised (Artificial Neural Networks, Bayesian Networks) through Semi-Supervised (Reinforcement Learning), to Unsupervised (Self-Organizing Maps). The application areas covered include image processing and pattern detection, natural language processing, knowledge extraction and interpretation, process control, navigation, and novel human-computer interfaces. Each contribution in this book is clear evidence of the tremendous potential of Machine Learning techniques to make the computers of tomorrow "smarter."

In summary, the information contained in this handbook makes it a valuable reference on exciting new real-world applications of Machine Learning and Intelligent Data Analysis methods.

Adam E Gaweda
University of Louisville, USA

Preface

What is Intelligent Data Analysis? The question is fully well-grounded, because the name itself is in some ways very ambiguous. The main idea lying under this definition is extracted knowledge from data.

This is now the Age of Information. Technology is ubiquitous, technology is cheap: technology is nowadays everything. Moore's Law has brought our world to the Technology Information Society, and even the most far away corner in the world is today covered by telecommunications technology. A high end technology cellular phone exhibits more computing power that the computer that drove man to the Moon 30 years ago. And we use it for playing bird-killing on-line games!

But with great power comes great responsibility, or it should. The cheap, powerful computing capabilities of nearly even appliance, the fast data highways that plough and fly through the Earth, and the nearly unlimited storage resources available everywhere, every time, are flooding us with digital data. The Age of Information could be also defined as the Curse of Data, because is quite cheap and easy to gather and store data, but people need information and chase knowledge. They have the haystack, but want the needle.

It is not easy to extract knowledge starting from raw data, and it is also not cheap. The curse of cheap hardware, cheap bandwidth, and cheap processors is an extraordinary large amount of data, a very large number of variables, and very little knowledge about what is cooking inside these data.

In the recent past, scientists and technologists have relied on traditional statistics to cope with the task of extracting information from data. Statistics building is deeply rooted in the ground of Mathematics since XVII Century but, during recent decades, this enormous amount of data and variables have overwhelmed the capabilities of classical statistics. There is no way for classical methods to deal with such amount of data; people cannot visualize even the lesser information. They are unable to extract knowledge form the radiant, brand-new gathered datasets.

Mathematics are also now coming to help, going beyond classical statistics and bringing tools that enable extraction of some information from these huge datasets. These new tools are collectively called "Intelligent Data Analysis." But Mathematics is not the only discipline involved in Data Analysis. Engineering, Computing Sciences, Database Science, Machine Learning, and even Artificial Intelligence are bringing their power to this newly-born data analysis discipline.

Intelligent Data Analysis could be defined as the tools that enable extracting information lying under very large amount of data, with very large amount of variables, data that represent very complex, non-linear, in two words, real-life problems, which are intractable with the old tools. People must be able to cope with high dimensionality, sparse data, very complex, unknown relationships, biased, wrong or incomplete data, or mathematics algorithms or methods that lie in the foggy frontier of Mathematics, Engineering, Physics, Computer Science, Statistics, Biology, or even Philosophy.

Moreover, Intelligent Data Analysis can help us in, starting from the raw data, coping with prediction tasks without knowing the theoretical description of the underlying process, classification tasks of new event in base of the past ones, or modeling the aforementioned unknown process. Classification, prediction, and modeling are the cornerstones that Intelligent Data Analysis can bring to us.

And in this Brave New Information World, information is the key. It is the key, the power and the engine that moves the economy. Because the world is moving with markets data, with medical epidemiologic sets, with Internet browsing records, with geological surveys data, complex engineering models, and so on. Nearly every digital activity nowadays is generating a big amount of data that can be easily gathered and stored, and the greatest value of the data is the information lying behind.

This book approaches Intelligent Data Analysis from a very practical point of view. There are many theoretical, academic books about theory on data mining and analysis. But the approach in this book comes from a real world view: solving common life problems with data analysis tools. It is a very "engineering" point of view, in the sense that the book presents a real problem, usually defined by complex, non-linear, and unknown processes, and offers a Data Analysis based solution, that gives the opportunity to solve the problem or even to infer the process underlying the raw data. The book discusses practical experiences with intelligent data analysis.

So this book is aimed to scientists and engineers carrying out research in very complex, non linear areas, as economics, biology, data processing, with large amount of data that need to extract some knowledge starting from the data, knowledge that can take the flavor of prediction, classification, or modeling. But this book also brings a valuable point of view to engineers and business men that work in companies, trying to solve practical, economical or technical problems in the field of their company activities or expertise. The pure practical approach helps to transmit the idea and the aim of the author of communicate the way to approach and to cope with problems that would be intractable in any other way. And at last, final courses of academic degrees in Engineering, Mathematics, or Business can use this book to provide students a new point of view for approaching and solving real, practical problems when underlying processes are no clear.

Obviously prior knowledge of statistics, discrete mathematics, and machine learning is desirable, although authors provide several references to help engineers and scientists to use the experience and the know-how described in every chapter to their own benefit.

The book is structured as follows. The first section of the book is about machine learning methods applied to real-world problems. In Chapter 1, "A Discovery Method of Attractive Rules from the Tabular Structured Data," Prof. Sakurai introduces an analysis method of transactions generated from the tabular structured data. The method focuses on relationships between attributes and their values in the data. The chapter introduces a processing method of transactions in which missing values occurs, an efficient discovery method of patterns, and their evaluation criteria. The topic of chapter 2, "Learning Different Concept Hierarchies and the Relations between them from Classified Data" by Benites and Sapozhnikova, is closely related to two fields of intelligent data analysis, namely to automatic ontology learning and multi-label classification. In the chapter, the authors investigate multi-label classification when the labels come from several taxonomies providing different insights into the data. It is a more interesting and less investigated task: finding interclass relationships may reveal new and unexpected links between different concept hierarchies. This enables the integration of multiple data sources, on the one hand, and improvement of the classification performance, on the other hand. Thus, the task is first to extract concept hierarchies by analyzing multi-labels in each label set and then to find hierarchical or so-called generalized association rules that describe the most important connections between different label sets. To be more precise, the co-occurrences of each label pair from two label sets are examined, taking into account the extracted hierarchies. This method is well validated by the experiments on real world data in the chapter. In Chapter 3, "Individual Prediction Reliability Estimates in Classification and Regression," Pevec, Bosnić, and Kononenko say that current machine learning algorithms perform well on many problem domains, but many experts are reluctant to use them because overall assessments of models do not provide them with enough information about individual predictions. The authors summarize the research areas that motivated the development of various approaches to estimating individual prediction reliability. Following an extensive empirical evaluation, the chapter shows the usefulness of these estimates in attempts to predict breast cancer recurrence, where reliability for individual predictions is of crucial importance. In Chapter 4, "Landmark Sliding for 3D Shape Correspondence," Dalal and Wang discuss shape correspondence in a population of shapes, which enables landmark recognition and classification. The discussion is centered on 3D Landmark Sliding method, with a measure based in Thin-plate splines and additional consistence restrictions. Chapter 5, titled "Supervised Classification with Bayesian Networks: A Review on Models and Applications," by Flores, Gámez, and Martínez, is about Bayesian Networks. Bayesian Network classifiers (BNCs) are Bayesian Network (BN) models specifically tailored for classification tasks. This chapter presents an overview of the main existing BNCs, especially semi-naïve Bayes, but also other networks-based classifiers, dynamic models, and multi-dimensional ones. Besides, mechanisms to handle numeric variables are described and analyzed. The final section of this chapter is focused on applications and recent developments, including some of the BNCs' approaches to the multi-class problem, together with other traditionally successful and cutting edge cases regarding real-world applications.

The second section groups the chapters on Machine Learning Applications in Computer Vision. Namely, Chapter 6, "Decay Detection in Citrus Fruits Using Hyperspectral Computer Vision" by Gómez, Olivas, Lorente, Martínez, Escandell, Guimerá, and Blasco, is about early automatic detection of fungal infections in post-harvest citrus fruits, which is especially important for the citrus industry because only a few infected fruits can spread the infection to a whole batch during operations such as storage or exportation. Penicillium fungi are among the main defects that may affect the commercialization of citrus fruits. Economic losses in fruit production may become enormous if an early detection of that kind of fungi is not carried out. Nowadays, this detection is carried out manually by trained workers illuminating the fruit with dangerous ultraviolet lighting. This work presents a new approach based on hyperspectral imagery and a set of machine learning techniques in order to detect decay caused by *Penicillium digitatum* and *Penicillium italicum*. The proposed system constitutes a feasible and implementable solution for the citrus industry, which has been proven by the fact that several machinery enterprises have shown their interest in the implementation and patent of the system. Chapter 7, "In-line Sorting of Processed Fruit Using Computer Vision: Application to the Inspection of Satsuma Segments and Pomegranate Arils," by Blasco, Aleixos, Cubero, Albert, Lorente, and Gómez, deals with the creation of a system for the in-line inspection of processed fruit based on computer vision that has been applied to the particular cases of pomegranate arils and satsuma segments ready for consumption. Computer vision system has been widely applied for the inspection of fresh fruit. However, due to the relative reduced market and the difficult of handling and analysing a very complex product such as minimally processed fruit, this technology it is being not already applied to this sector. This work shows the development of complete prototypes for the in-line and automatic inspection of this kind of fruit, including the development of the image processing algorithms. Once the images are captured, statistical methods based on the Bayes decision rule are used to achieve a decision about the quality of each object in order to classify and separate them into commercial categories. The prototypes have been tested in producing companies in actual commercial conditions. In Chapter 8, titled "Detecting Impact Craters in Planetary Images Using Machine Learning," Stepinski, Ding, and Vilalta, remark that robotic exploration of the Solar System over the past few decades has resulted in the collection of a vast amount of imagery data, turning traditional methods of planetary data analysis into a bottleneck from the discovery process. The chapter describes an application of machine learning to a particularly common and important approach for analysis of planetary images – detection and cataloging of impact craters. The chapter discusses how supervised learning can help in improving the efficiency and accuracy of crater detection algorithms. The first algorithm has been successfully applied to catalog relatively large craters over the entire surface of planet Mars, and the second algorithm addresses the need for detecting very small craters in high resolution images. In Chapter 9, "Integration of the Image and NL-text Analysis/Synthesis Systems," by Khakhalin, Kurbatov, Naidenova, and Lobzin, the authors describe an intelligent analytical system intended for combining image and natural text processing and modeling the interconnection of these processes in the framework of translating images into texts and vice versa. Plane geometry ("planimetry") has been selected as an applied domain of the system. The system includes the following subsystems: Image Analyzer, Image Synthesizer, Linguistic Analyzer of NL-text, Synthesizer of NL- text, and Applied Ontology. The ontology describes the knowledge common for these systems. The Analyzers use the applied ontology language for describing the results of their work, and this language is input for the Synthesizers. The language of semantic hypergraphs as a semantic network with the use of which n – dimensional relations are naturally represented has been selected for ontological knowledge representation. All principal questions of implementing enumerated subsystems are considered, including realization of key components of linguistic and image analysis, such as the parsing of complicated and elliptic clauses, the segmentation of complicated, complex, and compound sentences, machine learning in natural language processing, and some others.

The next section of the book groups the chapters under Other Machine Learning Applications. In Chapter 10, "Fault-Tolerant Control of Mechanical Systems Using Neural Networks," Sunan, Kok Kiong, and Tong Heng discuss about control techniques suitable to harsh environments. They propose a fault tolerant controller, based on Artificial Neural Networks, which can cope successfully with errors while keeping the system running continuously. The results can be applied to mechanical systems with probable component failures. Chapter 11 is titled "Supervision of Industrial Processes using Self Organizing Maps," written by Díaz, Cuadrado, Díez, Domínguez, Fuertes, and Prada. The chapter presents a corpus of visualization techniques based on the self-organizing map (SOM) to explore the behavior of industrial processes as well as to monitor its state. The chapter includes well established techniques, but also recent developments for novelty detection, correlation discovery, or visual analysis of process dynamics. The chapter illustrates these ideas with two application cases. In Chapter 12, "Learning and Explaining the Impact of Enterprises' Organizational Quality on their Economic Results," Pregeljc, Strumbelj, Mihelcic, and Kononenko present their study of 72 enterprises' economic results, illustrating the usefulness of machine learning tools in economic research. Prediction models are used to predict the enterprises' performance from various indicators of the enterprises' organizational quality. Furthermore, a novel post-processing method is used to aid the interpretation of the models' predictions, which provides useful economic insights, even in the case of more complex and non-transparent predictions models. In Chapter 13, "Automatic Text Classification from Labeled and Unlabeled Data," Professor Jiang presents a semi-supervised text classification system that integrates a clustering based Expectation-Maximization algorithm into radio basis function networks and can learn for classification effectively from a very small set of previously labeled samples and a largequantity of additional unlabeled data. In the last few years, there has been surging interest in developing semi-supervised learning models and these models are particularly relevant to many text classification problems where labeled training samples are limited in supply while relevant unlabeled data are abundantly available. The proposed system can be applied in many areas in information retrieval, document filtering, business intelligence mining andcustomer service automation. Chapter 14, "Agent Based Systems to Implement Natural Interfaces for CAD Applications" by Fernández, Aleixos, and Albert, is about CAS. CAS (Computer Aided Sketching) applications are intended to replace traditional menus with natural interfaces that support sketching for both commands and drawing, but the recognition process is very complex and not solved yet. This chapter gives an overview of the most important advances carried out in CAS field. The authors propose a solution for a CAS tool based on agents in the framework of CAD (Computer Aided Design) applications, proving that agent-based systems are valid for applications that require decision-making rules guided by knowledge, and also for these particular applications. The result is a paradigm based on agents that allows the user to draw freely no matter what he draws, the intended action, the number of strokes, or their sequence of introduction. Finally, some recommendations and future work are stated. Chapter 15, "Gaussian Process-based Manifold Learning for Human Motion Modeling," by Guoliang and Xin, studies human motion modeling using Gaussian Process-based manifold learning approaches. Specifically, the authors focused on the walking motion that is unique for every individual and could be used for many medical and biometric applications. The goal is to develop a general low-dimensional (LD) model from of a set of high-dimensional (HD) motion capture (MoCap) data acquired from different individuals, where there are two main factors involved, i.e., pose (a specific posture in a walking cycle) and gait (a specific walking style). Many Gaussian process (GP)-based manifold learning methods have been proposed to explore a compact and smooth LD manifold embedding for motion representation where only one factor (i.e., pose) is revealed explicitly with the other factor (i.e., gait) implicitly or independently treated. The authors recently proposed a new GP-based joint gait-pose manifold (JGPM) that unifies these two variables into one manifold structure to capture the coupling effect between them. As the result, JGPM is able to capture the motion variability both across different poses and among multiple gaits (i.e., individuals) simultaneously. In order to show advantages of joint modeling of combining the two factors in one manifold, the authors developed a validation technique to compare the proposed JGPM with recent GP-based methods in terms of their capability of motion interpolation, extrapolation, denoising, and recognition. The experimental results demonstrate advantages of the proposed JGPM for human motion modeling. Chapter 16, "Probabilistic Graphical Models for Sports Video Mining," by Guoliang and Yi, studies the application of probabilistic graphical models for sports video mining. The authors present a multi-level video semantic analysis framework that is featured by hybrid generative-discriminative probabilistic graphical models. A three-layer semantic space is introduced, by which the problem of semantic video analysis is cast into two inter-related inference problems defined at different semantic levels. In the first stage, a multi-channel segmental hidden Markov model (MCSHMM) is developed to jointly detect multi-channel mid-level keywords from low-level visual features, which can serve as building blocks for high-level semantic analysis. In the second stage, the authors propose the auxiliary segmentation conditional random fields (ASCRFs) to discover the game flow from multi-channel key-words, which provides a unified semantic representation for both event-based and structure-based semantic representation. The use of hybrid generative-discriminative approaches is proven to be effective and appropriate in two sequential and related stages of sports video mining. The experimental results from a set of American football video data demonstrate that the proposed method offers superior results compared with other traditional machine learning-based video mining approaches. The proposed framework along with the two new probabilistic graphical models has potential to be used in other video mining applications. In Chapter 17, "Static and Dynamic Multi-robot Coverage with Grammatical Evolution Guided by Reinforcement and Semantic Rules," Mingo, Aler, Maravall, and De Lope propose a method to solve multi-robot coverage problems in simulation by means of grammatical evolution of high-level controllers. Grammars are a valuable tool in order to create programs or controllers, because they allow users to specify a hierarchical structure for the behaviors instead of creating a monolithic whole system as other evolutionary approaches generally do. Using grammars, allows for developing solutions that are more readable and understandable than monolithic ones. Another advantage in the use of modular decomposition is the possible reuse of modules when new behaviors are being developed. Evolutionary algorithms implement a global search, and they are usually slow and do not scale well when the size of the problem grows. In order to improve the process, the proposed method includes two features: a learning process, and a formalism to allow semantic rules in the grammatical production rules. During the learning process, the algorithm can drive a local search and the semantic rules are a method for including common sense reasoning because the user can discard production rules in the process of building the controller when the production rules are semantically incorrect (although they are syntactically correct). This way, automatic high-level controllers can be built in fewer generations, and the solutions found are more readable as well. Besides, fewer individuals are needed in the population. The system proposed in the chapter is completely reactive, and it does consider neither communication among robots nor a map of the environment. In Chapter 18, "Computer-controlled Graphical Avatars and Reinforcement Learning," He and Tang talk about the resources of 3D graphical environments and avatars, which are growing at explosive speeds in the areas of World Wide Web and multimedia (e.g. MEPG-7). At the same time, the requirements of making 3D animations are growing much faster than the resources. However, the work of making high quality animations is difficult, because it can only be done by a small number of experts. To solve this problem, the authors present the method of bestowing 3D avatar intelligence to make them to adapt different circumstances automatically. Thus, machine learning is used in this area to achieve the goal - "Intelligent 3D avatars."

Rafael Magdalena-Bendito
University of Valencia, Spain

Marcelino Martínez-Sober
University of Valencia, Spain

José María Martínez-Martínez
University of Valencia, Spain

Pablo Escandell-Montero
University of Valencia, Spain

Joan Vila-Francés
University of Valencia, Spain

Section 1
Machine Learning Methods Applied to Real-World Problems

Chapter 1
A Discovery Method of Attractive Rules from the Tabular Structured Data

Shigeaki Sakurai
Tokyo Institute of Technology, Japan

ABSTRACT

This chapter introduces a discovery method of attractive rules from the tabular structured data. The data is a set of examples composed of attributes and their attribute values. The method is included in the research field discovering frequent patterns from transactions composed of items. Here, the transaction and the item are a receipt and a sales item in the case of the retail business. The method focuses on relationships between the attributes and the attribute values in order to efficiently discover patterns based on their frequencies from the tabular structured data. Also, the method needs to deal with missing values. This is because parts of attribute values are missing due to the problems of data collection and data storage. Thus, this chapter introduces a method dealing with the missing values. The method defines two evaluation criteria related to the patterns and introduces a method that discovers the patterns based on the two-stepwise evaluation method. In addition, this chapter introduces evaluation criteria of the attractive rules in order to discover the rules from the patterns.

DOI: 10.4018/978-1-4666-1806-0.ch001

INTRODUCTION

Owing to the progress of the computer environment and the network environment, it is easier and easier to collect and store large amounts of data. In the near future, we believe that many sensors are buried in real world environments and are attached to ourselves. Also, we believe that they compose huge sensor networks. The data related to our daily life will be easily collected and stored through the networks. We can anticipate that the analysis of the data leads to revise our daily life and to realize more smart society. Therefore, various types of the analysis have been aggressively studied since mid-1990s. The research field expands more and more. This is because there are various types of the data and there are various types of analysis needs. However, the analysis depends on both the data types and the needs to some extent. It is impossible to construct only one analysis method. This chapter focuses on the discovery of frequent patterns and association rules from the collected data as one of the analysis tasks. The patterns are frequently observed in the data. The rules are discovered from the patterns and represent characteristic combinations of items. Here, an item is a minimum element composing the data. The analysts can recognize relationships hidden in the data by checking the patterns and the rules. They can activate the patterns and the rules to their decision making. For example, in the case of the retail businesses, sales managers can use the patterns and the rules to decide how to display sales items. Also, in the case of the information security field, the system administrators can use the patterns and the rules to analyze attack methods of the crackers. On the other hand, the discovery of the patterns and the rules is a difficult task because we have to discover them from exponential combinations of items and to process large amounts of data. It is necessary to efficiently discover the patterns and the rules.

Thus, in the following, this chapter firstly introduces related works in this research field. It shortly introduces two representative discovery methods of frequent patterns. Next, it focuses on the discovery method of patterns from the tabular structured data. The data is a set of examples composed of attributes and their attribute values. The method focuses on relationships between the attributes and the attribute values in order to efficiently discover the patterns. Also, this method focuses on missing values in order to discover more valid patterns. In addition, this chapter introduces evaluation criteria in order to extract attractive rules from the patterns. Lastly, this chapter introduces the future trend of this research field.

BACKGROUND

Basket analysis of receipts collected from the retail business is the origin of the discovery of both frequent patterns and association rules. The rules are usually extracted from the discovered patterns. Therefore, it is important to efficiently discover the patterns. Each receipt is defined as a transaction in the analysis. Then, each transaction is composed of some items such sales items in the retail business. Each item is regarded as either of two cases in the transaction. That is, one case shows that the item is included in the transaction and the other case shows that the item is not included. Agrawal and Srikant (1994) and Han et al. (2000) propose representative discovery methods of frequent patterns using the monotonic property of the patterns. The property shows that if the pattern grows, its evaluation criterion monotonically decreases. It is called the Apriori property. On the other hand, Morzy and Zakrzewicz (1998) and Zaki et al. (1997) propose methods that speedily discover the patterns by devising storage methods for the data. Also, Koh et al. (2005) proposes a method that discovers association rules with low support but high confidence. Here, the support and the confidence are evaluation criteria of the patterns and the rules. Yan et al. (2005) proposes a discovery method of association rules based on a genetic method. The method regards the combination of an association rule including k items and the number of items in the condition part as a chromosome. It genetically discovers better association rules by using three genetic operators: select, crossover, and mutation.

These methods are expanded in order to discover the patterns and the association rules from the other types of the data. Numerical data is one of the types of data. Chen et al. (2008) proposes a method that discovers fuzzy association rules based on a genetic method. Here, the numerical data is represented by linguistic terms composed of fuzzy sets. The method adjusts the minimum support and the membership functions. Alcalá et al. (2007) proposes a method that discovers different types of fuzzy association rules. The numerical data is represented by 2-tuple linguistic representation. The representation is composed of linguistic term and its lateral displacement. The lateral displacement is adjusted based on a genetic method.

Tabular structured data is the other of the types of data. It is composed of examples. Each example is composed of attributes and attribute values. It is necessary for the discovery methods from the data to transform original values to items in the transaction. That is, the preprocessing method generates items by combining attributes with their attribute values. The number of generated items corresponds to the number of attribute values. The preprocessing method tends to generate many items. This is because an item is generated from an attribute value and each attribute can have two or more values. The tabular structured data can express more situations than the transaction data can. Therefore, it is especially important for the discovery methods to efficiently investigate the combination of items.

In addition, in the case of the tabular structured data, attributes do not always have their attribute values due to various problems related to the data collection and the data storage. Some attribute

values may not be collected or stored. The values are called missing values. The preprocessing method of the data is required in order to analyze the data in which the missing values occur. Either of three typical methods is usually used in order to preprocess the values. The first one gets rid of examples in which the missing values occur. The second one completes missing values by referring to distribution of attribute values related to the missing values (Song and Shepperd, 2007). The third one regards missing values as specific attribute values. These methods are efficient to some extent. However, the first method cannot use the information of remaining attribute values in examples in which the missing values occur. The second method may infer inappropriate attribute values and may assign wrong attribute values to the missing values. The wrong attribute values may discover wrong patterns and rules. The third method may discover patterns and rules whose meaning cannot be interpreted. This is because the third method equally deals with the missing values, even if the missing values originally have different meanings. Therefore, it is necessary to more efficiently deal with the missing values.

These methods are common preprocessing methods in the machine learning field. They do not always aim at the discovery of frequent patterns and association rules. Some methods have been proposed for their discovery. Ragel (1998) completes missing values by using association rules discovered from the data in which missing values occur. Ragel and Crémilleux (1998) divides a database composed of examples into the valid databases. Here, the database in which missing values do not occur is the valid database. In the valid database, the evaluation criteria of the patterns and the rules are redefined. The patterns and the rules are discovered based on the criteria. Calders et al. (2007) proposes an algorithm satisfying the Apriori property in the discovery of association rules from the data in which the missing values occur. Shen and Chen (2003) proposes a method that composes association rules and reuses them in order to improve the validity of both association rules and completed missing values. Shintani (2006) divides a database in which missing values occur into some databases in which missing values do not occur. It discovers association rules from the divided databases. Othman and Yahia (2006) introduces the concept of robustness for association rules. It aims to select robust association rules for the completion of the missing values. However, these methods based on the completion have the problem such as the second common preprocessing method. In addition, all introduced methods simply use the generation strategy of patterns. That is, the strategy corresponds to the one of the original data type. We can anticipate to more efficiently discover the frequent patterns and the association rules by using the relationships between attributes and attribute values. Thus, this chapter introduces the discovery method of the patterns incorporating the relationships (Sakurai et al., 2009) (Sakurai and Mori, 2010). Also, it introduces new criteria to extract attractive rules from the patterns.

DISCOVERY METHOD OF FREQUENT PATTERNS

This section defines frequent patterns and association rules based on two evaluation criteria: support and confidence. The frequent pattern is an item subset whose support is larger than or equal to the minimum support. Also, the association rule is an item subset which satisfies the following conditions. Then, the item subset can be exclusively divided into the condition part and the result part. Its support is larger than or equal to the minimum support and its confidence is larger than or equal to the minimum confidence. The support and the confidence are defined as shown in Formula (1) and Formula (2), respectively. We note that some association rules may be acquired from a frequent pattern. This is because there are some cases which divides the pattern into the condition

part and the result part. In these formulae, X and Y are item subsets, $n(X)$ shows the number of transactions including X and N_{all} is the number of all transactions.

$$supp(X \rightarrow Y) = \frac{n(X \cup Y)}{N_{all}} \qquad (1)$$

$$conf(X \rightarrow Y) = \frac{n(X \cup Y)}{n(X)} \qquad (2)$$

The association rules are discovered by the two-stepwise method. That is, the algorithm firstly discovers all frequent patterns from transactions. It uses the Apriori property to efficiently discover the patterns. Secondly, it discovers all association rules by evaluating the combinations of item subsets extracted from the patterns. The discovery of association rules depends on the discovery of frequent patterns. Therefore, the discovery of the frequent patterns is very important. Two representative methods have been proposed.

The first method is a discovery method based on the candidate pattern (Agrawal and Srikant, 1994). The method calculates supports of each item and identifies frequent items. It regards the frequent items as the first frequent patterns. Next, the i-th candidate patterns are generated by combining with two $(i-1)$-th frequent patterns as shown in Figure 1. Each $(i-1)$-th frequent pattern is composed of $(i-2)$ common items and a different item. Each i-th candidate pattern is composed of the common items and two different items. For example, (it_a, it_b) is a second candidate pattern when it_a and it_b are frequent items. Also, (it_a, it_b, it_c) is a third candidate pattern when (it_a, it_b) and (it_a, it_c) are second frequent patterns. We note that the common items do not exist in the case that i is equal to 2. The method calculates supports of the candidate patterns and identifies i-th frequent patterns. If all i-th candidate patterns are evaluated, the method adds 1 to i where the initialization value is 2. The expansion of patterns is repeated until

Figure 1. Generation of i-th candidate pattern

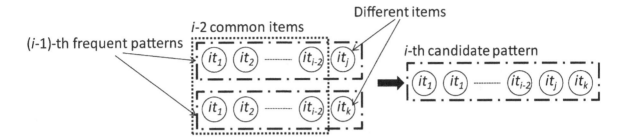

all frequent patterns discover. We note that it is not necessary for the method to investigate other candidate patterns. This is because if a pattern is not a frequent pattern, patterns completely including it, called supper patterns, cannot be frequent patterns due to the Apriori property. The method can avoid generating and identifying redundant candidate patterns.

The second method is a discovery method based on the Frequent Pattern-tree (FP-tree) (Han et al., 2000). The FP-tree expresses a transaction subset with the tree format. Each node except the top node of the tree is assigned an item name and its frequency. The top node is called the root node and is assigned ``null''. The method calculates item frequencies and identifies frequent items. The method picks up frequent items from each transaction and sorts them in descending order of their frequencies. It generates a selected and sorted transaction subset. Also, it generates an FP-tree from the subset by picking up items included in the subset one by one. That is, if the tree has the node including a picked-up item, the frequency of the node is updated by adding 1 to the frequency. Otherwise, a new node is generated and is registered in the tree. The node is assigned the item name and 1. On the other hand, the method selects an item and extracts a transaction subset with the frequency from parts of the FP-tree related to the item. The is, it searches nodes assigned the item. A path from each searched node to the root node is extracted from the FP-tree. The path is gotten rid of the searched node and the root node. The item subset in the remaining

path is regarded as a transaction. The transaction is assigned the frequency of the searched item as the frequency of the transaction. The subset of the transactions extracted from all searched nodes is a transaction subset conditioned by the item. The generation of the selected and sorted transaction subset, the FP-tree, and the transaction subset conditioned by the item are repeated in order. In the case of the method, the rows of the conditioned item express frequent patterns. Figure 2 shows the outline of the method. In this figure, the transaction set shows that the numbers of it_1, it_2, it_3, it_4, it_5, and it_6 are 5, 3, 3, 4, 3, and 2, respectively. Also, the total number of transactions is 6. If the minimum support is 0.33(=1/3), it_6 is not frequent and it_6 is removed from each transaction. The remaining items in each transaction are sorted in descending order of their frequencies. The FP-tree grows by picking up a selected and sorted transaction in order. Figure 3 shows parts of the growth. Lastly, the FP-tree in Figure 2 is generated from the selected and sorted transaction subset in Figure 2. On the other hand, if it_6 is picked up from the header table, the leftmost path it_5 - it_3 - it_2 - it_1 -*null* is extracted from the FP-tree. The subset (it_3, it_2, it_1) is extracted from the path and is assigned 1 as its frequency. The frequency corresponds to the frequency of it_5. Similarly, the subsets (it_4) and (it_1) are extracted from the paths it_5 - it_4-*null* and it_5 - it_1-*null*. Their frequencies are 1 and 1, respectively. These extracted subsets with their frequencies are a transaction subset conditioned by it_5.

Figure 2. An outline of the discovery method based on the FP-tree

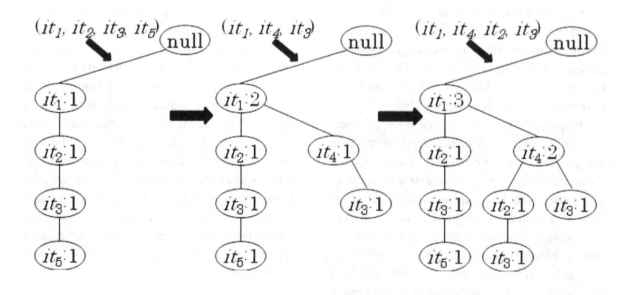

Transaction set
(it_1, it_2, it_3, it_5)
(it_1, it_3, it_4)
(it_1, it_2, it_3, it_4)
(it_1, it_2, it_4)
(it_4, it_5, it_6)
(it_1, it_5, it_6)

Selected and sorted transaction subset
(it_1, it_2, it_3, it_5)
(it_1, it_4, it_3)
(it_1, it_4, it_2, it_3)
(it_1, it_4, it_2)
(it_4, it_5)
(it_1, it_5)

header table

it_1	
it_4	
it_2	
it_3	
it_5	

FP-tree

null

$it_1{:}5$ $it_4{:}1$
$it_2{:}1$ $it_4{:}3$ $it_5{:}1$ $it_5{:}1$
$it_3{:}1$ $it_2{:}2$ $it_3{:}1$
$it_5{:}1$ $it_3{:}1$

Transaction subset conditioned by it_5
$(it_3, it_2, it_1){:}\ 1$
$(it_4){:}\ 1$
$(it_1){:}\ 1$

Figure 3. Growth of the FP-tree

(it_1, it_2, it_3, it_5) null
$it_1{:}1$
$it_2{:}1$
$it_3{:}1$
$it_5{:}1$

(it_1, it_4, it_3) null
$it_1{:}2$
$it_2{:}1$ $it_4{:}1$
$it_3{:}1$ $it_3{:}1$
$it_5{:}1$

(it_1, it_4, it_2, it_3) null
$it_1{:}3$
$it_2{:}1$ $it_4{:}2$
$it_3{:}1$ $it_2{:}1$ $it_3{:}1$
$it_5{:}1$ $it_3{:}1$

TABULAR STRUCTURED DATA

This section explains how to discover characteristic patterns from the tabular structured data. The characteristic patterns are frequent patterns reflecting on missing values.

Expression of Items

The tabular structured data is composed of examples. Each example corresponds to a transaction. Also, it is composed of attributes and attribute values. Each attribute can have three or more attribute values. If we try to discover patterns from the data, it is necessary to transform each attribute into items with two values based on the preprocessing method. For example, an attribute ``blood pressure" is given and it has three attribute values: ``high", ``normal", and ``low". The preprocessing method generates items from combinations of the attribute and its attribute values. That is, ``blood pressure: high", ``blood pressure: normal", and ``blood pressure: low" are regarded as items. In general, if an example of the data t is given by Formula (3), it is interpreted as items defined by Formula (4). Here, A_i, ($i=1, 2, ..., m$) is an attribute, $a_{ix(j)}$ is an attribute value of the attribute A_i, m is the number of attributes, and the combination of an attribute and an attribute value $A_i:a_{ix(j)}$ is an item.

$$\left(a_{1x(1)}, a_{2x(2),} \cdots, a_{mx(m)} \right) \tag{3}$$

$$\left(A_1 : a_{1x(1)}, A_2 : a_{2x(2),} \cdots, A_m : a_{mx(m)} \right) \tag{4}$$

Missing Values

This subsection introduces problems of missing values in the tabular structured data. It is introduced by using a data set as shown in Table 1. The data set is composed of 6 examples t_1 - t_6. Each example is composed of two attribute values cor-

Table 1. Tabular structured data 1 in which missing values occur

	A_1	A_2
t_1	a_{11}	a_{21}
t_2	a_{11}	-
t_3	a_{12}	a_{21}
t_4	-	a_{22}
t_5	a_{12}	a_{22}
t_6	a_{13}	a_{23}

responding to attributes A_1 and A_2, respectively. In this table, '-' shows a missing value. A missing value occurs in two examples t_2 and t_4. If the examples are deleted from the data, the number of remaining examples is 4 (=6-2). The numbers of attribute values a_{11}, a_{12}, and a_{13} are 1, 2, and 1. The numbers of attribute values a_{21}, a_{22}, and a_{23} are 2, 1, and 1. The supports of items $A_1:a_{11}$, $A_1:a_{12}$, $A_1:a_{13}$, $A_2:a_{21}$, $A_2:a_{22}$, and $A_2:a_{23}$ are 0.25, 0.50, 0.25, 0.50, 0.25, and 0.25, respectively. If the minimum support is 0.30, two patterns $A_1:a_{12}$ and $A_2:a_{21}$ are extracted as frequent patterns.

On the other hand, if only an attribute A_1 is focused, only an example t_4 is deleted. The number of remaining examples is 5 (=6-1). The numbers of attribute values a_{11}, a_{12}, and a_{13} are 2, 2, and 1. The supports of items $A_1:a_{11}$, $A_1:a_{12}$, and $A_1:a_{13}$ are 0.40, 0.40, and, 0.20, respectively. Two patterns $A_1:a_{11}$ and $A_1:a_{12}$ are extracted as frequent patterns. Similarly, if only the attribute A_2 is focused, two patterns $A_2:a_{21}$ and $A_2:a_{22}$ are extracted as frequent patterns. Therefore, 4 patterns are extracted due to the evaluation of individual attributes. The complete deletion of examples in which missing values occur and their partial deletion based on each attribute lead to different sets of frequent patterns. We can anticipate that the partial deletion discovers more valid patterns than the complete deletion does. This is because the partial deletion uses the information which is not used in the complete deletion. Thus, this section introduces two evaluation criteria based on the

Table 2. Tabular structured data 2 in which missing values occur

	A_1	A_2	A_3
t_1	a_{11}	a_{21}	a_{31}
t_2	a_{11}	a_{21}	a_{31}
t_3	a_{12}	a_{22}	-
t_4	a_{12}	a_{23}	a_{32}
t_5	a_{12}	a_{23}	a_{33}

partial deletion (Sakurai et al., 2009) (Sakurai and Mori, 2010). One criterion is the characteristic support. It focuses on such examples that all attribute values in a selected attribute subset are stored. The example and the subset are called the valid example and the attribute pattern, hereafter. The characteristic support is defined by Formula (5). In this formula, S_{XY} is an attribute pattern of the pattern XY and $N(S_{XY})$ is a function that calculates the number of valid examples corresponding to S_{XY}. The characteristic support is the same as the support redefined in (Ragel and Crémilleux, 1998). It can reflect on the effect of the partial deletion.

$$supp_{char}(X \rightarrow Y) = \frac{n(X \cup Y)}{N(S_{XY})} \qquad (5)$$

Unfortunately, the characteristic support does not satisfy the Apriori property. For example, we focus on a data set as shown in Table 2. The data set includes 5 examples t_1 - t_5. The number of examples including $(A_1:a_{11}, A_2:a_{21})$ is 2 in the data set. A missing value does not occur in the attribute pattern (A_1, A_2) and the number of valid examples is 5. Therefore, the characteristic support of $(A_1:a_{11}, A_2:a_{21})$ is 0.4 (=2/5). Also, the number of examples including $(A_1:a_{11}, A_2:a_{21}, A_3:a_{31})$ is 2. A missing value occurs in the attribute pattern (A_1, A_2, A_3) and the number of valid examples is 4. Therefore, the characteristic support of $(A_1:a_{11}, A_2:a_{21}, A_3:a_{31})$ is 0.5 (=2/4). The latter characteristic support is larger than the former characteristic

support regardless that $(A_1:a_{11}, A_2:a_{21}, A_3:a_{31})$ grows from $(A_1:a_{11}, A_2:a_{21})$. This case shows that the characteristic support does not satisfy the Apriori property.

On the other hand, the property is indispensable to efficiently discover all frequent patterns. Thus, the other criterion is introduced. It is the possible support defined by Formula (6).

$$supp_{pos}(X \rightarrow Y) = \frac{n(X \cup Y)}{N(S_{all})} \qquad (6)$$

In this formula, S_{all} is an attribute pattern in the case all attributes composing examples are selected. The possible support satisfies the Apriori property. This is because $N(S_{all})$ is fixed and the numerator monotonically decreases in the case that the patterns grow. Also, the possible support of a pattern is larger than or equal to its characteristic support. This is because $N(S_{XY})$ is larger than or equal to $N(S_{all})$. The possible support gives the upper bound of characteristic supports to supper patterns of the pattern.

In this chapter, a pattern whose characteristic support is larger than or equal to the minimum support is called the characteristic pattern. Also, a pattern whose possible support is larger than or equal to the minimum support is called the possible pattern. The minimum support is defined by the analysts. This chapter is interested in the efficient discovery method of all characteristic patterns. The method uses relationships between the characteristic support and the possible support. That is, the method calculates a possible support of a candidate pattern and evaluates whether the pattern is a possible pattern. If the candidate pattern is the possible pattern, it is kept regardless of its characteristic support. The pattern is used in order to create larger candidate patterns including the pattern. This is because even if the former candidate pattern is not a characteristic pattern, its supper patterns can be a characteristic pattern. Next, the method calculates a characteristic support of the candidate pattern and evaluates whether the candidate pattern is a characteristic pattern. The identified characteristic pattern is output. We can efficiently discover all characteristic patterns by using the two-stepwise evaluation method.

Generation of Candidate Patterns

This section explains a method that efficiently discovers all characteristic patterns from the tabular structured data. The method is based on the generation of the candidate pattern (Agrawal and Srikant, 1994). On the other hand, the method uses relationship between an attribute and its attribute values. In the following explanation, we anticipate that the attribute and the attribute values are arranged according to a criterion such as the alphabetic order. We can use the assumption without losing generality. Thus, we assume that $A_i < A_j$, $a_{ik} < a_{il}$, and $a_{ix} < a_{jy}$ for $i < j$ and $k < l$. The method is composed of two generation processes. The first process generates a larger attribute pattern by combining two smaller attributes patterns. The second process generates a larger attribute value pattern by combining two smaller attribute value patterns. Here, the attribute value pattern is a subset of attribute values included in an attribute pattern. Each process is similar to the generation of the candidate pattern. We explain each process in the following.

The first process generates all attribute patterns (A_i, A_j) including two attributes by combining two attribute patterns A_i and A_j as shown in Figure 4. In this figure, the first process generates an attribute pattern (A_1, A_2) from two attribute patterns A_1 and A_2. Also, it generates an attribute pattern (A_1, A_3) from two attribute patterns A_1 and A_3. Similarly, attribute patterns (A_1, A_4), ---, (A_1, A_m), (A_2, A_3), ---, (A_3, A_4), ---, and (A_{m-1}, A_m) are generated in order. We note that the generation is performed by using only two different attribute patterns. This is because a candidate pattern does not simultaneously include two items included in an attribute pattern due to the property of tabular structured

data. That is, patterns such as $(A_1: a_{11}, A_1: a_{12})$ and $(A_2: a_{21}, A_2: a_{22})$ are not candidate patterns. The first process has the same effect as the attribute constraint (Sakurai et al., 2008) without judging the attribute constraint. Here, the constraint expresses relationships among attributes and the patterns satisfying it are removed. Next, the first process generates all attribute patterns (A_i, A_p, A_q) including three attributes by combining two attribute patterns (A_i, A_p) and (A_i, A_q), where $i < p < q$. That is, it generates attribute patterns (A_1, A_2, A_3), (A_1, A_2, A_4), ---, (A_1, A_2, A_m), (A_2, A_3, A_4), ---, (A_3, A_4, A_5), ---, and (A_{m-2}, A_{m-1}, A_m) in order. In general, it generates all attribute patterns $(A_{i(1)}, A_{i(2)}, ---, A_{i(r-2)}, A_p, A_q)$ including r attributes by combining two attribute patterns $(A_{i(1)}, A_{i(2)}, ---, A_{i(r-2)}, A_p)$ and $(A_{i(1)}, A_{i(2)}, ---, A_{i(r-2)}, A_q)$ including $(r-1)$ attributes, where $i(1) < i(2) < --- < i(r-2) < p < q$. Each attribute pattern including $(r-1)$ attributes have the common $(r-2)$ attributes and a different attribute. In the generated attribute pattern, the common attributes are arranged before remaining deferent attributes.

If an attribute pattern is generated, the second process generates all attribute value patterns included in the attribute pattern. Its generation is similar to the first process. That is, it generates all attribute value patterns $(a_{ij(1)}, a_{ij(2)}, ---, a_{ij(r-2)}, a_{ip}, a_{iq})$ including r attribute values by combining two attribute value patterns $(a_{ij(1)}, a_{ij(2)}, ---, a_{ij(r-2)}, a_{ip})$ and $(a_{ij(1)}, a_{ij(2)}, ---, a_{ij(r-2)}, a_{iq})$ including $(r-1)$ attribute values, where $j(1) < j(2) < --- < j(r-2) < p < q$. Each attribute value pattern including $(r-1)$ attribute values have the $(r-2)$ common attribute values and a different attribute value. The common attribute values are arranged before remaining different attribute values. For example, the second process generates an attribute value pattern (a_{11}, a_{21}) including two attribute values by combining two attribute value patterns a_{11} and a_{21} including an attribute value. Also, it generates attribute value patterns (a_{11}, a_{22}), ---, $(a_{11}, a_{2m(2)})$, (a_{12}, a_{21}), --- in order. In addition, it generates an attribute value pattern (a_{11}, a_{21}, a_{31}) including three attribute

Figure 4. Generation of candidate patterns from the tabular structured data

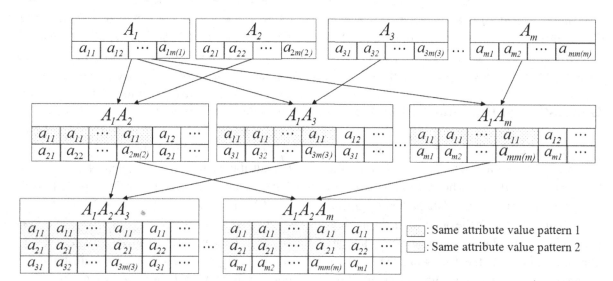

values by combining two attribute value patterns (a_{11}, a_{21}) and (a_{11}, a_{31}) including two attribute values. It generates the attribute value patterns $(a_{11}, a_{21}, a_{31}), (a_{11}, a_{21}, a_{32}), ---, (a_{11}, a_{21}, a_{3m(3)}), (a_{11}, a_{22}, a_{31})$ in order. A candidate pattern is generated from the combination of a generated attribute pattern and its attribute value pattern.

Growth Strategy

This section explains the growth strategy of candidate patterns. We can use the width-based method and depth-based method as the growth strategy. The width-based method generates candidate patterns according to small numbers of items in order. It can simultaneously calculate the numbers of examples including attribute value patterns related to a specific attribute pattern and the number of valid examples in the attribute pattern. Therefore, the method can efficiently calculate possible supports and characteristic supports of candidate patterns. Also, it can efficiently identify that each candidate pattern is either a possible pattern, a characteristic pattern, or the other pattern. On the other hand, the depth-based method generates candidate patterns related to specific

items or item sets in order. It can get rid of all possible patterns related to a specific item or a specific item set, if its discovery is over. It requires small memory space. Each of these methods has merits and demerits. Thus, this section uses the method combined the width-based method with the depth-based method by balancing the calculation speed and the memory space. That is, the combined method evaluates candidate patterns related to attribute patterns $A_1, A_2, ---$, and A_m in order. Next, it evaluates candidate patterns related to the attribute patterns $(A_1, A_2), (A_1, A_3), ---, (A_1, A_m)$ in order. It evaluates candidate patterns including attribute patterns $(A_1, A_2, A_3), (A_1, A_2, A_4), ---, (A_1, A_2, A_m)$ in order. The evaluation based on the width is repeated until all candidate patterns related to A_1 are evaluated. We note that it is not always necessary to evaluate all combinations of attributes related to A_1. This is because supper patterns of an attribute pattern are not evaluated when the attribute pattern does not have a possible attribute value pattern. If all candidate patterns related to A_1 are evaluated, the method begins to evaluate candidates patterns related to A_2 by the depth-based method. But, the candidate patterns related to A_1 is removed from the candidate patterns related to A_2. That is, the method evaluates candidate patterns including attribute patterns $(A_2, A_3), (A_2, A_4), ---, (A_2, A_m), (A_2, A_3, A_4), (A_2, A_3, A_5), ----, (A_2, A_3, A_m)$ in order. Similarly, candidate patterns related to $A_2, A_3, ---, A_{m-1}$ are evaluated in order. We note that candidate patterns related to A_m is not evaluated. This is because the candidate patterns are evaluated by the candidate patterns related to other attributes.

EVALUATION CRITERIA

The support is an evaluation criterion based on the frequency. Patterns discovered by the support are important patterns to some extent. However, we may still know the patterns because they are popular. Therefore, the other criteria are defined in order to discover more attractive patterns. The confidence defined by Formula (2) is one of the criteria. In the case of the tabular structured data, it is important to define the confidence reflecting on missing values. The confidence has two meanings. One is a conditional probability of a pattern in the case that a condition part is given. The other is the ratio of the support corresponding to the condition part to the support corresponding to the pattern. Therefore, we can define two types of confidences. In this section, the former one is probable confidence and the latter one is called characteristic confidence. They are defined as shown in Formula (7) and Formula (8), respectively.

$$conf_{prob}(X \rightarrow Y) = \frac{n(X \cup Y)}{n(X)} \quad (7)$$

$$conf_{char}(X \rightarrow Y) = \frac{supp(X \rightarrow Y)}{supp(X)}$$
$$= \frac{n(X \cup Y)}{n(X)} \cdot \frac{N(S_X)}{N(S_{XY})} \quad (8)$$

If there is not a missing value, the probable confidence is equal to the characteristic confidence. This is because the number of the valid examples is equal to the number of all examples. On the other hand, if there are missing values, the number of valid examples monotonically decreases as the patterns grow. Therefore, the second term in Formula (8) is larger than or equal to 1 and the characteristic confidence is larger than or equal to the probable confidence. The probable confidence is ranged in [0, 1], but the characteristic confidence may be larger than 1.

Next, this section introduces expanded lifts as the other criterion. The existing lift can evaluate the independence property between the condition part and the result part of a pattern. It shows that the pattern is attractive if the value is not close to 1. Also, it has two types of definitions. One is the ratio of the joint probability of the condition part and the result part to the product of respective probabilities. The other is the confidence weighted by the support of the result part. The existing lift is defined by Formula (9).

$$lift(X \rightarrow Y) = \frac{\dfrac{n(X \cup Y)}{N_{all}}}{\dfrac{n(X)}{N_{all}} \cdot \dfrac{n(Y)}{N_{all}}}$$
$$= \frac{\text{conf}(X \rightarrow Y)}{\text{supp}(Y)} \quad (9)$$

In the case of the tabular structured data, we can define two types of lifts. One is probable lift and the other is characteristic lift. The former one corresponds to the case of the joint probability and the latter one corresponds to the case of the weighted confidence. Fortunately, these definitions give the same values. These lifts are defined by Formula (10). We note that if there is not a missing value, the values of $N(X)$, $N(Y)$, and $N(X \cup Y)$ are equal to N_{all}. That is, the existing lift is equal to the probable lift and the characteristic lift.

Figure 5. Experimental results: the congressional data set

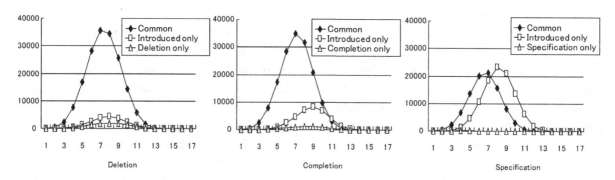

$$
\begin{aligned}
lift_{prob}(X \rightarrow Y) &= \frac{\dfrac{n(X \cup Y)}{N(X \cup Y)}}{\dfrac{n(X)}{N(X)} \cdot \dfrac{n(Y)}{N(Y)}} \\
&= \frac{conf_{char}(X \rightarrow Y)}{supp_{char}(Y)} \\
&= lift_{char}(X \rightarrow Y)
\end{aligned} \tag{10}
$$

The defined confidences and the defined lift are used in order to extract attractive rules from each characteristic pattern. That is, the characteristic pattern is divided into the condition part and the result part. It can have some combinations of the condition part and the result part. Each combination is calculated its characteristic confidence, its probable confidence, and its characteristic lift. It is identified whether it is an attractive rule by comparing them with the predefined thresholds. Here, the thresholds are predefined by the analysts. The evaluation is performed for all characteristic patterns. The attractive rules are acquired by the evaluation.

EXPERIMENTAL EVALUATION

This section introduces some experimental results (Sakurai and Mori, 2010) in order to verify the effect of the introduced discovery method from the tabular structured data. It focuses on the difference of patterns discovered by it and the discovery method incorporating three existing preprocessing methods of missing values: the deletion method, the completion method, and the specification method.

This section uses the congressional data set in the UCI machine learning repository (http://archive.ics.uci.edu/ml/). The data set includes 435 examples. Each example is composed of 17 attributes and each attribute is composed of two attribute values. The ratio of the missing values is 0.053. In this experiment, 0.10 is set as the minimum support. Figure 5 shows the results such that the introduced method is compared with three existing methods, respectively. In each graph, the horizontal axis is the length of patterns and the vertical axis is the number of discovered patterns. Each graph has three lines: "Common", "Introduced only", and "Deletion, Completion, or Specification only". "Common" shows the number of patterns discovered by both the introduced method and the respective existing methods. "Introduced only" does the one discovered by only introduced method, "Deletion, Completion, or Specification only" shows the one discovered by the respective existing methods.

The results show that introduced method discovers many patterns that the existing method cannot discover. We think that the patterns includes attractive patterns because the introduced method naturally deals with missing values.

FUTURE RESEARCH DIRECTIONS

In the near future of the pattern and the rule discovery from the tabular structured data, we have some research directions. That is, it is necessary to more strictly estimate the upper bound of the characteristic support or to approximately estimate it. This is because the number of valid examples tends to be small and many candidate patterns tend to be generated in the case that missing values frequently occurs. Also, it is necessary to consider the discovery method based on the FP-tree. This is because the discovery method based on the FP-tree is comparatively faster than the one based on the candidate patterns, even if the former one requires larger memory size in order to store many FP-trees at the same time. We can select an appropriate method by referring to the distribution of items and our computer environment if we can use two kinds of methods. In addition, we have many tabular structured data sets such as medical examination and demographic data of customers. We try to apply the introduced method to the data sets in order to acquire more valid patterns and rules.

On the other hand, the discovery of attractive rules is more and more important. This is because large amounts of data is easily generated by our daily actions and is easily collected according to the progress of the network environment and the computer environment. We think that it is necessary to deal with various types of data such as numerical values, texts, voices, static pictures, and dynamic pictures. The discovery method is required to simultaneously deal with the various data. Also, we think that the data is collected with different time span as second, minute, day, and week. The discovery method is required to reflect on the granularity of the time. In addition, the data is tied to the information related to the environments such as location, temperature, and humidity. The discovery method is required to reflect on them in the data analysis. Lastly, the discovery method can be applied to various fields such as Web, biology, and astronomy. We believe that the research filed of the discovery method expands more and more.

CONCLUSION

This chapter introduces a method of attractive rules from tabular structured data. The data is composed of examples including attribute and attribute values. In the case of the tabular structured data, it is necessary to deal with missing values. Also, it is necessary to reflect on a relationship between the attribute and the attribute values in order to efficiently discover patterns. In addition, this chapter introduces some evaluation criteria reflecting on the missing values. The criteria are used to extract attractive rules from the discovered patterns. The introduced discovery method can get rid of patterns including multiple same attributes as redundant patterns without calculating their frequencies. It can discover all frequent patterns with low calculation cost. Also, it sufficiently activates the remaining information of examples in which missing values occur. We can anticipate that the activation leads to the discovery of more valid patterns and rules. We believe that they can use in order to help our decision making in our daily life and daily business.

REFERENCES

Agrawal, R., & Srikant, R. (1994). Fast algorithms for mining association rules in large databases. *20th International Conference on Very Large Data Bases* (pp. 487-499).

Alcalá, R., Alcalá-Fdez, J., Gacto, M. J., & Herrera, F. (2007). Genetic learning of membership functions for mining fuzzy association rules. *16th IEEE International Conference on Fuzzy Systems* (pp. 1-6).

Calders, T., Goethals, B., & Mampaey, M. (2007). Mining itemsets in the presence of missing values. *2007 ACM Symposium on Applied Computing* (pp. 404-408).

Chen, C.-H., Hong, T.-P., & Tseng, V. S. (2008). A divide-and-conquer genetic-fuzzy mining approach for items with multiple minimum supports. *17th IEEE International Conference on Fuzzy Systems* (pp. 1231-1235).

Han, J., Pei, J., & Yin, Y. (2000). Mining frequent patterns without candidate generation. *ACM SIGMOD International Conference on Management of Data* (pp. 1-12).

Koh, Y. S., Rountree, N., & O'Keefe, R. (2005). Finding non-coincidental sporadic rules using apriori-inverse. *International Journal of Data Warehousing and Mining, 2*(2), 38–54. doi:10.4018/jdwm.2006040102

Morzy, T., & Zakrzewicz, M. (1998). Group bitmap index: A structure for association rules retrieval. *4th International Conference on Knowledge Discovery and Data Mining* (pp. 284-288).

Othman, L. B., & Yahia, S. B. (2006). Yet another approach for completing missing values. *4th International Conference on Concept Lattices and Their Applications* (pp. 155-169).

Ragel, A. (1998). Preprocessing of missing values using robust association rules. *2nd European Symposium on Principles of Data Mining and Knowledge Discovery* (pp. 414-422).

Ragel, A., & Crémilleux, B. (1998). Treatment of missing values for association rules. *2nd Pacific-Asia Conference on Research and Development in Knowledge Discovery and Data Mining* (pp. 258-270).

Sakurai, S., & Mori, K. (2010). Discovery of characteristic patterns from tabular structured data including missing values. *International Journal of Business Intelligence and Data Mining, 5*(3), 213–230. doi:10.1504/IJBIDM.2010.033359

Sakurai, S., Mori, K., & Orihara, R. (2009). Discovery of association rules from data including missing values. *International Conference on Complex, Intelligent and Software Intensive Systems* (pp. 67-74).

Shen, J.-J., & Chen, M.-T. (2003). A recycle technique of association rule for missing value completion. *17th International Conference on Advanced Information Networking and Applications,* (pp. 526-529).

Shintani, T. (2006). Mining association rules from data with missing values by database partitioning and merging. *5th IEEE/ACIS International Conference on Computer and Information Science and 1st IEEE/ACIS International Workshop on Component-based Software Engineering, Software Architecture and Reuse* (pp. 193-200).

Song, Q., & Shepperd, M. (2007). Missing data imputation techniques. *International Journal of Business Intelligence and Data Mining, 2*(3), 261–291. doi:10.1504/IJBIDM.2007.015485

Yan, X., Zhang, C., & Zhang, S. (2005). ARMGA: Identifying interesting association rules with genetic algorithms. *Applied Artificial Intelligence, 19,* 677–689. doi:10.1080/08839510590967316

Zaki, M. J., Parthasarathy, S., Ogihara, M., & Li, W. (1997). New algorithms for fast discovery of association rules. *3rd International Conference on Knowledge Discovery and Data Mining* (pp. 283-286).

ADDITIONAL READING

Agrawal, R., & Srikant, R. (1995). Mining sequential patterns. *11th International Conference on Data Engineering* (pp. 3-14).

Angryk, R. A., & Petry, F. E. (2005). Mining multi-level associations with fuzzy hierarchies. *14th IEEE International Conference on Fuzzy Systems* (pp. 785-790).

Ayouni, S., & Yahia, S. B. (2007). Extracting compact and information lossless set of fuzzy association rules. *16th IEEE International Conference on Fuzzy Systems* (pp. 1-6).

Borgelt, C., & Rodriguez, G. G. (2007). FrIDA - A free intelligent data analysis toolbox. *16th IEEE International Conference on Fuzzy Systems* (pp. 1-5).

Chakrabarti, D., & Faloutsos, C. (2006). Graph mining: Laws, generators, and algorithms. *ACM Computing Surveys, 38*(1), 1–69.

Chen, C.-H., Hong, T.-P., Tseng, V. S., & Lee, C.-S. (2007). A genetic-fuzzy mining approach for items with multiple minimum supports. *16th IEEE International Conference on Fuzzy Systems* (pp. 1-6).

Cheng, J., Ke, Y., & Ng, W. (2008). A survey on algorithms for mining frequent itemsets over data streams. *Knowledge and Information Systems, 16*(1), 1–27. doi:10.1007/s10115-007-0092-4

Dehaspe, L., & Toivonen, H. (1999). Discovery of frequent datalog patterns. *Data Mining and Knowledge Discovery, 3*(1), 7–36. doi:10.1023/A:1009863704807

Delavallade, T., & Dang, T. H. (2007). Using entropy to impute missing data in a classification task. *16th IEEE International Conference on Fuzzy Systems* (pp. 1-6).

Djouadi, Y., Redaoui, S., & Amroun, K. (2007). Mining association rules under imprecision and vagueness: Towards a possibilistic approach. *16th IEEE International Conference on Fuzzy Systems* (pp. 1-6).

Fiot, C., Laurent, A., & Teisseire, M. (2007). Approximate sequential patterns for incomplete sequence database mining. *16th IEEE International Conference on Fuzzy Systems* (pp. 1-6).

Fiot, C., Masseglia, F., Laurent, A., & Teisseire, M. (2008). TED and EVA: Expressing temporal tendencies among quantitative variables using fuzzy sequential patterns. *17th IEEE International Conference on Fuzzy Systems* (pp. 1861-1868).

Ganti, V., Gehrke, J., & Ramakrishnan, R. (2002). Mining data streams under block evolution. *ACM SIGKDD Explorations Newsletter, 3*(2), 1–10. doi:10.1145/507515.507517

Getoor, L., & Diehl, C. P. (2005). Link mining: A survey. *ACM SIGKDD Explorations, 7*(2), 3–12. doi:10.1145/1117454.1117456

Goebel, M., & Gruenwald, L. (1999). A survey of data mining and knowledge discovery software tools. *ACM SIGKDD Explorations, 1*(1), 20–33. doi:10.1145/846170.846172

Hotta, H., Takano, A., & Hagiwara, M. (2008). Mining KANSEI fuzzy rules from photos on the internet. *17th IEEE International Conference on Fuzzy Systems* (pp. 2242-2249).

Huang, Y.-P., & Kao, L.-J. (2005). A novel approach to mining inter-transaction fuzzy association rules from stock price variation data. *14th IEEE International Conference on Fuzzy Systems* (pp. 791-796).

Hüllermeier, E., Weskamp, N., Klebe, G., & Kuhn, D. (2007). Graph alignment: Fuzzy pattern mining for the structural analysis of protein active sites. *16th IEEE International Conference on Fuzzy Systems* (pp. 1-6).

Inokuchi, A., Washio, T., & Motoda, H. (2000). An apriori-based algorithm for mining frequent substructures from graph data. *4th Pacific-Asia Conference on Knowledge Discovery and Data Mining* (pp. 13-23).

Jiang, J.-Y., Lee, W.-J., & Lee, S.-J. (2005). Mining calendar-based asynchronous periodical association rules with fuzzy calendar constraints. *14th IEEE International Conference on Fuzzy Systems* (pp. 773-778).

Ling, C. X., & Li, C. (1998). Data mining for direct marketing: Problems and solutions. *4th International Conference on Knowledge Discovery and Data Mining* (pp. 73-79).

Lopez, F. J., Blanco, A., Garcia, F., & Marin, A. (2007). Extracting biological knowledge by fuzzy association rule mining. *16th IEEE International Conference on Fuzzy Systems* (pp. 1-6).

Nakata, K., Sakurai, S., & Orihara, R. (2008). Classification method utilizing reliably labeled data. *12th International Conference on Knowledge-Based and Intelligent Information & Engineering Systems* (pp. 114-122).

Pei, J., Han, J., Mortazavi-Asl, B., & Pinto, H. (2001). PrefixSpan: Mining sequential patterns efficiently by prefix-projected pattern growth. *17th International Conference on Data Engineering* (pp. 215-224).

Pei, J., Han, J., Mortazavi-Asl, B., Wang, J., Pinto, H., & Chen, Q. (2004). Mining sequential patterns by pattern-growth: The PrefixSpan approach. *IEEE Transactions on Knowledge and Data Engineering, 16*(11), 1424–1440. doi:10.1109/TKDE.2004.77

Pei, Z. (2008). Extracting association rules based on intuitionistic fuzzy special sets. *17th IEEE International Conference on Fuzzy Systems* (pp. 873-878).

Sakurai, S. (2010). An efficient discovery method of patterns from transactions with their classes. *2010 IEEE International Conference on Systems, Man and Cybernetics* (pp. 2116-2123).

Sakurai, S. (2011). Prediction of sales volume based on the RFID data collected from apparel shops. *International Journal of Space-Based and Situated Computing, 1*(2/3), 174–182. doi:10.1504/IJSSC.2011.040343

Sakurai, S., Kitahara, Y., & Orihara, R. (2008). A sequential pattern mining method based on sequential interestingness. *International Journal of Computational Intelligence, 4*(4), 252–260.

Sakurai, S., Kitahara, Y., & Orihara, R. (2008). Discovery of sequential patterns based on constraint patterns. *International Journal of Computational Intelligence, 4*(4), 275–281.

Sakurai, S., Kitahara, Y., Orihara, R., Iwata, K., Honda, N., & Hayashi, T. (2008). Discovery of sequential patterns coinciding with analysts' interests. *Journal of Computers, 3*(7), 1–8. doi:10.4304/jcp.3.7.1-8

Sakurai, S., & Suyama, A. (2005). An e-mail analysis method based on text mining techniques. *Applied Soft Computing, 6*(1), 62–71. doi:10.1016/j.asoc.2004.10.007

Sakurai, S., & Ueno, K. (2004). Analysis of daily business reports based on sequential text mining method. *2004 IEEE International Conference on Systems, Man and Cybernetics* (pp. 3279-3284).

Sakurai, S., Ueno, K., & Orihara, R. (2008). Discovery of time series event patterns based on time constraints from textual data. *International Journal of Computational Intelligence, 4*(2), 144–151.

Shankar, S., & Purusothaman, T. (2009). Utility sentient frequent itemset mining and association rule - mining: A literature survey and comparative study. *International Journal of Soft Computing Applications, 4*, 81–95.

Strike, K., Emam, K. E., & Madhavji, N. H. (2001). Software cost estimation with incomplete data. *IEEE Transactions on Software Engineering*, *27*(10), 890–908. doi:10.1109/32.962560

Xie, D. W. (2005). Fuzzy association rules discovered on effective reduced database algorithm. *14th IEEE International Conference on Fuzzy Systems* (pp. 779-784).

Yahia, S. B., & Nguifo, E. M. (2004). Contextual generic association rules visualization using hierarchical fuzzy meta-rules. *13th IEEE International Conference on Fuzzy Systems, 1*, (pp. 227-232).

KEY TERMS AND DEFINITIONS

Apriori Property: This is one of properties related to patterns. This property means that if a pattern is included in the other pattern, the frequency of the former one is larger than or equal to the frequency of the latter one. It is used to efficiently discover patterns.

Association Rule: This is a kind of rules composed of the condition part and the result part with relationships such as simultaneity and independence. The rule is discovered from frequent patterns by designating the condition part and setting thresholds of evaluation criteria.

Confidence: This is one of criteria which evaluate a pattern. It corresponds to the conditional probability in the case that a subset of items included in the pattern is designated as the condition part.

Frequent Pattern: This is a pattern whose support is larger than or equal to the threshold predefined by the analysts. It is composed of frequent items. In the frequent pattern discovery task, the pattern is discovered from a transaction set.

Item: This is one of basic elements in the frequent pattern discovery task. It is an element of a transaction. In the case of the retail field, each sales item is regarded as the item.

Lift: This is one of criteria which evaluate a pattern. It can evaluate the independence property between the condition part and the result part where these parts are subsets of the pattern. If the value is not close to 1, it shows that there is a specific relationship between them.

Missing Value: This is a value that is not acquired in the data collection phase or that is lost in the data storage phase. In the case of the data in which the value occurs, the value is complemented, it is regarded as a specific value, or the data is deleted.

Support: This is one of criteria which evaluate a pattern. It is the ratio of the number of transactions including the pattern to the number of all transactions. It satisfies the Apriori property.

Transaction: This is one of basic elements in the frequent pattern discovery task. It is composed of a set of exclusive items. In the case of the retail field, a receipt is regarded as the transaction.

Tabular Structured Data: This is data composed of examples. Each example is composed of attributes and their attribute values. In the frequent pattern discovery task, the combination of an attribute and its attribute value is regarded as an item.

Chapter 2
Learning Different Concept Hierarchies and the Relations Between them from Classified Data

Fernando Benites
University of Konstanz, Germany

Elena Sapozhnikova
University of Konstanz, Germany

ABSTRACT

Methods for the automatic extraction of taxonomies and concept hierarchies from data have recently emerged as essential assistance for humans in ontology construction. The objective of this chapter is to show how the extraction of concept hierarchies and finding relations between them can be effectively coupled with a multi-label classification task. The authors introduce a data mining system which performs classification and addresses both issues by means of association rule mining. The proposed system has been tested on two real-world datasets with the class labels of each dataset coming from two different class hierarchies. Several experiments on hierarchy extraction and concept relation were conducted in order to evaluate the system and three different interestingness measures were applied, to select the most important relations between concepts. One of the measures was developed by the authors. The experimental results showed that the system is able to infer quite accurate concept hierarchies and associations among the concepts. It is therefore well suited for classification-based reasoning.

DOI: 10.4018/978-1-4666-1806-0.ch002

INTRODUCTION

The complexity and amount of data on the Internet as well as in science and industry is growing rapidly. As a result of increased data complexity, it is becoming more and more difficult to find and manage relevant materials. A successful way to cope well with the enormous information flow is the use of taxonomies with hierarchically structured concepts which are usually called concept hierarchies or, more generally, ontologies, and are provided by domain experts. A common example may be a tourism ontology containing concepts such as accommodation, attractions and transport (where, for example, "hotel" and "youth hostel" are subcategories of "accommodation"). This kind of ontology formally specifies the concepts and their relationships in a domain and facilitates information search. Furthermore, ontologies are very useful for knowledge representation purposes, e.g. in the semantic Web, and therefore have become an active research field in the last few years. Unfortunately, manual creation of concept hierarchies is very cost-intensive and often impossible in face of the large scale of many domains. Additionally, it is expensive and tedious to maintain complex taxonomies manually when the data are changing frequently. For this reason, the acquisition of ontologies directly from raw text also known as ontology learning (Maedche & Staab, 2001) has recently emerged as an alternative to manual ontology building with the aim of assisting humans in ontology construction. This problem has been extensively studied in the past (Bendaoud, Hacene, Toussaint, Delecroix, & Napoli, 2007, Cimiano, Hotho, & Staab, 2005, Omelayenko, 2001).

As a subfield of text mining, these methods are closely related to the field of natural language processing. Some of them use available semantic knowledge such as the synonymous or antonymous relations between concepts. Another approach is represented by syntactical methods, which treat textual or other data as abstract structures.

Besides the domain-specific text corpora, other types of data like databases may also comprise hidden or implicit taxonomic information, which can be discovered in many applications from Web mining to bioinformatics. Syntactical data-driven methods for the automatic extraction of taxonomies and concept hierarchies have been shown to be successful in assisting knowledge engineers with ontology development (Majidian & Martin, 2009). In general, any classified data containing class labels are potential sources for inferring concept hierarchies. Our previous work (Brucker, Benites, & Sapozhnikova, 2011) has shown that it is possible to extract quite accurate taxonomies by analyzing co-occurrences between labels in multi-label classification, i.e. when an instance belongs to more than one class. A movie, for example, can be classified into crime, thriller, and horror genre categories simultaneously. The presented work extends the research area to the analysis of multiple class taxonomies.

Often several ontologies may exist for the same data, each of them representing a specific point of view on a certain domain. There are a lot of studies considering similar taxonomies where the tasks of ontology merging, mapping or alignment are often dealt with in order to unify available knowledge (Choi, Song, & Han, 2006). On the other hand, multiple taxonomies may be used either for specializing in sub-domains or for providing different perspectives (Wimalasuriya & Dou, 2009). In the latter case, which is the focus of our research, a movie, for example, can be classified either by its genre into a genre taxonomy or by the producing company in a taxonomy of producers. This task of relating the taxonomies of different natures is much less investigated. In such a case, the combination of information from taxonomies providing different insights into a problem domain can lead to the discovery of new knowledge. Solving this knowledge extraction task enables, for instance, the integration of evidence from multiple data sources and thus decreases the human effort required to create useful knowledge representations.

The objective of this chapter is to show how both important data mining tasks discussed above, automatic learning of concept hierarchies and relating them, can be effectively coupled with a multi-label classification task. To the best of the authors' knowledge, in the field of multi-label classification, there are still problems with multiple class taxonomies, which can complement each other, that have not been investigated yet. Thus our work aims at filling this deficiency and addresses both issues by extracting multiple class hierarchies from classified data and by finding one-to-one relationships between their classes. In addition to this goal, the subject of relating multiple taxonomies is also of interest to us because we intend to use discovered connections between the classes of different taxonomies to improve classifier predictions.

This work is part of the "DAMIART" project aimed at integrating multi-source and multi-taxonomy approaches into a single data mining system based on a neuro-fuzzy classifier in order to improve classification performance and knowledge extraction from the data. In contrast to the existing methods, which learn concept hierarchies directly from data and require a large amount of labeled instances, it can use predicted labels instead of original ones. While it is still affected by classifier accuracy, this approach allows the system to find relationships between classes automatically even when labeled data are sparse. A small training set can be used to learn the classifiers; if there are a large number of test instances a large number of predictions will be available for hierarchy extraction and concept relation. The goal is to combine multi-label classification, hierarchy extraction and concept relation and supplement them with the knowledge extraction from the classifier. The fuzzy rules extracted from the trained classifier can extend the body of discovered association rules by connecting them to the input space, which simplifies the plausibility check. When experts

subsequently interact with the system (see Fig. *1*), it should be possible to reveal conflicts in the classification rules and to correct them. In the data mining system, the hierarchies extracted from multi-labels could be additionally compared to the original hierarchy, if it exists, revealing concept drifting and changes in the rules.

To date, the developed data mining system performs multi-label classification, hierarchy extraction and discovers relationships between class hierarchies. The latter two steps are accomplished by means of association rule mining. Finding relations between concepts in our system is instance-based, which means that they are determined by data only and may change accordingly when the data change. For instance, a specific district in a city may be recognized as a shopping district and another district as an industrial area. Thus the relations between a particular shop and its location and a specific industrial company and its location are given for this city but do not necessarily exist in another city.

The proposed system was tested on two real-world datasets from different application domains. The data in each of them were labeled according to two predefined concept hierarchies. In order to evaluate the system, we conducted several experiments on hierarchy extraction and concept relation. In order to select the most important relations between concepts, three different interestingness measures were applied. Besides support and confidence many other measures have been proposed to assess the quality of harvested rules (Lallich, Teytaud, & Prudhomme, 2007, Tan, Kumar, & Srivastava, 2004). From these measures, the Jaccard coefficient was chosen because of its useful properties. Additionally, we developed a new interestingness measure which is especially well suited for hierarchically organized rules.

Our experimental results showed that the system is capable of inferring quite accurate concept hierarchies and associations among the concepts. It is therefore well suited for classification-based reasoning.

Figure 1. System

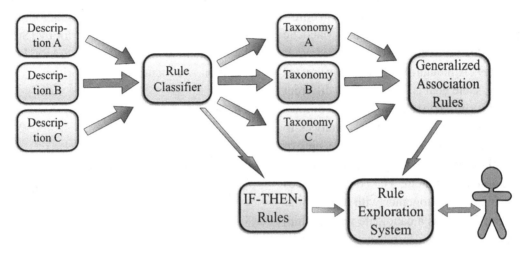

The rest of this chapter is organized as follows: First, we provide an overview about related work in Section **RELATED WORK**. Next, Section **APPROACH** explains our approach and is followed by Section **EXPERIMENTS** in which we present the experiments supporting our method. We finalize the chapter with the **CONCLUSION** where also future work is outlined.

RELATED WORK

As mentioned above, there is still no research on combining multi-label classification with relating different concept hierarchies. Work on multiple ontologies has started in the fields of ontology merging, mapping or alignment. Among the variety of proposed methods several are instance-based ones such as (Doan, Madhavan, Domingos, & Halevy, 2002, Rajan, Punera, & Ghosh, 2005, Takeda, Hideaki, & Shinichi, 2001). They are generally less relevant for us because they focus on similar taxonomies, while we are interested in analyzing connections between taxonomies of different types. More recent research directions include using multiple ontologies in web searches (Tomás & Vicedo, 2007) and information extraction (Wimalasuriya & Dou, 2009). In the

former study the goal is to classify a question in multiple taxonomies by a language model, but the authors do not concentrate on how the taxonomies are related to each other. Wimalasuriya and Dou argue that using multiple ontologies can improve the information extraction process as compared to the use of a single ontology. They demonstrate improvements on two real-world datasets where each dataset has two ontologies. Here again similar ontologies are used.

Another related topic is the use of ontologies as background knowledge for mining association rules in order to enhance knowledge discovery. Many research projects utilize generalized association rules (GARs), which were initially introduced in (Srikant & Agrawal, 1995). GARs enable identification of the appropriate level of abstraction at which relations between concepts should be established. The most recent studies consider fuzzy ontologies (Miani, Yaguinuma, Santos, & Biajiz, 2009), but they typically use a single ontology. An exception is presented in (T. Martin & Shen, 2009, T. P. Martin, Shen, & Azvine, 2008), which is similar to our own work. These papers focus on finding associations between multiple taxonomies with fuzzy categories in contrast to our case of crisp taxonomies.

The research field closest to our work focuses on discovering non-taxonomic relations in ontology learning by association rule mining (Maedche & Staab, 2000, Villaverde, Persson, Godoy, & Amandi, 2009). Although a single ontology is used in both papers, the goal is to connect its different parts, which is similar to relating different ontologies. The latter work uses linguistic analysis to find semantic relationships between concepts of a concept hierarchy denoted by the verbs usually employed to connect them. The co-occurrences of a pair of concepts together with a particular verb are considered as a candidate relationship, which should be validated by means of association rule mining. Only frequent co-occurrences in a domain-specific text corpus generate a set of association rules describing statistically significant non-taxonomic relationships between concepts of a concept hierarchy. Our approach differs by the absence of linguistic analysis and by the use of GARs for connecting hierarchies. Maedche and Staab (Maedche & Staab, 2000) also use GARs in order to mine co-occurrence among pairs of words in text. Although their algorithm claims to be built on the algorithm developed by (Srikant & Agrawal, 1995), it is in fact quite different. The rules are pruned in such a way that more general ancestral rules replace more specific ones due to their generally higher support and confidence. In contrast to this approach, we suggest discovering the most interesting rules by analyzing the difference between expected and actual support or confidence values as introduced by (Srikant & Agrawal, 1995).

APPROACH

In our setting, the concepts of different concept hierarchies are classes in (hierarchical) multi-label classification, represented by labels. Generally, the task is first to infer concept hierarchies by analyzing multi-labels (for more details see (Brucker et al., 2011)) and then to find GARs that describe the most interesting relations between two label sets. In order to discover one-to-one relations between concepts, we adapt the algorithm by (Srikant & Agrawal, 1995) for generating GARs. From this point on, we focus on this algorithm.

Notation

We are given a family of instances $(t^{(s)})_{s=1,..,n}$, and at least two families of multi-labels $(x^{(s)})_{s=1,..,n}$ and $(y^{(s)})_{s=1,..,n}$. Each family of multi-labels is based on a different label set, that is $x^{(s)} \subseteq \{1,...,q_1\} =: L_1$ and $y^{(s)} \subseteq \{q_1+1,...,q_1+q_2\} =: L_2$ for all $s=1,...,n$. Each of the label sets L_1 and L_2 has a hierarchical structure $H_i (i = 1, 2)$, where H_i refers to the *hierarchy* of L_i. A hierarchy H on L is considered as a rooted labeled directed tree, i.e. an arrangement of L in tree form. No assumptions concerning the origins of H_1 and H_2 are made, i.e. at this point it does not matter whether they are original hierarchies or extracted ones. The task is to infer relations between the different label sets, i.e. to find out how two labels $i \in L_1$ and $j \in L_2$ are related.

Hierarchical Multi-label

A hierarchy H is required to contain each label $i \in L$ exactly once. To simplify presentation it is further assumed that the root of the tree has the label $0 \in L$. Since mapping between hierarchy nodes and labels is one to one we usually do not distinguish between them. Thus H can be interpreted as a set of edges $H \subset (L \cup \{0\}) \times L$ where $(i,j) \in H$ if and only if i is the parent of j. The parent of i in H is denoted by $p_H(i)$.

The connection between multi-labels and a hierarchy H is as follows: If a multi-label m contains a certain label $i \in L$, it should also contain its parent and thus all its ancestors:

Table 1. Measures

Support(A,B)	$$\dfrac{\|\{t^{(s)} \mid A \in \mathrm{x}^{(s)} \wedge B \in y^{(s)}\}\|}{n}$$
Confidence(A,B)	$$\dfrac{\|\{t^{(s)} \mid A \in \mathrm{x}^{(s)} \wedge B \in y^{(s)}\}\|}{\|\{t^{(s)} \mid A \in \mathrm{x}^{(s)}\}\|}$$
Jaccard(A,B)	$$\dfrac{\|\{t^{(s)} \mid A \in \mathrm{x}^{(s)} \wedge B \in y^{(s)}\}\|}{\|\{t^{(s)} \mid A \in \mathrm{x}^{(s)} \vee B \in y^{(s)}\}\|}$$

$$p_H(i) \in m \text{ for all } i \in m \text{ if } p_H(i) \neq 0$$

Quality Measures for Association Rules

Association analysis measures co-occurrences of items in a transaction database and relates them. A transaction is a set of items which, for example, are purchased together. The most frequently co-occurring items build an association represented as a rule of the form $X \rightarrow Y$ where X and Y are sets of items (X is called the antecedent and Y is called the consequent). Although association rules can generally represent many-to-many relationships, we consider the special case of one-to-one relationships. In our setting, transactions are multi-label instances and an item is a single label. Therefore, the association rules output those pairs of classes or concepts for which some statistical relation has been found among them. Generally, association rule mining algorithms produce a large amount of rules and many of them may be redundant or not interesting. So, evaluation of their quality or interestingness is the main step in association analysis.

The common quality measures in association rule mining are support and confidence. In our task, support describes the fraction of multi-labels that belong to a given rule. Usually, obtained rules are pruned by support and confidence thresholds.

With support, one can estimate how important a rule is for the dataset, e.g. how many instances it covers. Confidence indicates the estimated conditional probability of a rule given the elements and the antecedent. Obviously, it is not symmetrical: Confidence (A,B) $\neq$ Confidence (B,A). The importance of an antecedent to the rule can be measured with confidence: the higher the confidence, the more important the antecedent is for the rule. Additionally, we employed the Jaccard measure. It is symmetrical and gives more value to rules where antecedent and consequent are equally important to a rule. This measure also possesses key properties examined in (Surana & Reddy, 2010) as essential for mining rare association rules. Since a large part of a label set can occur relatively infrequently, such sensitivity to rare association rules is valuable for our experiments.

Interestingness

In order to find the most interesting rules with respect to the hierarchy and not only the rules with a high confidence or support value, we developed a new method for calculating the interestingness of a GAR:

$$Int(i, j) = \frac{M(i, j)}{M(i, j) + M_E(i, j)}$$

where M can be either support, confidence or any other measure with M_E being its respective expectation as first defined in (Srikant & Agrawal, 1995). This is explained in more detail in the Section entitled **GAR Pruning** below. $Int \in [0,1]$ has high values if M is much higher than M_E. It achieves 0.5 when $M=M_E$ and is lower than 0.5 if $M<M_E$.

Algorithm

Our algorithm can be summarized in six steps. As input it takes multi-labels from two label sets L_1 and L_2. It creates association rules by connecting a label from L_1 to a label from L_2. Next, it prunes rules with respect to the thresholds for support and confidence as well as to the particular quality measure. The steps are as follows:

1. Create rules by calculating the support from the multi-labels for each label pair $l_i \in L_p : L_1 \times L_2$.
2. Remove those rules where a support value is below the user-specified minimum support threshold.
3. Calculate the confidence for the remaining rules.
4. Remove those rules where a confidence value is below the user-specified minimum confidence threshold.
5. Calculate the values of the selected quality measure for each remaining rule.
6. Prune rules where the values of the quality measure are below those of their ancestral rules with respect to the antecedent taxonomy. Here two methods are possible as described below.

Pruning

We used Pruning by Ancestral Rules (PAR), but the calculation of the interestingness measure defined above needs the expectation defined in **GAR Pruning** (GARP).

GAR Pruning

In GARP, we compare the value of an interestingness measure over the rule from a parent $p_H(i)$ to a consequent j with the value of a child rule $i{\rightarrow}j$ concerning the same consequent. If the child rule is better we keep that rule in the rule set. Here

"better" means that the rule's value corresponding to a given measure is greater by a predefined factor $\gamma > 1 : r_i > \gamma r_{p_H(i)}$. This is motivated by the fact that the important rules describe the relationships between the hierarchies and the less important rules can be deduced from the more important ones using the hierarchy. GARP was formalized in (Srikant & Agrawal, 1995) using expected values:

$$Sup_E(X,Y) = \frac{|X|}{|p_H(X)|} * P(p_H(X) \cap Y),$$

$$Conf_E(X,Y) = Conf(p_H(X), Y),$$

thus the measured value should be greater than its expectation. We already used the expectations in Section **Interestingness** to propose the interestingness measure. From their definitions it is clear that if only the antecedent is generalized, then using support or confidence to determine interestingness results in the same value. We use this variant in the experiments.

PAR

PAR, in turn, assures that only those rules are selected where the values of the chosen metric are greater than the corresponding values of all their ancestors. Such pruning differs from GARP in that it does not consider decreases and increases, in a wave-like manner, along a path. In (Srikant & Agrawal, 1995) the authors argue that rule pruning should only consider the closest ancestors (parents), but as we aim at selecting the most interesting rules preferably in lower hierarchy levels, we use ancestral pruning, i.e. a value of a rule must be greater than all values of rules of the antecedent's ancestors.

EXPERIMENTS

The main difficulty in evaluating our approach is that it is typically not known how many and what type of relationships between taxonomies should be discovered. To simplify evaluation, we chose two similar taxonomies for the first experiment, establishing a base line. In this case it is much easier to connect similar concepts manually, an approach which is often used to validate results (Doan et al., 2002, Maedche & Staab, 2000). In the second experiment, we investigated two different taxonomies and compared results obtained for true taxonomies with the results obtained for taxonomies extracted from classifier predictions. In both experiments, we examined which quality measure produces fewer rules that are still interesting.

Performance Measures

To assess the obtained results, two usual performance measures, known as recall and precision, were used:

$$R(A, B) = \frac{|A \cap B|}{|A|}, \quad P(A, B) = \frac{|A \cap B|}{|B|},$$

where A represents the set of true elements and B the set of found elements. In this work, elements were either the relations between concepts or multi-label instances. The F-measure is the harmonic mean between recall and precision. Both were macro-averaged over the instances to calculate the F-measure.

In (Maedche & Staab, 2000) an evaluation metric is introduced, known as Generic Relation Learning Accuracy (RLA). We have transformed it into RLA recall and RLA precision by focusing on the true rule set instead of the discovered one and building the sum over true rules instead

of averaging over found rules. RLA recall can be obtained by dividing the resulting sum by the number of true rules whereas RLA precision through division by the number of rules found. This is motivated by the fact that not only the discovered true rules are important but also the number of discovered irrelevant or redundant rules. It should be noted that RLA precision can become greater 1 because a smaller set of rules can cover a larger set of rules with good approximation, i.e. it is no longer normalized, and calculating an F-measure can lead to a very good value even if the recall is bad.

Data

The IMDb and Rotten Tomatoes (RT) dataset, used in (T. P. Martin et al., 2008), was kindly donated by Trevor Martin. From the roughly 90,000 movies of each database, we selected only those that have at least one genre assigned and that have an almost exact match in title and director in both datasets. This resulted in 3079 entries. We further enriched the dataset with data we collected from IMDb from August 2010 comprising about 390,000 movies. From these 390,000 IMDb entries we extracted the genres and keywords as labels and created two label sets, one which had classes with more than 250 entries (IMDb_large) and the other with classes with more than 600 entries (IMDb_small). Further, we deleted some redundancy and obvious dependencies reducing the label set to 88 labels for IMDb_large and 48 for IMDb_small about genre and keywords (like friend, friendship). We added their respective selected keywords and genres (labels) to the 3079 IMDb movies, creating the IMDb_large and IMDb_small multi-label dataset. After that, we created a hierarchy which we extracted with the Apriori algorithm and 0.4 confidence threshold (method described in (Brucker et al., 2011)) from the multi-labels for each label set. Further, we expanded the multi-labels by ancestry, i.e. parent labels were assigned to their respective child for each multi-label instance, and for each dataset/ hierarchy. The Rotten Tomatoes dataset had also two versions of the label set, one small (RT_small) with labels with more or equal 50 entries and one large (RT_large) with more or equal than 30 entries. The hierarchy was extracted from the labels with the Apriori and threshold also set to 0.4 for both RT datasets. With the extracted hierarchy we performed ancestor expansion on the multi-labels and removed label redundancy as in IMDb.

The WIPO-alpha dataset[1] is a collection of patent documents made available for research by the World Intellectual Property Organization (WIPO). The original hierarchy consists, from top to bottom, of 8 *sections*, 120 *classes*, 630 *subclasses* and about 69,000 *groups*. In our experiment, the hierarchy was only considered through to, and including, subclasses. Each document in the collection has one so-called *main code* and any number of *secondary codes*, where each code describes a subclass to which the document belongs. Both main and secondary codes were used in our experiment. We removed subclasses with fewer than 50 training and 50 test instances (and any documents that only belonged to such "small" subclasses). The remaining training and test documents were then combined to form a single dataset. The final dataset consisted of 62,587 records with a label set of size 273. For Wipo A, only branch A (Human Necessities) and for Wipo C, only branch C (Chemistry) (the branches which have most correlated documents (4146)) were used, which span only 89 nodes and have 26,530 documents.

Multi-label statistics about each dataset are depicted in Table 2. The datasets are quite different: Wipo A & C is not so dense and IMDb & RT is not as large as Wipo.

IMDb-RT (Small) Strong Associations

We compared the IMDb_small with the RT_small to find out if our method could find the same strong associations as Martin et al. found in (T.

Table 2. Multi-label statistics of datasets

	IMDb:RT small/large	Wipo A& C
# multi-labels	3079	27,483
Cardinality	8.1/9.5	4.0
Density	0.09/0.06	0.04
Multi-labels distinct	2616/2807	1325
Hierarchy depth	3:4/4:5	3

Martin, Shen, & Azvine, 2007). The rules were discovered by PAR using three different interestingness measures discussed above: Interestingness (*Int*), Confidence (*Conf*) and Jaccard (*Jac*), and a minimum confidence threshold of 0.2 (#rules 120), which was found experimentally. Minimum support threshold was not employed because the dataset was relatively small.

With the interestingness measure, we found 13 of the 17 strong associations found by Martin et al.[2] from 101 extracted connections. Examples of the found rules are:

- Horror → Horror/Suspense
- Documentary → Documentary
- War → Drama
- blood → Horror/Suspense
- Documentary → Education/General Interest

The main connections were discovered successfully. Some deviations can be explained by their redundancy with respect to the GARs. For example, IMDb Thriller could not be connected to RT Drama, since IMDb Thriller is a direct child of Drama (IMDb Drama → RT Drama is a strong bond therefore implying the rule left out). Similarly, Mystery could not be related to Horror/ Suspense since its direct parent, Thriller, was also strongly connected to it, and also Adventure → Action/Adventure because of Action → Action/ Adventure. Taking these rules into account, this sums up to a total of 16 rules covered by the method. Another connection Adult → Education/

Figure 2. Excerpt from the IMDb_small, genres are uppercase, keywords are in lowercase

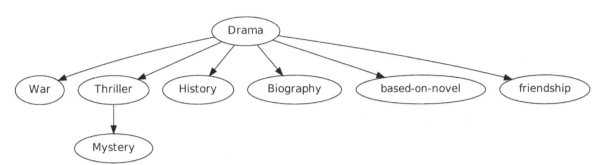

General Interest could not be discovered due to its relatively low confidence and support values, which indicates that the connection is noisy. This single deviation can also be explained by the dataset itself, since we did not use exactly the same dataset. Therefore, we can state that the interestingness had a very good rule recovery with a low number of irrelevant rules.

With confidence, 124 rules were extracted and the result was almost the same but instead of Mystery → Horror/Suspense, the rule that was not found was Mystery → Drama, again Thriller had a stronger connection to Drama, while Drama to Drama was even stronger (See Fig. 2). The difference can be explained by the fact that PAR with interestingness concentrates more on the relative increase of confidence, whereas PAR with confidence focuses on the absolute difference to ancestors. That means in this case that confidence had a greater increase from Drama → Horror/Suspense to Thriller → Horror/Suspense in comparison to Thriller → Horror/Suspense to Mystery → Horror/Suspense, although confidence for Mystery → Horror/Suspense was highest along its ancestor path. For Mystery → Drama, the highest confidence along the ancestor path was Drama → Drama, but there was an increase between Thriller and Mystery making it more interesting than the previous rule.

The association rules discovered by using the Jaccard measure did not match the rules we compared since the asymmetrical connections were

Table 3. Recall/precision for IMDb_small and RT_small rules compared to the strong associations from Martin et al.

Min. Conf.	*Int*	*Conf*	*Jac*
0	0.824/0.012	0.824/0.013	0.588/0.012
0.2	0.765/0.108	0.765/0.105	0.529/0.129

not discovered. For example, the relation War → Drama with confidence 0.6 and only 0.04 in the opposite direction (Drama → War) was not found.

Leaving out pruning with minimum confidence increased recall but decreased precision dramatically, as can be seen in Table 3. One can also see that the results of interestingness and confidence are comparable but precision was somewhat better in the former case. Jaccard had the worst recall but the best precision at 0.2 minimum confidence.

IMDb-RT (Large) Finding Manual Connections

In the next experiment 48 manual connections between the IMDb_large and RT_large hierarchies were created manually, e.g. Comedy → Comedy, Sci-Fi → Science Fiction and Fantasy, gangster → Organized Crime. We expected to discover as many hand-coded connections as possible, plus the connections which were not evident or redundant.

We compared our method with the method employed by (Maedche & Staab, 2000), which

Table 4. Recall/precision for PAR with interestingness, confidence and Jaccard for IMDb-RT (Large)

Conf	0.10			0.20			0.40		
Sup	*Int*	*Conf*	*Jac*	*Int*	*Conf*	*Jac*	*Int*	*Conf*	*Jac*
0	31/373	32/387	29/156	22/212	23/215	21/79	11/121	11/124	9/30
	0.65/0.08	0.67/0.08	0.6/0.19	0.46/0.10	0.48/0.11	0.44/0.27	0.23/0.09	0.23/0.09	0.19/0.30
0.002	29/327	30/338	28/143	22/204	23/208	21/79	11/113	11/117	9/30
	0.60/0.09	0.62/0.09	0.58/0.20	0.46/0.11	0.48/0.11	0.44/0.27	0.23/0.10	0.23/0.09	0.19/0.30
0.040	9/59	9/58	8/39	8/49	8/48	7/30	6/35	6/35	5/18
	0.19/0.15	0.19/0.16	0.17/0.21	0.17/0.16	0.17/0.17	0.15/0.23	0.12/0.17	0.12/0.17	0.10/0.28

consisted in pruning the rules by ancestral rules with higher or equal confidence and support. That is, a rule was selected only if its ancestors' confidence and support values were less than its own values. In contrast, we only used confidence pruning, since support pruning allowed only the top level classes to generate rules in our setup.

The manually generated relationships were symmetrical but we focused only on the IMDb to RT direction in this experiment. First, the pruning with minimum support and confidence set to 0 and 0.1, respectively, was examined. There were 31 rules found by using PAR with interestingness and 32 with confidence which corresponds to 65% and 67% accuracy, respectively. This result is comparable to the results achieved earlier in ontology mapping (Doan et al., 2002). Though some of the hand-coded relations were not found even when the minimum confidence was set to 0.1: singer → Musical and Performing Arts, sex → Erotic, policeman → Cops. PAR with interestingness did not find the rule wwii → World War II, because it was covered by the rule War → World War II. On the other hand, PAR with confidence could not find the sheriff → Western rule, which was subsumed by Western → Western. It should be noted that these relations had low confidence: For half of the not discovered manual rules, confidence was less than 10 percent.

A possible method to find more relations with less total rules would be to consider the inverse confidence (RT to IMDb) and to select only those

rules that have a sufficiently high confidence value in both directions. Setting support to 0 and confidence to 0.1 returned 1160 rules with 39 rules found. Although this method discovered seven more manual connections it had approximately three times more rules in total.

By increasing confidence to 0.4, the number of found relations rapidly decreased. This indicates that the movies in the datasets were labeled differently and inconsistently. Moreover, there were still many other rules found mostly because many keywords and genres were connected through the hierarchy, e.g. politics → Drama (*Conf* IMDb to RT:0.6, *Conf* RT to IMDb:0.03) is four times stronger than politics → Politics (0.15,0.18). In addition, connections from the bottom of IMDb to the top of RT occurred frequently indicating that the labeling and generalization was different in both label sets.

Wipo A & C

In the WIPO dataset hand-coded relations were not used for evaluation. It was difficult to create such connections because the branches of Wipo A & C are very different, and such manual mapping requires expert knowledge. The more appropriate way would be to discover the connections directly from the data. Since the proposed method of mining interesting associations between taxonomies worked well with the movie dataset of lower quality, it was natural to assume that

Table 5. Tree distances between the hierarchies extracted from the true and predicted multi-labels. In parentheses is the used confidence threshold.

Dataset	CTED	LCAP	TO
Wipo A	0.0732 (1)	0.0796 (1)	0 (1)
Wipo C	0.1250 (0.8)	0.1406 (0.8)	0 (0.8)
Wipo A& C	0.1236 (0.7)	0.1268 (0.7)	0 (0.8)

Table 6. RLA recall /RLA precision from rules extracted from predicted multi-labels to rules from the true multi-labels for WIPO

True AC	*Int*	*Conf*	*Jac*
True AC			
Int	1.00 1.00	0.94 1.04	0.96 0.76
Conf	0.93 0.85	1.00 1.00	1.00 0.71
Jac	0.80 1.01	0.86 1.21	1.00 1.00
Separately predicted A to C			
Int	0.65 0.93	0.63 1.00	0.67 0.76
Conf	0.62 0.82	0.64 0.93	0.68 0.70
Jac	0.55 1.01	0.56 1.15	0.64 0.93
Together predicted A to C			
Int	0.76 0.33	0.75 0.36	0.77 0.26
Conf	0.74 0.30	0.74 0.33	0.77 0.25
Jac	0.68 0.39	0.68 0.43	0.73 0.33

this method would also work successfully on the WIPO dataset with well labeled instances. The Wipo A & C was classified by ML-ARAM with 5-fold cross validation using labels from A only, labels from C only and labels from A & C. The parameters were chosen as in (Brucker et al., 2011): 9 voters, vigilance at 0.9 and a threshold of 0.002. Hierarchies were extracted from original multi-labels and from predicted multi-labels and the tree distances CTED, LCAPD and TO* were calculated similarly to (Brucker et al., 2011).

The macro averaged F1-measure value was 0.63, 0.57 and 0.46 for the predicted multi-labels for Wipo A alone, Wipo C alone and Wipo A & C together, respectively. The standard deviation was less then 0.001 for all three cases. Such results point to a relatively hard to predict dataset. Table 5 shows that the extracted hierarchies were very close to the original ones.

The next comparison concerns the rules discovered from the true labels and the rules discovered from the predicted labels. Using RLA recall and RLA precision revealed not only that all true rules were discovered, but also if the results contained uninteresting rules, in terms of the true rules among the discovered ones. Table 6 depicts the results for RLA recall and RLA precision of rules extracted from the predicted multi-labels covering rules extracted from the true multi-labels. The discovered rules from the true multi-labels were pruned by PAR with the true hierarchy, but for the rules discovered from the predicted multi-labels the extracted hierarchy was used. Next, the RLA recall and RLA precision values between these

two rule sets were calculated by means of the true hierarchy.

In the the top part of the table the discovered rules from the true multi-labels using three different interestingness measures were compared to each other. Although both rule sets extracted by using *Int* and *Conf* almost covered each other rule set, the set of rules discovered by *Int* had fewer number of rules, indicated by the RLA precision greater 1. *Jac* had few rules in total but the number of covered rules was lower.

The RLA recall from the separately predicted A to C rules was relatively low as compared with the case when they were predicted together. However RLA precision was close to 1 when they were predicted separately and was low when they were predicted together. This small increase of RLA recall indicates that the overlap between the rule sets was higher when the branches were predicted together, on the other side the large decrease of RLA precision points to a significant increase of the number of rules extracted from the predicted labels. This indicates that the predicted labels (for the "together" scenario) had multi-label combinations which did not happen in the true multi-labels, as expected. When the branches were predicted separately, the rule sets extracted were more compact but fewer rules from the true rule set were discovered, indicating that some multi-label combinations were not accurately enough predicted. Of all the measures, *Int* was the best with a higher RLA recall or at least a higher RLA precision as compared to *Conf. Jac* was not as good as *Conf* when the labels were predicted together and also in the case of true multi-labels against true multi-labels. We can conclude from the F1-measure values as well as from the RLA recall and RLA precision results that the branches had few strong correlations but also a certain amount of loose ones.

CONCLUSION

In this chapter, the extraction of concept hierarchies and finding relations between them was demonstrated in the context of a multi-label classification task. We introduced a data mining system, which performs classification and mining of generalized association rules. The proposed system was applied to two real-world datasets with the class labels of each dataset taken from two different class hierarchies. Using Pruning by Ancestral Rules, the majority of redundant rules could be removed leaving only very important rules. A new quality measure for generalized association rules was developed, which not only correlates very well with the confidence measure, but can be effectively used for pruning uninteresting rules with respect to the hierarchy. We also improved the RLA measure, relating it to recall and precision. There is still room for other improvements, for instance, by removing redundancy. For rule parents where the rule has just one child rule, i.e. $p(i) \rightarrow j$, and there is only one rule for $child(p(i)) \rightarrow j$ the $p(i) \rightarrow j$ rule can be erased. This becomes more important in deeper hierarchies. A subject of future work is to improve classification by means of discovered associations between taxonomies.

REFERENCES

Bendaoud, R., & Hacene, M. Rouane, Toussaint, Y., Delecroix, B., & Napoli, A. (2007). *Text-based ontology construction using relational concept analysis*. In International Workshop on Ontology Dynamics. Innsbruck, Austria.

Brucker, F., Benites, F., & Sapozhnikova, E. (2011). Multi-label classification and extracting predicted class hierarchies. *Pattern Recognition, 44*(3), 724–738. doi:10.1016/j.patcog.2010.09.010

Choi, N., Song, I. Y., & Han, H. (2006). A survey on ontology mapping. *SIGMOD Record, 35*(3), 34–41. doi:10.1145/1168092.1168097

Cimiano, P., Hotho, A., & Staab, S. (2005, August). Learning concept hierarchies from text corpora using formal concept analysis. *Journal of Artificial Intelligence Research, 24*, 305–339.

Doan, A., Madhavan, J., Domingos, P., & Halevy, A. (2002). Learning to map between ontologies on the semantic web. In *Proceedings of the 11th International Conference on World Wide Web* (pp. 662–673). New York, NY: ACM.

Lallich, S., Teytaud, O., & Prudhomme, E. (2007). Association rule interestingness: Measure and statistical validation. In Guillet, F., & Hamilton, H. (Eds.), *Quality measures in data mining* (*Vol. 43*, pp. 251–275). Berlin, Germany: Springer. doi:10.1007/978-3-540-44918-8_11

Maedche, A., & Staab, S. (2000). Discovering conceptual relations from text. In *Proceedings of the 14th European Conference on Artificial Intelligence (ECAI)* (pp. 321–325).

Maedche, A., & Staab, S. (2001, March). Ontology learning for the semantic web. *IEEE Intelligent Systems, 16*, 72–79. doi:10.1109/5254.920602

Majidian, A., & Martin, T. (2009). Extracting taxonomies from data - A case study using fuzzy formal concept analysis. In *WI-IAT '09: Proceedings of the 2009 IEEE/WIC/ACM International Joint Conference on Web Intelligence and Intelligent Agent Technology* (pp. 191–194). Washington, DC: IEEE Computer Society.

Martin, T., & Shen, Y. (2009, June). Fuzzy association rules in soft conceptual hierarchies. In *Fuzzy Information Processing Society, NAFIPS 2009* (p. 1 - 6).

Martin, T., Shen, Y., & Azvine, B. (2007). A mass assignment approach to granular association rules for multiple taxonomies. In *Proceedings of the Third ISWC Workshop on Uncertainty Reasoning for the Semantic Web*, Busan. *Korea & World Affairs*, (November): 12.

Martin, T. P., Shen, Y., & Azvine, B. (2008). Granular association rules for multiple taxonomies: A mass assignment approach. In *Uncertainty Reasoning for the Semantic Web I: ISWC International Workshops, URSW 2005-2007, Revised Selected and Invited Papers* (pp. 224–243). Berlin, Germany: Springer-Verlag. doi:10.1007/978-3-540-89765-1_14

Miani, R. G., Yaguinuma, C. A., Santos, M. T. P., & Biajiz, M. (2009). NARFO algorithm: Mining non-redundant and generalized association rules based on fuzzy ontologies. In Aalst, W. (Eds.), *Enterprise information systems* (*Vol. 24*, pp. 415–426). Berlin, Germany: Springer. doi:10.1007/978-3-642-01347-8_35

Omelayenko, B. (2001). Learning of ontologies for the Web: The analysis of existent approaches. In *Proceedings of the International Workshop on Web Dynamics, held in conj. with the 8th International Conference on Database Theory (ICDT'01), London, UK.*

Rajan, S., Punera, K., & Ghosh, J. (2005). A maximum likelihood framework for integrating taxonomies. In *AAAI '05: Proceedings of the 20th National Conference on Artificial Intelligence* (pp. 856–861). AAAI Press.

Srikant, R., & Agrawal, R. (1995). Mining generalized association rules. In *VLDB '95: Proceedings of the 21th International Conference on Very Large Data Bases* (pp. 407–419). San Francisco, CA: Morgan Kaufmann Publishers Inc.

Surana, A., Kiran, U., & Reddy, P. K. (2010). *Selecting a right interestingness measure for rare association rules.* In 16th International Conference on Management of Data (COMAD).

Takeda, I. R., Hideaki, T., & Shinichi, H. (2001). Rule induction for concept hierarchy alignment. In *Proceedings of the 2nd Workshop on Ontology Learning at the 17th International Joint Conference on Artificial Intelligence (IJCAI).*

Tan, P. N., Kumar, V., & Srivastava, J. (2004, June). Selecting the right objective measure for association analysis. *Information Systems, 29*, 293–313. doi:10.1016/S0306-4379(03)00072-3

Tomás, D., & Vicedo, J. L. (2007). Multiple-taxonomy question classification for category search on faceted information. In *TSD '07: Proceedings of the 10th International Conference on Text, Speech and Dialogue* (pp. 653–660). Berlin, Germany: Springer-Verlag.

Villaverde, J., Persson, A., Godoy, D., & Amandi, A. (2009, September). Supporting the discovery and labeling of non-taxonomic relationships in ontology learning. *Expert Systems with Applications, 36*, 10288–10294. doi:10.1016/j.eswa.2009.01.048

Wimalasuriya, D. C., & Dou, D. (2009). Using multiple ontologies in information extraction. In *CIKM '09: Proceeding of the 18th ACM Conference on Information and Knowledge Management* (pp. 235–244). New York, NY: ACM.

ADDITIONAL READING

Agrawal, R., Imieliński, T., & Swami, A. (1993). Mining association rules between sets of items in large databases. In *Proceedings of the 1993 ACM SIGMOD International Conference on Management of Data* (pp. 207–216). New York, NY: ACM.

Berardi, M., Lapi, M., Leo, P., & Loglisci, C. (2005). Mining generalized association rules on biomedical literature. In A. Moonis & F. Esposito, F. (Eds.), *Innovations in Applied Artificial Intelligence, Lecture Notes in Artificial Intelligence, 3353* (pp. 500–509). Springer-Verlag.

Berzal, F., Cubero, J.-C., Marin, N., Sanchez, D., Serrano, J.-M., & Vila, A. (2005). Association rule evaluation for classification purposes. In *Internacional Congreso Español de Informática (CEDI 2005)*. España.

Bodenreider, O., Aubry, M., & Burgun, A. (2005). Non-lexical approaches to identifying associative relations in the gene ontology. In *The Gene Ontology* (pp. 91–102). PBS. doi:10.1142/9789812702456_0010

Brijs, T., Vanhoof, K., & Wets, G. (2003). Defining interestingness measures for association rules. *International Journal of Information Theories and Applications, 10*(4), 370–376.

de Carvalho, V. O., Rezende, S. O., & de Castro, M. (2007). Evaluating generalized association rules through objective measures. In *AIAP '07: Proceedings of the 25th Conference on IASTED International Multi-Conference* (pp. 301–306). Anaheim, CA: ACTA Press.

Haehnel, S., Hauf, J., & Kudrass, T. (2006). *Design of a data mining framework to mine generalized association rules in a web-based GIS* (pp. 114–117). DMIN.

Harsh, K. V., Deepti, G., & Suraj, S. (2010, August). Article: Comparative investigations and performance evaluation for multiple-level association rules mining algorithm. *International Journal of Computers and Applications, 4*(10), 40–45. doi:10.5120/860-1208

Hong, T. P., Lin, K. Y., & Wang, S. L. (2003, September). Fuzzy data mining for interesting generalized association rules. *Fuzzy Sets and Systems, 138*, 255–269. doi:10.1016/S0165-0114(02)00272-5

Jalali-Heravi, M., & Zaïane, O. R. (2010). A study on interestingness measures for associative classifiers. In *Proceedings of the 2010 ACM Symposium on Applied Computing* (pp. 1039–1046). New York, NY: ACM.

Kunkle, D., Zhang, D., & Cooperman, G. (2008). Mining frequent generalized itemsets and generalized association rules without redundancy. *Journal of Computer Science and Technology, 23*, 77–102. doi:10.1007/s11390-008-9107-1

Marinica, C., & Guillet, F. (2010). Knowledge-based interactive postmining of association rules using ontologies. *IEEE Transactions on Knowledge and Data Engineering, 22*, 784–797. doi:10.1109/TKDE.2010.29

Natarajan, R., & Shekar, B. (2005). A relatedness-based data-driven approach to determination of interestingness of association rules. In *Proceedings of the 2005 ACM Symposium on Applied Computing* (pp. 551–552). New York, NY: ACM.

Pasquier, N. (2000). Mining association rules using formal concept analysis. In Stumme, G. (Ed.), *Working with Conceptual Structures. Contributions to ICCS 2000* (pp. 259–264).

Sánchez, D., & Moreno, A. (2008, March). Learning non-taxonomic relationships from web documents for domain ontology construction. *Data & Knowledge Engineering, 64*, 600–623. doi:10.1016/j.datak.2007.10.001

Sánchez Fernández, D., Berzal Galiano, F., Cubero Talavera, J. C., Serrano Chica, J. M., Marín Ruiz, N., & Vila Miranda, M. A. (2005). Association rule evaluation for classification purposes. In *Internacional Congreso Español De Informática (CEDI 2005)*. España.

Shaw, G., Xu, Y., & Geva, S. (2009). Interestingness measures for multi-level association rules. In *Proceedings of ADCS 2009*, School of Information Technologies, University of Sydney.

Shrivastava, V. K., Kumar, P., & Pardasani, K. R. (2010, February). Fp-tree and COFI based approach for mining of multiple level association rules in large databases. *International Journal of Computer Science and Information Security, 7*(2).

Sikora, M., & Gruca, A. (2010). Quality improvement of rule-based gene group descriptions using information about go terms importance occurring in premises of determined rules. *Applied Mathematics and Computer Science, 20*(3), 555–570.

Singh, L., Scheuermann, P., & Chen, B. (1997). Generating association rules from semi-structured documents using an extended concept hierarchy. In *Proceedings of the Sixth International Conference on Information and Knowledge Management* (pp. 193–200).

Stumme, G., Taouil, R., Bastide, Y., Pasquier, N., & Lakhal, L. (2001). Intelligent structuring and reducing of association rules with formal concept analysis. In Baader, F., Brewka, G., & Eiter, T. (Eds.), *KI 2001: Advances in Artificial Intelligence* (Vol. 2174, pp. 335–350). Berlin, Germany: Springer. doi:10.1007/3-540-45422-5_24

Toivonen, H., Klemettinen, M., Ronkainen, P., Hätönen, K., & Mannila, H. (1995). *Pruning and grouping discovered association rules.*

Tseng, M. C., Lin, W. Y., & Jeng, R. (2008). Updating generalized association rules with evolving taxonomies. *Applied Intelligence, 29*, 306–320. doi:10.1007/s10489-007-0096-5

Verma, H. K., Gupta, D., & Srivastava, S. (2010, August). Article: Comparative investigations and performance evaluation for multiple-level association rules mining algorithm. *International Journal of Computers and Applications, 4*(10), 40–45. doi:10.5120/860-1208

Wu, T., Chen, Y., & Han, J. (2010, November). Re-examination of interestingness measures in pattern mining: a unified framework. *Data Mining and Knowledge Discovery, 21*, 371–397. doi:10.1007/s10618-009-0161-2

Xu, Y., & Li, Y. (2007). Generating concise association rules. In *Proceedings of the Sixteenth ACM Conference on Conference on Information and Knowledge Management* (pp. 781–790). New York, NY: ACM.

Yang, L. (2005, January). Pruning and visualizing generalized association rules in parallel coordinates. *IEEE Transactions on Knowledge and Data Engineering, 17*, 60–70. doi:10.1109/TKDE.2005.14

Zhang, H., Zhao, Y., Cao, L., & Zhang, C. (2007). Class association rule mining with multiple imbalanced attributes. In *Proceedings of the 20th Australian Joint Conference on Advances in Artificial Intelligence* (pp. 827–831). Berlin, Germany: Springer-Verlag.

KEY TERMS AND DEFINITIONS

Association Rule: Connection between two items or item sets which occur frequently together in a given multiset of transactions. The connection strength is traditionally measured by confidence in order to find the most interesting associations, but it can also be assessed by any other interestingness measure.

Classification: The process of learning a function to map instances to classes, where each instance possesses a set of features. The instance

33

set is usually divided into a training set and a test set.

Cross Validation: A classification procedure with dividing the whole dataset into a number of small test sets and using the rest of the respective set to train the classifier.

Hierarchy: A tree-like structure of classes or concepts where each child class has exactly one parent class as opposite to a direct acyclic graph where a child class can have multiple parents. It is often used to ease and organize data.

Multi-Label Classification: Classification with not mutually exclusive classes when an instance can belong to multiple classes.

Non-Taxonomic Concept Relations: Associations between concepts (classes) which are not covered by a hierarchy. They can be either within a single label set or between several label sets.

Rule Pruning: Elimination of redundant association rules with the aim of selecting a small set of truly interesting rules containing useful knowledge.

ENDNOTES

[1]   http://www.wipo.int/classifications/ipc/
      en/ITsupport/Categorization/dataset/wipo-
      alpha-readme.html (retrieved August 2009)
[2]   We grouped some labels together, e.g. Comedies and Comedy.

Chapter 3
Individual Prediction Reliability Estimates in Classification and Regression

Darko Pevec
University of Ljubljana, Slovenia

Zoran Bosnić
University of Ljubljana, Slovenia

Igor Kononenko
University of Ljubljana, Slovenia

ABSTRACT

Current machine learning algorithms perform well in many problem domains, but in risk-sensitive decision making – for example, in medicine and finance – experts do not rely on common evaluation methods that provide overall assessments of models because such techniques do not provide any information about single predictions. This chapter summarizes the research areas that have motivated the development of various approaches to individual prediction reliability. Based on these motivations, the authors describe six approaches to reliability estimation: inverse transduction, local sensitivity analysis, bagging variance, local cross-validation, local error modelling, and density-based estimation. Empirical evaluation of the benchmark datasets provides promising results, especially for use with decision and regression trees. The testing results also reveal that the reliability estimators exhibit different performance levels when used with different models and in different domains. The authors show the usefulness of individual prediction reliability estimates in attempts to predict breast cancer recurrence. In this context, estimating prediction reliability for individual predictions is of crucial importance for physicians seeking to validate predictions derived using classification and regression models.

DOI: 10.4018/978-1-4666-1806-0.ch003

INTRODUCTION

In supervised learning, one of the goals is to achieve the best possible prediction accuracy with new and unknown examples. Reliability estimation is a rather contemporary field of machine learning whose origins lie in statistics (in the analysis of confidence intervals and levels of significance). Nevertheless, because current prediction systems do not provide sufficient information about single predictions, experts find it hard to trust them. Common evaluation methods used to validate classification and regression machine learning models indicate the average accuracy of the models, but in general, predictive models do not provide reliability estimates for individual predictions.

Methods of measuring the overall accuracy of a particular predictive model or of its individual predictions are founded on a quantitative description of the predictive model's properties or of the characteristics of the input space. Data noise and non-uniform distributions of examples represent a challenge for learning algorithms, yielding different levels of prediction accuracy in different parts of the problem space. Apart from the distribution of the learning examples, there are also other factors that influence the accuracy of prediction models, including generalisability, bias, resistance to noise, and avoidance of over-fitting. Because these model characteristics cannot be measured quantitatively, they cannot be used to construct quantitative measures for evaluating a model's accuracy.

The reliability estimates made in individual predictions are based on an analysis of the specific model and instance properties. In cases in which predictions may have significant consequences (e.g., in medical diagnosis, in the stock market, in navigation, and in control applications), traditional methods are insufficient because they do not validate individual predictions using more credible reliability statements. In such areas, appropriate reliability estimates may provide additional information about prediction correctness and enable users (e.g., medical doctor) to differentiate between more and less reliable predictions.

The next section summarizes the concepts from the relevant research areas that provide the motivation for developing approaches to individual prediction reliability estimation. We then describe the approaches themselves: inverse transduction and local sensitivity analysis, bagging variance, local cross-validation, local error modelling, and density estimation. An empirical evaluation and comparison of the approaches is conducted using 48 benchmark datasets. Finally, we present the results obtained by using these techniques with a hard real-world oncologic dataset and conclude.

MOTIVATIONS FROM THE FIELD OF MODEL ANALYSIS

An appropriate criterion for differentiating between various approaches is whether they target a specific predictive model or are model-independent. Many researchers are working to develop methods specific to the neural network model, but here, we focus on model-independent (i.e., "black box") approaches.

Model-independent approaches are based on exploiting general supervised learning framework parameters such as learning sets and attributes. These approaches include observing how a particular learning example locally influences a model, conducting local error modelling, and utilizing other properties of the input domain such as its density distribution. They are defined independently of any predictive model formalization. This assures greater generalisability because it offers users more freedom to choose the predictive model that suits the problem best. However, the reliability estimates based on these approaches are usually not probabilistically interpretable, meaning that they can take values from an arbitrary interval of numbers and are therefore harder to analytically evaluate.

In the following, we summarize the work in three related research fields that has motivated the development of the model-independent approaches. Fields that deal with perturbed data and the use of unlabelled examples in supervised learning are generally concerned with accuracy performance and with evaluating the whole predictive model. Both of these fields exploit variations in the original learning set to improve general model accuracy. Some of these methods also focus on weighing and analysing the role of individual examples in learning set variation. One way to further apply this approach is to use transduction and sensitivity analysis as a general framework, as indicated in the last portion of this section.

Perturbations of Learning and Test Examples

The group of approaches intended to improve the accuracy of predictive systems by perturbing learning data is general and model-independent. These approaches generate perturbations of learning data either by creating a new learning set by selecting learning examples with replacement or by assigning weights to particular examples.

One of the most well known methods, which generates multiple learning sets by sampling the original learning set with replacement, is *bagging* (Breiman, 1996). For each of the generated versions of the learning set, bagging builds a separate predictive model and uses it to calculate a prediction that represents a solution to a partial problem. The final solution is obtained by combining individual predictions into an aggregated one. Bagging has been shown to greatly reduce the variance while in most cases leaving the bias unchanged. Averaging individual predictions in aggregate therefore yields a smoothed prediction that is more stable. Thus, it is mostly effective when used in conjunction with decision and regression trees that exhibit high variance. Although this approach has proven effective, its downside is that

constructing the whole set of models requires a great deal of time and memory.

One of the latest methods involving model aggregation is *boosting* (Freund, 1997; Schapire, 1999). Its authors developed an algorithm that sequentially fits weak classifiers with different weightings of the examples in a dataset. The observations that the previous classifier poorly predicts receive greater weight in the next iteration. The final classifier is defined as a weighted average of all of the weak classifiers. The final classifier merge has proven an effective method of reducing bias and variance; it also decreases misclassification rates. Empirical evidence has shown that the base classifier can be fairly simplistic (i.e., shallow classification trees) but, when boosted, can capture complex decision boundaries. In later work, this approach was adapted and evaluated for use with regression problems (Drucker, 1997; Ridgeway, 1999). Similar approaches that involve fitting several models and merging the predictions that each model produces include *stacking* (Wolpert, 1992) and *bumping* (Tibshirani, 1999).

The *dual perturb and combine* algorithm (Geurts, 2001) is an approach that, unlike the previously described approaches, perturbs test examples. In the first stage of the algorithm, a single prediction model is generated that remains unchanged throughout the entire procedure. In the prediction stage, the attribute vector of a test example is perturbed several times using additive random noise. The predictions calculated for each of these perturbed test examples are then aggregated and averaged to obtain a more stable prediction for the original test example. Experiments on several data sets with decision trees have shown that this method yields significantly improved prediction accuracy that in some cases is comparable to the results obtained using bagging. However, unlike bagging, this approach only uses one model and delays the generation of multiple predictions until the prediction stage. Thus, this method preserves the interpretability and the computational efficiency of the original model.

Figure 1. Concept behind the expectation-maximization algorithm

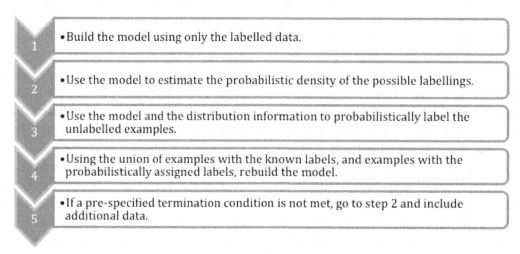

The data perturbation approach has been also used in unsupervised learning to obtain clustering reliability estimates and assess clustering stability (Kerr, 2000). The authors propose using bootstrapping to generate a large number of bootstrapped clusters. By analysing the frequency with which a particular example is included in each of these simulated clusters, the authors measure the reliability of the initial cluster. Such defined reliability estimates may also help to correct the clustering outcome for a given example (i.e., by assigning the example to another cluster if that example belonged to that cluster in the majority of the simulated cases).

All of the mentioned approaches iteratively modify the learning set and have been proven to improve general hypothesis accuracy scores. These results suggest that including or removing individual learning examples, while maintaining the accuracy of the final model, may also be utilized as an indicator of model stability for that individual example.

Use of Unlabelled Data in Supervised Learning

The core idea behind learning with unlabelled data is using unlabelled examples together with labelled

learning examples can significantly improve the accuracy of the predictive model (Seeger, 2000). Because the true labels of unlabelled examples are unknown, employing such examples does not directly contribute to our knowledge about the relationship between particular attributes and the dependent (predicted) value. Instead, using such examples in the learning process contributes supplemental information about the true example distribution in the problem space, which makes the outcome of the learning process more accurate.

Before the models can be improved by combining unlabelled and labelled examples, the unlabelled examples must be assigned dependent variable values. The well-known EM (Expectation - Maximization) algorithm (Dempster, 1977; Ghahramani, 1994) provides an approach to this task that can be summarized as shown in Figure 1.

Such approaches have been shown to provide added value in environments in which many unlabelled examples is available but it is impossible or too costly to label all of them and use them in a classical supervised learning scenario. This may occur with problems in medical domains that handle large amounts of data for undiagnosed patients but have no experts to systematically label them. It may also occur with image recognition problems, for which it may be very time consuming to process the graphical data. Adaptation of classifiers in the field of image classification (Baluja, 1998) has shown that this approach yields greater classification accuracy than does the traditional approach.

The following research is more focused on the use of unlabelled examples in the context of co-training, i.e., cases in which the description of each learning example can be partitioned into two independent and mutually redundant parts (Blum, 1998; Mitchell, 1999). Based on the assumption that each of the views is independently sufficient to solve the classification problem by itself, two separate learning sets are formed that include the same learning examples but are described with different attribute sets. By building classifiers for each of these two problems, one can use a classifier that was based on one view to classify unlabelled data presented using the other view. The resulting newly labelled examples can afterwards be included in the original learning set.

Similar approaches are also used in other fields. De Sa (1993) addresses the problem of learning from unlabelled data without any experience with previously labelled examples. The author proposes a form of *self-supervised* learning that partitions a problem into two independent problems as in (Blum, 1998) and processes it using two neural networks for each of the separated data sets. The outputs of both networks are then joined using the common output layer of neurons. The goal of this self-supervised learning process is to minimize the differences between the outputs of the two networks, making both networks classify two views of the same examples into the same two implicit classes. The proposed method does not perform as well as the standard supervised learning approaches, but nevertheless, it successfully and innovatively solves the problem of learning from completely unlabelled data.

The results attained using unlabelled data in supervised learning indicate that additional learning examples generated from the same original probabilistic distribution can be beneficially utilized to improve predictor accuracy. As seen from the variety of approaches developed in this field, the procedures used to incorporate additional learning examples and build new predictive models are performed in turn and in many iterations. This allows the predictive model to gradually increase in accuracy and makes it possible to more accurately label unlabelled examples that are yet to be included in later iterations. Because the model changes with each included example, it is important to evaluate the influence of the inclusion of a particular new example in the learning set. By observing the consequential changes in the predictive model, we can make inferences about the model's stability related to that individual example.

Transduction and Sensitivity Analysis

In past research, the notion of reliability estimation has most frequently appeared in conjunction with the notion of *transduction* or *transductive reasoning*. These terms may have different meanings in different environments, but essentially, transduction is an inference principle that reasons from particular to particular (Vapnik, 1995), unlike inductive learning, which aims to infer a general rule from particular data. Transductive inference therefore aims to make predictions from unlabelled examples without constructing a general predictive model. This definition closely relates transductive reasoning to instance-based learning and case-based reasoning (one of the most well known algorithms in this area is the k-nearest neighbours algorithm). However, the transductive methods constitute a wide family of approaches; the reasoning used can also be based on other criteria (e.g., the distribution of examples in the input space) and not only using the distance metrics and labels of the nearest neighbours. Transductive methods may also use only selected examples of interest and not necessarily the whole input space, which enables them to make other inferences apart from predicting labels. In the context of reliability estimation, such methods represent the basis for many approaches (Gammerman, 1998; Saunders, 1999; Li, 2005). Transductive reasoning is often used to construct reliability estimates that measure how the newly labelled example fits into the distribution of previously seen examples. The notion of transduction is also used in cases in which a hypothesis is needed only for examples of interest or for some other use apart from prediction. This might include the estimation of prediction reliability as conducted by Kukar (2002) and Bosnić (2003).

One possible way to analyse local particularities in data and predictive model properties is to conduct a *sensitivity analysis*. Sensitivity analyses are used to study the influence of model parameters and properties on its structure and outputs (Breierova, 1996). They are usually performed as a series of experiments in which the user systematically changes the input parameters and observes the dynamics of the changes in outputs. To use this technique, no knowledge of the model's mathematical properties is required. Hence, the model is basically used as a parameter of the method, presenting a black box with inputs and outputs (Kleijnen, 2001), which are the only parameters of interest. This approach has been most widely used in the areas of statistics, mathematical programming (Saltelli, 2003) and the natural sciences (Saltelli, 2005). The usage of sensitivity analyses with artificial neural networks (Hashem, sensitivity) and with Bayesian networks (Kjaerullf, 2000) has shown the potential applications of this approach to supervised learning algorithms.

Theoretical stability analyses of learning algorithms have been a focus of Bousquet and Elisseeff (2002). They defined notions of stability for learning algorithms and showed how to derive generalization error bounds based on empirical error and leave-one-out error. They also introduced the concept of β-stable learners, in which the expected loss function of the learned solution does not change more than β with small changes

in the training set. Bousquet and Elisseeff (2000) and Bousquet and Pontil (2002) applied these ideas to several learning models and showed how to obtain bounds on their generalization performance.

Similarly, Kearns and Ron (1997) define *hypothesis stability* as measuring how much the function that is learned by the algorithm will change when one point in the training set is removed. All mentioned studies focus on the dependence of error-bounds based on either the VC (Vapnik-Chervonenkis) theory (Vapnik, 1995) or the way the learning algorithm searches the space.

By proving the theoretical usefulness of the notion of *stability*, these approaches motivated empirical estimations of individual prediction reliability based on the local stability of the model. For use in machine learning, a framework has been proposed (Bosnić, 2007) for changing the input (i.e., the learning set) of the learning algorithm in a controlled way and observing the changes in the output (i.e., predictions) of the learning algorithm. This framework defines a systematic approach to modifying the learning set that induces a change in the input of the learning algorithm. If this change is small, then the change in the output prediction for the modified example is also expected to be small. Because the opposite scenario would indicate instability in the generated model, the magnitude of the output change may therefore be used as a measure of model instability for a modified example. The same reasoning is also used in other model-independent approaches in the field of individual prediction reliability estimation.

RELIABILITY ESTIMATION

Because the model-independent approaches are general, they cannot make use of parameters specific to a given predictive model. Rather, they focus on influencing the parameters available in the standard supervised learning framework (e.g., the learning set and attributes). Reliability estimators based on these approaches are defined as metrics over the observed learning parameters. Because reliability is based on a heuristic interpretation of the available data, these metrics can take values from an arbitrary interval of numbers. As such, those values have no probabilistic interpretation. In the regression case, the estimates take on an arbitrary real number, but we define the estimates such that 0 represents the most reliable prediction and all other values represent a degree of unreliability. In the classification case, it is possible to normalize the estimates so that 0 represents the most reliable prediction and 1 the most unreliable. We expect the reliability estimators to give insight into the prediction error, and we expect to find a positive correlation between the two.

In this section, we present methods inspired by and/or based on the topics covered in the previous section. The first two algorithms, based on inverse transduction and local sensitivity analysis, are based on the same concept of transduction, although the first can be used only with classification and the second only with regression models. Other algorithms are sufficiently general to require only minor adaptations, to be converted for use from regression to classification models, or vice-versa.

Inverse Transduction and Local Sensitivity Analysis

As previously stated, transduction is reasoning from particular to particular. This includes reasoning from the learning data to the dependent variable of a new instance. Transduction can be also used in the reverse direction to observe the model's behaviour when inserting modified learning instances for the unseen and unlabelled example (Kukar, 2001).

Let x represent the example's attribute vector (the domain) and y its known class (the co-domain). Let us denote the learning example with known label y as (x, y); $(x, \_)$ denotes the unseen and unlabelled example whose prediction reliability we wish to estimate. This prediction is computed

using a model built on the initial learning set (i.e., the initial prediction computed by the initial model), and we denote this prediction of the true label y by K.

Inverse transduction works in the classification setting when the classifier returns a class probability distribution. It is then possible to rank the model predictions and create the new modified learning instance in three distinct ways:

- Insert $(x, \_)$ into the learning set and label it the same class as the initial model predicts. The model should only reinforce its probability statement regarding the predicted class.

- Insert $(x, \_)$ into the learning set but label it with the first "losing" class, the second-ranked class in the initial model prediction. It is of interest how the model prediction will change with this slight adjustment.

- Insert $(x, \_)$ into the learning set and label it in the last-ranked class according to the initial model prediction. It should then be observed how the model prediction changes when the new example is most changed.

With the modified instance in the learning set, the model is rebuilt. The distance between the initial probability vector and the rebuilt model forms the reliability estimate. The three reliability estimators for the classification models are labelled $TRANS_{first}$, $TRANS_{second}$ and $TRANS_{last}$.

In the regression case, x still represents the example's attribute vector, but the co-domain is now continuous. Let us again denote the learning example with a known/assigned label y with (x, y) and let $(x, \_)$ represent the unseen and unlabelled example for which we wish to estimate the reliability of the prediction K. Having assigned the label $K + \delta$ (δ denotes some small additive change to K, which serves as an approximate true value) to the unlabelled example $(x, \_)$, we insert the newly generated example $(x, K + \delta)$ into the learning set and re-build the predictive model. We define

δ relative to the upper and lower bounds of the known label values (y_{max} and y_{min}, respectively). In particular, we define $\delta = \varepsilon(y_{max} - y_{min})$ where ε serves as a factor expressing the interval proportion. In this way, we obtain a sensitivity model that computes a sensitivity prediction K_ε for the example (x, _) and parameter ε.

By repeatedly modifying the learning set and obtaining sensitivity predictions from the acquired sensitivity models, we combine them into reliability estimates. Furthermore, by selecting different $\varepsilon \in \{\varepsilon_1, \varepsilon_2, ..., \varepsilon_m\}$, we iteratively obtain a set of sensitivity predictions

$$K_{\varepsilon_1}, \ K_{-\varepsilon_1}, \ K_{\varepsilon_2}, \ K_{-\varepsilon_2}, ..., \ K_{\varepsilon_m}, \ K_{-\varepsilon_m}.$$

Using these sensitivity predictions, we compute the differences $K_\varepsilon - K$, which are then combined into different reliability measures that indicate the stability of the model. The selected values of parameter ε influence the label and therefore indirectly define the magnitude of the induced change in the initial learning set. To widen the observation window in the local problem space and make the measures robust to local anomalies, the reliability measures use predictions from the sensitivity models that are obtained and averaged across different values of ε. The number of used ε values therefore represents a trade-off between gaining more stable reliability estimates and total computational time. Because we assume that the zero-difference between the predictions represents the maximum reliability, we also define the reliability measures so that value 0 indicates the most reliable prediction. In the experiments, the set of ε was {0.01, 0.1, 0.5, 1.0, 2.0}. For more details, refer to (Bosnić, 2007).

Let us assume that we have a set of non-negative ε values $E = \{\varepsilon_1, \varepsilon_2, ..., \varepsilon_{|E|}\}$. We define the estimates as follows:

- Estimate *SAvar* (Sensitivity Analysis local variance):

$$SAvar = \frac{\sum_{\varepsilon \in E}(K_\varepsilon - K_{-\varepsilon})}{|E|} \tag{1}$$

- In the case of reliable predictions, we expect that the change in the sensitivity model for K_ε and $K_{-\varepsilon}$ will be minimal (0 for the most reliable predictions). We define the reliability measure *SAvar* using the symmetric sensitivity predictions K_ε and $K_{-\varepsilon}$ to capture the model instabilities using the positive and negative change δ in the initial prediction K. The measure takes the average of the differences across all values of ε. Because the *SAvar* estimate represents the width of the interval between sensitivity predictions (defined using positive and negative values of a particular δ), it indicates the local variance.

- Estimate *SAbias* (Sensitivity Analysis local bias):

$$SAbias = \frac{\sum_{\varepsilon \in E}(K_\varepsilon - K) + (K_{-\varepsilon} - K)}{2|E|} \tag{2}$$

- Unlike *SAvar*, *SAbias* measures the difference between the predictions of the initial and sensitivity models. The estimate averages $K_\varepsilon - K$ and $K_{-\varepsilon} - K$, and therefore measures the average change in the prediction using positive and negative δ. Averaging across all ε parameters also stabilizes the defined estimate. *SAbias* estimates the skew (the asymmetry between the left and right subintervals) and therefore indicates local bias. It is noteworthy that *SAbias* can take either positive or values. Its sign carries information about the direction in which the predictor is less stable. In the following we refer to the signed and absolute value versions of the estimate as *SAbias-s* and *SAbias-a*, respectively.

The estimates *SAvar* and *SAbias* are very similar to the symmetrised form of the formula for computing the numerical derivative. The function derivative – i.e., the slope of a function – is an indicator of function sensitivity at the given point, which is consistent with our definition of reliability estimates.

Bagging Variance

The variance of predictions in bagged aggregates was first used to indirectly estimate the reliability of aggregated prediction with artificial neural networks. Because an arbitrary model can be used with the bagging technique, the technique was generalized and employed as a reliability estimate for use with other regression models (Bosnić, 2008). In related studies, the variance of predictions in the bagged aggregate of artificial neural networks has already been used to indirectly estimate the reliability of aggregated predictions (Heskes, 1997; Carney, 1999). The proposed reliability estimate is generalized for use with other models.

Again, let K be the predictor's prediction for a given unlabelled example $(x, \_)$. Given a bagged aggregate of m predictive models where each of the models yields a prediction B_k, $k = 1 \ldots m$, the reliability estimator *BAGV* is defined as the variance in the bagged predictions:

$$BAGV = \frac{1}{m} \sum_{k=1}^{m} \left(B_k - K \right)^2 . \qquad (3)$$

The algorithm was implemented for use with a bagged aggregate of 50 predictive models.

Local Cross-Validation

If applied to a local segment of the input space, cross-validation can be used to estimate local prediction error and therefore the reliability of the predictions for local examples. The *LCV* (local cross-validation) reliability estimate is computed using the local leave-one-out (LOO) procedure. Suppose that we are given an unlabelled example for which we wish to compute the prediction and the *LCV* estimate. Focusing on the subspace defined by k nearest neighbours (parameter k is selected in advance), we then generate k local models, each of them excluding one of the k nearest neighbours. Using the newly generated models, we compute the leave-one-out predictions K_i, $i = 1 \ldots k$, for each of the k nearest neighbours. Because the labels of these nearest neighbours are known, we mark them as C_i, $i = 1 \ldots k$, and we are then able to calculate the absolute local leave-one-out prediction error as the average of the nearest neighbours' local errors:

$$LCV = \frac{1}{k} \sum_{i} \left| C_i - K_i \right| . \qquad (4)$$

The procedure can be summarized using the following pseudo-code algorithm:

1. Define the set of k nearest neighbours $N = \{(x_1, C_1), \ldots, (x_k, C_k)\}$
2. For each (x_i, C_i) in N,
   a. generate model M_i on $N(x_i, C_i)$
   b. for (x_i, C_i), compute LOO prediction K_i with model M_i

   for (x_i, C_i), compute LOO error $e_i = |C_i - K_i|$

$$LCV = \frac{1}{k} \sum_{i} e_i \qquad (5)$$

In experimental work, we implemented the algorithm to be adaptive in size of the neighbourhood with respect to the number of examples in the learning set. The parameter k was designated as one tenth the size of the learning set.

Local Error Modelling

This approach to local estimations of prediction reliability is based on the nearest neighbours' labels. Given a set of k nearest neighbours where C_i is the true label of the i-th nearest neighbour, the estimate CNK ($N_{eighbours}$ - K) for the unlabelled example is defined as the difference between the average label of the k nearest neighbours and the example prediction K:

$$CNK = \frac{\sum_i C_i}{k} - K \ . \qquad (6)$$

CNK is obviously not a suitable reliability estimate for the *k*-nearest neighbours algorithm because they both work based on the same principle. In our experiments, we used 5 nearest neighbours to compute *CNK*. In regression tests, *CNK-a* denotes the absolute value of the estimate, whereas *CNK-s* denotes the signed value.

Density Based Estimation

This approach assumes that the error is lower for predictions made, for example, in denser problem subspaces (local parts of the input space with a higher number of learning examples), and higher for predictions made in sparser subspaces (local parts of the input space with fewer learning examples). A typical use of this approach involves decision and regression trees, where we trust each prediction with respect to the proportion of learning examples that fall in the same leaf of a tree as the predicted example. However, although this approach considers the quantity of available information, it also presents a disadvantage: it does not consider the labels of the learning example. This causes the method to perform poorly with noisy data and in cases in which the examples are not clearly separable.

The reliability estimator *DENS* is a value of the estimated probability density function for a given unlabelled example. To estimate the density, Parzen windows are used, taking the Gaussian kernel. The problem of computing the multidimensional Gaussian kernel was reduced to the task of computing the two-dimensional kernel using a distance function applied to pairs of example vectors. Given the learning set $L=\{(x_1,y_1), \ldots, (x_n, y_n)\}$, the density estimate for unlabelled example $(x, \_)$ is defined as

$$p(x) = \frac{1}{n} \sum_{l \in L} \kappa(x, l) \ , \qquad (7)$$

where κ denotes a kernel function (in our case Gaussian). Therefore the reliability estimate is given by

$$DENS = \max_{l \in L}\left(p(l)\right) - p(x) \ . \qquad (8)$$

EMPIRICAL EVALUATION OF ESTIMATORS

In this section we focus on evaluating the estimators. We sum up the empirical evaluations and compare the developed reliability estimators. The main question is whether the reliability estimates can tell us something about the prediction error associated with new and unseen individual examples. We test this relationship using correlation coefficients. There were 20 benchmark data sets used for the classification tests and 28 data sets used for the regression problems. Table 1 provides a brief description of the datasets used in the classification tests and Table 2 of those used in the regression datasets.

The evaluation was conducted on domains gathered from the UCI Machine Learning Repository (Asuncion & Newman, 2007) and from the StatLib DataSets Archive (Department of Statistics at Carnegie Mellon University, 2005).

Table 1. Basic description of the classification datasets

Data set	no. of examples	no. of discr. attr.	no. of cont. attr.	no. of classes
housevotes	435	1	14	2
wine	178	6	16	3
parkinsons	195	8	17	2
zoo	101	0	4	7
tictactoe	958	0	14	2
postoperative	90	0	8	3
monks	432	1	8	2
iris	150	2	4	3
glass	214	0	6	6
hungarian	294	0	2	2
ecoli	336	3	6	8
heart	270	1	1	2
haberman	306	2	5	2
flag	194	2	2	10
wdbc	569	0	3	2
bcw	699	7	6	2
sonar	208	7	2	2
soybean	47	1	1	4
hepatitis	155	4	7	2
lungcancer	32	56	0	3

To conduct performance evaluations for different models, we tested the estimators with eight regression and seven classification models, all using statistical package R. Testing was performed using the leave-one-out cross-validation procedure. For each learning example that was left out of the iteration, the prediction and all of the reliability estimates were computed. Once we had completed all iterations, the leave-one-out errors and estimates were computed for all available examples. The performance of the reliability estimates in the classification tests was measured by computing the Spearman's rank correlation coefficient of the reliability estimates and prediction errors. In regression tests, the Pearson correlation coefficient of the reliability estimate and the prediction error is the appropriate statistic.

The significance of the correlation coefficients was then statistically evaluated using a t-test.

The key properties of the used models are:

- **Decision trees (DT):** Trees (Breiman et al., 1984) with the *gini* index as the splitting criterion
- **Regression trees (RT):** Trees (Breiman et al., 1984) with the mean squared error used as the splitting criterion; the values in the leaves represent the average label of the corresponding training examples
- **Linear regression (LR):** Linear regression with no explicit parameters
- **Neural networks (NN):** Three-layered perceptron (Rumelhart et al., 1986) with 5 hidden neurons, an activation function

Table 2. Basic description of the regression datasets

Data set	no. of examples	no. of discr. attr.	no. of cont. attr.
autoprice	159	1	14
auto93	93	6	16
autohorse	203	8	17
baskball	96	0	4
bodyfat	252	0	14
brainsize	20	0	8
breasttumor	286	1	8
cloud	108	2	4
cpu	209	0	6
diabetes	43	0	2
echomonths	130	3	6
elusage	55	1	1
fishcatch	158	2	5
fruitfly	125	2	2
grv	123	0	3
hungarian	294	7	6
lowbwt	189	7	2
mbagrade	61	1	1
pharynx	195	4	7
pollution	60	0	15
pwlinear	200	0	10
pyrim	74	0	27
servo	167	2	2
sleep	58	0	7
transplant	131	0	2
triazines	186	0	60
tumor	86	0	4
wpbc	198	0	32

tanh, and a back-propagation learning algorithm using adaptive gradient descent

- **Bagging (BAG):** Bagging (Breiman, 1996) with 50 classification and regression trees
- **Support vector machines (SVM):** Classification and regression SVM (Vapnik, 1995; Smola & Schölkopf, 1998) implemented in the LIBSVM library (Christianini & Shawe-Taylor, 2000; Chang & Lin, 2001); we use the third-degree RBF kernel and a precision parameter of ε=0.1
- ***k*-nearest neighbours (KNN):** Use of the *k*-nearest neighbours classification algorithm with the Minkowski distance; the classification is made using the maximum of the summed kernel densities, and ordinal and continuous variables can be predicted

Table 3. Percentage of classification experiments exhibiting significant positive/negative correlation

method	TRANSfirst +/–	TRANSsecond +/–	TRANSlast +/–	BAGV +/–	LCV +/–	CNK +/–	DENS +/–
DT	35/0	43/8	47/3	85/5	75/4	72/6	15/15
NN	38/1	30/9	26/14	65/0	69/0	72/0	20/10
BAG	75/0	13/31	12/46	75/0	75/2	61/0	15/25
SVM	38/31	35/28	30/25	40/40	62/3	64/3	15/10
KNN	75/5	40/10	30/34	75/0	83/1	9/1	10/15
RF	77/0	13/45	13/41	65/0	64/4	55/2	10/25
NB	38/0	22/9	18/6	65/0	68/2	55/7	10/25
average	54/5	28/20	25/24	67/6	71/2	55/3	14/18

- **Locally weighted regression (LWR):** Local regression with Gaussian kernel for weighting examples by their distance
- **Random forests (RF):** Random forests (Breiman, 2001) with 100 trees
- **Naive Bayes (NB):** Standard use o of the classifier from the *e1071* library.
- **Generalized additive model (GAM):** Linear model (Wood, 2006; Hastie & Tibshirani, 1990) with no special parameters.

Based on the assumptions and the definitions of the estimates, the estimates are expected to positively correlate with the prediction error. This means that their higher absolute values represent less reliable predictions and their lower absolute values represent more reliable predictions; the lowest absolute value, 0, represents the reliability of the most reliable prediction.

Results

We now present the results of the testing procedure described in the previous section. After all reliability estimates and prediction errors were calculated, the correlation coefficients were calculated for the reliability estimates and prediction errors. The correlation coefficients were further tested for significance using the t-test. Table 3 presents the percentage of domains with a significant positive/negative correlation between the reliability estimates made for classification prediction purposes and the degree of prediction error. Table 4 presents the results of the same procedure conducted for regression tests. The last lines in Table 3 and Table 4 present the results averaged across all testing models.

The detailed results presented in Table 3 indicate that the performance of the *BAGV* estimates with the decision trees and the *LCV* estimates with the *k*-nearest neighbours stand out the most. The two sets of estimates are significantly positively correlated with the prediction error in 85% and 83% of the experiments but negatively correlated with the prediction error in 5% and 1% of experiments. The estimator *CNK* produced the second-best estimates; they were positively correlated with the prediction error in 55% to 72% of the classification test results, with negative correlation in up to 7% of cases. The exception is the KNN model, in which the estimates are not significantly different from the predictions. The estimates from $TRANS_{first}$ were almost as high quality as those of *CNK* and were better than those of *BAGV* in combination with the RF model.

Of the detailed regression test results (Table 4), those for the estimate *CNK-s* with the regression trees stands out the most. The estimate was significantly positively correlated with the pre-

Table 4. Percentage of regression experiments exhibiting significant positive/negative correlation

method	SAvar +/−	SAbias-s +/−	SAbias-a +/−	BAGV +/−	LCV +/−	CNK-s +/−	CNK-a +/−	DENS +/−
RT	46/0	82/0	50/0	64/0	36/0	86/0	68/0	36/4
LR	54/0	7/0	7/4	54/0	32/0	50/0	57/0	32/4
NN	39/4	18/4	29/4	50/0	36/0	36/4	39/4	25/4
BAG	46/4	21/0	11/0	57/0	50/0	25/0	46/0	36/7
SVM	46/4	36/7	25/0	46/0	61/0	29/11	36/0	39/4
LWR	39/7	4/7	11/7	46/0	46/0	25/11	32/0	43/7
RF	25/7	14/0	11/0	57/0	61/0	11/25	46/4	32/11
GAM	54/0	7/0	7/4	50/0	32/0	50/0	57/0	32/4
average	44/3	24/2	19/2	53/0	44/0	39/6	48/1	34/6

diction error in 86% of experiments and was not negatively correlated with the prediction error in any experiment. The estimate *SAbias*-s achieved similar performance; it was positively correlated with the prediction error in 82% of tests with the regression trees and negatively in 0% of tests. The *CNK-a* estimate achieved better performance with linear models (linear regression and generalized additive models) than did the *BAGV* estimate, which was the estimate with the highest number of significant positive correlations on average (53%).

The results are consistent with our expectation that the reliability estimates should be positively correlated with the prediction error. We can see in Tables 2 and 3 that the number of positive (desired) correlations dominates the number of negative (non-desired) correlations in all model/reliability estimate pairs. The only exception is the *DENS* estimates, with which we did not get separable results in the classification experiments. We can also see that the best results were achieved using *LCV, BAGV, CNK* and *TRANSfirst* in classification tests and *BAGV, CNK-a, LCV* and *SAvar* in regression tests (in decreasing order with respect to the percentage of significant positive correlations). Figure 2 and Figure 3 present these results graphically, showing the average performance of the reliability estimates ranked in decreasing

order with respect to the percentage of positive correlations.

The results indicate that the estimators *TRANSfirst, SAbias, CNK, BAGV* and *LCV* have good potential estimating prediction reliability. However, the results also show that these estimates perform differently with different classification and regression models. With DT and RT, the estimators exhibited the most consistent performance.

APPLICATION ON A MEDICAL DOMAIN

To test the usefulness of the reliability estimators, we applied them to a challenging medical problem for which the Institute of Oncology Ljubljana provided the initial dataset. The data consist of 1035 entries from breast cancer patients who had surgical treatment. Each patient entry includes data regarding a set of standard prognostic factors for breast cancer recurrence: 22 medical features recorded at the time of surgery and 10 features recorded during the patient's follow-up examination. The latter indicate whether the patient experienced a recurrence of breast cancer. If so, information is also included on when the recurrence happened. Alternately, if there was

Figure 2. Ranking of reliability estimators by the average percent of significant positive and negative correlation with the prediction error in classification experiments

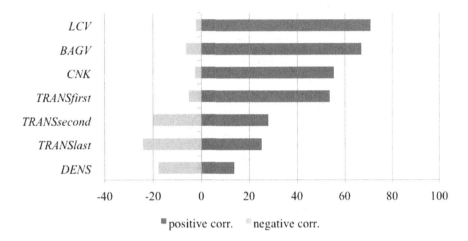

Figure 3. Ranking of reliability estimators by the average percent of significant positive and negative correlation with the prediction error in regression experiments

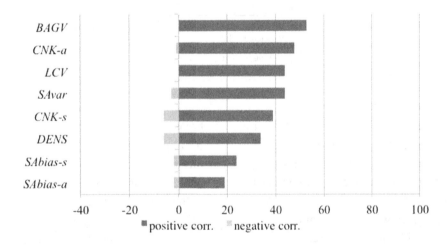

no recurrence, the follow-up duration and last recorded state of the patient are indicated.

Some of the 22 factors for which data are recorded during surgery are redundant, and not all are considered relevant for breast cancer recurrence. Furthermore, for several features, both numerical and discretised data were recorded. The oncologists conducted the discretisation based on how they use such information in their everyday medical practice. A preliminary analysis has shown that there is no significant difference between the degrees of prediction power when using numerical versions versus discretised ones. Hence, the numerical versions were removed. This cleaned dataset is named *oncologyBC*, has 13 features and is described in Table 5. Because we are interested in breast cancer recurrence, the follow-up features have been reduced to two relevant features. The first feature is binary and indicates whether a recurrence has occurred within 10 years of the

Table 5. Description of the features representing the oncologyBC dataset

Feature name	Feature description
menop	Menopausal status binary
stage	Tumor stage 1-4: ordered levels
grade	Tumor grade 1-3: ordered levels, 4: not applicable, 9: not determined
PgR	Level of progesterone receptors 0-1: ordered values, 9: unknown
invasive	Invasiveness of the tumor 0-4: ordered values
nLymph	Number of involved lymph nodes 0-3: ordered values
famHist	Medical history 0-5: categorical values, 9: not determined
LVI	Lymphatic or vascular invasion binary
ER	Level of estrogen receptors in tumor 1-4: ordered values, 9: not determined
maxNode	Diameter of the largest removed lymph node 1-3: ordered values
posRatio	Ratio between involved and total lymph nodes removed 1-4: ordered values
age	Patient age group 1-5: ordered values

surgery. Together with the features recorded at the time of surgery, this forms the classification dataset *oncologyBC10*. The second relevant follow-up feature is numerical and indicates the time of recurrence if the cancer recurred or the time of the last follow-up if the cancer did not recur. Together with the features recorded at the time of surgery, this forms the regression dataset *oncologyBCR*. Patients with a value larger than 10 years are considered to have experienced no recurrence. To accurately determine that there was no recurrence within 10 years of the surgery, the patient should have been observed for at least 10 years. 154 patients that did not have a recurrence but were observed for less than 10 years were removed from *oncologyBC10* and *oncologyBCR*.

The analysis has shown that this is a difficult prediction problem because the possibility of breast cancer recurrence is continuously present for almost 20 years after surgical treatment. Furthermore, the data present two prediction problems: a binary classification problem associated with the question of whether the condition will recur at all and a regression problem associated with the issue of predicting the time of recurrence.

The empirical analysis of the reliability estimates in previous studies showed that the correlation between the reliability estimates and the prediction error depends on the model used and on the particular problem domain. Further analysis showed that different numbers of estimates are significantly correlated with the prediction error in each of the testing domains, which enables us to rank the domains according to their difficulty. Here, "difficult" denotes those domains in which none or only a few sets of reliability estimates are

Table 6. Leave-one-out accuracy achieved with the oncologyBC10train dataset

model	DT	NN	BAG	SVM	KNN	RF	NB
LOO accuracy	73.03%	38.52%	69.96%	65.49%	66.67%	71.02%	72.44%

Table 7. Separability of correctly classified and misclassified learning examples. Checkmarks represent statistically significant separability and positive correlation, whereas minuses indicate significant separability but negative correlation. Insignificant results are left blank.

method\model	DT	NN	BAG	SVM	KNN	RF	NB
TRANSfirst							
TRANSsecond							
TRANSlast							
BAGV	✓	–	✓	✓	✓	✓	✓
LCV		–					
CNK		✓					
DENS		–					

Table 8. Achieved RMSE on the oncologyBCRtrain dataset

model	BAG	GAM	RF	LR	SVM	RT	LWR	NN
RMSE	0.790	0.791	0.801	0.806	0.838	0.852	0.862	0.955

positively correlated with the prediction error. To evaluate the reliability estimation difficulty for the oncology problem, we tested the performance of the reliability estimators in the same manner as in the previous section.

Table 6 presents the results obtained by testing different predictive models with the classification problem. The achieved LOO accuracy indicates that we should use models DT, NB or RF. We then computed the reliability estimates for all models and searched for statistically separable sets of estimates with α=0.05. The final results are presented in Table 7.

The table shows that *BAGV* produced separable estimates for all models except the NN model. For this model, only estimator *CNK* produced estimates that separated the learning in-

stances. With the NN model and estimators *BAGV, LCV* and *DENS*, the calculated correlation was significant but negative due to the poor accuracy of the prediction model (38.52%). The results show that the domain can be considered very hard.

The analysis was also conducted for the regression set *oncologyBCR* (to predict the mean recurrence time). Table 8 presents the ranking of the regression models in decreasing order of their performance, using ten-fold cross-validation. The table shows the relative mean squared error (RMSE) for each model.

For the regression test, the reliability estimates and prediction errors were computed using the leave-one-out procedure for all learning examples. The BAG model was employed for this purpose. Afterwards, the Pearson correlation coefficients

Table 9. Ranked correlation coefficients of the reliability estimates and the prediction errors for the BAG model. The significant coefficients (α=0.05) are presented in bold.

	SAvar	*BAGV*	*DENS*	*SAbias-s*	*CNK-s*	*CNK-a*	*SAbias-a*	*LCV*
corr. coef.	**0.274**	**0.274**	**-0.155**	**0.076**	0.036	0.035	0.035	0.030

were computed. The computed coefficients are shown in Table 9. The table shows the ranking of correlation coefficients together with their statistical significance. It suggests that *SAvar* or *BAGV* could be used.

Performance was then measured using the test data set. There were two sets of positively correlated estimates, those of *SAvar* and *BAGV*. Both are from the sub-set of estimators that were successful with the learning examples. The evaluation of the results achieved for the test examples revealed that both sets are still useful; the *SAvar* correlation coefficient was 0.234, and that of *BAGV* was 0.226.

By implementing the prediction system with the reliability estimator *SAvar* and comparing its predictions to those of experts, we concluded that the former were significantly correlated with the latter. Additionally, the reliability estimates provided the experts with validation information regarding the accuracy of the predictions. This was not possible before because the experts' subjective reliability measures were not significantly correlated with their prediction errors.

FUTURE RESEARCH DIRECTIONS

Further efforts were made to improve the performance of the reliability estimates. Automatic selection of the appropriate regression estimator was considered using meta-learning and internal cross validation. Mixed results were obtained by searching for the optimal combination of estimators. Additional research could be conducted in the emerging fields of data streams and on-line learning, in which the estimates could guide continuous learning. Further applications for these methods could be found in the fields of multi-label and multi-target learning. We have covered only point-wise estimation and not interval prediction; we believe that there remains much to be done in that area.

The following open questions remain:

- Is it possible to define reference estimates, with which it would be more natural to compare results across different models and datasets?
- How can the accuracy of the reliability estimates be further improved?
- How can the most appropriate estimator for a given data set be efficiently selected?

CONCLUSION

The chapter first summarizes the concepts that provide the motivation for developing approaches to individual prediction reliability. We covered why we seek model-independent approaches, the use of perturbations of learning and test examples, the use of unlabelled data and the concepts of transduction and sensitivity analysis. Model-independent approaches are defined independently of the predictive model formalizations, which ensures greater generality because it offers users more freedom in choosing the predictive model that suits the problem best. Approaches that aim to improve the accuracy of predictive systems via perturbations of learning and test examples are sufficiently general to be model-independent. The approaches that involve perturbing the test examples do so by modifying attribute vectors with the aim of estimating or improving accuracy for a particular test example.

The idea behind approaches that use unlabelled data is that the additional use of unlabelled examples together with the labelled learning examples can significantly improve the accuracy of the predictive model. Using such examples in the learning process contributes supplemental information about the true example distribution in the problem space, which should facilitate a more accurate learning process. Transduction and sensitivity analysis are foundational to the reliability estimators based on inverse transduction ($TRANS_{first}$, $TRANS_{second}$, $TRANS_{last}$) and on local sensitivity analysis ($SAvar$, $SAbias$).. Estimators based on bagging variance ($BAGV$), local cross-validation (LCV), local error modelling (CNK) and density-based estimation ($DENS$) were also covered.

The reliability estimates were empirically evaluated first on 48 benchmark datasets and then on a real-world hard dataset. The testing was performed using the leave-one-out cross-validation procedure. The performance of the reliability estimates was measured by computing the correlation coefficients of the reliability estimates and the predictions. The significance of the correlation coefficients was then statistically evaluated using a t-test. The statistical evaluation indicates promising results, especially for the use of estimators $BAGV$, LCV and CNK. The testing results also revealed that the reliability estimates exhibit different performance with different models and domains but were most consistent with the decision and regression trees.

We tested the individual prediction reliability estimators by applying them to the problem of predicting breast cancer recurrence. In this context, the estimation of prediction reliability estimates for individual predictions is of crucial importance for physicians seeking to validate their prediction systems. Our tests suggested the use of estimators $SAvar$ and $BAGV$, and by implementing the prediction system with these reliability estimators, we concluded that our predictions are significantly correlated with those of experts. The reliability estimates can also provide experts with validation information regarding prediction accuracy that was previously unavailable.

Advances in the reliability estimation of individual predictions will have a significant impact on areas in which current decision support tools are inadequate or even nonexistent. We believe that the results will widen the scope of machine learning, especially by increasing end user trust in machine predictions. The ultimate result will be the much wider application of machine learning methods in many different fields.

REFERENCES

Asunction, A., & Newman, D. J. (2007). *UCI Machine Learning repository*.

Baluja, S. (1998). Probabilistic modeling for face orientation discrimination: Learning from labelled and unlabelled data. In *Neural Information Processing systems (NIPS '98)*, (pp. 854–860).

Blum, A., & Mitchell, T. (1998). Combining labeled and unlabelled data with co-training. In *Proceedings of the 11th Annual Conference on Computational Learning Theory*, (pp. 92–100).

Bosnić, Z., & Kononenko, I. (2007). Estimation of individual prediction reliability using the local sensitivity analysis. *Applied Intelligence*, *29*(3), 187–203. doi:10.1007/s10489-007-0084-9

Bosnić, Z., & Kononenko, I. (2008). Comparison of approaches for estimating reliability of individual regression predictions. *Data & Knowledge Engineering*, *67*(3), 504–516. doi:10.1016/j.datak.2008.08.001

Bosnić, Z., Kononenko, I., Robnik-Šikonja, M., & Kukar, M. (2003). Evaluation of prediction reliability in regression using the transduction principle . In Zajc, B., & Tkalčič, M. (Eds.), *Proceedings of Eurocon 2003* (pp. 99–103). doi:10.1109/EURCON.2003.1248158

Bousquet, O., & Elisseeff, A. (2000). Algorithmic stability and generalization performance. In *Neural Information Processing Systems*, (pp. 196–202).

Bousquet, O., & Elisseeff, A. (2002). Stability and generalization. *Journal of Machine Learning Research*, 2, 499–526.

Bousquet, O., & Pontil, M. (2003). Leave-one-out error and stability of learning algorithms with applications . In Suykens, J. (Eds.), *Advances in learning theory: Methods, models and applications*. IOS Press.

Breierova, L., & Choudhari, M. (1996). *An introduction to sensitivity analysis*. MIT System Dynamics in Education Project.

Breiman, L. (1996). Bagging predictors. *Machine Learning*, 24(2), 123–140. doi:10.1007/BF00058655

Breiman, L. (2001). Random forests. *Machine Learning*, 45(1), 5–32. doi:10.1023/A:1010933404324

Breiman, L., Friedman, J. H., Olshen, R. A., & Stone, C. J. (1984). *Classification and regression trees*. Belmont, CA: Wadsworth International Group.

Carney, J., & Cunningham, P. (1999). Confidence and prediction intervals for neural network ensembles. In *Proceedings of IJCNN'99, The International Joint Conference on Neural Networks*, Washington, USA, (pp. 1215–1218).

Chang, C., & Lin, C. (2001). *LIBSVM: a library for support vector machines*. Retrieved from http://www.csie.ntu.edu.tw/~cjlin/libsvm/.

Christiannini, N., & Shawe-Taylor, J. (2000). *Support vector machines and other kernel–based learning methods*. Cambridge University Press.

de Sa, V. (1993). Learning classification with unlabelled data. In J. D. Cowan, G. Tesauro & J. Alspector, (Eds.), *Proceedings of NIPS'93, Neural Information Processing Systems*, (pp. 112–119). San Francisco, CA: Morgan Kaufmann Publishers.

Dempster, A. P., Laird, N. M., & Rubin, D. B. (1977). Maximum likelihood from incomplete data via the EM algorithm. *Journal of the Royal Statistical Society. Series B. Methodological*, 39(1), 1–38.

Department of Statistics at Carnegie Mellon University. (2005). *Statlib – Data, software and news from the statistics community*. Retrieved from http://lib.stat.cmu.edu/

Drucker, H. (1997). Improving regressors using boosting techniques. In *Proceedings of 14th International Conference on Machine Learning*, (pp. 107–115). Morgan Kaufmann.

Freund, Y., & Schapire, R. (1997). A decision-theoretic generalization of on-line learning and an application to boosting. *Journal of Computer and System Sciences*, 55(1), 119–139. doi:10.1006/jcss.1997.1504

Gammerman, A., Vovk, V., & Vapnik, V. (1998). Learning by transduction. In *Proceedings of the 14th Conference on Uncertainty in Artificial Intelligence*, (pp. 148–155). Madison, Wisconsin.

Geurts, P. (2001). Dual perturb and combine algorithm. In *Proceedings of the Eighth International Workshop on Artificial Intelligence and Statistics*, (pp. 196–201).

Ghahramani, Z., & Jordan, M. (1994). Supervised learning from incomplete data via an EM approach. *Advances in Neural Information Processing Systems*, 6, 120–127.

Hashem, H. (1992). Sensitivity analysis for feedforward artificial neural networks with differentiable activation functions. In *Proceedings of 1992 International Joint Conference on Neural Networks IJCNN92*, Vol. 1, (pp. 419–424).

Hastie, T., & Tibshirani, R. (1990). *Generalized additive models*. London, UK: Chapman and Hall.

Heskes, T. (1997). Practical confidence and prediction intervals. In M. C. Mozer, M. I. Jordan, & T. Petsche (Eds.), *Advances in Neural Information Processing Systems, 9*, 176–182. The MIT Press.

Kearns, M. J., & Ron, D. (1997). Algorithmic stability and sanity-check bounds for leave-one-out cross-validation. In *Computational Learning Theory*, (pp. 152–162).

Kerr, M., & Churchill, G. (2000). Bootstrapping cluster analysis: assessing the reliability of conclusions from microarray experiments. *Proceedings of the National Academy of Sciences of the United States of America, 96*, 8961–8965.

Kjaerulff, U., & van der Gaag, L. C. (2000). Making sensitivity analysis computationally efficient. In *Proceedings of the Sixteenth Conference on Uncertainty in Artificial Intelligence*, (pp. 317-325). San Francisco, CA: Morgan Kaufmann.

Kleijnen, J. (2001). Experimental designs for sensitivity analysis of simulation models. In *Proceedings of EUROSIM 2001.*

Kukar, M. (2001). *Estimating classifications' reliability and cost-sensitive combination of machine learning methods*. Unpublished doctoral dissertation, University of Ljubljana, 2001.

Kukar, M., & Kononenko, I. (2002). Reliable classifications with machine learning. In Elomaa, T., Manilla, H., & Toivonen, H. (Eds.), *Proceedings of Machine Learning: ECML-2002* (pp. 219–231). Helsinki, Finland: Springer Verlag. doi:10.1007/3-540-36755-1_19

Li, F., & Wechsler, H. (2005). Open set face recognition using transduction. *IEEE Transactions on Pattern Analysis and Machine Intelligence, 27*(11), 1686–1697. doi:10.1109/TPAMI.2005.224

Mitchell, T. (1999). The role of unlabelled data in supervised learning. In *Proceedings of the 6th International Colloquium of Cognitive Science*, San Sebastian, Spain.

Ridgeway, G., Madigan, D., & Richardson, T. (1999). Boosting methodology for regression problems . In Heckerman, D., & Whittaker, J. (Eds.), *Proceedings of Artificial Intelligence and Statistics* (pp. 152–161).

Rumelhart, D., Hinton, G., & Williams, R. (1986). *Learning internal representations by error propagation* (pp. 318–362). Cambridge, MA: MIT Press.

Saltelli, A., Ratto, M., Tarantola, S., & Campolongo, F. (2005). Sensitivity analysis for chemical models. *Chemical Reviews, 105*(7), 2811–2828. doi:10.1021/cr040659d

Saltelli, A., Tarantola, S., Campolongo, F., & Ratto, M. (2003). *Sensitivity analysis in practice: A guide to assessing scientific models*. London, UK: John Wiley & Sons Ltd.

Saunders, C., Gammerman, A., & Vovk, V. (1999). Transduction with confidence and credibility. In *Proceedings of IJCAI'99*, Vol. 2, (pp. 722–726).

Schapire, R. E. (1999). A brief introduction to boosting. In *International Joint Conferences on Aritifical Intelligence*, (pp. 1401–1406).

Seeger, M. (2000). *Learning with labeled and unlabelled data*. Technical report. Retrieved from http://www.dai.ed.ac.uk/~seeger/papers.html

Smola, A. J., & Schölkopf, B. (1998). *A tutorial on support vector regression*. NeuroCOLT2 Technical Report NC2-TR-1998-030.

Tibshirani, R., & Knight, K. (1999). Model search and inference by bootstrap bumping. *Journal of Computational and Graphical Statistics, 8,* 671–686.

Vapnik, V. (1995). *The nature of statistical learning theory.* Springer.

Wolpert, D. H. (1992). Stacked generalization. *Neural Networks, 5,* 241–259. doi:10.1016/S0893-6080(05)80023-1

Wood, S. N. (2006). *Generalized additive models: An introduction with R.* Chapman & Hall/CRC.

KEY TERMS AND DEFINITIONS

Classification: Supervised learning problem of predicting the categorical class labels of new observations.

Model-Independent Reliability Estimation: An approach that uses an arbitrary model and deals with it as a black box. This wrapper-like approach is more general, as it utilizes only general parameters available in the supervised learning framework.

Regression: Supervised learning problem of predicting the real-valued class labels of new observations.

Reliability Estimate: Any assessment of the reliability of an individual classification or regression prediction.

Reliability: Any qualitative property of the system, which is related to a critical performance indicator (positive or negative) of that system, such as accuracy, inaccuracy, availability, or downtime rate, responsiveness.

Sensitivity Analysis: An approach, which is used to study the influence of parameters and model properties to its structure and outputs.

Transduction: Means of inference; from particular to particular.

Chapter 4
Landmark Sliding for 3D Shape Correspondence

Pahal Dalal
University of South Carolina, USA

Song Wang
University of South Carolina, USA

ABSTRACT

Shape correspondence, which aims at accurately identifying corresponding landmarks from a given population of shape instances, is a very challenging step in constructing a statistical shape model such as the Point Distribution Model. Many shape correspondence methods are primarily focused on closed-surface shape correspondence. The authors of this chapter discuss the 3D Landmark Sliding method of shape correspondence, which is able to identify accurately corresponding landmarks on 3D closed-surfaces and open-surfaces (Dalal 2007, 2009). In particular, they introduce a shape correspondence measure based on Thin-plate splines and the concept of explicit topology consistency on the identified landmarks to ensure that they form a simple, consistent triangle mesh to more accurately model the correspondence of the underlying continuous shape instances. The authors also discuss issues such as correspondence of boundary landmarks for open-surface shapes and different strategies to obtain an initial estimate of correspondence before performing landmark sliding.

BACKGROUND

The Point Distribution Model (Cootes, 1995) has become a very popular tool for statistical shape analysis and has been widely used in various computer-vision and medical-imaging applica-

tions such as image segmentation and shape based diagnosis. The major challenge in constructing a Point Distribution Model (PDM), especially in 3D, is the step of landmark-based shape correspondence. Shape correspondence aims at identifying a set of accurately corresponding landmarks from a population of given shape instances. The non-linearity of the shape description and shape

DOI: 10.4018/978-1-4666-1806-0.ch004

Figure 1. Illustration of each representation of a shape instance: (a) Point cloud S_P representing the surface and the surface boundary S_B. (b) Landmark-based triangle mesh S_T where each vertex is a landmark in S_L. (c) Discrete triangle mesh S_M to approximate the surface S. Note that S_M and S_T are not the same.

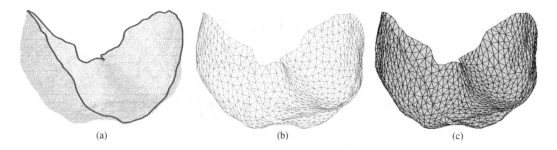

(a)   (b)   (c)

variation for most anatomical structures leads to a problem where it is very difficult to find an optimal solution.

Various 3D shape correspondence methods have been proposed for PDM construction. However, most of these methods are aimed at closed-surface shape correspondence. For example, both the *Minimum Description Length* (Davies, 2002; Heimann, 2005) and *Spherical Harmonics* (Brechbuhler, 1995; Gerig, 2001) methods map each shape instance to a sphere and reduce the shape correspondence problem to that of parameterizing the sphere. It is usually difficult to apply such a sphere-mapping step to open-surface shapes. Hence, we require a method that can perform 3D shape correspondence for both closed-surface and open-surface shapes.

PROBLEM FORMULATION

The aim of shape correspondence is to obtain a set of corresponding landmarks on a population of shape instances. As shown in Figure 1, we can represent each shape instance S as:

S_P, a dense point cloud defining the entire closed or open surface;

S_B, the subset of S_P that describe the closed boundary of the surface if S_P is an open surface (S_B is empty if S_P is a closed surface);

S_M, a triangle mesh constructed to approximate S;

S_L, the set of landmarks identified by the shape correspondence method;

S_T, the triangle mesh on S_L.

With correspondence across all shape instances, the triangle mesh S_T can be used to ensure topology consistency among all instances in the population. Different from S_L and S_T, S_M is constructed independently and may contain different number of vertices and triangles for each shape instance. Further, S_B is required to ensure that the landmarks along the boundary of an open-surface shape instance are correctly corresponded with points along the boundary of another instance in the population.

First we consider a simplified form of the shape correspondence where the population consists of only two instances: a *template U* and a *target V*. If we identify a set of landmarks U_L on the template, the problem then is to identify target landmarks V_L. Following this same method for a population of N instances, we can first select an instance as the template and identify template landmarks U_L. Then, we can construct corresponding landmarks on each target V_i in a pair-wise manner. In this way, corresponding landmarks can be identified on the entire population of shape instances. Note that these landmarks may not coincide with any anatomically significant locations or features.

LANDMARK SLIDING

Shape Correspondence Error

For shape correspondence, the major problem then is to define a shape correspondence error φ between U_L and V_L. This shape correspondence error must describe the underlying non-rigid deformation between the two shape instances represented by these landmarks. Further, the shape correspondence error must well-represent the entire target surface V and its properties. For example, we must ensure that landmarks along the boundary of U have corresponding landmarks along the boundary of V for open-surface shapes. To achieve these two goals, we can define the shape correspondence error as

$$\varphi(U_L, V_L) = d(U_L, V_L) + R(V_L)$$

where $d(U_L, V_L)$ quantifies the non-rigid shape deformation between U_L and V_L, and $R(V_L)$ is a regularization term to reflect the surface properties.

We use the 3D thin-plate splines to model the non-rigid deformation between the template and target surfaces and use the thin-plate bending energy as $d(U_L, V_L)$. In particular, the thin-plate spline finds a mapping $\mathbf{t} = (t_x, t_y, t_z)$ from U_L to V_L i.e., $v_{ix} = t_x(\mathbf{u}_i), v_{iy} = t_y(\mathbf{u}_i)$ and $v_{iz} = t_z(\mathbf{u}_i), i = 1, 2, ..., n$. The thin-plate bending energy, which measures the energy required to deform a volume to match these two sets of landmarks, is then characterized by

$$d(U_L, V_L) = \int \int \int_{-\infty}^{+\infty} (\mathbf{L}(t_x) + \mathbf{L}(t_y) + \mathbf{L}(t_z)) dx dy dz$$

where

$$\mathbf{L}(\cdot) = \left(\frac{\partial^2}{\partial x^2}\right)^2 + \left(\frac{\partial^2}{\partial y^2}\right)^2 + \left(\frac{\partial^2}{\partial z^2}\right)^2 + 2\left(\frac{\partial^2}{\partial x \partial y}\right)^2 + 2\left(\frac{\partial^2}{\partial y \partial z}\right)^2 + 2\left(\frac{\partial^2}{\partial z \partial x}\right)^2.$$

Expressed in a quadratic form, the bending energy can be defined as

$$d(U_L, V_L) = \mathbf{v}_x^T \mathbf{L} \mathbf{v}_x + \mathbf{v}_y^T \mathbf{L} \mathbf{v}_y + \mathbf{v}_z^T \mathbf{L} \mathbf{v}_z$$

where $\mathbf{v}_x, \mathbf{v}_y$ and $\mathbf{v}_z$ are the columnized vectors that contain the x, y and z coordinates of the landmarks in V_L, respectively. $\mathbf{L}$ is the $n \times n$ upper-left sub-matrix of

$$\begin{bmatrix} \mathbf{K} & \mathbf{D} \\ \mathbf{D}^T & 0 \end{bmatrix}^{-1}$$

where the $n \times n$ matrix $\mathbf{K}$ has element $k_{ij} = -\frac{1}{8\pi}\|\mathbf{u}_i - \mathbf{v}_i\|$, $n \times 4$ matrix $\mathbf{D} = \begin{bmatrix} 1_{n \times 1}, \mathbf{u}_x, \mathbf{u}_y, \mathbf{u}_z \end{bmatrix}$ with $\mathbf{u}_x, \mathbf{u}_y$ and $\mathbf{u}_z$ being the columnized vectors that contain the x, y, and z coordinates of the landmarks in U_L, respectively. The thin-plate bending energy is invariant to any affine transformation, i.e., if the mapping $\mathbf{t}$ is affine, the resulting bending energy is always zero.

For the regularization term $R(V_L)$ we discuss two strategies: (a) a strategy based on consistency in the distribution of landmarks between the template and target, and (b) a strategy for modeling the correspondence between boundaries of open-surface shapes. First, we note that the thin-plate spline based shape deformation measure $d(U_L, V_L)$ does not prevent the aggregation of target landmarks in a small region of the surface V. Since we wish to construct landmarks that represent the entire surface, we will ensure that the selected template landmarks U_L are uniformly (or nearly uniformly) distributed over U. Certainly, target landmarks V_L aggregated within a small region on V do not truly reflect the correspondence in the underlying surfaces U and V. The major reason is that the numeric value of $d(U_L, V_L)$ is dependent on the size of V_L. If all the coordinates of V_L are scaled to half their original values, $d(U_L, V_L)$ will be reduced to one-fourth of its original value. Therefore, if all the target landmarks are aggregated within a small region of V the value of $d(U_L, V_L)$ may become smaller. One way is to construct an initial estimate of V_L by co-aligning the template and target after removing their translation, rotation, and scaling difference, and then we can impose a distribution consistency between U_L and V_L by setting

$$R(V_L) = \sum_{i=1}^{n} \lambda_i \left\| \mathbf{v}_i - \mathbf{u}_i \right\|^2$$

where $\lambda_i > 0$ can be used to balance the terms $d(U_L, V_L)$ and $R(V_L)$ by setting $\lambda_1 = \lambda_2 = ... = \lambda_n$. On the other hand, the regularization term may be used to reflect a specific characteristic of the surface. For example, we can use $R(V_L)$ to reflect that boundaries of open-surface shapes must correspond to each other. More specifically, we can first consider only the template boundary landmarks $U_{BL} \subseteq U_L$ and use a contour correspondence method to obtain the *expected* target boundary landmarks. Then we can define

$$R(V_L) = \sum_{i=1}^{n} \lambda_i \left\| \mathbf{v}_i - \mathbf{v}_i^b \right\|$$

where $\mathbf{v}_i^b$ is the *expected* position of $\mathbf{v}_i$ based on the correspondence of only the boundary contour and $\lambda_i > 0$ if $\mathbf{v}_i$ is a boundary landmark, $\lambda_i = 0$

otherwise. In this way, the regularization term can be applied to selected landmarks to better reflect the underlying characteristics of the shape.

Topology Consistency

Using the thin-plate spline bending energy as the shape correspondence error does not guarantee the preservation of topology consistency between the template and the target. For example, in Figure 2, the landmarks V_L shown in (b) have a finite bending energy with the template landmarks U_L in (a). However, when we connect the landmarks V_L by following the same vertex connectivity as the template triangle mesh, we obtain a non-simple triangle mesh V_T with self intersections. Landmark topology consistency reflects the geometric homeomorphism between the template and the target shape instances. Hence, landmark topology consistency should be included as a critical constraint in shape correspondence and statistical shape modeling. Including such a constraint explicitly into the shape correspondence error may not be tractable. Instead, we may algorithmically ensure that topology consistency is maintained at each step in the construction of template and target landmarks. Note that we cannot redefine the connection order in V_T to remove self intersections because this connection order is defined by the template mesh U_T. In our experiments, we notice that topology consistency is generally not violated for closed-surface shapes but can be a very serious problem in open-surface shapes.

Template Landmarks and Initial Estimate of Target Landmarks

We construct the template and target landmarks in three steps. First, we construct the template landmarks, U_L independently of all other target instances. Second, we construct an initial estimate of target landmarks V_L. Finally, we apply a refinement step to minimize the shape correspondence error $\varphi(U_L, V_L)$ through landmark sliding. The

Figure 2. Illustration of inconsistency in topology of template landmarks U_L and target landmarks V_L: (a) Triangulation of template landmarks $\mathbf{u}_1, \mathbf{u}_2, \mathbf{u}_3, \mathbf{u}_4, \mathbf{u}_5, \mathbf{u}_6$. (b) Triangulation of corresponding target landmarks $\mathbf{v}_1, \mathbf{v}_2, \mathbf{v}_3, \mathbf{v}_4, \mathbf{v}_5, \mathbf{v}_6$ showing self-intersection.

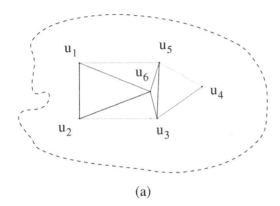 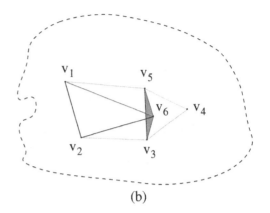

(a)   (b)

landmarks U_L must well-represent the entire template surface and hence be well-distributed on the surface U. We may impose a uniformly divided 3D grid on the template instance and select the point in U_P closest to the center of a cell as a template landmark. By tuning the size and number of cells in this 3D grid, we can change the number of template landmarks.

Another approach is to sample the points U_P using a method such as *k-mean clustering*. Using K-means clustering is certainly more flexible than the grid based method, since the number of landmarks can be directly specified. While the traditional K-means clustering method is suitable for closed-surface shapes, it may lead to the boundary of open-surface shapes not being represented sufficiently as shown in Figure 3(a). The major reason is that there may be no cluster centers along the boundary of the open-surface shape instance. To address this problem, we adapt the K-means clustering algorithm to a *constrained* K-means algorithm which identifies sufficient cluster centers from the surface boundary as shown in Figure 3(b). The approach is similar to the traditional K-means algorithm where clusters are iteratively identified and their centers are calculated by averaging the points in each cluster. For the constrained K-means clustering, we identify whether a cluster contains

any points in the template surface boundary U_B and if so, we calculate the center of such a cluster as the average of only the points that are in U_B. In this way, we can obtain well-distributed template landmarks U_L which include sufficient landmarks representing the boundary of the template surface.

To obtain the initial estimate of target landmarks V_L, we propose two strategies: the first is a general method applicable to both closed-surface and open-surface shapes, the second is aimed towards a better initial estimate of V_L for open-surface shapes. In the first strategy, the basic idea is to remove the location, scaling and rotation differences between the template and target represented by their triangle meshes U_M and V_M. We remove the location and scaling differences between U_M and V_M by moving their centers of mass to the origin and normalizing their sizes to be the same. We then remove the rotations between the template and the target by aligning their principal axes. Consider the template surface U_M as an example. Suppose the template triangle mesh U_M contains m triangle faces with areas $w_1, w_2, ..., w_m$, respectively. For each triangle, we calculate its centroid as the average of its three vertices. Denote the centroid of these m triangles as $\mathbf{c}_1, \mathbf{c}_2, ..., \mathbf{c}_m$ respectively. Denote $\mathbf{r}_i = \dfrac{w_i \mathbf{c}_i}{\sum_{j=1}^{m} w_j}$ and each

Figure 3. A simple 2D illustration of the constrained K-means clustering algorithm: (a) Traditional K-means clustering of S_p leads to well distributed cluster centers, but surface boundary points are not usually included as cluster centers. (b) Constrained K-means clustering with cluster centers along the boundary.

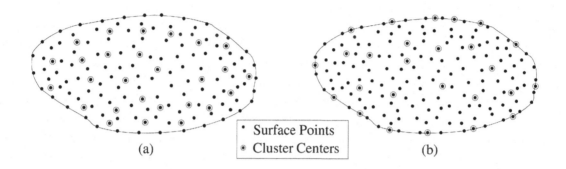

(a) • Surface Points • Cluster Centers (b)

$\mathbf{r}_i = \left(r_{ix}, r_{iy}, r_{iz}\right)^T$ is a 3D vector. We can then create a 3×3 covariance matrix

$$\begin{bmatrix} \sum_{i=1}^{m} r_{ix}^2 & \sum_{i=1}^{m} r_{ix}r_{iy} & \sum_{i=1}^{m} r_{ix}r_{iz} \\ \sum_{i=1}^{m} r_{ix}r_{iy} & \sum_{i=1}^{m} r_{iy}^2 & \sum_{i=1}^{m} r_{iy}r_{iz} \\ \sum_{i=1}^{m} r_{ix}r_{iz} & \sum_{i=1}^{m} r_{iy}r_{iz} & \sum_{i=1}^{m} r_{iz}^2 \end{bmatrix}$$

Applying eigenvalue decomposition to this matrix yields three orthogonal principal vectors $\mathbf{e}_1, \mathbf{e}_2,$ and $\mathbf{e}_3$ with three corresponding eigenvalues being sorted in a decreasing order. We then rotate the whole template shape surface so that $\mathbf{e}_1, \mathbf{e}_2$ are aligned with the x and y axes, respectively. However, we must determine whether to align $\mathbf{e}_1, \mathbf{e}_2$ to positive or negative direction of the x and y axes, so that they are consistent when processing both template and target surfaces. In order to address this problem, we calculate the sum of dot products $\sum_{i=1}^{m} w_i(\mathbf{e}_1 \cdot \mathbf{c}_i)$. If its value is positive, we align $\mathbf{e}_1$ to the positive direction of x axis. Otherwise, we align $\mathbf{e}_1$ to the negative direction of x axis. Similarly, we can use the same strategy to determine the unique rotation to align $\mathbf{e}_2$ to the y axis. For the target shape surface, we perform the same eigenvalue decomposition and axis rotations. This will make the template and target to have the same orientations. However, there are rare cases where such eigenvalue-decomposition and axis rotation strategy fail to work i.e. when any two eigenvalues of the covariance matrix are too close to each other and/or the value of $\sum_{i=1}^{m} w_i(\mathbf{e}_1 \cdot \mathbf{c}_i)$ or $\sum_{i=1}^{m} w_i(\mathbf{e}_2 \cdot \mathbf{c}_i)$ is very close to zero. However, for most shapes with certain amount of complexity, we find that this strategy can effectively remove the rotation transformations between two shape instances.

By removing the possible rotation, translation, and scaling transformations between the template and target, we can construct an initial estimate of the target landmarks V_L. We construct V_L by finding, from the target point cloud V_P, the points with smallest distance to the template landmarks U_L. Specifically, for each template landmark $\mathbf{u}_i$, we find from all the surface points in V_P the one with the smallest Euclidean distance as the initial estimate of the target landmark $\mathbf{v}_i, i = 1, 2, ..., n$ as shown in Figure 4. To avoid the possible problem of finding the same target surface point for two different template landmarks, we exclude a target surface point from the search space if it has been included in V_L in previous searches. Since the

Figure 4. An illustration of finding an initial estimate of the target landmarks V_L by co-aligning the template and target surfaces

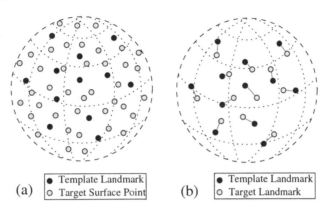

(a)

●	Template Landmark
○	Target Surface Point

(b)

●	Template Landmark
○	Target Landmark

template and the target shape surfaces are pre-aligned, this algorithm is able to find V_L that correspond roughly to U_L.

In the second strategy, which is applied only to open-surface shapes, we use shape matching based on geometric information along with conformal mapping to construct an initial estimate for the target landmarks V_L. First, we flatten the template triangle mesh U_T and target triangle mesh V_M to their 2D conformal representations $\tilde{U}_T$ and $\tilde{V}_M$ respectively, as shown in Figure 5(a) and (b). With the 2D conformal maps, we can easily build a 2D parameterization for the 3D surface. Second, we find a set of corresponding landmarks on the 3D boundary of U and V using a contour correspondence algorithm (Wang, 2004). By projecting these landmarks to their respective conformal mappings, we obtain $\tilde{U}_{BL}$ and $\tilde{V}_{BL}$ which are the 2D, conformal projections of the template and target boundary landmarks $U_{BL} \subseteq U_L$ and $V_{BL} \subseteq V_L$. We use $\tilde{U}_{BL}$ and $\tilde{V}_{BL}$ to eliminate the translation, rotation and scaling differences between the template and the target using *Procrustes* analysis on the 2D plane. We then use the shape-context method (Belongie, 2002) to find a matching between all the template landmarks $\tilde{U}_L$ (on the 2D plane) and $\tilde{V}_D$, a down-sampled subset of points on the target in the 2D plane. We use the

constrained K-means clustering method to preserve the boundary while constructing $\tilde{V}_D$. We only require that the number of points in $\tilde{V}_D$ be larger than or equal to the number of landmarks in $\tilde{U}_L$ so that each template landmark is assigned a corresponding target landmark. To enforce the requirement that template boundary landmarks $\tilde{U}_{BL}$ are corresponded to a point along $\tilde{V}_B$, we set the cost of matching boundary landmarks with non-boundary points to a very large number. After finding the matches of $\tilde{U}_L$ in $\tilde{V}_D$, we perform inverse conformal mapping to get a set of target landmarks on the 3D target surface. However, we cannot directly use this set of 3D landmarks on the target as the initial estimate of V_L. It may contain mismatches, because shape context only considers geometry information but not spatial topology, as shown in Figure 5(c). If we construct the triangle mesh V_T by connecting V_L using the same connection information as U_T, the mesh V_T may not be a simple mesh without self-intersections. We use statistical regression and develop a process of elimination to remove such pairs $(\mathbf{u}_i, \mathbf{v}_i)$. We then use the remaining matched pairs to establish a topologically consistent initial estimate for V_L.

Specifically, we define the regression cost function as

Figure 5. An illustration of conformal mapping and shape-context descriptor: (a) 3D mesh of the human diaphragm. (b) The conformal map of the 3D mesh. (c) The shape-context descriptor of a landmark $\mathbf{u}_i$.

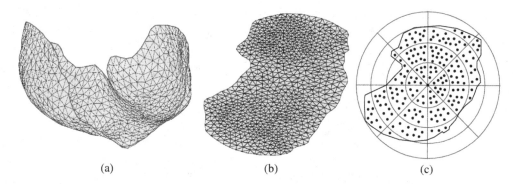

(a)	(b)	(c)

$$\psi = \sum_{i=1}^{n} \left\| \mathbf{v}_i - \hat{\mathbf{v}}_i \right\|^2 + v_x^T \mathbf{L} v_x + v_y^T \mathbf{L} v_y + v_z^T \mathbf{L} v_z$$

where $\mathbf{L}$ is the same thin-plate spline bending matrix as before. We calculate the optimal values of $\hat{\mathbf{v}}$ to minimize this cost by equating to 0 the partial derivative of ψ with respect to $\hat{\mathbf{v}}$. To identify the mismatched pairs $(\mathbf{u}_i, \mathbf{v}_i)$, we calculate the Euclidean distance between each $\mathbf{v}_i$ and $\hat{\mathbf{v}}_i$. Then, we sort the list of pairs $(\mathbf{u}_i, \mathbf{v}_i)$ by decreasing value of this Euclidean distance (worst matched pair to best) and discard the pair $(\mathbf{u}_i, \mathbf{v}_i)$ if it satisfies the following conditions:

The pair violates the topology consistency requirement. For example, in Figure 2 we discard the pair $(\mathbf{u}_6, \mathbf{v}_6)$.

They are not boundary landmarks. However, neighboring boundary landmarks may be switched to ensure topology consistency.

Worst 30% pairs of matches $(\mathbf{u}_i, \mathbf{v}_i)$ are considered as mismatches, but we do not remove all the landmarks on the same triangle in U_T.

By this process of elimination, we get U_R and V_R which are topologically consistent and representative landmarks. Finally, we calculate the 3D thin-plate transform between U_R and V_R, such that $V_R = \mathbf{t}(U_R)$ and apply this transform $\mathbf{t}$ to all landmarks in U_L to get the initial estimate for V_L

i.e. $V_L = \mathbf{t}(U_L)$. We now connect the landmarks in V_L using the same triangulation information as U_T to get V_T.

Landmark Refinement

The initial estimate V_L described above is constructed using only the geometry information, whether by co-aligning the template and target or using shape-context based matching for open-surface shapes. While it preserves the landmark-topology consistency, it may not minimize the 3D shape correspondence error. Hence, we adopt an iterative refinement procedure for V_L such that the shape correspondence error is minimized. In this algorithm, all landmarks in V_L are simultaneously and iteratively moved on the surface V to minimize the correspondence error. In an iteration, we first move each landmark on its tangent plane and then project the new landmarks back onto the surface V. More specifically, each landmark $\mathbf{v}_i \in V_L$ is moved to $\mathbf{v}'_i = \mathbf{v}_i + \alpha_i \mathbf{p}_i + \beta_i \mathbf{q}_i$ on the tangent plane, where $\mathbf{p}_i$ and $\mathbf{q}_i$ are linearly independent unit tangent vectors and α_i and β_i are the sliding distances along these two tangent vectors. The optimal sliding distances can be found by solving the following quadratic-programming problem

$$\min_{\alpha,\beta} \varphi(U_L, V_L; \alpha, \beta)$$

$$= \sum_{*\in\{x,y,z\}} (v_* + \mathbf{P}_*\alpha + \mathbf{Q}_*\beta)^T \mathbf{L}(v_* + \mathbf{P}_*\alpha + \mathbf{Q}_*\beta)$$

$$+ \sum_{i=1}^{n} \lambda_i \left\| \mathbf{v}_i + \alpha_i \mathbf{p}_i + \beta_i \mathbf{q}_i - \mathbf{v}_i^e \right\|^2$$

subject to constraints

$$|\alpha_i| \le \varepsilon, |\beta_i| \le \varepsilon$$

where,

$$\alpha = (\alpha_1, \alpha_2, ..., \alpha_n)^T, \beta = (\beta_1, \beta_2, ..., \beta_n)$$
$$\mathbf{P}_* = diag(\mathbf{p}_{1*}, \mathbf{p}_{2*}, ..., \mathbf{p}_{n*})$$
$$\mathbf{Q}_* = diag(\mathbf{q}_{1*}, \mathbf{q}_{2*}, ..., \mathbf{q}_{n*})$$

For closed-surface shapes, we may set $\mathbf{v}_i^e = \mathbf{u}_i$ where the regularization term $R(V_L)$ is used to ensure consistency in distribution of landmarks. For open-surface shapes we may set $\mathbf{v}_i^e = \mathbf{v}_i^b$ where $\mathbf{v}_i^b$ is the expected position of a boundary landmark based on its boundary contour correspondence. In the case of closed-surface shapes, we can then set $\lambda_1 = \lambda_2 = ... = \lambda_n$. On the other hand for open-surface shapes, we can set $\lambda_i > 0$ if $\mathbf{v}_i$ is a boundary landmark or $\lambda_i = 0$ otherwise. In this way, the second term of the cost function only considers the expected boundary landmarks since $\lambda_i = 0$ for all other landmarks in the case of open-surface shapes.

Usually ε may be set to a small value to avoid the landmarks from sliding too far from the surface. The major concern is that topology consistency may not be maintained for large values of ε. However, if we can ensure topology consistency, we may adopt an aggressive landmark sliding approach. First, we set ε to a large value and perform a step of landmark sliding. If the topology consistency is broken by the result of this

step of sliding, we set $\varepsilon = \dfrac{\varepsilon}{2}$ and redo the step of landmark sliding. We continue this process until a value for ε is reached such that the landmark sliding can be performed without violating the topology consistency or the value of ε becomes too small to perform any landmark sliding. For projecting $\mathbf{v}'_i$ back onto the surface V, we find, from the input dense point cloud V_P, a point that has the smallest distance to $\mathbf{v}'_i$. The resulting closest point is then used as $\mathbf{v}_i$ for the next iteration of landmark sliding.

Generally, it is very difficult to directly check the topology consistency of landmarks in 3D. We may use the 2D parameterization rendered by the conformal mapping for open-surface shapes and a conformal mapping to a canonical sphere for closed-surface shapes. Specifically, we find from triangle mesh V_M, the closest point to $\mathbf{v}'_i$. This point denoted as $\mathbf{v}''_i$, may be located within a triangle or along the sides of a triangle. Since $\mathbf{v}''_i, i = 1, 2, ..., n$ are on the triangle mesh V_M, we can apply the conformal mapping to find their mapping $\tilde{\mathbf{v}}''_i$ (to flat plane for open-surface shapes and sphere for closed-surface shapes). If the triangle mesh built on the point-set $\tilde{\mathbf{v}}''_i, i = 1, 2, ..., n$ using the same connection order as in U_T has any self-intersections; we know the landmark topology is inconsistent with the template.

Experiments

We implemented the proposed method in C++ and used two 3D data sets for testing its performance. The first data set contains 41 instances of closed-surface hippocampus shapes and the second contains 26 instances of open-surface human diaphragm shapes.

For the hippocampus data we set each $\lambda_i = 0.001, i = 1, 2, ..., n$ and $\varepsilon = 0.05$ to perform a version of landmark sliding referred to as SLIDE. Specifically, this method uses co-alignment for initial estimate of V_L and does not explicitly check

Figure 6. Quantitative evaluation of MDL, SPHARM and SLIDE methods on the hippocampus data: (a) compactness measure, (b) generality measure, (c) specificity measure, and (d) total CPU time taken by each method for corresponding all 41 hippocampus shape instances. Note that, for the measures shown in (a), (b) and (c), the smaller the better.

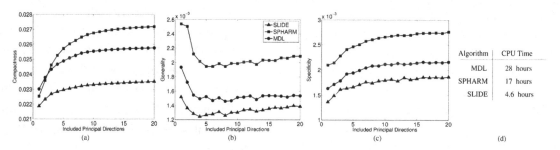

for topology consistency since ε is set to a very small value. We identify the initial estimate of landmark correspondence by eliminating translation, rotation, and scaling differences between the template and target. After performing the landmark sliding to refine this initial estimate, we construct a point distribution model (PDM) and use the *compactness*, *generality*, and *specificity* measures (Styner, 2003) to evaluate the performance of shape correspondence. Particularly, compactness evaluates the amount of variance in the PDM. Generality uses a leave one out test to evaluate a PDM's capability to describe unseen shape instances outside of the training set. Specificity evaluates a PDM's capability to represent only valid shapes. Note that, the smaller these measures the better the shape correspondence. We test the proposed method on 41 hippocampus instances. Each hippocampus shape instance contains 8,000 to 10,000 surface points. We compare the performance of the proposed method with the MDL method using the implementation based on gradient-descent algorithm (Heimann, 2005) and SPHARM methods (Brechbuhler, 1995; Gerig, 2001). For a fair comparison we identify 642 corresponding landmarks on this population of hippocampus instances using each of the three methods. The resulting PDMs for each method are shown in Figure 7 by considering the first two principal directions, where SLIDE indicates the

result of the proposed method. Further, the compactness, generality, and specificity measures are shown in Figure 6. These results show that the proposed method outperforms both MDL and SPHARM in terms of compactness, specificity, and generality. In addition, the proposed method requires much less CPU time than MDL and SPHARM.

For the diaphragm data, we perform experiments on 26 instances, each described by approximately 100,000 to 250,000 points. Since both MDL and SPHARM are not able to correspond open-surface shapes, we compare the correspondence results of the landmark sliding method without any consideration for open-surfaces or enforcement of topology consistency (SLIDE), and a version that ensures boundaries are corresponded and topology consistency is maintained between template and target (SLIDE-T). In SLIDE-T, we set $\varepsilon = 50$ and $\lambda_i = 1$ for boundary landmarks and $\lambda_i = 0$ for all others. Using these settings, we identify 842 corresponding landmarks to construct and evaluate the point distribution model (PDM) derived from the correspondence results for SLIDE-T. To perform a fair comparison, we identify 842 landmarks on the same dataset using SLIDE. In Figure 8, we show a few significant instances from the deformable shape space described by the PDMs constructed using SLIDE and SLIDE-T. Particularly,

Figure 7. Qualitative evaluation of MDL, SPHARM and SLIDE method on the hippocampus data. "0" indicates the mean shape.

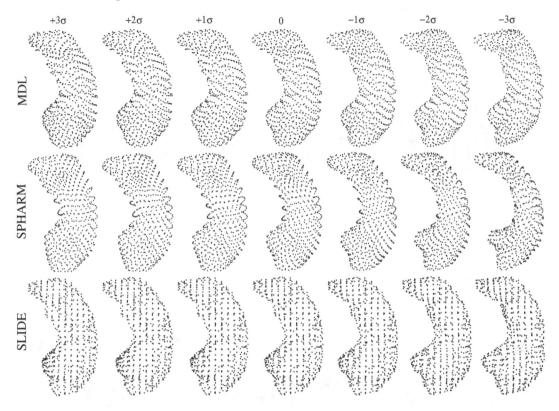

we show the shape instances after deforming the mean shapes along their first two principal directions, respectively. It is clear that the two PDMs describe similar shape spaces, but differ in two aspects. First, the shape space described by the PDM of SLIDE allows shape instances with self-intersecting surfaces and unnatural folding in some regions, while SLIDE-T always leads to a simple triangle mesh with no self intersections. Second, it can be observed that the boundary of the diaphragm shape is not well described by the PDM constructed using SLIDE and shows some folding, while SLIDE-T leads to a smooth boundary. We introduce two new measures to check whether the identified landmarks can well represent the topology and the boundary of each diaphragm shape instance. Without correct topology and good representation of the boundary, the identified landmarks cannot well represent the

shape instance. First, we define the *topology error* as:

Δ_t = Number of triangles in V_T that are not topologically consistent with U_T.

This measure evaluates the ability of a method to correctly represent the topological homeomorphism of the underlying shape. Second, we define the *boundary error* as:

$$\Delta_b = \sum_{\mathbf{v}_i \in V_{BL}} \left\| \mathbf{v}_i - \mathbf{v}^{(i)} \right\|$$

where $\mathbf{v}^{(i)}$ is the closest point along V_B to $\mathbf{v}_i$. This measure evaluates the ability of a shape correspondence method to represent the boundary of an open-surface shape. We apply these two new

Figure 8. Comparison of SLIDE and SLIDE-T: (First Row, M=1) Shape space of the PDM created using SLIDE (top) and SLIDE-T (bottom) for M=1. (Second Row, M=2) Shape space of the PDM created using SLIDE (top) and SLIDE-T (bottom) for M=2. M = 1, 2 are the two principal directions, μ is the mean shape and σ is the standard deviation along a principal direction.

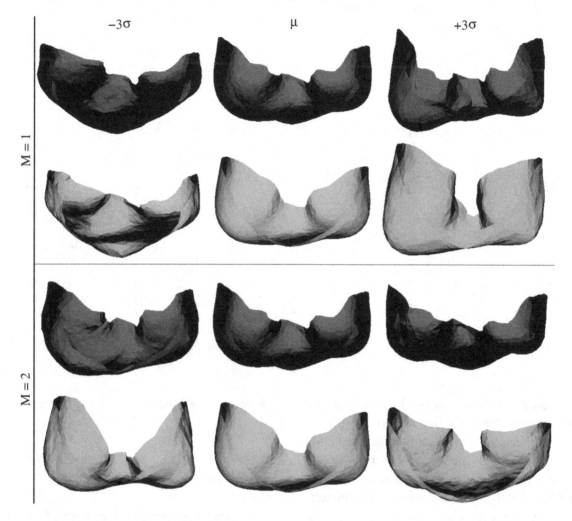

measures to all 26 shape instances and show them in Figure 9. It is clear that SLIDE-T performs better than SLIDE.

In addition to these new measures of shape correspondence evaluation, we find the compactness, generality and specificity measure for SLIDE and SLIDE-T. As shown in Figure 10, SLIDE leads to better performance on the compactness, generality and specificity measures compared to SLIDE-T. This is in contrast to what we obtained above. The major reason is that, without a refer-

ence to any ground truth, these three measures only evaluate the properties of the resulting PDM and do not check whether the resulting PDM can really represent the underlying shape. In other words, these three measures are only meaningful when the identified landmarks can well represent the original shape instances, both topologically and geometrically. More specifically, we can clearly see from Figure 11(a) that landmarks identified by SLIDE do not correctly model the whole diaphragm by missing the area near the

Figure 9. Comparison of SLIDE and SLIDE-T: Measures of topology error and boundary error. $\Delta_t = 0$ *for all instances in SLIDE-T which is represented by the horizontal axis. The horizontal axis represents the 26 shape instances.*

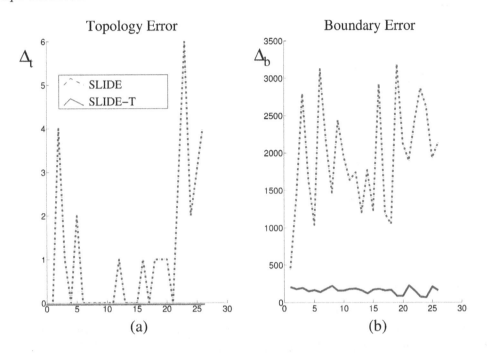

(a)   (b)

Figure 10. Compactness, generality, and specificity measures for SLIDE and SLIDE-T

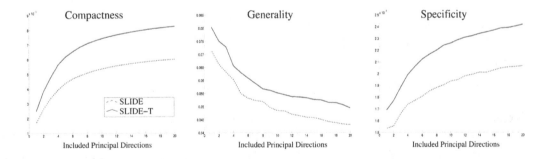

boundary; leading to a PDM with lesser variation and hence a better compactness measure. This also makes the size of the mean shape resulting from SLIDE smaller than that from SLIDE-T along the vertical direction, as shown in Figure 11(b), which gives SLIDE an undesirable advantage in terms of these three measures. As mentioned above, in this case, the correspondence results from SLIDE are in fact incorrect and the results from these three measures are misleading.

CONCLUSION

In this chapter, we have described a landmark sliding method to address the important problem of 3D shape correspondence for both closed-surface shapes and open-surface shapes. This method can identify corresponding landmarks on a population of shape instances with high accuracy such that they are topologically consistent. In this method, the 3D thin-plate spline bending energy is used to

Figure 11. (a) The PDM resulting from SLIDE is unable to model the shape boundary correctly. (b) The mean shape resulting from SLIDE (red) and SLIDE-T (green) have the same size in the horizontal and depth directions but not the vertical direction; giving SLIDE an advantage in the values of compactness, generality, and specificity.

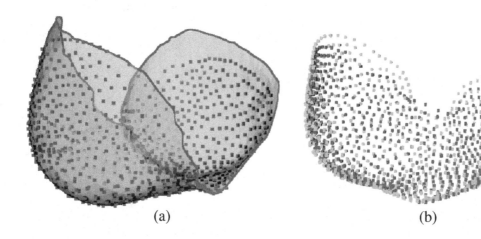

(a)   (b)

model the landmark correspondence error and an efficient, iterative landmark refinement process is developed. For the closed-surface shapes, experiments reveal that the landmark sliding method leads to better shape correspondence results compared to MDL and SPHARM methods. Further, the introduction of topology consistency significantly improves the shape correspondence results of the landmark sliding method for open-surface shapes.

REFERENCES

Belongie, S., Malik, J., & Puzicha, J. (2002). Shape matching and object recognition using shape contexts. *IEEE Transactions on Pattern Analysis and Machine Intelligence*, *4*(24), 509–522. doi:10.1109/34.993558

Brechbuhler, C., Gerig, G., & Kubler, O. (1995). Parametrization of closed surfaces for 3-D shape description. *Computer Vision Graphics and Image Processing*, *61*, 154–170. doi:10.1006/cviu.1995.1013

Cootes, T., Taylor, C., Cooper, D., & Graham, J. (1995). Active shape models - Their training and application. *Computer Vision and Image Understanding*, *61*(1), 38–59. doi:10.1006/cviu.1995.1004

Dalal, P., Ju, L., McLaughlin, M., Zhou, X., Fujita, H., & Wang, S. (2009). 3D open-surface shape correspondence for statistical shape modeling: Identifying topologically consistent landmarks. In *IEEE International Conference on Computer Vision*, (pp. 1857-1864).

Dalal, P., Munsell, B., Wang, S., Tang, J., Oliver, K., & Ninomiya, H. … Fujita, H. (2007) A fast 3D correspondence method for statistical shape modeling. In *IEEE Conference on Computer Vision and Pattern Recognition*, (pp. 1-8).

Davies, R., Twining, C., Cootes, T., Waterton, J., & Taylor, C. (2002). A minimum description length approach to statistical shape modeling. *IEEE Transactions on Medical Imaging*, *21*(5), 525–537. doi:10.1109/TMI.2002.1009388

Gerig, G., Styner, M., Jones, D., Weinberger, D., & Lieberman, J. (2001) Shape analysis of brain ventricles using spharm. In *Mathematical Methods in Biomedical Image Analysis*, (pp. 171–178).

Heimann, T., Wolf, I., Williams, T., & Meinzer, H.-P. (2005). 3D active shape models using gradient descent optimization of description length. In *Information Processing in Medical Imaging, LNCS 3565*.

Styner, M., Rajamani, K., Nolte, L.-P., Zsemlye, G., Szekely, G., Taylor, C., & Davies, R. (2003). 3D correspondence methods for model building. In *Proceedings of Information Processing in Medical Imaging* (pp. 63–75). Evaluation of. doi:10.1007/978-3-540-45087-0_6

Wang, S., Kubota, T., & Richardson, T. (2004). Shape correspondence through landmark sliding. In *IEEE Conference on Computer Vision and Pattern Recognition*, (pp. 143–150).

Chapter 5
Supervised Classification with Bayesian Networks:
A Review on Models and Applications

M. Julia Flores
University of Castilla – La Mancha (UCLM), Instituto de Investigación en informática de Albacete, Spain

José A. Gámez
University of Castilla – La Mancha (UCLM), Instituto de Investigación en informática de Albacete, Spain

Ana M. Martínez
University of Castilla – La Mancha (UCLM), Instituto de Investigación en informática de Albacete, Spain

ABSTRACT

Bayesian Network classifiers (BNCs) are Bayesian Network (BN) models specifically tailored for classification tasks. There is a wide range of existing models that vary in complexity and efficiency. All of them have in common the ability to deal with uncertainty in a very natural way, at the same time providing a descriptive environment. In this chapter, the authors focus on the family of semi-naïve Bayesian classifiers (naïve Bayes, AODE, TAN, kDB, etc.), motivated by the good trade-off between efficiency and performance they provide. The domain of the BNs is generally of discrete nature, but since the presence of continuous variables is very common, the chapter discusses more classical and novel approaches to handling numeric data. In this chapter the authors also discuss more recent techniques such as multidimensional and dynamic models. Last but not least, they focus on applications and recent developments, including some of the BNCs approaches to the multi-class problem together with other traditionally successful and cutting edge cases regarding real-world applications.

DOI: 10.4018/978-1-4666-1806-0.ch005

INTRODUCTION

The task of classification is one of the most popular and, therefore, important tasks in data mining, as it is applied in many real applications. In this context, the basic *classification* task involves learning a model (or generalization) from a set of labelled data, in order to assign one label to every new example. The model learning phase can be more or less complex, to such a degree that most of the work might be carried out in the assignation phase (as in *lazy classifiers*) or, often simply called, classification phase. As world is not deterministic, we will have to manage with uncertainty in classification.

Formally, a model is learnt from a dataset with *t* examples and *n* attributes, all of them with known labels given by a special attribute called *class*, *C*. Hence it is also often referred to as *supervised classification* in contrast to *unsupervised classification* or *clustering*, where the labels are not known a priori. For every example of the type $\vec{e} = \{a_1, a_2 \ldots, a_n\}$, where each a_i is the value for the attribute A_i, a typical classifier would assign a label c_i from a finite set Ω_C of possible labels. Note that we are referring here to a finite set of labels, if the class to predict is of a continuous type it becomes a problem of *regression*, which is out of the scope of this chapter.

There exist multiple paradigms for classification, such as Bayesian networks, decision trees, rule induction, artificial neural networks, genetic programming, support vector machines, etc. In this chapter we focus on the first of these, which might be seen as a combination of statistical techniques and graphical models. BNs provide several advantages to the classification task:

- The networks store information about dependencies existing among the variables involved, which makes them capable of inherently dealing with uncertainty, very frequently present in real world.

- The graphical representation through the Bayesian network facilitates the interpretation and formulation of conclusions about the domain of study.

- In addition, Bayesian network classifiers can combine causal relationships with probabilistic logic, which helps to incorporate expert knowledge into the model.

Thus, one of the greatest advantages of the BNs is that they can represent both the qualitative and the quantitative aspect of the problem. The former is encoded in a directed acyclic graph (DAG), whereas the latter involves storing a probability table for every node conditioned on its parents. Even though the conditional probability distribution can be represented in several ways, the most common representation is the use of tables, i.e. conditional probability tables (CPT).

In a DAG, each node represents a variable; an arc represents a direct dependence between the pair of nodes connected. If there is a directed arc from *X* to *Y*, it means that *X* is the *parent* of *Y* and *Y* is *child* of *X*. Furthermore, if there exists a directed path from *X* to *Z*, it implies that *X* is an *ancestor* of *Z*, while *Z* is a *descendant* of *X*.

Through the property of *conditional independence*, which states that a node is conditionally independent of its non-descendant given its parents, we can represent the joint probability distribution of a Bayesian network by the product of the CPTs associated with each of its nodes.

In classification, we want to obtain $p(c \mid \vec{e}) \ \forall c \in \Omega_C$, i.e. the conditional probability for *C* given $\vec{e}$. The accurate estimation of the probabilities a posteriori for every combination of the class labels and the values of the attributes is unfeasible in practice, as it requires a large amount of training data even with a moderate number of attributes. That is why it is convenient to resort to the Bayes theorem:

$$p(c \mid \vec{e}) = \frac{p(\vec{e} \mid c)p(c)}{p(\vec{e})}. \qquad (0.1)$$

When the probabilities a posteriori are compared for the different class labels, the denominator is constant and can be ignored. The search for the label c^* that maximises these probabilities is called Maximum a posteriori (MAP) rule:

$$\begin{aligned} c^* &= arg\ max_{c \in \Omega_C}\ p(c \mid \vec{e}) \\ &= arg\ max_{c \in \Omega_C}\ \left(p(c)p(\vec{e} \mid c) \right). \end{aligned} \qquad (0.2)$$

The prior probability $p(c)$ can be easily estimated from training data by calculating the fraction of examples that belong to each class. In order to estimate the probabilities conditioned to the class $p(\vec{e} \mid c)$ different approximations can be used and depend on structure of the DAG learnt.

The MAP rule in this case is equivalent to the 0/1 *loss function* defined as:

$$c^* = arg\ min_{c \in \Omega} \sum_{c' \in \Omega} L(c, c')P(c' \mid \vec{e}),$$

where $L(c,c') = 0$ if c=c' and 1 otherwise.

In this chapter we are not covering general BN structure learning. Learning the structure of a network can take a long time and effort, especially if we think of datasets of high dimensionality. That is why it is often convenient to consider a partially or totally pre-fixed structure from which the CPTs are learnt. The most simple of these structures is the one used by the naïve Bayes (NB) classifier, that assumes all the attributes are independent given the class. In spite of its naïve assumption, it performs surprisingly well in certain domains. Hence, numerous techniques have been proposed that aim to improve the accuracy of NB by alleviating the attribute interdependence problem. We refer to them as semi-naïve Bayesian network classifiers, a term introduced by Kononenko, I. (1991). They all have one thing in common, either they do not perform structural search or it is very simple.

The natural domain of Bayesian networks are the discrete variables, hence, we will assume these property for all the variables in the dataset except in the section devoted to numeric variables.

It is also often the presence of missing values in the dataset, and even if there exist several methods to replace these values (*imputation* of single or multiple values, via mean substitution or linear interpolation for example), the direct way to proceed in a BNC is ignoring the affected counting in every CPT where the attribute whose value is missing appears, which is called *available-case analysis*. Note that this is not the same as ignoring the whole instance (*aka complete-case analysis*), which is in turn necessary when the class label is missing. It is not clear which is the best way to proceed; it partially depends on the number of samples and proportion of cases with missing data. For more information on how to deal with missing values please refer to (Hongwei Zhang & Lu, 2002).

SEMI-NAÏVE BAYESIAN NETWORK CLASSIFIERS

NB (Duda, Hart, & Stork, 1973) is the most simple of the Bayesian network classifiers. It assumes that all attributes are conditionally independent given the class, which implies the following factorization for the joint probability distribution:

$$p(C, A_1, A_2, \ldots, A_n) = p(C)\prod_{i=1}^{n} p(A_i \mid C).$$

This independence assumption translates into a simple Bayesian network with a fixed structure having exactly n edges, which point from the class to each predictive attribute; see Figure 1(a). Therefore, only parameter estimation is needed: a marginal (multinomial) probability distribution for the class variable, $p(C)$; and a conditional probability distribution for each predictive attribute given the class, $p(A_i \mid C)$. In this case, a multinomial or Gaussian (Normal) distribution is

Figure 1. Example of network structures with 4 predictive attributes for Naïve Bayes, TAN, kDB and AODE

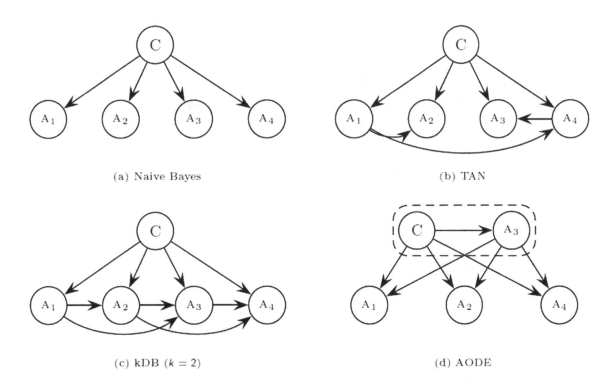

(a) Naive Bayes

(b) TAN

(c) kDB ($k = 2$)

(d) AODE

estimated for each value c of C, depending on the nature of A_i: discrete or numeric respectively. Although different estimation procedures have been proposed, usually maximum likelihood estimation or any smoothed method (e.g. Laplace correction or m-estimation) is applied.

This approach is more feasible than others, as a large training set is not required to obtain acceptable probability estimation.

Here, the MAP rule in this case, given an instance $\vec{e}$, chooses the class label $c *$ such that:

$$c^* = argmax_{c \in \Omega_C}\ p(c \mid \vec{e}) = argmax_{c \in \Omega_C} \left[p(c)\prod_{i=1}^{n} p(a_i \mid c) \right]$$
(0.3)

NB is a very efficient algorithm which has time complexity $\mathcal{O}(tn)$ to induce the classifier over a dataset with t instances and c classes, and complexity $\mathcal{O}(cn)$ to classify a new instance. The

space complexity is $\mathcal{O}(cnv)$, where v is the average number of values per attribute.

Despite its simplicity and unrealistic independence assumption, the performance of the NB classifier is remarkably successful in practice (Domingos & Pazzani, 1996; P. Langley, Iba, & Thompson, 1992).

It is also well known that NB is very sensitive to the presence of redundant and/or irrelevant attributes. The presence of redundant (highly correlated) attributes can bias the decision taken by the NB classifier (Pat Langley & Sage, 1994). On the other hand, NB should be robust regarding irrelevant variables because, in this case, $P(A_i \mid C = c)$ should be equal for all values of $c \in \Omega$. However, because of the small sample effect and the presence of noise, this is not true in general, and thus, in the case of high-dimensional datasets, where hundreds or thousands of irrelevant variables are present, irrelevant vari-

Supervised Classification with Bayesian Networks

Algorithm 1. The TAN algorithm

1:	Calculate $MI(A_i, A_j; C)$ for each pair of attributes $(i < j)$ where $i, j = \{1, ..., n\}$)
2:	Build a complete undirected graph (UG) with all the attributes
3:	$\forall$ arc connecting A_i and A_j assign the weight $MI(A_i, A_j; C)$
4:	**{CHOW AND LIU ALGORITHM: Maximum Weight Spanning Tree (Chow & Liu, 1968)}**
5:	Add the two arcs with maximum weight
6:	**while** (arcs in BN $\leq$ (n-1)) **do**
7:	Add the arc with maximum weight if not cycle in BN
8:	**end while**
9:	Transform the UG into a directed graph (DG) selecting a root
10:	Complete the DG adding C and arcs from C to A_i, $\forall i$
11:	Compute the CPTs

ables can also hurt the precision of the NB classifier.

In order to overcome NB's weaknesses, different approaches, known as semi-naïve classifiers, have been proposed. We include some of the most successful below.

Tree Augmented Naïve Bayes

The Tree Augmented Naïve Bayes (TAN) model (Friedman, Geiger, & Goldszmidt, 1997) relaxes the conditional independence restriction without a large increase in the complexity of the construction process. The idea behind TAN entails learning a maximum weighted spanning tree based on the conditional mutual information between two attributes given the class label, choosing a variable as root and completing the model by adding a link from the class to each attribute (see Algorithm 1 for more details).

The mutual information between two discrete variables: A_i and A_j conditioned to the class C can be defined as:

$$MI(A_i, A_j; C) =$$

$$\sum_{i=1}\sum_{j=1}\sum_{r=1} p(a_i, a_j, c_r) \frac{\log p(a_i, a_j, c_r)}{p(a_i \mid c_r)p(a_j \mid c_r)}. \quad (0.4)$$

Chow and Liu's algorithm guarantees that the tree learned from the training data is the optimal one, i.e. it is the best possible probabilistic representation from the available data as a tree.

TAN becomes a structural augmentation of NB where every attribute has the class variable and at most one other attribute as its parents, see Figure 1(b). It is considered a fair trade-off between model complexity and model accuracy.

At training time TAN generates a three-dimensional table, with a space complexity $\mathcal{O}(c(nv)^2)$. The time complexity of forming the three-dimensional probability table is $\mathcal{O}(tn^2)$ and $\mathcal{O}(cn^2v^2)$ of creating the parent function. A maximal spanning tree is then generated, with time complexity $\mathcal{O}(n^2 \log n)$. At classification time TAN only needs to store the probability tables, with space complexity $\mathcal{O}(cnv^2)$. The time complexity of classifying a single example is $\mathcal{O}(cn)$.

In fact, the TAN classifier can be considered a particular case of the **Forest Augmented Naïve**

Bayes (FAN) (Lucas, 2004). This classifier aims to alleviate TAN's limitation that comes from the fact that some arcs may imply the insertion of noise, as the number of arcs in the tree has to be $n - 1$ (where n is the number of attributes). In FAN, a maximum spanning forest is learnt, which implies to form a forest of trees with a disjoint set of attributes. The number of arcs to include must be previously specified so that it is possible to ignore certain arcs, hence, becoming a more flexible model than TAN.

k-Dependence Bayesian Classifier

Sahami (1996) introduced the notion of k-dependence estimators, through which the probability of each attribute value is conditioned by the class and, at most, k other attributes. Throughout the kDB algorithm, it is possible to construct classifiers across the whole spectrum from the NB structure to the full BN structure by varying the value of k, i.e. the maximum number of parents that every attribute can have.

The kDB algorithm selects, per descending order of mutual information with the class, the different predictive attributes. Then, it adds k parents to each feature depending on the conditional mutual information for each pair of attributes (see Algorithm 2 for more details). It is possible to add these parents only when this conditional mutual information surpasses a given threshold. This avoids including dependences that do not appear to exist when the value of k is set too high.

The advantage of this type of classifiers compared with TAN is their flexibility. In TAN, a variable can have, at most, one other feature variable for its parent besides the class, see Figure 1(c). This restriction on the number of parents strongly constrains the dependencies that can be modeled between the groups of features.

Computing the actual network structure with the kDB algorithm requires $O(n^2 tcv^2)$ time and calculating the conditional probability tables

within the network takes $O(n(t + v^2))$ time, where v here is the maximum number of values that an attribute may take. Classification time would require $O(nck)$.

Averaged One-Dependence Estimators

AODE (Webb, Boughton, & Wang, 2005) is considered an improvement on NB and an interesting alternative to other attempts such as Lazy Bayesian Rules (LBR) (Z. Zheng & Webb, 2000) and Super-Parent TAN (SP-TAN) (Keogh & Pazzani, 1999) since they offer similar accuracy values, but AODE is significantly more efficient at classification time compared with the first one and at training time compared with the second. In order to maintain efficiency, AODE is restricted to exclusively use 1-dependence estimators. Specifically, AODE can be considered as an ensemble of SPODEs (Superparent One-Dependence Estimators), because every attribute depends on the class and another shared attribute, designated as superparent.

Graphically, every SPODE used in AODE will have a structure such as the one depicted in Figure 1(d), where AODE combines all possible classifiers with this pattern structure. Hence, AODE computes the average of the n possible SPODE classifiers (one for each attribute in the database):

$$c^* =$$

$$argmax_{c \in \Omega_C} \left(\sum_{j=1, N(a_j) > m}^{n} p(c, a_j) \prod_{i=1, i \neq j}^{n} p(a_i \mid c, a_j) \right),$$
(0.5)

where the condition $N(a_j) > m$ is used as a threshold to avoid making predictions from attributes with few observations.

At training time, AODE has $\mathcal{O}(tn^2)$ time complexity. The resulting time complexity at

Algorithm 2. The kDB algorithm

1:	Calculate $MI(A_i; C)$ for all attributes.
2:	Calculate $MI(A_i, A_j; C)$ for each pair of attributes $(i \neq j)$.
3:	Let the used variable list $V = \varnothing$
4:	Nodes in BN $= \{C\}$
5:	**while** $(\exists A_i \notin V)$ **do**
6:	$\quad A_{max} = max_i MI(A_i; C), \forall A_i \notin V$
7:	$\quad$ Nodes in BN = Nodes in BN $\cup A_{max}$
8:	$\quad$ Add an arc from C to $A_{max} \in$ BN
9:	$\quad$ m=min($|V|$, k)
10:	$\quad$ Let the auxiliary variable list $Q = \varnothing$
11:	$\quad$ **while** (m > 0) **do**
12	$\quad\quad A_{max2} = max_j MI(A_{max}, A_j; c), \forall A_j \in V \wedge A_j \notin Q$
13	$\quad\quad$ Add an arc from A_{max2} to A_{max}
14	$\quad\quad Q = Q \cup A_{max2}$
15	$\quad$ **end while**
16	$\quad V = V \cup A_{max}$
17	**end while**
18	Compute the CPTs

classification time is $\mathcal{O}(kn^2)$, while the space complexity is $\mathcal{O}(k(nv)^2)$.

AODE offers an attractive alternative to other approaches that aim to improve NB maintaining its efficiency, as it provides competitive error rates with an efficient profile (F. Zheng & Webb, 2005).

There exists an interesting modification of AODE, where the different models, instead of being averaged are weighted according to the mutual information between the superparent and the class, known as WAODE (Jiang & Zhang, 2006).

Other Semi-Naïve Bayesian Classifiers

Apart from the classifiers mentioned above, there exist other not-so-well-known approaches that should also be taken into account. We indicate some of them here:

Hidden Naïve Bayes (HNB) (Harry Zhang, Jiang, & Su, 2005): this classifier creates a hidden parent for each attribute that aims to combine the influences from all other attributes by considering the following classification rule:

$$c^* =$$

$$argmax_{c \in \Omega_C} \left(p(c) \prod_{i=1}^{n} \sum_{i=1, i \neq j}^{n} W_{ij} p(a_i \mid a_j, c) \right), \quad (0.6)$$

Where $W_{ij} = \dfrac{MI(A_i, A_j; C)}{\sum_{j=1, j \neq i}^{n} MI(A_i, A_j; C)}$. The

HNB is similar in idea to AODE but it has higher training time $O(tn^2 + kv^2 n^2)$.

Hidden One-Dependence Estimator (HODE) (M. J. Flores, Gámez, A. M. Martínez, & Puerta, 2009b): This classifier considers a single hidden variable joined to the classification class to be estimated using the Expectation-Maximization algorithm. It is an interesting alternative as it offers similar results to AODE with a lower space demand, which makes it more suitable for high-dimensional datasets at the expenses of a longer training time overall (of same complexity order as AODE though).

Full Bayesian Network Classifier (FBNC) (Su & Zhang, 2006): this Bayesian classifier assumes a full BN and learns a decision tree for each CPT with a novel and more efficient algorithm. The authors claim that it is quadratic in training time $O(tn^2)$, and linear in classification time $O(n)$, providing competitive results with other state-of-the-art learning algorithms.

Bayesian Network Augmented Naïve-Bayes (BAN) (Friedman, et al., 1997): The BAN classifier further relaxes the independence assumption as it creates a BN among the attributes, while it maintains the class variable as a parent of each attribute. The posterior probability is of these classifiers is formulated as:

$$c^* = argmax_{c \in \Omega} p(c) \prod_{i=1}^{n} p(a_i \mid pa(a_i), c) \quad (0.7)$$

where $p(a_i)$ are the parents of A_i. It is the empty set for NB, it is a set with one single parent for TAN, and it is an unlimited parent set for BAN.

MULTI-DIMENSIONAL BAYESIAN NETWORKS CLASSIFIERS

In previous sections of this chapter we have dealt with standard classification problem, where our goal is to induce a function f, such that $f : X_1 \times X_2 \times \ldots \times X_n \to C$. However in this section we deal with a different classification problem known as multi-dimensional, in which more than one class variable are included. Thus, our goal is to induce a function h, such that:

$$h : X_1 \times X_2 \times \ldots \times X_n \to C_1 \times C_2 \times \ldots \times C_d.$$

This is a problem with many application domains: a book or a film can be classified regarding different targets (genre, expected public, age suitability, etc.), a patient may suffer from multiple diseases, a tumour can be described attending to different parameters (shape, volume, stage, etc.), a gene can have multiple biological functions, etc.

In multi-dimensional classification, given an input instance $(x_1, \ldots, x_n)$, our goal is not to obtain a single value c_i, but a vector $(c_1, \ldots, c_d)$. Of course, this point makes a great difference not only in the classification problem but also in the validation one. That is, by using the 0-1 loss function the predicted vector $(c_1^1, c_2^1, c_3^2, c_4^3)$ will count +1 when calculating accuracy if this is in fact the correct assignment, however the following two vectors will count 0 even their similarity to the correct one is too different: $(c_1^1, c_2^1, c_3^2, c_4^1)$ and $(c_1^2, c_2^2, c_3^1, c_4^1)$. Therefore, multi-dimensional classification requires different evaluation metrics than those used in traditional single-class problems. Some of the metrics proposed in the literature can be found in the surveys done by (Larrañaga, 2010; Tsoumakas & Katakis, 2007).

Approaches to multi-dimensional classification can be grouped into two main categories: problem transformation methods and algorithm adaptation methods. The first one contains those methods that transform the multi-dimensional classification problem either into one or more single-class problems. One of the most used problem transformation method is to consider d independent single-class problems:

$$(X_1,...,X_n,C_1),(X_1,...,X_n,C_2),...,(X_1,...,X_n,C_d).$$

Each single-class problem is solved independently (e.g. using a BNC) and the solution to the multi-dimensional problem is obtained by assembling a d-dimensional vector with the obtained 1-dimensional solutions. Some other problem transformation methods can be found in the literature (Larrañaga, 2010; Tsoumakas & Katakis, 2007).

The main drawback of the problem transformation approach is that interactions between the class variables are lost or the problem complexity is largely increased (e.g. considering a single-class variable where the class is the Cartesian product of the $d$class variables in the original multi-dimensional problem). Because of this, here we focus on the adaptation approach, that is, methods that extend specific learning algorithms (BNCs in our case) in order to handle multi-dimensional data directly.

In this (brief) review of multi-dimensional BNCs (MDBNCs) we follow the definition given (van der Gaag & de Waal, 2006), later refined by (Bielza, Li, & Larrañaga, 2011). In that definition, a MDBNC is a BN with restricted topology, where its directed acyclic graph is divided into three sub-graphs:

- class subgraph: contains the arcs between the class variables.
- feature subgraph: contains the arcs between the features or predictive attributes.
- bridge subgraph: contains the arcs from the class variables to the feature variables.

Depending on the type of graph (empty, tree, polytree, kDB or DAG) allowed in the class/feature subgraph we can have different families of MDBNCs, e.g. empty-empty, empty-tree, tree-empty, tree-tree, etc. The following figure shows an example where the class subgraph is a tree and the feature subgraph has a kDB structure (k=2).

The first approach in the literature dealing with MDBNCs is due to (van der Gaag & de Waal, 2006). In this paper they provide the general setting of MDBNCs and focus on the problem of efficient learning of tree-tree MDBNCs. They use a score+search approach based on MDL (Minimum Description Length) score, and prove that for a given bridge subgraph, the class and feature subgraph (tree) can be optimally learnt independently. Thus, the class subgraph (tree) is first learnt by using Chow-Liu algorithm (Chow & Liu, 1968), and then assuming the bridge subgraph is known, again Chow-Liu is used but considering conditional mutual information (as in TAN) as weight for candidate edges between features. The conditioning set for each pair of features is given by the fixed bridge subgraph. The global algorithm is guided by a wrapper strategy that tries to identify the bridge sugraph that leads to a whole structure maximizing accuracy.

Later, the same authors extend this study to the polytree-polytree MDBNC (de Waal & van der Gaag, 2007). This time the authors focus on a theoretical study to identify the conditions required for the optimal recovery of both polytree structures (class and feature subgraphs). However, the proposal does not include how to identify the bridge subgraph.

Recently, (Bielza, Li, & Larrañaga, 2011) proposed a unified framework for MDBNCs allowing any Bayesian network structure in the two main subgraphs of the model. This is a really strong paper where several learning and inference algorithms are developed. Regarding learning, three algorithms are proposed:

- A **pure filter algorithm** based on the use of an ancestral ordering between the class and feature variables in order to reduce computations. The idea is similar to the one proposed by (van der Gaag & de Waal, 2006), that is, first the class subgraph is learnt, and then the feature subgraph is learnt for a given bridge subgraph. However both algorithms differ because now any DAG can be learn (not only a tree) and the bridge subraph is learnt in a filter way by using a decomposable score and a best-first search algorithm. Concretely, K2 algorithm (Cooper & Herskovits, 1992) is used to learn the class and feature networks, restricted to the given ordering and current bridge subgraph.

- A **pure wrapper algorithm** guided by accuracy. A greedy (hill climbing) algorithm is used that at each step tries to add or delete each possible arc, provided that the topology of a MDBNC is respected. The algorithm stops when no arc can be added or deleted to the current structure to improve the global accuracy.
- A **hybrid algorithm**. The same as pure filter algorithm, but now decision on the bridge subgraph is based on accuracy instead of using the filter score.

Bielza, Li, & Larrañaga (2011) also pay attention to the inference problem in MDBNCs. In fact, this is a complex problem, because the configuration of maximal probability must be identified for the class variables. This leads to a MPE (Most Probable Explanation) or total abduction problem in BNs if there are no missing values in the instance to be classified, or to a MAP or partial abduction problem if there is missing values. Both problems are NP-hard, however MAP remains exponential even for those cases in which MPE can be solved in polynomial time, see e.g. (Gámez, 2004) for details about abductive inference in BNs). In their proposal, Bielza et al. introduce two improvements for inference:

- By exploiting the specific structure of MDBNCs and using gray code, a new

way of moving in the space of joint configurations of the class variables is defined, which allows to reduce the number of computations required to compute (by exhaustive enumeration) the MPE.
- A new type of MDBNCs is introduced, *class-bridge decomposable* MDBNCs that allows to factorize the MPE in a set of subconfigurations that can be obtained independently, alleviating in this way the computational burden for MPE computations.

In a related work, (Borchani, Bielza, & Larrañaga, 2010), take advantage of the class-bridge decomposability property in the induction/learning step. The idea is to induce CB-decomposable MDBNCs in order to obtain structures for which MPE computation can be done efficiently. Thus, the algorithm first greedily identifies the bridge and feature subgraphs, and then iteratively merges components if an improvement is obtained. Each time two components are merged (arcs are added between the class variables) the bridge and feature subgraph are updated.

Zaragoza et al. (2011) also present a hybrid algorithm that combines filter and wrapper techniques. Their algorithm has two stages. In the first one a MDBNC is learnt in a filter way by using mutual information. Tree-like structures are learnt independently by using Chow and Liu algorithm. Then, all the possible pairs between a class variable and a feature one are scored by using mutual information. Those arcs corresponding to pairs whose mutual information exceeds a fixed threshold are added to the bridge subgraph from higher to lower mutual information. In a second step new arcs are added to the bridge subgraph by using accuracy as the score to be optimized.

Finally, Rodríguez & Lozano (2008) present a method for learning kDB-kDB MDBNCs. The proposal however is rather different to the aforementioned ones because of two reasons: (1) evolutionary algorithms are used to discover the kDB+bridge+kDB structure minimizing the classification error and, (2) a multi-objective approach is used that considers the accuracy of each class variable separately as the function to optimize. The solution returned is then the Pareto set of non-dominated MDBNCs and their accuracy rates for the different class variables. It is the decision maker who must choose the classifier that best suits the particular problem.

OTHER NETWORKS-BASED PROBABILISTIC CLASSIFIERS

Although the most common probabilistic graphical models used in network-based probabilistic classifiers are Bayesian (or Gaussian) networks, in the literature we can find probabilistic classifiers based on alternative probabilistic graphical models. In this section we review some of them.

Bayesian Multinets (BMs) were first introduced by Geiger & Heckerman (1996) and then studied by (Friedman, et al., 1997) as classifiers. In a BM the dataset is partitioned into $|C|$ datasets, each one containing those instances labelled with class state c_i. Then a BN B_i over all the predictive attributes is learnt for each projected dataset. Finally the prior probability of C is estimated according to the frequency of its labels in the original dataset. Thus, a multinet M defines the following joint distribution:

$$P_M(C, X_1, \ldots, X_n) =$$
$$P(C) \cdot P_{B_i}(X_1, \ldots, X_n) \text{ when } C = c_i.$$

Multinets are useful for representing contextual independence assertions. For example, in a classification context we may directly represent the (possibly different) independence relations over the predictive attributes for each of the class values. Consequently a multinet classifier is expected to have a higher, or at least the same, representational power than that of a single BN classifier. Notice also, that the type of graph learnt

for each class state can be restricted to be a tree, chain, kDB, etc.

Dependency networks (DNs) were introduced by (Heckerman, Chickering, Meek, Rounthwaite, & Kadie, 2001) and its main difference with respect to BNs is the fact that they allow directed cycles. Structural learning can therefore be performed very efficiently, since the node families can be learned independently of each other. Because of the presence of cycles general inference must be done in approximate way (usually Gibbs sampling is used), however, as in classification only the class variable is unknown, inference can be carried out as efficiently as in BNs. (Gámez, Mateo, Nielsen, & Puerta, 2008; Gámez, Mateo, & Puerta, 2006, 2007) propose different approaches for DN-based classifiers.

- In Gámez et al. (2006) a filter algorithm is presented based on the use of χ^2 test in order to iteratively obtain the parent set for each variable. This algorithm is comparable to other BNCs like TAN and BAN, and as parent sets are learnt independently for each variable, scalability is its main merit.

- A different approach is followed in (Gámez, et al., 2007). Three different algorithms are proposed to efficiently learn DNs classifiers based on the kDB algorithm. Then, the obtained DN classifier is translated into a BN classifier (BAN). The translation method is just a wrapper algorithm which behaves greedily by removing at each step the link (from those that belong to any cycle) whose elimination yields the best classifier according to accuracy.

- Finally DN-multinets are proposed in (Gámez, et al., 2008). The idea is not only to replicate Bayesian multinets, but also to reduce learning time and improve robustness when dealing with data sparse classes, by designing methods for reusing calculations across mixture components.

Probabilistic decision graphs (PDGs) were introduced by (Jaeger, 2004) and are a kind of probabilistic graphical model that efficiently captures certain context specific independencies that are not easily represented by other graphical models traditionally used for classification. This means that the PDG model can capture some distributions using fewer parameters than classical models. (Nielsen, Rumí, & Salmerón, 2009) propose to apply the PDG model for supervised classification. They propose two different algorithms:

- Transformation of a previously obtained FAN classifier into a PDG model that later is refined. The authors show that a FAN can be translated into a PDG without increasing the number of parameters. Then, the PDG classifier is refined by merging nodes which allow to (1) reduce the number of parameters and (2) to take fully advantage of PDG expressiveness. This refinement (merging) phase is done in a wrapper way, using accuracy as the score to optimize.
- Direct learning of a PDG-based classifier from a dataset of labelled data. The algorithm works incrementally by adding predictive attributes to the variable tree structure with root C guided by classification accuracy on a hold-out set. Merging is again used, and two nodes are collapsed into a single one if doing so increases classification accuracy measured on the hold-out data.
- From the experiments can be concluded that the proposed models are competitive with the state-of-the-art BN classifiers.

Dynamic Bayesian networks (DBNs) are time-sliced BNs in which the following assumptions are usually done: (1) the structure of the BN included in each slice is always the same, (2) the model is Markovian, that is, the future is independent of the past given the present, and (3) the

process is stationary, that is, the transition probabilities and so the arcs connecting nodes between two consecutive slices are always the same. Dynamic Bayesian network classifiers are an adaptation of DBNs to the supervised classification problem for those cases in which time plays an important role in the process (e.g. gesture recognition). In the literature we can find several approaches based on Naïve Bayes(Avilés-Arriaga & Sucar, 2002; Avilés-Arriaga, Sucar, & Mendoza, 2006; M. Martínez & Sucar, 2008; Palacios-Alonso, Brizuela, & Sucar, 2010). In (Avilés-Arriaga & Sucar, 2002; Avilés-Arriaga, et al., 2006)the structure included in each slice is a NB, and the only transition relation allowed is modelled by adding an arrow from the class in time t to the class in time $t+1$, that is, $P(C_{t+1} \mid C_t)$. In (M. Martínez & Sucar, 2008; Palacios-Alonso, et al., 2010), the general structure is the same but now the predictive attributes are a subset of the available ones plus some combinations (Cartesian product) as in semi-NB model proposed by Pazzani (1996).

A richer model is introduced in (Zhong, Martínez, Nielsen, & Langseth, 2010) where transition relation are allowed between predictive attributes and also a hidden variable is included to gather some dependences. Obviously, the learning process is much more complex than in NB-based models.

HOW TO HANDLE NUMERIC VARIABLES

So far, we have just considered that all the attributes in the dataset of interest are of a discrete (nominal) type. However, in many real applications the input data are of a continuous nature. Unfortunately, at the moment of writing, there is not a clear guideline on the best way to handle these numeric attributes when learning a Bayesian model.

In general, Bayesian methods make use of multinomial distributions, which assume all the variables are discrete. Hence, the more direct way to proceed in order to be able to treat these numeric attributes is discretization. Even though it entails an unavoidable loss of information, it can be a good (or even the best) alternative in many domains. Other techniques to directly deal with the original numeric values implies assuming that these attributes follow a known parametric distribution, such as Gaussians, Kernels or mixtures of truncated exponentials.

There exist other alternatives, and it is not always clear which is the best option. The first question raised is whether discretization is suitable for our purposes or we should directly assume our samples follow a known parametric distribution. But even if it was clear that discretization is the best option, the type of discretization along with its configuration values should be set. On the other hand, if no discretization is performed, one or more probability distributions must be selected. The best decision to make is not always clear, that is why in the following sections we pretend to provide an overview of the most common procedures in Bayesian classifiers.

Discretization

Every discretization process involves the transformation of continuous domains into discrete counterparts. It implies an unavoidable loss of information, since from the infinite number of continuous values provided as original input, "only" a finite set of values is kept.

In this context, we consider discretization as a data pre-processing technique that transforms a quantitative attribute into a qualitative one. In practice, the discretization process can be viewed as a method for reducing data dimensionality, as input data is transformed from a huge range of continuous values into a much smaller subset of discrete ones. Although we can find a considerable variation in the terminology used to refer to

this these types of attributes (Yinh, 2003), in this chapter, we will refer to attributes for which no arithmetic operations can be applied as 'discrete', and the rest as 'continuous' or 'numeric'.

The necessity of applying discretization on the input data can be due to different reasons. Firstly, many powerful classification and modelling algorithms only operate on categorical or nominal data, and therefore discretization is a prerequisite if we wish to apply these algorithms (e.g. certain Bayesian methods). In other cases, discretization improves the run time for the given algorithms, such as decision trees, as the number of possible partitions to be evaluated is drastically decreased.

Also, discrete values for a variable may on many occasions provide a higher interpretability of the models. Finally, there are cases where discretization is simply a pre-processing step with the aim of obtaining a reduction in the value set and, thus, a reduction in the noise which is quite possibly present in the data.

Many different taxonomies for dividing and organizing the various discretization techniques can be found in the literature (Liu, Hussain, Tan, & Dash, 2002), the most commonly used being the one which distinguishes between **unsupervised** (e.g. equal frequency or width, k-means) and **supervised** (such as those based on entropy, 1R algorithm) methods. This distinction is made depending on whether or not the method takes class information into account in order to find proper intervals.

Traditionally, supervised discretization techniques have been believed to be especially suitable for classification tasks. Nevertheless, some recent experiments on several semi-naïve classifiers comparing some unsupervised methods vs. the minimum description length supervised technique show that unsupervised division techniques by equal frequency generally provide better results in some semi-naïve Bayesian classifiers (M.J. Flores, Gámez, A.M. Martínez, & Puerta, 2011). This could be explained by the good trade-off between discretization bias and variance achieved.

Another way of categorizing discretization methods is by considering whether variables are discretized independently, known as **univariate** (and also as local), or if not, we have the **multivariate** methods (also referred to as global, although we prefer the former nomenclature to avoid ambiguity), which take into consideration the relationships among attributes during discretization. It has been proven that multivariate techniques can produce better discretizations, since the joint information measures are much more powerful (Chmielewski & Jerzy, 1996). Also, optimization methods such as evolutionary computation techniques can be used in this multivariate scheme (J. L. Flores, Inza, & Larrañaga, 2007). However, these methods cannot be considered under time restrictions, and their complexity increases dramatically with the number of attributes. Thus, the main drawback is that they are much more costly in resource consumption than classical approaches. This fact makes them less attractive for the semi-naïve family of BNCs considered in this chapter.

Furthermore, for a particular classifier (or family of classifiers) it is possible to construct *ad hoc* discretization methods, which could be categorized as tailored methods. In this category, we could place two discretization techniques proposed in (Yang & Webb, 2009) designed to fit NB's needs. These two techniques though, provided overall worse results for other classifiers belonging to the semi-naïve family (M.J. Flores, et al., 2011).

Nonetheless, all the discretization techniques taken into account so far formed non-overlapping intervals for numeric attributes. A novel type of discretization was proposed also for NB by Webb and Yang, called Non-disjoint discretization, which creates bins that overlap. This technique has also been tested on the classifiers AODE and HAODE providing promising results (A.M. Martínez, Webb, Flores, & Gámez, 2011).

Gaussian Density Estimation

The Gaussian distribution (also known as normal) is one of the most frequently found distributions in real phenomena. The graph of the associated probability density function is "bell"-shaped, and is known as the **Gaussian function** or **bell curve** (see Figure 2, right graph). It can be entirely defined by its density functions: through its mean, μ, and variance, σ^2.

Every continuous node in a BN can be modelled through a Gaussian distribution function. Likewise, every continuous node can have a Gaussian distribution for every configuration of its discrete parents. The estimated probability that a discrete variable takes a certain value is equal to its sample frequency, the maximum likelihood estimates of the mean and standard deviation of a normal distribution are the sample average and the sample standard deviation. Then, the 'adaptation' of Eq. (0.10) is straightforward, as (Cowell, Dawid, Lauritzen, & Spiegelhalter, 2003; De-Groot, 2004; Geiger & Heckerman, 1996):

$$p(X = x \mid pa(X) = q) \sim \mathcal{N}(x; \mu_q, \sigma_q) \quad (0.8)$$

where μ_q and σ_q are the mean and standard deviation of X conditioned on the value of its parents, all of them of discrete type; and:

$$\mathcal{N}(x; \mu, \sigma) = \frac{1}{\sqrt{2\mu\sigma}} e^{-\frac{(x-\mu)^2}{2\sigma^2}} \quad (0.9)$$

These would be sufficient for some classifiers, such as naïve Bayes, as the numeric attributes are exclusively class-conditioned, i.e, so far, we have just considered that $pa(x)$ are of type discrete. But what happens if the numeric variable to model has one or more continuous parents? In this case we have to resort to the use of the Conditional Gaussian Networks.

Figure 2. Tree-kDB MDBNC. Arrows of class subraph are in blue (tree). Arrows of feature subgraph are in green (kDB with k=2 and X1,..,X5 as ordering). Arrows of bridge subgraph are in black.

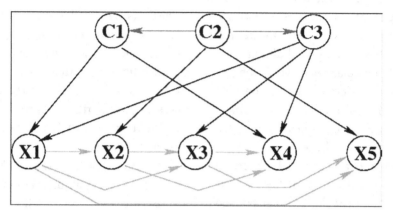

In a **Conditional Gaussian Network (CGN)** (Lauritzen, 1992; Lauritzen & Jensen, 2001; Lauritzen & Wermuth, 1998; Olesen, 1993; Shachter & Kenley, 1989) the mean of a numeric node is linearly dependent of the states of its continuous parents and the variance.

In general, each node stores a local density function (lineal regression model) where the distribution for a continuous variable X with discrete parents Y and continuous parents Z is a univariate Gaussian distribution, conditioned on the values of its parents (DeGroot, 1970):

$$f(X \mid Y = y, Z = z) =$$
$$\mathcal{N}(\mu_X(y) + \sum_z b_{XZ}(y)(z - \mu_Z(y)), \sigma^2_{X|Z}(y))$$

$$(0.10)$$

where:

- $\mu_X(y)$ is the mean of X with the configuration of its discrete parents Y.
- $\mu_Z(y)$ is the mean of Z_j with the configuration of its discrete parents Y.
- $\sigma^2_{X|Z}(y)$ is the conditional variance of X over its continuous parents Z and also according to the configuration $Y=y$. It is calculated as $\sigma^2_X(y) - b^2_{XZ}(y)\sigma^2_Z(y)$.

- $b_{XZ}(y)$ is a regression term that individually measures the strength of the connection between X and every continuous parent (it will be equal to 0 if there is not an edge between them). It is calculated as $\dfrac{\sigma_{XZ}(y)}{\sigma^2_Z(y)}$.

The local parameters are given by $\Theta = (\mu_x(y), b_x(y), \sigma_{X|Z}(y))$, where $b_X(y) = (b_{XZ_1}(y), \ldots, b_{XZ_s}(y))^t$ is a column vector. Hence, even if $pa(x)$ contains numeric variables, we can still apply equation (0.10) considering the mean and variance as specified above.

In (Pérez, Larrañaga, & Inza, 2006), the authors show how to adapt different classifiers, in which we find NB, TAN, kDB and semi naïve Bayes, and other proposals based on feature selection from these classifiers, to the conditional Gaussian network paradigm, along with the corresponding empirical evaluation. It is also interesting to note their proposition to calculate the mutual information between every pair of continuous predictive variables conditioned on the class.

AODE has also been tested under numeric and hybrid domains with the GAODE (Gaussian AODE) and HAODE (Hybrid AODE) classifiers(M. J. Flores, Gámez, A.M. Martínez, & Puerta, 2009a). The former, makes use of the

CGNs in order to deal with exclusively numeric datasets. The latter uses the discretized version of the superparent (the node which is parent of all the other attributes, apart from the class), both in the learning and classification process, so that it is not required to resort to CGNs, but instead, simple Gaussian and multinomial distributions are estimated. Note that, when every node plays the role of a child, its numeric version, if given, is utilized. Empirical results show that HAODE provides surprisingly good results, especially on numeric datasets, compared with the other classifiers.

So far, we have just considered how to model continuous variables conditioned on either discrete or continuous variables as well, but how can we face discrete variables with continuous parents? Unfortunately, CGN cannot provide any help in this situation, hence being only useful when exclusively numeric data are considered.

Furthermore, CGNs should be preferably used when Gaussian data is provided. In principle, it may seem easy to determine whether the data of interest follows a Gaussian distribution and hence, deciding whether or not to use CGN for our classifiers. As a matter of fact, there exist several statistical tests to check normality such as Kolmogórov-Smirnov or Shapiro–Wilk available through all kinds of tools. Nevertheless, it is important to take into account the structure of the BN we are considering for classification and performing multivariate normality tests according to it.

Kernel Density Estimation

Modelling all the attributes in a dataset through Gaussian estimations entails a clear problem, as the group of samples for many of them may not follow a normal distribution. A possible solution to this problem is the use of **histograms**, as they are considered the most simple non-parametric density estimators. Unlike the parametric estimators, where the estimator has a prefixed function

and the parameters of that function are the only information to store, the non-parametric estimators do not have a prefixed structure and depend on all the samples to provide estimation. In order to build a histogram, the range of the data is divided into subintervals of equal size (bins), and they are represented in the X-axis. For every sample belonging to a specific bin, the corresponding block in the Y-axis is incremented by one unit.

Nevertheless, the use of histograms has several problems, such as the lack of smoothing, the dependence of the bin-width and the final points selected. In order to ameliorate these issues, we can resort to the use of **density estimators based on kernels** (Silverman, 1986).

With the aim of relieving the dependence on the final points selected for each bin, estimations based on kernels build a kernel function for every sample. It is possible to smooth density estimation by using an smoothed kernel function; hence avoiding two out of the three problems existing in histograms. The bin-width issue can also be solved, as we will introduce below.

Formally, kernel estimations smooth the contribution of each sample according to the points in its neighborhood. The contribution of the point $x(i)$ on the estimation of other point x depends on how separate they are. The scope of this contribution also depends on the shape and width adopted by the kernel function K. The estimated density in the point x is defined through the following equation:

$$\hat{f}(x) = \frac{1}{th} \sum_{i=1}^{n} K\left(\frac{x - x(i)}{h}\right)$$

(0.11)

where $h > 0$ is a smoothing parameter called the bandwidth. Intuitively one wants to choose h as small as the data allows, however there is always a trade-off between the bias of the estimator and its variance.

Gaussian kernels are the most well known, but there exist other options, such us uniform kernels, triangulars', Epanechnikov's, etc... Even though the selection of K determines the shape of the density to estimate, the literature suggests that this selection is not critical, at least among the most common ones (Deaton, 1997). It is believed that the specification of the bandwidth is even more important: the bigger the value of h, the greater the smoothing factor, being important to find the optimal value.

From its definition one can deduce that both temporal and space complexity in kernel estimations may be too high to consider along with the semi-naïve Bayesian classifiers proposed in this chapter, where keeping these two factors under control is one of the main goals.

Still, we can find studies in literature that successfully apply kernel estimations to semi-naïve Bayesian classifiers, in the sense that if no constrains in terms of space or time are imposed, the results are generally much better than other alternatives. In (John & Langley, 1995) the authors introduce the notion of *flexible classifier*, that aims to be similar to NB except for the method used for density estimation on continuous variables. They particularly investigate kernel density estimation with Gaussian kernels selecting $h = \sigma_c = \dfrac{1}{\sqrt{t_c}}$ as bandwidth, where t_c is the number of training instances with class c.

It is in (Pérez, Larrañaga, & Inza, 2009), where the generalization of these notion of flexible naïve Bayes is proposed, extended to other paradigms such as TAN, kDB or even the complete graph classifier. It is also interesting to note the new definition for an estimator of the mutual information based on kernels.

Mixtures of Truncated Exponentials

Even though conditional Gaussian networks (CGNs) offer a frame where it is possible to guarantee the exactitude in the inference under time constrains, there exists a serious restriction: it is not possible to model discrete variables with continuous parents. Furthermore, this model is especially useful in those situations where the joint distribution of the continuous variables given the configuration of the its discrete parents follows a multivariate Gaussian; nevertheless, it is possible to find, in practice, scenarios where this hypothesis is not accomplished. In order to overcome this problem there is a relatively new alternative that is becoming more and more popular, the use of Mixtures of Truncated Exponentials (MTEs) (Moral, Rumí, & Salmerón, 2001). MTE can be an attractive alternative to discretization, as discretization can be seen as an approximation to a density function with a mixture of uniforms, being the use of exponentials a more accurate estimation.

Following the former notation, where $Y = \{Y_1, \ldots, Y_d\}$ is the set of discrete variables and $Z = \{Z_1, \ldots, Z_c\}$ the set of continuous variables, and T both, with $d + c = n$. Considering that for the classification task $Y \neq \varnothing$, as at least the class variable is discrete, a function $f : \Omega_T \mapsto \Re_0^+$ is and MTE potential if for each value $y \in \Omega_Y$, the potential over the continuous variables Z is defined as follows:

$$f_y(z) = a_0 + \sum_{i=1}^{m} a_i\, exp\left\{\sum_{j=1}^{c} \mathbf{b}_i^T \mathbf{z}\right\} \qquad (0.12)$$

where all $\mathbf{z} \in \Omega_{\mathbf{z}}$, where $a_i \in \mathbb{R}$ and $b_i \in \mathbb{R}^c, i = 1, \ldots, m$. We also say that f is an MTE potential if there is a partition $D_1, \ldots, D_k$ of $\Omega_{\mathbf{z}}$ into hypercubes and in each partition, f is defined as in Eq. (0.12). An MTE potential is an **MTE density** if it integrates to 1.

In a Bayesian network, two types of densities can be found:

- $f(x)$ for each variable X with no parents.

- A conditional density $f(x \mid pa(x))$ for each variable X with parents $pa(X)$.

A conditional density $f(x \mid pa(x))$ is an MTE potential that obtains a density function for X when the possible values for $pa(X)$ are fixed. Note that either X or its parents can be discrete or continuous.

Estimations of Univariate and Conditional MTEs

If we restrict the definition of an MTE potential to a variable with no parents and restricted to a single constant term and two exponentials, we obtain the following densities:

$$f^*(x) = k + a\ exp\{bx\} + c\ exp\{dx\} \qquad (0.13)$$

The estimation of the parameters $(\hat{a}, \hat{b}, \hat{c}, \hat{d}, \hat{k})$ of a univariate MTE density function is carried out through the MTE-fitting algorithm, described in (Rumí, Salmerón, & Moral, 2006). However, this method is not valid for the conditional case, as more restrictions should be considered over the parameters in order to force the integration of the MTE potential for each combination of the values for $pa(X)$.

Precisely, the use of conditional distributions through MTEs applied to the learning phase in a Naïve Bayes classifier is shown in (Rumí, et al., 2006). In this case, the adaptation of the MTE-fitting algorithm is straightway, as it is called for every class value and the marginal function of the class is estimated according to its frequency. Nevertheless, this method is just valid if the variable whose distribution we want to estimate has only discrete parents. Hence, it is not extendable to appearance of numeric parents.

This problem was solved in (Moral, Rumí, & Salmerón, 2003), where the authors propose to partition at the domain of the conditioning variables and adjust the univariate density function

for each part using the MTE-fitting algorithm. More precisely, the algorithm learns a mixed tree whose leaves contain MTE densities that only depend on the child variable (or node), and that represent the density for the corresponding branch in the mixed tree. The tree is learnt in such a way that the leaves discriminate as much as possible, following a scheme similar to that carried out by decision trees (Quinlan, 1986). In order to do so, the following steps must be followed:

1. Selection of the variable to expand from $pa(X)$ by means of the splitting gain.
2. Determination of the splits of the selected variable (for example equal frequency intervals can be used).
3. Learning the MTE. There exists a criterion to stop branching the tree by means of a threshold given by the user.
4. Pruning the tree.

Equation (1.1) shows an example of a possible conditional MTE density for Y given X (both of them continuous variables).

$$f(y \mid x) =$$
$$\begin{cases} 1.26 - 1.15e^{0.006y} & \text{if } 0.4 \leq x < 5, 0 \leq y < 13, \\ 1.18 - 1.16e^{0.0002y} & \text{if } 0.4 \leq x < 5, 13 \leq y < 43, \\ 0.07 - 0.03e^{-0.4y} + 0.0001e^{0.0004y} & \text{if } 5 \leq x < 19, 0 \leq y < 5, \\ -0.99 + 1.03e^{0.001y} & \text{if } 5 \leq x < 19, 5 \leq y < 43. \end{cases}$$
$$(1.1)$$

Most of the work published so far concerning semi-naïve Bayesian classifiers with MTEs is more focussed on *regression* (Fernández & Salmerón, 2008) rather than *classification* (Flesch, Fernández, & Salmerón, 2007), i.e. the class variables to predict are numeric instead of discrete. It makes sense, since MTEs are a good alternative especially in that domain. Nevertheless, the inference mechanisms are similar, and we believe, that the results can also provide an idea on those that would be obtained in the classification domain.

Figure 2 shows the graphical results of using the different methods described above to handle a numeric attribute called *waiting*, which represents the waiting time between eruptions for the Old Faithful geyser in Yellowstone National Park, Wyoming, USA. The graph on the left hand side shows the average of the values placed in the same bin when applying equal frequency discretization with 5 bins. The graph on the right hand side shows the Gaussian, Kernel and MTE estimations.

APPLICATIONS

Generally speaking, Bayesian technology has become popular and well-established, as demonstrated by the numerous companies specialising in this formalism. Just to give a few examples, we can find enterprises such as Agenarisk (http://www.agenarisk.com/), BayesiaLab (http://www.bayesia.com/) or Bayesian Intelligence (http://www.bayesian-intelligence.com/). This *commercial* interest on BNs suggests they are useful in real applications. In this section we describe some domains where BN classifiers have been successfully applied with fruitful results.

Computing and Robotics

It is quite logical and natural that Bayesian networks Classifiers (BNCs), developed by computing researchers, were firstly applied to solve certain tasks related to computers such as e-mail services (Sahami, Dumais, Heckerman, & Horvitz, 1998), web/text classification (Jiang, Zhang, Cai, & Su, 2005) or artificial vision (Rehg & Murphy, 1999). We can even find a chess *player*, BayesChess (Fernandez & Salmeron, 2008). BNCs have also been successfully included for fault detection in networking systems, with similar aims as those applied in Medicine (next subsection).

BNCs have been so broadly used in spam filters that many of the commercial-use programs are based in this technology. We can therefore speak about an outstanding family called *Bayesian spam filtering*. These filters can be integrated into the mail client or be separately installed in a filtering software package, for instance SpamAssassin (http://spamassassin.apache.org/) and SpamBayes (http://spambayes.sourceforge.net/).

Just to mention in more detail one of the numerous applications, we have selected BayesChess, mainly because of its originality. This is not the most powerful chess player if we compare it with other current programs as, for example, *Fritz*, Software product commercialised by ChessBase (http://www.chessbase.com). However, it presents a very interesting novelty: BayesChess is able to adapt its game strategy to its opponent, as well as to adapt the evaluation function that guides the search process according to its playing experience. These adaptive and learning abilities BNCs are achieved by implementing BNCs. Interested readers can download this program from http://programo.albacete.org/?seccion=recursos. Figure 4 shows a fragment of one of the classifiers that BayesChess uses to refine the parameters in the heuristic defined to play chess. Another is used to determine the opponent's style. Notice that this classifier is based on the Naïve Bayes structure, but with the difference that instead of one class variable, in this case there are two of them: the current game stage (opening, middle-game or end-game) and the result (win, lose, draw). In fact this is a multi-dimensional model, empty-empty type (see Sec. Multi-dimensional BNCs), though this is not used in that way in this work. Note that in the figure only a few of the 838 feature variables are depicted. Those 838 variables, used in the heuristic function, correspond to the value for each piece on the board, the value of setting the opponent's king under check and the number stored in the 8 x 8 matrices. See Sec. 3 in (Fernandez & Salmeron, 2008) for more detail.

So, the classifier in Figure 4 obtains the best configuration for the heuristic that BayesChess will use in chess playing, which is at the same time necessary for the min-max algorithm. The

Figure 3. The figure on the left hand side shows the original data points along with the corresponding equal frequency discretization with 5 bins. The figure on the right hand side shows the histogram of the original data along with: the Gaussian estimate, the Kernel estimate and the estimated function using Mixtures of Truncated Exponentials.

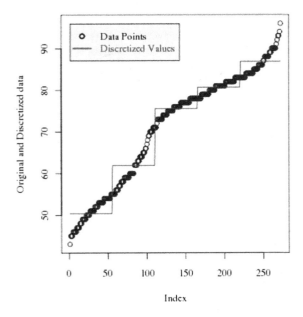
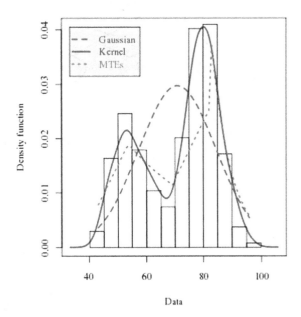

high number of variables meant that a more complex structure in the classifier had to be avoided, so that time for exploring the search tree is not drastically increased. The drawback of this choice is that the independence assumption can be little realistic, but this is compensated for the reduction in the number of free parameters that have to be estimated from data. Experiments with a database of 2000 chess games have proved that BayesChess succeeds in its adaptive behavior.

Medicine and Healthcare

Artificial Intelligence has been broadly applied to medical areas through the use of Decision Support Systems, and classification is not an exception (Kammerdiner, Gupal, & Pardalos, 2007). BNCs have been proved a very useful tool for many aspects of medicine, including heart diseases (Qazi et al., 2007), cancer diagnosis (Antal, Fannes, Timmerman, Moreau, & DeMoor, 2003), gene

identification (Armañanzas, Inza, & Larrañaga, 2008) and human biology (Morales, Bengoetxea, & Larrañaga, 2008).

For example, Armañanzas, et al. (2008) applied BNCs to the search of gene interaction networks. These are used to map relationships of the genes in a genomic study. The interactions induced by BNCs are based both on the expressions levels and on the phenotype information. This work proposes a Data Mining approach which also involves variable selection. Figure 5 shows an example classifier they obtained for a particular problem, but they also experiment with three other genomic datasets. In particular, this DNA microarray study-case involves the analysis of different cells coming from a variety of lymphoma tumors. The genes in Figure 5 named gyyyyX (y being a digit) are those considered relevant by their dependency model. In this problem there are 9 diagnostic classes corresponding to different lymphocyte cell types. This application provides

Figure 4. BN classifier used in BayesChess for learning the heuristic (© 2008, Elsevier, Used with permission)

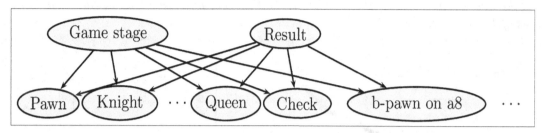

Figure 5. Example of the graphical structure of the network classifiers in (Armañanzas, et al., 2008) representing the model structure for the Lymphoma using high-confidence dependences (© 2008, Elsevier, Used with permission)

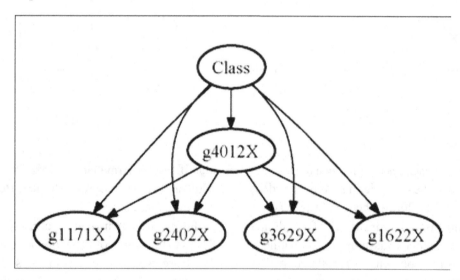

a new set of tools to help understand complex diseases, by showing relationships of different degrees among the involved genes.

Economy, Finance, and Banking

Businesses and governments must often assess and manage risk in areas where there is little or no direct historical data to draw upon, or where relevant data is difficult to identify. In many cases banks need to assess credit or market risk, which is possible since there are sufficient data for prediction and mitigation of risk, but it can

be even more important to attain the capability of predicting the operational risk, that is, the results of failures in everyday operational processes (Fenton & Neil, 2007). One of the strengths present in BNs and its family of classifiers is their potential for modelling relationships between variables. Finding these dependencies is not an easy task, but achieving the goal of discovering relationships can be extremely useful for those activities highly related to economy. For example, BNCs had been applied to assess risk in certain operations such as credit approval or deciding whether to invest in a particular area or enterprise.

Figure 6. TAN classifier used in (Pavlenko & Chernyak, 2010) to design a credit risk model (© 2010, Wiley & Sons, Used with permission)

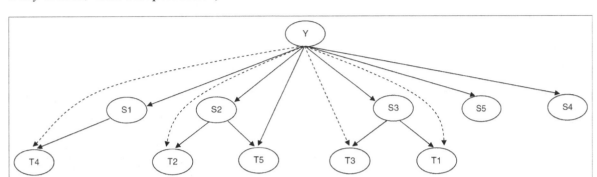

Pavlenko & Chernyak (2010) worked with data from a private midsized bank in Ukraine whose aim was to design a credit risk model in which a particular role of the related borrowers exposure can be analyzed as a risk-aggregating factor. Figure 6 illustrates the classifier obtained by means of an analytical process to get real data. This is made up of the following nodes, $\{X = Y, S_1, \ldots, S_5, T_1, \ldots, T_5\}$, and edges represent direct dependencies between the nodes in accordance with credit experts evaluation. Y denotes the bankruptcy status of the bank, S_i denotes the solvency status of the i-th Financial Institution, being $i = 1, \ldots, 5$, and T_j denotes the solvency status of j-th private enterprise, $j = 1, \ldots, 5$.

Recall that a BNC provides not only a structure but also the probabilistic information in terms of $P(X_i \mid pa(X_i))$ since the Joint Probability Distribution can be obtained from the multiplication of all conditional probabilities tables (CPTs) for all variables. For example, for the previously depicted classifier original CPTs are shown in Figure 7. Note that CPTs can be automatically learned, but also elicited from the expert (as in this case) or even a combination of both.

This model (expressed by Figure 6 and Figure 7) is initially constructed using a classical BNC and also with the collaboration of experts. Afterwards it is also validated and it could be updated according to the results of the assessment process.

In the same work kDB is also explored. As the authors state, BNCs provide the ability to integrate uncertain expert knowledge (e.g. expert estimates of the risk exposure of a group of related borrowers) with data. This potentially provides economists with the ability to update prior knowledge with new information as it is learned, and to build a solution of increasing scope and complexity. Another advantage of the BN modeling approach is that both the graph structure and probability parameter estimate can easily be updated on a periodic basis. So, these are two reasons that reinforce the use of BNCs in this area of knowledge.

In Chapter 7 of (Korb & Nicholson, 2010) other examples of credit risk assessment with BNs are reviewed.

Environmental Science

Environmental science is another area where BNCs have been successfully applied in the past, and, in fact, the interest in these Bayesian structures has increased enormously during the last five years. Reviewing the literature we can find relevant works in ecology, microbiology (Wang, Garrity, Tiedje, & Cole, 2007), fish recruitment (Fernandes et al., 2010), and fish classification (Axelson, Standal, Martinez, & Aursand, 2009).

BNCs provide two main utilities: their descriptive side, which allows the discovery of relation-

Figure 7. Conditional probabilities tables estimated for the TAN classifier in Figure 6

$P(Y=b)$	$P(Y=nb)$
0.5	0.5

	$y=nb$	$y=b$
$P_{S_1|Y}(s|y)$	0.7	0.2
$P_{S_1|Y}(ns|y)$	0.3	0.8
$P_{S_2|Y}(s|y)$	0.7	0.2
$P_{S_2|Y}(ns|y)$	0.3	0.8
$P_{S_3|Y}(s|y)$	0.6	0.3
$P_{S_3|Y}(ns|y)$	0.4	0.7
$P_{S_4|Y}(s|y)$	0.8	0.1
$P_{S_4|Y}(ns|y)$	0.2	0.9
$P_{S_5|Y}(s|y)$	0.6	0.3
$P_{S_5|Y}(ns|y)$	0.4	0.7

	$x=s$	$x=ns$
$P_{T_1|S_3}(s|x)$	0.6	0.3
$P_{T_1|S_3}(ns|x)$	0.4	0.7
$P_{T_2|S_2}(s|x)$	0.6	0.3
$P_{T_2|S_2}(ns|x)$	0.4	0.7
$P_{T_3|S_3}(s|x)$	0.55	0.25
$P_{T_3|S_3}(ns|x)$	0.45	0.75
$P_{T_4|S_1}(s|x)$	0.65	0.3
$P_{T_4|S_1}(ns|x)$	0.35	0.7
$P_{T_5|S_2}(s|x)$	0.52	0.45
$P_{T_5|S_2}(ns|x)$	0.48	0.55

	$y=nb$	$y=b$
$P_{T_1|Y}(s|y)$	0.5	0.3
$P_{T_1|Y}(ns|y)$	0.5	0.7
$P_{T_2|Y}(s|y)$	0.5	0.4
$P_{T_2|Y}(ns|y)$	0.5	0.6
$P_{T_3|Y}(s|y)$	0.5	0.35
$P_{T_3|Y}(ns|y)$	0.5	0.65
$P_{T_4|Y}(s|y)$	0.6	0.5
$P_{T_4|Y}(ns|y)$	0.4	0.5
$P_{T_5|Y}(s|y)$	0.6	0.3
$P_{T_5|Y}(ns|y)$	0.4	0.7

ships among variables, and also their predictive value. It is from this second feature that many applications in meteorology have benefitted from BNCs, such in the work by (Hruschka Jr., Hruschka, & Ebecken, 2005) where "wet fog" conditions in a Brazilian airport were predicted by BNs. Notice that BNCs have also been used in this paper for data preparation (feature selection and imputation of missing values).

BNCs have been used in habitat characterization and conservation planning, such as the recent paper by (Aguilera, Fernández, Reche, & Rumí, 2010). Geographical Information Systems and mapping have also been attracted by the application of BNCs. Porwal, Carranza & Hale (2006) applied both NB classifier and TAN to generate a favorability map that identifies the mineralization of certain areas in western India where NB is proven as an efficient tool. In the same direction, BNCs have contributed to the classification of land use, for example Park & Stenstrom (2008) describe a study case where Bayesian networks have been used to accurately classify urban land use from Landsat imagery.

There has also been research applying BNCs to agricultural domain. For instance, Zaffalon (2005) uses Naïve Credal Classifiers, which extends NB to credal sets, to a dataset related to grass grub population and pasture damage levels. Bressan, Oliveira, Hruschka Jr., & Nicoletti (2009) use BNCs for risk detection, but this time for weed infestation in a corn-crop. In the work by Ordoñez, Matias, Rivas & Bastante (2009) BNCs serve as a guideline for the reforestation of deforested areas. Their results demonstrated that the predictive capacity of the BNs is comparable to that of the best available techniques used to date, with the added advantages of interpretability and a posteriori inferential ability. We note that BNCs can be used for monitoring tasks, for instance, Ammar, McKee & Kaluarachchi (2011) studied its use for groundwater quality monitoring.

The relevance of BNs in the environmental field can also been deduced from a whole book very recently published dedicated to the application of Bayesian inference to ecological problems (Link & Barker, 2010). Note, however, that this book is focused on Bayesian statistics but it does not use the valuable support of graphical models that clearly enrich and facilitate the model construction and understanding.

Others

It is challenging to choose which domains to cover in this section, since BNCs have been used in many distinct areas and tasks, and their application is growing rapidly.

There are also multidisciplinary areas that could be described in two of the previous subsections. Just as an example bioinformatics has a computing side, but also its biological component can be sometimes directed to ecology and some others to medicine. Bioinformatics deserves a mention since it combines many disciplines and have been developed thanks to the new technological improvements. In this area BNCs have also been applied very frequently. The PhD thesis by Armañanzas (2009) presents a broad review and a set of developed algorithms to this particular field.

In order to give just a few examples of applications in other fields not previously mentioned, we have selected the use for traffic and transportation described by Boyles & Waller (2007). They developed a probabilistic model based on NB classifier to assist with prediction of incident duration in transportation. Another even more curious, and very recent, study case is the one that attempts to tackle the Sentiment Analysis problem in text: (Ortigosa-Hernandez et al., 2011). This is also an example of multi-dimensional classification, also seen in the previous section. In this innovative work, the authors solve a real problem consisting of the characterization for the attitude of a customer when he writes a post about a particular topic in a specific forum. The three differently related dimensions (classes) were: Will to Influence, Sentiment Polarity and Subjectivity. In order to give an overview of the problem we show the distribution of the working dataset obtained from the authors, which will be the input for learning the multi-dimensional classifier in Figure 8.

With this section covering applications we have provided an overview of how BNCs have already been used, as well as emphasizing the generally good results attained by them. We can see that Naïve Bayes stands out, probably because it appeared first and due to its simplicity and efficiency. However, current technology is ready to apply more complex BNCs that are able to model relationships between predictive attributes. Naïve Bayes' popularity is followed by that of the TAN classifier. We should remember that semi-Naïve classifiers are still very competitive in terms of computation time. As already explained, multi-dimensional classifiers are also a very promising technology when the problem naturally presents several class variables. Finally, we would like to encourage researchers in any area coping with a classification problem to test BNCs, as they have been proved to be a very promising tool that offers extra capabilities such as uncertainty management, ease at updating models or understandability for the expert in contrast to other *black-box* system classifiers.

CONCLUSION

In this chapter we have presented an overview of the state-of-the-art for Bayesian Network Classifiers. Apart from the most known and simple as Naïve Bayes and its extensions (semi-Naïve), we have covered other possibilities which have reached high relevance in the last years such as multi-dimensional classifiers. There are also some related issues that need to be covered such as how to handle numeric attributes, and we have given a review on distinct ways to work with this special kind of variables.

BNCs have been applied in numerous domains and we have also provided an overview of this practical aspect with a double purpose: (1) show the interested reader how BNCs had successfully been integrated to solve real problems and (2) inspire researchers and companies to consider this technology when tackling a classification task that could fit in a Bayesian structure model.

The reader interested in a deeper knowledge in this topic should read/study the following references (Duda, Hart, & Stork, 1973), (Domingos & Pazzani, 1996), (Sahami, 1996), (Friedman, et al., 1997), (Lucas, 2004), (Webb, et al., 2005) and (F. Zheng & Webb, 2005).

Figure 8. Distribution of the labels of the three class variables over the labelled subset. The marginal distributions of Will to Influence, Sentiment Polarity, and Subjectivity are represented as bar diagrams (left) and the joint distribution is represented in a table (right). From (Ortigosa-Hernandez et al., 2011). Used with permission.

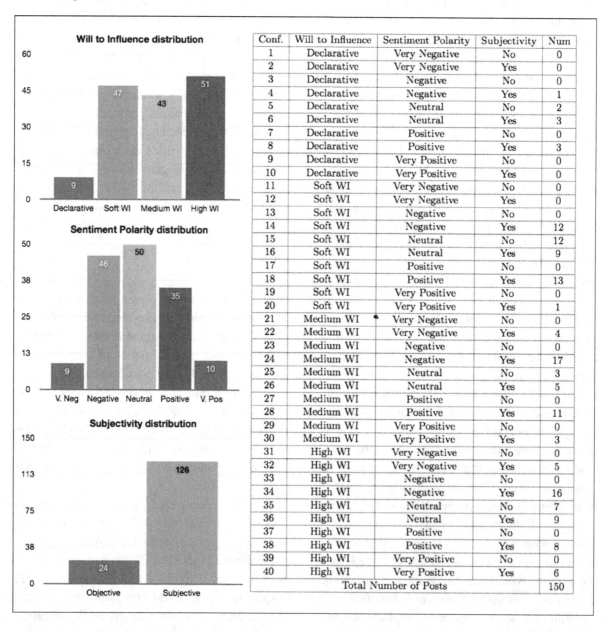

REFERENCES

Aguilera, P. A., Fernández, A., Reche, F., & Rumí, R. (2010). Hybrid Bayesian network classifiers: Application to species distribution models. *Environmental Modelling & Software, 25*(12), 1630–1639. doi:10.1016/j.envsoft.2010.04.016

Ammar, K., McKee, M., & Kaluarachchi, J. (2011). Bayesian method for groundwater quality monitoring network analysis. *Journal of Water Resources Planning and Management, 137*(1), 51–61. doi:10.1061/(ASCE)WR.1943-5452.0000043

Antal, P., Fannes, G., Timmerman, D., Moreau, Y., & DeMoor, B. (2003). Bayesian applications of belief networks and multilayer perceptrons for ovarian tumor classification with rejection. *Artificial Intelligence in Medicine, 29*, 39–60. doi:10.1016/S0933-3657(03)00053-8

Armañanzas, R. (2009). *Consensus policies to solve bioinformatic problems through Bayesian network classifiers and estimation of distribution algorithms.* Department of Computer Science and Artificial Intelligence, University of the Basque Country.

Armañanzas, R., Inza, I., & Larrañaga, P. (2008). Detecting reliable gene interactions by a hierarchy of Bayesian network classifiers. *Computer Methods and Programs in Biomedicine, 91*(2), 110–121. doi:10.1016/j.cmpb.2008.02.010

Avilés-Arriaga, H. H., & Sucar, L. E. (2002). Dynamic Bayesian networks for visual recognition of dynamic gestures. *Journal of Intelligent and Fuzzy Systems, 12*(3-4), 243–250.

Avilés-Arriaga, H. H., Sucar, L. E., & Mendoza, C. E. (2006). Visual recognition of similar gestures. *Proceedings of the 18th International Conference on Pattern Recognition - ICPR'06.*

Axelson, D. E., Standal, I. B., Martinez, I., & Aursand, M. (2009). Classification of wild and farmed salmon using Bayesian belief networks and gas chromatography-derived fatty acid distributions. *Journal of Agricultural and Food Chemistry, 57*(17), 7634–7639. doi:10.1021/jf9013235

Bielza, C., Li, G., & Larrañaga, P. (2011). Multi-dimensional classification with Bayesian networks. *International Journal of Approximate Reasoning, 52*(6). doi:10.1016/j.ijar.2011.01.007

Borchani, H., Bielza, C., & Larrañaga, P. (2010). Learning CB-decomposable multi-dimensional Bayesian network classifiers. *Proceedings of the 5th European Workshop on Probabilistic Graphical Models (PGM'10).*

Boyles, S. F. D., & Waller, S. T. (2007). *A naïve Bayesian classifer for incident duration prediction.* TRB - Transportation Research Board - Annual Meeting, Washington D.C.

Bressan, G. M., Oliveira, V. A., Hruschka, E. R. Jr, & Nicoletti, M. C. (2009). Using Bayesian networks with rule extraction to infer the risk of weed infestation in a corn-crop. *Engineering Applications of Artificial Intelligence, 22*(4-5), 579–592. doi:10.1016/j.engappai.2009.03.006

Chmielewski, M. R., & Jerzy. (1996). Global discretization of continuous attributes as preprocessing for machine learning. *International Journal of Approximate Reasoning, 15*(4), 319–331. doi:10.1016/S0888-613X(96)00074-6

Chow, C. I., & Liu, C. N. (1968). Approximating discrete probability distributions with dependence trees. *IEEE Transactions on Information Theory, 14*, 462–467. doi:10.1109/TIT.1968.1054142

Cooper, G. F., & Herskovits, E. (1992). A Bayesian method for the induction of probabilistic networks from data. *Machine Learning, 9*, 309–347. doi:10.1007/BF00994110

Cowell, R. G., Dawid, P. A., Lauritzen, S. L., & Spiegelhalter, D. J. (2003). *Probabilistic networks and expert systems (information science and statistics).* Springer.

de Waal, P. R., & van der Gaag, L. C. (2007). Inference and learning in multi-dimensional Bayesian network classifiers. *European Conference on Symbolic and Quantitative Approaches to Reasoning with Uncertainty* (Vol. 4724, pp. 501-511).

Deaton, A. (1997). *The analysis of household surveys: A microeconometric approach to development policy. World Bank.* Baltimore, MD: Johns Hopkins University Press.

DeGroot, M. H. (1970). *Optimal statistical decisions.* New York, NY: McGraw-Hill.

DeGroot, M. H. (2004). *Optimal statistical decisions.* Wiley-Interscience. doi:10.1002/0471729000

Domingos, P., & Pazzani, M. J. (1996). *Beyond independence: Conditions for the optimality of the simple Bayesian classifier.* International Conference on Machine Learning.

Duda, R. O., Hart, P. E., & Stork, D. G. (1973). *Pattern classification and scene analysis.* New York, NY: Wiley.

Fenton, N. E., & Neil, M. (2007). *Managing risk in the modern world: Bayesian networks and the applications.* London, UK: London Mathematical Society, Knowledge Transfer Report.

Fernandes, J. A., Irigoien, X., Goikoetxea, N., Lozano, J. A., Inza, I., & Perez, A. (2010). Fish recruitment prediction, using robust supervised classification methods. *Ecological Modelling, 221*(2), 338–352. doi:10.1016/j.ecolmodel.2009.09.020

Fernandez, A., & Salmeron, A. (2008). Bayes-Chess: A computer chess program based on Bayesian networks. *Pattern Recognition Letters, 29*(8), 1154–1159. doi:10.1016/j.patrec.2007.06.013

Fernández, A., & Salmerón, A. (2008). Extension of Bayesian network classifiers to regression problems. *Proceedings of the 11th Ibero-American conference on AI: Advances in Artificial Intelligence.*

Flesch, I., Fernández, A., & Salmerón, A. (2007). Incremental supervised classification for the MTE distribution: A preliminary study. *Actas de Simposio de Inteligencia Computacional, SICO'2007.*

Flores, J. L., Inza, I., & Larrañaga, P. (2007). Wrapper discretization by means of estimation of distribution algorithms. *Intelligent Data Analysis, 11*(5), 525–545.

Flores, M. J., Gámez, J. A., Martínez, A. M., & Puerta, J. M. (2009a). *GAODE and HAODE: Two proposals based on AODE to deal with continuous variables.* International Conference on Machine Learning - ICML.

Flores, M. J., Gámez, J. A., Martínez, A. M., & Puerta, J. M. (2009b). *HODE: Hidden one-dependence estimator.* European Conference on Symbolic and Quantitative Approaches to Reasoning with Uncertainty.

Flores, M. J., Gámez, J. A., Martínez, A. M., & Puerta, J. M. (2011). Handling numeric attributes when comparing Bayesian classifiers: Does the discretization method matter? *Applied Intelligence, 34*(3), 372–385. doi:10.1007/s10489-011-0286-z

Friedman, N., Geiger, D., & Goldszmidt, M. (1997). Bayesian network classifiers. *Machine Learning, 29*, 131–163. doi:10.1023/A:1007465528199

Gámez, J. A. (2004). *Abductive inference in Bayesian networks: A review. Advances in Bayesian Networks* (pp. 101–120). Springer Verlag.

Gámez, J. A., Mateo, J. L., Nielsen, T. D., & Puerta, J. M. (2008). Robust classification using mixtures of dependency networks. *Proceedings of the Fourth European Workshop on Probabilistic Graphical Models (PGM08).*

Gámez, J. A., Mateo, J. L., & Puerta, J. M. (2006). Dependency networks based classifiers: Learning models by using independence. *Proceedings of the 3rd European Workshop on Probabilistic Graphical Models.*

Gámez, J. A., Mateo, J. L., & Puerta, J. M. (2007). Learning Bayesian classifiers from dependency network classifiers. *Proceedings of the 8th International Conference on Adaptive and Natural Computing Algorithms (ICANNGA-07).*

Geiger, D., & Heckerman, D. (1996). Knowledge representation and inference in similarity networks and Bayesian multinets. *Artificial Intelligence, 82*, 45–74. doi:10.1016/0004-3702(95)00014-3

Heckerman, D., Chickering, D. M., Meek, C., Rounthwaite, R., & Kadie, C. (2001). Dependency networks for inference, collaborative filtering, and data visualization. *Journal of Machine Learning Research, 1*, 49–75.

Hruschka, E. R., Jr., Hruschka, E. R., & Ebecken, N. F. F. (2005). *Applying Bayesian networks for meteorological data mining.* SGAI International Conference on Artificial Intelligence.

Jaeger, M. (2004). Probabilistic decision graphs - Combining verification and AI techniques for probabilistic inference. *International Journal of Uncertainty, Fuzziness and Knowledge-Based Systems, 12*(Supplement-1), 19-42.

Jiang, L., & Zhang, H. (2006). Weightily averaged one-dependence estimators. *Proceedings of the 9th Pacific Rim International Conference on Artificial Intelligence.*

Jiang, L., Zhang, H., Cai, Z., & Su, J. (2005). Learning tree augmented naïve Bayes for ranking. *Database Systems for Advanced Applications, 3453*, 992–992. doi:10.1007/11408079_63

John, G. H., & Langley, P. (1995). Estimating continuous distributions in Bayesian classifiers. *Conference on Uncertainty in Artificial Intelligence.*

Kammerdiner, A. R., Gupal, A. M., & Pardalos, P. M. (2007). Application of Bayesian networks and data mining to biomedical problems. *AIP Conference Proceedings.*

Keogh, E., & Pazzani, M. (1999). Learning augmented Bayesian classifiers: A comparison of distribution-based and classification-based approaches. *Proceedings of the 7th International Workshop on AI and Statistics* (pp. 225-230).

Kononenko, I. (1991). Semi-naive Bayesian classifiers. *EWSL, 1991*, 206–219. doi:10.1007/BFb0017015

Korb, K. E., & Nicholson, A. E. (2010). *Bayesian artificial intelligence,* 2nd ed. Chapman & Hall/CRC Computer Science & Data Analysis.

Langley, P., Iba, W., & Thompson, K. (1992). An analysis of Bayesian classifiers. *Proceedings of the Tenth Annual Conference on Artificial Intelligence.*

Langley, P., & Sage, S. (1994). Induction of selective Bayesian classifiers. *Tenth Conference on Uncertainty in Artificial Intelligence.*

Larrañaga, P. (2010). Multi-label classification. *International Journal of Data Warehousing and Mining, 3*(3), 1–13.

Lauritzen, S. L. (1992). Propagation of probabilities, means and variances in mixed graphical association models. *Journal of the American Statistical Association, 87*, 1098–1108.

Lauritzen, S. L., & Jensen, F. (2001). Stable local computation with conditional Gaussian distributions. *Statistics and Computing, 11*(2), 191–203. doi:10.1023/A:1008935617754

Lauritzen, S. L., & Wermuth, N. (1998). Graphical models for associations between variables, some of which are qualitative and some quantitative. *Annals of Statistics, 17*(1), 31–57. doi:10.1214/aos/1176347003

Link, W. A., & Barker, R. J. (2010). *Bayesian inference: With ecological applications.* Elsevier.

Liu, H., Hussain, F., Tan, C. L., & Dash, M. (2002). Discretization: An enabling technique. *Data Mining and Knowledge Discovery, 6*(4), 393–423. doi:10.1023/A:1016304305535

Lucas, P. (2004). Restricted Bayesian network structure learning. *Studies in Fuzziness and Soft Computing, 49,* 217–232.

Martínez, A. M., Webb, G. I., Flores, M. J., & Gámez, J. A. (2011). *Non-disjoint discretization for aggregating one-dependence estimator classifiers.* (Submitted): University of Castilla-La Mancha, Computing Systems Department.

Martínez, M., & Sucar, L. E. (2008). Learning dynamic naïve Bayesian classifiers. *Proceedings of the Twenty-First International Florida Artificial Intelligence Research Society Conference (FLAIRS)* (pp. 655-659).

Moral, S., Rumí, R., & Salmerón, A. (2001). *Mixtures of truncated exponentials in hybrid Bayesian networks.* Paper presented at the ECSQARU '01: 6th European Conference on Symbolic and Quantitative Approaches to Reasoning with Uncertainty.

Moral, S., Rumí, R., & Salmerón, A. (2003). *Approximating conditional MTE distributions by means of mixed trees.* Paper presented at the ECSQARU.

Morales, D. A., Bengoetxea, E., & Larrañaga, P. (2008). Selection of human embryos for transfer by Bayesian classifiers. *Computers in Biology and Medicine, 38,* 1177–1186. doi:10.1016/j.compbiomed.2008.09.002

Nielsen, J. D., Rumí, R., & Salmerón, A. (2009). Supervised classification using probabilistic decision graphs. *Computational Statistics & Data Analysis, 53*(4), 1299–1311. doi:10.1016/j.csda.2008.11.003

Olesen, K. G. (1993). Causal probabilistic networks with both discrete and continuous variables. *IEEE Transactions on Pattern Analysis and Machine Intelligence, 15*(3), 275–279. doi:10.1109/34.204909

Ordoñez, C., Matias, J. M., Rivas, T., & Bastante, F. G. (2009). Reforestation planning using Bayesian networks. *Environmental Modelling & Software, 24*(11), 1285–1292. doi:10.1016/j.envsoft.2009.05.009

Ortigosa-Hernandez, J., Rodriguez, J. D., Alzate, L., Lucania, M., Inza, I., & Lozano, J. A. (2011). *Approaching sentiment analysis by using semi-supervised learning of multidimensional classifiers.* Department of Computer Science and Artificial Intelligence. University of the Basque Country.

Palacios-Alonso, M. A., Brizuela, C. A., & Sucar, L. E. (2010). Evolutionary learning of dynamic naïve Bayesian classifiers. *Journal of Automated Reasoning, 45*(1), 21–37. doi:10.1007/s10817-009-9130-0

Park, M.-H., & Stenstrom, M. K. (2008). Classifying environmentally significant urban land uses with satellite imagery. *Journal of Environmental Management, 86*(1), 181–192. doi:10.1016/j.jenvman.2006.12.010

Pavlenko, T., & Chernyak, O. (2010). Credit risk modeling using Bayesian networks. *International Journal of Intelligent Systems, 25,* 326–344.

Pazzani, M. J. (1996). Searching for dependencies in Bayesian classifiers. *Learning from Data: Artificial Intelligence and Statistics, V,* 239–248.

Pérez, A., Larrañaga, P., & Inza, I. (2006). Supervised classification with conditional Gaussian networks: Increasing the structure complexity from naïve Bayes. *International Journal of Approximate Reasoning, 43*(1), 1–25. doi:10.1016/j.ijar.2006.01.002

Pérez, A., Larrañaga, P., & Inza, I. (2009). Bayesian classifiers based on kernel density estimation: Flexible classifiers. *International Journal of Approximate Reasoning, 50,* 341–362. doi:10.1016/j.ijar.2008.08.008

Porwal, A., Carranza, E. J. M., & Hale, M. (2006). Bayesian network classifiers for mineral potential mapping. *Computers & Geosciences, 32,* 1–16. doi:10.1016/j.cageo.2005.03.018

Qazi, M., Fung, G., Krishnan, S., Rosales, R., Steck, H., Rao, R. B., et al. (2007). Automated heart wall motion abnormality detection from ultrasound images using Bayesian networks. *Proceedings of the 20th International Joint Conference on Artifical Intelligence.*

Quinlan, J. R. (1986). Induction of decision trees. *Machine Learning, 1*(1), 81–106. doi:10.1007/BF00116251

Rehg, J. M., & Murphy, K. P. (1999). Vision-based speaker detection using Bayesian networks. In Workshop on Perceptual User-Interfaces.

Rodríguez, J. D., & Lozano, J. A. (2008). Multi-objective learning of multi-dimensional Bayesian classifiers. *Proceedings of 8th International Conference on Hybrid Intelligent Systems (HIS 2008).*

Rumí, R., Salmerón, A., & Moral, S. (2006). Estimating mixtures of truncated exponentials in hybrid Bayesian networks. *TEST: An Official Journal of the Spanish Society of Statistics and Operations Research, 15*(2), 397–421.

Sahami, M. (1996). Learning limited dependence Bayesian classifiers. *Proceedings of the 2nd International Conference on Knowledge Discovery in Databases* (pp. 335-338).

Sahami, M., Dumais, S., Heckerman, D., & Horvitz, E. (1998). *A Bayesian approach to filtering junk e-mail.* AAAI Workshop on Learning for Text Categorization.

Shachter, R. D., & Kenley, C. R. (1989). Gaussian influence diagrams. *Management Science, 35*(5), 527–550. doi:10.1287/mnsc.35.5.527

Silverman, B. W. (1986). *Density estimation for statistics and data analysis.* Chapman & Hall/CRC.

Su, J., & Zhang, H. (2006). Full Bayesian network classifiers. *Proceedings of the 23rd International Conference on Machine Learning.*

Tsoumakas, G., & Katakis, I. (2007). Multi-label classification: An overview. *International Journal of Data Warehousing and Mining, 3*(3), 1–13. doi:10.4018/jdwm.2007070101

van der Gaag, L. C., & de Waal, P. R. (2006). *Multi-dimensional Bayesian network classifiers.* Third European Workshop on Probabilistic Graphical Models.

Wang, Q., Garrity, G. M., Tiedje, J. M., & Cole, R. J. (2007). Naïve Bayesian classifier for rapid assignment of rRNA sequences into the new bacterial taxonomy. *Applied and Environmental Microbiology, 73*(16), 5261–5267. doi:10.1128/AEM.00062-07

Webb, G. I., Boughton, J. R., & Wang, Z. (2005). Not so naïve Bayes: Aggregating one-dependence estimators. *Machine Learning, 58*(1), 5–24. doi:10.1007/s10994-005-4258-6

Yang, Y., & Webb, G. I. (2009). Discretization for naïve-Bayes learning: Managing discretization bias and variance. *Machine Learning, 74*(1), 39–74. doi:10.1007/s10994-008-5083-5

Yinh, Y. (2003). *Discretization for naïve-Bayes learning.* PhD. Thesis, Monash University.

Zaffalon, M. (2005). Credible classification for environmental problems. *Environmental Modelling & Software, 20*(8), 1003–1012. doi:10.1016/j.envsoft.2004.10.006

Zaragoza, J., Sucar, E., & Morales, E. (2011). *A two-step method to learn multidimensional Bayesian network classifiers based on mutual information measures.* Twenty-Fourth International Florida Artificial Intelligence Research Society Conference - FLAIRS24.

Zhang, H., Jiang, L., & Su, J. (2005). Hidden naïve Bayes. *Proceedings of the 20th National Conference on Artificial intelligence - Volume 2* (pp. 919-924). AAAI Press.

Zhang, H., & Lu, Y. (2002). Learning Bayesian network classifiers from data with missing values. *TENCON '02 Proceedings, IEEE Region 10 Conference on Computers, Communications, Control and Power Engineering.*

Zheng, F., & Webb, G. I. (2005). A comparative study of semi-naïve Bayes methods in classification learning.*Proceedings of 4th Australasian Data Mining Conference (AusDM05.* Zheng, Z., & Webb, G. I. (2000). Lazy learning of Bayesian rules. *Machine Learning, 41*(1), 53–84. doi:10.1023/A:1007613203719

Zhong, S., Martínez, A. M., Nielsen, T. D., & Langseth, H. (2010). Towards a more expressive model for dynamic classification. *Proceedings of the Twenty-Third International Florida Artificial Intelligence Research Society Conference (FLAIRS).*

Section 2
Machine Learning Applications in Computer Vision

Chapter 6
Decay Detection in Citrus Fruits Using Hyperspectral Computer Vision

Juan Gómez-Sanchis
Intelligent Data Analysis Laboratory, Universidad de Valencia, Spain

Emilio Soria-Olivas
Intelligent Data Analysis Laboratory, Universidad de Valencia, Spain

Delia Lorente-Garrido
Instituto Valenciano de Investigaciones Agrarias, Spain

José M. Martínez-Martínez
Intelligent Data Analysis Laboratory, Universidad de Valencia, Spain

Pablo Escandell-Montero
Intelligent Data Analysis Laboratory, Universidad de Valencia, Spain

Josep Guimerá-Tomás
Intelligent Data Analysis Laboratory, Universidad de Valencia, Spain

José Blasco-Ivars
Instituto Valenciano de Investigaciones Agrarias, Spain

ABSTRACT

The citrus industry is nowadays an important part of the Spanish agricultural sector. One of the main problems present in the citrus industry is decay caused by Penicillium digitatum and Penicillium italicum fungi. Early detection of decay produced by fungi in citrus is especially important for the citrus industry of distribution. This chapter presents a hyperspectral computer vision system and a set of machine learning techniques in order to detect decay caused by Penicillium digitatum and Penicillium italicum fungi that produce more economic losses to the sector. More specifically, the authors employ a hyperspectral system and artificial neural networks. Nowadays, inspection and removal of damaged citrus is done manually by workers using dangerous ultraviolet light. The proposed system constitutes a feasible and

DOI: 10.4018/978-1-4666-1806-0.ch006

implementable solution for the citrus industry; this has been proven by the fact that several machinery enterprises have shown their interest in the implementation and patent of the system.

INTRODUCTION

The citrus industry, with an annual production over 89 million tons, is the most important of the World regarding fruits and vegetables production, giving an idea of its relevance on the World economy. It is relevant too on the European Union, where its production arises sums around 10 million tons, of which the 35% is produced on the Valencian Region.

In fact, Spain is the first World fresh citrus exporter, with the 34% of the global market, and the fourth in production level. According to sources of the *Generalitat Valenciana*, during the 2006-2007 season, the valencian citrus production increased to 4.2 tons (Figure 1), which represents the 80% approximately of the total citrus production in Spain. If only the data of the most important citrus is observed, the *Comunitat*

Valenciana exported the 89% of the oranges and the 97% of the mandarins.

Of these exportations, the 82% approximately is addressed to European Union countries, while the rest is exported to so different countries as Japan or Canada, where the valencian citrus have strongly penetrated and have a market more and more important. As an example, the exportations to a so demanding market as the United States of America have risen from 4,200 to 80,000 tons in the last 10 years. This fact is due to the effort done by the producers in order to offer products of greater quality and by the researches, both from the point of view of the fruit, and from the technology for its cultivation.

The most of this effort has been focused on getting varieties resistant to plagues or illnesses or varieties marketable out of its usual period, on the biological fight against plagues and on

Figure 1. Estimation and balance of the production of citrus

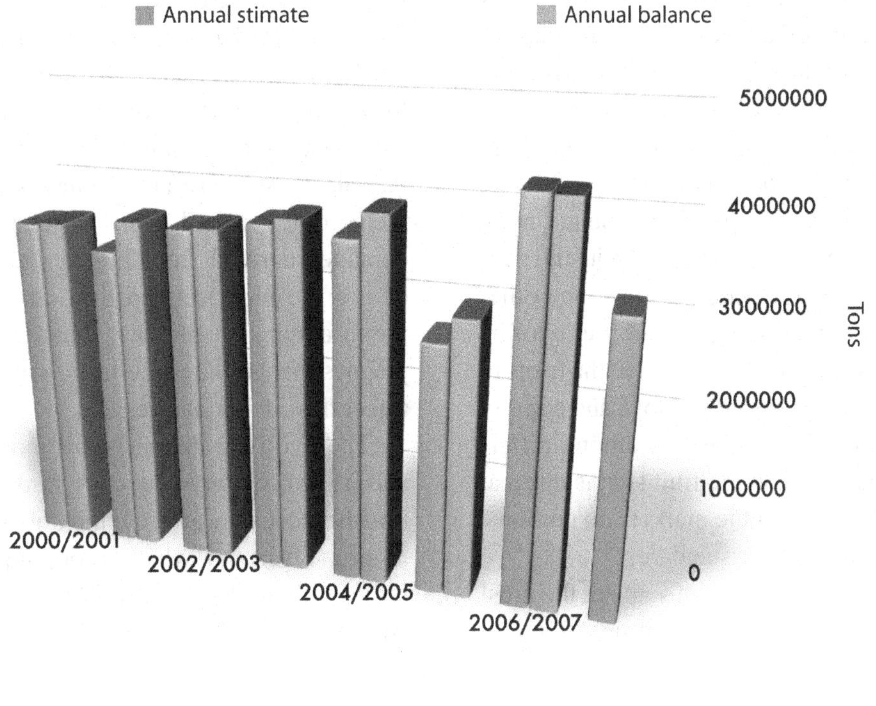

Figure 2. Common defects produced on citrus by: branching (a), peduncle loss (b), peduncle puncture (c), phytotoxicity (d), trips (e), Oystershell Scale (f), sooty mould (g), cold (h), oleocelosis (i), Penicillium digitatum(j), antracnosis (k), and fly bite (l).

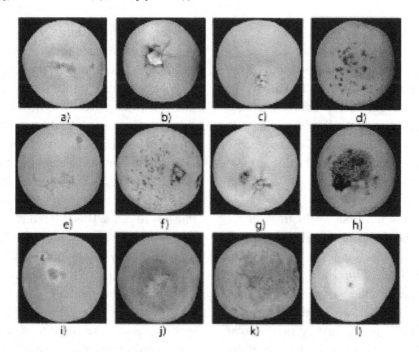

new technologies on post-cultivation treatments, especially in automatic quality estimation and detection of damaged and ill fruits systems.

One of the fundamental requirements for a fruit to be exportable is that there is no appreciable damage on it. It must have the suitable size and colour and, furthermore, have a completely damage free skin. These machines, which technology for the candidate system has been in research for more than 15 years, allow to estimate in an individual way the quality of each fruit, classifying and separating it depending on, among other factors, the presence, quantity and severity of its damages. These machines ensure that the fruits in the market are in the best conditions and comply all the standards. The distinction among different kinds of damages on the fruit skin is of great importance, because all the markets do not have the same requirements or standards.

Figure 2 shows examples of some of the most common damages that appear in citrus. Attending to the economic losses that they could generate, the damages on the citrus skin can be classified into two categories: defects that continue evolving once the fruit has been recollected and defects that do not evolve. The defects that do not evolve are those that cause an aesthetic damage and thus, they reduce the value of the product but do not hamper its commercialization in second markets. Among these there are: damages produced by meteorology as hail, wind or persistent raining, damages derived from biochemical alterations due to the incorrect fertilization, watering and phytosanitary treatments, damages caused by plagues that colonize the fruit surface but do not affect the intern qualities, etc.

The evolving damages are more dangerous and it is absolutely necessary to detect them on time because they affect to the organoleptic quality of the fruit and, what is more important, there is a risk of transmission to other undamaged fruits. Among the evolving defects there are, all the damages produces by fungi responsible of diverse decay. These fungi penetrate into the fruit taking advantage of any injury or bruise of the fruit that supposes a break in its skin and extending the infection over all the fruit, arriving to a complete degradation. Particularly dangerous is the damage caused by the Mediterranean fly, which deposits its eggs into the fruit and they hatch after a time, causing a posterior infection. An idea of the importance of this damage is seen in the rejection rate of the year 2001 to the Spanish citrus exportation due to the presence of fly larva in the exported fruit that supposed economic losses over 6 million Euros. Due to this problem, the United States of America imposed a veto to the Spanish exportations that lasted until the year 2003, generating a huge and a very important problem to the economy of the farmers.

Among the decay that causes all these serious damages, the green and the blue decay, originated by the *Penicillium digitatum* and *Penicillium italicum* fungi respectively, are highlighted due to their economical importance and because they affect to the fruits in their post-recollection, including the commercialization process. Economic losses caused by these fungi are very important, calculating, in generic terms, a contribution from 10% to 15% regarding the total value of the product (Eckert and Eaks, 1989). To this problem has to be added the fact that a reduced number of infected fruits could disseminate the infection to a full citrus consigment, producing huge economic losses, especially when the fruit is stored for long periods of time as is the case of exportations to far countries as USA or Japan (Wills et al., 1998).

Apart from the economic losses, the image that offers a high number of rotten fruit in the destination disrepute the spanish production, thus it is critical to ensure that this does not happen. There are two processes going on in order to prevent the appearance and extension of the rotten fruit. The detection and elimination of these fruits in order to prevent the extension of the infection, and the treatment with chemical fungicides in

post-collection that delay or prevent the appearance of the fungi. The fungicide treatment is harmful to the environment and reduce its use to the minimal is very important but in order to achieve it, the detection of the maximal of infected fruits as soon as possible is important. Nowadays there are no systems in the market that permit its automatic detection. This task is done manually taking advantage of the essential oils fluorescence phenomena, liberated due to the decay, when ultraviolet (UV) light is applied. This inspection is done by especially trained operators in small rooms especially enabled to that purpose, known popularly as "clubs" (see Figure 3). In these rooms, the fruits are illuminated with UV light and the operators refuse that ones presenting fluorescence. This manual operation mode presents serious problems due to the usage of UV lights is harmful for the human skin, so the operators can only stay in the room for a limited amount of time, doing short duration shifts (15 minutes).

The automation of this task shows obvious advantages. On one hand, the quality of the work of these operators will be improved being done automatically, limiting the operators' task to supervise the correct behavior of the technology through the control monitors. On the other hand, it will assure an objective detection and with a uniform quality, avoiding the subjectivity introduced by tiredness, fatigue and bad conditions in which manual detection is done. A possible solution to automate the problem could come from the development of techniques based on computer vision, specifically created to this purpose. Nevertheless, it is not a simple task, due to the existence of many varieties and species of citrus and each of them with its particularities that do it especial for the design of an automated system. Different sizes, textures and shapes in which the fluorescence is manifested, complicate the process. Defects less important that occasionally also can cause the fluorescence phenomena and some particular decay which fluorescence is hardly perceptible, impede the creation of a simple sys-

Figure 3. Decay inspection UV room in the citrus industry

Figure 4. Inspection lines capable of analyzing several fruits per second

tem, i.e., based on threshold levels. It is, precisely, this variability and complexity the cause of the existence in the market of systems capable of the slightly important damages detection and, however, this is yet an unsolved problem.

Computer vision systems are an increasingly importance part in the automation of the process in the farming (Kim et al., 2005) and an absolutely necessary element in the fresh fruit inspection tasks (Blasco et al., 2003), where maintaining the quality of a high production requires the

individual inspection of several tons of fruits per hour (see Figure 4).

This technological point is which nowadays can confer a competitive advantage to our producers against other countries that base its force in low production costs. Thus, it is of great importance the constant research in artificial vision systems applied to the fresh fruit inspection in order to achieve them to be more advanced and to adapt them to the necessities and particularities of our producers, which only could be achieved creating self-technology.

One of the main problems that the automatic vision systems have to face analyzing the fruits comes by the difficulty of distinguishing the real defect in some other natural part of the product, as the calyx or the peduncle. Bennedsen et al. (2005) developed an image processing system that could identify the defects and distinguish them from the calyx and the peduncle on apples, reducing to the minimal the false positives through the analysis of some images. The images were captured using two optical filters centered at 740 and 950 nm while the apples rotated. Unay and Gosselin (2007) compared different classification algorithms, as the discriminant analysis, the nearest neighbor or support vector machines, in order to study the peduncle and calyx recognition in *Jonagold* apples. Given that this apples variety shows a two-coloured skin, they use four filters centered at the visible and near infrared (NIR). Once the peduncle and calyx are detected, they compared various methods for the segmentation of different kind of defects in multispectral images (Unay and Gosselin, 2006), the studied methods were k-means, neural networks and self-organizing maps. Xing et al. (2007) identified some visible and NIR wavelengths for the distinction of the healthy skin peduncle and calyx and defects in apples by means of a hyperspectral system, applying PCA in order to reduce the high dimensionality of the data and to detect the most relevant lengths.

Vision systems commonly used in automatic inspection tasks, similarly to the human eye, use the radiation emitted by the bodies in three concrete wavelengths, centered at red, green and blue, and combine them in order to obtain the colour images that we see. One of the great advantages that the artificial vision systems present is that they are not limited to the visible spectrum, as it happens at the human eye. When acquiring and combining images only with these three wavelengths a lot of the reflectance information of the fruits on the other wavelengths apart of the visible range and other regions of the electromagnetic spectrum, as the infrared or ultraviolet, the defects are better appreciated in other intermediate and concrete wavelengths, away from red, green or blue.

Gaffney (1973) demonstrated that different kind of the citrus external defects present a different reflectance for each wavelength, making possible to detect which kind of defect it is by means of spectrometric methods. Later, Blasco (2001) tried to appreciate these differences through images captured using different interferometric filters placed at the optics of different ultraviolet, visible and near infrared sensible cameras. The main disadvantage of these filters is the impossibility of doing frequency sweeps (obtaining a set of monochromatic images of the scene), given that they only allow the propagation of the light in a concrete wavelength and it is necessary to change the optic filter in order to obtain images at different wavelengths, so they do not allow finding which of all the wavelengths are more relevant. This problem is solved by the hyperspectral image acquisition systems.

Hyperspectral image systems arise from the research field of remote sensing by means of multi and hyperspectral sensors for the Earth observation (Goetz et al., 1985), expanding, as its prize has been reduced, to other diverse science fields like the alimentary technology (Park et al., 2002) or the precision farming (Erives and Fitzgerald, 2005). The use of this kind of systems for the damage detection in fruits has undergone an important increase in the last years. One of its great advantages is, precisely, the possibility of detection of defects that are difficult to distinguish with colour images, like some types of decay. These dangerous damages are difficult to detect in citrus due to the colour and texture are similar in healthy and infected fruits.

Figure 5 compares images of oranges with different acquired defects with a standard monochromatic camera (upper) and a hyperspectral system at concrete wavelengths (lower). Using specific wavelengths (Figure 5 lower), damages appear more contrasted, which simplifies its detection by an automatic system.

Figure 5. Citrus images with different extern defects acquired with a monochromatic camera (upper) and the same fruit acquired at particular wavelengths (lower). From left to right 450 nm, 720 nm and 520 nm, 480 nm.

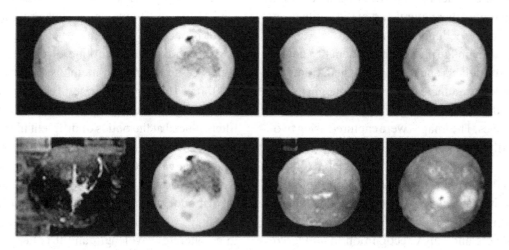

A drawback of these systems is the huge information that they provide and that has to be managed. The size of data sets generated by hyperspectral image techniques increases significantly and, therefore, the capacity and difficulty of designing systems for detection and classification also increases. Several methods have been investigated in order to select particular wavelengths to the solution that allows the development of viable systems for the online product inspection. This is the Lefcourt et al. (2006) aim, who developed a robust method for the wavelength selection for the multispectral detection of fecal contamination in apples from the hyperspectral data. ElMasry et al. (2009) obtained five optimal wavelengths for the cold defect detection in *Red Delicious* apples with artificial neural networks. Gowen et al. (2009) detected and classified damaged by freezing mushrooms selecting some wavelengths in the range from 400 to 1000 nm. With the aim of finding the optimal bandwidth in order to detect cucumber harvesting damage, Ariana et al. (2006) acquired cucumber hyperspectral images with damages caused by mechanical harvesting. Qin et al. (2009) differentiated red grapefruit affected by cranker of those

affected by other common damages by means of the divergence spectral information classification method. This procedure was based on the quantification of spectral similarities, using a predetermined reference spectrum from 450 to 930 nm.

The hyperspectral systems are characterized by acquiring a wide number of monochromatic images in the same scene in a wide and consecutive set of wavelengths (Figure 6).

These images are characterized by providing spatial information (like classical vision systems) and spectral information of the scene. Hyperspectral vision systems generally consist of two parts: an acquisition system (a camera) and a system that selects the wavelength of the radiation (a filter) that comes into contact with the camera. The fundamental characteristic of these filters is its ability to control the frequency of the transmitted radiation.

There are several kinds of filters, the most remarkable are image spectrophotometers, AOTF (Acoustic-Optic Tunable Filters) and LCTF (Liquid Crystal Tunable Filter). Spectrophotometers base their operation on the dispersion characteristics of electromagnetic waves in material medium. They are often used in applications where

Figure 6. A RGB image only gives information at three spectral bands of the visible range. However a hyperspectral image gives spectral information in all the system range.

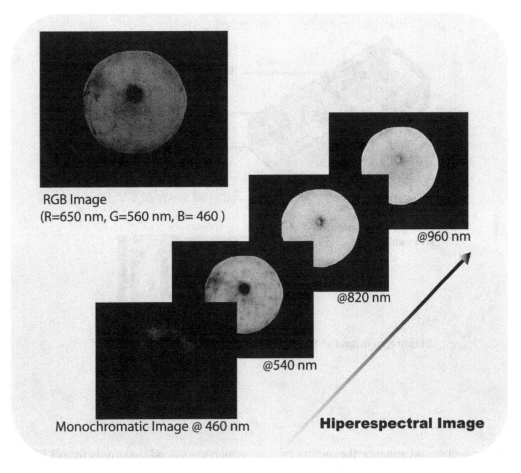

the image acquisition is done line by line, that is, each image captured by the camera contains the spectral information of one line of the scene. The main drawback of this type of frequency selection system is that it requires the relative motion of the scene acquired on the acquisition system. By contrast, the AOTF and LCTF are able to acquire a complete monochromatic image of the scene, without requiring a full frequency sweep. The devices of frequency selection used in this study are liquid crystal tunable filters, also called LCTF. They base their operation on the combination of Lyot filters. These filters are made of a sandwich structure with a plate of liquid crystal and a quartz plate between two linear polarizers. The plates of

quartz and liquid crystal constitute a retarder. The main success of the Lyot filter is to electronically control the desired frequency selectivity in the transmitted radiation (Hetchs, 1998). A LCTF consists of a series of stacked Lyot filters to get the range and frequency selectivity desired.

OBJECTIVE

The objective of this study is to investigate and develop technology for automatic detection of decay in citrus fruits. Such a system would avoid the current exposure of operators to ultraviolet light, would reduce the need for fungicides in the

Figure 7. 3D design of the filter holder box

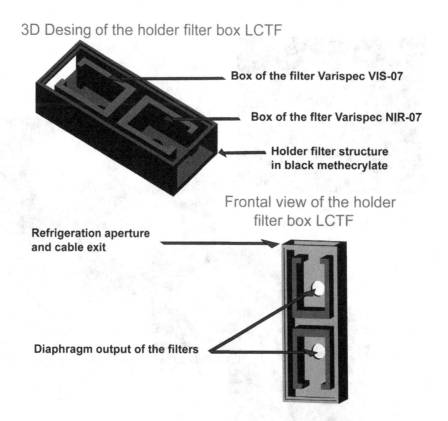

citrus industry and would enhance the quality of the products. For this, it has been studied the application of a hyperspectral image system in order to determine the most important wavelengths in the process. However, to reach this step, it is very important to develop classification methods that allow, from the sets of obtained images, obtaining the desired results.

HYPERSPECTRAL VISION SYSTEM

The hyperspectral vision system used in this work is based on the use of liquid crystal tunable filters (LCTF). The set of monochromatic images acquired by this system constitutes a hyperspectral image. The system consists of a high-resolution monochrome camera Photometrics CoolSnap ES,

which has a good sensitivity from 320 nm to 1020 nm. The system was adjusted to acquire images of 651 x 801 pixels, with a spatial resolution of 4.32 pixels / mm.

The camera transfers the images to a personal computer via a data acquisition card with PCI technology, proprietary of the camera. The control of the system was carried out with a personal computer with Intel Core Duo processor 1.67 GHz and 2 GB RAM. The lens used has a uniform focus capacity between 400 nm and 1000 nm (Schneider Xenoplan 1,4 / 17 mm). The frequency selection stage has been carried out using two liquid crystal tunable filters, one sensitive in the visible spectrum (460 nm - 720 nm, Varispec VIS07) and other sensitive in the near infrared region of the electromagnetic spectrum (730 - 1020 nm, Varispec NIR07). The two tunable filters are placed

Figure 8. Hyperspectral vision system for decay detection in citrus fruits

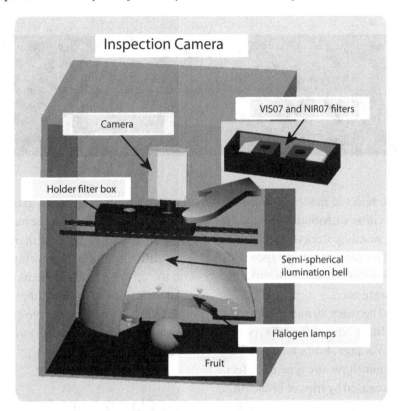

in a special holder designed by the authors of this paper (Figure 7).

Each fruit is individually illuminated by indirect lighting provided by 12 halogen lamps 20 W, arranged inside a hemispherical aluminium bell of diffusing light. The lighting system was plugged to a 12 V DC power supply, capable of providing an output of 350 W, thus ensuring that the lighting system provides a uniform response from the temporal point of view. The sum of the luminous efficiency of each part of the developed system (camera, lens, filters and lighting system) is different in each wavelength at which the system is able to acquire. The acquisition time for each band was obtained employing a certified reference white. This process was carried out with the aim that the spectral system response was uniform. The full hyperspectral vision system was placed inside a bell inspection of stainless steel to avoid the influence of ambient light. Figure 8 shows a schematic of the different parts of the developed system.

VEGETAL MATERIAL

For the experiments, mandarins from clemenules cultivation with two types of damage were used: 1) superficial scars that do not evolve with time produced by trips and by rubbing the fruit with the branches due to the wind (branching). The visual appearance of both damages is very similar, 2) infections that evolve over time produced by fungi belonging to the genus *Penicillium digitatum* (green rottennes) and *Penicillium italicum* (blue decay). Damages caused by trips or branching are visible to the naked eye. By contrast, the appearance of the decay, in early stages, is similar to the colour of the healthy skin and visual discrimination is not possible. The fruits affected by the first

Figure 9. RGB images of 4 mandarins, one healthy and the rest affected by trips/branching, P. digitatum, and P. itallicum

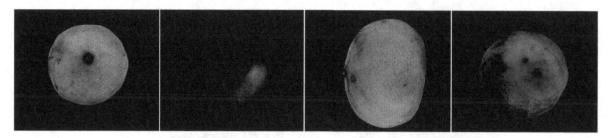

type of defects were selected randomly from the production line of citrus distribution company, while the damage caused by decay in fruits was induced by controlled inoculation of spores of each fungus. A total of 160 fruits with different stages of maturity were used.

Citrus size varied between 80 and 110 mm. At the same time, the fruits have different types of colour from green to orange. From the total fruit set, 40 samples did not show any type of defect, other 40 had defects caused by trips or branching, other 40 were inoculated with a solution of spores of *Penicillium digitatum* and the remaining 40 were inoculated with a solution of spores of *Penicillium italicum*. The inoculation was carried out using, in both cases, a solution of spores in suspension with a concentration of 106 spores / ml (Palou et al., 2001). The fruits were stored for three days in a controlled atmosphere at 25 ° C and a relative humidity of 99%. After this period, all mandarins inoculated with spores of both fungi showed initial symptoms of infection. The damaged surface area varied between 15 mm and 45 mm. Hyperspectral images were acquired for each fruit, from 460 nm to 1020 nm with a spectral resolution of 10 nm. The constructed database consisted of 9120 monochrome images of 160 citrus. Figure 9 shows colour images of four fruit: the first (left) depicts a healthy fruit and the remaining three are mandarins affected by trips / branching, *Penicillium digitatum* and *Penicillium italicum* respectively. From Figure 9, it can be compared the damages produced by trips/branching with a healthy skin.

By contrast, in fruits with green and blue decay is difficult to distinguish the healthy areas and the areas affected by fungi. Furthermore, it highlights the difficulty in distinguishing a type of fungus on the other, which can be important in order to plan strategies to combat fungi in the next season. All acquired images were pre-processed using the method of correction proposed in (Gomez-Sanchis et al., 2008a).

LABELLED DATA SET

The set of supervised techniques (both feature selection and segmentation) used in the trials of this work has motivated the construction of a set of labelling data. The data set is formed from 58 features associated with each pixel. Specifically, 57 spectral features (reflectance level of every pixel in each of the bands acquired) and one feature of type class. The data set was formed manually labelling regions of variable size of the acquired images and it is composed from 60000 pixels classified into 5 different classes. These classes are "Trips/Branching damage" (TB), "green healthy skin" (GS), "*Penicillium digitatum* damage" (PD), "*Penicillium italicum* damage" (PI) and "orange healthy skin" (OS). Each pattern contains 57 reflectance values and a class assigned manually by an expert. It has been included a class "background" because background pixels were previously segmented in the preprocessing stage. The labelled group was divided into three sets: a training set consisting of 20% of the pixels, a validation set consisting of other 20% of the pixels and a test set consisting of the remaining 60%. The first two subsets were used to build the models of segmentation and to feature selection. The third subset was used to evaluate the techniques developed to segment images. With the aim of verifying the generalization ability of the models, a high percentage of pixels was included in the test set.

ARTIFICIAL INTELLIGENCE ALGORITHMS: NEURAL NETWORKS

There is no general definition of artificial neural network, it is possible to find different definitions depending on the consulted bibliography. However, most definitions relate artificial neural networks to biological neurons. These networks are similar to the biological neural networks in the sense that operations are performed collectively and in parallel by the basic units, called neurons. These units are interconnected through a series of connections that, continuing the biological analogy, are known as synaptic weights. Thus, we can define the network learning as the process that changes the connections between neurons (synaptic weights) to perform a given task. We will see below the different types of learning that exist. The computational power of a neural network derives mainly from the structure of distributed computing.

The main advantages offered by neural networks are the following (Haykin, 1999):

- **Nonlinearity.** In a general definition, a neuron is a nonlinear element. Hence, a neural network formed from the interconnection of neurons will also be a nonlinear system processing. Nonlinearity is a highly important property, since it allows the modeling of nonlinear and chaotic systems.

- **Fault tolerance.** A neural network, has the potential to be inherently fault tolerant. Due to the distributed nature of the system, the failure of individual elements (neurons) does not significantly changes the total system response.

- **Adaptivity.** Neural networks have a built-in capability to adapt their synaptic weights to changes in the surrounding environment (changes in the inputs, presence of noise, etc.). However, if this adaptivity is too large, the system could tend to respond to spurious disturbances causing a drastic degradation in the system performance. This problem is known as the stability-plasticity dilemma.

- **Establishing nonlinear relationships between dependent and independent variables.** Neural networks are able to relate two sets of variables. Compared to traditional statistical methods, they have the advantage that the data does not need to meet the requirements of linearity, Gaussianity and stationarity (Proakis, 1997).

Artificial neural networks consist of some individual process elements called neurons, which are arranged in series of layers. Layers are connected together to give rise to neural structures. These structures are known as network architecture. In this paper, architectures with one and two hidden layers have been used. The neural network used in this work was the multilayer perceptron (MLP). This kind of network is the most popular artificial neural net and has been successfully applied in many problems. Its history begins in 1985 when Rosenblatt published the first works in a neural model called perceptron. The multilayer perceptron is a network composed of an input layer, at least one hidden layer and an output layer. Figure 10 shows the structure of a multilayer perceptron. The presence of hidden layers allows the MLP to perform nonlinear classification problems. The number of neurons forming the input and output

Figure 10. Scheme of the MPL architecture

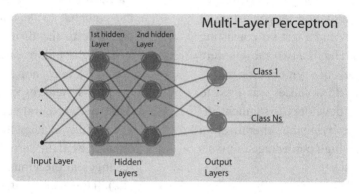

layers is determined by the problem characteristics. In this study, the number of inputs matches the 57 acquired spectral bands. However, in this work it has been used only 10 neurons (of possible 57) in the input layer in order to improve the system performance and reduce the number of acquired monochrome images. These 10 neurons correspond with the 10 most important bands for decay detection problem obtained by Gomez-Sanchis et al., (2008b). Table 1 shows the included bands. In the output layer 5 neurons were employed, corresponding with the number of classes of the proposed segmentation problem.

The remaining architecture parameters (number of hidden layers and number of neurons in each layer) are not defined by the problem or any theoretical rule. Hence, the designer should choose these parameters depending on the application.

It is only shown that, given a set of related data, a single layer neural network is able to establish a relationship between that data set, although the required number of nodes is not specified. If the set is not related, it is necessary at least two hidden layers (Kolmogorov, 1957). For this reason, architectures with one and two hidden layers were evaluated. Intuitively, it is logical to think that,

given these drawbacks, the ideal solution is to implement a network with many hidden layers and a large number of neurons in each of them. However, this solution is not always appropriate because it may decrease the generalization capabilities of the network; that is, its ability to produce accurate results on patterns that have not been used to build the models. The solution used to determine the number of neurons in the hidden layers was to evaluate architectures with different number of neurons. In particular, architectures with 10 to 20 neurons in each hidden layer were tested, whose values were determined through preliminary tests. The learning algorithm used to train the model is known as backpropagation, the network synaptic weights were initialized randomly (50 times) and the constant adaptation of the neural network was determined by the algorithm proposed in (Silva and Almeida, 1990).

SEGMENTATION MODELS BASED ON NEURAL NETWORKS

There have been evaluated 5500 neural models produced from different architectures and differ-

Table 1. Employed bands for the decay detection

Employed bands for the segmentation of hyperespectral images
480 nm, 560 nm, 600 nm, 630 nm, 730 nm, 760 nm, 820 nm, 880 nm, 960 nm, 1010 nm

Table 2. Confusion matrix provided by the winner segmentation model based on one MLP with 1 hidden layer and 17 neurons in the training and validation data sets

MLP with one hidden layer of 17 neurons Training and validation sets.					
Classification/Class (%)	Trips/Branch.	Green skin	P. digitatum	P. italicum	Orange slin
Trips/Branch.	100	0	0	0	0
Green skin	0	98,6	0	0	0
P. digitatum	0	0	98,2	0,2	0
P. italicum	0	0	1,8	99,8	0,9
Orange skin	0	1,4	0	0	99,1
K=0,991 OA=99,31%					

Table 3. Confusion matrix provided by the winner segmentation model based on one MLP with 1 hidden layer and 17 neurons in the test set

MLP with one hidden layer of 17 neurons Test set.					
Clarification/ Class (%)	**Trips/Branc.**	**Green skin**	**P. digitatum**	**P. italicum**	**Orange skin**
Trips/Branching	99,9	0	0	0	0
Green skin	0	98,58	0,02	0	0,24
P. digitatum	0	0,19	97,07	2,08	0,68
P. italicum	0,1	0	2,33	97,52	0,59
Orange skin	0	1,23	0,58	0,41	98,50
K=0,979 OA=98,30%					

ent weights initializations, 500 with one hidden layer (10 configurations in the hidden layer * 50 initializations) and 5000 with two hidden layers (100 configurations in hidden layer * 50 initializations). After analysing all the models from the point of view of accuracy -OA- (Overall accuracy) and bias of the classifier -estimated parameter kappa (K) in the test set-, it has been concluded that the classifier that provides better results is a neural network with one hidden layer of 17 neurons.

Nevertheless, this fact is justified from the point of view of the generalization capacity. The training of the model has been stopped by cross validation; this means that the model is built from the training data set and it is stopped when the validation error is minimum. Finally, from all the built models, there were selected those that

provided the minimum error. It was observed that the two layers architectures provided lower errors in training and validation, and higher in test. This fact indicates that the two layers models have higher capacity for "memorizing" the training data, but they behave worst in front of a never-seen situation.

Table 2 shows the confusion matrix, for both sets used to construct the model and the used in their validation. Similarly, Table 3 shows the results of the segmentation model used to evaluate the generalization capacity (test). The accuracy of the segmentation model is OA = 99.31% in training and OA = 98.30% in test. The tendency of the estimated kappa parameter is the same, K = 0.991 for training and K = 0.979 in test.

Figure 11. Example of segmentation of two mandarins cv. clemenules. The first damaged by trips / branching and the second without any kind of defect. On the left are the RGB images and on the right the segmentation produced by the model based on neural networks.

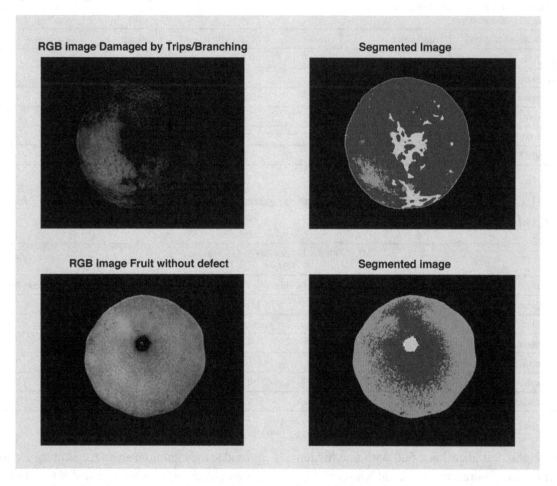

Looking at Tables 2 and 3 it is confirmed that the training and test results are very similar, showing an excellent generalization capability of the best model of segmentation. The test set confusion matrix shows that classification errors occur mainly due to the confusion between classes of rotten PD and PI, which was expected given the similarity between the damage produced by both fungi. However, even with all, errors are relatively low. It is worth noting the low percentage of healthy pixels (GS and OS) classified as rotten (PD and PI) and, even more important, the absence of error due to the classification of rotten as healthy, since the tolerances allowed by standards allow

an error due to the inclusion of healthy and damaged fruit, but not vice versa. In view of the results obtained, it is observed that the proposed segmentation model is clearly able to differentiate the two kinds of decay present, despite the similarity of the damage that both produce, and distinguish these from the fruit without damage.

SEGMENATION OF COMMON DAMAGE AND DECAY

After obtaining the segmentation model winner and analysing the confusion matrices, we worked

Figure 12. Example of segmentation of two mandarins cv. clemenules. The first damaged by trips/ branching and the second without any kind of defect. On the left are the RGB images and on the right the segmentation produced by the model based on neural networks.

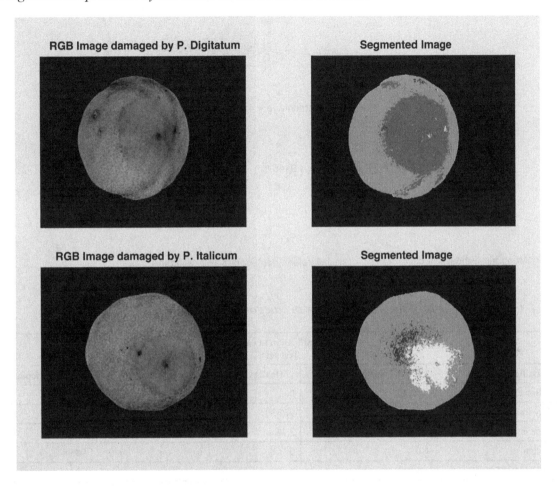

on the segmentation of images. Figure 11 shows examples of segmented images of healthy fruit and fruit damaged by trips / branching. In the left column, the citrus colour image is shown, and in the right one, the segmented image with the model presented in the previous section. The green and orange colours correspond to the PV and NP classes respectively; the brown colour corresponds to the TR class and the colours red and yellow to PD and PI classes respectively. In the pictures above it can be observed that the proposed segmentation strategy is able to distinguish the damage caused by trips / branching. Although there is a small number of pixels classified as PI

and PD, these pixels can be considered as noise classification and practically it is not perceived in the segmented images. It is worth pointing out that in the examples shown, the pixels of the peduncle of the fruit are classified as trips / branching, since a specific class in the segmentator has not been included, and the peduncle pixels are coloured similar to the TR class. However, this would not be a problem when classifying the fruit since the size of the peduncle is relatively smaller than most of defects caused by trips / branching, which would facilitate their discrimination. However, the discrimination of morphological damage, while important, is not in the scope of this study.

Figure 13. Decision tree for fruit classification. If the condition is satisfied the pattern shifts to the left.

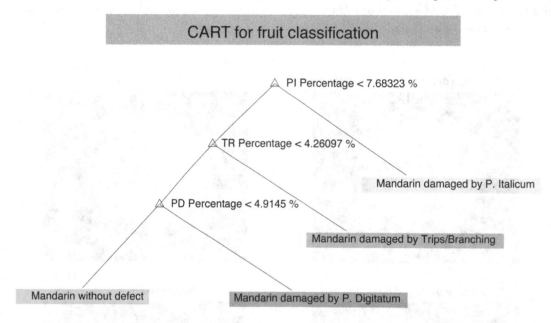

Table 4. Confusion matrix of the fruit classifier in categories

Fruit classification in categories Test set				
Classification/Class (%)	Trips/Branch.	Healthy fruit	P. digitatum	P. italicum
Trips/Branch.	82,35	0	0	0
Healthy fruit	8,84	97,33	0	0
P. digitatum	8,82	2,77	100	1,02
P. italicum	0	0	0	98,98
K=0,910 OA=93,06%				

Figure 12 shows two segmentation examples of both mandarins that have infections that evolve over time caused by *Penicillium digitatum* and *Penicillium italicum*. The top image corresponds to a fruit affected by *Penicillium digitatum* and the bottom one to a fruit affected by *Penicillium italicum*. The colour coding used in the segmented images is the same as that used in Figure 11. The colour images show the similarity of the damage produced by both types of decay in the visible spectrum and the difficulty to distinguish visually healthy skin. However, the segmented images show how the segmentation model is able to clearly differentiate one kind of decay from another in fruit with different colours, which is an added difficulty. Result is consistent with good segmentation results shown in Tables 2 and 3.

FRUIT CLASSIFICATION

After hyperspectral images segmentation, we have worked on the part of the system that must decide whether a fruit is damaged or not, and in case of being damaged, which type of defect presents. This is the ultimate goal of a fruit inspection system and therein lies its practical interest, in being able to classify the fruit and distinguish those that are commercially viable (and its quality) from which are not. To determine the ability of the system proposed in this regard, we used a decision tree (CART) with the 4 classes described above.

The classifier input features are: 1) Percentage of pixels segmented as trips / branching (PTR). 2) Percentage of pixels segmented as green healthy skin (PSV). 3) Percentage of pixels segmented as healthy skin orange (PSN). 4) Percentage of pixels segmented as P. digitatum (PPD). 5) Percentage of pixels segmented as P. italicum (PPI).

These percentages have been obtained from the segmented images as explained in the previous section. CART-based model was trained using a random selection of 40% of vegetable material used in this trial, 60% of the remaining fruit was used to validate the model.

Figure 13 shows the resulting classification tree, with thresholds (in percentage) for each damage on the segmented image resulting in the classification. One of the main advantages of the CART method is that the results provided are subject to interpretation, since the thresholds obtained in the decision nodes provide an idea of the minimum size of damage present in the database. Observing the figure, it can be seen that at any decision node appears the input feature PSV or PSN, which indicates that calculating these features is not obligatory and enables an improvement of the classification speed of the algorithm. Table 4 shows the classification results of the test set grouped by category. As principal result, we emphasize that healthy citrus are correctly classified almost in the entire test set (97.33%). The percentage of rotten fruit by both fungi classified as healthy is 0%.

This result is crucial from the point of view of the quality standards imposed by the citrus indus-

try. The classifier has a slight tendency (1%) to classify fruit rotted by *Penicillium italicum* and *Penicillium digitatum*. This low rate of false positives is not a serious problem for this class since the citrus industry discards any rotted fruit of any kind.

CONCLUSION

The detection of rotten fruits before they reach the market is of vital importance to the citrus industry, since this type of defect causes serious economic losses, and a significant decline in the prestige of the product itself and of the producer. This importance becomes harder when it is about fruit that is exported, because it represents their storage during transport and the possibility that the infection has spread to a large number of fruit when the fruit reaches its final destination.

Currently, the method of detection is based on manual inspection, which is dangerous to humans because the lighting systems used in the detection rooms employ UV light. This paper presents an important step in that direction. It has been developed, implemented and tested the effectiveness of a system of automatic detection of decay that sets the stage for the development of automatic sorting machines that can run online. The developed system allows early identification without user intervention with a high degree of accuracy supported by the tests and experiments, which shows that it is an alternative with high potential for use in industry. It must be taken into account that for obtaining these results were used advanced acquisition imaging systems based on hyperspectral imaging as well as more advanced artificial intelligence techniques (machine learning); so this system is at the forefront of expert systems applied in the food industry.

REFERENCES

Ariana, D., Lu, R., & Guyer, D. (2006). Near-infrared hyperspectral reflectance imaging for detection of bruises on pickling cucumbers. *Computers and Electronics in Agriculture, 53*(1), 60–70. doi:10.1016/j.compag.2006.04.001

Bennedsen, B. S., Peterson, D. L., & Tabb, A. (2005). Identifying defects in images of rotating apples. *Computers and Electronics in Agriculture, 48*, 92–102. doi:10.1016/j.compag.2005.01.003

Blasco, J. (2001). *Concepción de un sistema de visión artificial multiespectral para la detección e identificación de daños en cítricos*. PhD thesis, Valencia.

Blasco, J., Aleixos, N., & Moltó, E. (2003). Machine vision system for automatic quality grading of fruit. *Biosystems Engineering, 85*(4), 415–423. doi:10.1016/S1537-5110(03)00088-6

Eckert, J., & Eaks, I. (1989). *Postharvest disorders and diseases of citrus. The citrus industry*. University California Press.

ElMasry, G., Wang, N., & Vigneault, C. (2009). Detecting chilling injury in Red Delicious apple using hyperspectral imaging and neural networks. *Postharvest Biology and Technology, 52*, 1–8. doi:10.1016/j.postharvbio.2008.11.008

Erives, H., & Fitzgerald, G. (2005). Automated registration of hyperspectral images for precision agriculture. *Computers and Electronics in Agriculture, 47*, 103–119. doi:10.1016/j.compag.2004.11.016

Gaffney, J. (1973). Reflectance properties of citrus fruit. *Transactions of the ASAE. American Society of Agricultural Engineers, 16*(1), 310–314.

Generalitat Valenciana. (2008). *Aforos estadísticos*. Consellería Agricultura Ganadería i Pesca.

Goetz, A., Vane, G., Solomon, J., & Rock, B. (1985). Imaging spectrometry for Earth remote sensing. *Science, 228*, 1147–1153. doi:10.1126/science.228.4704.1147

Gómez-Sanchis, J., Camps-Valls, G., Moltó, E., Gómez-Chova, L., Aleixos, N., & Blasco, J. (2008b). Lecture Notes in Computer Science: *Vol. 5112. Segmentation of hyperspectral images for the detection of rotten mandarins* (pp. 1071–1080).

Gómez-Sanchis, J., Moltó, E., Camps-Valls, G., Gómez-Chova, L., Aleixos, N., & Blasco, J. (2008a). Automatic correction of the effects of the light source on spherical objects. An application to the analysis of hyperspectral images of citrus fruits. *Journal of Food Engineering, 85*(2), 191–200. doi:10.1016/j.jfoodeng.2007.06.036

Gowen, A. A., Taghizadeh, M., & O'Donnell, C. P. (2009). Identification of mushrooms subjected to freeze damage using hyperspectral imaging. *Journal of Food Engineering, 93*, 7–12. doi:10.1016/j.jfoodeng.2008.12.021

Haykin, S. (1999). *Neural networks: A comprehensive foundation*. Prentice-Hall.

Hetchts, E. (1998). *Optics* (3rd ed.). Addison Wesley Longman.

Kim, M., Leftcourt, A., Chao, K., & Chen, Y. (2005). Statistical and neural network classifiers for citrus disease detection using machine vision. *Transactions of the ASAE. American Society of Agricultural Engineers, 48*(5), 2007–2014.

Kolmogorov, A. (1957). On the representation of continuous functions of several variables by superposition of continuous functions of one variable and addition. *Doklady Akademii Nauk, 114*, 953–956.

Lefcourt, A. M., & Kim, M. S. (2006). Technique for normalizing intensity histograms of images when the approximate size of the target is known: Detection of feces on apples using fluorescence imaging. *Computers and Electronics in Agriculture, 50*, 135–147. doi:10.1016/j.compag.2005.10.001

Palou, L., Smilanick, J., Usall, J., & Viñas, I. (2001). Control postharvest blue and green molds of oranges by hot water, sodium carbonate, and sodium bicarbonate. *Plant Disease, 85*, 371–376. doi:10.1094/PDIS.2001.85.4.371

Park, B., Lawrence, K., Windhand, W., & Buhr, R. (2002). Hyperspectral imaging for detecting fecal and ingesta contaminants on poultry carcasses. *Transactions of the ASAE. American Society of Agricultural Engineers, 45*(6), 2017–2026.

Proakis, J. G. (1997). *Tratamiento digital de señaales: Principios, algoritmos y aplicaciones.* Prentice-Hall.

Qin, J., Burksa, T., Ritenourb, M., & Bonn, W. (2009). Detection of citrus canker using hyperspectral reflectance imaging with spectral information divergence. *Journal of Food Engineering, 93*(2), 183–191. doi:10.1016/j.jfoodeng.2009.01.014

Silva, M., & Almeida, L. (1990). Acceleration techniques for the backpropagation algorithm. *Lecture Notes in Computer Science. Neural Networks, 412*, 110–119. doi:10.1007/3-540-52255-7_32

Unay, D., & Gosselin, B. (2006). Automatic defect segmentation of 'Jonagold' apples on multi-spectral images: A comparative study. *Postharvest Biology and Technology, 42*, 271–279. doi:10.1016/j.postharvbio.2006.06.010

Unay, D., & Gosselin, B. (2007). Stem and calyx recognition on 'Jonagold' apples by pattern recognition. *Journal of Food Engineering, 78*, 597–605. doi:10.1016/j.jfoodeng.2005.10.038

Wills, R., Maglasson, W., Graham, D., & Joice, D. (1998). *Postharvest. Introduction to the physiology and handling of fruits, vegetables and ornamentals* (4th ed.). CAB International.

Xing, J., Jancsók, P., & De Baerdemaeker, J. (2007). Stem-end/calyx identification on apples using contour analysis in multispectral images. *Biosystems Engineering, 96*(2), 231–237. doi:10.1016/j.biosystemseng.2006.10.018

Chapter 7

In-line Sorting of Processed Fruit Using Computer Vision:
Application to the Inspection of Satsuma Segments and Pomegranate Arils

J. Blasco
Instituto Valenciano de Investigaciones Agrarias, Spain

N. Aleixos
Instituto en Bioingeniería y Tecnología Orientada al Ser Humano, Universitat Politècnica de València, Spain

S. Cubero
Instituto Valenciano de Investigaciones Agrarias, Spain

F. Albert
Instituto en Bioingeniería y Tecnología Orientada al Ser Humano, Universitat Politècnica de València, Spain

D. Lorente
Instituto Valenciano de Investigaciones Agrarias, Spain

J. Gómez-Sanchis
Intelligent Data Analysis Laboratory, Universitat de València, Spain

ABSTRACT

Nowadays, there is a growing demand for quality fruits and vegetables that are simple to prepare and consume, like minimally processed fruits. These products have to accomplish some particular characteristics to make them more attractive to the consumers, like a similar appearance and the total absence of external defects. Although recent advances in machine vision have allowed for the automatic inspection of fresh fruit and vegetables, there are no commercially available equipments for sorting of minority processed fruits, like arils of pomegranate (Punica granatum L) or segments of Satsuma mandarin (Citrus unshiu) ready to eat. This work describes a complete solution based on machine vision for the automatic inspection and classification of these fruits based on their estimated quality. The classification is based on morphological and colour features estimated from images taken in-line, and their analysis using statistical methods in order to grade the fruit into commercial categories.

DOI: 10.4018/978-1-4666-1806-0.ch007

INTRODUCTION

The habits of the consumers are constantly changing and nowadays there is a growing demand for quality fruits and vegetables that are simple to prepare and consume. Minimally processed fruits are fresh products that are slightly processed, with the aim of providing a food ready to eat and with characteristics similar to whole fresh products. Consumers expect that these products are free of defects, an optimum degree of ripeness and a high organoleptic and nutritional quality, along with a guarantee of hygienic safety.

The minimum processing of fresh fruit includes various operations that, in general, include several operations such as pre-cut, sliced, portioned or pre-packed in consumer retail packs. After these operations, the expected product has to accomplish some particular characteristics to make them more attractive to the consumer, like similar size, shape, colour or the total absence of discolorations or external defects. Moreover, the maker needs to be sure that foreign objects like seeds, leaves, pieces of skin, etcetera that could be released during the processing, are detected and removed from the product line. Traditionally, manual inspection has been the unique chance to ensure the quality of this kind of products but, as the decisions made by operators are affected by psychological factors such as fatigue or acquired habits, there is a high risk of human error in the evaluation or sorting processes. This is one of the most important drawbacks that can be prevented by automated inspection systems based on computer vision. A study carried out with different varieties of apples, where various shape, size and colour parameters were compared by trained operators, showed the limited human capacity to reproduce the estimation of quality, which the authors defined as 'inconsistency' (Paulus et al., 1997). Moreover, as the number of parameters considered in a decision-making process increases, so does the error of classification.

Although the recent advances in machine vision for the automatic inspection of fresh fruit and vegetables, there are no commercially available equipments for sorting some particular and minority processed fruits, like arils of pomegranate (*Punica granatum* L) or segments of Satsuma mandarin (*Citrus unshiu*) ready to eat. Hence, it is important for this industry to research in new specific devices to handle and physically separate these kinds of products, and specific image processing techniques and data analysis to sort them in quality categories. The objective of this chapter is to describe a complete solution based on machine vision for the automatic inspection and classification of two kinds of minimally processed fruit based on their estimated quality: Satsuma segments and pomegranate arils. The inspection is based on the extraction of morphological and colour features from images taken in-line, and their analysis using some statistical methods in order to grade the fruit in commercial categories.

BACKGROUND

The application of machine vision in agriculture has increased considerably in recent years. There are many fields in which computer vision is involved, including terrestrial and aerial mapping of natural resources, crop monitoring, precision agriculture, robotics, automatic guidance, non-destructive inspection of product properties, quality control and classification on processing lines and, in general, process automation. This wide range of applications is a result of the fact that machine vision systems provide substantial amounts of information about the nature and attributes of the objects present in a scene. One field where the use of this technology has spread rapidly is the inspection of agri-food commodities and particularly the automatic inspection of fruits and vegetables (Cubero et al., 2010), since it is more reliable and objective than human inspection. The quality of a particular fruit or vegetable is defined by a series of physicochemical characteristics which make it more or less attractive to the consumer, such as its ripeness, size, weight, shape, colour, the presence of blemishes and diseases, the presence or absence of fruit stems, the presence of seeds, its sugar content, and so forth. These characteristics cover all of the factors that exert an influence on the product's appearance, on its nutritional and organoleptic qualities or on its suitability for preservation. Most of these factors have traditionally been assessed by visual inspection performed by trained operators, but nowadays many of them are estimated with commercial vision systems (Sun, 2007).

The recent advances in the technology allow creating automatic alternatives based on artificial vision to perform this inspection. However, automated inspection of agricultural produce shows certain particularities and problems that are not present in other fields due to their biological nature. While manufactured products often present similar colours, shapes, sizes and other external features, fruit and vegetables may show very different characteristics from one item to another. Most of the applications concerning machine vision for the inspection of fruits or vegetables have been implemented for the quality control of fresh fruits, mainly apples (Throop et al., 2005, Xiao-bo et al., 2010) but also for the automatic analysis of other products like citrus fruits (Pydipaty et al., 2006, Blasco et al., 2009a), banana (Quevedo et al., 2008), Tomato (Polder et al., 2003), avocado (Karimi et al., 2009), potatoes (Al-Mallahi et al., 2010) or strawberry (ElMasry et al., 2007) have been reported. In this kind of fruit, it is essential that the presence of stem-ends, leaves, dirt or any extraneous material be identified and not confused with true skin defects (Unay & Gosslein, 2007). On the contrary, the relative low production of processed fruit compared to the fresh fruit has caused that the industry have not been interested in invest in the development of complex and very specific systems to automate the product quality. Nowadays, in most industries, this task

is still done by trained operators. However, this process is particularly inaccurate in the cases of pomegranate arils because the low size and high number of units to be inspected and expensive in the case of Satsuma segments since the speed of the production line must be very slow to allow a detailed inspection by several operators.

A key difference between both kinds of products fresh and processed is the singulation. An automatic system usually requires and individual inspection of each unit which implies a previous singulation of all pieces. In the case of fresh fruit this is done relatively easy by mechanical means, but in the case of some processed fruit it can be a very complex task. Added difficulties are the range of possible colours, the high speed of the conveyor belts, and the bright spots produced by water on the processed product, which complicates colour estimation. Table olives are an example of minimally processed fruit that can be isolated and transported individually to be inspected by an automatic system (Díaz et al., 2004) but they are whole and regular shaped fruits. Other works related with machine vision systems for processed and small fruit have been reported for raisins (Huxoll et al., 1995), sweet cherry (Beyer et al., 2002), apples (Fernández et al., 2005), dates (Lee et al., 2008) or strawberry (Liming & Yanchao, 2010). On the other hand, Satsuma segments and pomegranate arils are examples of small, irregular and sticky processed products very difficult to handle Blasco et al. (2009b, 2009c).

In all cases, the data obtained thorough the analysis of the images have to be processed very fast in order to determine the quality and classify the product in real-time operation. Supervised segmentation techniques based on statistics, such as Bayesian methods, can facilitate image analysis (Blasco et al., 2003, Marchant, & Onyango, 2003), although they require the participation of an expert to train the system properly. Simpler techniques, such as thresholding provide faster image segmentation, but they can be used only if the colours of the objects belonging to the different classes are distinctive and well defined (Obenland & Neipp, 2005; Bennedsen & Peterson, 2005; Baranowsky et al., 2008). Markets demand very fast image processing and for this reason a trade-off between speed and accuracy must be found. A commonly used approach for sorting the objects in these applications comes from the discriminant analysis based on the Bayesian theory.

Learning techniques can be used to understand meaningful and complex relationships automatically in a set of training data, and to produce a generalisation of these relationships in order to infer interpretations for new test data (Mitchell et al., 1996). As an example of this, Bayesian theory provides a probabilistic approach to inference, which proves successful both for segmentation of images and classification of objects in computer vision. This approach is aimed at estimating the probabilities of an observed pattern's belonging to each of some pre-defined classes in a classification problem, and then assigning the pattern to the class to which it is most likely to be a member. This set of probabilities, which henceforth are called *a posteriori* probabilities, is determined using the Bayes theorem, expressed in equation (1). The Bayes theorem calculates the *a posteriori* probability, $P(\Omega_i|x)$, that an observed pattern x, constituted by a series of j features ($x_1 .. x_j$), belongs to class Ω_i from the *a priori* probability of this class, $P(\Omega_i)$, and the conditional probabilities $P(x|\Omega_i)$, which are the probabilities of finding this pattern in class Ω_i.

$$P(\Omega_i|x) = \frac{P(x|\Omega_i)P(\Omega_i)}{P(x)} \tag{1}$$

Where $P(x)$ is the probability that a pattern x is present throughout the population data, and this probability can be determined from the total probability theorem as:

$$P(x) = \sum_{i=1}^{N} P(x|\Omega_i)P(\Omega_i) \tag{2}$$

The Bayes theory assumes that a pattern x, whose class is unknown, belongs to the class Ω_i, as follows:

$$x \in \Omega_i \Leftrightarrow \max_{r=i}\{P(\Omega_r|x)\} \tag{3}$$

From equation (2), we can consider that $P(x)$ is only a factor of scale for the *a posteriori* probabilities to be standardized between 0 and 1. This factor is essential for normalization of $P(\Omega_i|x)$ and for verification of probability axiomatic principles. Discriminant functions $f_i(x)$ are calculated from the *a priori* probabilities and the conditional *probabilities*, $P(x|\Omega_i)$. A discriminant function f_i that minimizes the error probability of classification can be calculated for each class Ω_i from the following set of equations:

$$f_i(x) = \ln\left[p(x|\Omega_i)\right] + \ln\left[P(\Omega_i)\right] \tag{4}$$

Once the values of the discriminant functions have been calculated for the observed pattern (which are sometimes called *scores*), the decision rule consists in assigning it to the class whose discriminant function has the highest value (*score*).

In any case, the probability distribution of patterns in each class $P(x|\Omega_i)$ and the *a priori* probability of classes $P(\Omega)_i$ have to be known in order to build the decision rule, but in many real-world problems they are unknown. In these cases, a labelled training set is used to estimate them. This training set is a dataset of observed patterns in which the class of each of the patterns is known. The way to estimate the above-mentioned probabilities is the basis of the different implementations of the Bayesian classifiers found in the literature. This technique is employed in this chapter by using the colour information (the RGB coordinates) of each pixel as input of the Bayesian

Figure 1. Prototype for sorting minimally processed fruit

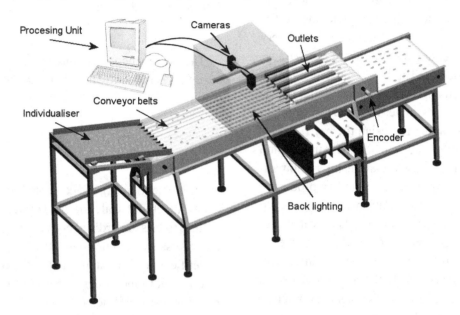

model in the case of pomegranate arils and some parameters obtained from the processing of the contour of the objects in the case of the Satsuma segments.

DESCRIPTION OF THE INSPECTION MACHINE

This chapter presents a possible solution to the automatic inspection and sorting of processed fruit based on computer vision. The prototype created for this purpose is described detailing all the essential components and how they work, including the description of the image processing algorithms and also the data extraction and analysis. The prototype consisted of essentially three main parts: the feeding, inspection and sorting units (Figure 1) that include as the principal elements the conveyor belts, the illumination system, the cameras, the air ejectors, the outlets, the machine vision algorithms and the synchronisation protocol. These are described below.

Individualisation and Transport of the Objects

Raw product to be sorted falls down into a vibrating and tilting plate. The inclination of the plate and its vibrating movement make the material to spread while it reaches to the end of the plate. The frequency and slope of this unit must be adjusted for each product. In the following step, it is split into several narrow conveyor belts that move forward at a relatively higher speed (0.75-1.25 m/s). Ideally, this action should produce an individual separation of the different objects that compose the raw input which is decisive for success of subsequent processes, since it allows the system to use simple image analysis techniques, hence speed up the inspection, and to expel each object to its corresponding outlet. The narrow size of the belts avoids large accumulations of material and facilitates the separation of the objects.

The colour of the conveyor belts is chosen in each case to enhance the contrast between background and product in order to make easier the segmentation of the images (the separation of the objects of interest from the rest of the image). To choose the appropriated, conveyor belts having different colours have been tested before being installed on the prototype. These preliminary tests consisted in the automatic image analysis of product of different categories and other foreign material like pieces of skin or internal membranes, placed over conveyor belts in several colours, including a semi-transparent one, and then obtaining the success ratio of the classification.

In the case of pomegranate arils, the conveyor belts were chosen in blue colour since it enhanced the contrast between the colour of the objects (mostly red and white) and the background. On the other hand, in the case of Satsuma segments it was chosen a semi-transparent conveyor belt to allow the backlighting of the product in order to silhouette the product and make easier the analysis of the shape the feature.

Computer Vision System and Image Acquisition

The data acquisition is done through two progressive scan cameras that acquire RGB (Red, Green and Blue) images with a size of 512 x 384 pixels and approximately 0.70 mm/pixel resolution. Both cameras are connected to a personal computer by means of a single frame grabber that digitise the images and store them in the computer's memory. The lighting system is composed of 12 compact fluorescent tubes (Osram Dulux L36 W/954) located above the conveyor belts. The tubes are powered by high frequency electronic ballast (Osram Quicktronic professional QTP5) to avoid the flicker effect caused by the standard frequency of light. This arrangement illuminates uniformly the product from the top and do not produce shadows, having at the same time an acceptable colour reproduction. The influence of bright spots in the scene caused by directional lighting on the wet surface of the product can alter the perception of the colour by the inspection system, hence it is minimised by using cross polarisation, placing polarising filters in front of the lamps and on the camera lenses.

The machine for inspecting segments includes a secondary lighting systems consisting in fluorescent tubes placed just below each individual conveyor belt. Since they are semi-transparent, illuminating from below enhance the contrast between the segments and the background and facilitates the detection of pips inside the segments, which are one of the defects that the system must find out and remove, and enhance the . The scene captured by each camera has a length of approximately 360 mm along the direction of the movement of the objects. All the system is arranged inside a stainless steel chamber.

As already stated, it is possible to acquire images from two cameras at the same time, but the vision computer has to serialise the processing of each image, queuing one while it processes the other. Therefore, since the acquisition of the images is a very time consuming process (40 ms per image) it is necessary to optimise this operation to achieve real-time operation. Therefore, the strategy employed consists of processing the image captured by one camera at the same time another image is being acquired from the second camera. The overlap in the time between the processing of one image and the acquisition of the next allows saving time and optimising the operation.

The Sorting Unit: Quality Grading

The data collected from each object is used to sort them in different commercial categories. This means a physical separation that is done by the machine just after the inspection. Attending to commercial parameters, three outlets were placed on one side of each conveyor belt and another at the end. In front of each outlet, at the other side the conveyor belt, the air ejectors are placed to expel the arils when they passed by the assigned outlet. The air flow is regulated by electro-valves that are controlled directly by the control computer using two auxiliary parallel ports (each electro-valve is connected to an output pin of the parallel port). When the computer estimates that a specific object is going to pass by the chosen outlet, it activates the appropriate pin of the parallel port. Then, the electro-valve is activated and the object is moved to the outlet.

Synchronisation

Algorithms to control the prototype were programmed using the C programming language and implemented in the control computer. This computer controls the movement of the conveyor belts by means of an encoder that is attached to the shaft of the carrier roller and connected to the parallel port of the computer. This encoder has a resolution of three pulses mm-1, which means that for every mm the conveyor belts advance, the encoder gives three pulses to a specific input of the parallel port. The computer reads the parallel port and from the number of pulses can calculate the exact position of the conveyor belts.

Using these pulses, the control software synchronises the camera acquisition with the movement of the conveyor belts. By knowing the size (in mm) of the scene captured by the cameras it is possible to know the number of pulses the system has to wait between two consecutive acquisitions, being independent of the conveyor belt speed and avoiding overlapping or gapping between two consecutive images.

The pulse corresponding to the moment in which an image is captured is stored and related with the position of the objects found in it. The distance in pulses between the scene and each outlet is also known so it is possible to calculate the distance in pulses between each object and the outlet in which it has to be removed. For each object found in the image a pulses account is created initialised to the original distance between the object and the outlet assigned by the sorting algorithm. Each time a pulse is read, all these counters are decreased. When a counter of a particular object reaches a value of zero, the computer opens the

assigned electro-valve to activate the air ejector. This process is done by a digital card with 32 outputs that manages the air ejectors.

CASE STUDY 1: POMEGRANATE ARILS

Pomegranate is a highly seasonal product with a high level of production that must be marketed in a relatively short period of time. Before being harvested this fruit is affected by particular problems, such as the so-called sunburn (Melgarejo et al. 2004), which does not influence the internal quality, but prevents the marketing of the fruits affected because it degrades the external appearance. On the other hand, there is the difficulty of peeling the fruit and manually extracting the arils, which produces rejection by the consumer in favour of other fruits that are easier to prepare. Following estimations by the pomegranate producer Santiago Mira, S.L., about 300 Mg of fresh pomegranates are trashed every year because they are affected by external damage, although the fruit itself preserves all its quality and nourishing properties. One solution for this fruit could be the marketing of pomegranate arils ready for consumption. This would allow the introduction of a new product, with a high added value, onto a market in which consumers' interest for this type of products is increasing.

Since the colour is the natural sense we use to make our first evaluation of the quality of fruits, most of the inspection systems use only this feature to segment the images (León et al., 2006; Mendoza et al.; 2006; Blasco et al., 2007). The usual colour of the arils that are fit for consumption varies from white to red, depending on the variety and growing conditions. They can also be a brownish colour which indicates flawed arils. In order to make a product that is more attractive to consumers, all the arils in the same package should have a homogeneous colour and there should be no membranes or foreign objects; to achieve this,

Figure 2. Screen capture from the interface of the automatic sorting application based on machine vision

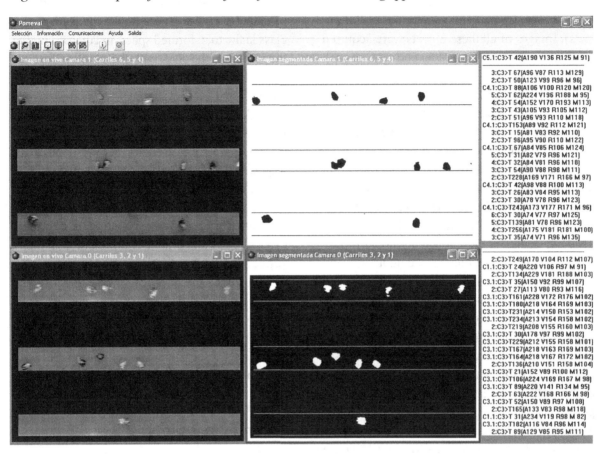

the automatic inspection and classification of the arils would be necessary.

The prototype described has been used to inspect and separate pomegranate arils automatically depending on their quality estimated from the data acquired through image analysis. Foreign objects, such as pieces of skin or inner membranes can be also detected and separated from the good arils.

System Setup

Our solution was tested using pomegranates cv. Mollar de Elche. The automatic prototype captured images of arils while they passed under the camera at a high speed, separates the arils from the background and estimates their individual averaged colour coordinates to sort them into commercial categories. The colour of the arils ranged from white-pink (predominant at the beginning of the season) to red-brown (more frequent at the end of the season).

Training and validation sets of objects were built from samples obtained from the extracting machine. These objects were sorted in five categories by experienced workers. Following the quality standards of the company, these categories depend on the colour of the objects, and were named: white aril, pink aril, red aril, brown (rotten) aril and undesired material. This last category was composed mainly by the internal membranes, which were mostly white and bigger than the arils. The training set was composed by 100 arils of each colour category and 50 membranes (a total of 550 objects). The validation set was composed by independent samples of 400 arils of each category and 100 membranes (1700 objects). Images of all these objects were acquired using the prototype. The colour and class of each object were stored. Different methods were used to define the colour of the objects; all of them based on the average RGB values of their pixels: the average RGB values themselves, the R/G ratio, the R value and the G value.

During the normal use of this kind of sorting machines in the industry, changes caused by the evolution of the colour of the arils along the season require frequent re-training of the machine vision system. But these machines are normally handled by workers without any computer vision knowledge nor statistical experience and they need a fast way to adapt the inspection software to the evolution of the colour of the product. Colour thresholds are intuitive and easy to implement by means of virtual switches in the graphical user interface. For this reason, this technique was one of the methods chosen to be implemented in the prototype.

Thresholds for each of the object classes were established from percentile 10% and 90% of each of the colour descriptors in each class. When gaps or overlapping between categories were found, the central value of the gap or the overlap was used to define the borders of each class.

Percentiles 10% and 90% overlapped only for the red and brown categories, which could cause the confusion between these categories.

However, a simple technique like this is not always the optimal solution for a problem and we decided to compare it with the results obtained with a widely used statistical method, such as Bayesian linear discriminant analysis (LDA). LDA is a commonly used statistical technique for data classification and dimensionality reduction that has been applied in agro-industrial applications based on computer vision (Blasco et al., 2009d). This supervised method is focused on finding linear projections to a lower dimensional space where the class separation is maximised. The

class membership of a sample can be predicted by calculating the distance to the centroid of each class in the transformed space and then assigning the sample to the class with the smallest distance to it. LDA has no free parameters to be tuned and the extracted features are potentially interpretable under linearity assumptions. Furthermore, LDA is closely related to principal component analysis (PCA). The main difference between both techniques is that LDA explicitly attempts to model the difference between the classes of data. PCA on the other hand does not take into account any difference in class. These capabilities lead to its extensive use and practical exploitation in many application fields where classification is needed as is this case. In our practical case the observed vector has three dimensions (the average RGB values of an object), the number of classes is five, the a priori probability was considered to be the same for each class) and the conditional density function of the RGB values for each class was assumed as Gaussian with equal covariance matrix.

Testing the Prototype

The testing prototype was installed in the commercial facility of a collaborative company. It was configured to separate the arils as described above. The prototype was tested in commercial conditions between October and November 2007. The assessment of the two classification methods was performed by implementing all the classification functions in the image analysis software and automatically classifying all the objects of the validation set accordingly. These results were then compared with the classification made by human experts, in order to build the confusion matrix of each method. Tests were performed along the season to observe if there were changes in the performance of the classification algorithms.

Table 1. Average success of the classification on the validation set using thresholds on the different colour descriptors

Category	R	G	B	R/G
White aril	48.6%	68.1%	69.9%	92.0%
Pink aril	41.8%	54.7%	64.8%	91.4%
Red aril	58.1%	73.1%	62.6%	89.2%
Brown aril	49.6%	61.1%	58.0%	89.0%
Undes. mat.	88.9%	100%	83.7%	98.3%
Total	52.4%	67.0%	60.9%	89.9%

Results and Discussion

The main result of this work is that we have provided an engineering solution for sorting pomegranate arils under commercial conditions whose results that have been statistically evaluated. The development of this automatic inspection machine constitutes itself an important engineering achievement. Following we will describe other important partial results that led to this development.

Table 1 shows the average success obtained on the validation set when using the defined thresholds on single R, G, B values and on the R/G ratio to distinguish between white, pink, red and brown arils and undesired material. Average success was low (52%) when using the R values alone. This may indicate that all the categories have relatively high red components, which increased the confusion between categories and was not apparent before conducting the experiments. Average success was also low when suing the R and G bands alone, reaching 61% and 67% respectively. Although the five categories presented different average values for R, G, B values, the high variability of values within the categories avoided their automatic separation by this simple method. However, the use of the R/G ratio improved considerably the results (90% success).

Table 2 shows the confusion matrix on the validation set using thresholds in the R/G ratio. It is clear that undesired material was the class in which best correct classification obtained (98%) which can be easily explained because the colour and the size of foreign material is normally very different from those of the arils (the sorting algorithm considered both parameters to produce the final decision of the class). Most sensitive classes from the commercial point of view were red and brown aril with a success classification of about 86%. Confusion between these two classes is higher than for any other pair of classes, probably due to the overlapping colour values. Better results were obtained for the pair of classes white and pink. It has to be taken into account that arils experience a global darkening as pomegranates ripen along the season, although this fact has not been quantitatively demonstrated in this work. This could explain the augment of the confusion between both pair of classes in the last experiment.

Results of classifying the validation set based on LDA on the average RGB values of the object are shown in Table 3. In general, all categories were well classified, and detection of undesired material reached 99% success, although 1% of white arils were wrongly classified in this class. There was a small confusion between white and pink arils, but it has to be taken into consideration that pink and white are secondary qualities. Around 6% confusion was found between red and brown classes that should be minimised. The average success of this method was close to 92% along the season.

Table 2. Confusion matrix of the classification using thresholds on the R/G ratio. Results refer to the validation set.

Classified as / Actual	White	Pink	Red	Brown	Und. mat.
White aril	90.7%	5.6%	0.0%	2.4%	1.3%
Pink aril	2.7%	89.8%	1.6%	5.9%	0.0%
Red aril	0.0%	2.6%	87.4%	9.4%	0.0%
Brown aril	1.4%	5.0%	8.4%	85.7%	0.0%
Undes. mat.	1.7%	0.0%	0.0%	0.0%	98.3%

Table 3. Confusion matrix of the classification using LDA on the average RGB values of the objects. Results refer to the validation set.

Classified as / Actual	White	Pink	Red	Brown	Und. mat.
White aril	92.3%	4.8%	0.0%	1.8%	1.0%
Pink aril	2.5%	90.8%	3.0%	4.1%	0.0%
Red aril	0.0%	3.6%	90.3%	6.1%	0.0%
Brown aril	1.1%	3.7%	6.8%	88.4%	0.0%
Undesired material	0.3%	0.1%	0.0%	0.0%	99.6%

Since the average success rate of both methods (multiple thresholds on the R/G ratio and LDA on average values of objects) were similar (they differed about 1% in each category), it can be recommendable to use the simplest one for industrial purposes; thresholds are easier to tune by the operators when they want to change the results of the sorting in real time.

CASE STUDY 2: SATSUMA SEGMENTS

Mandarin segments can be canned and sold as ready to eat food. In modern factories, mandarins are peeled and segments are roughly separated using specific machinery. In a subsequent step, an automated enzymatic process removes the skin of the segments, almost completely separating them. All these tasks use water to transport the product. Before being canned, the product has to be inspected and sorted, and undesirable material such as membranes, broken segments, remnants of skin, non-separated segments or segments with pips must be removed. First quality cans are those that contain less than 5% of partially broken segments, while second quality may include a high proportion of broken segments. Pips are not allowed in any of them. Although preliminary tasks are performed automatically, inspection and sorting are currently carried out manually.

In this stage, segments are particularly difficult to handle because they are a wet and sticky product, which makes them very difficult to separate. Currently, operators have to detect broken segments or those that contain pips as they travel in front of them on a conveyor belt. When a defective segment is identified, it is removed from the conveyor belt manually. Subjectivity, fatigue or the disparity of standards among operators when it comes to establishing objective criteria on exactly how broken a segment is are factors that decrease the quality of the inspection and, consequently, the final product. Since manual inspection is too expensive and subjective, computer vision opens up the possibility of constructing an automatic machine.

Shape analysis for the in-line inspection of agricultural products has been approached from different angles. Commonly, the techniques employed are easy to implement and fast to execute in order to obtain real-time performance. Morphological parameters such as area, perimeter, compactness, major and minor axis length, aspect ratio, compactness, convexity roundness or derivate ratios are the most common features extracted from shape to classify or identify the product. Sakai et al. (1996) used them to distinguish between four different varieties of rice, and Shouche et al. (2001) employed them to discriminate between 15 varieties of wheat. The application to fruits has also been investigated for estimating volume or for classification purposes. Koc (2007) estimates the volume of water melon through an ellipsoid created from the major and minor diameters of the fruit. Fourier descriptors have also been widely used for image compression and for the classification of regular shapes (Osowski & Nghia, 2002); they are invariant to size and rotation and have been successfully applied to describe the shape of agricultural products (Lootens et al., 2007).

This work focuses on the image processing algorithms developed for the analysis of the shape of segments of Satsuma mandarin in real-time, and describes the machinery that was developed to individually isolate, transport and separate the segments into four commercial categories. The solution proposed has been implemented on the described prototype to sort all the objects into four categories. Computer vision algorithms had to estimate the shape of each object individually, and had to be capable of discriminating between segments and other undesirable material, mainly composed of pieces of skin or seeds.

System Setup

Once the image has been acquired, the first step is segmentation. Segmentation consists in determining which regions of the image correspond to background and which represent objects of interest. The lighting setup allowed the system to acquire well-contrasted images thanks to the tubes situated under the belts, but colour was also preserved thanks to the upper tubes. Segments appeared in the images in a translucent orange colour. Seeds inside the segments appeared as dark regions, while raw material was shown as irregular objects with a colour that varied from translucent orange to dark. Figure 3 shows an example of an image processed by the system.

In order to get real-time performance, a simple but effective technique had to be implemented. In a first step, the background was removed. When backlit, objects contrasted sharply against the translucent conveyor belts thanks to their relative smaller blue component with respect to the background. The great difference between the almost saturated blue value of the background (practically equal to 255) and the average blue component of the objects (36) made practically any value threshold valid for detecting background pixels (it was set to 150 during the experiments). Objects found in this way included segments, seeds or pieces of skin. A second segmentation within the area of these objects was performed to sort them. Because seeds and skin pieces are more opaque than segments, they showed lower values of the red component. In the case of segments, 95% of the red values of the pixels were in the 160-255 range, while 95% of the values of pixels belonging to seeds or skins were in the range of red values 45-112 (a red level average of 204 versus 78). This second step also detected double segments whose red values ranged from 127 to 154. This process was fast and very effective because of the great differences in colour levels between the different categories of objects of interest and the background.

Figure 3. Image of objects to be analysed (left) and image after segmentation (right)

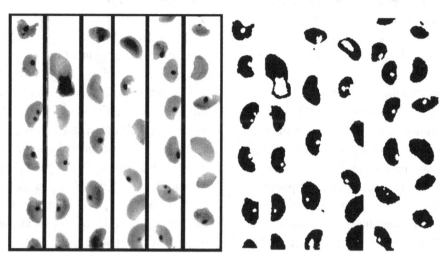

Undesirable material and segments with seeds must be rejected at the same outlet. However, in this work both types of objects were tagged differently for statistical purposes. Seeds are normally smaller than pieces of skin, which makes them easy to identify. Double segments are normally detected as large opaque objects inside an area having a colour close to that of the individual segments. The area of each object is estimated by counting the number of pixels belonging to it. In a further step, morphological operations are applied only to objects that are candidates to be segments. The contours of the remaining objects are analysed to estimate morphological features that allow the system to determine whether they are complete, broken or small pieces of segments.

Morphological Parameters Studied

Several morphological parameters of the segments are extracted and analysed and used in a statistical model to classify the segments in different quality categories (Figure 4). The image processing starts with the extraction of the perimeter (P) of the object, which is formed by those pixels belonging to the object that have some neighbour belonging to the background. The geometric centre is then calculated as the average x and y coordinates of

Figure 4. Some morphological parameters estimated in the model

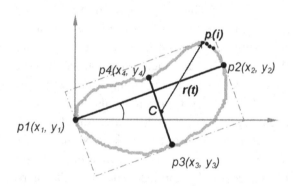

the pixels in the perimeter. The area (A) is calculated as the number of pixels inside the perimeter. The moments of inertia are calculated to obtain the principal axes of inertia (Tanenbaum, 2004), which are used to estimate the length and the orientation of the object.

In the next step the elongation (E) is calculated using the ratio between the length (L) and width (W) of the object. A circularity shape factor (CS) is calculated to estimate the relative shape of the object against a circumference with a perimeter equal to the object. The value of this factor ranges between 0 and 1 and was calculated using equation 5 (Throop & Aneshanesly, 1995).

$$CS=4\pi A/P^2 \qquad (5)$$

The compactness (CM) is used to analyse the presence of concavities and convexities in the contour caused by breakages in the segment. It is calculated using equation 6 (Gonzalez & Woods, 2002).

$$CM=P^2/A \qquad (6)$$

It is to be supposed that a complete segment is more symmetric than a broken one. The estimation of the distribution of the mass on both sides of the secondary axis of inertia can be used as an estimation of the symmetry (S). The ratio between the number of pixels having a symmetric pixel on the other side and the total area of the segment is calculated. Finally, the contour is coded using the polar signature, which is a one-dimensional array containing the Euclidean distance $r(i)$ between the geometric centre of the object (C) and each of the i points of the contour $p(i)$; $i=[0,P]$ (Figure 4). The fast Fourier transform (FFT) of this signature is then calculated because it provides information about its profile that can be used as an estimation of the shape of the objects. The whole sequence of the shape analysis is shown in Figure 5.

Testing the Prototype

Once the prototype was ready, it was installed in commercial facilities for industrial testing between October and December 2006, during the producing season in Spain. It was configured to separate segments and undesirable material. Segments with seeds, double segments and undesirable material are identified in a first step. Then, sound, broken and half segments were classified by means of a statistical model based on Bayesian discriminant analysis. In order to generate this model, a set of 620 segments were randomly chosen from the production line, labelled as good, broken or half segments, and imaged. The morphological parameters described above (shape factor, compactness,

elongation, length, area, symmetry) plus the first 10 harmonics of the FFT of the polar signature (Tao et al., 1995) were calculated for each of these segments. Standard non-linear Bayesian discriminant analysis was used to calculate the classification functions. For this practical case, the observed vector had 16 dimensions (all the features calculated for the segment), the number of classes was five, the *a priori* probability was considered to be the same for each class and, finally, we assumed that all of density functions were Gaussian with different covariance matrices in each class.

During the season, two tests were performed: one consisting in the in-line analysis of 10 sets of 3 kg of segments (about 6000 segments) that were randomly chosen from the producing line and classified by the automatic system. An expert from the quality control laboratory of the producer company analysed the results of the outlets of the machine just after the inspection to obtain the actual performance of the machine.

For the second tests, due to the high production rate, individual in-line inspection of all the production of the machine by experts was unfeasible. Therefore, off-line test were done. More than 15000 images of mandarin segments of all classes were taken and stored along the tests, each image containing a random number of segments. The segments in these images (more than 100.000) were classified by the system using the model described and the classification was compared with the one performed by human experts by visualising the images.

Results and Discussion

Regarding the first test, the evaluation performed in-line by the expert of the company gave similar results to the ones obtained in the second test, intended to know the actual performance of the statistical model.

For the second test, the system classified the segments contained in the 15000 images using the

137

Figure 5. Algorithm of extraction and data analysis for the sorting of Satsuma segments

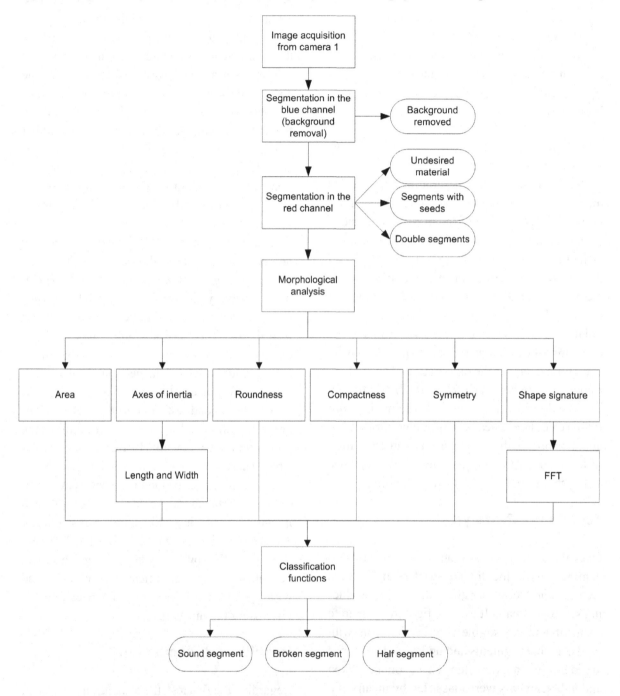

model generated based on discriminant analysis. These segments were previously classified by experts in order to obtain the confusion matrix and the success ratios for each category showed in Table 4.

The system was capable of detecting correctly 96% of the segments that contained pips and pieces of skin that were travelling on the conveyor belt. The algorithms' rate of success in separating out sound segments was 93% while

Table 4. Confusion matrix of the classification obtained by the automatic system

Category	Complete	Broken	Half segments	Seeds	Skins	Doubles
Complete	93.2%	5.8%	0.3%	0.7%	0.0%	0.0%
Broken	9.9%	83.4%	6.7%	0.0%	0.0%	0.0%
Half segments	1.1%	4.7%	94.2%	0.0%	0.0%	0.0%
Seeds	2.5%	0.9%	0.3%	96.3%	0.0%	0.0%
Skins	1.1%	1.5%	1.2%	0.0%	96.2%	0.0%
Doubles	10.0%	3.3%	0.1%	0.0%	4.2%	82.4%

Table 5. Averaged correct classification obtained using each single variable (Fast Fourier transform, Compactness, Perimeter, Area, Circularity shape factor, Symmetry, Elongation)

Variable	FFT	C	P	A	CS	S	E
Global success	36%	48%	69%	66%	48%	50%	32%

the detection of broken ones was only 83% due mainly to the fact that most of the breakages in many segments correspond to small fragments at one end, which the present system has difficulty in detecting. Specific algorithms have to be developed in order to detect these small breakages. Most of the confusion that arises between these two classes occurs with the 'half segments' class. Since there is no objective criterion for separating broken from half segments, confusion increases. However, from the commercial point of view, this confusion is not as critical as that which occurs between complete and broken segments because both types of objects belong to secondary categories. Furthermore, half segments are confused with good small ones. Segments with seeds inside and pieces of skin also belong to the same category and are rejected through the same outlet; however, there is no confusion between these two classes. The overall average successful detection reached by the prototype is about 90%. The results were similar for both tests, for those obtained by the company experts from the analysis of the outlets and for the ones obtained through the off-line analysis of the images of the segments, being the percentages very close for all categories.

Regarding the discriminant power of the variables employed in the classification, a test was performed consisting in classifying the segments using only each single variable, resulting that most discriminant variables were A and P who reach 66% and 69% of correct classification respectively. The results of this test are shown in Table 5.

FUTURE TRENDS

Computer vision provides to the food industry a reliable, robust and objective alternative for automate the process of quality inspection of food. These processes are done manually in many cases, which introduce error factors such as fatigue or subjectivity of the operators, in addition to higher production costs. This technology has entered strongly in recent years in the industry for the inspection of fresh fruit or vegetables. However, in other minority sectors such as processed fruit has not yet been implemented due either to seasonal factors (production in a period short time of the year) or due to a relatively low production that would make difficult to amortize the equipment.

The reduction of the prices of the vision technology together with the use of new cameras with additional capabilities will help in the incorporation of the technology in this promising market. Smart cameras that incorporate image processors or hyperspectral cameras are now common in other research fields and their use will probably become widespread in the next few years. Stereo vision or 3-D imaging will open up the possibility of inspecting not only the shape of products but also the volume, making the process more accurate. Moreover, UV and NIR acquisition systems are more readily available. In all these technological advances, a compromise between the increase in performance and costs will have to be found in the coming years.

Moreover, the trend is toward increasing of the consumption of this type of fruit ready to eat, which opens up a interesting future for this sector that need to be automated eventually. Real-time systems offer the advantage of high production but are geared towards the management of fruit relatively easy to handle, very different from the case of processed fruit, very fragile, sometimes wet and difficult to individualise and handle. New transportation systems and separation of fruit, and more powerful image processing techniques should be created for this specific purpose. The increase in computational capacity stimulates the development of more powerful software that can be used for real-time image processing. Adaptive algorithms have yielded promising results in other fields. Computer vision-based inspection systems in agriculture must adapt to objects and circumstances that constantly change (i.e. size, colour or shape of the produce throughout the harvesting season). New developments in pattern recognition and massive data processing will also necessarily be included in future machine vision applications to increase the robustness and accuracy of the decisions.

CONCLUSION

This work shows an engineering solution for the automatic inspection of the quality of processed fruit, applied to very fragile products like mandarin segments or pomegranate arils. A prototype for inspecting and sorting this fragile product has been developed and tested, proving that it was capable of reaching commercial performance with the current configuration. The inspection unit, which had two cameras connected to a single computer vision, had sufficient capacity to achieve real-time specifications and enough accuracy to fulfil the commercial requirements. In both cases, image processing algorithms particularly implemented to tackle this problem. Intensive testing under commercial conditions yielded good results throughout one season.

In the case of pomegranate arils, the algorithms allowed estimating the averaged colour of each individual fruit. Using the RGB colour coordinates two approaches are investigated, one using a ratio based in R/G coordinates and other using a linear discriminant analysis with the aim of sort the arils in colour categories. The statistical model reaches better results than the thresholding using the ratio. However, the improvement is limited and the easiness of using ratios in a human interface prepared for non-trained operators in comparison of making statistical models makes adopt the decision of using the ratios in the industrial application.

On the other hand, the sorting of Satsuma segments is more complex and cannot be managed using thresholds from the basic parameters. Instead, morphological information of the product obtained in real-time is analysed using a Bayesian discriminant model in order to sort them into commercial categories. In general, sound product is classified with a success of about 90% being the confusion mostly done between adjoining categories. Discriminant analysis is therefore a technique that fits well with this kind of problems that deals with the inspection and classification of agricultural products and can be used for real-life applications needing real-time.

REFERENCES

Al-Mallahi, A., Kataoka, T., Okamoto, H., & Shibata, Y. (2010). Detection of potato tubers using an ultraviolet imaging-based machine vision system. *Biosystems Engineering*, *105*(2), 257–265. doi:10.1016/j.biosystemseng.2009.11.004

Baranowski, P., Lipecki, J., Mazurek, W., & Walczak, R. T. (2008). Detection of watercore in 'Gloster' apples using thermography. *Postharvest Biology and Technology*, *47*, 358–366. doi:10.1016/j.postharvbio.2007.07.014

Bennedsen, B. S., & Peterson, D. L. (2005). Performance of a system for apple surface defect identification in near-infrared images. *Biosystems Engineering*, *90*(4), 419–431. doi:10.1016/j.biosystemseng.2004.12.005

Beyer, M., Hahn, R., Peschel, S., Harz, M., & Knoche, M. (2002). Analysing fruit shape in sweet cherry (*Prunus avium* L.). *Scientia Horticulturae*, *96*, 139–150. doi:10.1016/S0304-4238(02)00123-1

Blasco, J., Aleixos, N., Cubero, S., Gómez-Sanchis, J., & Moltó, E. (2009b). Automatic sorting of Satsuma (*Citrus unshiu*) segments using computer vision and morphological features. *Computers and Electronics in Agriculture*, *66*, 1–8. doi:10.1016/j.compag.2008.11.006

Blasco, J., Aleixos, N., Gómez-Sanchis, J., Guerrero, J. F., & Moltó, E. (2009d). A survey of Bayesian techniques in computer vision for agricultural and agro-industrial applications. In Soria, E., Martín, J. D., Magdalena, R., Martínez, M., & Serrano, A. J. (Eds.), *Handbook of research on machine learning applications and trends: Algorithms, methods and techniques* (pp. 482–498). Hershey, PA: IGI Global. doi:10.4018/978-1-60566-766-9.ch023

Blasco, J., Aleixos, N., Gómez-Sanchis, J., & Moltó, E. (2009a). Recognition and classification of external skin damage in citrus fruits using multispectral data and morphological features. *Biosystems Engineering*, *103*, 137–145. doi:10.1016/j.biosystemseng.2009.03.009

Blasco, J., Aleixos, N., & Moltó, E. (2003). Machine vision system for automatic quality grading of fruit. *Biosystems Engineering*, *85*(4), 415–423. doi:10.1016/S1537-5110(03)00088-6

Blasco, J., Aleixos, N., & Moltó, E. (2007a). Computer vision detection of peel defects in citrus by means of a region oriented segmentation algorithm. *Journal of Food Engineering*, *81*, 535–543. doi:10.1016/j.jfoodeng.2006.12.007

Blasco, J., Cubero, S., Gómez-Sanchis, J., Mira, P., & Moltó, E. (2009c). Development of a machine for the automatic sorting of pomegranate (*Punica granatum* L) arils based on computer vision. *Journal of Food Engineering*, *90*, 27–34. doi:10.1016/j.jfoodeng.2008.05.035

Cubero, S., Aleixos, N., Moltó, E., Gómez-Sanchis, J., & Blasco, J. (2010). Advances in machine vision applications for automatic inspection and quality evaluation of fruits and vegetables. *Food and Bioprocess Technology*, *4*(4), 487–504. doi:10.1007/s11947-010-0411-8

Díaz, R., Gil, L., Serrano, C., Blasco, M., Moltó, E., & Blasco, J. (2004). Comparison of three algorithms in the classification of table olives by means of computer vision. *Journal of Food Engineering*, *61*, 101–107. doi:10.1016/S0260-8774(03)00191-2

ElMasry, G., Wang, N., ElSayed, A., & Ngadi, M. (2007). Hyperspectral imaging for nondestructive determination of some quality attributes for strawberry. *Journal of Food Engineering*, *81*, 98–107. doi:10.1016/j.jfoodeng.2006.10.016

Fernández, L., Castillero, C., & Aguilera, J. M. (2005). An application of image analysis to dehydration of apple discs. *Journal of Food Engineering*, *67*, 185–193. doi:10.1016/j.jfoodeng.2004.05.070

Gonzalez, R. C., & Woods, R. E. (2002). *Digital image processing*. Prentice Hall.

Huxoll, C. C., Bolin, H. R., & Mackey, B. E. (1995). Near infrared analysis potential for grading raisin quality and moisture. *Journal of Food Science*, *60*(1), 176–180. doi:10.1111/j.1365-2621.1995.tb05632.x

Karimi, Y., Maftoonazad, N., Ramaswamy, H. S., Prasher, S. O., & Marcotte, M. (2009). Application of hyperspectral technique for color classification avocados subjected to different treatments. *Food and Bioprocess Technology*, *5*(1). doi:doi:10.1007/s11947-009-0292-x

Koc, A. B. (2007). Determination of watermelon volume using ellipsoid approximation and image processing. *Postharvest Biology and Technology*, *45*(3), 366–371. doi:10.1016/j.postharvbio.2007.03.010

Lee, D.-J., Schoenberger, R., Archibald, J., & McCollum, S. (2008). Development of a machine vision system for automatic date grading using digital reflective near-infrared imaging. *Journal of Food Engineering*, *86*, 388–398. doi:10.1016/j.jfoodeng.2007.10.021

León, K., Domingo, M., Pedreschi, F., & León, J. (2006). Color measurement in L*a*b* units from RGB digital images. *Food Research International*, *39*, 1084–1091. doi:10.1016/j.foodres.2006.03.006

Liming, X., & Yanchao, Z. (2010). Automated strawberry grading system based on image processing. *Computers and Electronics in Agriculture*, *71*(S1), S32–S39. doi:10.1016/j.compag.2009.09.013

Lootens, P., Van Waes, J., & Carlier, L. (2007). Description of the morphology of roots of *Chicorium intybus* L. partim by means of image analysis: Comparison of elliptic Fourier descriptors classical parameters. *Computers and Electronics in Agriculture*, *58*(2), 164–173. doi:10.1016/j.compag.2007.03.014

Marchant, J. A., & Onyango, C. M. (2003). Comparison of a Bayesian classifier with a multilayer feed-forward neural network using the example of plant/weed/soil discrimination. *Computers and Electronics in Agriculture*, *39*(1), 3–22. doi:10.1016/S0168-1699(02)00223-5

Melgarejo, P., Martínez, J. J., Hernández, F., Martínez-Font, R., Barrows, P., & Erez, A. (2004). Kaolin treatment to reduce pomegranate sunburn. *Scientia Horticulturae*, *100*(1), 349–353. doi:10.1016/j.scienta.2003.09.006

Mendoza, F., Dejmek, P., & Aguilera, J. M. (2006). Calibrated color measurements of agricultural foods using image analysis. *Postharvest Biology and Technology*, *41*, 285–295. doi:10.1016/j.postharvbio.2006.04.004

Obenland, D., & Neipp, P. (2005). Chlorophyll fluorescence imaging allows early detection and localization of lemon rind injury following hot water treatment. *HortScience*, *40*(6), 1821–1823.

Osowski, S., & Nghia, D. D. (2002). Fourier wavelet descriptors fro shape recognition using neural networks – A comparative study. *Pattern Recognition*, *35*, 1949–1957. doi:10.1016/S0031-3203(01)00153-4

Paulus, I., De Busscher, R., & Schrevens, E. (1997). Use of image analysis to investigate human quality classification of apples. *Journal of Agricultural Engineering Research*, *68*, 341–353. doi:10.1006/jaer.1997.0210

Polder, G., van der Heijden, G. W. A. M., Keizer, L. C. P., & Young, I. T. (2003). Calibration and characterization of spectral imaging systems. *Journal of Near Infrared Spectroscopy, 11*, 193–210. doi:10.1255/jnirs.366

Pydipati, R., Burks, T. F., & Lee, W. S. (2006). Identification of citrus disease using color texture features and discriminant analysis. *Computers and Electronics in Agriculture, 52*, 49–59. doi:10.1016/j.compag.2006.01.004

Quevedo, R., Mendoza, F., Aguilera, J. M., Chanona, J., & Gutiérrez-López, G. (2008). Determination of senescent spotting in banana (*Musa cavendish*) using fractal texture Fourier image. *Journal of Food Engineering, 84*, 509–515. doi:10.1016/j.jfoodeng.2007.06.013

Sakai, N., Yonekawa, S., Matsuzaki, A., & Morishima, H. (1996). Two-dimensional image analysis of the shape of rice its application to separating varieties. *Journal of Food Engineering, 27*(4), 397–407. doi:10.1016/0260-8774(95)00022-4

Shouche, S. P., Rastogi, R., Bhagwat, S. G., & Sainis, J. K. (2001). Shape analysis of grains of Indian wheat varieties. *Computers and Electronics in Agriculture, 33*(1), 55–76. doi:10.1016/S0168-1699(01)00174-0

Sun, D.-W. (Ed.). (2007). *Computer vision technology for food quality evaluation*. London, UK: Academic Press, Elsevier Science.

Tanenbaum, R. A. (2004). *Fundamentals of applied dynamics*. New York, NY: Springer-Verlag.

Tao, Y., Morrow, C. T., Heinemann, P. H., & Sommer, H. J. (1995). Fourier-based separation technique for shape grading of potatoes using machine vision. *Transactions of the ASAE. American Society of Agricultural Engineers, 38*(3), 949–957.

Throop, J. A., Aneshansley, D. J., Anger, W. C., & Peterson, D. L. (2005). Quality evaluation of apples based on surface defects: Development of an automated inspection system. *Postharvest Biology and Technology, 36*(3), 281–290. doi:10.1016/j.postharvbio.2005.01.004

Throop, J. A., Aneshansley, D. J., & Upchurch, B. L. (1995). An image processing algorithm to find new old bruises. *Applied Engineering in Agriculture, 11*(5), 751–757.

Unay, D., & Gosselin, B. (2007). Stem and calyx recognition on 'Jonagold' apples by pattern recognition. *Journal of Food Engineering, 78*, 597–605. doi:10.1016/j.jfoodeng.2005.10.038

Xiao-Bo, Z., Jie-Wen, Z., Yanxiao, L., & Holmes, M. (2010). In-line detection of apple defects using three color cameras system. *Computers and Electronics in Agriculture, 70*, 129–134. doi:10.1016/j.compag.2009.09.014

ADDITIONAL READING

Abe, N., Kudo, M., Toyama, J., & Shimbo, M. (2000). A divergence criterion for classifierindependent feature selection. *Advances in Pattern Recognition. Lecture Notes in Computer Science, 1876*, 668–676. doi:10.1007/3-540-44522-6_69

Aleixos, N., Blasco, J., Navarrón, F., & Moltó, E. (2002). Multispectral inspection of citrus in real time using machine vision and digital signal processors. *Computers and Electronics in Agriculture, 33*(2), 121–137. doi:10.1016/S0168-1699(02)00002-9

Ariana, D. P., & Lu, R. (2010). Hyperspectral waveband selection for internal defect detection of pickling cucumbers and whole pickles. *Computers and Electronics in Agriculture, 74*(1), 137–144. doi:10.1016/j.compag.2010.07.008

Basseville, M. (1989). Distance measures for signal processing and pattern recognition. *Signal Processing, 18*(4), 349–369. doi:10.1016/0165-1684(89)90079-0

Battiti, R. (1994). Using mutual information for selecting features in supervised neural net learning. *IEEE Transactions on Neural Networks, 5*(4), 537–550. doi:10.1109/72.298224

Blasco, J., Aleixos, N., Gómez, J., & Moltó, E. (2007b). Citrus sorting by identification of the most common defects using multispectral computer vision. *Journal of Food Engineering, 83*(3), 384–393. doi:10.1016/j.jfoodeng.2007.03.027

Cheng, X., Chen, Y., Tao, Y., Wang, C., Kim, M. S., & Lefcourt, A. (2004). A novel integrated PCA and FLD method on hyperspectral image feature extraction for cucumber chilling damage inspection. *Transactions of the ASAE. American Society of Agricultural Engineers, 47*(4), 1313–1320.

Choi, E., & Lee, C. (2003). Feature extraction based on the Bhattacharyya distance. *Pattern Recognition, 36*(8), 1703–1709. doi:10.1016/S0031-3203(03)00035-9

Du, C.-J., & Sun, D.-W. (2006). Learning techniques used in computer vision for food quality evaluation: A review. *Journal of Food Engineering, 72*, 39–55. doi:10.1016/j.jfoodeng.2004.11.017

Duda, R., Hart, P., & Stork, D. (2001). *Pattern classification* (2nd ed.). New York, NY: John Wiley Sons, Inc.

Egmont-Petersen, M., de Ridder, D., & Handels, H. (2002). Image processing with neural networks - A review. *Pattern Recognition, 35*(10), 2279–2301. doi:10.1016/S0031-3203(01)00178-9

Fisher, R. (1936). The use of multiple measurements in taxonomic problems. *Annals of Eugenics, 7*, 179–188. doi:10.1111/j.1469-1809.1936.tb02137.x

Gestal, M., & Rivero, D. (Eds.). (2011). *Soft computing methods for practical environmental solutions: techniques and studies*. Hershey, PA: IGI Global.

Gómez-Sanchis, J., Gómez-Chova, L., Aleixos, N., Camps-Valls, G., Montesinos-Herrero, C., Moltó, E., & Blasco, J. (2008a). Hyperspectral system for early detection of rottenness caused by Penicillium digitatum in mandarins. *Journal of Food Engineering, 89*(1), 80–86. doi:10.1016/j.jfoodeng.2008.04.009

Gómez-Sanchis, J., Moltó, E., Camps-Valls, G., Gómez-Chova, L., Aleixos, N., & Blasco, J. (2008b). Automatic correction of the effects of the light source on spherical objects. An application to the analysis of hyperspectral images of citrus fruits. *Journal of Food Engineering, 85*(2), 191–200. doi:10.1016/j.jfoodeng.2007.06.036

Guyon, I., & Elisseeff, A. (2003). An introduction to variable and feature selection. *Journal of Machine Learning Research, 3*, 1157–1182.

Hair, J., Black, W., Babin, B., Anderson, R., & Tatham, R. (2005). *Multivariate data analysis* (6th ed.). Prentice Hall.

Huang, Y., Kangas, L. J., & Rasco, B. A. (2007). Applications of artificial neural networks (ANNs) in food science. *Critical Reviews in Food Science and Nutrition, 47*(2), 113–126. doi:10.1080/10408390600626453

Jolliffe, I. T. (2002). *Principal component analysis* (2nd ed.). New York, NY: Springer-Verlag.

Kondo, N., Ahmad, U., Monta, M., & Murase, H. (2000). Machine vision based quality evaluation of Iyokan orange fruit using neural networks. *Computers and Electronics in Agriculture, 29*(1-2), 135–147. doi:10.1016/S0168-1699(00)00141-1

Lee, J. A., & Verleysen, M. (2007). *Nonlinear dimensionality reduction*. New York, NY: Springer-Verlag. doi:10.1007/978-0-387-39351-3

Li, S., Liao, C., & Kwok, J. (2006). Gene feature extraction using T-test statistics and Kernel partial least squares. *Lecture Notes in Computer Science, Neural Information and Processing, 4234*, 11–20.

Martinez, A. M., & Kak, A. C. (2004). PCA versus LDA. *IEEE Transactions on Pattern Analysis and Machine Intelligence, 23*(2), 228–233. doi:10.1109/34.908974

McLachlan, G. J. (2004). *Discriminant analysis and statistical pattern recognition*. Wiley-Interscience.

Plaza, A., Benediktsson, J. A., Boardman, J. W., Brazile, J., Bruzzone, L., & Camps-Valls, G. (2009). Recent advances in techniques for hyperspectral image processing. *Remote Sensing of Environment, 113*(1), S110–S122. doi:10.1016/j.rse.2007.07.028

Rodgers, J. L., & Nicewander, A. W. (1988). Thirteen ways to look at the correlation coefficient. *The American Statistician, 42*(1), 59–66. doi:10.2307/2685263

Shih, F. Y. (2010). *Image processing and pattern recognition: Fundamentals and techniques*. New York, NY: Wiley-IEEE Press. doi:10.1002/9780470590416

Sierra, A. (2002). High-order Fisher's discriminant analysis. *Pattern Recognition, 35*, 1291–1302. doi:10.1016/S0031-3203(01)00107-8

Soria, E., Martín, J. D., Magdalena, R., Martínez, M., & Serrano, A. J. (Eds.). (2009). *Handbook of research on machine learning applications and trends: Algorithms, methods and techniques*. Hershey, PA: IGI Global.

Sun, D.-W. (Ed.). (2010). *Hyperspectral imaging for food quality analysis and control*. London, UK: Academic Press, Elsevier Science.

Vinzi, V., Chin, W. W., Henseler, J., & Wang, H. (Eds.). (2010). *Handbook of partial least squares*. Berlin, Germany: Springer-Verlag. doi:10.1007/978-3-540-32827-8

Wang, S., Li, D., Song, X., Wei, Y., & Li, H. (2011). A feature selection method based on improved Fisher's discriminant ratio for text sentiment classification. *Expert Systems with Applications, 38*(7), 8696–8702. doi:10.1016/j.eswa.2011.01.077

Zude, M. (Ed.). (2008). *Optical monitoring of fresh and processed agricultural crops*. CRC Press LLC.

KEY TERMS AND DEFINITIONS

Automatic In-Line Inspection: Quality inspection where singulated objects are transported by a conveyor belt or similar. A camera captures images of the moving objects that are processed in order to obtain features used to sort the objects into commercial categories.

Pomegranate Aril: Are the seeds of pomegranate. Each aril is between 5 to 14 mm in size and is surrounded be a water-laden pulp ranging in colour from white to deep red or purple. The seeds are embedded in a white, spongy, astringent pulp that can drop together with the arils during automatic peeling.

Real-Time Processing: In the case of pomegranate arils or satsuma segments it means to process about 5-6 images per second, containing an average of 50 objects each.

Satsuma Segment: Segments of satsuma mandarin that are peeled and commercialised canned in syrup.

Chapter 8
Detecting Impact Craters in Planetary Images Using Machine Learning

T. F. Stepinski
University of Cincinnati, USA

Wei Ding
University of Massachusetts Boston, USA

R. Vilalta
University of Houston, USA

ABSTRACT

Prompted by crater counts as the only available tool for measuring remotely the relative ages of geologic formations on planets, advances in remote sensing have produced a very large database of high resolution planetary images, opening up an opportunity to survey much more numerous small craters improving the spatial and temporal resolution of stratigraphy. Automating the process of crater detection is key to generate comprehensive surveys of smaller craters. Here, the authors discuss two supervised machine learning techniques for crater detection algorithms (CDA): identification of craters from digital elevation models (also known as range images), and identification of craters from panchromatic images. They present applications of both techniques and demonstrate how such automated analysis has produced new knowledge about planet Mars.

INTRODUCTION

Impact craters are structures formed by collisions of meteoroids with planetary surfaces. They are common features on all hard-surface bodies in the Solar System, but are most abundant on bodies such as the Moon, Mercury, or Mars where they can accumulate over geologically long times due to slow surface erosion rates. The importance of impact craters stems from the wealth of information that detailed analysis of their distributions and morphology can bring forth. In particular, in the absence of in situ measurements, crater counting is the only technique for establishing relative

DOI: 10.4018/978-1-4666-1806-0.ch008

chronology of different planetary surfaces (Wise & Minkowski, 1980) (Tanaka, 1986). Simply put, heavily cratered surfaces are relatively older than less cratered surfaces. Thus, surveying impact craters is one of the most fundamental tools of planetary geology science (Hartmann, Martian cratering VI: Crater count isochrons and evidence for recent volcanism from Mars Global Surveyor, 1999) (Hartmann & Neukum, 2001).

Presently, all such surveys are done manually via visual inspection of images. Manually compiled databases of craters are either spatially comprehensive, but restricted to only the largest craters (Barlow, 1988) (Rodionova, et al., 2000) (Andersson & Whitaker, 1982) (Kozlova, Michael, Rodinova, & Shevchenko, 2001), or size comprehensive, but limited to only narrowly defined geographical locations. Using spatially comprehensive catalogs of only the largest craters allows for establishing relative chronology on large spatial scale and coarse temporal resolution. This is because large craters are rare, so their counts must be collected from spatially extended regions in order to accumulate a sufficient number of samples for accurate statistics (cumulative distribution of crater sizes is well approximated by a power law with index equal to -2). A finer spatial resolution of the stratigraphy can only be obtained from statistics of much more numerous smaller craters. Compiling global or regional catalogs of small craters, however, would be a very laborious process, ill-suited for the standard technique of manual visual detection.

Advances in gathering planetary data by space probes has resulted in a deluge of high resolution images that show craters as small as 100 m in diameter, and can be combined into mosaics covering entire surfaces of planets such as Mars, the Moon, and soon the Mercury. It is now clear that, if left to manual surveys, the fraction of cataloged craters to the craters actually present in the available and forthcoming imagery data will continue to drop precipitously. Progress in measuring surface relative chronology with

increasing spatial and temporal accuracies can only be achieved by automating the process of crater surveying. Because of the importance of craters to the field of planetary science, there have been numerous attempts to develop a "crater detection algorithm" (CDA). Despite a large body of work, practitioners of planetary science continue to count craters manually, resulting in a lack of progress (relative to available data) in improving the surface chronology. This is because most approaches to CDA are restricted to demonstration that a particular algorithm achieves high accuracy on a particular image or set of images containing relatively simple "textbook" craters, whereas practitioners of planetary science are looking for a robust algorithm having a decent performance on all possible surfaces. In reality, craters are rarely simply circular on a relatively uniform background; craters appearance in an image depends on their level of degradation, on their internal morphologies, on the degree of overlapping with other craters, on image quality (illumination angle, surface properties, atmospheric state), and on their sizes, that may differ by orders of magnitude. Thus the construction of a robust and practical CDA stands as a significant challenge to the scientific community.

Because of a large variety of crater forms, as well as diversity of backgrounds, we contend that a CDA must be based on machine learning principles, in order to be robust enough for actual application. An objective of this chapter is to describe our research on machine learning applied to robust crater detection. We start by reviewing the existing literature on CDA, emphasizing the difference between semi-automatic approaches, based purely on image processing which identify circular features in an image leaving actual decision of whether a structure is indeed a crater to an analyst, and fully automatic approaches, based on a combination of image processing and machine learning which make their own decisions about structures being craters. We then proceed to describe two different families of machine-based

CDAs, one constructed for identification of craters from digital elevation models (also known as range images), and another constructed for identification of craters from panchromatic images. We present applications of both CDAs and demonstrate how such automated analysis led to new knowledge about planet Mars. We finish with enumerating existing challenges and indicating future research directions.

APPROACHES TO AUTO-DETECTION OF CRATERS

Because of the importance of craters for planetary science, the literature on crater detections algorithms is extensive (Salamuniccar & Loncaric, GT-57633 catalogue of martian impact craters developed for evaluation of crater detection algorithms, 2008) (Salamuniccar & Loncaric, 2008). Since 2008, there has been a further increase in publications on auto-cataloging of craters; (Salamaniccar & Loncaric, 2010) provides extensive references for those newer works. From the data source point of view, the CDAs can be divided into those that detect craters from images (most often panchromatic images), and those that detect craters from digital elevation models (DEMs). DEM is a raster-type dataset that stores the value of elevation in each cell.

Image-based crater-detection approaches could be divided into those that dispense with machine learning and those that exploit it. The first class of methods rely exclusively on pattern recognition techniques to identify crater rims having circular or elliptical features in an image (for example, (Barata, Alves, Saraiva, & Pina, 2004) (Cheng, Johnson, Matthies, & Olson, 2002) (Honda, Iijima, & Konishi, 2002) (Kim, Muller, S., J., & Neukum, 2005) (Leroy, Medioni, & Matthies, 2001) (Salamaniccar & Loncaric, 2010) (Salamuniccar & Loncaric, 2008) (Salamuniccar & Loncaric, 2008). The general idea of such methods is to first preprocess an image to enhance the edges of the

crater rims, and then to detect the craters using variants of the Hough Transform (Hough V, 1962), genetic algorithms (Honda, Iijima, & Konishi, 2002), or the radial consistency algorithm (Earl, Chicarro, Koeberl, Marchetti, & Milnes, 2005) that identifies regions of rotational symmetry.

The second class of methods (for example, (Burl, Stough, Colwell, Bierhaus, Merline, & Chapman, 2001) (Plesko, Brumby, Asphaug, Chamberlain, & Engel., 2005) (Vinogradova, Burl, & Mjolsness, 2002) (Wetzler, Honda, Enke, Merline, Chapman, & Burl, 2005) utilize machine learning to facilitate crater detection. In a learning phase, the training set of images containing craters labeled by domain experts is fed to an algorithm. In the detection phase, the previously trained algorithm detects craters in a new, unlabeled set of images (Burl, Stough, Colwell, Bierhaus, Merline, & Chapman, 2001); (Vinogradova, Burl, & Mjolsness, 2002) used a continuously scalable template-model technique to achieve detection. (Wetzler, Honda, Enke, Merline, Chapman, & Burl, 2005) tested a number of machine learning algorithms and reported that support vector machines achieve the best rate of crater detection. (Plesko, Brumby, Asphaug, Chamberlain, & Engel., 2005) used a genetic programming to generate a population of random-detection algorithms whose performance is iteratively improved using a training set as selection criteria.

Image-based CDAs must employ multistep algorithms to combat inherent limitations of imagery data (see previous section). (Honda, Iijima, & Konishi, 2002) first clusters the set of images from which craters are to be detected with respect to image quality and apply separate, optimized detection algorithm to each cluster. (Kim, Muller, S., J., & Neukum, 2005) verified detected craters by template matching and employed neural networks to remove false detections. In spite of such measures, image-based crater-detection algorithms had only limited success. When applied to imagery data, the machine learning-based CDA algorithms work well for small craters (Plesko, Brumby, Asphaug,

Chamberlain, & Engel., 2005), our papers) and/or for relatively simple terrain, but their efficiency drops in proportion to the complexity of the terrain (Vinogradova, Burl, & Mjolsness, 2002). Methods that don't employ machine learning work well in the limited context of an autonomous spacecraft navigation system (Cheng, Johnson, Matthies, & Olson, 2002) because of the relative simplicity of asteroid surfaces.

For several planets (Mars, the Moon, and soon Mercury) high resolution DEMs with near global coverage are available. DEMs are much more fundamental descriptors of planetary surfaces than images. They are suitable for a quantitative geomorphic analysis and are well suited for automated identification of craters. Some authors (Salamaniccar & Loncaric, 2010) (Salamuniccar & Loncaric, 2008) (Salamuniccar & Loncaric, 2008) (Stepinski, Mendenhall, & Bue, Robust automated identification of martian impact craters, 2007) identify craters in a DEM in a manner similar to the identification of craters in an image – through rim detection. Alternatively, (Stepinski, Mendenhall, & Bue., 2009) fully utilize tree-dimensional character of the DEM data and identify craters from DEM as round-shaped depression of certain depth. Overall, it is preferable to detect craters from DEMs than from images. However, DEMs are still limited in availability and resolution, so detecting craters from images is still necessary.

TOWARD ROBUST DETECTION OF CRATERS

Crater Detection Algorithms Design Issues

Crater detection may be an interesting computer science challenge, but ultimately any CDA algorithm must address the needs of the end user – a planetary scientist that needs to survey craters over some extent of planetary surface. Most needed are CDAs capable of global surveys of small craters;

such algorithms are required to identify up to millions of craters from large collections of images (or DEMs) in a robust manner and with minimal involvement from an analyst. Because of the sheer size of the task, a practical algorithm must rely on machine learning. Algorithms based exclusively on pattern recognition are not discriminating enough to have sufficient accuracy and human examination of the results, and are out of question for tasks involving thousands to millions of craters. The overall design architecture for a robust CDA consists of three components: (1) identification of crater candidates (pattern recognition task), (2) binary classification of crater candidates into craters and non-craters (machine learning task), and (3) an ability to adjust a classifier to a new type of surface in order to maintain its performance while minimizing the cost of adjustment to an analyst.

The design of some CDAs combines the first two components; crater candidates are not calculated, instead a decision about a block of image being a crater is done directly on the basis of its pattern. In our experience, such approach results in either high computational cost or inferior accuracy. For example, a viable CDA design may be based on a combination of texture features (Papageorgiou, Oren, & Poggio, 1998) and boosting algorithm (Viola & Jones, 2004). This is an example of a design that concentrates on machine learning at the expense of image processing. In such a CDA, implemented by (Rodionova, et al., 2000), an exhaustive search generates blindly "crater candidates" consisting of square image blocks of all possible sizes centered on all possible locations in an image. Each block is classified as either containing a crater or not by boosting a classifier on the basis of its grayscale texture. Such design is capable of yielding a CDA of sufficient accuracy, however, at a large computational cost. This is because a classifier needs to evaluate a very large number of image blocks, the overwhelming majority of which contain no craters or only fragments of craters. An opposite design approach, one that concentrates on image processing at the expense of machine learning, was introduced by (Urbach & Stepinski, 2009). They detect craters efficiently taking advantage of the fact that photographic imprint of a crater contains crescent-like highlight and shadow regions. Their CDA utilizes methods of mathematical morphology (Serra, 1982) to design scale-invariant and rotation-invariant shape filters for identification of crescent like regions. Because a single application of shape filter to an entire image identifies all craters irrespective of their sizes and orientation, such CDA is very efficient. The lack of a machine learning component in deciding which shapes to include in the filters, however, results in poor crater identification accuracy. Our point of view is that separating identification of crater candidates (for example, by means of mathematical morphology with relatively relaxed shape criteria) with machine learning (for example a boosting algorithm applied only to crater candidates and not to all conceivable image blocks) offers the best possible design that optimizes both performance and accuracy.

Identification of Craters from Topography

For planet Mars and the Moon, global–scale datasets of topography exist in the form of DEMs. Mars was the first planet for which such dataset existed, so much of our effort focuses on auto-surveying craters on Mars, however the methodology can be applied without systemic changes to the Moon; the only change necessary is the training set, as the Martian and lunar craters have somewhat different character and shape.

Our algorithm for automatic identification of craters from Martian topographic data (Urbach & Stepinski, 2009) is designed to have separate modules for identification of crater candidates and for the final classification. Such modular architecture separates the two major challenges facing all feature-finding algorithms, completeness (minimization of false negative detections)

and accuracy (minimization of false positive detections). In the present context, false negatives are craters not identified by the algorithm, and false positives are non-crater features identified by the algorithm as craters. The module for identification of crater candidates is designed to address the completeness issue; its input is the topographic dataset (hereafter referred to as a *site* to underscore its geographical meaning), and its output is a list of crater candidates containing, as its subset, the true craters. The module for final classification of crater candidates is designed to address the accuracy issue. This is why it is based on machine learning; its input is the list of crater candidates, and its output is the same list but with labels indicating whether a given depression is a crater or not

The core concept behind the "candidates" module is that, in the topographic data, craters are depressions. Thus, the role of the candidate-finding module is to identify all topographic depressions in a given dataset. The challenge is to identify all depressions including superposed depressions and irregular depressions. In principle, depressions in topographic dataset could be identified by the "flooding" algorithm (O'Callagnan & Mark, 1984). The flooding algorithm identifies depressions in the DEM by raising elevation of pixels within them to the level of the lowest pour point. However, (Stepinski, Mendenhall, & Bue, 2007) have pointed out that flooding algorithms cannot be utilized as an accurate depression-finder in actual Martian landscapes because superposed depressions, common in such landscapes, are identified as a single depression by the flooding algorithm.

In our algorithm, the problem of nested depressions is addressed by first identifying only the smallest depressions, then proceeding to identification of successively larger depressions in subsequent steps. In order to separate depressions of different scales, we introduce a function that transforms the original landscape (as given by the DEM) into an artificial landscape optimized for identification of depressions having a given

Figure 1. Visualizing crater detection from topographic data. Martian surface topography is illustrated by gradients of colors from light (low elevations) to dark (high elevations). (Left) Outlines indicate depressions (crater candidates). (Right) Outlines indicate craters.

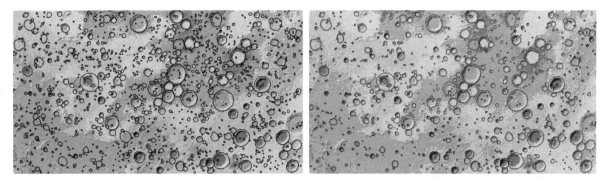

length scale. This transformation calculates the degree to which elevation gradients anchored to pixels in the given-scale neighborhood of the focal pixel are aligned to point toward that pixel (for details see (Urbach & Stepinski, 2009). Such transformation preserves depressions of a given scale, however, features having smaller scale are smoothed out, and features having larger scale bigger are suppressed. Topographic depressions in the transformed landscape are identified as upward-concave regions. Concativity is determined by calculating the discrete second derivative in principal directions; the single-connected regions of upward-concave pixels mark individual topographic depressions of a given scale. This depression-finding procedure is repeated using a transformation with increasingly larger spatial scale in order to identify increasingly larger depressions. All identified depressions are crater candidates; for each of them we calculate five features: diameter, depth, depth/diameter ratio, and two features describing a planar shape of the depression (elongation and lumpiness).

The machine learning module uses the C4.5 decision tree algorithm (Quinlan, 1993) as implemented in the software package WEKA (Witten & Frank, 2005). Because a crater's morphology depends on its size, we have acquired three different training sets for three different sizes of craters

(large, medium, and small). With the resolution of the grid being about 0.5 km, the small craters are those having diameter of about 5 km, medium are those having diameters between 5 and 10 km, and large are those having diameter larger than 10 km. The training sets are constructed iteratively. First a relatively small number of crater candidates is hand-labeled by a human expert and a classifier is built based on this initial training set. This classifier is then applied to all crater candidates in a given site and the results are visually reviewed and corrected if necessary. The corrected results constitute a new, much larger training set. This procedure is repeated for a number of sites. The final three training sets contain 5970, 1010, and 431 labeled examples, respectively. The final pruned decision tree constructed on the basis of 5970 examples and pertaining to identification of smallest craters has 59 nodes and 30 leaves; its expected accuracy is 96.2%. The final pruned decision tree constructed on the basis of 1010 and pertaining to identification of medium-size craters has 25 nodes and 13 leaves; its expected accuracy is 90.1%. Finally, the decision tree constructed on the basis of 431 examples and pertaining to large craters has 15 nodes and 8 leaves; its expected accuracy is 89%. Accuracies are measured using 10-fold cross-validation (Kohavi, 1995). In order to visualize the process of crater detection, Figure

Figure 2. Map of craters relative depths created using attributes of 75,919 craters automatically detected by the crater detection algorithm. Color gradient from dark to light indicates deep to shallow craters.

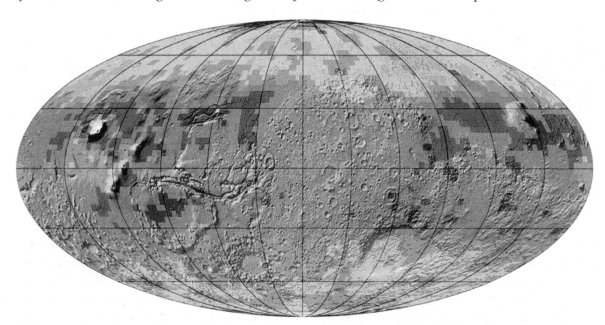

1 shows a small portion of the entire Martian surface with (Left) crater candidates indicated by black outlines and (Right) craters indicated by red outlines.

The methodology described above was used to conduct automatic survey of craters over the entire surface of planet Mars (Stepinski & Urbach, 2009). The result of this survey is a catalog of 75,919 craters (ranging in size from 1.36 km to 347 km.) listing coordinates of the center of each crater, its diameter (D) and depth estimate (d). This survey constitutes a major progress in the study of Martian surface. A "carpet coverage" of Mars surface by 75,919 craters with estimated depths makes, for the first time, possible construction of planet-wide maps showing geographical distribution of depths for craters of different sizes. These maps led to an independent confirmation of the notion that ice exists just beneath the surface at the higher latitudes of the planet but not in its equatorial regions. Figure 2 shows a map of crater relative depths (d/D) for a subset of our auto survey restricted to craters in the 5-10

km size range. It shows that the craters are deeper at the equator than at higher latitude regions. Because craters of the same size should be equally deep, this result indicate that craters at high latitudes experiences some process subsequent to their formation that led to their shallow nature. The best interpretation is that these craters were emplaced in a ground rich in ice, a substance that undergoes a shape relaxation on geologic times. The craters located near the equator preserved their original depths indicating lack of ice there.

Identification of Craters from Images

Presently, topographic data is too coarse for identification of craters that are smaller than about 1 km in diameter. However, those small craters are most useful for improvements in surface chronology. Auto-surveys of craters from topography offers unique capabilities for estimating crater depths and may lead to knowledge discovery (see previous sub-section), but for improved accuracy of surface chronology, where only size and not the depth of the crater is required, image-based auto-surveys are necessary. In planetary context, high resolution images are panchromatic (grayscale), so the task is to find craters in grayscale images. Our approach to image-based crater detection is consistent with our philosophy that the process works best if divided into two parts: identification of crater candidates, and finding true craters from amongst the candidates. In application to image-based crater detection, these modules are based on different principles when compared to topography-based detection (discussed above). This is because craters in images look different than craters in 3-D terrains.

The core concept behind the "candidates" module is that, in the imagery data, a small crater appears as a pair of semi-circular of crescent-like highlight and shadow regions. Thus, (Urbach & Stepinski, 2009) proposed identifying small craters utilizing tools of mathematical morphology (Serra, 1982). Rotation and shape invariant filters can be constructed for identification of crescent-like regions in an image. Because a single application of shape filter to an image identifies all crater candidates irrespective of their sizes (within a limit) and orientation, the shape-based method is very efficient and thus well suited for detecting small crater candidates in large images. However, craters are not the only features on planetary surfaces that may have such a double crescent imprint in an image. Thus, a mathematical morphology-based algorithm is not a very accurate stand-alone crater detection algorithm, but it is a very efficient crater candidate finding algorithm. The efficiency of identifying crater candidates in an image using our algorithm becomes clear if one considers alternatives. The only alternative is to use exhaustive search of sub-windows of different sizes and locations within an image. There are many orders of magnitude more such sub-windows than actual craters; mathematical morphology identifies number of crater candidates that is about the same order of magnitude as the number of craters.

The output of the crater candidate detection module is a list of shapes (each containing a pair of crescent-like shadow and highlight regions). This list constitutes the input to a machine learning module. The first design choice is to select image features as discriminants between craters and other surface objects on the list of candidates. Unlike the case of topographic data, no clear, physics-based features are available, because image is not a physical reality of the surface but rather its projection into 2-D space under given illumination. We encode images of crater candidates in terms of texture features (Ding, et al., 2011). First, each candidate (irregular fragment of an image) is embedded in a square image block, centered on the location of the candidate and having a dimension twice the diameter of the candidate. Second, texture features are extracted from the image block using a simple geometrical technique for texture feature extraction first proposed in (Papageorgiou, Oren, & Poggio, 1998), and popularized by (Viola & Jones, 2004) in the context of face recognition. Figure 2A illustrates the construction of such features; only one of possible mask sizes and one mask location are shown. Such texture features are broadly utilized for object detection and have proven to work well for crater detection (Martins, Pina, Marques, & Silveira., 2008). Overall, we represent each crater candidate by 1089 texture features; see (Ding, et al., 2011) for details. A large number of features restricts our choices of a learning algorithm; for example, decision trees or support vector machines would be ineffective in such context. We need to select automatically only those features that are most useful in discriminating between craters and non-craters. We use a variant (Viola & Jones, 2004) of AdaBoost algorithm (Freund & Schapire, 1995) that simultaneously selects the best features and trains the classifier.

We evaluated our approach to image-based crater detection using high resolution (12.5 meters/

Figure 3. (A) The concept of texture features. Different shape masks used to calculate texture features are shown on the left. The value of a particular mask-feature is obtained by placing the mask over a selected part of an image block and subtracting the sum of grayscale values of the pixels covered by black sectors of the mask from the sum of grayscale values of the pixels covered by white sectors of the mask. (B) Positive examples of craters. (C) Negative examples of craters.

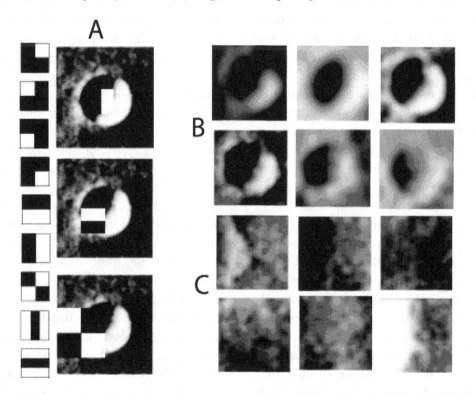

pixel) images of Mars taken by the High Resolution Stereo Camera (HRSC) on-board the Mars Express spacecraft. In this site an analyst has manually cataloged 1937 craters having diameters larger than 16 pixels in size but smaller than 400 pixels. These craters are deemed "detectable" by our method and serve as the ground truth.

The deep valley passes through the middle of the image introducing heterogeneity of the terrain. In order to account for this heterogeneity in the evaluation of our algorithm, we divided the image into three sections (West, Central, and East). Our experimental setup corresponds to the likely use of an algorithm by a planetary scientist who is expected to have a small image annotated (ground truth), but wants to find the craters in a different, larger image. Note that an alternative (not likely to

be of practical importance in planetary research) is to have a training set scattered across the large image. Applying the crater candidate finding module to the test site results in the identification of 14,004 crater candidates. We have chosen 633 candidates, all located in the northern half of the East section of the test site, to constitute the training set; 211 of them are true craters and 422 are non-crater objects. Figure 3B and 3C shows few of the positive and negative examples. In the training phase of the classification module the AdaBoost algorithm ranks the features by their importance in distinguishing between craters and non-craters and establishes the minimum number of features (about 100) required number for classification phase. The selected features focus on detecting a

Figure 4. Fragment of the grayscale image used to evaluate our image-based CDA. Found and missed craters are shown as indicated.

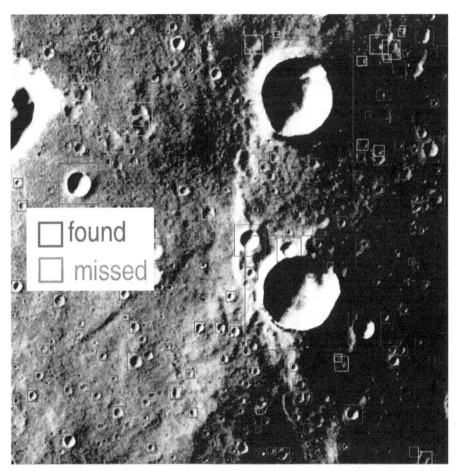

boundary between the shadow and the highlight portions of a crater.

We use the trained classifier to detect the craters in the entire image. Overall the detection rate is 81% compared with 64% for an algorithm based on mathematical morphology alone. Thus application of supervised learning improved the performance of the classifier by 17%. Moreover, the detection rate in the East section of an image (from where training set was sampled) is 87%. However, detection rate in West and central sections, which did not contribute to the training set) is about 79%. Figure 4 shows a fragment of the entire image with found and missed craters indicated by different color outlines. This is because

the West and Central regions contain crater candidates having character unaccounted for in the training set. We could remedy this drop in performance by selecting candidates from the West and Central region to the training set. However, this would be contrary to our overall approach to testing carter detection methods in accordance with how they are expected to be used by planetary scientists (see above). Future research should incorporate techniques of transfer learning and active learning in order to allow the user to modify (with minimum necessary effort) the training set to take into account changing character of craters at different images. The focus of such effort should be on intelligent selection of new samples that exemplify differences between existing training set and the character of new candidates.

Solutions and Recommendations

Automatic crater detection is very likely to become the first popular tool for a planetary scientist that employs supervised learning. The technology has still some way to go before delivering a robust and usable implementation of a crater detection algorithm. In many ways the problem is similar to face detecting algorithms but the technology may take longer to develop because of lower demand and, consequently, fewer resources devoted to the research. The most promising approach to automate crater detection is to find them from topographic data. We expect that the first truly robust crater detector will be based on the high resolution DEMs which are in the process of being obtained for the Moon and planet Mercury. No new topography data gathering mission to the planet mars is planned, so we are likely to be stuck with currently available medium resolution DEMs, although higher resolution DEMs may be constructed locally from stereo pair images. Detecting craters from images will need to be done for planets where high resolution topography data is not available.

Irrespectively of the data type used, we advocate a two-step design for crater detection algorithm. Such design separates the process of finding crater candidates from the process of labeling the candidates. Both steps require further research, although it is the first step (finding the candidates) that can benefit most from further research. Existing supervised learning techniques appear sufficient for the second step of CDA, however further research is needed for identification of the best set of features. More work is necessary on how to assess the accuracy of CDAs. There are problems with the ground truth as well as with the process of matching finds with the ground truth. Unlike the case of human faces, what is and what is not a crater is sometimes debatable, and experts may differ in their opinions. Thus, in the crater detection problem, there is no such thing as a completely objective ground truth. Moreover, the ground truth not only consists of the presence/absence of the crater but also of the size of the crater. Measuring the size of the crater is not as straightforward as it may appear and there is no guarantee that expert collected measurements are always accurate. Thus comparing craters identified by a CDA with ground truth requires a certain degree of flexibility with respect to position and size; finding the best, standard way to do it remains a challenge.

FUTURE RESEARCH DIRECTIONS

The most important challenge in designing a robust and usable CDA is how to maintain high accuracy throughout changing images (or DEMs) without significant additional training. The character of planetary surface changes with location and so does the appearance of craters embedded in those surfaces. Planetary scientist expects to obtain a CDA and use it "out of the box" without training or with minimal training. A CDA that requires extensive training will not be accepted by the planetary community. A solution to this problem is to collect an extensive training set that reflects many known types of surfaces. However, there is a great variety of planetary surfaces and not all of them could be anticipated by CDA designers. This is why future research must concentrate on incorporating elements of active learning, semi-supervised learning, and learning transfer methods to offer adaptation of CDA to different datasets. First attempts (Ding W. S., 2010) (Ding, et al., 2011) on incorporating transfer learning to crater detection show some promise but much more work is necessary.

CONCLUSION

Crater survey is an important task in the field of planetary science, which until now has been performed manually. With increasing amount of available images and other planetary data, this task is ripe for automation via machine learning techniques. In this chapter we have given an overview of the field, pointing the readers to the existing literature and presenting our own contribution to designing and implementing crater detection algorithms. Our approach is underpinned by the philosophy that an efficient and accurate CDA needs to be divided into a step that finds crater candidates, and a step that narrows the field of crater candidates to just craters. Within this flexible framework we demonstrated two different algorithms, one for detection of craters from topographic data, and another for detection of craters from images. Although the two algorithms share our design philosophy, they differ very much in particularities. We have also demonstrated, using Mars as an example, how obtaining a global catalog craters can lead to knowledge discovery.

The algorithms presented here give reasonably accurate surveys of craters, but can benefit from better training sets. We suggest that the most important challenge of CDA is to incorporate elements of transfer learning and/or machine learning to allow for efficient addition of training samples as the need arises.

ACKNOWLEDGMENT

This work was supported by National Science Foundation under grants IIS-0812372 and IIS-1103684.

REFERENCES

Andersson, L. B., & Whitaker, B. A. (1982). *NASA catalogue of lunar nomenclature* (p. 1097). NASA Reference Publication.

Barata, T., Alves, E. I., Saraiva, J., & Pina, P. (2004). Automatic recognition of impact craters on the surface of Mars. *ICIAR, 2,* 489–496.

Barlow, N. G. (1988). Crater size-distributions and a revised martian relative. *Icarus, 75*(2), 285–305. doi:10.1016/0019-1035(88)90006-1

Burl, M. C., Stough, T., Colwell, W., Bierhaus, E. B., Merline, W. J., & Chapman, C. (2001). Automated detection of craters and other geological features. *International Symposium on Artificial Intelligence, Robotics, and Automations in Space,* Montreal.

Cheng, Y., Johnson, A. E., Matthies, L. H., & Olson, C. F. (2002). Optical landmark detection for spacecraft navigation. *The 13th Annual AAS/AIAA Space Flight Mechanics Meeting,* (pp. 1785-1803). Puerto Rico.

Ding, W., Stepinski, T., Mu, Y., Bandeira, L., Vilalta, R., Wu, Y., et al. (2011). Sub-kilometer crater discovery with boosting and transfer learning. *ACM Transactions on Intelligent Systems and Technology, 2*(4).

Ding, W. S. (2010). *Automatic detection of craters in planetary images: An embedded framework using feature selection and boosting.* The 19th ACM International Conference on Information and Knowledge Management, Toronto, Canada.

Earl, J., Chicarro, A. F., Koeberl, C., Marchetti, P. G., & Milnes, M. (2005). *Automatic recognition of crater-like structures in terrestrial and planetary images.* 36th Annual Lunar and Planetary Science Conference, League City.

Freund, Y., & Schapire, R. (1995). A decision-theoretic generalization of on-line learning and an application to boosting. *Computational Learning Theory: Eurocolt*, (pp. 23-37).

Hartmann, W. K. (1999). Martian cratering VI: Crater count isochrons and evidence for recent volcanism from Mars Global Surveyor. *Meteoritics & Planetary Science, 34*(2), 166–177. doi:10.1111/j.1945-5100.1999.tb01743.x

Hartmann, W. K., & Neukum, G. (2001). *Cratering chronology and evolution of Mars* (pp. 165–194). Chronology and Evolution of Mars.

Honda, R., Iijima, Y., & Konishi, O. (2002). *Mining of topographic feature from heterogeneous imagery and its application to lunar craters.* Progress in Discovery Science, Final Report of the Japanese Discovery Science Project.

Hough, V. P. C. (1962). *United States Patent.*

Kim, J., & Muller, J.-P., S., V. G., J., M., & Neukum, G. (2005). Automated crater detection: A new tool for Mars cartography and chronology. *Photogrammetric Engineering and Remote Sensing, 71*, 1205–1217.

Kozlova, E. A., Michael, G. G., Rodinova, J. F., & Shevchenko, V. V. (2001). *Compilation and preliminary analysis of a catalogue. Lunar and Planetary Science* (p. 1231). XXXII.

Leroy, B., Medioni, G., & Matthies, E. J. (2001). Crater detection for autonomous landing on asteroids. *Image and Vision Computing, 19*, 787–792. doi:10.1016/S0262-8856(00)00111-6

Martins, R., Pina, P., Marques, J. S., & Silveira, M. (2008). Crater detection by a boosting approach. *IEEE Geoscience and Remote Sensing Letters, 6*(1), 127–131. doi:10.1109/LGRS.2008.2006004

O'Callagnan, J., & Mark, D. (1984). The extraction of drainage networks from digital elevation data. *Computer Vision Graphics and Image Processing, 28*, 328–344.

Papageorgiou, C., Oren, M., & Poggio, T. (1998). A general framework for object detection. *Sixth International Conference on Computer Vision,* (pp. 555-562).

Plesko, C., Brumby, S., Asphaug, E., Chamberlain, D., & Engel, T. (2005). Automatic crater counts on Mars. *Lunar and Planetary Science,* XXXV.

Quinlan, J. R. (1993). *C4.5: Programs for machine learning.* San Francisco, CA: Morgan Kaufmann Publishers.

Rodionova, F. J., Dekchtyareva, K. I., Khramchikhin, A., Michael, G. G., Ajukov, S. V., & Pugacheva, S. G. (2000). *Morphological catalogue of the craters of Mars.* ESA-ESTEC.

Salamaniccar, G., & Loncaric, S. (2010). Method for crater detection from martian digital topography data using gradient value/orientation, morphometry, vote analysis, slip tuning, and calibration. *IEEE Transactions on Geoscience and Remote, 48*(5).

Salamuniccar, G., & Loncaric, S. (2008). GT-57633 catalogue of martian impact craters developed for evaluation of crater detection algorithms. *Planetary and Space Science, 56*(15). doi:10.1016/j.pss.2008.09.010

Salamuniccar, G., & Loncaric, S. (2008). Open framework for objective evaluation of crater detection algorithms with first test-field subsytem based on MOLA data. *Advances in Space Research, 42,* 6–19. doi:10.1016/j.asr.2007.04.028

Serra, J. (1982). *Image analysis and mathematical morphology.* Academic Press.

Stepinski, T. F., Mendenhall, M. P., & Bue, B. D. (2007). Robust automated identification of martian impact craters. *Lunar and Planetary Science,* XXXVIII.

Stepinski, T. F., Mendenhall, M. P., & Bue, B. D. (2009). Machine cataloging of impact craters on Mars. *Icarus*, *203*(1), 77–87. doi:10.1016/j.icarus.2009.04.026

Stepinski, T. F., & Urbach, E. R. (2009). *The first automatic survey of impact craters on Mars: Global maps of depth/diameter ratio.* 40th Lunar and Planetary Science Conference, (Lunar and Planetary Science XL), The Woodlands.

Tanaka, K. L. (1986). The stratigraphy of Mars. *Journal of Geophysical Research*, *91*(B13), 139–158. doi:10.1029/JB091iB13p0E139

Urbach, E. R., & Stepinski, T. F. (2009). Automatic detection of sub-km craters in high resolution planetary images. *Planetary and Space Science*, *57*, 880–887. doi:10.1016/j.pss.2009.03.009

Vinogradova, T., Burl, M., & Mjolsness, E. (2002). Training of a crater detection algorithm for Mars crater imagery. *IEEE Aerospace Conference Proceedings, 7,* (pp. 3201-3211).

Viola, P., & Jones, M. J. (2004). Robust real-time face detection. *International Journal of Computer Vision, 57,* 147–154. doi:10.1023/B:VISI.0000013087.49260.fb

Wetzler, P., Honda, R., Enke, B., Merline, W., Chapman, C., & Burl, M. (2005). Learning to detect small impact craters. *Seventh IEEE Workshops on Application of Computer Vision, 1,* 178–184.

Wise, U. D., & Minkowski, G. (1980). *Dating methodology of small, homogeneous crater populations applied to the tempe-utopia trough region on Mars. Goddard Space Flight.* Greenbelt, MD: NASA.

Witten, I. H., & Frank, E. (2005). *Data mining: Practical machine learning tools and techniques* (2nd ed.). San Francisco, CA: Morgan Kaufmann.

Chapter 9
Integration of the Image and NL–text Analysis/ Synthesis Systems

Gennady K. Khakhalin
Freelancer, Russia

Sergey S. Kurbatov
Research Centre of Electronic Computing Engineering (RCECE), Russia

Xenia A. Naidenova
Research Centre of Military Medical Academy (RCMMA), Russia

Alex P. Lobzin
Research Centre of Electronic Computing Engineering (RCECE), Russia

ABSTRACT

A complex combining multimodal intelligent systems is described. The complex consists of the following systems: image analyzer, image synthesizer, linguistic analyzer of NL-text, and synthesizer of NL-text and applied ontology. The ontology describes the knowledge common for these systems. The analyzers use the applied ontology language for describing the results of their work, and this language is input for the synthesizers. The language of semantic hypergraphs has been selected for ontological knowledge representation. It is an extension of semantic networks. Plane geometry (planimetry) has been selected as an applied domain of the complex. The complex's systems and their interaction are described.

DOI: 10.4018/978-1-4666-1806-0.ch009

INTRODUCTION

A complex combining multimodal intelligent systems is described. The complex consists of the following systems: Image Analyzer, Image Synthesizer, Linguistic Analyzer of NL-text, Synthesizer of NL- text and Applied Ontology.

The ontology describes the knowledge common for these systems. The Analyzers use the applied ontology language for describing the results of their work, and this language is input for the Synthesizers.

The language of semantic hypergraphs has been selected for ontological knowledge representation. It is an extension of semantic networks with the use of which n – dimensional relations are naturally represented.

Plane geometry ("planimetry") has been selected as the applied domain of the complex. This field has a rich arsenal of both images (the plane figures, children's pictures) and text descriptions of plane geometry constructions.

The Image Analyzer is considered as a hybrid system consisting of two subsystems one of which is intended for recognizing (in classical sense) simple objects and the second subsystem is intended for conceptual analyzing simple and complex objects and situations, represented by the applied ontology. The conceptual analysis is contextual and goal-directed.

The system of conceptual synthesis of graphic images is not an alternative to the traditional methods of machine drawing, but it is a superstructure above them having some additional possibilities. The Image Synthesizer produces, on the basis of ontological descriptions, the graphic objects and situations.

The Linguistic Analyzer of NL-text solves two basic problems: the resolution of all possible uncertainties in texts and the representation of text information (explicit or implicit) in the applied ontology language.

A method of contextual fragmenting similar to the augmented transition networks is used for analyzing the texts. The Linguistic Analyzer ensures the translation of complete simple sentences as well as elements of connected text, in particular, complicated, complex and elliptical sentences from the NL to the ontology language.

The task of NL-text synthesis consists in generating texts according to ontological image descriptions. But this task is still insufficiently studied. For the synthesis, a "pattern" method is usually used, when the previously elaborated templates (answers, questions, explanations) with the specific "lacunas" are embedded into the system. During the process of synthesis, the Synthesizer of NL-text finds the appropriate template and fulfills it.

The different system interaction schemes are examined, for example: analyzing an image and checking, by an expert, the descriptions of synthesized geometry situations; generating text according to a picture; creating a picture and its transforming to the text; paraphrasing a text (text analysis/synthesis) and some others.

The possibility of machine learning application in functioning of the complex is also considered.

APPLIED ONTOLOGY

By ontology, we imply a conceptual "model of world". Applied ontologies include concepts related both to ontology of tasks and ontology supporting knowledge representation in some practical application. Ontological engineering embraces: introducing classes of concepts and concept taxonomies, developing concept structures and situations, giving concept properties (attributes) and their ranges, working out inference procedures based on ontology and procedures of transforming concept relations into ontology.

If ontology is taken as an interface of integrated systems, then two problems arise. The first problem concerns the choice of ontological knowledge representation language such that this language would subsequently make it possible

Figure 1. General form of a hypergraph

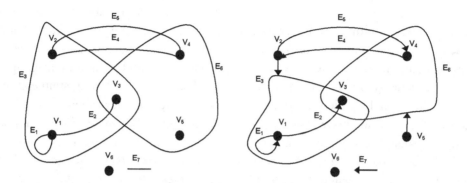

"to immerse" in it the required expansions, for example, fuzzy knowledge, cognitive procedures, etc. The second problem relates to the development of general applied ontology, capable, at the conceptual level, to integrate heterogeneous entrances for the synthesizers and outputs of the analyzers of the integral system. It is, of course, assumed that "inside" each sub-system there can be appropriate knowledge representation languages and bases of "internal" knowledge. For example, the Image Analyzer uses specific procedures or rules for extracting "non-derivative" (= primitive) objects; the Analyzer of NL-text uses specific methods for morphological, syntactical, and semantic NL-language processing.

Knowledge Representation Language

For different subject areas and for different tasks, there is a spectrum of knowledge representation languages (Bashmakov, 2006). From our point of view, the most adequate language of conceptual knowledge representation for heterogeneous information is the language of hypergraphs as an expansion of semantic networks for representing n-dimensional relations. This language makes it possible to assign not only attributes of objects, but also to represent structural, "integral" objects' descriptions with the interrelations between their components.

It is known (Zykov, 1974; Vizing, 2007) that hypergraph H is defined by a pair (V, E), where V is a set of *vertices*, $V = \{v_i\}$, $i \in I = \{1, 2, ..., n\}$, and E is a set of *edges*, $E = \{e_j\}$, $j \in J = \{1, 2, ..., m\}$. Every edge represents a subset of V. Vertex v and edge e are called *incidental* if $v \in e$. Denote by $d(v)$ the number of edges incidental to vertex v and by $r(e)$ the number of vertices incidental to edge e; $d(v)$ is the *vertex degree of v*.

A hypergraph H is *r-uniform* if all its hyperedges have the same cardinality r (have size r). In other words, it is a collection of sets of size r. So a 2-uniform hypergraph is a graph, a 3-uniform hypergraph is a collection of triples, and so on.

A hypergraph (V', E') is called *subhypergraph of (V, E)* if $V' \subseteq V$, $E' \subseteq E$, and v, e are incidental in (V', E') iff they are incidental in (V, E).

The hypergraphs can be *directed* and *undirected*. The edges of undirected hypergraph are called *branches* (*undirected edges*). An edge $e \in E$ of directed hypergraph is called *a directed edge* (*hyperarc*, or *arc*, for short) and it can be represented by an ordered pair (h, T), where $h \in V$, $T \subseteq V \backslash \{h\}$, $T \neq \emptyset$, h is called the *beginning* of the *arc* e, and every vertex from T is called the *terminal vertex* of the *arc* e. The arc e is said to *go out* of vertex h and *comes into* every vertex of the set T. A hypergraph is called a *mixed one* if in it there are branches and hyperarcs. In Figure 1, a non-uniform undirected hypergraph and a non-uniform directed hypergraph are presented.

Figure 2. Structural description of a triangle concept in terms of semantic hypergraph

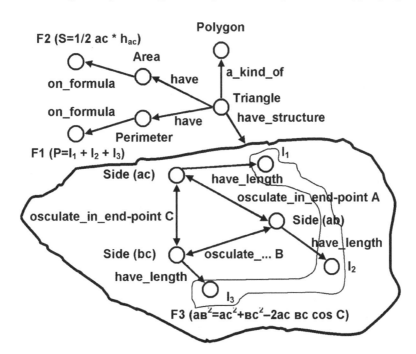

A weighted, labeled hypergraph is a hypergraph whose edges and vertices come along with labels, and with one or more numbers that are generically called weights. The labels can be considered as the names of concepts and relations of an ontology represented by the labeled hypergraph. That hypergraph is called a *semantic hypergraph* (Khakhalin, 2009). The semantic hypergraph for the concept of "Triangle" is given in Figure 2.

The complete description of knowledge representation language and its program support are presented in (Kurbatov, 2011). An example of real semantic hypergraph representation (see, please Figure 2) in the form of program structure of knowledge representation language is shown in Box 1.

Experimental Application Domain

The application domain 'Planimetry' is chosen due to its fitness to modeling image perception, image synthesis, and analysis/synthesis of natural language texts too. We plan also in the future to model the processes of planimetry task decision planning, answering questions, explaining results based on plausible inference, and machine learning as an imitation of human learning based on an experience in geometrical task solving.

The planimetry (plane geometry) figures are the following ones: line segment, triangle, trapezium, ellipse, circle, angle, median etc. We include also plane «child»'s pictures (a childish little ship, toy house, and little locomotive and similar figures) in the set of considered objects.

The ship is an equilateral trapezium ("the frame of ship") on larger base of which a perpendicular (a segment of line) is dropped ("the mast of ship"). A parallelogram intersecting the mast is a "sail". To the upper part of the mast, a triangle is fastened ("flag"). The images (pictures) can contain some fragments of texts in the form of inscription (denotation of object sides, object names and so on).

```
Box 1.

("OBJ_1"  "hypergraph "  ""  ""  "fgr_155"  "cntx_55"
   "name=Structure of triangle ")
("OBJ_2"  "edge HG"  ""  ""  "fgr_155"  "cntx_55"
   "name=E1"  "ext_name=have_structure")
("REL_1"  " belongs to HG"  ""  ""  "fgr_155"  "cntx_55"
   "set=OBJ_1"  "subset=OBJ_2")
("OBJ_3"  "edge HG"  ""  ""  "fgr_155"  "cntx_55"
   "name=E2"  "ext_name=have_length")
("REL_2"  "belongs to HG"  ""  ""  "fgr_155"  "cntx_55"
   "set=OBJ_1"  "subset=OBJ_3")
("OBJ_4"  "edge HG"  ""  ""  "fgr_155"  "cntx_55"
   "name=E3"  "ext_name=have_length")
("REL_3"  "belongs to HG"  ""  ""  "fgr_155"  "cntx_55"
   "set=OBJ_1"  "subset=OBJ_4")
("OBJ_5"  "edge HG"  ""  ""  "fgr_155"  "cntx_55"
   "name=E3"  "ext_name=have_length")
("REL_4"  "belongs to HG"  ""  ""  "fgr_155"  "cntx_55"
   "set=OBJ_1"  "subset=OBJ_5")
("OBJ_20"  "vertex HG"  ""  ""  "fgr_155"  "cntx_55"
   "name=V1"  "ext_name=Triangle")
("REL_21"  "belongs to AR"  ""  ""  "fgr_155"  "cntx_55"
   "set=OBJ_2"  "subset=OBJ_20")
```

A plane geometry situation is defined as a subset of interrelated planimetric objects. The situations can be expressed both by the aid of images and by the aid of NL-texts.

The plane geometry relations have diverse nature. For example, relations of adjoining (be contiguous with, next to), space relations (more to the right, to the right below, it follows), metric relations (it has a length, it has a thickness) and many others.

The NL-texts in our domain application contain not only rather clear formulations of planimetric tasks (although there are many uncertainties in them), but also the descriptions of pictures such as "a little ship" in which the "variability and arbitrariness" of expressions are sufficiently wide. As far as the vocabulary, it is determined by the domain application; the sense of words is consid-ered to be more or less single-valued; there are no metaphors, associations etc. However, we observe many natural language phenomena in textual geometric task descriptions such that homonymy, polysemy, complicated and compound sentences, incomplete constructions (elliptical and anaphoric sentences), errors, special impregnations (formula, geometric and mathematical signs), etc. Some examples of diverse geometric tasks with different complexities and uncertainties are given below:

'The perimeter of a right triangle is equal to 132, and the sum of second degree of its sides - 6050. Find the sides. (Here the dash stands instead of "equals", and in the sentence "Find the sides" the word "triangle" is omitted).

'Prove that the second degree of the area of a quadrilateral circumscribed about a circle is equal to abcd $\sin^2 (\beta + \delta) / 2$ (a formula appears in the text).

'Divide a given triangle into two isometric parts by the straight line, parallel one of the sides' (isometric = having equal areas). The word 'divide' is a many-valued one.

An analysis of linguistic difficulties in geometrical tasks is done in (Naidenova et al., 2011).

Structure of the Applied Ontology

The applied ontology of 'Planimetry' is developed based on common principles of constructing ontology (Hovy, 1998). The formalism of semantic hypergraph makes it possible to determine ontology in the form:

$$O\ (H(X, R),\ I,\ P),$$

where $H(X, R)$ – semantic hypergraph, X – the set of problem domain concepts with proper structures and properties, R is the set of relationships between concepts, I is the set of concept and relationship names, and P is the set of inference procedures with the use of ontology.

A vertex in semantic graph can be associated with a logical, arithmetic or another expression. In this case, the graph's fragment connected with the vertex will contain formulas for calculating the values of some properties of geometrical figures. The vertex of graph will contain also the values of calculated results, for example, the vertices *Difference*, *Sum*, *Perimeter*, *and Area* use the attached procedures (methods).

The concept set X is open, i.e., it can be enlarged if necessary.

The relations between classes, subclasses (super classes) of concepts are organized in taxonomic hierarchies. For a taxonomy representation, the relation *A_Kind_Of* is used.

It is necessary to define in advance the list of base (main) relationships for domain ontology. Currently, there are not a conventional complete

enumeration of relations with exception of several ones (for example, *A_Kind_Of*, *Part_Of*, *Have_Value*, *Have_Structure* and the others).

In our complex, several groups of relations are used: *generally significant* relations, *arithmetical* relations, *logical* relations, *functional* relations and *domain or subject* relations. Note that the set R of relations is also an open set.

Some relations have declarative character: they serve for inferring required knowledge. The arithmetical, logical, functional, and domain relations can be interpreted as declarative ones or as procedures. The procedural interpretation means that the name of a relation is associated with an attached procedure. For example, the relation *to be_contiguous_in_the end_point* is interpreted by the Image Analyzer as an attached procedure allowing finding the contact point of figures in the image. The Synthesizer of NL-text will consider the relation *to_divide_into_two_equal_parts* as declarative description.

The names of concepts and relations of ontology (the set I) are selected both on the basis of terminology, corresponding with the natural-lingual reality in the application domain and in order to simplify the process of ontology development by the expert and the knowledge engineer.

But there is not a completed standardization of terms in this area of investigation and each developer of ontology, as far as possible, uses the conventional terminology (for the names of concepts) and its own preferences - for the names of relations. The concepts and relations in plane geometry are designated via the chains of symbols similar with the NL-words.

The set P of procedures of inferring on ontology is in detail described in (Khakhalin, 2009).

A fragment of plane figure ontology with taxonomy, incomplete structures of figures, and properties of concepts in the language of hypergraphs is given in Figure 3.

Usually, the situations in ontology do not have the status of concepts due to their temporary character. Sometimes a situation (let us say, de-

Figure 3. Fragment of ontology 'plane figure' with the taxonomy, figure structure, and concept properties

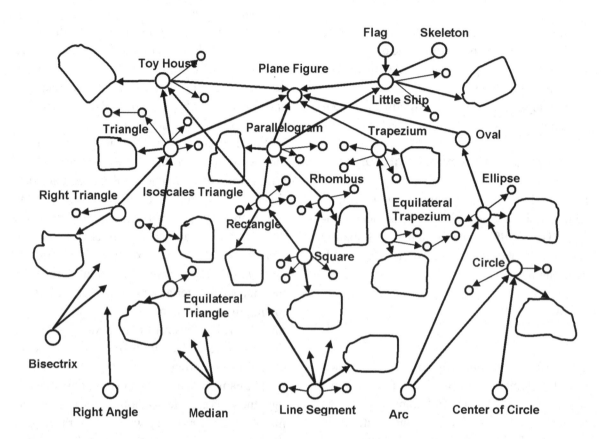

pending on the frequency of its appearance) can take the status in ontology as a certain complex concept. The examples of such situations are: the side of rectangle coincides with the hypotenuse of a given triangle; a fir tree is located near the house and to the right of it; a circle, inscribed into a triangle, etc.

An instance (exemplar, copy) of object in ontology is a structure with in full or in part designated parameters.

HYBRID SYSTEM OF IMAGES ANALYSIS

The task of the Image Analyzer is not only to recognize plane geometry objects but to describe these objects and their location in an image in terms of the applied ontology. The result of analyzing must contain exemplars of all recognized objects, descriptions of their characteristics and relations between them. The completeness of image description depends on some external criteria and the goal of analysis.

The complete image analysis tends to integrate traditional sufficiently effective process of pattern recognition (using "discriminant" methods) for extracting objects (directly from images), their class memberships and feature descriptions, with an effective conceptual image analysis for understanding structure and meaning of image as a whole.

This integration implies creating some hybrid analysis system based on the traditional methods and the methods of using application domain knowledge.

Therefore the Image Analyzer is considered as a hybrid system consisting of the recognition subsystem (in classical sense) for extracting non-derivative objects and the subsystem of conceptual analysis of simple and complex objects and situations, represented by the applied ontology. The conceptual analysis is contextual and goal-directed. It supports and enlarges image processing making it more reliable resolving uncertainties and correcting results of previous steps in pattern recognition.

Recognition of Non-Derivative Objects

We consider the program 'MyScript Notes' of the firm VisionObjects (MyScript Notes, 2007) as an example of recognizing primitive or non-derivative objects. This program recognizes geometric figures drawn by stylus in one window and the having been recognized figures are copied and represented in the second window with the larger clearness and the smoothness of their tracing.

The system recognizes circle, ellipse, rectangle, rhombus, triangle, arc, and line segments, straight and bent arrows (but not a trapezium).

The file obtained as a result of recognition contains information in digital form (in the language of data representation). This information is accessible for the use (for an export, for example). Besides the name of identified class of figure, the program fixes the values of figure's parameters (coordinates of the point of intersection of pairs of lines, center and radius of a circle, etc).

The general structure of object description in the output file is the following one:

```
<the name of the figure> <the prob-
ability of identification> <parameter
1 of the figure> … <parameter n of
the figure>.
```

The information about the possible candidates for recognized objects with the appropriate prob-

abilities of their identification is assigned for each image in the output file. For example, for the image 'a ship with the flag' in Figure 4, the distribution of candidates appears as shown in Box 2.

The names of figure classes (isolated with medium boldface type) with the appropriate parameters are the results of recognition: parallelogram, line segments and arrow.

Conceptual Goal-Directed Analysis of Images

Any closed pattern recognition system has some drawbacks, for example, the quality of recognition depends greatly on the information gain of feature space; adding a new class of objects leads to retraining of the system; a preliminary image processing is accomplished on entire image, etc. Naturally, the pattern recognition system must be open and work in collaboration with a system of goal-directed conceptual analysis.

Baikov et al., (1980) advanced a concept of so called ontology of structural descriptions in order to organize the process of goal-directed analysis of images. Structural object description implies that an object as a whole consists of parts, connected together by certain space relations. The structural descriptions support the analysis of images as well as their synthesis.

Such descriptions must be complete. The independence of descriptions (due to their completeness) determines the open nature of structural ontology: it is easy to add descriptions of new objects, to correct already represented descriptions, to carry out all possible connections between objects without the disturbance of ontological integrity.

With each structural element, a procedure is associated for extracting this element directly on the image. The alphabet of initial "non-derivative" (primitive) and "derivative" elements includes such concepts as *point, segment of line, curved line, triangle, trapezium, circle, ellipse, arc, ship, toy house*, etc. The alphabets of elements and

Figure 4. Example of recognizing "childish little ship with little flag"

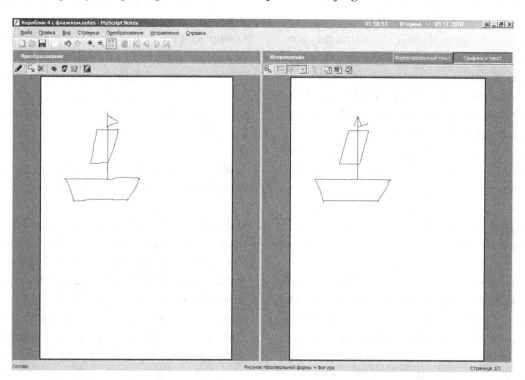

```
Box 2.

parallelogram 0.841063 528.52 912.446 747.868 908.344 840.673 554.967 621.324
559.07
triangle 0.31167 497.79 1142.93 906.228 557.91 608.597 556.68
ellipse 0.290373 685.072 726.389 211.211 122.372 -1.14976
arc 0.290167 685.072 726.389 211.211 122.372 -1.14976 0 6.28319
line 0.731522 353.853 1307.62 956.88 1293.76
arc 0.100776 636.153 1305.02 253.049 6.93823 -0.0208331 2.56482 6.28319
arrow 0.58867 728.269 1086 728.952 513.004 724.757 405.722 719.983 536.781
838.554 471.303 0
arc 0.155304 771.232 752.132 371.109 59.9316 1.55854 0.503146 3.89018
line 0.834599 261.09 1084.42 1079.87 1067.7
arc 0.125702 660.368 1072.95 392.703 6.51846 -0.00942964 -1.11674 3.12932
line 0.436261 267.309 1072.13 362.242 1311.92
arc 0.201896 307.866 1192.53 118.11 9.32409 1.19305 3.09251 6.28319
arc 0.340376 946.813 1303.56 8.19667 4.2457 -1.11007 2.76117 6.35682
line 0.400571 724.831 518.537 838.117 480.311
arc 0.121137 784.761 499.124 52.1676 3.29824 -0.349319 3.12932 7.20357
line 0.424352 957.14 1296.5 1085.65 1070.8
arc 0.159768 1017.81 1180.51 114.253 7.37352 -1.03893 -0.638136 3.14159
```

relations are open and can be extended without the readjustment of the image analysis system.

The structure of ontology supports, in image processing, a goal-directed interaction of the following strategies: from the results of non-derivative object recognition to the ontology, "from top to bottom" (from the ontology to an image), and "from bottom to top" (from an image to the ontology). Therefore the system of conceptual analysis can work both independent of the pattern recognition system and on the basis of its results. Usually, the interaction of these systems occurs.

The process of image contextual analysis has an iterative nature:

- Hypotheses are generated about the presence of an object and its location on the image;
- Testing the advanced hypotheses;
- Decision making (intermediate or terminal) is performed on the validity of each hypothesis.

Generating and testing hypotheses are governed by the current context, formed by the current result of contextual analysis, the information from the applied ontology, and the prior information.

Testing hypotheses is reduced to a goal-directed search for a collection of elements on the image such that these elements satisfy the structural description of analyzed objects.

The solution about accepting a hypothesis can be reviewed in the subsequent stages of image analysis, if the higher level context connected with this hypothesis will require it.

We illustrate the stages of contextual analysis of object '*small ship with the flag*' (see Figure 4). Let the structure of concepts *trapezium*, *ship*, and *ship with the flag* be present in the ontology (see Figure 3).

If a *parallelogram* and several *line segments* will be discovered on the image, then the structure of a *ship* will be selected as a structure-hypothesis. The comparison of the ontological structure of ship

with the results of recognition yields the positive results: four line segments (with the coordinates of their end points) compose a trapezium, an isolated line segment corresponds with a mast, and the identified parallelogram corresponds with a sail).

But since some not yet identified elements (*an arrow* and *small 'tail' – some line segments*, see, please, the image) remained, the system searches for the context of higher level containing the concept '*ship*'. This context contains the concept '*ship with the flag*'. Now the system of image analysis will perform a goal-directed search for the additional parts of the object '*ship with the flag*' on the image, already knowing, where approximately to search for and what to search for (let us note that such a strategy solves the problem of image segmentation too).

The region of search is determined by the coordinates of objects '*arrow*' and '*tail*' (see, please, these parameters in Figure 4). A '*flag*' will be the object of searching for (= triangle). If '*flag*' is correctly identified, then the result of the entire image analysis will be a designated copy of the ontological structure of concept '*ship with the flag*'. Its description can be synthesized as a variant of NL-text. Let a brief version of the text be: '*On the image, a ship with the flag is located in the left upper part of the screen*'.

SYSTEM OF THE CONCEPTUAL IMAGE SYNTHESIS

The system of conceptual synthesis of plane geometry graphic images (the Image Synthesizer) is not an alternative to traditional methods of computer graphics but it is a superstructure above them guaranteeing additional possibilities (Vlasov at al., 1988).

The task of Image Synthesizer consists in transforming complete or partial signified ontological object descriptions into their graphical visualizations.

The ontological descriptions (synonym of conceptual descriptions) are based on the structural models of plane geometrical objects and links between them. The object model in which all vertices' values have been assigned is the description of a concrete instance of object. Thus an object instance has the name, structure, and parameters whose values have been calculated.

For visualizing an object instance, it is necessary to construct a description of this exemplar required by one of the computer graphical programs. Traditionally, these programs create images from line segments approximating given plane geometrical objects. A special program, the Planner of Image, makes all required calculations. The Planner is a universal instrument with respect to all object models.

It is important that the visualization system could discover the discrepancy of data, i.e., the impossibility of single-valued calculation of an exemplar of object.

SYSTEM OF THE NL-TEXT LINGUISTIC ANALYSIS

Usually, in NL-text processing, the linguistic analysis is considered as a task solving two basic problems: resolving ambiguities appearing in texts and representation of text information (explicit and implicit) in the language of applied ontology.

Let T be the set of all NL-sentences and M be the set of semantic descriptions of all situations in an applied ontology. The linguistic analysis solves the task of mapping Ψ: $T{\rightarrow}M$, allowing for a given sentence $t_i \in T$ constructing corresponding description $m_i \in M$. This mapping must resolve the uncertainties of surface and deep levels of NL (homonymy, homography, polysemy, incompleteness, incorrectness, irregularity and other non-factors), reducing them to the single-valued semantic representation.

The mapping Ψ can be considered as a realization of three language processes: grammar analysis, semantic interpretation, and semantic analysis. Grammar analysis includes morphological analysis and syntactic analysis. Semantic interpretation performs "translating" text's fragments into corresponding fragments of ontological descriptions directed by syntactic rules. Semantic analysis gives the complete ontological description of plane geometrical situation generated by NL-descriptions of these fragments.

The morphological analysis (in the case of procedural embodiment) performs the analysis of internal structure of word form (determining its stem and inflexions), the search for the stem in the dictionary and, according to the obtained lexical article, the adding to the word form the corresponding grammatical categories (markers). There is a certain set of the morphological analyzers, from which it is possible to use any one, for example, (Mal' kovsky, 1985).

The variety of syntactic analyzers "strikes imagination". But majority of them uses one of the following methods: the consistency tree, the tree of dependences, and the augmented transition networks. Constant disputes about the advantages of each of these methods are conducted among the developers. We use an approach nearest to the apparatus of augmented transition networks, realized in the translator Systran (Flanagan et al., 2002).

The semantic interpretation practically is not separated as a special stage. Sometimes it partially (in the limits of surface semantics) "is hidden" in the syntactic analysis.

The semantic analysis, to a certain degree, is included in the practical systems of NL-access to the data bases (Popov, 1982; Narin'jany, 1995).

The Linguistic Analyzer of NL-text, in our integral complex, is based on a method of contextual fragmentation (Khakhalin at al., 2006). It contains two components: a base one and extended one. The base component performs translating complete simple phrases (syntactic constructions) and sentences from the NL into the ontology language. The extended component is intended for translating connected texts, in particular, the complicated, complex, compound and elliptical sentences.

Base Component of Linguistic Analysis

An NL-sentence t_i will be considered as a graph $t_i(x_j^k)$, where x_j^k - elements of this sentence (upper index gives the ordering of words in the sentence). The elements of sentence are considered to be word forms, punctuation marks, brackets, abbreviations, and other "impregnations" in NL-text obtained after graphematic analysis (in this work, it is not considered).

Full linguistic analysis consists in sequential performing morphological and syntactical analysis, semantic interpretation, and semantic analysis. Each stage of linguistic analysis is maintained by its proper model. The morphological analysis uses a morphological data base (morphological lexicon). The syntactic analysis is supported by a special ontology "the syntax of NL" constructed with the use of semantic hypergraph based on the same principles that the applied ontology "Planimetry" exploits, where the roles of objects and relations play the elements of natural language syntax. The semantic interpretation is based on a production type model that "translates" syntactically correct fragments of text into fragments of the applied ontology. The semantic analysis is realized via the applied ontology with the aid of all the subsystems of integrated complex. Consider the characteristics of the models enumerated above.

Grammatical Ontology

The grammar model (= syntactic ontology) is constructed by analogy with the applied ontology and we have as a result a "syntactic hypergraph". Syntactic information is represented in the form of fragments called contexts or contextual rules. The contexts form a hierarchic structure determined recursively by a set of hypergraphs of different levels with syntactic relations.

The contextual rules are given at the levels of word forms, stems, lexemes, classes of objects, etc. The contexts can be the templates for extracting from texts, for example, dates, numbers, names of files, geographical names, surnames, etc.

The semantic features can be added to the contexts, if the possibility of their extracting from text is provided, for example, they can be used by the so-called role structures.

The nomenclature and content of contextual rules depend on the developer of syntactic part of grammar ontology and his membership to a certain linguistic school. A fragment of syntactic ontology in the form of hypergraph is given in (Kuzin at al., 1989).

Model of Semantic Interpretation

For each lexical element of natural language, "the nest" of productions is assigned as follows (Pospelov, 1990):

```
(i); Q₁; P₁; A₁ ⇒ B₁; N₁
     Q₂; P₂; A₂ ⇒ B₂; N₂
     ................
     Qₙ; Pₙ; Aₙ ⇒ Bₙ; Nₙ
```

Here **(i)** is a unique name of production. As the name of production, words, combination of words, punctuation marks can be used, etc, if they reflect the essential content of this production.

The element **Q** characterizes the application sphere of production or the theme of a text. The theme of text can be dynamically determined by well-known statistical methods. An original method of extracting the theme of text is given in (Naidenova, 2006).

The main element of production is its core $A \Rightarrow B$, where **A** is an ordered set of contextual syntactic rules; **B** is a corresponding with **A** fragment of the applied ontology. For text's elements not having an interpretation, the set $\mathbf{B} = \varnothing$.

The element **P** is the condition of applicability (pre-condition) of production core, and it is defined via the membership of an analyzed word to a certain part of speech.

The element **N** describes the post-conditions of production. The post-conditions are actualized if the core of production has been extracted from text. The post-conditions describe the actions and procedures performed after the realization of **B**.

The model of interpretation is a "vocabulary" of system containing the way of "translating" a text fragment into a fragment of the semantic ontology depending on the syntactic rules.

Semantic Model or Applied Ontology

The model of language semantics is considered as a part of the applied ontology (see, please Section 1.3). Names of concepts and relations can be the NL-words, fulfilling the nominative function. They are used for simplification and convenience in the processes of development, filling and checking the semantic models. The information described in the applied ontology language is expressed explicitly, even if it is implicitly represented in the text. For example, if, in the text, there is the word combination *the altitude of triangle*, then, in the ontology language, this combination will be represented as follows: (*triangle*) (*include*) (*the altitude*).

Grammatical Analysis

The morphological analysis on the basis of a declarative or procedurally assigned morphological lexicon prescribes a set of grammatical characteristics to each word of sentence.

Syntactic parsing t_i will consist in searching for a set $\{f_{ij}\}$ of fragments of t_i such that to cover completely t_i and to form a connected (coherent) structure of fragments. But in many cases, it is possible to speak only of partial syntactic analysis.

The process of complete parsing has an iterative character. It includes the following steps:

choosing context-hypotheses by the use of a set of context rules, comparing these contexts with t_i, and extracting connected fragments.

The process of searching for and choosing a relevant (suitable) context for t_i is determined by a selected word and by the successfully matched contexts. The necessary information is drawn from the syntactic ontology according to the relations *"A Kind Of"*, *"it enters into the structure"*. With the successfully selected context of the current level, the next hypothesis is generated about a set of contexts of the following level with the use of the inclusion relation given on the set of contexts.

Let f_{ij} be a selected fragment of t_i. If the condition of connectivity of it with the already chosen fragments for t_i is satisfied, then it supplements the connected structure of fragments.

The analysis continues for the next word, which did not enter the connected structure of chosen fragments. If f_{ij} is an isolated fragment, then it is memorized for its possible entering the fragments' structures at subsequent iterations and the analysis is performed for the next word.

Thus, the process is repeated until obtaining the complete parsing. The parsing graph τ_i, as a collection of connected fragments' graphs, with the information of matching contexts and t_i will be the result of this process.

If it is not possible to obtain the complete and connected covering of a sentence, then we assume that the parsing goes on the false branch (in the sentence, there are uncertainties), the sentence is incomplete or it is incorrect with respect to the given syntactic model.

Semantic Interpretation

The languages for describing semantic and syntax are different and this fact implies the difference of text fragmentations resulted from syntactic and semantic parsing. The lexicon of M-language (an applied ontology language) consists of a set of problem-oriented concepts and relations. Given a hypergraph of grammar analysis, the semantic interpretation deals with obtaining an ordered set of ontological fragments with associated presuppositions, determined by the interpretation models. This set is called 'the result of linear translation" (RLT).

The presupposition contains explicitly the information, which is implicitly contained in the fragments of a sentence, but in the applied ontology, must be recorded explicitly. The semantic interpreter constructs RLT, with the use of a production system, iteratively performing semantic disambiguation in all parts of RLT.

The semantic disambiguation in RLT is produced with the use of intersecting the interpretations of words and word combinations. If the result of intersection is unique, then the presuppositions of intersected fragments are united. If it is impossible to obtain a single-valued interpretation, then the sentence is considered to be semantically incorrect in the framework of this interpretation.

The single-valued RLT is viewed as a hypergraph of sentence t_i.

Semantic Analysis of Sentences

The output of the semantic interpreter for a sentence is the set of fragmental semantic descriptions of a plane geometry situation represented in this sentence. These fragments are connected in an integral ontological description by the Semantic Analyzer. The Semantic Analyzer performs testing both the completeness and correctness of ontological descriptions. The semantic analysis is analogous to the complete grammar analysis. It results in obtaining ontological descriptions of plane geometry situations represented in a given analyzed text.

The algorithm of linguistic analysis described above is intended for simple complete sentences. Translation of connected texts' elements (elliptical, complicated, complex and compound sentences and clauses) is realized by an Extended Component of the Linguistic Analyzer.

An Extended Component of Linguistic Analyzer

This extended analyzer divides any complex and compound sentence (clause) into simple phrases and each phrase is translated into ontological description by the base component of Linguistic Analyzer. It is necessary to view together the parsing of complicated and elliptic clauses, because the segmentation of complicated, complex and compound sentences leads often to obtaining incomplete phrases which must be linked with the other phrases in text or fragments of the same sentence. There is also an independent task of analyzing separate incomplete NL-sentences.

Translation of the Elliptic Sentences

Ellipsis is characterized by the incompleteness. Formally, it is possible to assume that an ellipsis may appear both at the syntactical and semantic level.

We shall think of syntactic ellipsis as of such correctly constructed sentence t_i, that there exists at least one word x_i^k for which it is impossible to find a fragment f_{ij} extending connected structure of syntactical fragments of this sentence. The analogous consideration is true for semantic ellipsis.

Processing the ellipsis consists of two stages: the restoration of it to complete phrase due to discourse and translation of restored phrases with the use of the base component of the linguistic analyzer. We use a local discourse (for complex and compound sentences) and global discourse (for simple incomplete sentences). The absence of discourse or the impossibility to resolve ellipsis testifies a disturbance of NL-text connectivity or incompleteness of the Linguistic Analyzer's model.

The ellipsis reconstruction includes the search for analogous fragments of discourse and ellipsis; then it is performed the adding of missing elements to ellipsis from discourse with their correcting if it is necessary. For example, let the following text be entered the Linguistic Analyzer:

What formula is used for calculating the area of triangle? And for rectangle?

The second sentence is a syntactic ellipsis. Matching discourse and ellipsis gives the following correspondence: *triangle ↔ rectangle*. And the incomplete phrase will be reconstructed as follows:

What formula is used for calculating the area of rectangle?

Translation of the Compound and Complex Sentences

The translation of complex and compound sentences is based on two component of the Linguistic Analyzer: a) for complete phrase and b) for dealing with ellipsis for incomplete phrases. This translation consists of the following stages: segmentation of complex and compound sentences into phrases with respect to the characteristics of their structural complexity; constructing current phrase structure of the sentence with its subsequent refinement; iterative translation of each extracted phrase and joining their ontological descriptions into a single whole structure.

In correctly constructed complicated, complex and compound sentences there are always the indicators "of their complexity": conjunctions, conjunction words, punctuation marks, etc. For each NL, the set of the complex and compound sentence types is limited. It permits simplifying the grammar model of translation by introducing the concepts and structures of a "binding". The number of such binding structures for Russian Language is about 250-300 (Rozental' at al, 1995).

All structures are naturally "immersed" in a certain connected model, in which there are relations of the type "*A Kind Of*", "*to enter into structure*", etc, and with the aid of which it is possible to accomplish the search for and comparison of the binding structures with a given sentence.

The elements of the binding structures can be concrete word forms, lexemes, parts of speech, punctuation marks and their different combinations with their syntactic and geometric interrelations.

Each structural binding (connector) has its unique name (in a given model) and possesses some properties (the properties characterize the type of connector complexity, for example, "complex definitive type" or "introductory construction", etc.

The process of fragmentation includes the following stages: choosing a set of structural connectors; matching these structural connectors with a NL-sentence; extracting the connecting parts of sentence, and constructing phrases iteratively.

The positive result of comparing the structure of connector with a sentence gives the possibility to determine the type of complex and compound sentence in question.

This fragmentation of complex and compound sentence into the phrases takes into account the plurality of the interrelating of each word with different phrases, i.e., a certain word can be connected with several phrases simultaneously. For example, let the following sentence be given:

Find area of the equilateral triangle, side of which equals 15 cm, and altitude 12 cm,

As a result of the fragmentation, we will obtain three phrases:

Find area of the equilateral triangle | triangle, side of which equals 15 cm | altitude 12 cm.

The second phrase under translation will be equivalent to the phrase *the side of the triangle equals 15 cm* (on the basis of the anaphoric conversions).

Figure 5. The representation of a situation, described by the NL-text of the geometric task, in the form of semantic hypergraphs

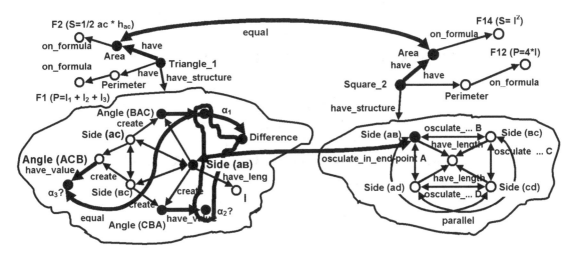

The third phrase is elliptic and it can be restored as follows:

Altitude of the triangle equals 12 cm.

On the basis of the binding structures, utilized for the sentence fragmentation, we obtain the phrase structure of the entire sentence: it is subordinate attributive sentence, where the subordinate part is a compound phrase.

It is worth noting that the obtained phrase structure is not a tree structure (in contrast to the system of constituents or the dependency tree).

We give an example of translating the text of a geometrical task into ontological description. The text of task is the following:

'Area of a triangle, one of the angles of which equals the difference of two the others is equal to the area of a square, the side of which coincides with one of the sides of this triangle. Find the angles of this triangle'.

The description of plane geometrical situation in the language of semantic hypergraph with the designated elements (marked vertices and bold edges) is given in Fig 5.

SYSTEM OF THE NL-TEXT LINGUISTIC SYNTHESIS

The task of NL-text synthesis consists in generating the text according to the structural ontological descriptions. The complete synthesis of NL-phrases assumes the stages of semantic synthesis, syntactic interpretation, syntactic synthesis, morphological synthesis and formatting (graphematic synthesis).

It should be noted that the synthesis of NL-sentences from the level of ontology is still insufficiently studied. Usually with the synthesis, a "pattern" method is used, when the previously specified templates (answers, questions, explanations) with previously specified "lacunas" are embedded into the system.

As an example of using the complete scheme of synthesizing NL-sentences from the level of applied ontology (model of domain application) can serve the system "POET" (Popov, 1982).

Figure 6. Scheme of the system interaction

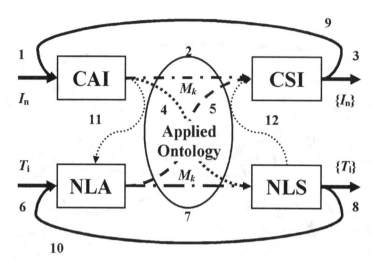

The synthesis from the syntactic (superficially-semantic) level is sufficiently described in the literature, for example, in (Apresjan at al., 1988).

SYSTEM INTERACTION SCHEME

The dynamics of artificial intelligence systems and methods of their development makes it possible to assume that obtaining a new qualitative result in constructing intelligent computer systems is currently determined via integrating already existent intelligent systems solving different complex tasks.

However the main problem of this integration is the realization of interacting between these intelligent systems. Clearly, all the systems of our integrated complex participate in the process of understanding texts and images. The common result of all complex's systems is represented in the applied ontology. Figure 6 illustrates the interaction of all these systems. Each act of the interaction has the name and a sequence of steps.

(**CAI** is image's conceptual analysis system. **CSI** is image's conceptual synthesis system. **NLA** is NL-analysis system. **NLS** is NL-synthesis system. I_n denotes input/output images. $\{I_n\}$ de-

notes a set of images. T_i denotes NL-text. $\{T_i\}$ denotes a set of NL-texts (periphrases). M_k specifies description of object or situation in terms of semantic hypergraphs.)

1. Analysis/understanding of an image.
   {1, 2} – input: an image; in ontology – names of object or situation classes; description of image – assigned structures of objects and situation in the ontology language.
2. Analysis of an image and testing the ontological descriptions of geometric situation from the side of an expert (Analysis/synthesis of an image).
   {1, 2, 3} – input: an image; in ontology – the ontological description of image situation; output: a set of instances of identified image situation.
3. Generation of text according to a given figure.
   {1, 4, 8} – input: an image; in ontology – the ontological description of situation on the image; output – the NL-text describing geometric situation on the image.
4. Generation of images according to a given text.

{6, 5, 3} – input: – a NL-text; in ontology – the semantic description of text in the ontology language; output – a set of images illustrating the text.

5. Paraphrase of input text (text analysis/synthesis).

{6, 7, 8} – input: – a NL-text; in ontology – the semantic description of the text in the ontology language; output – a set of NL texts describing the situations identified in the input text (paraphrases).

6. An image and its text description.

{1, 2; 6, 7} – input: – an image; the ontological description of image situations; – input: the NL-text describing the image; the semantic description of geometrical situations represented by the text in the ontology language; A goal function is comparing the descriptions.

The remaining interactions relate to the following cases: a) the result is formed in the applied ontology; b) a text is a fragment of image, and some others.

The interactions of the systems are examined under the assumption that the applied ontology is constructed on the comprehensive and exhaustive information. It is obvious that to construct by hand all ontological knowledge even for one application domain is practically impossible. Some methods of automated formation of knowledge base have been proposed in (Kurbatov, 2010). The complex must also use some machine learning methods both inductive and deductive ones.

MACHINE LEARNING IN NATURAL LANGUAGE PROCESSING

The application of machine learning techniques to natural language processing (NLP) is dramatically increased in recent years. There is now a variety of work on applying learning methods to almost all aspects of language processing including morphological and syntactic analysis, semantic disambiguation, semantic interpretation, discourse processing, segmentation of long sentences (Kim et al., 2001), categorization instances with regard to an ontology (Cimiano et al., 2004), ontology learning from text (Cimiano, 2006) and many others. The machine learning methods in linguistics embrace a collection of diverse problems from low-level analysis to high level of NLP (Cardie, 1999). At lexical level, these methods cover part-of-speech tagging and noun phrase chunking. At high level, the problems of syntactic parsing, text categorization and clustering, extracting information on a particular topic, extracting patterns from text, text segmentation, extracting text structure and content are supported by machine learning techniques.

Unfortunately, in machine learning application to NLP, a somewhat narrow focus prevails on feature-vector classification problem or learning classification of objects, represented by their descriptions in a feature space. The goal of learning is to obtain necessary and sufficient rules or 'concept descriptions' with the use of which it can be performed the classification of new objects familiar with those belonging to a training set of object instances. In this case, we deal with learning from examples or supervised learning. This mode of learning requires a lot of human efforts in preparing data to learning experiments. This work includes:

- Choice and formation of feature space;
- Checking hypotheses related to the similarity-distinction of objects and their classes; defining the binary operations for determining the similarity-distinction relationships between objects and between classes of objects;
- Forming a training set of object examples;
- Forming a control set of object examples;
- Choice of an adequate learning algorithm.

The choice of feature space determines a learning task with respect to its content and the type of learning algorithm. The formation of training and control sets of object examples in the case of supervised learning determines the accuracy, rapidity and effectiveness of learning.

However the implementation of the complex of multimodal intelligent systems requires modeling human associative thinking. The extraction of associations from the data becomes one of the most urgent tasks of the intelligent system automated construction. We mean the associative connections of different kind: associations between words in a text, between sentences and fragments of a text, associations between ontological or semantic graphs, and association of the type "image ↔ ontological description of image ↔ NL-description of image".

To associative thinking can be attributed also reasoning by analogy and determining the similarity between any objects, situations, complex structures. In our program complex, it is very important to find similar images, similar ontological descriptions, similar graphs (trees) of syntactic parsing, and similar textual descriptions of geometrical tasks. Machine learning procedures mine associations in data and knowledge in order to use them in the organization of system reasoning.

Another mode of machine learning is related to learning chains or sequences of procedures on the basis of given examples with memorizing the associations between tasks and these sequences of procedures.

We give some examples of machine learning applications with respect of our tasks of geometry text analysis. Plane geometry tasks are divided into separate classes. There are tasks related to proving assertions, constructing figures, calculating elements or properties of figures, testing theoretical knowledge of students. In geometry handbooks, the tasks exist directed toward the study of only one plane geometry figure, for example, "inscribed and circumscribed triangles", "the area of circle",

or a class of relationships, for example, "the metric relationships in triangle".

The structure of task's text and its lexical-syntactic features substantially depend on the class of this task. Therefore one of the necessary functions of multimodal intelligent system in question is recognizing the class of proposed task. This function gives the possibility to choose the necessary fragment of ontological knowledge.

It is useful to recognize the similarity of tasks with respect to their content: a figure and some calculated relationships corresponding to a task can be used for analyzing and solving similar tasks.

For the recognition of tasks' content similarity, it is insufficient to establish only their text similarity. A problem appears to recognize the semantic equivalence of sentences or text fragments. The concept itself of "understanding text" requires refinement and constructive determination. In our work, it is proposed to transform text to a certain "canonical" form describing objects, their designation (in a figure), properties and situations (what they make and what is done with them) in the form trinomial simple propositions.

For the semantic analysis, it is possible to use the models of context on the basis of syntactic connections in sentences, as it is examined in (Stepanova & Emelyanov, 2007).

The system of synonymous conversions above deep syntactic structures is examined in (Mikhaylov, & Emelyanov, 2010). In the same work, it is solved the problem of clustering texts on the basis of syntactic contexts of noun. All these problems are maintained by machine learning techniques.

For mining associations from NL-texts, we develop a system SMAT (System Mining Associations from Text). A dictionary is formed of words, entering a given text. Text is considered as a totality of sentences, sentence is considered as a totality of words. All words and sentences are indexed. Each sentence is associated to the list of indices of dictionary words entered this sentence. For each word, it is formed the list of indices of the sentences, in which it is contained.

The set-theoretical operations are assigned on the set of all subsets of indices. With the aid of these operations the inclusion relations between the subsets of indices are established.

One of the tasks solving by the SMAT is forming the themes and contexts of themes related to a given text (Naidenova, 2006). Let j be the index of sentence, *word* (j) be the list of words of sentence j, the entries of which into the text are equal to or more than two, and *list* (*word* (j)) be the united list of the entries of words of *word* (j) into the other sentences of the text. *Word* (j) is called the core of sentence j or the theme of it. The set of sentences corresponding with *list* (*word* (j)) is called the development of theme or its context.

The theme or the collection of words from *word* (j) is converted to a minimal connected text, extracted from sentence j. Thus, each sentence "is compressed" in accordance with its theme. The choice of theme determines its context; the text generates a set of various contexts.

The SMAT uses a set of original algorithms for mining the word and sentences associations from NL-texts (Naidenova & Shagalov, 2009).

CONCLUSION

The concept of an artificial intelligence integral system is represented in this chapter. The different parts of this integral system are in different stage of development. The program system of supporting the semantic hypergraph language for knowledge representation is being developed. Some components of linguistic translator for analyzing text in Russian language have already implemented.

The adjustment of the discriminant recognition system to the system of goal-directed image analysis is being performed.

The upper level system of image synthesis according to ontological image descriptions is currently realized and this system is united with a system of machine drawing.

An experimental applied ontology "Planimetry" is also constructed and tested currently. This ontology is intended for modeling the interaction processes of the complex systems.

For the complete realization of integrated systems, it is required conducting further studies of theoretical as well as practical artificial intelligent tasks.

REFERENCES

Apresjan, J. D. (Ed.). (1988). *Linguistic supporting of the system STAGE-2*. Moscow, Russia: Science. (in Russian)

Baikov, A. M., Kuzin, E. S., Khakhalin, G. K., & Shamis, A. L. (1980). The context task-oriented analysis of images in terms of semantic network. *Questions of Radio Electronics* [in Russian]. *Topical GT, 1*, 50–58.

Bashmakov, A. I., & Bashmakov, I. A. (2006). *Intellectual information technologies*. Moscow, Russia: Published by Moscow State Technical University. (in Russian)

Cardie, C. (1999). Guest editors' introduction: Machine learning and natural language. *Machine Learning, 34*, 5–9. doi:10.1023/A:1007580931600

Cimiano, P. (2006). *Ontology learning and population from text. Algorithms, evaluation and applications*. Springer Science+Busivess Media, LLC.

Cimiano, P., Handschuh, S., & Staab, S. (2004). Towards the self-annotating Web. In S. Feldman, M. Uretski, M. Najork, & C. Wills (Eds.), *Proceedings of the 13th World Wide Web Conference* (pp. 462-471). ACM.

Emelyanov, G. M., & Mikhailov, D. V. (2005). Updating the language knowledge base in the problem of equivalence analysis of semantic images of statements. *Pattern Recognition and Image Analysis, 15*(2), 384–386.

Flanagan, M., & McClure, S. (2002). SYSTRAN and the reinvention of MT. *IDC Bulletin #26459.*

Hovy, E. (2005). Methodologies for the reliable construction of ontological knowledge. In Dau, F., Mugnier, M.-L., & Stumme, G. (Eds.), *Conceptual structures: Common semantics for sharing knowledge* (pp. 91–107). Berlin, Germany: Springer-Verlag. doi:10.1007/11524564_6

Khakhalin, G. K. (2009). Applied ontology in terms of hypergraph. *Proceedings of II All-Russian Conference Knowledge-Ontology-Theory (KONT-09)* (pp. 223-231). Novosibirsk, Russian Federation: Published by Sobolev Institute of Mathematics, Siberian Department of RAN (In Russian).

Khakhalin, G. K., & Voskresenskiy, A. L. (2006). The contextual fragmentation in the linguistic analysis. *Proceedings of 10th National Conference on Artificial Intelligence* (pp. 479-488). Moscow, Russia: Publishing House of Physical-Mathematical Literature (in Russian).

Kim, S.-D., Zhang, B.-T., & Kim, Y.-T. (2001). Learning-based intra-sentence segmentation for efficient translation of long sentences. *Machine Translation, 16*, 151–174. doi:10.1023/A:1019896420277

Kurbatov, S. S. (2010). The high-level heuristics for automated formation of knowledge base. *Proceedings of XII National Conference on Artificial Intelligence: Vol. 1* (pp. 231-239). Moscow, Russia: Publishing House of Physical-Mathematical Literature (in Russian).

Kurbatov, S. S. (2011). *A tool of support of knowledge representation language* (in Russian). Retrieved from http://eia--dostup.ru/exp_anal.htm

Kurbatov, S. S., Naidenova, X. A., & Khakhalin, G. K. (2010). On interacting scheme of integrated program complex "Analysis and synthesis of natural language and images". *Proceedings of XII National Conference on Artificial Intelligence: Vol. 1* (pp. 234-242). Moscow, Russia: Publishing House of Physical-Mathematical Literature (in Russian).

Kuzin, E. S., Roitman, A. I., Fominikh, I. B., & Khakhalin, G. K. (1989). *Computer intellectualization.* Moscow: Publishing House of Higher School: Future Considerations of Computation Engineering Series (in Russian).

Mal'kovsky, M. G. (1985). *The dialogue with AI system.* Moscow, Russia: Moscow State University. (in Russian)

MyScript Studio. (2010). Retrieved from http://www.visionobjects.com/en/webstore/myscript-studio/description/

Naidenova, X. A. (2006). *The role of machine learning in mining natural language texts.* Retrieved from http://www.dialog-21.ru/dialog2006/materials/html/Naidenova.htm

Naidenova, X. A., Khakhalin, G. K., & Kurbatov, S. S. (2011). Semantic-syntactic analysis of NL-texts of plane geometry tasks. *System Analysis and Semiotic Modeling: The Materials of the First All-Russian Scientific Conference with the International Participations* (SASM'2011) (pp. 184-191). Kazan, Russia: "Fen" the Academy of Science of Republic Tatarstan (in Russian).

Naidenova, X. A., & Nevzorova, O. A. (2008). Machine learning in tasks of NL-processing: Survey of state-of-the-art investigations. [in Russian]. *News Kazan University, 1*, 3–24.

Naidenova, X. A., & Shagalov, V. L. (2009). Diagnostic test machine. In M. Auer (Ed.), *Proceedings of the ICL'2009 – Interactive Computer Aided Learning Conference* (pp. 505-507). Kassel, Germany: Kassel University Press. ISBN: 978-3-89958-481-3

Narin'jany, A. S. (1995). The understanding problem of data-base queries was decided. In R. C. Bukharajev, et al. (Eds.), *DIALOG'95: Computational Linguistics and its Applied Computing, Proceedings of International Seminar* (pp. 206-215). Kazan, Tatarstan: Kazan University Press (in Russian).

Popov, E. V. (1982). *Communication with computer on natural language*. Moscow, Russia: Nauka. (in Russian)

Pospelov, D. A. (Ed.). (1990). *Artificial intelligence*. Moscow, Russia: Radio and Communication. (in Russian)

Rozental, D. E., Golub, I. B., & Telenkova, M. A. (1995). *Modern Russian*. Moscow, Russia: Foreign Relations. (in Russian)

Stepanova, N., & Emelyanov, G. (2007). Knowledge acquisition process modeling for question answering systems. In V. Soloviev, R. Potapova, & V. Polyakov (Eds.), *Cognitive Modeling in Linguistics*: *Proceedings of IX International Conference* (344-354). Kazan, Tatarstan: Kazan University Press (in Russian).

Vizing, V. G. (2007). On incidentor colouring in hypergraph. [in Russian]. *Sampling Analysis and Operations Research, 14*(3), 40–45.

Vlasov, A. V., & Aredova, I. I. (1988). Experimental system of the synthesis of graphic images according to their description in the terms of geometric concepts. *Material of the Conference on Development of Intellectual Possibility of Modern and Perspective Computers* (pp. 123-132). Moscow, Russia: Moscow House of Scientific and Technical Propaganda (MHSTP) (in Russian).

Zykov, A. A. (1974). Hypergraphs. *Russian Mathematical Surveys, 29*(6), 89. doi:10.1070/RM1974v029n06ABEH001303

ADDITIONAL READING

Adorni, G., Manzo, M. D., & Giunchiglis, F. (1984). Natural language driven image generation. *Proceedings COLING '84 of the 10th International Conference on Computational Linguistics* (pp. 495-500). Association for Computational Linguistics Stroudsburg, PA, USA. doi>10.3115/980491.980597

Apresjan, Y. D., Boguslavsij, I. M., & Iomdin, L. L. (1992). *A linguistic processor for complex information systems*. Moscow, Russia: Nauka. (in Russian)

Berge, C. (1989). *Hypergraphs: The theory of finite sets*. Amsterdam, The Netherlands: North-Holland.

Berwick, R. C. (1984). Bounded context parsing and easy learnability. *Proceedings COLING '84 of the 10th International Conference on Computational Linguistics* (pp. 20-23). Association for Computational Linguistics Stroudsburg, PA, USA. doi>10.3115/980431.980497

Bronevich, A., & Melnichenko, A. (2011). Automatic image annotation based on low-level features and classification of the statistical classes. In Kuznetsov, S. O. (Eds.), *Rough Sets, Fuzzy Sets, Data Mining and Granular Computing, LNAI 6743* (pp. 314–321). Berlin, Heidelberg: Springer-Verlag. doi:10.1007/978-3-642-21881-1_49

Clark, A., Fox, C., & Lappin, S. (Eds.). (2010). *The handbook of computational linguistics and natural language processing*. Blackwell Publishing Ltd. doi:10.1002/9781444324044

Deb, S. (Ed.). (2004). *Multimedia systems and content-based image retrieval*. Hershey, PA: IGI Global.

Deselaers, T., Müller, H., Clough, P., Ney, H., & Lehmann, T. M. (2007). The CLEF 2005 automatic medical image annotation task. *International Journal of Computer Vision, 74*, 51–58. doi:10.1007/s11263-006-0007-y

Duda, R. O., & Hart, P. E. (1973). *Pattern classification and scene analysis.* A Wiley-Interscience Publication.

Duygulu, p., Barnard, K., de Freitas, J. F. G., & Forsyth, D. (2002). Object recognition as machine translation: Learning a lexicon for a fixed image vocabulary. In A. Heyden, G. Sparr, M. Nielsen & P. Johansen (Eds.), *ECCV 2002, LNCS 2353* (pp. 97-112). Heidelberg, Germany: Springer.

EasyDone System. (1996-2011). Retrieved from http://www.recsoft.com

Emelichev, V. A., Mel'nikov, O. I., Sarvanov, V. I., & T'ischkevich, R. I. (2009). *Lectures on graph theory.* Moscow, Russia: Science ("Nauka") (in Russian).

Fu, K. S. (1974). *Syntactic methods in pattern recognition.* Academic Press.

Gavrilova, T. A., & Khoroschevsky, V. F. (2000). *Knowledge base of intelligence systems.* St. Petersburg, Russia: Piter. (in Russian)

Graeme, H. (1987). *Semantic interpretation and the resolution of ambiguity.* Cambridge University Press.

Hanbury, A. (2008). A survey of methods for image annotation. *Journal of Visual Languages and Computing, 19*(5), 617–627. doi:10.1016/j.jvlc.2008.01.002

Hède, P., Moëllic, P.-A., Bourgeoys, J., Joint, M., & Thomas, C. (2004). Automatic generation of natural language descriptions for images. In C. Fluhr, G. Grefenstette, & W. B. Croft (Eds.), *Proceedings of Computer-Assisted Information Retrieval (Recherche d'Information et ses Applications) - RIAO 2004, 7th International Conference* (pp.306-313). Publisher CID 2004.

Herzog, G., & Wazinski, P. (1995). Visual translator: Linking perceptions and natural language descriptions. In Mc Kevitt, P. (Ed.), *Integration of natural language and vision processing: Computational models and systems* (*Vol. 1*, pp. 83–95). Dordrecht, The Netherlands: Kluwer. doi:10.1007/BF00849073

Itskovich, L., & Kuznetsov, S. (2011). Machine learning methods in character recognition. In Kuznetsov, S. O. (Eds.), *Rough Sets, Fuzzy Sets, Data Mining and Granular Computing, LNAI 6743* (pp. 322–329). Berlin, Germany: Springer-Verlag. doi:10.1007/978-3-642-21881-1_50

Jia, Z., Amselang, L., & Gros, P. (2008). Content-based image retrieval from a large image database. *Pattern Recognition, 11*(5), 1479–1495. doi:10.1016/j.patcog.2007.06.034

Khakhalin, G. K. (2002). *Intelligence systems, part 1. Models of the knowledge representation, image analysis and intellectual graphics.* Moscow, Russia: Moscow Automobile & Road Institute (State University) (in Russian).

Kim, D. S., Barker, K., & Porter, B. (2010). Improving the quality of text understanding by delaying ambiguity resolution. In C.-R. Huang & D. Jurafsky (Eds.), *Proceedings of the 23rd International Conference on Computational Linguistics (Coling 2010)*, (pp. 581-589). Tsinghua University Press.

Knoth, P., Novotny, J., & Zdrahal, Z. (2010). Automatic generation of inter-passage links based on semantic similarity. In C.-R. Huang & D. Jurafsky (Eds.), *Proceedings of the 23rd International Conference on Computational Linguistics (Coling 2010)*, (pp. 590–598). Tsinghua University Press.

Konar, A. (2000). *Artificial intelligence and soft computing: Behavioral and cognitive modeling of the human brain.* Boca Raton, FL: CRC Press.

Kong, F., Zhou, G., Qian, L., & Zhu, Q. (2010). Dependency-driven anaphoricity determination for coreference resolution. In C. R. Huang & D. Jurafsky (Eds.), *Proceedings of the 23rd International Conference on Computational Linguistics* (Coling 2010), (pp. 599–607). Tsinghua University Press.

Koval, S. A. (2005). *Linguistic problems of computer morphology.* St. Petersburg, Russia: St. Petersburg State University. (in Russian)

Kozlov, V. N. (2001). *Elements of visual perception mathematical theory.* Moscow, Russia: Mechanics-Mathematical Department of Moscow State University. (in Russian)

Lehmann, T. M., Güld, M. O., Thies, C., Fischer, B., Spitzer, K., & Keysers, D. (2004). Content-based image retrieval in medical applications. *Methods of Information in Medicine, 43,* 354–361.

Leont'eva, N. N. (2006). *Automatic understanding of text: Systems, models, resources.* Moscow, Russia: Academy. (in Russian)

Névéol, A., Deserno, T. M., Darmoni, S. J., Güld, M. O., & Aronson, A. R. (2009). Natural language processing versus content-based image analysis for medical document retrieval. *Journal of the American Society for Information Science and Technology, 1,* 123–134. doi:10.1002/asi.20955

Poliakov, I. V. (1987). *Linguistics and structured semantics.* Novosibirsk, Russia: Science ("Nauka"), Siberian Department (In Russian).

Pospelov, D. A. (1996). Situation control: An overview. In R. J. Strohl (Ed.), *Proceedings of Workshop on Russian Situation Control and Cybernetic/Semiotic Modeling* (pp. 7-37). Columbus, OH: Published by the. Battelle.

Pospelov, D. A., Ehrlich, A. I., & Osipov, G. S. (1995). Semiotic modeling and situation control. *10ᵗʰ IEEE International Symposium on Intelligent Control, Proceedings of ISIC Workshop on Architectures for Semiotic Modeling and Situation Analysis in Large Complex Systems* (pp. 127-129). Bala Cynwyd, PA: AdRem, Inc.

Potapov, A. S. (2007). *The pattern recognition and machine perception.* Moscow, Russia: Polytechnics. (in Russian)

Reilly, R. G. (1984). A connectionist model of some aspects of anaphor resolution. *Proceedings COLING '84 of the 10th International Conference on Computational Linguistics* (pp. 144-149). Stroudsburg, PA: Association for Computational Linguistics. doi>10.3115/980431.980522

Rui, Y., Huang, T., & Chang, S. F. (1999). Image retrieval: Current techniques, promising directions and open issues. *Visual Communication and Image Representation, 10,* 39–62. doi:10.1006/jvci.1999.0413

Russ, J. (2007). *The image processing handbook* (5th ed.). Boca Raton, FL: CRC Press.

Russell, S., & Norvig, P. (2010). *Artificial intelligence: A modern approach.* Prentice-Hall, Inc.

Savchenko, A. V. (2011). Image recognition with a large database using method of directed enumeration alternatives modification. In Kuznetsov, S. O. (Eds.), *Rough Sets, Fuzzy Sets, Data Mining and Granular Computing, LNAI 6743* (pp. 338–341). Berlin, Germany: Springer-Verlag. doi:10.1007/978-3-642-21881-1_52

Schamis, A. L. (2005). *Behavior, perception, thinking: Problems of artificial intelligence development.* Moscow, Russia: URSS. (in Russian)

Sosnowski, Ł., & Ślęzak, D. (2011). Comparators for compound object identification. In Kuznetsov, S. O. (Eds.), *Rough Sets, Fuzzy Sets, Data Mining and Granular Computing, LNAI 6743* (pp. 342–349). Berlin, Germany: Springer-Verlag. doi:10.1007/978-3-642-21881-1_53

Sowa, J. F. (2006). Worlds, models, and descriptions. *Studia Logica. Special Issue Ways of Worlds II, 84*(2), 323–360.

Stefanjuk, V. L. (2004). *On-site organization of the intelligence system*. Moscow, Russia: Publishing House of Physical-Mathematical Literature. (in Russian)

Tel'nov, J. F. (2004). *Intellectual information systems*. Moscow, Russia: Moscow International Institute Econometrics, Informatics, Finances, and Law. (in Russian)

Theodoridis, S., & Koutroumbas, C. (2009). *Pattern recognition* (4th ed.). Amsterdam, The Netherlands: Elsevier.

Tulip, D. A. (2003). A huge graph visualisation framework. In Mutzel, P., & Jünger, M. (Eds.), *Graph drawing softwares, mathematics and visualization* (pp. 105–126). Springer-Verlag.

van Bommel, P. (Ed.). (2005). *Transformation of knowledge, information and data: Theory and applications*. Hershey, PA: Information Science Publishing (an Imprint of Idea Group Inc.).

Wang, J., Markert, K., & Everingham, M. (2009). *Learning models for object recognition from natural language descriptions*. Presented at the 20th British Machine Vision Conference (BMVC2009). School of Computing University of Leeds.

Winston, P. H. (1992). *Artificial intelligence* (3rd ed.). Reading, MA: Addison Wesley.

Zhuravljev, Y. I., Rjazanov, V. V., & Sen'ko, O. V. (2005). *Recognition; mathematical methods; program system; practical use*. Moscow, Russia: Fazis. (in Russian)

KEY TERMS AND DEFINITIONS

Applied Ontology: It is conceptual knowledge formalization of application domains, presented on a single knowledge representation language (semantic hypergraph). Applied ontology is used to reason about the objects and relations between them in a given application domain.

Association: Association or Association Rule connects a pair of observations (situations, objects, images, texts, or any entities) such that the set of occurrences of one of these observations is included in the set of occurrences of the other observation. It is said that one of these observations is accompanied very often by the occurrence of the other observation. Searching for frequent associations in a given set of observations is one of the tasks of unsupervised symbolic machine learning.

Conceptual Goal-Directed Analysis of Images: The structural object description implies that an object as a whole consists of parts, connected together by certain space relations. The ontology structure supports, during image processing, a goal-directed analysis of images when an already recognized object or part of object initializes, via its structural connections, searching for another certain object or part of object.

Conceptual Synthesis of Graphic Images: It is the process of transforming complete or partial ontological object descriptions into their graphical visualizations. This task is performed by the system of Image Synthesizer.

Hybrid System of Images Analysis: It consists of two subsystems one of which is intended for recognizing (in classical sense) simple (non-derivative) objects and the second subsystem is intended for conceptual analyzing simple and complex objects and situations, represented by the applied ontology.

Linguistic Analysis of NL-Sentences: This analysis includes the following basic problems: the resolution of all possible uncertainties in texts, extraction of information (explicit or implicit) contained in text about some target objects and situations, and translation of extracted knowledge in the applied ontology language.

NL-Text Synthesis: The task of NL-text synthesis consists in generating texts according to ontological image descriptions. For the synthesis, a "pattern" method is usually used, when the previously elaborated templates (answers, questions, explanations) with the specific "lacunas" are embedded into the NL-Text Synthesis System. During the process of synthesis, the Synthesizer of NL-text finds the appropriate template and fulfills it.

Non-Derivable (Non-Derivative) Object: Object, which is recognized by a recognition system as a whole, not decomposed in elementary (atomic) parts.

Semantic Hypergraph: Knowledge representation language by the use of which conceptual knowledge of several intelligent systems can be integrated. It is generalization of semantic network.

Section 3
Other Machine Learning Applications

Chapter 10
Fault–Tolerant Control of Mechanical Systems Using Neural Networks

Sunan Huang
National University of Singapore, Singapore

Kok Kiong Tan
National University of Singapore, Singapore

Tong Heng Lee
National University of Singapore, Singapore

ABSTRACT

Due to harsh working environment, control systems may degrade to an unacceptable level, causing more regular fault occurrences. In this case, it is necessary to provide the fault-tolerant control for operating the system continuously. The existing control techniques have given some ways to solve this problem, but if the system behaves in an unanticipated manner, then the control system may need to be modified, so that it handles the modified system. In this chapter, the authors are concerned with how this control system can be done automatically, and when it can be done successfully. They aimed in this work at handling unanticipated failure modes, for which solutions have not been solved completely. The model-based fault-tolerant controller with a self-detecting algorithm is proposed. Here, the radial basis function neural network is used in the controller to estimate the unknown failures. Once the failure is detected, the re-configured control is activated and then maintains the system continuously. The fault-tolerant control is illustrated in two cases. It is shown that the proposed method can cope with different failure modes which are unknown a priori. The result indicates that the solution is suitable for a class of mechanical systems whose dynamics are subject to sudden changes resulting from component failures when working in a harsh environment.

DOI: 10.4018/978-1-4666-1806-0.ch010

INTRODUCTION

Control systems include many components, such as transducers, sensors, actuators and mechanical parts. These components are required to be operated under some specific conditions. However, due to prolonged operations or harsh operating environment, the properties of these devices may degrade to an unacceptable level, causing more regular fault occurrences. It is therefore necessary to provide the fault-tolerant control which compensates for the fault of the component by substituting a configuration of redundant elements so that the system continues to operate satisfactorily (Patton, Frank and Clark, 1989).

Traditionally, the fault-tolerant control is achieved through the use of hardware redundancy (Sun, Wang, Howe & Jewell, 2008). Multiple hardware elements are distributed spatially around the system to provide protection against system failures. The major problems encountered with hardware redundancy are the extra cost and space requirement. To overcome the problems, at least in part, software control approaches based on signal processing technique have been developed and reported during the last two decades. In Hamada, Shin & Sebe (1998), a design method for fault-tolerant multivariable control systems is proposed. In Aberkane, Sauter & Ponsart (2007), a static feedback controller is designed for a class of nonlinear stochastic discrete system subject to random failures. In Deutsch (2008), a fault-tolerant control system for a linear combustion engine is designed subject to system failures. In Rothenhagen & Fuchs (2009), a bank of observers is used to reconfigure the drive and reenter closed-loop control to a doubly fed induction generator. In Kambhampati, Perkgcz, Patton & Ahamed (2007), a reconfigured network control strategy is designed based on the fault isolation information. The advantage of this work is that the fault location information can be incorporated into the reconfigured controller. In recent years, intelligent techniques have grown to an important field in fault-tolerant control and to a certain extent, is being fueled by advancements in computing technology. Examples of intelligent techniques include expert systems (Visinsky, Cavallaro & Walker, 1994), fuzzy systems (Diao, Passino, 2001; Zhang, Huo, & Zhang, 2008; Visinsky, Cavallaro & Walker, 1995; Wang, Tong & Tong, 2007; Tong, Wang & Zhang, 2008), and artificial neural networks (Polycarpou & Helmicki, 1995; Polycarpou, 2001; Liu, Wu & Zhang, 2008; Farrell, Berger & Appleby, 1993).

This chapter further expands on these reported works. We propose and develop a set of schemes suitable for fault-tolerant control of mechanical systems. The basic idea of the proposed method is to use the information provided by the neural networks to accommodate faults in order to permit continued operation of the system. First, a model-based fault detection is designed based on a nominal system model. The fault detection embedded into the controller is carried out by comparing the states with their signatures. Secondly, if the fault is detected, the controller is reconfigured by incorporating with neural networks which are used to capture the nonlinear characteristics of unknown faults. Finally, the case studies are conducted based on real-time machine actuation systems, while most of existing results are simulated ones. Unlike the existing neural network fault-tolerant control (Polycarpou and Helmicki, 1995; Polycarpou, 2001; Liu, Wu, Shi & Zhang, 2008; Farrell, Berger & Appleby, 1993)., the proposed controller can achieve the automated fault-tolerance using a deadzone operator.

SYSTEM MODEL AND CONTROL OBJECTIVE

Consider the following mechanical system described by

$$\ddot{q} = M^{-1}(q)[u - V_m(q, \dot{q}) - H(\dot{q}) - H_G(q) - \tau_d] \\ + B(t - T)\zeta(x) \tag{1}$$

where $q = [q_1, q_2, ... q_m]^T$ are the joint position of the subsystems, $M(q)$ are the symmetric positive definite inertia matrix; $V_m(q, \dot{q})$ represent Coriolis and centripetal forces; $H(\dot{q})$ are the dynamic frictional force matrix; τ_d are a load disturbance matrix; $H_G(q)$ are the potential energy terms; u denote generalized input control of the system applied at the joints. Since the friction matrix $H(\dot{q})$ may be unknown accurately, we define a nominal matrix $\bar{H}(\dot{q})$ and then the uncertain matrix is $H(\dot{x}) - \bar{H}(\dot{q})$.

The system (1) can also be written as a compact form

$$\begin{aligned} \dot{x} &= A_0 x + b[F(x) + G(q)u + \eta(x, t) \\ &\quad + B(t - T)\zeta(x)] \\ y &= Cx + B_y(t - T_y)\vartheta(x) \end{aligned} \tag{2}$$

where

$$x = [q_1, \dot{q}_1, q_2, \dot{q}_2, ..., q_m, \dot{q}_m]^T \tag{3}$$

$$A_0 = diag\{A_{01}, A_{02}, ..., A_{0m}\} \tag{4}$$

$$b = diag\{b_1, b_2, ..., b_m\} \tag{5}$$

$$F = -M^{-1}(q)[V_m(q, \dot{q}) + \bar{H}(\dot{q}) + H_G(q)] \tag{6}$$

$$\begin{aligned} G &= M^{-1}(q), \eta \\ &= -M^{-1}(q)[H(\dot{q}) - \bar{H}(\dot{q}) + \tau_d] \end{aligned} \tag{7}$$

$$C = diag\{C_1, C_2, ..., C_m\} \tag{8}$$

$$A_{0i} = \begin{bmatrix} 0 & 1 \\ 0 & 0 \end{bmatrix}, b_i = \begin{bmatrix} 0 \\ 1 \end{bmatrix}, C_i = [c_1, c_2]. \tag{9}$$

where y is the system output vector. The nonlinear fault vector ζ characterizes the deviation in the dynamics of the system due to a state fault and ϑ expresses the change in the output equation characteristics due to an output fault. In a practical system, ζ can represent mechanical or actuator faults, while ϑ can represent sensor failures. Mechanical faults are, for example, caused by wear, switch, relay, control valve, missing lubrication, or other malfunctions of components such as springs, bearings, or gears.

We consider faults with time profiles modeled by

$$B(t - T) = diag\{\beta_1(t - T), ..., \beta_m(t - T)\},$$
$$\beta_i(t - T) = \begin{cases} 0 & t < T \\ 1 - e^{-\theta_i(t-T)} & t \geq T \end{cases}, \tag{10}$$

$$B_y(t - T_y) =$$
$$diag\{\beta_{y1}(t - T_y), ..., \beta_{ym}(t - T_y)\}, \tag{11}$$
$$\beta_{yi}(t - T_y) = \begin{cases} 0 & t < T_y \\ 1 - e^{-\theta_{yi}(t-T_y)} & t \geq T_y \end{cases},$$

where T and T_y are unknown times of occurrence of state and output faults, respectively, and $\theta_i, \theta_{yi} > 0$ are unknown constants that represent the rate at which the fault in states and outputs evolve.

The goal of the chapter is to control the system continously when working in a harsh environment, i.e., the controller can handle the failures when the system fails to function normally.

The basic assumptions for the problems stated are

Figure 1. Structure of a multi-layered neural network

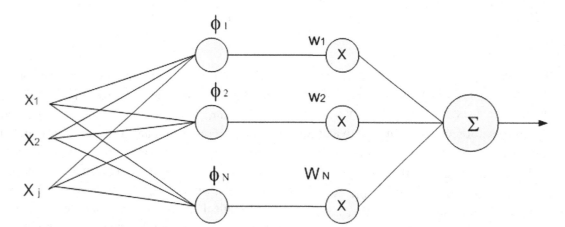

A1) The modeling uncertainties $\eta(x,t) = [\eta_1(x,t), \eta_2(x,t), ..., \eta_m(x,t)]^T$ are bounded by

$$\| \eta(x,t) \| \leq \overline{\eta}. \tag{12}$$

where $\overline{\eta}$ is a known bound.

A2) The desired position trajectories $q_d = [q_{d1}, q_{d2}, ..., q_{dm}]^T$ are known bounded functions of time with bounded known derivatives.

NEURAL NETWORK FUNDAMENTALS

In the case of neural networks, an explicit attempt is made to draw inspiration from nature and biology. It borrows ideas from how biological systems solve problems and extends them to cope with the nonlinear identification and control problems (e.g., the use of neural networks for control). This methodology is more acceptable of making heuristics and nonlinear approximations, as compared to the rest of the approaches in the modern control field.

Neural Network Model

Initially, neural network model came from the biological system. Now, it has been developed to many types of nonlinear models for reflecting the various attempts to design models that closely resemble biological neural networks and their attributes. A typical neural network model is structured in layers of neurons. Some have one layer, i.e., single-layer neural networks and some have more layers, i.e., multilayer neural network. In this chapter, we focus on multilayer neural network.

Multi-layer feedforward neural network, or commonly known as multi-layer perceptron (MLP) has become very popular for scientists in recent years. In this network, it is supposed that a number of node element layers exist. One layer of nodes then forms the input layer which is used to input data, while the another forms the output layer which is used to produce the network responses, with a number of intermediate or hidden layers existing between them. Figure 1 shows a general MLP network which is composed of many simple perceptrons in a hierarchical structure forming a feedforward topology with one or more hidden layers between the input and output layers. MLP structure is strictly feedforward and can be fully or partially connected. To design a MLP, the develop-

Figure 2. Structure of learning

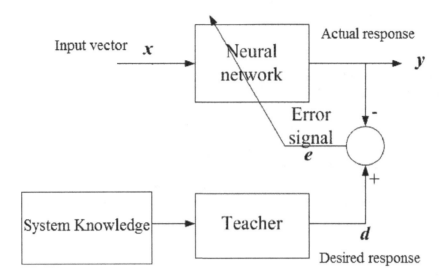

ers will have to determine how many layers and how many neurons per layer should be selected for their application.

Learning Method

Learning in a neural network is performed to simulate the behavior of its biological counterpart. Through learning, a neural network is able to adapt itself and subsequently improve its biological characteristics gradually. In this section, the concept of the learning method presented in the chapter will be described.

It is well known that learning is known as `Learning with a teacher'. Figure 2 shows the structure of this kind of learning. The teacher has the system knowledge of the plant. To begin with learning process, we have to provide a training set, comprising of an input vector x and the corresponding desired output vector d. During the training, the teacher gives the neural network with desired responses for the set of training vectors. The learning aims at making the neural network to emulate the teacher. This results in output y produced by the network. During the whole process, the parameters of the network is

adjusted by the error information $e = d - y$, so that the neural network emulates the teacher more and more closely.

MAIN FOCUS OF THE CHAPTER

Problems with Fault-Tolerant Control

Fault-tolerant control has been the subject of intensive research for more than thirty years. Extensive results are now available. As described in the introduction Section, the soft control methods have become the main stream in this subject. The key issue dealing with fault-tolerant control is data analysis. This involves the fault diagnosis and control: the fault diagnosis uses the input-output data to identify system failures, while the control uses the feedback information to accommodate the failures. Most soft methods in fault diagnosis are focused on off-line data analysis, i.e., using the off-line information to obtain the failure features. The main problem with this type of methods is the lack of current dynamical information, thereby resulting the missed detection. On-line data analysis for fault diganosis issue has played an important role in the reconfigurable controller design, and in turn, in the overall performance of the fault-tolerant control. Challenges in this area may include (1) how to deal with the nonlinearities in proposed algorithms;(2) how to make thresholds for fault detection on-line. For accommodating failures, existing problems is how to reconfigure the controller with consideration of some practical issues such as memory limitation and implementaton of data processing algorithm in a real-time system. In this chapter, we try to use neural network technique to solve the above challenging issues and implement the fault-tolerant control in a real control environment.

Fault-Tolerant Control with Neural Networks

In this section, the proposed fault-tolerant control algorithm and its constituent components will be elaborated in detail. The design of the self-detecting algorithm is first considered. Later, the fault-tolerant control algorithm is developed to handle the system failures when receiving an alarm from the fault detection system.

Consider the following fault detection algorithm

$$\dot{x} = A_0 x + b[F(x) + G(q)u] + Kx, \qquad (13)$$

$$\hat{y} = Cx \qquad (14)$$

where $x = [\hat{x}_{11}, \hat{x}_{12}, \hat{x}_{21}, \hat{x}_{22}, ..., \hat{x}_{m1}, \hat{x}_{m2}]^T$ denotes the estimated state vector of x, the state error is defined as $x = x - x$, and K is a constant matrix. The next step in the construction of the fault detection scheme is the design of the algorithm for monitoring a fault occurrence.

Combining (13) with (2), we have the following error equation

$$\dot{x} = \bar{A}_0 x + b[\eta(x,t) + B(t - T)\zeta(x)], \qquad (15)$$

$$\tilde{y} = Cx + B_y(t - T_y)\vartheta(x) \qquad (16)$$

where $\bar{A}_0 = A - K$. Note that K should be designed so that $\bar{A}_0$ is stable. Based on the residual signal $\tilde{y}_i(t) = y_i - \hat{y}_i, i = 1, 2, ..., m$, a fault monitoring algorithm is presented. Since $B(t - T)\zeta(x)$ and $B_y(t - T_y)$ are zero when $t < T_0 = [0, min(T, T_y)]$, the solution of the state estimation error between (2) and (13) is given by

$$\tilde{y}(t) = Ce^{\bar{A}_0 t}x(0)$$
$$+ C\int_0^t e^{\bar{A}_0(t-\tau)}b\eta(x,\tau)d\tau, \, t < T_0. \qquad (17)$$

The time-varying threshold bound ϖ is chosen as follows,

$$\varpi = \| Ce^{\bar{A}_0 t}x(0) \| + \int_0^t \| Ce^{\bar{A}_0(t-\tau)}b \| \bar{\eta}d\tau. \qquad (18)$$

It should be noted that the time-varying signal ϖ is a stable bound. This is because $\bar{A}$ is a stable matrix and there exist α_0 and β_0 such that $\| e^{\bar{A}_0 t} \| \le \alpha_0 e^{-\beta_0 t}$. This implies that

$$\varpi \le \| C \| \alpha_0 e^{-\beta_0 t} \| x(0) \|$$
$$+ \int_0^t \| C \| \alpha_0 e^{-\beta_0(t-\tau)} \| b \| \bar{\eta}d\tau$$
$$\le \| C \| \alpha_0 e^{-\beta_0 t} \| x(0) \|$$
$$+ \frac{\| C \| \| b \| \alpha_0 \bar{\eta}}{\beta_0} \qquad (19)$$

This also implies that

$$lim_{t \to \infty} \varpi \le \frac{\| C \| \| b \| \alpha_0 \bar{\eta}}{\beta_0}.$$

When monitoring the system, using the model (13), a fault has occurred is made if the estimation error $\| \tilde{y}(t) \|$ exceeds its corresponding threshold bound ϖ.

On the basis of the obtained online fault detection information, we can design a fault-tolerant controller to guarantee stability in the presence of faults. We begin by considering the following filtered error equation.

Let the errors $e_i(t) = q_i - q_{di}$. Then, we define the filtered tracking errors as

$$r_1 = k_1 e_1 + \dot{e}_1, ..., r_m = k_m e_m + \dot{e}_m, \qquad (20)$$

where $k_1, ..., k_m$ are positive constants to be selected. Thus, the system equation can be written as

$$\dot{R}(t) = F(x) + G(q)u + \sigma - q_d^{(2)} \\ + \eta(x,t) + B(t-T)\zeta(x), \qquad (21)$$

where

$$R = [r_1, r_2, ..., r_m]^T, q_d^{(2)} = [q_{d1}^{(2)}, q_{d2}^{(2)}, ... q_{dn}^{(2)}]^T,$$

and $\sigma = [\sigma_1, \sigma_2, ..., \sigma_m]^T$ with $\sigma_i = k_i \dot{e}_i$. In this system, the controller design has to handle the unknown fault function $\zeta(x)$. In this section, a two-layer neural network (NN) will be used to approximate the fault function. It has been proven that NN satisfies the condition of the Stone-Weierstrass Theorem and can approximate any continuous function over a compact set. Consider the neural network, which can be seen as a two-layered processing structure, as shown in Figure 1. The hidden layer consists of an array of computing units (i.e., $\varphi_1, \varphi_2, ..., \varphi_N$). These hidden units provide a set of basis functions of

the input vectors (i.e., $x_1, x_2, ..., x_J$) as they are expanded into the higher dimension hidden-unit space. The mapping from the input vectors to the outputs of the hidden units is nonlinear, whereas the mapping from the hidden units to the final output of the neural network is linear. Let $f(\chi)$ be a smooth function. Then, given a compact S and a positive number ε_M, there exists an ideal RBF system such that

$$f(\chi) = W\Phi(\chi) + \varepsilon, \qquad (22)$$

where W is the representative value vector and $\Phi(\chi)$ is the NN basis function, and ε is the NN approximation error satisfying $\| \varepsilon \| \leq \varepsilon_M$ with ε_M constant for all $\chi \in S$. This approximation is considered with the linear RBF network.

Since the fault function is unknown, NN approximator can be used to solve this problem, i.e., the fault function $\zeta(x)$ is approximated by a general one layer neural network as

$$\zeta(x) = W^{*T}\Phi(x) + \xi, \qquad (23)$$

where W^* is the ideal weight of the network and the bounded function approximation error ξ satisfies $\| \xi \| \leq \xi_M$ with constant ξ_M. The NN approximation error ξ represents the minimum possible deviation between the unknown function and the function estimation. In general, increasing the NN node number reduces the error ξ. The ideal weights W^* are unknown and need to be estimated for controller design. Let $\hat{W}$ be estimates of the ideal W^*. Then, an estimate $\hat{\zeta}(x)$ of $\zeta(x)$ can be given by

$$\hat{\zeta}(x) = \hat{W}^T\Phi(x). \qquad (24)$$

Figure 3. Flow diagram of proposed fault-tolerant control scheme

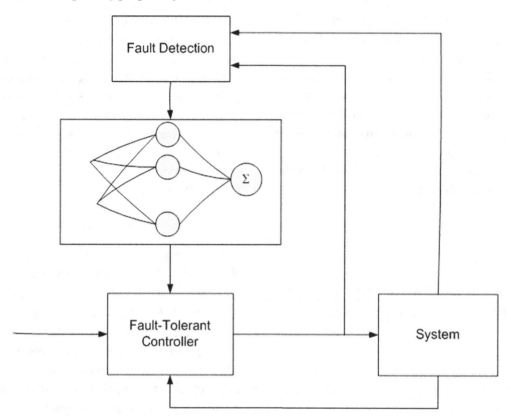

Therefore, the fault-tolerant control law is given by

$$u =$$
$$G^{-1}(q)\left\{-F(x) - \sigma - \Lambda R - D[||\, \tilde{y}\, ||]\hat{W}^T\Phi(x)\right\}, \quad (25)$$

where $\Lambda > 0$ is the gain matrix which is determined by users, and D[.] is the dead-zone operator, defined as

$$D[||\, \tilde{y}\, ||] = \begin{cases} 0 & if \;||\, \tilde{y}\, ||\leq \varpi \\ 1 & otherwise \end{cases} \quad (26)$$

The RBF network learning law is given by

$$\dot{\hat{W}} = \Upsilon[\Phi(x)R^T - \rho(\hat{W} - W_a)]D[||\, \tilde{y}\, ||], \quad (27)$$

where $\Upsilon = \Upsilon^T > 0, \rho > 0$, and W_a is a design constant matrix. The dead-zone operator prevents adaptation of the NN weights when the output estimation error $\tilde{y}$ is below its corresponding threshold, thereby preventing any false action.

Remark. The gain Λ should be chosen such that the nominal system is stable. This implies that the choice of the control gain should be made when the system is operating in a normal case. A simple way is to choose Λ as a diagonal matrix, i.e., $\Lambda = diag\{\lambda_1, \lambda_2, ..., \lambda_m\}$, where λ_i should be chosen so that its corresponding control loop is stable.

When a fault occurs, the fault-tolerant control is applied to the system. A summary of the proposed scheme found under the mentioned circumstances is depicted in Figure 3. In this case, substituting the control law (25) into the system (21), we have

$$\dot{R} = -\Lambda R + \eta - q_d^{(2)}$$
$$+ B(t-T)\zeta(x) - \hat{W}^T \Phi(x).$$

The term $B(t-T)\zeta(x) - \hat{W}^T\Phi(x)$ will satisfy the following relationship

$$B(t-T)\zeta(x) - \hat{W}^T\Phi(x)$$
$$= \tilde{W}^T\Phi(x) - \Theta(t)W^{*T}\Phi(x) + B(t-T)\xi, \tag{28}$$

Where

$$\tilde{W} = W^* - \hat{W}, \Theta(t)$$
$$= diag\{e^{-\theta_1(t-T)}, e^{-\theta_2(t-T)}, ..., e^{-\theta_m(t-T)}\}.$$

Note that $B(t-T)$ is bounded, therefore, $\| B(t-T)\xi \| \leq \xi_M$. Utilizing these results and Lyapunov theory, we establish the theorem 1.

Theorem 1 Consider the system (1) in the presence of faults and the accommodation control described by (25) and (27). Suppose Assumptions **A1- A2** are satisfied. Then, the tracking error R and RBF network weights $\tilde{W}$ are uniformly ultimately bounded (UUB).

Proof. Define the Lyapunov function

$$V = R^T R + tr(\tilde{W}^T \Upsilon^{-1}\tilde{W}). \tag{29}$$

The time derivative of V is given by

$$\dot{V} \leq -2\lambda_{min}(\Lambda) \| R \|^2 + 2\rho tr[\tilde{W}^T(\hat{W} - W_a)]$$
$$+2R^T[\eta - q_d^{(2)} + B(t-T)\xi - \Theta(t)W^{*T}\Phi]. \tag{30}$$

where $\lambda_{min}(\Lambda)$ is the minimum eigenvalue of Λ. By completion of squares, it follows that

$$2tr[\tilde{W}^T(\hat{W} - W_a)]$$
$$= 2tr[\tilde{W}^T(\hat{W} - W^* + W^* - W_a)]$$
$$\leq -2 \| \tilde{W} \|_F^2 + 2 \| \tilde{W} \|_F \| W^* - W_a \|_F$$
$$\leq - \| \tilde{W} \|_F^2 + \| W^* - W_a \|_F^2, \tag{31}$$

where $\| \cdot \|_F$ is the Frobenius norm. Using the inequalities

$$2\alpha^T\beta \leq \frac{\lambda_{min}(\Lambda)}{4}\alpha^T\alpha + 4\lambda_{min}^{-1}(\Lambda)\beta^T\beta, \tag{32}$$

we have

$$2R^T B(t-T)\xi \leq \frac{\lambda_{min}(\Lambda) \| R \|^2}{4} + \frac{4\xi_M^2}{\lambda_{min}(\Lambda)}$$

$$-2R^T\Theta(t)W^{*T}\Phi \leq \frac{\lambda_{min}(\Lambda) \| R \|^2}{4}$$
$$+ \frac{4max_{1\leq i \leq n}[e^{-2\theta_i(t-T)}] \| W^{*T}\Phi \|^2}{\lambda_{min}(\Lambda)}$$

$$-2R^T q_d^{(2)} \leq \frac{\lambda_{min}(\Lambda)}{4} \| R \|^2 + \frac{4q_{dM}^2}{\lambda_{min}(\Lambda)}$$

$$2R^T\eta \leq \frac{\lambda_{min}(\Lambda)}{4} \| R \|^2 + \frac{4\bar{\eta}^2}{\lambda_{min}(\Lambda)}$$

where $q_{dM} = max\{\| q_d^{(2)} \|\}$. Notice that in general the RBF basis function $\Phi(x)$ is bounded, i.e., $\| \Phi(x) \| \leq \bar{\Phi}$. It should also be noted that for the term $max_{1\leq i \leq n}[e^{-2\theta_i(t-T)}] \| W^* \|^2 \bar{\Phi}^2$ for a given small number ρ, there exists a $T_1 > T$ such that $max_{1\leq i \leq n}[e^{-2\theta_i(t-T)}] \| W^* \|^2 \bar{\Phi}^2 \leq \rho$ for $t \geq T_1$. Substituting the above inequalities into (30) yields

$$\dot{V} \leq -\lambda_{min}(\Lambda) \| R \|^2 - \rho \| \tilde{W} \|_F^2$$
$$+ \rho \| W^* - W_a \|_F^2 + \mu \tag{33}$$

Figure 4. Control testbed

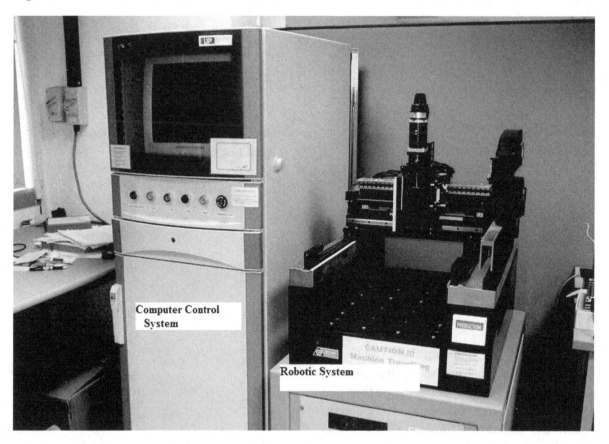

where

$$\mu = 4\lambda_{min}^{-1}(\Lambda)\xi_M^2 + 4\rho\lambda_{min}^{-1}(\Lambda)$$
$$+ 4\lambda_{min}^{-1}(\Lambda)q_{dM}^2 + 4\lambda_{min}^{-1}(\Lambda)\bar{\eta}^2. \tag{34}$$

Hence, we obtain the following conditions for $\dot{V} \leq 0$

$$\| R \| > \sqrt{\frac{\rho \| W^* - W_a \|_F^2 + \mu}{\lambda_{min}(\Lambda)}},$$
$$or, \| \tilde{W} \|_F > \sqrt{\frac{\rho \| W^* - W_a \|_F^2 + \mu}{\rho}}.$$

for $t \geq T_1$, where W_a may choose a rough estimate of W^* to reduce the size of the bound. This demonstrates that $R, \tilde{W}$ are UUB.

CASE STUDIES

The purpose of this section is to illustrate the usefulness of the proposed fault-tolerant control in the presence of the system failures.

Case 1

Real-time experiments are carried out on a Cartesian robotic system (see Figure 4) manufactured by Anorad Co., USA. The dSPACE control development and rapid prototyping system, in particular, the DS1103 board, is used. Due to the system working in MATLAB environment, the proposed algorithm can be implemented on a Simulink platform. The following model is built for this machine:

$$\ddot{x} = \left. \begin{array}{l} -2.110\dot{x} + 0.058u - 0.166sgn(\dot{x}) \\ -0.121e^{-\frac{\dot{x}^2}{0.001^2}}sgn(\dot{x}) + \eta(x,t) \end{array} \right\}$$

(35)

The function $\eta(x,t)$ is the remaining nonlinear uncertainty and bounded by 1.2. The fault monitoring used is given by

$$\dot{\hat{x}} = \begin{bmatrix} 0 & 1 \\ 0 & 0 \end{bmatrix}\hat{x} + \begin{bmatrix} 0 \\ 1 \end{bmatrix}\left[\begin{array}{l} 0 \\ -2.110\dot{x} \end{array} \right.$$

$$+0.058u - (0.166 + 0.121e^{-\frac{\dot{x}^2}{0.001^2}})sgn(\dot{x}) \Big]$$

$$+ \begin{bmatrix} 50 & 0 \\ 100 & 2.11 \end{bmatrix}\begin{bmatrix} \tilde{x} \\ \dot{\tilde{x}} \end{bmatrix}$$

From the formula (18), the threshold value of the residual signal can be derived as

$$\varpi = \frac{1}{43.5137}\int_0^t 1.2\Big[e^{-4.2982(t-\tau)} - e^{-47.8119(t-\tau)}\Big]d\tau$$

$$\leq 0.0046 \times 1.2 = 0.0055$$

since the initial states are zero. In the experiment, the linear motor follows the trajectory $x_d = 0.02sin(wt)$ where $w = 2rad/sec$. The parameters in the controller are chosen as $k = 10, \Lambda = 100$. To apply the controller, the radial basis function (RBF) neural networks are designed to approximate the unknown failures. Theoretically speaking, a large RBF size can improve performance of the learning system, but not too large due to memory limit and computa-

tional load. In our experiments, each RBF network used is chosen as $\hat{W}^T\Phi(x) = \sum_{i=1}^{10}\hat{w}_i\varphi_i(x)$, i.e., 10 units, where $\hat{w}_i$ is the representative value and $\varphi_i(x)$ is the radial basis function. Here,

$$\varphi_i = exp(-\parallel x - a_i \parallel^2 / b_i^2), i = 1, 2, ..., 10.$$

where $x = [x, \dot{x}]^T$,

$$a_i \in \{[0.001\ 0.01]^T, [0.005\ 0.05]^T, [0.01\ 0.1]^T,$$
$$[0.05\ 0.5]^T, [0.1\ 1]^T, [-0.001\ -0.01]^T,$$
$$[-0.005\ -0.05]^T, [-0.01\ -0.1]^T,$$
$$[-0.05\ -0.5]^T, [-0.1\ -1]^T\}$$

and $b_i = 0.5$. The learning algorithm (27) is used for tuning the RBF weights. The block diagram of the fault-tolerant control is shown in Figure 5. Now, we consider a mechanical fault due to obstruction from the cable protection chain which consists of many chain links. Due to prolonged high speed operation, one or several of the chain links are jammed which obstruct the motor movement. Figure 6 shows the response due to the fault occurrence. It is observed that the fault monitoring signal is beyond its threshold. It should be noted that the tracking performance is degraded due to fault occurrence. In this case, the RBF fault-tolerant control (25) is used to deal with the failure. Figures 7-8 show the control performance and adaptive RBF compensation signal respectively. It is observed that once the monitoring signal exceeds the threshold value, the RBF fault-tolerant control is triggered to compensate the effects of the fault. The results show that the control performance is improved following the adaptive RBF learning.

Figure 5. Block diagram of fault-tolerant control

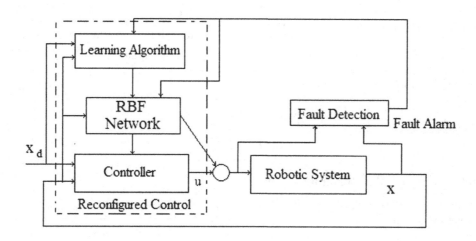

Figure 6. Tracking performance and fault monitoring signal when the fault occurs, where T is the fault occurrence time

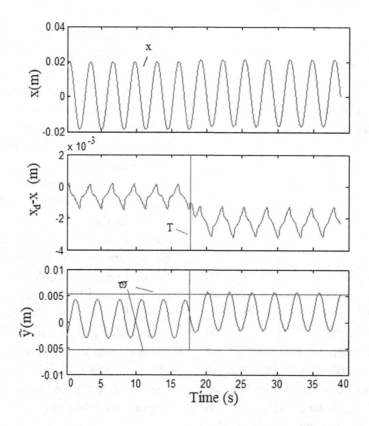

Figure 7. Tracking performance and residual signal under RBF fault-tolerant control

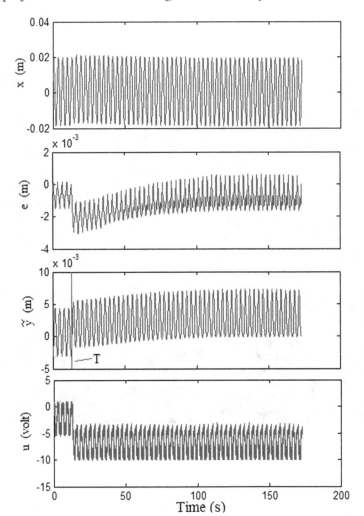

Figure 8. Adaptive RBF output signal

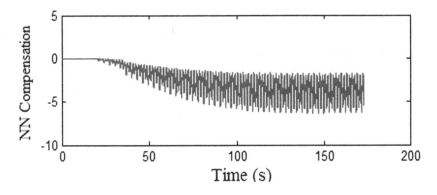

Figure 9. Experimental set-up

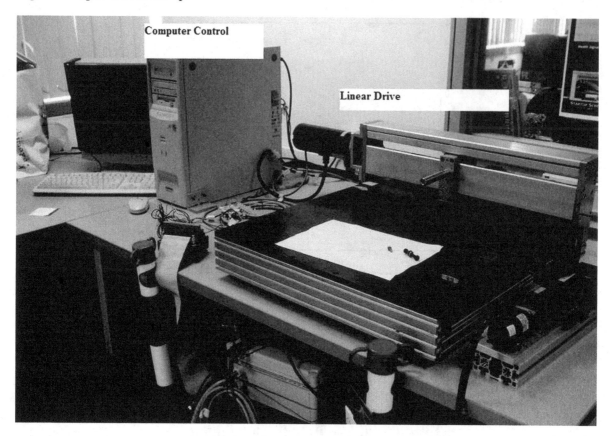

Case 2

In this subsection, the proposed control is applied to the motion control of the linear drive, which has a travel length of 200mm. The experimental setup is shown in Figure 10. The system consists of the linear motion mechanism, encoder system, a amplifier and a PC with dSPACE card 1102. MATLAB/SIMULINK can be used from within dSPACE environment. The entire control system is written into a Simulink object. The sampling period for our test is chosen as 0.001sec.

A motor model which will be used for the observer design, is given by

$$\dot{v} = -3.690v + 0.294u$$
$$- 0.0564sgn(v) - T_l \tag{36}$$

where v is the speed, u is the input voltage, and T_l is the disturbance. Based on this model, the monitoring design is given by

$$\dot{\hat{v}} = -3.690\hat{v} + 0.2940u$$
$$- 0.0564sgn(v) + 15\tilde{v} \tag{37}$$

From experimental results, the disturbance is bounded by 0.29. The monitoring threshold can be computed from (18), that is

$$\omega = e^{-18.692t} \mid \tilde{v}(0) \mid + \int_0^t e^{-18.692(t-\tau)}[0.0564 + 0.29]d\tau$$
$$\leq e^{-18.692t} \mid \tilde{v}(0) \mid + 0.0185 \tag{38}$$

The initial state can be set to zero and then the threshold is 0.0185. The monitoring system will

Figure 10. Tracking performance when a fault occurs without fault tolerant control: Tracking error (top), Monitoring signal (middle), Control signal (bottom)

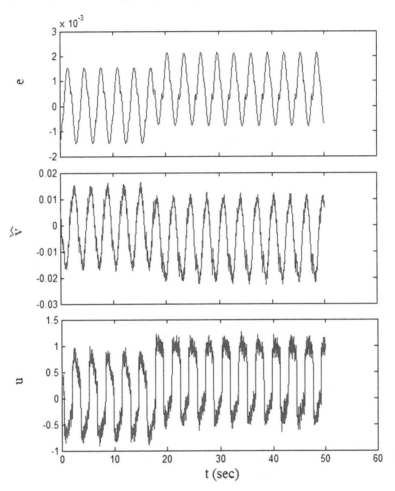

check the residual value against the threshold. The fault-tolerant controller is designed according to (25). In the controller design, the values of k, Λ are chosen as 8, 20 respectively. The control signal is given by

$$u = \frac{3.692v + 8e + 0.0564sgn(v) + 20R + D[\bullet]\hat{W}^T\Phi(x,v)}{0.294}$$

to follow the desired trajectory $x_d = 0.05sin(2t)$. A seven units RBF network is used in this experiment, where

$$\Phi(x,v) = [\varphi_1(x,v),...,\varphi_7(x,v)]^T$$

with

$$\varphi_1 = exp(-\mid [x\ v] - [0.001\ 0.01]\mid^2),$$
$$\varphi_2 = exp(-\mid [x\ v] - [0.005\ 0.05]\mid^2),$$
$$\varphi_3 = exp(-\mid [x\ v] - [0.01\ 0.1]\mid^2),$$
$$\varphi_4 = exp(-\mid [x\ v] - [0.05\ 0.5]\mid^2),$$
$$\varphi_5 = exp(-\mid [x\ v] - [0.1\ 1]\mid^2),$$
$$\varphi_6 = exp(-\mid [x\ v] - [-0.001 - 0.01]\mid^2),$$
$$\varphi_7 = exp(-\mid [x\ v] - [-0.005; 0.05]\mid^2).$$

The initial $\hat{W}(0)$ are simply set to zeros. In this paper, we consider a mechanical fault arising

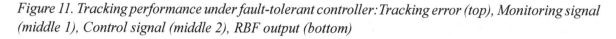

Figure 11. Tracking performance under fault-tolerant controller: Tracking error (top), Monitoring signal (middle 1), Control signal (middle 2), RBF output (bottom)

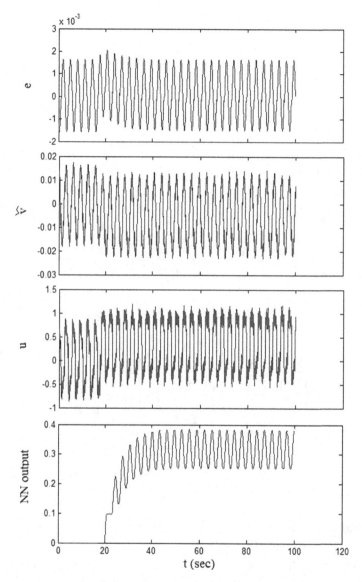

due to mechanical impedance from the ball screw. Figure 10 shows the position control when the fault occurs without fault-tolerant scheme. It is observed that the tracking error is satisfactory when without the fault occurrence, that is 1.65×10^{-3}, but the tracking performance is degraded after the fault occurrence and the maximum error is increased to 2.50×10^{-3}. From the second plot, it is seen that the fault is de-

tected by the monitoring system since the residual signal exceeds its corresponding threshold 0.0185. Now, we repeat the same experiment with the failure and apply the proposed fault-tolerant controller to the system. Figure 11 shows the experimental results. It is observed that when the monitoring signal exceeds its corresponding threshold, the fault-tolerant controller with an adaptive neural network is activated to compensate the effects of the fault. The variation of the tracking error, monitoring signal, and actual control signal are shown in Figure 11. In particular, the RBF output signal added to the controller is also shown in Figure 11, which is used to compensate the effect of the fault adaptively. It is observed that after t=40sec the tracking error is reduced from 2.50×10^{-3} m to $1.65 \times 10^{-3} m$ following the adaptive compensation.

FUTURE RESEARCH DIRECTIONS

Although this chapter has reported important progress in fault-tolerant control, many open questions remain for future research. We give below two desirable objectives for the near future.

1) Reliability analysis of fault-tolerant control Systems

Research on fault-tolerant control has now reached a relatively mature stage. The important factors for stability have been employed to develop a range of fault-tolerant controllers. However, from a practical viewpoint, it is quite important to give analysis and assessment for reliability of fault-tolerant control system. In this regard, a lot of tests should be made and statistic analysis tools should be used to give a confidence level of the proposed fault-tolerant control.

2) Integration of the fault-tolerant control with associated techniques.

Fault-tolerant control is multi-disciplinary and interdisciplinary research across mathematics, control, risk analysis, computing, communication, and hardware implementation. With rapid development in microelectronics and mechatronics technologies, it is possible to implement an intelligent fault-tolerant control platform in conjunction with techniques in these area.

CONCLUSION

In this chapter, fault-tolerant algorithm has been proposed for mechanical systems. Using a model-based observer, the self-detecting technique is designed to send out a warning signal to the controller when a fault is detected. The threshold of detecting failures has been discussed based on the model and residual information. Utilizing neural networks, fault-tolerant control can accommodate the failures and achieve stable control. Two examples have been studied to show how to select the neural network node number and implement the proposed algorithm in a real-time control system. The results have confirmed that the designed controller can improve the tracking performance against the failure. In future, we will conduct a detailed test by comparison with existing fault-tolerant controllers.

REFERENCES

Aberkane, S., Sauter, D., & Ponsart, J. C. (2007). Output feedback stochastic H stabilization of networked fault-tolerant control systems. *Systems and Control Engineering, 221*, 927–935. doi:10.1243/09596518JSCE352

Deutsch, P. (2008). Fault tolerant control system for linear combustion engine. *The 34th Annual Conference on Industrial Electronics* (pp. 198-203). Orlando, FL, USA

Diao, Y., & Passino, K. M. (2001). Stable fault-tolerant adaptive fuzzy/neural control for a turbine engine. *IEEE Transactions on Control Systems Technology, 9*, 494–509. doi:10.1109/87.918902

Farrell, J. A., Berger, T., & Appleby, B. D. (1993). Using learning techniques to accommodate unanticipated faults. *IEEE Control Systems Magazine, 13*, 40–49. doi:10.1109/37.214943

Hamada, Y., Shin, S., & Sebe, N. (1998). A design method for fault-tolerant multivariable control systems—A condition for l-partial integrity. *SICE Transactions*, *34*(9), 1184–1190.

Kambhampati, C., Perkgoz, C., Patton, R. J., & Ahamed, W. (2007). An interaction predictive approach to fault-tolerant control in network control systems. *Systems and Control Engineering*, *221*, 885–894. doi:10.1243/09596518JSCE377

Liu, X., Wu, Y., Shi, J., & Zhang, W. (2008). Adaptive fault-tolerant flight control system design using neural networks. *The 2008 IEEE International Conference on Industrial Technology*, (pp. 1-5). Chengdu, China.

Patton, R., Frank, P., & Clark, R. (1989). *Fault diagnosis in dynamic systems*. Prentice Hall.

Polycarpou, M. M. (2001). Fault accommodation of a class of multivariable nonlinear dynamical systems using a learning approach. *IEEE Transactions on Automatic Control*, *46*, 736–742. doi:10.1109/9.920792

Polycarpou, M. M., & Helmicki, A. J. (1995). Automated fault detection and accommodation: A learning systems approach. *IEEE Transactions on Systems, Man, and Cybernetics*, *25*, 1447–1458. doi:10.1109/21.467710

Rothenhagen, K., & Fuchs, F. W. (2009). Doubly fed induction generator model-based sensor fault detection and control loop reconfiguration. *IEEE Transactions on Industrial Electronics*, *56*(10), 4229–4238. doi:10.1109/TIE.2009.2013683

Sun, Z., Wang, J., Howe, D., & Jewell, G. (2008). Analytical prediction of the short-circuit current in fault-tolerant permanent-magnet machines. *IEEE Transactions on Industrial Electronics*, *55*(12), 4210–4217. doi:10.1109/TIE.2008.2005019

Tong, S., Wang, T., & Zhang, W. (2008). Fault tolerant control for uncertain fuzzy systems with actuator failures. *International Journal of Innovative Computing and Information Control*, *4*(10), 2461–2474.

Visinsky, M. L., Cavallaro, J. R., & Walker, I. D. (1994). Expert system framework for fault detection and fault olerance in robotics. *Computers & Electrical Engineering*, *20*, 421–435. doi:10.1016/0045-7906(94)90035-3

Visinsky, M. L., Cavallaro, J. R., & Walker, I. D. (1995). A dynamic fault tolerance framework for remote robots. *IEEE Transactions on Robotics and Automation*, *11*, 477–490. doi:10.1109/70.406930

Wang, T., Tong, S., & Tong, S. C. (2007). Robust fault tolerant fuzzy control for uncertain fuzzy systems with actuator failures. In *Proceedings of the 2nd International Conference on Innovative Computing and Information Control*, Kumamoto, Japan, (p. 44).

Zhang, Z., Huo, Z., & Zhang, L. (2008). *Fault-tolerant control research for networked control systems based on quasi T-S fuzzy models*. The 2008 IEEE International Conference on Industrial Technology, (pp. 1-4). Chengdu, China.

ADDITIONAL READING

Agrawal, H., DeMillo, R. A., & Spafford, E. H. (1993). Debugging with dynamic slicing and backtracking. *Software, Practice & Experience*, *23*(6), 589–616. doi:10.1002/spe.4380230603

Bonivento, C., Marconi, L., & Paoli, A. (2003). Fault-tolerant control of the ship propulsion system benchmark. *Control Engineering Practice*, *11*, 483–597. doi:10.1016/S0967-0661(02)00095-3

Chen, M. Y., Kiciman, E., Fratkin, E., Fox, A., & Brewer, E. (2002). Pinpoint: Problem determination in large, dynamic internet services. In *Proceedings of the 2002 International Conference on Dependable Systems and Networks*, (pp. 595–604). Washington, DC: IEEE Computer Society.

De Persis, C., & Isidori, A. (2001). A geometric approach to nonlinear fault detection and isolation. *IEEE Transactions on Automatic Control*, *AC-46*, 853–865. doi:10.1109/9.928586

Frank, P. (1990). Fault diagnosis: A survey and some new results. *Automatica*, *26*(3), 459–474. doi:10.1016/0005-1098(90)90018-D

Gertler, J. (1988). Survey of model-based failure detection and isolation in complex plants. *IEEE Control Systems Magazine*, *8*, 3–11. doi:10.1109/37.9163

Gertler, J. (1997). Fault detection and isolation using parity relations. *Control Engineering Practice*, *5*, 653–661. doi:10.1016/S0967-0661(97)00047-6

Gertler, J. (1998). *Fault detection and diagnosis in engineering systems*. New York, NY: Marcel Dekker.

Gupta, N., He, H., Zhang, X., & Gupta, R. (2005). Locating faulty code using failure- inducing chops. In *Proceedings of the 20th IEEE/ACM international Conference on Automated Software Engineering*, (pp. 263–272). Long Beach, CA: ACM Press.

Isermann, R. (1989). A review on detection and diagnosis illustrate that process faults can be detected when based on the estimation of unmeasurable process parameters and state variables. *Automatica*, *20*(4), 387–404. doi:10.1016/0005-1098(84)90098-0

Lunze, J. (1999). A timed discrete-event abstraction of continuous-variable systems. *International Journal of Control*, *72*, 1147–1164. doi:10.1080/002071799220317

Manders, E. J., Mosterman, P. J., & Biswas, G. (1999). Signal to symbol transformation techniques for robust diagnosis in TRANSCEND. *Tenth International Workshop on Principles of Diagnosis*, (pp. 155-165). Loch Awe, Scotland

Mauss, J. (1995). Diagnosis by algebraic modeling and fault-tree induction. In *Proceedings 6th International Workshop Principles Diagnosis*, Oct. 1995, (pp. 73–80). Goslar, Germany

Mosterman, P. J., & Biswas, G. (1999). Diagnosis of continuous valued systems in transient operating regions. *IEEE Transactions on Systems, Man, and Cybernetics*, *29*(6), 554–565. doi:10.1109/3468.798059

Sampath, M., Sengupta, R., Lafortune, S., Sinnamohideen, K., & Demosthenis, T. C. (1996). Failure diagnosis using discrete-event models. *IEEE Transactions on Control Systems Technology*, *4*, 105–124. doi:10.1109/87.486338

KEY TERMS AND DEFINITIONS

Control: It uses a command to drive a system approaching a desired trajectory closely.

Fault: A fault is a sensor, actuator, or mechanical part which cannot work properly.

Fault Detection: A control system can monitor and find a fault occurrence.

Fault Diagnosis: It is concerned that a control system can identify when a fault has occurred and point out the type of fault and its location.

Fault Tolerant Control: it is concerned that a control system can accommodate a fault and continue to work properly when a fault has occurred.

Neural Network: It is used to refer to a network or circuit of biological neurons which is composed of nodes.

System Model: It is used to model the behaviour of the system in response to external and internal events.

Chapter 11
Supervision of Industrial Processes using Self Organizing Maps

Ignacio Díaz
Universidad de Oviedo, Spain

Manuel Domínguez
Instituto de Automática y Fabricación,
Universidad de León, Spain

Abel A. Cuadrado
Universidad de Oviedo, Spain

Juan J. Fuertes
Instituto de Automática y Fabricación,
Universidad de León, Spain

Alberto B. Diez
Universidad de Oviedo, Spain

Miguel A. Prada
Instituto de Automática y Fabricación,
Universidad de León, Spain

ABSTRACT

The objective of this chapter is to present, in a comprehensive and unified way, a corpus of data and knowledge visualization techniques based on the Self-Organizing Map (SOM). These techniques allow exploring the behavior of the process in a visual and intuitive way through the integration of existing process-related knowledge with information extracted from data, providing new ways for knowledge discovery. With a special focus on the application to process supervision and modeling, the chapter reviews well known techniques –such as component planes, u-matrix, and projection of the process state– but also presents recent developments for visualizing process-related knowledge, such as fuzzy maps, local correlation maps, and model maps. It also introduces the maps of dynamics, which allow users to visualize the dynamical behavior of the process on a local model basis, in a seamless integration with the former visualizations, making it possible to confront all them for discovery of new knowledge.

DOI: 10.4018/978-1-4666-1806-0.ch011

INTRODUCTION

Knowledge of the industrial process is a key factor in today's industry. Quality and production standards increasingly require a better knowledge about its behavior in order to optimize its performance, productivity and quality. Many industrial processes, however, are complex, due to both the number of variables and states and also due to the diverse and coupled nature of the physical, chemical, algorithmic, biological, etc. sub-processes. Such processes may have a large number of strongly coupled variables –from tens to thousands– whose relationships may be partially or completely unknown. In the last years, dramatic drops in the cost of technologies for data acquisition and storage have allowed the creation of huge databases containing useful information about the process. On the other hand, prior knowledge is often available in really diverse ways: *rules* at different levels of detail, ranging from vague descriptions to well defined expressions, *models* –e.g. physical equations– describing the whole process or parts of it, *cases* consisting of subsets of data related to a known occurrence, *correlations* between certain variables, etc. In sum, the process engineer often faces scenarios with large amounts of information in terms of raw data from process sensors and heterogeneous kinds of knowledge about the process, which should be connected.

This chapter will cover the following topics. First, a background on supervision of industrial processes using SOM will be provided along with a literature review on the topic. The main focus of the chapter will be devoted to describe the existing and some novel methods to represent information and knowledge about the process from a unified viewpoint. This section will be divided into two main parts: methods to represent knowledge about the *process behavior* providing insight into the process nature, which are the basis for process optimization and decision making; and methods to represent the current *process state*, understood here as the set of variables that define its work-

ing condition, being the basis for monitoring and fault detection and isolation methods. Next, the chapter describes briefly two application cases of industrial supervision using SOM. Finally, sections on future research directions and concluding remarks are included.

BACKGROUND

In the last decade, there has been an increasing interest in visualization techniques for multidimensional data (Card et al., 1999; Vesanto, 1999; Keim, 2002; Ferreira de Oliveira et al.; 2003; Kreuseler et al., 2002). Information visualization approaches have been successfully used in scenarios similar to that described in the introduction, allowing to integrate vast amounts of data with available prior knowledge in a user centric fashion, by transforming data and information into a visual representation to exploit the pattern recognition capabilities of the human visual system.

One approach for multidimensional data visualization is the so-called *dimensionality reduction* (DR) approach. The DR approach consists of obtaining a dimension reduction mapping which projects, in a continuous way, points from the data space onto a 2D or 3D space, which can be visualized, without losing significant information. Once all information is presented in a visual way, the human ability for detection, reasoning and inference with complex patterns can be exploited for process understanding and discovery of new knowledge. These mappings serve as a bridge between the high dimensional space of process data and 2D visualizations –actually *maps* of the process–, that allow the human to operate with reasoning tools valid in the data space, such as rules or theoretical models –e.g. mechanical or electrical equations– in an insightful way, boosting his ability to find new relationships and, in sum, to discover new knowledge.

The challenge of complex process optimization using large amounts of data and sparse heteroge-

Figure 1. SOM mapping

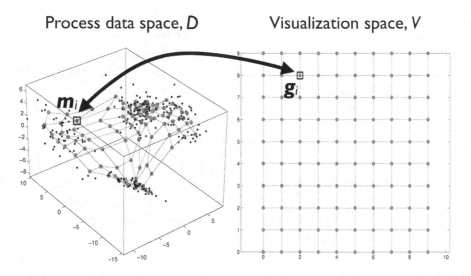

Process data space, *D*   Visualization space, *V*

neous knowledge has been actively investigated. Visual Data Mining methods have been used in industry for fault detection and improvement of both quality and process performance. In (Grishin et al., 2003), a visual method that exploits the human abilities of pattern recognition for the monitoring and diagnosis of very complex systems is described. The visual approach was also used for the improvement of manufacturing processes according to (Porzio et al., 2003). In (Albazzaz et al., 2006), Independent Component Analysis for dimension reduction and parallel components for visualization, are combined in a Statistical Process Control approach, which is applied in a case study with data from a wastewater treatment plant. In (He et al., 2009), it is shown how data mining techniques are used to solve problems related to product quality in manufacturing.

Particularly, the Self-Organizing Map (SOM) (Kohonen, 2001; Vesanto, 1999) has proved to be a powerful tool for process analysis and supervision. In (Harris, 1993) and (Alhoniemi et al., 1999), applications of SOM as a data mining tool for fault detection, monitoring, modeling and regression for quality prediction of complex industrial processes have been described.

The ideas described in this chapter share several of the above-mentioned approaches but make a special stress in the integration of process-related knowledge using the SOM as the main foundation element. In the next section, the basics of the SOM are explained.

The SOM Algorithm

The Self-Organizing Map (SOM) (Kohonen et al., 1996) is a type of artificial neural network able to learn a low-dimensional, discretized representation of a high-dimensional input dataset, with powerful visualization capabilities. It has become increasingly used in the scope of process monitoring and optimization due to its ability to exploit the existing knowledge and to discover new knowledge about the process, as well as to show up its working state in a flexible, dynamic and real-time way. It has also been integrated into many supervision and monitoring systems.

The SOM can be seen as a set of elements called *units* or *nodes* with a topological structure of lateral connections that typically form a lattice. Each unit i –see Figure 1– has associated a codebook vector $\mathbf{m}_i$ in the *data space D*, and a position vector $\mathbf{g}_i$ on a grid or lattice defined in a

Figure 2. SOM properties. Left and center images describe PCA approximation and 1D-SOM approximation. The SOM captures the low dimensional structure of data in a much more efficient way than PCA. The rightmost figure describes how the SOM is able to capture the density distribution of data.

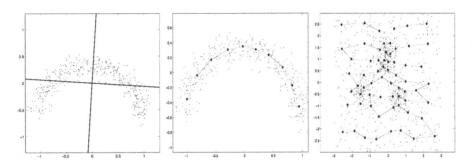

low dimensional *visualization space V* –typically 2D–, meant for visualization purposes. This defines a correspondence or *mapping* between the codebook vectors and the grid positions

$$\mathbf{m}_i \leftrightarrow \mathbf{g}_i \qquad (1)$$

This association is the basis for SOM visualization. A simple functional mapping $\mathcal{S} : \mathbb{R}^n \to \mathbb{R}^2$ allows to extend this to all points in D

$$\mathbf{x} \to \mathcal{S}(\mathbf{x}) = \mathbf{g}_c, \quad \text{where}$$
$$c = \arg\min_i \{\|\mathbf{x} - \mathbf{m}_i\|\} \qquad (2)$$

that is, each data vector $\mathbf{x}$ of the process –composed of measurements or features– can be assigned to a 2D position $\mathbf{g}_c$ corresponding to the closest prototype $\mathbf{m}_c$ to $\mathbf{x}$ in D. To be useful for visualization, the mapping S($\cdot$) must satisfy the following properties, which are illustrated in Figure 2:

1. It must capture the low dimensional structure of process data in D.
2. It must be a good approximation of the process data distribution in D. The representative element according to the model, that is, the closest codebook vector $\mathbf{m}_c$, should be close enough to $\mathbf{x}$.

3. The mapping must be smooth and ordered, ensuring that close points in V represent neighbor states in D.

Kohonen (Kohonen, et al., 1996) summarized these properties in a cost function that represents the previous constraints,

$$E = \int \sum_i h_{ci} f\left(\|\mathbf{x} - \mathbf{m}_i\|\right) p(\mathbf{x}) d\mathbf{x} \qquad (3)$$

where $p(\cdot)$ represents the joint probability density function (pdf) of $\mathbf{x}$ in the data space D, $f(\cdot)$ is a monotonically increasing function and h_{ci} describes the proximity of unit i to the winner unit c in the visualization space V according to a predefined topology.

Kohonen proposed in the early 80's a competitive-cooperative algorithm –see (Kohonen, 2001)– that approximately minimized the previous cost function. The SOM algorithm adapts a set of codebook vectors $\mathbf{m}_i$ in D, placing them in such a way that they span the geometry of process data $\mathbf{x}_k$ and, in addition, preserve a previously defined topology –typically a rectangular 2D lattice, albeit other topologies such as toroids, spheres, etc. have been described–, so that close units $\mathbf{g}_i$, $\mathbf{g}_j$ in the lattice correspond to close codebook vectors $\mathbf{m}_i$, $\mathbf{m}_j$ in D, resulting in a smooth ordered mapping suitable for visualization. The SOM algorithm is surprisingly simple and takes two steps:

Initialize the codebook vectors $\mathbf{m}_i$ using a random Gaussian or a 2D PCA approximation of the input data.

1. Given an input point $\mathbf{x}_k$ in D, get the index of the closest prototype, also called best matching unit (BMU),

$$c = \arg\min_i \|\mathbf{x}_k - \mathbf{m}_i(t)\| \quad (4)$$

2. Adapt the best matching unit, but also the units close to it by slightly moving them towards $\mathbf{x}_i$

$$\mathbf{m}_i(t+1) = \mathbf{m}_i(t) + \alpha(t)h_{ci}(t)[\mathbf{x}_k - \mathbf{m}_i(t)] \quad (5)$$

Repeat steps 1 and 2 $\forall \mathbf{m}_i, \forall \mathbf{x}_k \in D \subset \mathbb{R}^n$ for a given number of epochs.

The neighborhood function h_{ci} is generally a smoothly decreasing function with distance between units c and i in the lattice. Typically, $h_{ci}(t) = \exp(-\|\mathbf{g}_c\text{-}\mathbf{g}_i\|^2/\sigma^2)$ where $\sigma(t)$ is the kernel width and $\| . \|$ can be the Euclidean or link distance in the SOM topology. This ensures large learning rates for units close to the winner in the lattice and small ones for faraway units, so, after training, nearby units will have received similar adaptation patterns and will end up in similar positions. Finally, to provide a global learning at the beginning and a fine and local tuning at the end, both the width factor $\sigma(t)$ and the learning factor $\alpha(t)$ are usually made to decrease monotonically with time. A computationally efficient version of the original SOM algorithm is the *batch version*:

Initialize the codebook vectors $\mathbf{m}_i$ using a random Gaussian or a 2D PCA approximation of the input data.

1. Get the indices of winner units for each sample vector $\mathbf{x}_k$

$$c(k) = \arg\min_i \|\mathbf{x}_k - \mathbf{m}_i(t)\|, \quad k = 1, 2, ..., N \quad (6)$$

2. Obtain the new codebook vectors $\mathbf{m}_i(t+1)$ as a weighted mean

$$\mathbf{m}_i(t+1) = \frac{\sum_k h_{c(k)i} \cdot \mathbf{x}_k}{\sum_k h_{c(k)i}} \quad (7)$$

Repeat steps 1 and 2 with a monotonically decreasing width σ in $h_{ci}(t)$ for a given number of epochs.

VISUALIZING PROCESS-RELATED KNOWLEDGE WITH THE SOM

The SOM algorithm, described in the previous section, allows defining a *map* of the process data that has a strong analogy with a typical cartographic map, where process conditions composed of similar or related process states, are mapped to specific regions that can be labeled on the map. However, the basic SOM algorithm is unsupervised and produces a "blind map". To be useful, this map has to be labeled using the available process-related knowledge.

Fortunately, such mapping encloses an extraordinary potential to represent the available knowledge. The SOM is actually a model of the process data distribution. Due to its ability to discover low dimensional structures in data, it is actually a simplified description of the process that provides a one-to-one association between a set of representative states of the process –the codebook vectors, $\mathbf{m}_i$– and a 2D visualization,

Figure 3. Representation of a property p by means of a plane

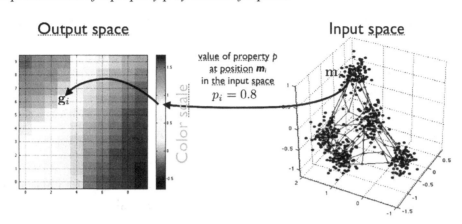

where any physical properties considered or evaluated in the process data space, can be translated to the 2D space, where they become visual. This translation to a visual space brings together the physical intuition about the process and the power of the human visual system to establish relationships and detect complex patterns, laying the basis to build and discover new knowledge upon the available one. Using the proper knowledge representation techniques, this results in a *unified* representation that brings the user a comprehensive visual description of the process nature as well as an intuitive way to monitor its current state of operation.

This section describes several ways to represent process-related knowledge on the SOM mapping including cases, models, rules, correlations and also the dynamical states of the process. All these kinds of information are represented in the same map and can be compared in a consistent way, exactly in the same fashion as meteorological maps of pressures, temperatures or winds of a country.

DEFINITION OF A PLANE

In a general sense, a *plane* of a scalar property or feature p can be defined by the following elements

$$\{\mathbf{g}_i, p_i\}_{i=1...N} \tag{8}$$

where $\mathbf{g}_i$ are the coordinates of unit i in the visualization space, N is the total number of SOM units and p_i is the value of a scalar property of the process evaluated or measured at a state defined by $\mathbf{m}_i$. An efficient representation for a plane –see Figure 3– consists in associating a color level to p_i and displaying it at position $\mathbf{g}_i$, typically using a pixel or a glyph. If the SOM lattice has a rectangular shape the result is a rectangular image showing a colored pattern that describes the distribution of property p as a function of the process states. Thanks to the topology preservation property of the SOM, the resulting color distribution is smooth and gradual, being suitable for visual analysis. Planes can efficiently represent very different kinds of process-related knowledge, in terms of cases, sets of rules –including fuzzy–, mathematical models or correlations. Moreover, since all planes represent exactly the same map of the process states, all of them are visually comparable, allowing to find connections between different forms of knowledge for discovering new one, thus making it a powerful tool for process data analysis.

In the following subsections some methods to represent a wide range of process-related types of knowledge, all of them based on the previous definition of plane, will be described.

VISUALIZATION OF PROCESS VARIABLES

Process variables can be efficiently visualized using the so-called *component planes*. The component plane of the *j*th process variable is defined by $\{\mathbf{g}_i, m_{ij}\}$ for $i = 1, 2, ..., N$. Component planes, already described in (Kohonen, et al., 1996), are interpreted in a similar way as typical weather maps –pressures, rains or temperatures– of a country, and trigger similar kinds of understanding mechanisms about the process as these about weather. Component planes have been the main tools for process analysis in many applications of SOM –see e.g. (Alhoniemi, et al., 1999; Abonyi et al., 2003; Laiho et al., 2005; Díaz et al., 2006; Rendueles et al., 2006)–, showing the behavior of the process variables with respect to the process states. Looking at component planes the user can easily find correlations among process variables, just by finding similar looking planes, as well as identify and label regions in the visualization space that define different process states using prior knowledge about the process.

CLUSTER VISUALIZATION

A key task to characterize a process through a map is to delimit regions corresponding to different process conditions. This is sometimes difficult using the component planes alone. Obtaining precise borders between regions is possible by defining planes that reveal the average distance of every codebook vector $\mathbf{m}_i$ to its neighbors, since they get closer to their neighbors in regions –clusters– with a high density of data –see Figure 2. The u-matrix visualization (Ultsch, 2003), computes for each unit i the sum of distances to the codebook vectors in the neighborhood. A slightly

more general formulation can be obtained defining planes given by $\{\mathbf{g}_i, D_i\}$ computing the weighted mean distances between $\mathbf{m}_i$ and $\mathbf{m}_j$, according to their neighborhood distance h_{ij},

$$D_i = \frac{\sum_j h_{ij} d(\mathbf{m}_i, \mathbf{m}_j)}{\sum_j h_{ij}} \qquad (9)$$

Additionally, supervised classifiers $f_C: D \rightarrow \{0,1,2,... M\}$ trained in D –e.g. support vector machines– can be used to assign a class label $1,... M$ to each unit $\mathbf{m}_i$ leading to a *class map* $\{\mathbf{g}_i, f_C(\mathbf{m}_i)\}$ that reveals classes of process data in V. A good reference on SOM clustering can be found in (Vesanto et al., 2000).

CASE BASED REASONING

Process-related knowledge is often available in terms of *cases* given by subsets of process data $S = \{\mathbf{x}_k\}_{k \in I_S}$, where I_S is an index set, with some associated *prior knowledge* as, for instance, a label ("fault type 1") or any other kinds of metadata. It is possible to obtain the region in V described by case S by means of a plane $\{\mathbf{g}_i, A_i\}$ that shows a weighted histogram of hits

$$A_i = \frac{\sum_{k \in I_S} h_{c(k)i}}{\sum_j h_{ij}} \quad \text{where} \qquad (10)$$

$$c(k) = \arg\min_i \{d(\mathbf{x}_k, \mathbf{m}_i)\}, \; k \in I_S$$

where h_{ij} is the neighborhood distance between units i and j, and $c(k)$ represents the winner unit for sample $\mathbf{x}_k$. Note that the A_i compute the hits on unit i but also hits on neighbor units.

VISUALIZATION OF MODELS

Prior knowledge about a process is often given in terms of models expressed as functional relationships between variables x_1, x_2, ..., x_n. Such models often define new variables from the existing ones as $y_j = f_j(x_1, x_2, ..., x_n) = f_j(\mathbf{x})$. The j-th *virtual plane* can be defined as $\{\mathbf{g}_i, f_j(\mathbf{m}_i)\}$, which can be interpreted in the same manner as component planes. Also, closed expressions of the existing process variables that must hold under certain –known– hypotheses can be expressed in implicit form $g_j(x_1, x_2, ..., x_n) = 0$. A very simplified example of the first class would be obtaining a new variable "power" $P(t)$ in terms of voltage $V(t)$ and current $I(t)$. An example of the second case, would be based on the certainty that

$$P(t) = V(t)I(t) \rightarrow P(t) - V(t)I(t) = 0 \qquad (11)$$

that is

$$f(x_1, x_2, x_3) = f(V, I, P) = 0 \qquad (12)$$

To show in the map states where the process does not behave as expected, a map of residuals $\epsilon_j \{\mathbf{g}_i, \epsilon_j\}$ can be defined, being $\epsilon_j = f_j(x_1, x_2, ..., x_n)$ the j-th model residual.

VISUALIZATION OF RULES

The SOM can be used to visualize process-related knowledge in terms of rules. *Fuzzy inference systems* (FIS) use fuzzy sets theory to compute the degree of membership to a class from a set of fuzzy rules (Lin et al., 1996). FIS make it possible to exploit linguistic knowledge about the process through three steps, namely, fuzzification, rule inference and defuzzification. In particular, a FIS can be defined to obtain the memberships μ_j of a given data vector $\mathbf{x}$ to, say, m classes –that can be e.g. fault conditions– from a set of fuzzy rules

expressed in vague terms and a set of membership functions that define belongingness of the process measurements or features x_i to known classes. Such a FIS can be seen as continuous function $f_C: D \rightarrow [0,1]^m$. Taking each of the m outputs independently we have

$$\mu_j = \mathcal{F}_j(x_1, x_2, ...x_n) \qquad j = 1, ..., m \qquad (13)$$

that gives the memberships for the consequents μ_1, ..., μ_n given a set of input variables x_1, ..., x_n, a set of fuzzy rules and a set of membership functions. A *fuzzy map* for the j-th consequent can be defined as

$$\{\mathbf{g}_i, \mathcal{F}_j(\mathbf{m}_i)\} \qquad (14)$$

The resulting maps are therefore visual representations of linguistic knowledge about the process expressed in terms of rules. These maps are directly comparable to the other planes, making them a very powerful tool to combine different kinds of process-related knowledge.

CORRELATION DISCOVERY

In nonlinear processes, correlations among variables depend on the working point. *Global* correlations –evaluated for all working points– may produce misleading results since they can differ substantially from *local* correlations, evaluated around operating points. Local correlations can be represented by means of SOM, defining a *neighborhood function* $w_{ij} = e^{-\frac{1}{2}\|\mathbf{x}_i - \mathbf{m}_j\|^2 / \sigma^2}$, which describes the proximity of a data vector $\mathbf{x}_i$ to unit $\mathbf{m}_j$ in D. For every unit j, the *local mean vector* μ^j and the *local covariance matrix* $\mathbf{C}^j$ are defined as

213

Figure 4. Illustrative example

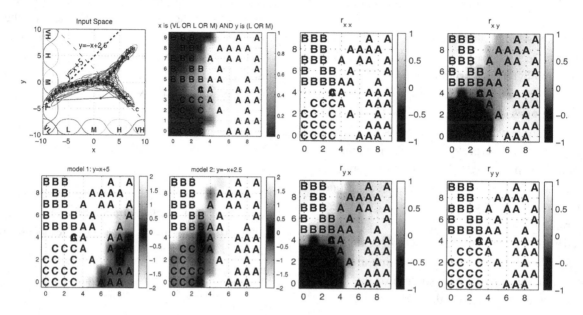

$$\mu^j = \frac{\sum_i \mathbf{x}_i \cdot w_{ij}}{\sum_i w_{ij}} \quad (15)$$

$$\mathbf{C}^j = \frac{\sum_i [\mathbf{x}_i - \mu^j][\mathbf{x}_i - \mu^j]^T \cdot w_{ij}}{\sum_i w_{ij}} \quad (16)$$

The $n \times n$ components (c^j_{ab}) of the local covariance matrix $\mathbf{C}^j$, describe the local dependency between variables x_a and x_b of the process. A *local correlation matrix* around unit j, which is more appropriate for correlation analysis, can be defined as

$$\mathbf{R}^j = (r^j_{ab}) \quad where, \quad r^j_{ab} = \frac{c^j_{ab}}{\sqrt{c^j_{aa} c^j_{bb}}}. \quad (17)$$

Its $n \times n$ components (r^j_{ab}) represent the local correlation coefficient between variables x_a and x_b and always lie in the interval $[-1, +1]$, being $+1$ full correlation, 0 uncorrelation, and -1 full inverse correlation. Accordingly, $n \times n$ planes called *cor-*

relation maps can be defined as $\{\mathbf{g}_j, r^j_{ab}\}$. These planes reveal how x_a and x_b are *locally* correlated on a working point basis, and in a consistent way with the other SOM planes, providing insight about correlation dependencies.

Illustrative Example: A simple example illustrates some of the previously described visualizations. Let's consider the 2D data described in Figure 4. As seen, this dataset has a different local correlation structure –positive, negative or zero correlations–, depending on the location. Let's also consider the following two models defined in D

model 1: $y = x + 5$
model 2: $x + y = 2.5$

Finally, let's consider a set of membership functions described in the figure and a rule that defines the points labeled with an "A"

x is (VL OR L OR M) AND y is (L OR M)

A 10x10 SOM was trained to learn the data structure. As seen in Figure 4, correlation map r_{xy} describes the changing local correlations between variables x and y, showing up three different regions (A with a mild positive correlation, B with a strong positive correlation and C with a strong negative correlation). Also the fuzzy map for the previous rule clearly reveals the A points as fulfilling the rule. Finally the map for model 2 (expressed in explicit form: $y=-x+2.5$) shows that only the C points fit to it. It is important to note that all representations are consistent and allow combination of substantially different kinds of knowledge

VISUALIZATION OF PROCESS DYNAMICS

The techniques described in the previous sections present a great potential to visualize knowledge and information about the process. However, they only model static relationships among the process variables that might be related in a dynamical way –e.g. through a differential equation.

The SOM algorithm has ideal properties for visualization of the dynamical relationships of systems. Its ability to obtain smooth 2D maps that preserve distances makes it possible to group the dynamical models according to their similarity in the visualization and paves the way for building approximations of the global dynamics by creating several simpler local models.

Several approaches were reported in the literature using SOM for modeling the dynamic behavior of both processes and time series (Guimarães et al., 2003; Barreto, 2007). Based on the argument that certain time features are better understood in the frequency domain, other methods were proposed based on training a SOM in parameter spaces or descriptors of the dynamics, such as wavelet coefficients (Moshou et al., 2000) or energies in frequency bands (Díaz Blanco et al., 2003). However, maybe the most rigorous approach from a theoretical point of view and with better results in identification and control is the use of local dynamic models associated to each

unit of the SOM. In (Kohonen, 2001) the concept of *operator map* is described, in which each unit of the SOM is associated to a parametric model that allows analysis of non-stationary processes. This idea or related approaches were used for the analysis of 3G cellular networks in (Lehtimäki et al., 2003), for predicting time series (Vesanto, 1997) and for nonlinear system identification and control (Principe et al., 1998; Cho et al., 2006).

Surprisingly, none of the above methods has been explicitly conceived for visualization. A method for the visualization of dynamical processes was proposed in (Díaz Blanco et al., 2008), where a SOM is trained in a space of parameters of a dynamical model $y(k) = f(\varphi(k),\mathbf{p})$ that describes the dynamical relationships between two variables $u(k)$, $y(k)$, being $\varphi(k) = [y(k-1), y(k-2), ..., y(k-n), u(k), ..., u(k-m)]^T$ an embedded vector that contains delayed outputs $y(k)$ and inputs $u(k)$. The method builds N subsets of pairs $\{y(k), \varphi(k)\}$ containing, respectively, data close to N representative operating points –or, alternatively, using N time-shifted windows, if the process dynamics changes smoothly over time– and estimating N parameter vectors $\mathbf{p}_i$ using least squares. Then, a SOM is trained on N extended vectors $\mathbf{q}_i = [p_1, p_2, ... p_n, x_1, x_2, ..., x_n]^T$, $i=1, ..., N$, that contain the parameters of the dynamic model obtained from subset i and representative values of the operating point for this subset –typically the means over the subset samples. This results in codebook vectors $\mathbf{m}_i = [\mathbf{m}^i_p | \mathbf{m}^i_x]$ where the $\mathbf{m}^i_p$ part describes a local dynamic model and the $\mathbf{m}^i_x$ contains its "companion" operating point. This allows the simultaneous visualization of dynamic properties and the operating point, opening a wide range of possibilities for the exploration of the dynamic behavior of the process.

Process Monitoring using SOM

In the previous section, a number of visualizations were defined using always the same principle. This allows different kinds of knowledge to be represented in a unified way that admits pairwise comparisons among them, resulting in a powerful way to discover correlations and new knowledge about the process.

In addition to *explore the nature* of the process, the SOM allows *tracking its state* in a number of ways. Moreover, these representations are also compatible –and comparable– to those defined in the previous section.

PROJECTION OF STATE TRAJECTORY

Let $\mathbf{x}(t) = [x_1(t), \ldots, x_n(t)]^T$ be the current measurement vector of the process. A simple mapping from the data space D to the visualization space V can be defined as follows

$$S_{D \to V}(\mathbf{x}(t)) = \mathbf{g}_{c(t)} \quad \text{where}$$
$$c(t) = \arg \min_i \{\|\mathbf{x}(t) - \mathbf{m}_i\|\} \tag{18}$$

that is, mapping $\mathbf{x}(t)$ to the position of the best matching unit $c(t)$ in the 2D lattice defined in V. Thus, a trajectory of process states in D, $\{\mathbf{x}(t_1), \mathbf{x}(t_2), \ldots, \mathbf{x}(t_n)\}$ will induce a 2D trajectory in V, $\{\mathbf{g}_{c(t1)}, \mathbf{g}_{c(t2)}, \ldots, \mathbf{g}_{c(m)}\}$ that can be efficiently visualized.

Since the regions of V represent process conditions, the current projection $\mathbf{g}_{c(t)}$ displayed over one –or more– of the previous planes shows up in a straightforward way the current process condition, just by visually matching the current region on which it lies. This idea is described in Figure 5.

ANALYSIS OF THE TRAJECTORY

This method is based on the analysis of the trajectory created by the projection of the temporal sequence of process states on the 2-dimensional clustered SOM grid (Fuertes et al., 2010; Domínguez González et al., 2005). Each of the neurons of the grid has information about the cluster (process condition) that it belongs to. The analysis of the trajectory makes it possible to determine which process conditions are reachable from a certain cluster and which are not. To build the *dynamic model of transitions*, the transition probability between a given pair of process conditions, i and j, is computed as,

$$p_{ij} = \frac{n_{ij}}{\displaystyle\sum_{k=1}^{n_t} n_{ik}} \tag{19}$$

where n_{ij} is the number of transitions of the trajectory which exist from the process condition i to j and n_t is the number of conditions determined in the SOM clustering. The resulting model can be used to detect abnormal sequences of states (Fuertes et al., 2010) and can be interpreted as a Petri net (Murata, 1989) or a Markov chain (Norris, 1997), where the process conditions are the *places* (represented by a circle) whereas the *transitions* –related to the probabilities p_{ij}– describe the reachable conditions from a given one. This representation, similar to a flowchart, is useful to show the system evolution and to make the analysis of the model easier.

NOVELTY DETECTION AND VISUALIZATION

Since the SOM is a model of the joint pdf, new data from the process can be confronted to the model to check if it lies on the regions spanned by the process data. Besides being a low dimensional mapping the SOM, can be made to work as an auto-associative model in a similar way:

$$S_{D \to D}(\mathbf{x}(t)) = \mathbf{m}_{c(t)} \quad \text{where}$$
$$c(t) = \arg \min_i \{\|\mathbf{x}(t) - \mathbf{m}_i\|\} \tag{20}$$

Figure 5. Visualization of process state trajectory. The top left figure describes data and a process trajectory in D along with the SOM approximation. The top right one shows the corresponding SOM lattice and the projected trajectory in V. The four bottom figures describe the component planes for variables x_1, x_2 and x_3 as well as the distance map D_i that reveals the cluster structure of the original data space.

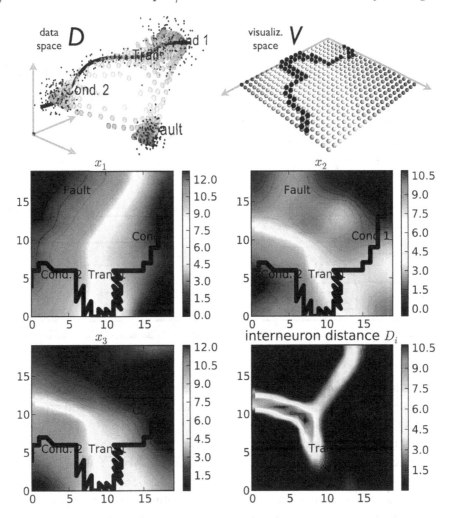

The resulting point $\mathbf{m}_{c(t)}$ of D can be interpreted as the best estimation of the current data vector $\mathbf{x}(t)$ by the SOM. If a novelty occurs in the process, that is, if a measurement vector $\mathbf{x}(t)$ lies outside the joint pdf of the normal process data, the SOM estimation will be inaccurate and the distance $q(t) = \|\mathbf{x}(t) - \mathbf{m}_{c(t)}\|$ will indicate a novel condition. Such quantity is called *quantification error* and fault detection schemes have been proposed based on thresholds on $q(t)$ –an early application of this can be found in (Vapola et al., 1994).

A vector measure of the divergence of the process from its expected behavior can be defined as $\mathbf{r}(t) = \mathbf{x}(t) - \mathbf{m}_{c(t)}$ called *vector of residuals*. Individual components of $\mathbf{r}(t)$, the residuals, can be used as individual indicators of faults in a per-variable basis, providing information on the nature of the fault by checking the faulty residuals. The selection of the winner unit can be constrained to the reachable conditions according to the dynamic model of transitions, obtained from the analysis of trajectories described in the previous section. This

*Figure 6. Visualization of the residual vector **r**(t). The y-axis describes the residuals for several harmonics of vibrations and currents. The x-axis represents time. A color scale represents the magnitude and sign of the residuals.*

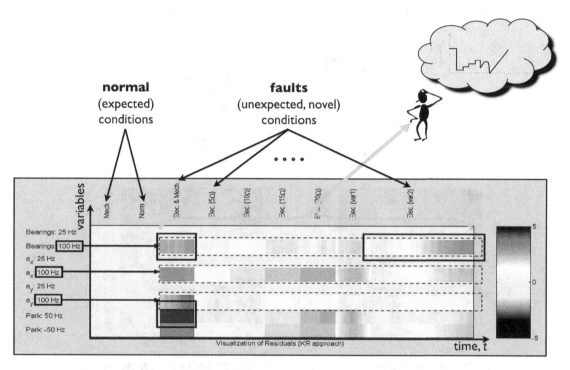

approach contributes to indicate more accurately the variables associated to the fault.

The vector of residuals **r**(t) can be efficiently visualized using a 2D image, using the horizontal axis to represent time, and the vertical axis to represent the residuals, whose values are represented using a color scale. An example is shown in Figure 6. This visualization shows the residuals of some harmonics in a 4kW induction motor for normal condition as well as for several fault conditions –mechanical asymmetry and electrical supply imbalance– in different degrees. This kind of visualization shows up, in a single snapshot, the variables involved in a novel condition and simultaneously their evolution in time, allowing to account for periodicities regularities, trends, etc. that can help to diagnose a fault condition. Finally, it can also be used as a "diff tool", specially in batch processes, allowing to compare one or

more groups of items, making it also a useful tool for visual exploration and process data mining.

DISSIMILARITY MAPS

An intuitive idea to compare different SOM-based models is to compare the codebook vectors of their neurons. Let us consider two processes A and B, where process A is the *reference process*, and process B is the *monitored process* which will be compared to process A. Given the SOM models for both processes, $\{\mathbf{m}_{Ai}\}_{i=1\ldots K}$ and $\{\mathbf{m}_{Bi}\}_{i=1\ldots K}$ are, respectively, the codebook vectors of model A and B whereas $\{\mathbf{g}_{Ai}\}_{i=1\ldots K}$ and $\{\mathbf{g}_{Bi}\}_{i=1\ldots K}$ are the location vectors of those models in V. The *dissimilarity vector function* of those models, $D_{BA} : \mathbb{R}^2 \to \mathbb{R}^n$ is defined for each unit i as

$$D_{BA_i} = \mathbf{m}_{B_i} - \mathbf{m}_{A_{c_i}} \quad \text{where}$$

$$c_i = \arg\min_j \left\{ \left\| \mathbf{m}_{B_i} - \mathbf{m}_{A_j} \right\|^2 \right\} \tag{21}$$

This function assigns the difference between the corresponding codebook vector $\mathbf{m}_{Bi}$ and its closest codebook vector in the model A, $\mathbf{m}_{Aci}$ to every position $\mathbf{g}_{Bi}$ in the lattice.

Dissimilarity maps are used to visualize this function in all the state space by assigning a pseudocolor to each neuron $\mathbf{g}_{Bi}$ in the 2D visualization lattice of model B proportional to the value of the magnitude of the dissimilarity function at that point. Therefore, colors representing values near 0 correspond to zones in the state space where model B remains unaltered compared to the reference one, i.e., model A. In contrast, colors representing non-null values identify zones where the behavior of the processes is different. As a consequence of the vectorial nature of the dissimilarity function, n different *dissimilarity component planes* can be displayed. To define such maps, a pseudocolor proportional to the k_{th} component of the dissimilarity function at that point, is assigned for each node position $\mathbf{g}_{Bi}$ in the 2D lattice of model B. These planes have a physical meaning since they show the deviations of a physical variable in the model B with regard to the same variable in the model A. These maps are useful to compare different runs or implementations of an industrial process in order to obtain the existing deviations between them, what makes it particularly useful for batch process monitoring.

APPLICATION CASES

Monitoring and Fault Detection of an Industrial Pilot Plant

The SOM has been used to monitor and detect faults in an industrial pilot plant (Domínguez González et al., 2004, Fuertes, et al., 2010). This plant is composed of a process main circuit and two utility circuits, associated to the temperature variable: the heating circuit and the cooling circuit. The process circuit controls four physical variables (pressure, flow, level and temperature) with recirculation. It is composed of two cascade tanks of 5 and 6.5 l each, which are associated to the level control loops.

In normal operation, the industrial plant runs a sequence of operations with all the aforementioned control loops. The control and data acquisition system is a DCS (distributed control system). Process data are sampled every 150ms and stored in a database by a link service. The SOM was trained for 50 epochs with the stored data, using the batch algorithm. The input space was made up of the 26 variables of the industrial process. The SOM had a 40×40 grid with a rectangular topology and a Gaussian neighborhood whose width decreased monotonically from 10 to 1.

After clustering, the SOM identified 17 different process conditions and the possible transitions between them (see Figure 7). After training, another sequence of operation of the plant was run to obtain a test data set. The direct projection of test data on the distance map followed sequentially the 17 clusters, in agreement to the transitions determined by the model, and the residual vectors remained near zero for all the process variables. This situation reveals that the test execution was very similar to the modeled one. Therefore, the model is self-consistent.

The online monitoring of the industrial plant is based on the direct projection of the current input sample onto the distance map, and the representation of its residual $\mathbf{r}(t) = \mathbf{x}(t) - \mathbf{m}_{c(t)}$ in the residual plot (Domínguez González et al., 2007). The selection of the winner unit was constrained to the reachable conditions according to the dynamic model of transitions. Figure 7, on the top rightmost corner, shows the evolution of the industrial plant through the four first process conditions. Since all those conditions are accessible according to the dynamic model, the evolution of

Figure 7. Picture of the industrial pilot plant and distance map with possible transitions between clusters (top) and residual representation (bottom)

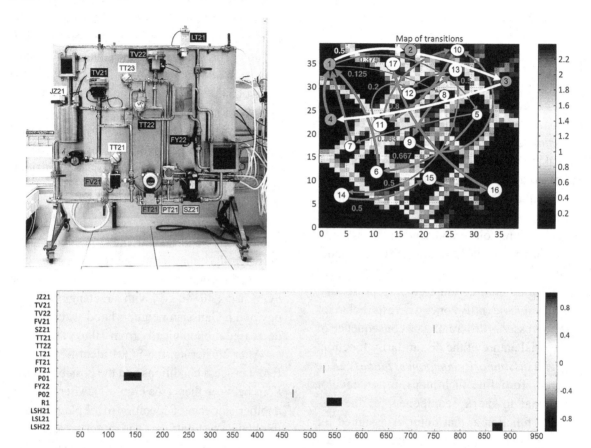

the process during this period was considered normal. However, in order to assess the usefulness of the dynamic model for fault detection, a sequence of faults was induced in the industrial scale model:

- Fault 1: heating circuit pump (P01)
- Fault 2: heating resistor (R1)
- Fault 3: Tank-4 switch (LSH22)

In the bottom part of Figure 7, it can be seen how the computation of residuals detects correctly all the faults around time samples 125, 525 and 860. The model identifies these situations as abnormal and associates them to the variables that actually caused the faults.

SUPERVISION OF A COLD ROLLING MILL

Some of the ideas described in this chapter were implemented in a visualization application –see Figure 8– for both offline and online analysis of coil data, which was conceived to help in the supervision and optimization of the performance of a cold rolling mill (Polzer et al., 2009). The application allows first to carry out an offline iterative analysis procedure on coil data previously stored in a database including the extraction of relevant features (static and dynamic features, including energies at configurable band frequencies). This analysis can be done in a completely interactive way, allowing visual selection of subsets of the

Figure 8. Screenshots of SOM-based data analysis and online monitoring applications analyzing rolling data from a cold rolling mill

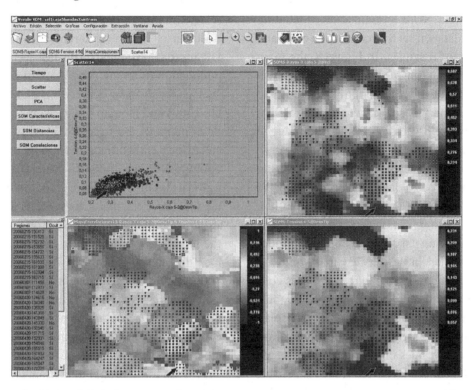

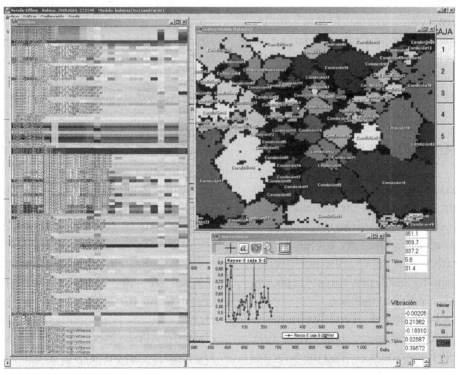

process data or features, along with a simultaneous display of different visualizations, such as scatter plots, PCA and SOM visualizations including component planes, u-matrix, correlation maps and visualization of residuals. In Figure 8, the main window of the data analysis application is shown displaying a scatter plot (left top), a correlation map (left bottom) and two component planes (right).

This iterative process allows to fine-tune the whole workflow (raw data → features → visualizations) that can be later exploited online, using coil and other process data acquired in real time for online monitoring and supervision. In Figure 8 the monitoring application deploys a SOM plane (right top) showing the different conditions identified and labeled in the process map, together with a pointer signaling the current process condition (bigger circle) and previous process conditions (smaller faded circles). It can also display a residual graph (left) which in online mode shows current residual values on its right and discards old values on its left, like a set of moving strips, one per feature.

This system is an important tool in a rolling mill at a factory of flat products of a large steel company, and is currently being used to assess the state of the rolls and to help deciding roll changes when they are considered defective.

FUTURE RESEARCH DIRECTIONS

The SOM-based process analysis methodology described here is rooted on the dimensionality reduction paradigm. There are two main questions on which advances can be very useful: 1) new projection methods that improve the quality of the projection mapping and 2) new ways to represent knowledge in an efficient manner.

There is a large branch of the literature devoted to methods for dimensionality reduction. Already in 1901, Pearson described the principal component analysis (PCA) method that led to a vast amount of works and still today is a refer-

ence method. Other approaches such as multidimensional scaling (MDS) (Togerson, 1958) and related methods (Sammon, 1969) have been also widely used. However, a renewed interest on the DR approach emerged on the last decade upon the publication of a new generation of DR methods such as local linear embedding LLE (Roweis et al., 2000) and Isomap (Tenenbaum et al., 2000). Such methods led to a new class of algorithms called local embeddings that involve a local model optimization for subsets of k nearest neighbors and a global alignment to obtain global coordinates for the local models, that usually leads to a singular value decomposition (SVD) problem. Some of the most known algorithms in this category are local linear embedding (LLE) (Roweis & Saul, 2000), ISOMAP (Tenenbaum, et al., 2000), Laplacian eigenmaps (LE) (Belkin et al., 2003), local tangent subspace alignment (LTSA) (Zhang et al., 2004), or Hessian eigenmaps (HE) (Donoho et al., 2003). Such methods allow projecting very large dimensional data points (such as, for instance, complete images stripped into a single vector) being able to capture the low dimensional structure of data. However, their application to real problems is still in a very immature state, particularly in the field of engineering applications. Many problems related to process supervision such as fault detection and identification, modeling or control can be reformulated in terms of very large dimensional vectors. One example of this can be found in batch processes, where data information of a whole batch could be included in a single vector for further projection.

Regarding visualization of knowledge, perhaps one of the most fertile and rather unexplored fields is the visualization of process dynamics. In this chapter a first approach for visualization of process dynamics using SOM was briefly described. However many issues remain open, such as the class of nonlinear processes that can be efficiently visualized by means of local models and the conditions required on the excitation signal (persistence of excitation) for a proper identification. On the other hand, it offers many exciting new research lines on visualization methods themselves, including analysis of MIMO systems (e.g. mapping the directionality of the responses with respect to operating point), visualization of novelties of dynamical behavior of the process (i.e., visualizing and tracking only the differences between the best model approximation by the SOM and the actual model of the process), or applications in control system design, such as developing maps of robustness properties or other performance indices of the control loop with respect to the working point, the control parameters or process parameters.

CONCLUSION

In this chapter a corpus of visualization tools based on the DR approach, some of them known and others newly developed by the authors, along with a methodology for process analysis and supervision has been presented. The proposed techniques make it possible to join around a single type of visualization (the plane) many different kinds of process related knowledge such as physical models, rules, cases, correlations and dynamical behavior. All these techniques are based on the dimension reduction principle, by which the states of the process are represented on a single 2D map. Since the representation of all these kinds of knowledge converge on a single space, the user can easily find connections among pieces of available knowledge of the process that were formerly sparse. The relationships between complementary sources of knowledge and information are indeed new knowledge.

ACKNOWLEDGMENT

This work was supported in part by the Spanish *Ministerio de Ciencia e Innovación* (MICINN) and with European FEDER funds under grants DPI2009-13398-C02-01 and DPI2009-13398-C02-02.

REFERENCES

Abonyi, J., Nemeth, S., Vincze, C., & Arva, P. (2003). Process analysis and product quality estimation by self-organizing maps with an application to polyethylene production. *Computers in Industry*, *52*(3), 221–234. doi:10.1016/S0166-3615(03)00128-3

Albazzaz, H., & Wang, X. Z. (2006). Historical data analysis based on plots of independent and parallel coordinates and statistical control limits. *Journal of Process Control*, *16*(2), 103–114. doi:10.1016/j.jprocont.2005.05.005

Alhoniemi, E., Hollmén, J., Simula, O., & Vesanto, J. (1999). Process monitoring and modeling using the self-organizing map. *Integrated Computer-Aided Engineering*, *6*(1), 3.

Barreto, G. A. (2007). Time series prediction with the self-organizing map: A review. *Perspectives of Neural-Symbolic Integration*, *77*, 135–158. doi:10.1007/978-3-540-73954-8_6

Belkin, M., & Niyogi, P. (2003). Laplacian eigenmaps for dimensionality reduction and data representation. *Neural Computation*, *15*(6), 1373–1396. doi:10.1162/089976603321780317

Card, S., Mackinlay, J., & Shneiderman, B. (1999). *Readings in information visualization. Using vision to think.* San Francisco, CA: Morgan Kaufmann Publishers.

Cho, J., Principe, J. C., Erdogmus, D., & Motter, M. A. (2006). Modeling and inverse controller design for an unmanned aerial vehicle based on the self-organizing map. *IEEE Transactions on Neural Networks*, *17*(2), 445–460. doi:10.1109/TNN.2005.863422

Díaz, G., Díaz Blanco, I., Arboleya, P., & Gómez-Aleixandre, J. (2006). Zero-sequence-based relaying technique for protecting power transformers and its performance assessment using unsupervised learning ANN. *European Transactions on Electrical Power, 16*(2), 147–160. doi:10.1002/etep.72

Díaz Blanco, I., Cuadrado Vega, A. A., Diez González, A. B., Loredo, L. R., Carrera, F. O., & Rodríguez, J. A. (2003). Visual predictive maintenance tool based on SOM projection techniques. *Revue de Metallurgie-Cahiers d Informations Techniques, 103*(3), 307–315.

Díaz Blanco, I., Domínguez González, M., Cuadrado, A. A., & Fuertes Martínez, J. J. (2008). A new approach to exploratory analysis of system dynamics using SOM. Applications to industrial processes. *Expert Systems with Applications, 34*(4), 2953–2965. doi:10.1016/j.eswa.2007.05.031

Domínguez González, M., Fuertes, J. J., Reguera, P., González, J. J., & Ramón, J. M. (2004). Maqueta industrial para docencia e investigacion. *Revista Iberoamericana de Automática e Informática Industrial, 1*(1), 58–63.

Domínguez González, M., Fuertes Martínez, J. J., Reguera, P., Díaz Blanco, I., & Cuadrado Vega, A. A. (2007). Internet based remote supervision of industrial processes using self organizing maps. *Engineering Applications of Artificial Intelligence, 20*(6), 757–765. doi:10.1016/j.engappai.2006.11.017

Domínguez González, M., Reguera, P., & Fuertes, J. J. (2005). Laboratorio Remoto para la Enseñanza de la Automática en la Universidad de León (España). *Revista Iberoamericana de Automática e Informática Industrial, 2*(2), 36–45.

Donoho, D. L., & Grimes, C. (2003). Hessian eigenmaps: Locally linear embedding techniques for high-dimensional data. *Proceedings of the National Academy of Sciences of the United States of America, 100*(10), 5591. doi:10.1073/pnas.1031596100

Ferreira de Oliveira, M. C., & Levkowitz, H. (2003). From visual data exploration to visual data mining: a survey. *IEEE Transactions on Visualization and Computer Graphics, 9*(3), 378–394. doi:10.1109/TVCG.2003.1207445

Fuertes, J. J., Domínguez, M., Reguera, P., Prada, M. A., Díaz, I., & Cuadrado, A. A. (2010). Visual dynamic model based on self-organizing maps for supervision and fault detection in industrial processes. *Engineering Applications of Artificial Intelligence, 23*(1), 8–17. doi:10.1016/j.engappai.2009.06.001

Grishin, V. G., Sula, A. S., & Ulieru, M. (2003). Pictorial analysis: A multi-resolution data visualization approach for monitoring and diagnosis of complex systems. *Information Sciences, 152*, 1–24. doi:10.1016/S0020-0255(03)00044-6

Guimarães, G., Sousa-Lobo, V., & Moura-Pires, F. (2003). A taxonomy of self-organizing maps for temporal sequence processing. *Intelligent Data Analysis, 4*, 269–290.

Harris, T. (1993, October). *A Kohonen SOM based, machine health monitoring system which enables diagnosis of faults not seen in the training set.* Paper presented at the Neural Networks, IJCNN '93-Nagoya.

He, S.-G., He, Z., Wang, G. A., & Li, L. (2009). *Data mining and knowledge discovery in real life applications: IN-TECH.*

Keim, D. A. (2002). Information visualization and visual data mining. *IEEE Transactions on Visualization and Computer Graphics, 8*(1), 1–8. doi:10.1109/2945.981847

Kohonen, T. (2001). *Self-organizing maps (Vol. 30)*. Berlin, Germany: Springer.

Kohonen, T., Oja, E., Simula, O., Visa, A., & Kangas, J. (1996). Engineering applications of the self-organizing map. *Proceedings of the IEEE, 84*(10), 1358–1384. doi:10.1109/5.537105

Kreuseler, M., & Schumann, H. (2002). A flexible approach for visual data mining. *IEEE Transactions on Visualization and Computer Graphics, 8*(1), 39–51. doi:10.1109/2945.981850

Laiho, J., Raivio, K., Lehtimäki, P., Hätönen, K., & Simula, O. (2005). Advanced analysis methods for 3G cellular networks. *IEEE Transactions on Wireless Communications, 4*(3), 930–942. doi:10.1109/TWC.2005.847088

Lehtimäki, P., Raivio, K., & Simula, O. (2003). Self-organizing operator maps in complex system analysis. *Lecture Notes in Computer Science*, 622–629. doi:10.1007/3-540-44989-2_74

Lin, C.-T., & Lee, C. S. G. (1996). *Neural fuzzy systems. A neuro-fuzzy synergism to intelligent systems*. Prentice Hall.

Moshou, D., Hostens, I., Papaioannou, G., & Ramon, H. (2000). *Wavelets and self-organising maps in electromyogram (EMG) analysis*. Laboratory of Kinesiology, Katholieke Universiteit Leuven.

Murata, T. (1989). Petri nets: properties, analysis, and applications. *Proceedings of the IEEE, 77*(4), 541–580. doi:10.1109/5.24143

Norris, J. R. (1997). *Markov chains*. Cambridge University Press.

Polzer, J., Markworth, M., Jelali, M., Redueles, J. L., Sanfilippo, F., & Lupinelli, M. … Cuadrado, A. (2009). *Intelligent soft-sensor technology and automatic model-based diagnosis for improved quality, control and maintenance of mill production lines (Softdetect)*. Research Fund for Coal and Steel. European Commission. ISBN: 978-92-79-11980-4

Porzio, G. C., & Ragozini, G. (2003). Visually mining off-line data for quality improvement. *Quality and Reliability Engineering International, 19*(4), 273–283. doi:10.1002/qre.588

Principe, J. C., Wang, L., & Motter, M. A. (1998). Local dynamic modeling with self-organizing maps and applications to nonlinear system identification and control. *Proceedings of the IEEE, 86*(11), 2240–2258. doi:10.1109/5.726789

Rendueles, J., L., González, J. A., Díaz Blanco, I., Diez González, A. B., Seijo, F., & Cuadrado Vega, A. A. (2006). Implementation of a virtual sensor on a hot dip galvanizing line for zinc coating thickness estimation. *Revue de Metallurgie-Cahiers d Informations Techniques, 103*(5), 226–232.

Roweis, S. T., & Saul, L. K. (2000). Nonlinear dimensionality reduction by locally linear embedding. *Science, 290*, 2323–2326. doi:10.1126/science.290.5500.2323

Sammon, J. W. (1969). A nonlinear mapping for data structure analysis. *IEEE Transactions on Computers, C-18*(5), 401–409. doi:10.1109/T-C.1969.222678

Tenenbaum, J. B., de Silva, V., & Langford, J. C. (2000). A global geometric framework for nonlinear dimensionality reduction. *Science, 290*, 2319–2323. doi:10.1126/science.290.5500.2319

Torgerson, W. (1958). *Theory and methods of scaling*. Wiley.

Ultsch, A. (2003). *U*-Matrix: A tool to visualize clusters in high dimensional data*. Dept. of Mathematics of Computer Science, University of Marburg.

Vapola, M., Simula, O., Kohonen, T., & Meriläinen, P. (1994, May). *Representation and identification of fault conditions of an anaesthesia system by means of the self organizing map*. Paper presented at the International Conference on Artificial Neural Networks (ICANN'94), Sorrento, Italy.

Vesanto, J. (1997, May). *Using the SOM and local models in time-series prediction.* Paper presented at the Workshop Self-Organizing Maps (WSOM), Helsinki University of Technology, Finland, June 4-6.

Vesanto, J. (1999). SOM-based data visualization methods. *Intelligent Data Analysis, 3*(2), 111–126. doi:10.1016/S1088-467X(99)00013-X

Vesanto, J., & Alhoniemi, E. (2000). Clustering of the self-organizing map. *IEEE Transactions on Neural Networks, 11*(3), 586–600. doi:10.1109/72.846731

Zhang, Z., & Zha, H. (2004). Principal manifolds and nonlinear dimension reduction via local tangent space alignment. *SIAM Journal on Scientific Computing, 26*(1), 313–338. doi:10.1137/S1064827502419154

ADDITIONAL READING

Corona, F., Mulas, M., Baratti, R., & Romagnoli, J. A. (2010). On the topological modeling and analysis of industrial process data using the SOM. *Computers & Chemical Engineering, 34*(12), 2022–2032. doi:10.1016/j.compchemeng.2010.07.002

Gertler, J. J. (1988). Survey of model-based failure detection and isolation in complex plants. *IEEE Control Systems Magazine, 8*(6), 3–11. doi:10.1109/37.9163

Haykin, S. (1999). *Neural networks: A comprehensive foundation.* Prentice-Hall, Inc.

Himberg, J., Ahola, J., Alhoniemi, E., Vesanto, J., & Simula, O. (2001). *The self-organizing map as a tool in knowledge engineering.*

Isermann, R. (1997). Supervision, fault-detection and fault-diagnosis methods. An introduction. *Control Engineering Practice, 5*(5), 639–652. doi:10.1016/S0967-0661(97)00046-4

Isermann, R. (2005). Model-based fault-detection and diagnosis-status and applications. *Annual Reviews in Control, 29*(1), 71–85. doi:10.1016/j.arcontrol.2004.12.002

Jamsa-Jounela, S.-L., Vermasvuori, M., Endén, P., & Haavisto, S. (2003). A process monitoring system based on the Kohonen self-organizing maps. *Control Engineering Practice, 11*(1), 83–92. doi:10.1016/S0967-0661(02)00141-7

Kaski, S. (1997). *Data exploration using self-organizing maps.* Helsinki University of Technology.

Kasslin, M., Kangas, J., & Simula, O. (1992). *Process state monitoring using self-organizing maps.*

Kohonen, T. (1990). The self-organizing map. *Proceedings of the IEEE, 78*(9), 1464–1480. doi:10.1109/5.58325

Markou, M., & Singh, S. (2003a). Novelty detection: A review. Part 1: Statistical approaches. *Signal Processing, 83*(12), 2481–2497. doi:10.1016/j.sigpro.2003.07.018

Markou, M., & Singh, S. (2003b). Novelty detection: A review. Part 2: Neural network based approaches. *Signal Processing, 83*(12), 2499–2521. doi:10.1016/j.sigpro.2003.07.019

Patton, R. J., & López-Toribio, C. J. (1998, October). *Artificial intelligence approaches to fault diagnosis.* Paper presented at the IEE Colloquium on Update on Developments in Intelligent Control (Ref. No. 1998/513).

Ritter, H., Martinetz, T., Schulten, K., Barsky, D., Tesch, M., & Kates, R. (1992). *Neural computation and self-organizing maps: An introduction.* Addison Wesley Longman Publishing Co., Inc.

Simula, O., & Alhoniemi, E. (1999). SOM based analysis of pulping process data. *Proceedings the Engineering Applications of Bio-Inspired Artificial Neural Networks, International Work-Conference on Artificial and Natural Neural Networks, IWANN'99, Vol. 2, Lecture Notes in Computer Science 1607,* Berlin, Germany.

Sorsa, T., Koivo, H. N., & Kovisto, H. (1991). Neural networks in process fault diagnosis. *IEEE Transactions on Systems, Man, and Cybernetics*, *21*(4), 815–849. doi:10.1109/21.108299

Tryba, V., & Goser, K. (1991). *Self-organizing feature maps for process control in chemistry.* Paper presented at the Artificial Neural Networks, Amsterdam, Netherlands.

Ultsch, A., & Siemon, H. P. (1990). *Kohonen's self organizing feature maps for exploratory data analysis.* Paper presented at the INNC Paris 90.

Venkatasubramanian, V., Rengaswamy, R., Yin, K., & Kavuri, S. N. (2003). A review of process fault detection and diagnosis. Part I: Quantitative model-based methods. *Computers & Chemical Engineering, 27*(3), 293–311. doi:10.1016/S0098-1354(02)00160-6

Vesanto, J. (2002). *Data exploration process based on the self-organizing map.* Helsinki University of Technology, Department of Computer Science and Engineering. FIN-02015 HUT. Finland.

Ypma, A., & Duin, R. P. W. (1997). Novelty detection using self-organizing maps. *Progress in Connectionist-Based Information Systems, 2,* 1322–1325.

KEY TERMS AND DEFINITIONS

Dimensionality Reduction (DR): This term describes a paradigm for which a high dimensional data set is transformed on a low dimensional space (generally 2D or 3D for visualization), without significant loss of information, by exploiting the fact that input data in many problems present low-dimensional structures due to physical relationships and constraints.

Industrial Processes: In this chapter, this term is considered from a systems theory point of view, as a combination of different types subsystems, often including mechanical, chemical, electrical and/or computational ones. Industrial processes often present a complex behavior resulting from coupling of subsystems as well as from the large number of variables and modes of operation. This fact often makes it difficult to explain certain behaviors using only first principles models, being necessary to use methods for experimental and data-based models and techniques, such as data mining and/or visualization.

Novelty Detection: This term refers to the identification of new or unknown behaviors of the process according to a given model.

Process State: The values of a minimum set of variables (known as state variables) that allow determining the evolution of the process outputs in the future with the knowledge about the evolution of the inputs. In complex processes it is generally not possible to consider all the state variables because its number is very high or they cannot be obtained, so a simplifying assumption is made and a set of measures that is considered to summarize the process state is taken instead.

Self-Organizing Map (SOM): The SOM is an unsupervised algorithm that produces a low dimensional, discrete and smooth mapping from high dimensional input data.

Supervision: This term is understood in a general sense, involving the use of methods and techniques aiming to obtain information about the process for further improving. Supervision can be carried out in two complementary manners: a) to track the process state; this involves monitoring, fault detection and identification, quality control, etc., and b) to get insight on the process nature, involving process modeling in all its forms, looking for ways to modify the process for better performance.

Visual Data Mining: Data mining is a class of procedures to extract useful information and knowledge from data. With the visual approach, the user is directly involved in the data mining process, which takes advantage of the human perceptual abilities by means of visual tools or techniques.

Chapter 12
Learning and Explaining the Impact of Enterprises' Organizational Quality on their Economic Results

Marko Pregeljc
University of Ljubljana, Slovenia

Erik Štrumbelj
University of Ljubljana, Slovenia

Miran Mihelčič
University of Ljubljana, Slovenia

Igor Kononenko
University of Ljubljana, Slovenia

ABSTRACT

The authors employed traditional and novel machine learning to improve insight into the connections between the quality of an organization of enterprises as a type of formal social units and the results of enterprises' performance in this chapter. The analyzed data set contains 72 Slovenian enterprises' economic results across four years and indicators of their organizational quality. The authors hypothesize that a causal relationship exists between the latter and the former. In the first part of a two-part process, they use several classification algorithms to study these relationships and to evaluate how accurately they predict the target economic results. However, the most successful models were often very complex and difficult to interpret, especially for non-technical users. Therefore, in the second part, the authors take advantage of a novel general explanation method that can be used to explain the influence of individual features on the model's prediction. Results show that traditional machine-learning approaches are successful at modeling the dependency relationship. Furthermore, the explanation of the influence of the input features on the predicted economic results provides insights that have a meaningful economic interpretation.

DOI: 10.4018/978-1-4666-1806-0.ch012

INTRODUCTION

The central question of this article is whether the novel intelligent data analysis methods can provide insight into the connections between the quality of an organization and its economic performance. We adopt the definition of an organization as a set of relationships between members of a formal social unit that are characteristics of the social unit and that ensure its existence, development, and rational achievement of the enterprise's goals (Mihelčič, 1992a). According to this definition, at the core of an organization there are organizational relationships; therefore, it is logically assumed that the very same relationships determine the quality of the organization.

As the analysis of Mihelčič (1992b) argues, the most relevant goal-oriented relationships can be divided into five basic types: technical, personnel, coordinative, communicational, and motivational. These relationships and their implementation should be evaluated, either directly through different aspects of the relationships' conditioned organizational life or indirectly through organizational contextual factors. Whichever approach is used, particular interdependent indicators as measures of organizational quality can be derived (e.g. value or worth, orientation towards people or technique, reliability, commitment, consistency, and provision of information). When such indicators of organizational quality are determined, we can explore their connections with the enterprise's economic results.

In our study, we determined the organizational quality and economic results of 72 Slovenian enterprises. The resulting data are suitable for intelligent data analysis, using traditional statistical and machine-learning methods. We used Logistic Regression, Naïve Bayes, Random Forests, and Artificial Neural Networks to evaluate the extent to which economic results can be predicted from indicators of organizational quality. Although our results reveal that the indicators of organizational quality have predictive power, the best perform-

ing model for a particular indicator of economic performance is often complex and difficult to interpret. Exploring the data with different types of models also makes comparison across models very difficult. To deal with these issues, we take advantage of a novel general explanation method (Štrumbelj & Kononenko, 2010). This method can be applied to any type of prediction model in a uniform way to provide insight into how the input features influence the model's prediction. This also simplifies the comparison of different types of models.

The remainder of this chapter is dedicated to explaining the economic background, with an emphasis on measuring organizational quality, and to describing our economic data. In the following sections, we first provide some background on general explanation methods and describe the explanation method we used in our study. This is followed by a description and the results of two sets of experiments that illustrate the usefulness of the explanation method and how it was successfully applied in our study. Before we conclude the chapter, we provide some ideas for further research.

BACKGROUND

Organizational Outcomes and their Measures

Observing the roles of members in an enterprise can lead to five fundamental relationships, defined as technical, personnel, coordinative, communicational and motivational issues, which can be arranged in pairs of relationships, as a cluster, a honeycomb or a wedge, or an inverted pyramid, as shown on Figure 1 (Mihelčič, 2007).

As part of the method of assessing the quality of organization of enterprise, known as MUKOZ (Mihelčič, 1992b), an extensive list of aspects of relationships was developed as distinct expressions of organizational events, acts, and conse-

Figure 1. Organization as a structure of relationships (adapted from: Mihelčič, 2007)

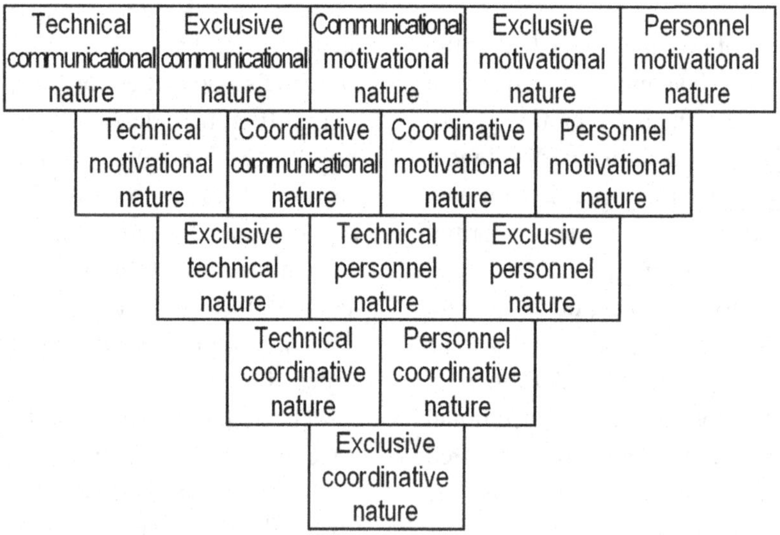

Technical communicational nature	Exclusive communicational nature	Communicational motivational nature	Exclusive motivational nature	Personnel motivational nature

Technical motivational nature	Coordinative communicational nature	Coordinative motivational nature	Personnel motivational nature

Exclusive technical nature	Technical personnel nature	Exclusive personnel nature

Technical coordinative nature	Personnel coordinative nature

Exclusive coordinative nature

quences of activities. For practical evaluation, the list was narrowed down to the 10 most significant aspects of each of 15 relationships, i.e. to a total of 150 aspects. For each aspect, a scale of corresponding descriptions of six quality states or levels of these aspects from 0 to 5 was prepared, like in an EFQM model from European Foundation for Quality Management. Level 0 denotes the worst state, where it is not possible to speak of the quality of the observed aspect at all, while Level 5 is the ideal state of the aspect. The calculation of an average mark for a particular relationship from all of its aspects reflects the full spectrum of quality (Dutton & Ragins 2007, 3).

It is also possible to calculate this grade by estimating the quality of the contextual factors, which occur in these aspects with different degrees of importance. The contextual factors of relationships are particular elements or factors appearing within different organizational arrangements (or settings), which influence and define the type of relationship in this particular classification of relationships. Thus far, the list of contextual factors in the aforementioned MUKOZ method contains 49 such factors (see Table 1).

Assessing the quality of relationships through organizational aspects or through contextual factors yields the six indicators of the quality of the organization: the organization's "value or worth" indicator, the organization's "reliability" indicator, the organization's "orientation" indicator, the "organizational commitment" indicator or "level of identification", the "organizational consistency" indicator and the "informational supply" or "information provision" indicator. The calculation of these is presented next.

The "Organization's Value or Worth" Indicator

The calculation of organization's value (v) is based on the sum of the marks for the fifteen relationships, using the following equation:

$$v = \left[\sqrt[4]{\left(\frac{n}{75} \right)^5} \right] \cdot 100, \tag{1}$$

where v stands for the "organization's value" indicator (or worth) and n stands for the sum of the

Table 1. List of contextual factors of relationships

achievements (individual)	communication channels	customer	group work	managers	problems	tasks assignments
achievements (of group)	enterprise's members	databases	groups	means of production	receivers of messages	technology
authority	enterprise's goals	distribution and assembly of work	incentives	members' variety of skills (competence fields)	results	training
business process	control	disturbance (in the enterprise)	innovations	messages	sanctions	values
business process elements	co-operator	disturbance (in the environment)	interests	organizational levels	senders of messages	work stations
business results	creativity	environment	jobs	organizational rules	span of control	working conditions
changes in the environment	criteria	equality of employees	knowledge of staff	organizational units	tasks	working time

marks for all fifteen relationships. The maximum value possible is 100. Eq. (1) has the following background:

- Division by 75 normalizes the maximum value of 75 (in the case of an ideal organization) to 100 as a generally accepted value of perfection.
- Mathematical reason for the fifth power and the fourth root is the ratio of 100/75 (abbreviated to the 4/3) and then adding 1 in the numerator as well as in the denominator (well-known approach from estimators in statistics).
- A power function deliberately emphasizes that in the beginning (from 0 onwards) value increases at a slower rate (compared to simple linear dependence), then faster (when closer to the ideal sum of 75). This is similar as the resonance in physics – the organization is gaining its acceleration (and hence value) when more and more of its components are closely to their maximum. For more information see (Mihelčič, 2008).

The "Organization's Reliability" Indicator

The calculation of "organization's reliability" (*or*) is based on the calculation of the standard deviation of the marks for individual relationships from the highest possible value (M=5):

$$or = \left[5 - \sqrt{\frac{1}{N} \cdot \sum (x - M)^2} \right] \cdot 20. \qquad (2)$$

In this calculation, N denotes the number of data (N=15 relationships).

Experiments show that this indicator would be better compared with other indicators if its value is patched with the following formula:

$$or_{c(omparable)} = \sqrt[4]{\left(\frac{or}{100} \right)^5} \cdot 4. \qquad (3)$$

The maximum possible value is 100.

The "Organization's Orientation" Indicator

The calculation of the "organization's orientation" indicator O is based on adding together all the grades of relationships located on the left side of the cluster (emphasize on the technique and communication), and summing up all grades of relationships from the right side of the cluster (emphasize on employees and their motivation). Finally, both totals are included in the following formula:

$$O = 90 + \frac{(n_l - n_r) \cdot 180}{60}, \qquad (4)$$

where n_l denotes the sum of the grades of relationships from the left side of the cluster and n_r denotes the sum of the grades of relationships from the right side of the cluster. The range of possible values is between 45° and 135°.

The "Organizational Commitment" Indicator or "Level of Identification"

To obtain the value of the "organizational commitment" indicator, all five grades for motivational relationships (exclusive motivational and combined with other four relationships) are added, and this sum is patched (multiplied) with a normalization factor (3 because the total number of relationships is three times more) and finally this value should be included as n in the basic Eq. (1), the maximum possible value for the "organizational commitment" indicator or "level of identification" is 100.

The "Organizational Consistency" Indicator

To obtain the value of the "organizational consistency" indicator, the grades of all five co-ordinative relationships (exclusive coordinative and com-

bined with other four relationships) are summed up, and the result is corrected (multiplied) with a normalization factor (3 in this case, because we again have five coordinative relationships, but fifteen in total) and finally this value should be inserted as n in the basic Eq. (1), the maximum possible value for the "organizational consistency" indicator is 100.

The "Informational Supply" or "Information Provision" Indicator

The last indicator of the MUKOZ methodology is the "informational supply" or "information provision" indicator. All five communicational relationships' (exclusive communicational and combined with the other four relationships) are summed up, and this sum is then corrected (multiplied) with a normalization factor (3, because besides the five communicational relationships we have in total fifteen relationships i.e. three times more). This corrected value is finally inserted as n in the basic Eq. (1). The maximum possible value for the "informational supply" or "information provision" indicator is 100.

Data Description

In our experiment, the connections between the organizational quality of enterprises and their economic results are explored. For this purpose, 72 Slovenian enterprises' organizational quality were assessed in 2007 according to the MUKOZ methodology (Mihelčič, 1992b). We also gathered publicly accessible economic indicators for the 2006, 2007, 2008 and 2009 business years. In this sense, the research has a longitudinal character.

Economic data for the assessed enterprises were collected through the Agency of the Republic of Slovenia for Public Legal Records and Related Services (AJPES). The following economic indicators were observed: total operating efficiency, business operating efficiency, capital profitability, net profitability of revenues, profitability of operating revenues, profitability of assets, value added per employee, proportion of fixed assets in assets, proportion of current assets in assets, proportion of investments in assets, average monthly wage per employee.

Data about the quality of the organization were obtained with the MUKOZ methodology through a survey in the form of a questionnaire. Due to timing reason, the original questionnaire was halved, i.e., 75 organizational aspects (5 organizational aspects for each of the 15 relationships) were measured instead of 150. In addition, the respondents assessed the quality of the organization of their enterprises through the evaluation of 49 organizational factors in the form of the frequency of agreement for their enterprise (six levels from "never applies" to "always applies"). Estimations obtained from both sources were averaged and used to calculate the six previously described indicators of organizational quality.

We used (separately) all three sets of input features: the six indicators of organizational quality, the originally surveyed scores of 15 organizational relationships, and the scores of 49 organizational contextual factors. All input features were treated as continuous variables. Target economic indicators were indexed with the average in the branch and discretized into three classes of equal frequency (low, medium, high).

The three sets of features and 11 economic indicators over four years resulted in a total of 132 classification data sets. However, the focus of this chapter is the use of a general explanation method. Therefore, in the experimental part, we have omitted the results for most of these data sets and limited ourselves to two sets of examples, which effectively illustrate the explanation method.

GENERAL EXPLANATION METHOD AND VIZUALIZATION

In a typical machine learning scenario a machine learning algorithm is used to construct a model of the relationships between the input features and the target variable with the purpose of predicting the target variable for new instances. Explaining the learned relationships is also an important part of machine learning. Some models, such as additive models and small decision trees, are inherently transparent and require little or no additional postprocessing (Becker et al., 1997; Jakulin et al., 2005; Možina et al., 2004; Szafron, 2006). Other, more complex and often better performing models are non-transparent and require additional explanation. Therefore, model-specific methods have been developed for models such as artificial neural networks and Support Vector Machines SVM (see Additional Reading section).

In practice (especially for users without a background in intelligent data analysis, such as economists, medical experts, etc...) dealing with several different explanation methods requires undesirable additional effort and also makes it difficult to compare models of different types. To address this issue, general explanation methods are used – methods, which treat the model as a black-box and can be used independent of the model's type. Most general explanation methods are based on computing the marginal effect of features (Lemaire, 2008; Zien, 2009). This approach is computationally efficient. It is also effective as long as the model is additive (that is, as long as the features do not interact). However, several widely-used machine learning models are not additive, which leads to misleading and incorrect explanations of the importance and influence of features (Štrumbelj & Kononenko, 2010).

Unlike existing general explanation methods, our method takes into account not only the marginal effect of a single feature at a time but also the effect of every subset of features. The idea behind the method is to compute the contributions of individual features to the model's prediction for a particular instance by decomposing the difference between the model's prediction for the given instance and the model's expected prediction, that is the model's predictions if none of the features' values are known.

We adopt, with only minor modifications for classification, the notation used in (Štrumbelj & Kononenko, 2011). Let $A = A_1 \times A_2 \times ... \times A_n$ be our feature space, where each feature A_i is a set of values. Let p be the probability mass function defined on the sample space A. Let $f_c: A \to [0,1]$ describe the classification model's prediction for class value c. Our goal is a general explanation method which can be used with any model, so no other assumptions are made about f_c. Therefore, we are limited to changing the inputs of the model and observing the outputs.

Let $S = \{A_1,..., A_n\}$ be the set of all features. The influence of a certain subset Q of S in a given instance $x \in A$ is defined as:

$$\Delta(Q)(x) = E[f \mid values\ of\ features\ in\ Q\ for\ x] - E[f] \quad (5)$$

The value of the above function for the entire set of features S is exactly the difference between the model's prediction for a given instance and the model's expected prediction that we wish to decompose. Note that we omit the class value in the notation of f.

Suppose that for every subset of features Q the value of $\Delta(Q)$ is known. The goal is to decompose $\Delta(S)$ in a way that assigns to each feature a contribution that is fair with respect to the features influence on the model's prediction. In (Štrumbelj & Kononenko, 2010) a solution is proposed that is equivalent to the Shapley value (Shapley, 1956) for the coalitional game with the n features as players and Δ as the characteristic function. The contribution of the i-th feature is defined as follows:

$$\phi_i(x) = \sum_{Q \subseteq S\{i\}} \frac{|Q|!(|S|-|Q|-1)!}{|S|!} (\Delta(Q \cup \{i\})(x) - \Delta(Q)(x)). \quad (6)$$

These contributions have some desirable properties. Their sum for a given instance x equals $\Delta(S)$, which was our initial goal and ensures implicit normalization. A feature that does not influence the prediction in any way will be assigned a 0 contribution. And, features that influence the prediction in a symmetrical way will be assigned equal contributions. For more information on the Shapley value and its applications see (Moratti & Patrone, 2008).

The computation of Eq. (6) is infeasible for large n as the computation time grows exponentially with n. The following approximation algorithm is proposed in (Štrumbelj & Kononenko, 2010). Assume that p, the probability distribution of instances, is such that individual features are mutually independent. For a discussion of the effect of this assumption see (Štrumbelj & Kononenko, 2011). This assumption allows us to transform Eq. (5) into

$$\Delta(Q)(x) = \sum_{y \in A} p(y)(f(\tau(x,y,Q)) - f(y)) \quad (7)$$

Here $\tau(x,y,W) = (z_1, z_2,..., z_n)$, where $z_i = x_i$ if $i \in W$ and $z_i = y_i$, otherwise. Eq. (7) says that if individual features are distributed independently then the expectation, conditional to some features' values being known, can be expressed as the average across all instances while the known features' values remain fixed. We use an alternative formulation of the Shapley value

$$\phi_i(x) = \frac{1}{n!} \sum_{O \in \pi(n)} \left(\Delta(\mathrm{Pr}^i(O) \cup \{i\})(x) - \Delta(\mathrm{Pr}^i(O))(x)\right), \quad (8)$$

where $\pi(n)$ is the set of all permutations of n and $Pr^i(O)$ is the set of features which precede the i-th feature in permutation $O \in \pi(n)$. The equivalence of Eq. (6) and Eq. (8) can easily be proven by counting the number of appearances of the term

$\Delta(\mathrm{Pr}^i(O) \cup \{i\})(x)$ and the term $\Delta(\mathrm{Pr}^i(O))(x)$ on the right hand side of Eq. (6) and Eq. (8). Combining Eq. (7) and (8) gives

$$\phi_i(x) =$$
$$\frac{1}{n!} \sum_{O \in \pi(n)} \sum_{y \in A} p(y) \cdot (f(\tau(x, y, \mathrm{Pr}^i(O) \cup \{i\})) - f(\tau(x, y, \mathrm{Pr}^i(O)))) \tag{9}$$

which facilitates random sampling.

For a global overview of a feature's contribution, we first define the contribution of the *i*-th feature's value *j* as the expected value of that feature's contribution when its value is *j* (see Eq. (9)):

$$\psi_{i,j} = \sum_{x \in A, x[i]=j} p(x)\phi_i(x) = \sum_{x \in A} p(x)\phi_i(x) =$$

$$= \frac{1}{n!} \sum_{O \in \pi(N)} \sum_{x \in A} p(x)(f(x') - f(x)) \tag{10}$$

$$= \sum_{x \in A} p(x)(f(x') - f(x))$$

where *x'* is instance *x* with the *i*-th feature's value set to *j*. While Eq. (6) (or, equvalently Eq. (8)) is a feature value's contribution in a particular instance, Eq. (10) is the expected contribution of a value across all instances. Visualizing this expected contribution across all values of a feature provides information about the feature's influence on the model. Again, random sampling can be used to approximate Eq. (10) as illustrated with the following algorithm:

Approximating $\psi_{i,j}$, the global importance of the *i*-th feature's value *j* for model *f*. Take *m* samples.

$\psi_{i,j} \leftarrow 0$,
for k=1 to m do
select (at random) instance $y \in A$
$x_i \leftarrow$ set *i*-th feature to *j*, take other values from

    y
$\psi_{i,j} \leftarrow \psi_{i,j} + f(x_1) - f(y)$
end for

$$\psi_{i,j} \leftarrow \frac{\psi_{i,j}}{m}$$

Note that "at random" in the above algorithm refers to constructing an instance by drawing the value of each feature according to its distribution, usually by sampling from the data set.

Let us illustrate the use of the features' local and global contributions (see Eq. (9) and (10)) using a simple data set with 5 numerical features $A_1,..., A_5$ with unit domains [0,1]. The binary class value equals 1 if $A_1 > 0.5$ or $A_2 > 0.7$ or $A_3 > 0.5$. Otherwise, the class value is 0. Therefore, only the first three features are relevant for predicting the class value.

This problem can easily be modeled with a decision tree. Figure 2 shows the results of explaining such a decision tree.

The global contributions of each feature's values are plotted separately. The black points are obtained by running the approximation algorithm for the corresponding feature and its value that corresponds to the value on the x-axis. The lighter line corresponds to the standard deviation of the samples across all values of that particular feature and can therefore be interpreted as the overall importance of the feature. The lighter lines reveal that only the first three features are important. The black lines reveal the areas where features contribute towards/against class value 1. For example, if the value of feature A_1 is higher than 0.5 it strongly contributes towards class value being 1. If it is lower, it contributes against class value being 1.

For example, the instance *x = (0.47, 0.82, 0.53, 0.58, 0.59)* belongs to class 1, which the decision tree correctly predicts. The visualization in Figure 3 shows the individual features' contributions for this instance (Eq. (9)).

The last two features have a 0 contribution. The only feature value that contributes towards class = 1 is $A_2 = 0.82$, while the remaining two features' values have a negative contribution.

Figure 2. Explanation of a decision tree

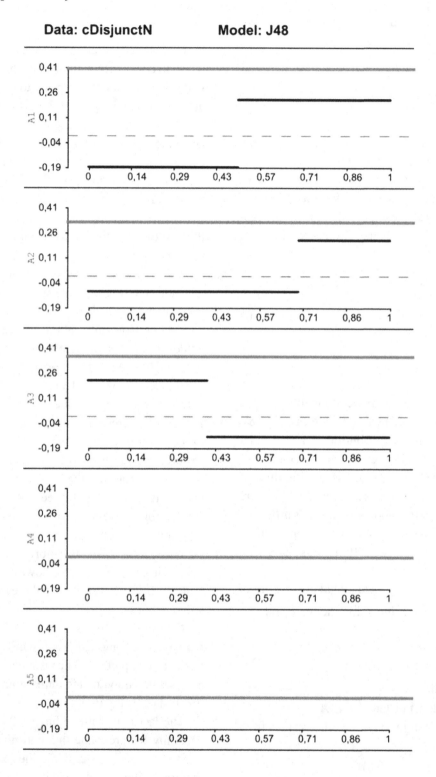

Figure 3. Visualization of the individual features' contributions for particular instance

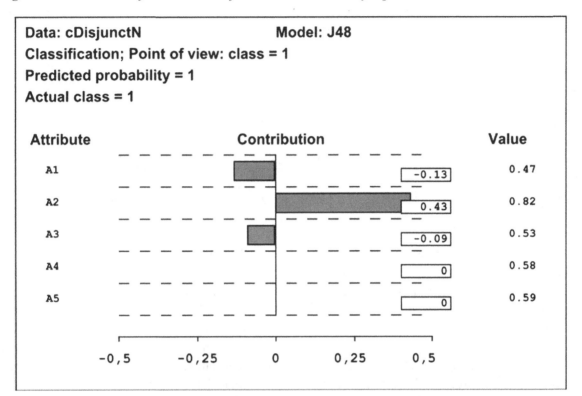

Results and Economic Interpretation

In this section, we use two sets of examples to illustrate the advantages of the described explanation method and how we used the method for the purposes of our study. The first set of examples is based on the data set with the quality of organization indicators as input features and the indicator of economic profitability index for the years 2008 and 2009 (separately) as the target variable. The second set of examples is based on the data set with 49 organizational factors as input features and the economic indicator of business operating efficiency index for 2009 as the target variable. We will refer to the first and second set of examples as Experiment 1 and Experiment 2, respectively.

In both experiments, we used the following well-known classification models: Naïve Bayes, Logistic Regression, **R**andom **F**orests (RF), and a Multilayer Perceptron artificial neural network.

To construct the models, we used the Weka (Hall et al., 2009) Java library. Table 2 shows the estimated generalization errors for all classification models and both experiments.

The Random Forest classifier is the best performing classifier for both years in Experiment 1. It is the most accurate and has the lowest Brier score. The Random Forest classifier is a less transparent model, making it difficult to interpret the connection between the input features and the target variable. However, using the described explanation method (using High as the target class value; see Section 2), provides us with some insight into the importance and influence of the input features. We can also inspect whether and how the latter changed between the years 2008 and 2009 (see Figures 4 and 5).

Figures 4 and 5 illustrate the interpretation of the RF model for the two consecutive years, how the indicators of the quality of the organization

Table 2. Classifier accuracy and Brier score (or loss) obtained with 10-fold cross-validation. The accuracy and Brier score of predicting according to the class value distribution on the training folds are included as a baseline for comparison (default).

	Experiment 1				Experiment 2	
	2008		2009		2009	
	Accuracy	Brier	Accuracy	Brier	Accuracy	Brier
Logistic Regression	0.358	0.2517	0.407	0.2554	0.533	0.2061
Multilayer Perceptron	0.313	0.2479	0.373	0.2505	0.667	0.1675
Naive Bayes	0.284	0.2942	0.237	0.2968	0.450	0.2282
Random Forest	0.493	0.2091	0.492	0.2280	0.450	0.2298
Default	**0.343**	**0.2287**	**0.339**	**0.2295**	**0.343**	**0.2295**

of the enterprise affect the achievement of the (index) indicator of economic profitability of operating revenues, which is defined as the ratio between operating profit/operating loss and total revenues.

A comparison between the interpretations of the findings of the RF model in both years yields the following conclusions about how the six organizational indicators influence the model's prediction for high economic profitability of operating revenues:

- An organization's high value or worth contributes to high profitability in both years. The interpolated global trend is positively oriented. An organization's low value or worth predicts relatively low profitability, whereas an organization's high value or worth predicts comparatively higher profitability of operating revenues (Figure 4 and 5 at the top). That conclusion is more pronounced in the first year (Figure 4) than in the other (Figure 5), which logically reflects the decline in the expressive power of the organization's state through time (the state of the quality of the organization was recorded only once, then it was compared with the economic results through several successive years).

- The indicator of the orientation exposes in the first year the finding that for high profitability the most favorable orientation is around 95° (degrees). That is, an organization labeled as limited self-initiative with focus more on technology and technique than on people. In the year of the global financial crisis (2009) it moved to 90°, where personnel and technical relationships are balanced or even with a slight emphasis on human resources and motivational relationships (an organization labeled as promoted self-initiative with more emphasis on people than on the technique). That finding indicates the crucial importance of motivational mechanisms in crisis times, together with confidence in people.

- The importance of commitment increases in the crisis year (2009) with regard to the previous year (2008). This again confirms, from a different perspective, the importance of motivational mechanisms for achieving a high profitability of operating revenues in crisis times and situations. When most other resources in crisis times are limited, the importance of people and their motivation increases.

- Greater consistency has a negative impact, which is reduced in the following year (2009). A strict and consistent approach,

Figure 4. Visualization of how the Random Forest's predictions of economic profitability of operating revenues in 2008 are influenced by organizational quality feature

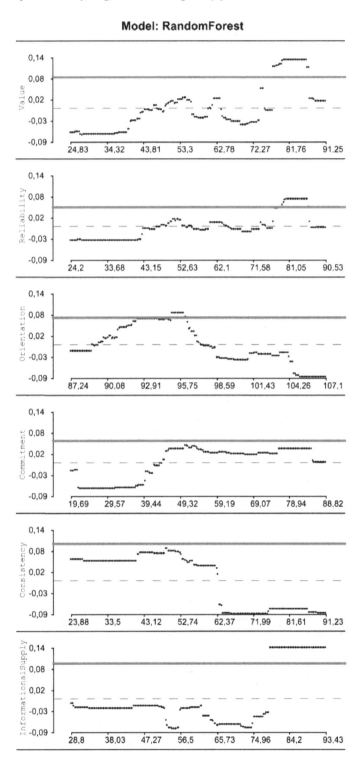

Figure 5. Visualization of how the Random Forest's predictions of economic profitability of operating revenues in 2009 are influenced by organizational quality feature

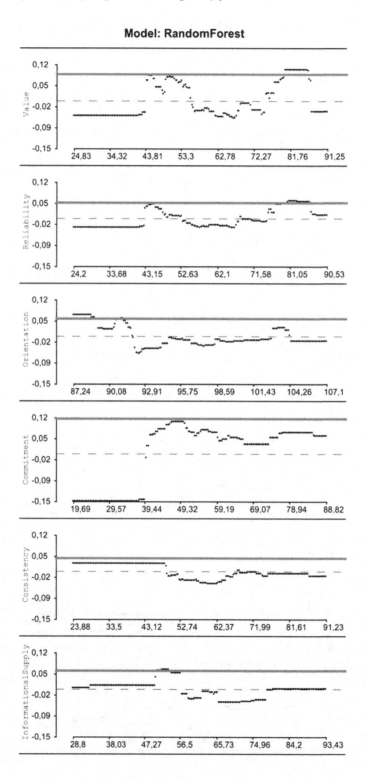

perhaps even extremely bureaucratic, does not have a favorable effect towards high profitability. The collected data show that it is better to allow at least some creative disorder. In the following year (2009), the impact of the consistency is reduced due to decreasing of expressive power of the once-recorded image of the quality of the organization. Furthermore, in a crisis, the mix of many other external influences in environment correspondingly reduces the influence of such internal factors.

- High informational supply has a positive effect, which is reduced in the following year (2009). The interpolated general trend is increasingly linearly positive. It is interesting to note that in order to achieve good economic results, the worst approach is semi-efficient information. This is in accordance with the theory of communications: without proper confidence, which requires further verification of the correctness of information, we cause unnecessary system load and consequently worse outcomes.

- An organization's higher reliability indicator has a positive impact in both years. An organization's low reliability in general leads to lower profitability. An organization's high reliability leads to higher profitability of operating revenues. In the organization's reliability indicator, the congruent ordering of all organizational elements is composed (technical, personnel, communications, coordination and motivation). The calculation of an organization's reliability indicator is based on the deviations between them. However, the curves of both years conclude with a warning that over-congruity (without deviations and accentuations) is not optimal, suggesting a slight decrease at the highest levels. This supports the theoretical basis of unfavorable sleepy non-responsive 'perfect'

organizations in the case of over-harmony, which is especially critical for responsiveness in crisis times. This experimental result is in accordance with Herbert Simon's theory about the inappropriateness of perfectionism.

In Experiment 2, all four classifiers are more accurate than default predictions. The Multilayer Perceptron performs best, while Logistic Regression is also more accurate than the remaining two classifiers. Note that we used ReliefF (Robnik-Šikonja & Kononenko, 2003) to preprocess the data set for Experiment 2 and select a subset of relevant features. Out of 49 organizational factors, the following four relevant input features were included: Organizational Rules, Technology, Creativity, and Staff Knowledge.

Logistic Regression is a generalized additive classifier, which makes it relatively easy to interpret; we can plot each feature's marginal effect function (see, for example, Jakulin et al., 2005; Možina et al., 2004). Therefore, in situations where interpretability is important, we might prefer Logistic Regression over the better-performing but non-transparent Multilayer Perceptron artificial neural network. However, the explanation method allows us to explain both models in the same way, which makes the Multilayer Perceptron more transparent and facilitates comparison.

The effect of the four input features on both models and the differences between the two models offer insight into the relationship between organizational factors and business operating efficiency (see Figures 6 and 7).

A comparison of interpretations by the various models in the same year yields to the following conclusions about the effect of individual input features on the likelihood of greater business operating efficiency:

- The predicted probability of high efficiency decreases with increasingly regularized organizational rules. Very strict organiza-

Figure 6. Visualization of how the organizational factors affect the the Multilayer Perceptron model's prediction of business operating efficiency in 2009

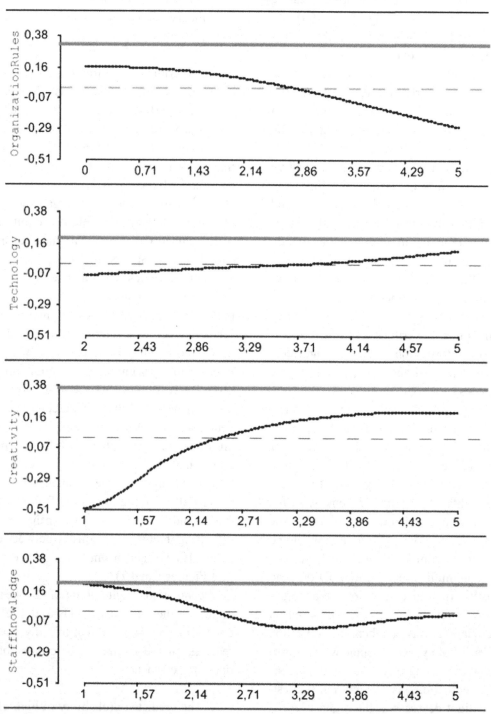

Figure 7. Visualization of how the organizational factors affect the the Logistic Regression model's prediction of business operating efficiency in 2009

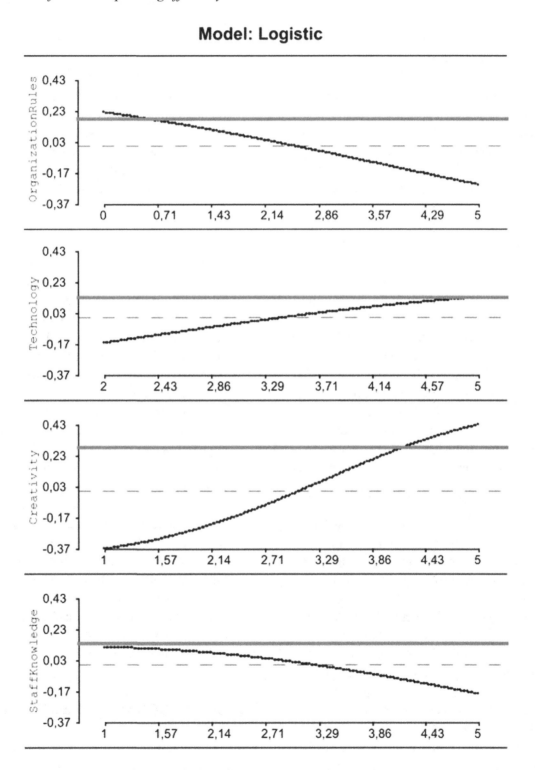

tional rules do not result in high efficiency, but have an opposite effect. Less strict organizational rules leave more space for creativity and initiative, so the potential for efficiency is higher.

- Business operating efficiency increases with improved technology equipment, i.e. better and more appropriate technological equipment leads to higher efficiency. This is an experimental confirmation of theoretical laws of the importance of starting technical relationships; if the enterprise is not in the very beginning capable of producing a technically viable product with proper technology, all consecutive organizational upgrades are fruitless.

- The business operating efficiency grows with creativity, which is the most important feature for both models. This is in accordance with the theoretical background of the importance of such organizational arrangements, which should not be too rigid, but should leave enough space for employees' creative freedom.

- Business operating efficiency decreases with staff knowledge. This is a very surprising finding, which also has an interesting shape of the curve. A possible explanation would be that with low (routine) knowledge of staff it is still possible to achieve high business operating efficiency (especially if the managers challenged with shortcomings in the personnel structure deliberately apply some other organizational mechanisms to successfully replace the shortfall reflected here). However, in addition to staff knowledge, many other internal and external factors in a complex mixture might have some impact, so more research has to be done.

- It is more reasonable for business-operating efficiency to start growing more at the beginning and then not so intensively (as interpreted by the neural network multilayer

perceptron), but not linearly (as explained by logistic regression): this is related to the economic laws expressed in the form of a power functions; thus the interpretation of neural networks is more consistent than a linear dependence of logistic regression, since creativity starts with high enthusiastic impulse and later reaches the natural limits of its own growth, not increasing with the same starting intensity.

- With regard to the theoretical background, it makes more sense that the medium-high knowledge of the staff has the most negative impact for business operating efficiency (as interpreted by the neural network multilayer perceptron), rather than almost linearly decreasing (as explained by logistic regression). The unusual form of the curve of impact of knowledge of staff on business operating efficiency can be explained with the fact that in extreme positions managers are more aware of the (limited) position of their personnel structure in terms of knowledge of staff and accordingly react with other organizational approaches. Staff knowledge at both extremes exerts influence upon the achievement of high business operating efficiency. The most disadvantaged state is the intermediate state of the average knowledge of the staff, which in its unrecognized state does not allow breaking through to the high business operating efficiency. Considering that the enterprises in the area of the average level of knowledge of staff are numerous, the competition in this domain lowers the economic performance.

FUTURE RESEARCH DIRECTIONS

From an economic-research perspective the explanation method and its visualizations were a helpful tool for interpreting less-transparent models, confirming known dependency relationships, and identifying new hypotheses. Our findings support the idea of the importance of quality of organization for enterprises, in ensuring not only their long-term survival, but also growth and further development. Further research on the interdependencies between organization quality and economic results is required to cross-examine our findings. Because of the use of self-assessment techniques in evaluating various organizational aspects in enterprises, the active co-operation of top managers as estimators of organization variables is inevitable. Therefore, to evaluate newly found hypotheses and extend our work, additional experiments with more data should be performed – both quantitatively, with more enterprises, and qualitatively, with more top managers among the assessors.

The general explanation method's efficiency can be improved. Possible improvements include the use quasi-random sampling (as opposed to pseudo-random sampling), which would improve the convergence rate, and selective sampling (that is, taking more samples for higher-variance input features). Although the explanation method takes into account all interactions between input features, these are aggregated into a single effect function. The end-user would benefit from an additional visualization of second-order interactions (interactions between pairs of features) and/or a list of the most influential second – (or higher) order interactions.

CONCLUSION

The novel general method for visualization and explanation of prediction models model was successful at providing useful insight into the often complex connection between organizational quality and economic results of enterprises. The interesting economic relationships and successful predictions come mostly from complex models such as Random Forests and artificial neural net-

works. Without proper visualization, these models are often discarded in favor of perhaps weaker, but more transparent models. Experts from the economic-organizational field, which reviewed and interpreted the results, also agree that such an explanation and visualization is useful and facilitates comparative analysis across different types of models. We conclude that the explanation method is a useful tool for both machine learning experts and non-experts from another field. We recommend its use in any setting which includes the use of complex machine learning models and/or one or more different types of prediction models, regardless of the nature of the problem domain.

REFERENCES

Becker, B., Kohavi, R., & Sommerfield, D. (1997). *Visualizing the simple Bayesian classier.* In KDD Workshop on Issues in the Integration of Data Mining and Data Visualization. Menlo Park, CA: AAAI Press.

Dutton, J. E., & Ragins, B. R. (2007). Positive relationships at work: An introduction and invitation. In *Exploring positive relationships at work: Building a theoretical and research foundation* (pp. 3–25). Mahwah, NJ: Lawrence Erlbaum Associates Publishers.

Hall, M., Frank, E., Holmes, G., Pfahringer, B., Reutemann, P., & Witten, I. H. (2009). The WEKA data mining software: An update. *SIGKDD Explorations, 11*(1), 1–3. doi:10.1145/1656274.1656278

Jakulin, A., Možina, M., Demšar, J., Bratko, I., & Zupan, B. (2005). Nomograms for visualizing support vector machines. In *KDD '05: ACM SIGKDD* (pp. 108–117). New York, NY: ACM.

Lemaire, V., Feraud, V., & Voisine, N. (2008). Contact personalization using a score understanding method. In *International Joint Conference on Neural Networks (IJCNN)* (pp. 649-654). Hong Kong: IEEE Xplore.

Mihelčič, M. (1992a). Focusing on relationships as a means of accelerating organizational improvement. In Geschka, H., & Huebner, H. (Eds.), *Innovation strategies - Theoretical approaches - Experiences - Improvements - An international perspective* (pp. 141–152). Amsterdam, The Netherlands: Elsevier.

Mihelčič, M. (1992b). Interdependency between perceived quality of companies' organization (organizational excellence) and performance: Some assumptions of correlational study. *Slovenska Ekonomska Revija, 43*(1), 67–81.

Mihelčič, M. (2007). Could learning about the structure of relationships lead either to a breakthrough or synthesis in organization theory? In *Proceedings: Beyond Waltz – Dances of Individuals and Organization, 23rd EGOS Colloquium,* Vienna, 4-7 July 2007. London, UK: Sage Publications.

Moretti, S., & Patrone, F. (2008). Transversality of the Shapley value. *Top (Madrid), 16,* 1–41. doi:10.1007/s11750-008-0044-5

Možina, M., Demšar, J., Kattan, M., & Zupan, B. (2004). Nomograms for visualization of naive Bayesian classifier. In *PKDD 2004* (pp. 337–348). Berlin, Germany: Springer - Verlag. doi:10.1007/978-3-540-30116-5_32

Robnik-Šikonja, M., & Kononenko, I. (2003). Theoretical and empirical analysis of ReliefF and RReliefF. *Machine Learning Journal, 53,* 23–69. doi:10.1023/A:1025667309714

Shapley, L. S. (1953). A value for n-person games. In Kuhn, H. W., & Tucker, A. W. (Eds.), *contributions to the theory of games (Vol. II)*. Princeton, NJ: Princeton University Press.

Štrumbelj, E., & Kononenko, I. (2010). An efficient explanation of individual classifications using game theory. *Journal of Machine Learning Research, 11,* 1–18.

Štrumbelj, E., & Kononenko, I. (in press). A general method for visualizing and explaining black-box regression models. *International Conference on Adaptive and Natural Computing Algorithms, ICANNGA 2011.*

Szafron, D., Poulin, B., Eisner, R., Lu, P., Greiner, R., & Wishart, D. ... Anvik, J. (2006). Visual explanation of evidence in additive classifiers. In *Proceedings of Innovative Applications of Artificial Intelligence – Volume 2*. Menlo Park, CA: AAAI Press.

Zien, A., Krämer, N., Sonnenburg, S., & Rätsch, G. (2009). The feature importance ranking measure. In *ECML PKDD 2009: Part II* (pp. 694–709). Berlin, Germany: Springer-Verlag.

ADDITIONAL READING

Achen, C. H. (1982). *Interpreting and using regression*. Newbury Park, CA: Sage Publications.

Alvarez, I. (2004). Explaining the result of a decision tree to the end-user. In R. L. Mantaras & L. Saitta (Eds.), *Proceedings of the 16th European Conference on Artificial Intelligence* (pp. 411–415). Amsterdam, The Netherlands: IOS Press.

Andrews, R., Diederich, J., & Tickle, A. B. (1995). Survey and critique of techniques for extracting rules from trained artificial neural networks. *Knowledge-Based Systems, 8,* 373–389. doi:10.1016/0950-7051(96)81920-4

Barney, J. B. (1991). Firm resources and sustained competitive advantage. *Journal of Management, 17,* 99–120. doi:10.1177/014920639101700108

Berscheid, E. (1999). The greening of relationships science. *The American Psychologist, 54*(4), 260–266. doi:10.1037/0003-066X.54.4.260

Blanchard, J., Guillet, F., & Briand, H. (2003). A user-driven and quality-oriented visualization for mining association rules. In *ICDM '03: Proceedings of the Third IEEE International Conference on Data Mining* (p. 493). Washington, DC: IEEE Computer Society.

Blanchard, J., Guillet, F., & Briand, H. (2007). Interactive visual exploration of association rules with rule-focusing methodology. *Knowledge and Information Systems, 13*, 43–75. doi:10.1007/s10115-006-0046-2

Bojarczuk, C. C., Setembro, A. S. D., Lopes, H. S., Freitas, A. A., & Conceio, R. I. (1999). Discovering comprehensible classification rules using genetic programming: A case study in a medical domain. In W. Banzhaf, J. Daida, A. E. Eiben, M. H. Garzon, V. Honavar, M. Jakiela, & R. E. Smith (Eds.), *Proceedings of the Genetic and Evolutionary Computation Conference GECCO-99* (pp. 953-958). San Francisco, CA: Morgan Kaufmann Publishers.

Cabrera, Á., & Cabrera, E. F. (2002). Knowledge-sharing dilemmas. *Organization Studies, 23*(5), 687–710. doi:10.1177/0170840602235001

Cano, J. R., Herrera, F., & Lozano, M. (2007). Evolutionary stratified training set selection for extracting classification rules with trade off precision-interpretability. *Data & Knowledge Engineering, 60*(1), 90–108. doi:10.1016/j.datak.2006.01.008

Craven, M. W., & Shavlik, J. (1994). Using sampling and queries to extract rules from trained neural networks. In W. W. Cohen & H. Hirsh (Eds.), *Proceedings of ICDM* (pp. 37–45). San Francisco, CA: Morgan Kaufmann Publishers.

Dehuri, S., Patnaik, S., Ghosh, A., & Mall, R. (2008). Application of elitist multi-objective genetic algorithm for classification rule generation. *Applied Soft Computing, 8*(1), 477–487. doi:10.1016/j.asoc.2007.02.009

Falco, De I., Cioppa, D. A., Iazzetta, A., & Tarantino, E. (2005). An evolutionary approach for automatically extracting intelligible classification rules. *Knowledge and Information Systems, 7*, 179–201. doi:10.1007/s10115-003-0143-4

Hastie, T., & Tibshirani, R. (1986). Generalized additive models. *Statistical Science, 1*, 297–310. doi:10.1214/ss/1177013604

Kononenko, I., & Kukar, M. (2007). *Machine learning and data mining – Introduction to principles and algorithms*. Chichester, UK: Horwood Publishing.

Lipovec, F. (1987). *Razvita teorija organizacije (The Developed Theory of Organization)*. Maribor, Slovenia: Obzorje.

Madigan, D., Mosurski, K., & Almond, R. G. (1997). Graphical explanation in belief networks. *Journal of Computational and Graphical Statistics, 6*, 160–181.

Martens, D., Baesens, B., Van Gestel, T., & Vanthienen, J. (2007). Comprehensible credit scoring models using rule extraction from support vector machines. *European Journal of Operational Research, 183*(3), 1466–1476. doi:10.1016/j.ejor.2006.04.051

Mc Auley, J., Duberley, J., & Johnson, P. (2007). *Organization theory, challenges and perspectives*. Harlow, UK: Prentice Hall.

Mihelčič, M. (2008). *Organizacija in ravnateljevanje (Organization and Management)*. Ljubljana, Slovenia: Založba FE in FRI.

Mihelčič, M., Gabrijelčič, J., Kline, M., Šček, J., & Štucin, I. (1988). *Metodologija ugotavljanja kakovosti ali popolnosti organizacije (gospodarskih) združb (Methodology of assuming the quality of firms' organization), research paper*. Ljubljana, Slovenia: Chamber of Economy of Slovenia.

Nayak, R. (2009). Generating rules with predicates, terms and variables from the pruned neural networks. *Neural Networks, 22*(4), 405–414. doi:10.1016/j.neunet.2009.02.001

Pregeljc, M. (2004). Why and how to assess the quality of organization? In *Proceedings: The Organization as a Set of Dynamic Relationships* 20th EGOS Colloquium, Ljubljana, 1-3 July 2004. London, UK: Sage Publications.

Ridgeway, G., Madigan, D., & Richardson, T. (1998). Interpretable boosted naïve Bayes classification. In R. Agrawal & P. Stolorz (Eds.), *4th International Conference on Knowledge Discovery and Data Mining - KDD98* (pp 101-104). Menlo Park, CA: AAAI Press.

Rozman, R. (2006, July). *Relationships dynamics: Organization conflicts and coordination process.* Paper presented in Sub-theme 27, Dynamic Relationships between People as the Connecting Fabric of Organizations and Society, 22nd Annual EGOS Colloquium, Bergen, Norway.

Santana, de A. L., Frances, C., Rocha, C. A., Carvalho, S. V., Vijaykumar, N. L., Rego, L. P., & Costa, J. C. (2007). Strategies for improving the modeling and interpretability of Bayesian networks. *Data & Knowledge Engineering, 63*(1), 91–107.

Towell, G., & Shavlik, J. W. (1993). Extracting refined rules from knowledge-based neural networks, machine learning. *Machine Learning, 13,* 71–101. doi:10.1007/BF00993103

Ustün, B., Melssen, W., & Buydens, L. (2007). Visualisation and interpretation of support vector regression models. *Analytica Chimica Acta, 595*(1-2), 299–309. doi:10.1016/j.aca.2007.03.023

Zhang, Y., Su, H., Jia, T., & Chu, J. (2005). Rule extraction from trained support vector machines. In T. B. Ho, D. Chenung, & H. Liu (Eds.), *Advances in Knowledge Discovery and Data Mining, 9th Pacific-Asia Conference, PAKDD 2005,* Hanoi, Vietnam, May 2005 (pp. 61–70). Berlin, Germany: Springer-Verlag.

KEY TERMS AND DEFINITIONS

Additive Models: A class of models which can be written as a sum of the features' marginal effects and are thus easier to interpret.

Coalitional Game: A cooperative game of a set of players where the worth of each subset (coalition) is given. The main goal is to divide the value of the grand coalition between the players.

Economic Results: Measures of attaining economic goals, expressed by comparing different economic yields (output) against different economic input.

Feature Contribution: A value assigned to a feature's value that is proportional to the feature's share in the model's prediction for an instance.

Marginal Effect: The marginal effect of an input feature is model's prediction against this input feature, holding all other input features constant.

Organization: A set of relationships between members of a formal social unit that are characteristics of the social unit and that ensure its existence, development, and rational achievement of the enterprise's goals.

Organizational Quality: Quality of organization ie. relationships' quality, where the most relevant goal-oriented relationships can be divided into technical, personnel, coordinative, communicational, and motivational.

Prediction Explanation: Information which clarifies the causal relationship between the input features and the model's predictions.

Chapter 13
Automatic Text Classification from Labeled and Unlabeled Data

Eric P. Jiang
University of San Diego, USA

ABSTRACT

Automatic text classification is a process that applies information retrieval technology and machine learning algorithms to build models from pre-labeled training samples and then deploys the models to previously unseen documents for classification. Text classification has been widely applied in many fields ranging from Web page indexing, document filtering, and information security, to business intelligence mining. This chapter presents a semi-supervised text classification framework that is based on the radial basis function (RBF) neural networks. The framework integrates an Expectation Maximization (EM) process into a RBF network and can learn for classification effectively from a very small quantity of labeled training samples and a large pool of additional unlabeled documents. The effectiveness of the framework is demonstrated and confirmed by some experiments of the framework on two popular text classification corpora.

DOI: 10.4018/978-1-4666-1806-0.ch013

INTRODUCTION

Automatic text classification refers to the process of applying information retrieval technology and machine learning algorithms to build models from pre-labeled training samples and deploy the models to previously unseen documents for classification. With the rapid growth of the Internet and advances of computer technology, more textual documents than ever before have been digitized, and digital libraries and encyclopedias have become increasingly valuable information resources. Recently, Google announced (Google, 2010) that, as part of the Google Books project that started in 2004, they have successfully scanned more than 15 million books from more than 100 countries in over 400 languages. Text classification has been widely applied in many areas that include Web indexing, document filtering and management, information security, business and marketing intelligence mining, and customer service automation. Text classification has played and will continue to play an important role in this digital phenomenon.

Over the years, a number of machine learning algorithms have been successfully used in building text classification models (Sebastiani, 2002). Among these algorithms, naïve Bayes (Sahami et al., 1998), nearest neighbor (Aha & Albert, 1991), decision trees with boosting (Schapier et al., 2000), SVM (Christianini & Shawe-Taylor, 2000) are the most cited. As one of the most popular supervised learning applications, the algorithms require a pre-labeled training dataset and, in general, the quantity and quality of the training data can have an impact on model classification effectiveness. Specifically, given a sufficient number of training samples, this supervised modeling process can produce reasonably good classification results. However, it may perform inadequately when there is only a limited number of labeled training data on hand. In many real-world applications, hand-labeling a large quantity of textual data could be labor-intensive or extremely difficult. For instance,

text classification can be used to develop personal software agents that automatically capture, filter and route relevant Web news articles to individual online readers based on their collected reading interests. Such products would likely require a few hundred or more user-labeled training articles in order to achieve acceptable accuracy (Nigam et al., 2000). Although this particular labeling task is doable, it can still be very tedious, undesirable and time-consuming. Web page categorization is another example in this context. Given the rapid proliferation of online information and its dynamic nature, accurately categorizing all available Web pages is indeed an invaluable yet very challenging task. But any attempt to classify this gigantic information database, even it is limited only to some specific topics, would need a set of labeled training pages with the size that might be too large to be manually accomplishable.

In the last few years, there has been surging interest in developing semi-supervised learning models that are capable of learning from both labeled training samples and additional (relevant) unlabeled data. The semi-supervised learning paradigm is particularly pertinent to many text classification problems where labeled training samples are limited in supply while unlabeled relevant documents are abundantly available. This chapter presents a semi-supervised text classification framework that integrates a clustering based Expectation Maximization (EM) process into the radial basis function (RBF) neural networks. The framework can learn for classification effectively from a very small number of labeled samples and a large quantity of additional unlabeled documents. Briefly, the framework first trains a RBF network by applying a clustering algorithm to both labeled and unlabeled data iteratively for computing the RBF middle layer network parameters, and then by using a regression model for determining the RBF output layer network weights. It uses the known class labels in the training data to guide the clustering process and can also apply a weighting scheme on unlabeled data to balance predictive values between labeled and unlabeled data. This balanced use of both labeled and unlabeled data helps improve classification accuracy.

Throughout this chapter, we use $D = \{d_1, d_2, ..., d_n\}$ to denote a set of training samples with size n and $C = \{c_1, c_2, ..., c_m\}$ the document classes (in D) with size m. We assume each document d_i can be expressed as a numeric vector representing the weighted terms or features t_j, i.e., $d_i = (t_1, t_2, ..., t_m)$ (see the section "Data Preprocessing and Representation" for detail).

The rest of the chapter is organized as follows. First, some background of semi-supervised learning algorithms for text classification and RBF neural networks are briefly described. Several data preprocessing procedures, including feature selection and document representation, are also discussed. Next, a detailed description of the RBF based semi-supervised classification framework is presented. It is followed by some experiments of the framework that demonstrate its classification effectiveness. Finally, a few concluding remarks are provided.

BACKGROUND

Over the years, several semi-supervised learning methods have been proposed for text classification. A co-training algorithm, for instance, was proposed in (Blum & Mitchell, 1998) that assumes the data to be learned can be represented by two separate feature sets and it subsequently builds two models, one for each feature set. Then using these two models, the algorithm works to augment labeled samples with unlabeled data. Another classification model, referred to as transductive support vector machine (TSVM), was introduced in (Joachims, 1999). A TSVM model takes into account a particular test set in constructing hyperplane margins and tries to improve the classification accuracy for the test set. In (Nigam et al., 2000), an Expectation-Maximization (EM) (Dempster et al., 1977) algorithm for training

a naïve Bayes classifier from both labeled and unlabeled data was presented. The algorithm first trains a classifier based on only labeled samples and then probabilistically labels the unlabeled documents. Both originally and newly labeled documents together participate in building a new classifier and the process repeats until it converges. A comprehensive survey on learning algorithms with labeled and unlabeled data can be found in (Seeger, 2001).

The well-known radial basis function networks can also be used in developing an effective semi-supervised classifier. Before we discuss a RBF based classification framework, we provide a brief overview of RBF networks below.

A RBF neural network has a feed-forward connected structure of three layers: an input layer, a hidden layer of nonlinear processing neurons and an output layer (Bishop, 1995). For classification problems with m distinct classes, the input layer of the network has n neurons and it takes input training samples d_i. The hidden layer contains k computational neurons; each neuron can be mathematically described by a radial basis function ϕ_i that maps a distance between two vectors in the Euclidean norm into a real value:

$$\phi_p(x) = \phi(\| x - a_p \|), p = 1, 2, ..., k \qquad (1)$$

where a_p are the RBF centers in input sample space and, in general, k is less than the size of training samples. The output layer of the network has m neurons and it produces target classes c_j according to

$$c_j = \sum_{i=1}^{k} w_{ij}\phi_i(x), j = 1, 2, ..., m \qquad (2)$$

where w_{ij} is the weight on the link connecting the ith neuron in the hidden layer to the jth neuron in the output layer. The neuron activation ϕ_i is a nonlinear function of the vector distance; the closer the distance, the stronger the neuron activation. The most commonly used basis function is the Gaussian function

$$\varphi(x) = e^{-\frac{x^2}{2\sigma^2}} \qquad (3)$$

where σ is a width parameter that controls smoothness properties of the basis function.

A RBF SEMI-SUPERVISED CLASSIFICATION FRAMEWORK

In this section we describe the major components of a RBF network based semi-supervised classification framework, including data preprocessing and representation, a two-stage network training procedure, a centroid clustering method, and two EM integrated learning algorithms that utilize both labeled and unlabeled training data.

Data Preprocessing and Representation

For text classification, appropriate feature or attribute selection can be very useful to aid in classification performance. A term or feature is referred to as a word, a number, or a symbol in a document. For a given set of training documents, features from the documents are selected according to their contributions to profiling the documents and the classes to which they belong. The remaining unselected features are then removed from the set for model learning and deploying. The objectives of feature selection are twofold. On one hand, it is designed for dimensionality reduction on document feature space. Dimensionality reduction aims to trim down the number of features to be modeled while the content of individual documents

is still preserved. It generally helps speed up a model training process. On the other hand, feature selection intends to filter out irrelevant features, thus helping build an accurate and effective model for classification. This is particularly valuable to certain machine learning algorithms such as RBF networks, which treat all data features equally in their distance computations and therefore are somewhat incapable of distinguishing relevant features from irrelevant ones.

Two steps of feature selection are used in the classification framework to be presented. First, for a given set of training documents, features are extracted and selected by an unsupervised setting. It is done by removing the stop or common words and applying a word stemming procedure. Then, the features with low document frequencies or low corpus frequencies are eliminated from the training set, as these features may not help much in differentiating documents for classes, and instead they can add some obscuring noises in document classification. The selection process also removes the features with very high corpus frequencies in the training data, as many of those features can distribute almost equally among document classes and may not be valuable in characterizing document classes. Next, features are selected by their frequency distributions among training documents of different classes. Using those labeled training samples, this supervised feature selection procedure intends to further identify the features that distribute most differently among the classes.

There have been several supervised feature selection methods that are widely used in text classification (Sebastiani, 2002). They include the chi-square statistic (CHI), information gain (IG) and odds ratio (OR) criteria. The IG criterion quantifies the amount of information gained for class prediction by the knowledge of the presence or absence of a feature in a document. More precisely, Information Gain of a feature t about a class c can be expressed as

$$IG(t,c) =$$

$$\sum_{c'\in(c,\overline{c})} \sum_{t'\in(t,t')} P(t',c') \log \frac{P(t',c')}{P(t')P(c')} \qquad (4)$$

where $P(c')$ and $P(t')$ denote the probability that a document belongs to class c' and the probability of feature t' occurs in a document, respectively, and $P(t',c')$ is the joint probability of t' and c'. All probabilities can be estimated by frequency counts from training data. Another popular feature selection method is the Chi-square statistic. It measures the lack of independence between the occurrence of feature t and the occurrence of class c. In other words, features are ranked with respect to the quantity:

$$CHI(t,c) =$$

$$\frac{n[P(t,c)P(\overline{t},\overline{c}) - P(t,\overline{c})P(\overline{t},c)]^2}{P(t)P(\overline{t})P(c)P(\overline{c})} \qquad (5)$$

where n is the size of training dataset D and the probability notations have the similar interpretations as in Equation (4). For instance, $P(\overline{c})$ represents the probability that a document does not belong to class c. The third feature selection criterion, odds ratio, has also been used in text classification. It measures the ratio of the odds of feature t occurring in a document of class c to the odds of the feature not occurring in c and, using the corresponding conditional probabilities, it can be defined as:

$$OR(t,c) = \frac{P(t \mid c)(1 - P(t \mid \overline{c}))}{(1 - P(t \mid c))P(t \mid \overline{c})} \qquad (6)$$

The effectiveness of feature selection methods for text classification has been discussed in previous studies (Yang & Pederson, 1997). Among several feature selection methods (including those described above), our experiments

suggest that the IG measure produces reasonably stable classification results and we use it in the framework. Through feature selection, the feature dimensionality of a training dataset can be reduced significantly.

After feature selection, each document is encoded as a numeric vector whose elements are the values of the retained features. Each feature value is associated with a local and global feature weight, representing the relative importance of the feature in the document and the overall importance of the feature in the corpus, respectively.

There are a few choices to weight a feature locally and globally based on its frequencies. For a given term t and a document d, the traditional *log (tf)-idf* term weight is defined as:

$$w_{t,d} = \log(1 + tf_{t,d}) \log \frac{|D|}{df_t} \qquad (7)$$

where $tf_{t,d}$ is the term frequency (tf) of t in d, df_t is the document frequency of t, representing the number of documents in a dataset D that contains t, and $|D|$ is the size of the dataset. The second component on the right hand side of Equation (7) is the inverse document frequency (idf) of t. This term weighting scheme is used in the framework.

Network Training

One typical approach for training RBF networks is to use some comprehensive optimization algorithms that determine parameters of the network through all connected neuron activations and the weights between network layers. This approach, however, is computationally expensive for dealing with text classification problems due to their high feature dimensionality. An alternative and also more computationally efficient approach is to use a two-stage training procedure to train the networks (Bishop, 1995). Specifically, the first stage of training is to form a representation of the density distribution of input document space in terms of the parameters of RBF basis functions. The network centers a (in Equation (1)) and widths σ (in Equation (3)) are determined by some relatively fast and unsupervised algorithms, clustering each document class independently to obtain k basis functions for the class. In general, the larger the value of k, the better the classification outcomes and, of course, the higher cost it carries in network training. Once the centers and widths for the hidden layer are estimated and fixed, the second stage of training computes the weights of the output layer by a regression model such as logistic regression. After the network training is completed and all network parameters are determined, the network can be deployed to the target documents for classification, and the classification outcomes from the network are computed by a weighted sum of the hidden layer activations, as is shown in Equation (2).

Integrating Unlabeled Data

For many text classification problems, especially those involving online databases, collecting relevant (unlabeled) documents is fairly straightforward whereas hand-labeling a large number of training samples can be labor-intensive and also prone to human errors. Therefore, developing semi-supervised learning algorithms that are capable of integrating additional unlabeled data into the RBF network learning is very meaningful and practical. Further, it is also desirable if the algorithms can perform well for the situations where there are only a small number of labeled training samples.

The two-stage network training procedure described in the previous section is well structured for augmenting additional unlabeled data, which represents a significant advantage over other multiplayer neural network alternatives. In principle, we do not require the data used in the first training stage, for determining all basis functions in the network's hidden layer, to be labeled because this

stage is carried out through a clustering algorithm. For the second training stage, however, we need some labeled samples for finding the weights of the network output layer.

The unsupervised clustering process in the first training stage can be performed by a centroid based clustering algorithm. For a given group or cluster of documents G and a vector representation of documents d_i, the centroid a of the cluster is defined as

$$a = \frac{1}{|G|} \sum_{d_i \in G} d_i \qquad (8)$$

where $|G|$ is the size of the cluster. The centroid is computed by averaging the feature weights of all documents in G. Since the clustering process is performed after feature selection on documents, the centroid can be viewed as an encoded content vector representing the most important topics within G. Therefore, we can use the centroid based clustering to group documents by topics where some underlying semantic term and document correlations are likely to be present.

For the classification framework, we use a variant of the well-known k-means clustering algorithm (Witten & Frank, 2005) in the first training stage, clustering each document class independently to obtain k basis functions. In practice, the number of clusters to be formed may vary depending on the characteristics from training data (such as the dimensionality of document feature space). Once all centroids of document classes are determined, we can use them to classify the unlabeled documents into classes.

A basic semi-supervised RBF training algorithm is summarized in Table 1.

The RBF training algorithm described in Table 1. is capable of incorporating both labeled and unlabeled data for classification. It has been applied to spam email filtering, an important and special two-category text classification problem

Table 1. A basic semi-supervised RBF training algorithm

Input: a set of labeled document vectors L and a set of unlabeled document vectors U
Output: a semi-supervised RBF text classifier
• Collect all labeled documents of class c_j in L to form L_j, $j = 1, 2, ..., m$
• Compute cluster centroids a_{jp} of L_j using Equation (8), $j = 1, 2, ..., m$, $p = 1, 2, ..., k$
• Set unlabeled documents U_j of class c_j to empty, $j = 1, 2, ..., m$
• For each unlabeled document d_i in U
   o Compute its normalized distances from all centroids a_{jp}, $j = 1, 2, ..., m$, $p = 1, 2, ..., k$
   o Include d_i in U_j if the distance between d_i and a_{jp} is minimal, $p = 1, 2, ..., k$
   o Update cluster centroids a_{jp} of $L_j \cup U_j$ using Equation (8), $j = 1, 2, ..., m$, $p = 1, 2, ..., k$
   o Estimate other parameters of network basis functions ϕ_{jp}, $j = 1, 2, ..., m$, $p = 1, 2, ..., k$
   o Determine weights w_{pj}, $p = 1, 2, ..., k$, $j = 1, 2, ..., m$, of the network output layer by logistic regression on set L

(Jiang, 2008). It has also been demonstrated that the RBF network training with additional augmented unlabeled data can generally help boost email classification accuracy, even for the cases where there are only very limited labeled email messages. In addition, comparing with some other popular classification algorithms such as naïve Bayes and SVM, this RBF network approach is effective in learning to classify spam email based on content.

Improving Learning with Unlabeled Data

The experiments reported in (Jiang, 2008) have also indicated that, while the basis functions of RBF networks can be estimated by applying a clustering process on combined labeled and unlabeled data as shown in Table 1, a RBF network can deliver substantially higher classification accuracy if the clustering process is performed iteratively and also guided by the labeled training samples. This should be reasonably expected because, in the context of text classification, the class information embedded in the labeled samples can be useful in producing accurate clusters for network parameter estimation.

A natural way for finding cluster centroids in this direction is to apply the well-known Expectation Maximization (EM) algorithm. EM is in general used to iteratively estimate the maximum

likelihood of hidden parameters for problems with incomplete data (Dempster et al., 1977). When we consider the labels of unlabeled data as unknown or missing entries, EM can be applied to estimate these class labels. A similar approach that combines EM with the naïve Bayes classifier was proposed in (Nigam et al., 2000).

Specifically, for a given dataset that combines labeled samples and unlabeled documents, we first start with a number of initial document clusters, one or more clusters for each document class, which are constructed by only the labeled samples. Then, we use these initial cluster centroids to classify the unlabeled documents. Next, we combine the newly classified documents and those originally labeled samples to form a new set of expanded document clusters and then compute their cluster centroids. This cluster expansion or refining process with updated centroids is repeated until all clusters are stabilized.

Another improvement we can make in regard to RBF network learning is to impose and adjust the weights for unlabeled data. When we use a very small number of labeled samples and many-order-of- magnitude more unlabeled data to train a RBF network, it may lead to inaccurate estimates of network parameters. The imbalance in count between labeled and unlabeled data can make the EM iteration process almost like performing unsupervised clustering (Nigam et al., 2000) and unlabeled data can potentially play a dominant role in parameter estimation. In general, when the natural clusters of the combined training data are in correspondence with the class labels, the unsupervised clustering on a large number of unlabeled data will produce the parameter estimates that are helpful for classification. However, when the natural clustering of the data generates parameter estimates that are not in correspondence with the class labels, then these estimates are likely to be destructive to classification accuracy.

In order to modulate the influence of unlabeled data in parameter estimation, we introduce a weighted centroid algorithm for the EM process. Let β_1 be a parameter, $0 \leq \beta_1 \leq 1$, L_p and U_p the labeled and unlabeled document set in the pth cluster, respectively, the weighted cluster centroid a_p is computed as:

$$a_p = \frac{1}{|L_p| + \beta_1 |U_p|} (\sum_{d_i \in L_p} d_i + \beta_1 \sum_{d_i \in U_p} d_i)$$

(9)

where $|L_p|$ and $|U_p|$ are the size of L_p and U_p, respectively. It is a weighted average of labeled and unlabeled documents in the cluster.

Once the EM iteration process is converged, we compute the mean and standard deviation for each cluster. For this computation, we use another separate weighting parameter β_2, $0 \leq \beta_2 \leq 1$, to provide some additional control of the influence of unlabeled data on the final estimation of network basis functions. The cluster's mean is computed by a similar formula as Equation (9) and the cluster's standard deviation is evaluated by

$$\sigma_p^2 =$$
$$\frac{1}{|L_p| + \beta_2 |U_p|} (\sum_{d_i \in L_p} (d_i - a_p)^2 + \beta_2 \sum_{d_i \in U_p} (d_i - a_p)^2)$$

(10)

Note that when both parameters β_1 and β_2 take small values that are near to zero, the unlabeled data will have little influence on the parameter estimation of basis functions. In particular, when both parameters are set to zero, we will only use labeled data to conduct the entire network training and, in this case, the training process effectively reduces to a supervised RBF approach. On the other hand, when both parameters are set to one, we assign each unlabeled document the same weight as a labeled one and in this case, the process simply applies a traditional centroid clustering algorithm.

In the proposed semi-supervised classification framework, we can set the weighting parameters β_1 and β_2 to some fixed values and, alternatively, we can also set them to the values that maximize classification accuracy among a limited number of trials. The experimental results presented in the next section indicate that, by setting both weighting parameters to some values between 0 and 1, additional unlabeled data can almost always help aid in classification, even when their natural clustering, without weight adjusting, would produce less accurate classification.

Table 2 summarizes an updated semi-supervised RBF training algorithm that includes various improvement strategies on unlabeled data that we have just discussed.

EXPERIMENTS

In this section, we provide the empirical results and analysis of the semi-supervised RBF classification framework with two text classification corpora. We show that unlabeled data can be incorporated into the framework to improve classification accuracy, in particular when available labeled training samples are very limited. We also compare the classification results obtained from the framework with different settings on the weighting parameters.

Table 2. An improved semi-supervised RBF training algorithm

Input: a set of labeled document vectors L and a set of unlabeled document vectors U
Output: a semi-supervised RBF text classifier
• Collect all labeled documents of class c_j in L to form L_j, $j = 1, 2, ..., m$
• Compute the initial cluster centroids a_{jp} of L_j, $j = 1, 2, ..., m$, $p = 1, 2, ..., k$
• Loop
• Set unlabeled documents U_j of class c_j to empty, $j = 1, 2, ..., m$
• For each unlabeled document d_i in U
    o Compute its normalized distances from all centroids a_{jp}, $j = 1, 2, ..., m$, $p = 1, 2, ..., k$
    o Include d_i in U_j if the distance between d_i and a_{jp} is minimal, $p = 1, 2, ..., k$
    o Update the cluster centroids a_{jp} of $L_j \cup U_j$ using Equation (9), $j = 1, 2, ..., m$, $p = 1, 2, ..., k$
    o If there is no change on cluster centroids, then forward to the next step; otherwise repeat the loop
    o Estimate the final parameters of network basis functions of $L_j \cup U_j$ using Equation (9) (but substituting β_1 with β_2) and Equation
(10), $j = 1, 2, ..., m$, $p = 1, 2, ..., p$
    Determine the weights w_{pj}, $p = 1, 2, ..., k$, $j = 1, 2, ..., m$, of the network output layer by logistic regression on set L

Datasets and Experiment Settings

The first corpus, WebKB is a collection of 8,145 web pages gathered from university computer science departments. It has 7 different classes: student, faculty, project, course, department, staff and other. The data from the first four classes are used in our experiments and they consist of 4,199 pages. Using a random partition, we created its training set of 2,803 pages and its testing set of 1,296 pages.

For the second data corpus, we considered Reuters 21578. It contains 21,578 articles and 135 topic categories from the Reuters newswire in 1978, and the standard "ModApte" training-testing split is typically used (Cohen & Sebastiani, 2004). Note that in this collection the distribution of documents across the categories is highly uneven and some of the documents are assigned to multiple categories or to no category at all. For our experiments, we use a subset of Reuters 21578 called R8 that contains the articles from the top eight most popular categories and with a single label (i.e., belonging to one category) (Cardoso-Cachopo & Oliveira, 2007). These categories are: acq, crude, earn, grain, interest, money-fx, ship and trade. We further partitioned R8 into its training set with 5,485 documents and its testing set with 2,189 documents.

Text classification performance can be evaluated by the precision (p) and recall (r) metrics. For a classifier and with respective to a class c, if the number of true positive, false positive and false negative decisions of the classifier on class c is tp, fp and fn respectively, then its precision and recall can be defined as:

$$p = \frac{tp}{tp + fp}$$
$$r = \frac{tp}{tp + fn} \tag{11}$$

In brief, the precision metric is gauged by the percentage of documents classified to c that actually belong to the class, whereas the recall is quantified by the percentage of documents from c that are predicted by the classifier. Clearly, these two metrics trade off against each other and one single metric that balances both is the F measure, which is the weighted harmonic mean of precision and recall. With an equal weight for both precision and recall, we have the commonly used F_1 measure:

$$F_1 = \frac{2pr}{p + r} \tag{12}$$

The F_1 measure in Equation (12) can be extended to the classification problems with multiple document classes: c_1, c_2, ..., c_m. Since some of the datasets used in our experiments have very unevenly distributed classes, we use the micro-averaged F_1 measure, which is a weighed average over all classes (Zeng et al., 2003). Assume tp_i, fp_i and fn_i denote the true positive, false positive and false negative decisions on class c_i, respectively, the micro-averaged F_1 measure is defined as

$$P = \frac{\sum_{i=1}^{m} tp_i}{\sum_{i=1}^{m}(tp_i + fp_i)}$$

$$R = \frac{\sum_{i=1}^{m} tp_i}{\sum_{i=1}^{m}(tp_i + fn_i)} \quad (13)$$

$$F_1(micro - averaged) = \frac{2PR}{P + R}$$

For the proposed classification framework, we are particularly interested in its effectiveness of semi-supervised learning with very small numbers of labeled samples. In the experiments, we considered different numbers of labeled training samples per class that range from 1 to 5, with an increment of 1, for both datasets and then from 10 to 70 for WebKB and from 10 to 40 for R8, with an increment of 10. The reason for having a smaller range with R8 is that one of the categories (grain) in the dataset contains only 41 labeled samples.

With a given training set, we first randomly selected a specified number of labeled samples from the set. Then, from the remaining training data we selected at random a subset of the data as unlabeled documents. The labels of these designated unlabeled documents are ignored in model learning. In addition, we used a fixed size of unlabeled data and specifically 5,000 unlabeled documents for R8, and 2,500 for WebKB. The results presented in this section are the average classification accuracy values over five repeated experiments; each experiment independently selected its own labeled and unlabeled data sets.

Experiments with Unlabeled Data

We first evaluate the use of additional unweighted unlabeled data for the semi-supervised RBF framework. We assume each unlabeled document has the same weight (i.e. $\beta_1 = \beta_2 = 1$) as a labeled sample in model training. Figure 1 shows the classification accuracy (or micro-averaged F_1) results of the framework on R8, trained with both labeled and unlabeled data (as *combined data* in the figure) and with only labeled (as *labeled data only* in the figure). Similarly, Figure 2 displays the classification results obtained from the framework on WebKB. The horizontal axis in the figures is the number of labeled samples per class used in training and the vertical axis is the micro-averaged F_1 values on the corresponding test set.

Both Figure 1 and Figure 2 indicate that, for the RBF network training, additional unlabeled documents are helpful in boosting classification accuracy at small numbers of labeled data (which are fewer than five). However, when more labeled samples become available, the advantage of augmenting unlabeled data in training seems vanishing; in fact, the supervised RBF network, trained only with labeled data, significantly outperforms the semi-supervised counterpart based on combined training data. This observation coincides with some previous studies such as (Nigam et al., 2000), and it suggests that unlabeled data may not always help improve classification performance. When the size of labeled training data for a document class is extremely small, the data may not be able to accurately represent the data distribution of the class; the data can carry a large variance towards parameter estimates of the network model. Using additional unlabeled data to augment the very limited labeled data could help improve the estimates. On the other hand, when

Figure 1. Classification accuracy results of RBF on R8 trained with labeled data only and with combined data

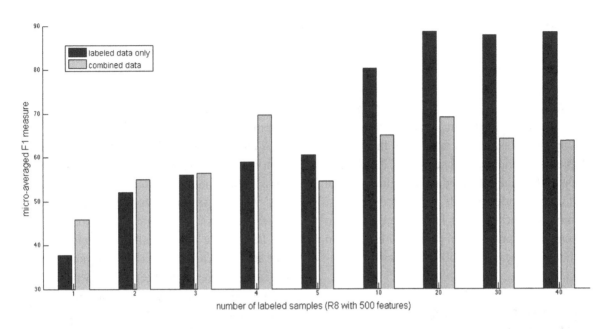

Figure 2. Classification accuracy results of RBF on WebKB trained with labeled data only and with combined data

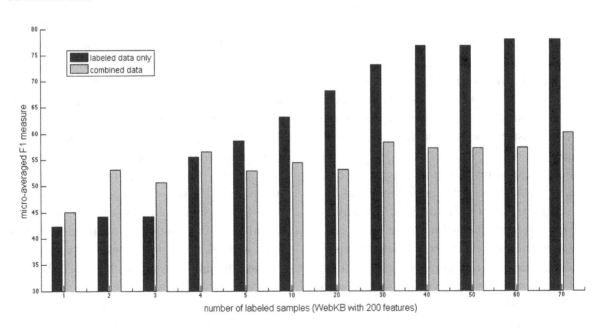

Table 3.

Number of labeled	1-4	5	10	20	30	40	50-70 (if applicable)
β_1 / β_2 value	1/1	.1/.001	.05/.001	.01/.001	.005/.001	.001/.001	.0005/.001

we use a relatively large number of labeled samples in training, a stronger data representation of document classes generated from the labeled samples is anticipated. Subsequently, the clustering on additional unlabeled data might not be in good correspondence with the labeled samples; this inconsistency between labeled and unlabeled data can cause problems in parameter estimation and hence decrease network classification accuracy.

Experiments with Weighted Unlabeled Data

As we have discussed, unlabeled data can have some significant influence on performance of the semi-supervised RBF framework. In order for the framework to fully utilize both types of data (labeled and unlabeled) and to modulate the impact of unlabeled data on the training (especially in the case when the ratio of labeled to unlabeled data is very small), we have introduced two weighting parameters β_1, β_2 and use them in updating cluster centroids in the EM iterations and in computing the final cluster means and standard deviations, respectively.

For the experiments with weighted unlabeled data, we set the values for β_1 and β_2 by two weighting schemes: *fixed weights* and *selected weights*. The *fixed weights* scheme simply sets one to both parameters when the number of labeled samples per class is less than five and as the size of labeled data increases, it assigns a gradually deceased value to β_1 while always keeping a fixed value for parameter β_2 (i.e., 0.001). This heuristic approach that has a decreasing pattern for β_1 intends to reduce the influence of unlabeled data on network

training. The parameter setting of this weighting scheme is summarized in Table 3.

A more general or ideal approach for setting such model parameters should use an independent cross-validation dataset and choose the parameters' values that maximize the classification accuracy on the set. This approach, however, would not be feasible when available labeled training data are very scarce, which is the primary problem we aim to address with the semi-supervised RBF framework. Alternatively, we can build several trial models with different parameter settings, and then select the values for β_1 and β_2 that maximize the classification accuracy from the trials. The *selected weights* scheme uses this approach. More specifically, using one out of seven possible values for the parameters: 0.0005, 0.001, 0.005, 0.01, 0.05, 0.1 and 1.0, we create a total of fourteen different combinations or trials. The initial reason for using this weights scheme was to verify whether there ever exist some values for β_1 and β_2 that can further improve performance of the semi-supervised RBF framework. As part of future work, we plan to look into methods to dynamically setting the weighting parameters.

Figure 3 shows and compares the classification accuracy results on R8 between the semi-supervised RBF framework, which is equipped with the weighting schemes (*fixed* and *selected*) on unlabeled data, and the corresponding supervised network using only labeled data. Figure 4 displays the similar results with WebKB. We can observe from the figures that the semi-supervised framework can achieve better classification performance in most cases if the *fixed weights* scheme is applied and in all cases if the *selected weights* scheme is used. Some significant improvement

Figure 3. Classification accuracy results of RBF on R8 trained with labeled data only and with combined data (When using combined data, the fixed and selected weighting schemes are applied to unlabeled documents)

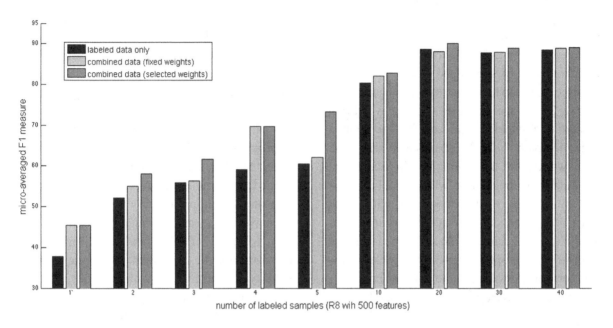

Figure 4. Classification accuracy results of RBF on WebKB trained with labeled data only and with combined data (When using combined data, the fixed and selected weighting schemes are applied to unlabeled documents)

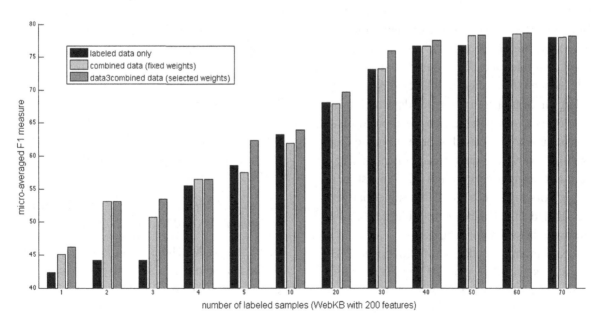

can be attained for the semi-supervised model with small numbers of labeled samples. For instance, using just four labeled samples per class with R8, the supervised RBF has an accuracy of 59% while the semi-supervised RBF achieves 69.7%. This represents a 26% reduction in classification error for the semi-supervised model.

In comparison to the results from Figure 1 and Figure 2, we see that the adjusted weighting method on unlabeled data is useful. The method can effectively help the semi-supervised RBF framework avoid the degradation in accuracy at large sizes of labeled data, whereas still preserving the benefits of the framework with small sizes of labeled data. In addition, the consistently superior accuracy values obtained from the *selected weights* option suggest that the classification performance of the framework can be further enhanced by developing improved methods of setting the weighting parameters.

CONCLUSION

This chapter has presented a semi-supervised text classification framework that integrates a clustering based EM algorithm into radial basis function (RBF) networks and can learn for classification effectively from a very small set of labeled samples and a large quantity of unlabeled data. Since the number of unlabeled data can be so large in comparison to labeled data, their influence on network parameter estimation needs to be adequately modulated in order to make them useful. Towards this direction, a generalized centroid clustering algorithm has been investigated in this work to balance predictive values between the labeled and unlabeled training data and to improve classification accuracy.

Experiments of the semi-supervised RBF framework with two popular text classification corpora have shown that, with proper use of additional unlabeled data, the framework can achieve classification error reduction by up to

26%. In addition, some appropriate settings on the weighting parameters for the framework can further improve its classification accuracy.

As future work we plan to improve the semi-supervised RBF framework in several directions. Currently in our system we use the simple and fixed weighting parameters to modulate the impact of unlabeled data in network learning. We plan to develop methods for dynamically adjusting the parameter values in EM iterations and for improving the estimates of network basis functions. Another area we plan to work on relates to the feature dimensionality of data. It has been indicated by our preliminary experiments on the framework that selecting an appropriate feature dimensionality, for the data to be learned, can help improve the framework's classification capability. We plan to study more in this area and investigate a mechanism for the framework that can correlate the setting of feature dimensionality to classification accuracy as well as the size of the labeled training data.

ACKNOWLEDGMENT

The author would like to thank two anonymous reviewers for their helpful comments on an earlier version of the chapter.

REFERENCES

Aha, W., & Albert, M. (1991). Instance-based learning algorithms. *Machine Learning*, 6, 37–66. doi:10.1007/BF00153759

Bishop, C. (1995). *Neural networks for pattern recognition*. Oxford University Press.

Blum, A., & Mitchell, T. (1998). Combining labeled and unlabeled data with co-training. *Proceedings of 11th COLT Conference* (pp. 92-100).

Cardoso-Cachopo, A., & Oliveira, A. (2007). Semi-supervised single-label text categorization using centroid-based classifiers. *ACM Symposium on Applied Computing* (pp. 844-851).

Christianini, B., & Shawe-Taylor, J. (2000). *An introduction to support vector machines and other kernel-based learning methods*. Cambridge University Press.

Cohen, F., & Sabastiani, F. (2004). An analysis of the relative hardness of reuters-21578 subsets. *Journal of the American Society for Information Science and Technology, 56*(6), 584–596.

Dempster, A., Laird, N., & Rubin, D. (1977). Maximum likelihood from incomplete data via the EM algorithm. *Journal of the Royal Statistical Society. Series B. Methodological, 39*, 1–38.

Google. (2001). *Inside Google Books*. Retrieved March 15, 2011, from http://booksearch.blogspot.com/ 2010/10/on-future-of-books.html

Jiang, E. (2008). Integrating background knowledge into text classification. In Li, H. (Eds.), *Information retrieval technology* (pp. 61–70). Berlin, Germany: Springer. doi:10.1007/978-3-540-68636-1_7

Joachims, T. (1999). Transductive inference for text classification using support vector machines. *Proceedings of 16th ICML Conference* (pp. 200-209).

Nigam, K., McGallum, S., Thurn, S., & Mitchell, T. (2000). Text classification from labeled and unlabeled documents using EM. *Machine Learning, 39*(2/3), 103–134. doi:10.1023/A:1007692713085

Sahami, M., Dumais, S., Heckerman, D., & Horvitz, E. (1998). A Bayesian approach to filtering junk e-mail. *Proceedings of AAAI Workshop* (pp. 55-62).

Schepier, R., & Singer, Y. (2000). BoosTexer: A boosting-based system for text categorization. *Machine Learning, 39*(2/3), 135–168. doi:10.1023/A:1007649029923

Sebastiani, F. (2002). Machine learning in automated text categorization. *ACM Computing Surveys, 1*, 1–47. doi:10.1145/505282.505283

Seeger, M. (2001). *Learning with labeled and unlabeled data. Technical Report*. Edinburgh University.

Witten, I., & Frank, E. (2005). *Data mining* (2nd ed.). Morgan Kaufmann.

Yang, Y., & Pederson, J. O. (1997). A comparative study on feature selection in text classification. *Proceedings of 14th International Conference on Machine Learning* (pp. 412-420).

Zeng, H., Wang, X., Chen, Z., Lu, H., & Ma, W. (2003). CBC-clustering based text classification requiring minimal labeled data. *Proceedings of 3rd International Conference on Data Mining* (pp. 443-450).

KEY TERMS AND DEFINITIONS

Artificial Neural Network: A computational model that is inspired by the structure and functionality of human brains. Artificial neural networks can be used to model complex relationships between data inputs and outputs through an interconnected set of artificial neurons.

Cross-Validation: A commonly used technique for assessing how the results of a computer learning model will generalize to an independent dataset. It involves partitioning a dataset into two complementary subsets, building the model on one subset and validating the model on the other subset. To reduce variability, multiple rounds of cross-validation can be performed using different partitions, and the validation results are averaged over the rounds.

Labeled Data: A set of training examples used for building computer learning models; each example is a pair consisting of an input object and an output label or value.

Radial Basis Function Neural Network: An artificial neural network that uses radial basis functions in computing its network activations.

Semi-Supervised Learning: A class of computer learning techniques that make use of both labeled and unlabeled training data. It falls between supervised learning and unsupervised learning.

Stop/Common Words: The words that are filled out prior to, or after, processing of natural language text. Any group of words can be chosen as the stop words for a given purpose. For information retrieval, the stop words are some of the most common, short function words, such as the, of, is.

Supervised Learning: A class of computer learning techniques that infer a function from labeled training data. Each labeled training ex-ample is a pair consisting of an input object and a desired output label or value. In supervised learning, a supervised learning algorithm analyzes the training data and produces an inferring function that should predict the correct output value for any valid input object.

Text/Document Classification: A computer learning process of assigning a digital document into one or more classes, based on its contents.

Unlabeled Data: A set of training examples used for building computer learning models; each example is an input object and it does not have an output label or value.

Unsupervised Learning: A class of computer learning techniques that intend to find hidden structure or patterns from unlabeled training data. This is different from supervised learning, and all training data do not carry any output labels or values.

Chapter 14
Agent Based Systems to Implement Natural Interfaces for CAD Applications

Daniel García Fernández-Pacheco
Universidad Politécnica de Cartagena, Spain

Nuria Aleixos Borrás
Instituto Interuniversitario de Investigación en Bioingeniería y Tecnología Orientada al Ser Humano, Universitat Politècnica de València, Spain

Francisco Albert Gil
Instituto Interuniversitario de Investigación en Bioingeniería y Tecnología Orientada al Ser Humano, Universitat Politècnica de València, Spain

ABSTRACT

Currently, important advances are being carried out in CAD (Computer Aided Design) applications; however, these advances have not yet taken place for CAS (Computer Aided Sketching) applications. These applications are intended to replace complex menus with natural interfaces that support sketching for commands and drawing, but the recognition process is very complex and doesn't allow its application yet. So, although natural interfaces for CAD applications have not yet been solved, works based on sketching devices have been explored to some extent. In this work, the authors propose a solution for the problem of recognition of sketches using an agent-based architecture, which distributes the agents hierarchically to achieve the best decision possible and to avoid reliance on of the drawing sequence.

INTRODUCTION

Two recent studies (Barr, 2004; Rose, 2005) concluded that within the field of graphic communication, the "ability to create solid 3D models on a computer" and the "ability to produce free-

hand sketches of engineering objects" are the two most highly valued skills that engineering students should be competent in. Other authors (Plimmer & Apperley, 2002; Tversky, 2002) have analysed the important role played by the use of sketches during the process of developing new industrial products, concluding that the main advantages of using sketches are the low cost of materials

DOI: 10.4018/978-1-4666-1806-0.ch014

involved, the simplicity of the interface tool and the ease of editing.

The arrival of CAD (Computer Aided Design) had a deep effect on several phases of the product design process but had a poor impact on the conceptual design phase (the initial stage), where ideas are expressed and sketches with pencil and paper are still used. The main reason for this is the lack of the CAS (Computer Aided Sketching) tools provided with CAD applications, where recognisers have limited capabilities (as for instance the strictness in the drawing sequence order or the low success recognition ratio) and, therefore, they do not improve the traditional sketching carried out on paper.

Multiple techniques are used in sketch recognition to detect symbols, diagrams, geometric shapes and other user command gestures. With a classic linear discriminator, Rubine (1991) calculates features in order to classify single-stroke sketches as digits, letters and basic commands. Also based on similar features Apte, Vo, and Kimura (1993) distinguish five simple geometric shapes basing their classification on thresholds to the ratio filters established, and Paulson and Hammond (2008) implement the PaleoSketch recognizer which classify between eight primitive forms. Gross (1994) describes a prototype for the recognition of glyphs, but his algorithm requires sketching in a strict order. Other features that remain invariant with rotation, such as convex hull, perimeter and area scalar ratios, were studied by Fonseca and Jorge (2000), who use ratio values in fuzzy sets to recognize some shapes. Methods based on Fourier descriptors achieve better results than methods based on shape descriptors as presented above. In this field, Zhang and Lu (2002) use Fourier descriptors to retrieve images from databases. Fourier descriptors were also used by Harding and Ellis (2004) for recognizing hand gesture movements. Other examples of applications that use Fourier descriptors are the detection of users' hand movement in a system to achieve an augmented reality tool (Licsar & Sziranyi, 2004).

Park and Park (2005) use Fourier transform to describe fingerprints that are classified by means of non-linear discriminant analysis.

Hence, the challenge of replacing conventional pencil and paper sketches with a digital sketching environment exists. This new environment must be designed in such a way that it favours a "natural" process that does not hinder the user and permits producing an output that can be reused in the remaining phases of the design process. These kinds of environments are known as natural or calligraphic interfaces.

Attending the classification of the different types of sketches that engineers/designers use in the course of creating a product, the one proposed by Ferguson (1994) has been followed. Thus, we distinguish between "thinking sketches," which are used to focus and guide non-verbal thought; "talking sketches," which provide a support for the considerations about the design that take place between colleagues; and "prescriptive sketches," which convey instructions to the draughts person, who is responsible for producing the final version of the engineering drawings. This work is focused on the thinking sketches. The field of Sketch-Based Interfaces and Modelling (SBIM) is an emerging area of research. Proof of this is the fact that, in Europe, the forum specialized in this field was only set up 6 years ago. We are referring to the SBIM workshop, whose current objectives are still changing wide-ranging, the creation of 3D models from thinking sketches being one of the most active areas of work.

There are two approaches to the problem of transforming a thinking sketch into a 3D model within the context of the development of industrial products, namely, those based on geometric reconstruction techniques (that remains out of this paper's scope) and the so-called gesture-based modelling methods based on interaction with the user through gestures that are recognized as commands to generate solids from 2D sections, such as the GIDeS (Pereira, Jorge, Branco, & Nunes, 2000), TEDDY (Igarashi, Matsuoka, &

Tanaka, 1999) or SKETCH (Zeleznik, Herndon, & Hughes, 1996) systems for example.

Automatic gesture recognition is a complex task since the same symbols can be drawn by different users with a different shape, orientation or size. For this reason, current recognizers present several limitations: they are not robust and can present ambiguity in the results depending on the user, the change between different operating modes (e.g. geometric or command modes) normally requires specific menu buttons, the input sequence of the stroke is previously fixed, and the size of the dictionary is usually limited.

For this reason, a methodology change in recognizers is needed in order to distinguish and classify sketches like a human person would do, that is to say, using context information and being flexible at middle and final decisions. This way of behaviour can be assigned to the recognizers by the use of expert systems, object based systems, and agent-based systems, among others.

In the case of agent-based systems, they have been widely used in applications for process simulation and control, such as algorithms to obtain the optimal path for the refuse collection lorries (Pérez-Delgado & Matos-Franco, 2009), face recognizers (Chetty & Sharma, 2006), and software applications for management of tourist reserves by means of an iPhone (Palanca, Aranda, & García-Fornes, 2009). However, their use is being extended more and more to recognition processes for supporting natural interfaces. The main benefits we can take advantage of are the flexibility of these systems and the autonomy of agents. According to Wooldridge and Jennings (1995), these agents must be autonomous (acting by themselves without human intervention), reactive (perceiving the environment and responding to changes), pro-active (being able to lead the way and establish the objectives) and social (interacting with other agents to achieve a common problem, as well as helping the rest in their tasks).

The main objective of this chapter is to propose an agent-based architecture to support the interface of a recognizer that allows to generate geometry from sketches, to consider command gestures and other standardized symbols. This environment will take into account context information and will have a flexible structure in order to increase easily the number of symbols in the dictionary. Furthermore, the annoying change of mode currently implemented in most CAD applications by a button is eliminated, and no fixed input sequence is required in order to get the gesture correctly identified.

The chapter is organized as follows. In the next section we present some applications carried out in the field of natural sketch recognition, as well as applications for the same purpose using agents. Then, an overview of the proposed agent-based architecture for recognition of free-hand sketches is described in detail. Finally, some future trends are outlined and conclusions stated.

BACKGROUND

Some works based on the interaction between the user and the application by means of gestures, which are recognized as commands to generate solids from 2D sections (Figure 1), can be found in the literature. In this kind of project, we must take into account that recognition is usually simplified, forcing the user to introduce the input following a determined sequence. One example can be given for illustration: drawing a line from the top down is not the same as drawing from the bottom up, since the recogniser differentiates, for example, the direction for extrusion. Many works that base their gesture recognition process on this principle limit the user's way of drawing, providing a non intuitive and rigid interface.

According to these kind of systems based on a "gestural interface," the SKETCH system (Zeleznik et al., 1996) can be given as an example. Basically, this application is guided by architectural shapes, where the geometry modelling process is defined by the use of gestures and

Figure 1. Interface of SKETCH system for thinking sketches

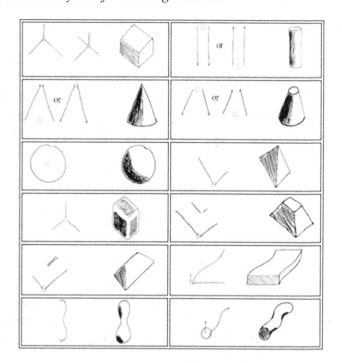

conventionalisms based on the drawing of simple lines. Another application as an extension of the SKETCH system is "JavaSketch," which allows to create three dimensional models through cubes and lines.

Another example is the SKETCH-N-MAKE system (Bloomenthal et al., 1998), which attempts to facilitate the computer numerically controlled machining of simple pieces modelled by means of a gestural interface. Moreover, the TEDDY system (Igarashi et al., 1999) allows to model freeform three-dimensional surfaces using a very simple interface. The method starts with the sketched shape that represents an object silhouette and automatically proposes a polygonal surface that fits on the contour. Later, Alexe, Gaildrat, and Barthe (2004) present another freeform surface modeller based on some algorithms developed by Igarashi et al. (1999).

In addition, the GIDeS system (Pereira et al., 2000) takes just one unique perspective projection as input for constructing accurate designs from

ambiguous drawings. The system has of a gesture alphabet that identifies a basic set of modelling primitives. However, the dynamic recognition of these modelling gestures is interrupted by the offering of a context window with icons, which forces the user to confirm his intention if it were needed.

At the moment, several CAD applications to create 2D and 3D simple models can be found in the market. Nevertheless, many of them make use of the term "sketching" to designate the conceptual development process, employing a series of buttons and icons that enable the different actions of the software. This concept is wrongly used, since the term "sketch" is normally assigned to a quick free-hand drawing without the need of any buttons or restrictions that can disturb the idea of the designer. Thereby, several commercial applications to develop both 2D and 3D geometry can be found, such as Autocad®, Pro/Engineer®, Solidworks®, Sketch Up!®, or Catia®, among others. These applications make the creation of any model possible by means of buttons and menus. However, they do not allow to create sketches in a quick and intuitive manner, requiring long learning times that encourage the user to operate with the traditional pencil and paper tools during the design conceptual stage. The Catia® software, developed by Dassault Systems, is the only one which, in case of detecting its execution on a Tablet PC, offers the possibility of employing a reduced gestural command set. Anyhow, several attempts are needed in order to get a positive recognition, and therefore it is more difficult than using the button associated to the desired action directly.

The employment of the Microsoft.Ink library (Jarrett & Su, 2002), is also worth highlighting, which implements diverse applications in several programming languages which take advantage of the characteristics of a Tablet PC, such as the pointer caption, the detection of the pressure level of the pointer, and other interesting parameters.

In addition, several programmers develop low cost software (or freeware) to create sketches on an iPhone, a Tablet PC, or even a computer with the aid of a mouse. For example, the "Sketches 2" commercial tool from the Latenitesoft company, designed for the iPhone and the iPod-Touch, which allows to write notes and diagrams, and drawing and garnishing images with different kinds of figures. Another application developed by Autodesk for the iPhone to be considered is the "SketchBook Pro" software, which enables drawing on an iPhone in an artistic way, achieving striking results.

In short, the cited applications offer the possibility of creating a sketch easily by using a touching device. Nevertheless, the obtained sketch is treated as an image composed of pixels, with no detection of the entities or the existing relations between the identified elements. For this reason, the MIT Research Group have developed a sketching application over an interactive digital blackboard named "MagicPaper," where the different elements are recognized and some physical properties are assigned to them.

Applications for Natural Sketch Recognition Using Agents

Although agent-based technology has been mainly used in applications for process simulation, management and control, its use is being extended more and more to processes in artificial vision environments, image analysis, and recognition tasks, such as sketch interpretation for supporting natural interfaces. There are multiple propositions regarding the structure, which a multi-agent system should implement. For example, the "Impact" collaborative system proposed by Rogers, Ross, and Subrahmanian (2000) for creating agent-based applications, or the "LADDER" sketch language defined by Hammond and Davis (2005) for user interface developers. Julian, Carrascosa, Rebollo, Soler, and Botti (2002) also present the "ARTIS" multi-agent architecture, which warranties communications among agents satisfying the critical time restrictions of a real time environment.

Juchmes, Leclercq, and Azar (2005) justify the use of multi-agent systems for free-hand sketch interpretation through the following affirmations: 1) a multi-agent system allows to divide the existing problem into easier sub-objectives, and 2) it is designed to be easily adapted taking account of the possible changes. They also present the EsQUIsE sketch interpretation tool for conceptual architectural design, in which a calligraphic interface composed of a pencil and a digital tablet is employed. The system is able to capture lines and interpret them in real time, constructing progressively the technological and functional models of the building that is being designed. The system structure is mainly formed by two stages: a graphic recognition and a semantic analysis of the detected elements.

In other respects, Achten and Jessurum (2002) present the theoretical model of a multi-agent platform capable of recognizing graphic units in technical drawings. The proposed structure consists of singular agents that are specialized in the recognition of graphic units. These agents communicate among themselves and establish negotiating mechanisms that will allow to resolve ambiguous cases. However, the authors only propose the system structure, without managing its implementation.

A similar structure is presented by Azar, Couvreury, Delfosse, Jaspartz, and Boulanger (2006), who propose and implement a multi-modal interface for architectural sketches interpretation based on a multi-agent architecture. In this case, the system is composed of several graphic agents which are in charge of recognizing basic graphic elements (such as lines and circles), and other more complex ones (such as doors or stairs), all of which belong to the architectural design. They also implement a series of "vocal" agents that will recognize the dimensions and commands introduced with the help of a microphone.

Other authors such as Mackenzie and Alechina (2003) choose to apply a multi-agent architecture to a recognizer for child-like sketches of animals, such as dogs, cats, fishes, and so on. The classification process has three main stages: a first stage where the sketch is parsed into a set of likely meaningful components on the basis of their geometry; a second one where the matching of those components to generalised animal body parts (head, legs, tail, etc.) contained in a database is carried out; and a third stage where the relationships among the detected entities are analyzed and the introduced sketch is finally classified. To achieve this classification the authors define an "arena" for the agent system. In this arena, the potential features extracted from the graph are added, and each agent tries to find some specific high-level features that allow it to achieve its objective, defining in this way a confidence level for each agent.

In turn, Flasinski, Jurek, and Myslinski (2009) present a multi-agent system based on a syntactic pattern recognition approach, which is used to classify hand postures of the Polish Sign Language. Due to the variety of styles of performing hand postures depending on the user, the construc-

tion of a grammar which can be divided into sub-grammars and distributed to several agents is required. These agents will be in charge of detecting if the introduced hand posture belongs to them, obtaining a positive matching.

It is apparent that the extraction of the context information is needed in order to get a correct recognition, since it also allows to resolve some ambiguity problems. This is precisely the case of the recognizer of UML Use Case Diagrams based on an agent-based framework and proposed by Casella, Deufemia, Mascardi, Costagliola, and Martelli (2008). The recognition process is carried out by a series of "intelligent agents" which are in charge of recognizing the sketched symbols and coordinate among themselves to get an efficient and precise interpretation of the introduced sketch.

It is also worth highlighting the work by Alhajj and Elnagar (2005), who develop a multi-agent system aimed at treating the problem of separating handwritten connected digits as a matter of a bad sketching, or the work by Saeed (2000), who implements through agents an application for recognizing Arabic characters, as well as the "AgenTrac" multiagent framework developed by Bryll, Rose, and Quek (2005) for vision-based tracking of conversational gestures.

According to the mentioned works, as well as the one presented by the authors below, agent-based applications provide obvious advantages over the traditional programming platforms, such as flexibility, information management, hierarchy, autonomy and adaptability of the implemented code, discussion and agreement in decision-making, facility for assessing the context, and so on. In the next section, a new agent-based architecture for recognition of free-hand sketches is presented in detail.

Figure 2. Dictionary of implemented symbols

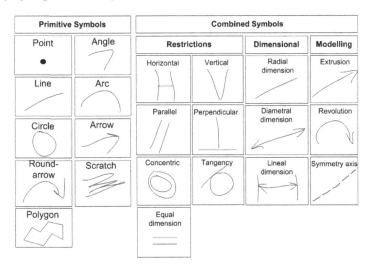

AN AGENT-BASED ARCHITECTURE FOR SUPPORTING NATURAL INTERFACES

At this point, a recognition process has been formulated in order to take advantage of the flexibility and autonomy of a multi-agent hierarchical architecture (Fernández-Pacheco, Conesa, and Aleixos, 2010), which is also considered as an extension of a previous proposal (Fernández-Pacheco, Conesa, Aleixos, Company, and Contero, 2009). In this work, a comparison between the graphical and spoken languages is performed, and a hierarchical breakdown of the graphical symbols is defined in such a way that the symbols (as though they were "words" of a dictionary) are made up of one or several simple strokes (as though they were "phonemes" of an alphabet). One or several phonemes or simple strokes (defined from now on as "primitive symbols") make, in turn, a word or complex symbol (considered from now on as "combined symbol") which belongs to a set of accepted words (our dictionary). In this hierarchical architecture, phonemes remain in a lower level than words, so the recognition process has to be arranged into two levels: a lower level

where the phonemes are recognized, and an upper level where the words are deduced.

Figure 2 shows a dictionary of common symbols that are frequently used in modelling tasks. This allows the user to build parametric geometry from sketches and to create basic solid models: modelling commands (such as extrusion, revolution, etc.), symbols to indicate geometrical restrictions (like concentric, parallel, etc.), annotations (like radial dimension, etc.) and other basic symbols are included.

Thus, an agent architecture has been designed to work on three levels: a low level for the Basic Agents, which are responsible for the interface, pre-processing and feature extraction; an intermediate level for the Primitive Agents responsible for syntactic meaning of every single stroke; and the upper level that holds the Combined Agents which have responsibility for semantic meaning of several strokes forming a symbol. Also in the lower level is the Broker Agent that centralizes the information and delivers the tasks to the respective agents. All agents in the system are executed in parallel.

As the functional diagram of the architecture shows in Figure 3, when a user draws a stroke, the Interface Agent (IA) sends the digitalized

Figure 3. Operating mode of the agent-based architecture

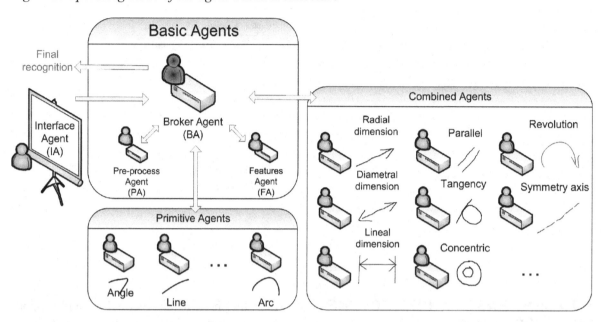

points to a data structure. The Broker Agent (BA) receives the notification and sends these points to the Preprocessing Agent (PA). The Preprocessing Agent (PA) must filter and eliminate the noise from the introduced stroke in order to get a beautified stroke ready for the recognition process (the points should be uniformly distributed as well as the drawing which should be lightly smoothed to get rid of trembling and halting). Later, the BA requests the Feature Agent (FA) to extract and send back the main features of the stroke. The FA has a sequential operating mode, in which two processes can be easily distinguished. On the one hand, a segmentation of the stroke is carried out to fit the stroke to geometric entities. This segmentation process is achieved by means of the TCVD (Tangent and Corner Vertices Detection) algorithm (Fernández-Pacheco, 2010), whose segmentation parameters are previously optimized by means of the Simulated Annealing technique (Fernández-Pacheco, Albert, Aleixos, Conesa, and Contero, 2011). On the other hand, interesting invariant to scale, position and orientation features from the stroke are obtained. These features are the Fast Fourier Transform (FFT) (Tao, Morrow, Heine-

mann, and Sommer, 1995) of two signatures: the radius signature and the arc length versus cumulative turning angle signature. These signatures are used as input variables of a non-linear Bayesian discriminatory analysis (Fernández-Pacheco, Contero, Naya, and Aleixos, 2008) in order to get a value from a maximization function.

Once these features are extracted by the FA, the BA sends this information to the primitive agents, which will send back the results after the first recognition stage is accomplished. If the input sketch matches with a primitive symbol, the BA sends the results to the Combined Agents, and the second recognition stage is executed. Finally, the Combined Agents send back their results to the Broker Agent, which will take the final decision for the recognition process.

The proposed architecture (Figure 4) has been implemented on top of the JADE agent-based platform (Bellifemine, Poggi, and Rimassa, 2000). Messages for communications are encoded following the FIPA-ACL standard (FIPA ORG, 2002), which is a communication language natively supported by JADE. The JADE platform makes it possible to send and receive messages,

Figure 4. Agent-based architecture

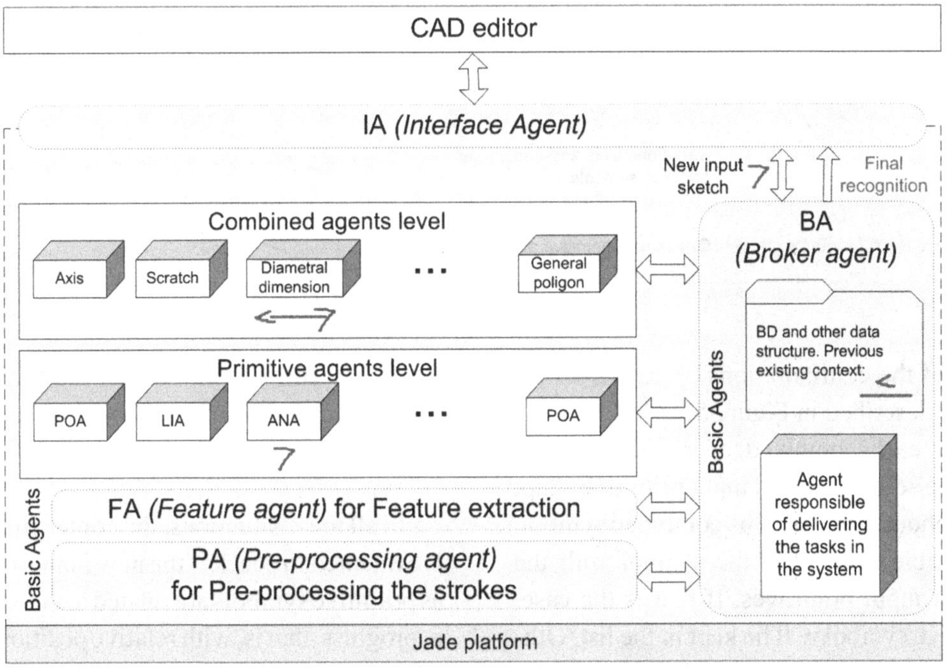

in a way that is transparent to the agent developer, maintaining a private queue of incoming ACL messages per agent and allowing the MAS (Multi-Agent System) developer to monitor the transit of messages.

The Primitive Agents

With the data from the Feature Agent (FA), all the Primitive Agents try to recognise the primitive symbol they are in charge of. At least, one agent for each primitive symbol has been implemented. A primitive agent will use the information that it considers significant in order to recognise the primitive symbol which it is dealing with. So, each primitive agent evaluates the stroke introduced and quantifies its information from two processes. A first process where a recognition based on the segmentation of the stroke is carried out, returning a positive or negative match (Match or No_match of the found vertices and the approximated primitives). And a second process, where the result of the discriminatory analysis is used to evaluate and

quantify this match. The results of both processes are sent to the Broker Agent, which will decide if the syntactic recognition has a valid candidate.

The Combined Agents

Once the first recognition stage is finished and the Broker Agent has sent the information to the Combined Agents, each one of these agents look for the semantic recognition of the combined symbol they deal with, using the provided information (results from Primitive Agents). These combined agents manage new results with stored information from previous recognitions until a full semantic meaning is reached, that is, a complete combined symbol can be confirmed.

Regarding the semantic interpretation, it is important to consider that a stroke can either represent a symbol by itself or be part of a more complex symbol made up of different primitive symbols. For instance, the Extrusion/Radial-dimension combined symbol can be recognized

Figure 5. Possible inputs for extrusion/radial-dimension combined symbol

Extrusion/Radial-dimension Combined Symbol	Different inputs (no matter the sequence)		
	Set of three 'line' primitive symbols		
	Set of one 'line' and one 'angle' primitive symbols		
	One 'arrow' primitive symbol		

from one of the configurations of primitives (in any order) described in Figure 5.

Briefly, each combined agent will analyse whether the set of previous input primitives kept in the storehouse identifies its combined symbol, or if it is able to identify the symbol with the subsequent input primitives. If that is the case, the primitive symbol will be kept in the list. Otherwise it will be rejected. Therefore the system checks out the following situations:

1. If the stroke has a full meaning by itself, that is, it does not pertain to any more complex symbol, the recognition process finishes.
2. If it is possible that the stroke belongs to a more complex symbol or symbols which are formed by several strokes, it is kept in a storehouse and the system waits for the following stroke:
    ◦   If the following stroke can form a combined symbol with the strokes previously introduced and a full meaning is raised, then the actual recognition concludes, updating the status of the symbol to "accepted."
    ◦   If the following stroke can form a combined symbol with the strokes previously introduced and a full meaning is not reached, then it is stored and the status of the symbol remains "in process."
    ◦   If the consecutive stroke is not in the dictionary of primitive symbols, the

current symbol will be "accepted" if it has a full meaning by itself and otherwise "rejected."

In all these situations, the context information is evaluated to check if the new inputs recognised as primitive symbols are related to the recognition in progress, that is, with relative position, size and orientation. If the current input is rejected, the system checks the possibility of being sketched geometry, otherwise the input is definitely rejected.

In the example of Figure 6, the recognition of a diametral dimension combined symbol is performed. The figure shows the system agents being activated as the strokes are being introduced. Initially, when a line stroke is introduced, all the combined agents that are able to include lines are activated. Then, the second stroke is introduced and an angle primitive symbol is recognized. Only combined agents relative to combined symbols for Extrusion/Radial-dimension, diametral and Lineal dimension are still "in process." Later, when the third stroke is introduced, an Angle primitive symbol is recognized again and consequently combined agents for diametral and lineal dimension symbols remain "in process." Depending on the next input stroke several possibilities can be achieved. If the next input is a Circle primitive symbol the combined symbol is recognised as the diametral dimension symbol and a new process recognition starts. On the contrary, if the next input is a line primitive symbol, only the lineal dimension combined symbol is possible. If a subsequent

Figure 6. Example of a recognition process

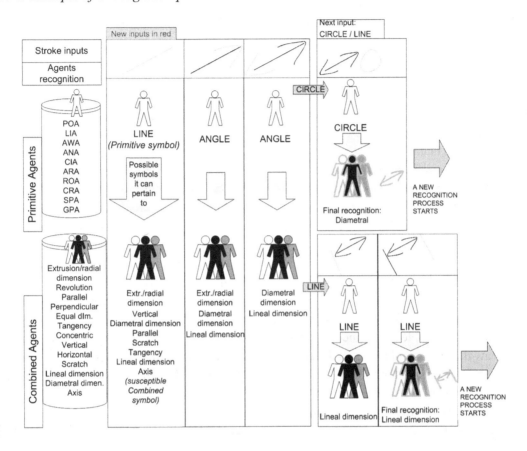

line primitive symbol is sketched, then the final recognition will return a lineal dimension matching and a new recognition process will take place.

Experimental Work and Results

The architecture proposed in this chapter has been implemented and evaluated in two different stages: a first stage, where the syntactic recognition is carried out by the primitive agents, and a second stage where the semantic recognition is performed by the combined agents. Then, the final result is provided by the Broker Agent.

In the tests performed to evaluate the first stage of recognition, about 2200 primitive symbols with different orientations and sizes have been used. The results of this first recognition stage show an average success ratio in classification for each phoneme of 96.41%. Main errors in classification correspond to cases in which the sketched symbol is wrongly digitized or poorly sketched. Also, errors can be due to symbols that are wrongly interpreted as for instance: an unclosed circle that can be confused with an arc; an arc with high radius value that can be converted to a line; an arrow or round-arrow symbol that can be confused depending if the main long stroke is more or less curved, independently of the user intention. On the other hand, the tests for the evaluation of the second recognition stage (final recognition), were carried out with a total of 2500 combined symbols with different orientations and sizes. For the evaluation of the recogniser, any possibility of the combined symbols was allowed, with a random sequence of introduction of strokes. The results show an average success ratio of 96.8%.

According to obtained results, the implementation of the proposed architecture makes the correct classification of the sketched symbols in a natural interface possible, with the exception of those cases in which the sketched form is not recognized as a word from the dictionary and consequently is classified as geometry. In this case the user should delete it and sketch again the intended form more accurately. Anyway, thanks to the cues extracted by the Feature Agent and the primitive agents, and the context information analyzed by the combined agents, the consideration of the non-intended "no gesture" possibility, impossible to detect by other recognizers, has been solved.

Solutions and Recommendations

Recognition of free-hand sketches has not yet been solved due to its complexness, since different users can draw the same symbol with a different sequence, shape, size, orientation and way of drawing (p.e. shaky drawing). Also, there are several limitations associated to traditional techniques, as for instance: a) they are not robust and can present ambiguity in the results depending on the user; b) a previous stage of training is normally needed; c) the number of sketched strokes is usually limited and the input sequence is previously set, reducing the freedom of the designer; or d) sketches are always classified even if they are not in the dictionary and consequently execute a non intended action.

Although these problems still remain, some works that use agent based technology are giving promising results in this field. The main difference of this technology from traditional techniques such as fuzzy logic, neural networks or other statistical learning is the implementation of specific algorithms to solve different problems, that is, the technique utilized is adaptable. Additionally, traditional techniques are more rigid since they use the same classification method to recognise different symbols, that is, the same neural network or the same discriminant analysis is executed to classify different objects, whereas in case of using agents, the classification method is customized for each type of symbol to be recognised, resulting in a higher success ratio.

Besides, agents are also autonomous and adaptative, and are therefore capable of changing their decision depending on the context or even if an interesting cue is found during the recognition process. Another benefit of using agents is the flexibility of this kind of system. In the particular case of the presented sketch recognizer, the implemented architecture allows the adding of new primitive ("phonemes") or combined ("words") symbols to the dictionary just by adding the corresponding Primitive Agent or Combined Agent respectively. Also, an improvement could be made by extending the architecture to a more hierarchical one, where other agents supervise the recognition process at every step, and distributing the architecture by modules, which could help to arrange the flow of the system more efficiently.

FUTURE RESEARCH DIRECTIONS

As has been shown in the previous sections, traditional techniques present important limitations in applications related to recognition of user sketches. Even so, they are still used nowadays. In parallel, alternative techniques that are now emerging like technology based on agents, which provides other functionality like flexibility, robustness, adaptability, running in parallel, and so on, are being applied more and more.

In a traditional environment the recognition process is carried out sequentially. However, in agent-based systems the specific tasks of the recognition process can be assigned to different agents that can act independently, avoiding the sequential process and executing the recognition process in parallel, as well as interacting among themselves and making reasoning together to achieve the best result. In light of the aforementioned, the solution of recognition of free-hand sketches implies the use of agent-based technology or others with similar features. In short, with proper technology, it is possible that this kind of interface is not an unachievable objective. And, however, although the use of this kind of system opens a new possibility for resolving the current problems in recognition, there is still much work to be done in this field.

CONCLUSION

A novel agent-based recognition architecture for a freehand-sketch interface has been proposed. The main recognition process is supported by two levels of agents: Primitive Agents which are in charge of the syntactic recognition, and Combined Agents which carry out the semantic recognition using contextual information. The proposed recognizer has the advantage of being easily extensible by means of new primitive or combined agents, so the addition of new gestures/symbols to the dictionary can be done with minimal intrusion to the designed system. The recognizer is not dependent on the number of strokes or on the sketching sequence order of user inputs, and the interface menus have been reduced to a minimum set. The agent-based architecture of the recognition system has been implemented in a Java platform, obtaining a success ratio of 96.41% for primitive symbols and 96.8% for the combined ones. These results reveal the relevancy of the proposed architecture for a sketch-based environment.

In summary, this work develops the algorithms, methods and tools needed to provide a parametric design environment based on sketches with the possibility of introducing the geometry and control parameters directly, without interference from handwritten menus, providing the same functionality than traditional tools of pen and paper, and other obvious advantages, such as reusing the sketches for the later stages of conceptual design.

There is evidence that agent-based systems are valid for applications that require decision-

making rules guided by knowledge, and also for these particular applications, where it is important to have the context information available to make decisions that guide the recognition process. This has been possible through the use of reasoning techniques, similar to those used by expert systems for changing decisions based on different possibilities, allowing the user to draw freely no matter what he draws, the intended action, the number of strokes or their sequence of introduction.

REFERENCES

Achten, H. H., & Jessurun, A. J. (2002). An agent framework for recognition of graphic units in drawings. In *Proceedings of 20th International Conference on Education and Research in Computer Aided Architectural Design in Europe* (pp. 246-253). Warsaw.

Alexe, A., Gaildrat, V., & Barthe, L. (2004). Interactive modelling from sketches using spherical implicit functions. In *Proceedings of the 3rd International Conference on Computer Graphics, Virtual Reality, Visualisation and Interaction in Africa* (pp. 25-34). Stellenbosch, South Africa: ACM.

Alhajj, R., & Elnagar, A. (2005). Multiagents to separating handwritten connected digits. *IEEE Transactions on Systems, Man, and Cybernetics. Part A, Systems and Humans, 35*(5), 593–602. doi:10.1109/TSMCA.2005.843389

Apte, A., Vo, V., & Kimura, T. D. (1993). Recognising multistroke geometric shapes: An experimental evaluation. In *Proceedings of the ACM (UIST'93)* (pp. 121-128). Atlanta, Georgia.

Azar, S., Couvreur, L., Delfosse, V., Jaspart, B., & Boulanger, C. (2006). An agent-based multimodal interface for sketch interpretation. In *IEEE Workshop on Multimedia Signal Processing* (pp. 488-492). New York, NY: IEEE.

Barr, R. E. (2004). The current status of graphical communication in engineering education. In *34th ASEE/IEEE Frontiers in Education Conference: Vol. 3* (pp. S1D8-S1D13). Savannah.

Bellifemine, F., Poggi, A., & Rimassa, G. (2001). Developing multi-agent systems with JADE. In *Intelligent Agents VII Agent Theories Architectures and Languages* (*Vol. 1986*, pp. 42–47). Berlin, Germany: Springer. doi:10.1007/3-540-44631-1_7

Bloomenthal, M., Zeleznik, R., Cutts, M., Fish, R., Drake, S., Holden, L., & Fuchs, H. (1998). Sketch-n-make: Automated machining of CAD sketches. In *Proceedings of ASME Design Engineering Technical Conferences, Computers in Engineering* (pp. 1-11).

Bryll, R., Rose, R. T., & Quek, F. (2005). Agent-based gesture tracking. *IEEE Transactions on Systems Man and Cybernetics Part a-Systems and Humans, 35*(6), 795-810.

Casella, G., Deufemia, V., Mascardi, V., Gennaro, C., & Martelli, M. (2008). An agent-based framework for sketched symbol interpretation. *Journal of Visual Languages and Computing, 19*(2), 225–257. doi:10.1016/j.jvlc.2007.04.002

Chetty, G., & Sharma, D. (2006). Distributed face recognition: A multiagent approach. In. *Proceedings of Knowledge-Based Intelligent Information and Engineering Systems, 4253*, 1168–1175. doi:10.1007/11893011_148

Ferguson, E. S. (1994). *Engineering and the mind's eye*. The MIT Press.

Fernandez-Pacheco, D. C., Conesa, J., Aleixos, N., Company, P., & Contero, M. (2009). An agent-based paradigm for free-hand sketch recognition. In *AI*IA 2009* (*Vol. 5883*, pp. 345–354). Emergent Perspectives in Artificial Intelligence. doi:10.1007/978-3-642-10291-2_35

Fernandez-Pacheco, D. G. (2010). *Aplicación para reconocimiento de bocetos basada en sistemas multi-agente*. Unpublished Doctoral dissertation, Technical University of Valencia, Valencia.

Fernández-Pacheco, D. G., Albert, F., Aleixos, N., Conesa, J., & Contero, M. (2011). Automated tuning of parameters for the segmentation of freehand sketches. In *Proceedings of the International Conference on Computer Graphics Theory and Applications (GRAP 2011)* (pp. 321-329). Algarve, Portugal.

Fernandez-Pacheco, D. G., Conesa, J., & Aleixos, N. (2010). A new agent-based paradigm for recognition of free-hand sketches. In *Proceedings of International Conference on Computational Science - ICCS 2010: Vol. 1* (pp. 2007-2016).

Fernandez-Pacheco, D. G., Contero, M., Naya, F., & Aleixos, N. (2008). A calligraphic interface in a sketch-based modelling environment. In *20° Congreso Internacional de Ingenieria Grafica INGEGRAF*. Valencia.

FIPA, O. R. G. (2002). *FIPA ACL message structure specification*.

Flasinski, M., Jurek, J., & Myslinski, S. (2009). Multi-agent system for recognition of hand postures. In *Computational Science* (*Vol. 5545*, pp. 815–824). ICCS. doi:10.1007/978-3-642-01973-9_91

Fonseca, M. J., & Jorge, J. (2000). Using fuzzy logic to recognise geometric shapes interactively. In *Proceedings of 9th IEEE Conference on Fuzzy Systems: Vol. 1* (pp. 291-296). San Antonio, Texas.

Gross, M. D. (1994). Recognising and interpreting diagrams in design. In *Proceedings of ACM (AVI'94)* (pp. 88-94). Bari, Italy.

Hammond, T., & Davis, R. (2005). LADDER, a sketching language for user interface developers. *Computers & Graphics-UK, 29*(4), 518–532. doi:10.1016/j.cag.2005.05.005

Harding, P. R. G., & Ellis, T. J. (2004). Recognising hand gesture using Fourier descriptors. In *Proceedings of the 17th International Conference on Pattern Recognition: Vol. 3* (pp. 286-289).

Igarashi, T., Matsuoka, S., & Tanaka, H. (1999). Teddy: A sketching interface for 3D freeform design. In *Siggraph 99 Conference Proceedings* (pp. 409-416). New York, NY: Association for Computing Machinery.

Jarrett, R., & Su, P. (2002). *Building tablet PC applications*. Microsoft Press.

Juchmes, R., Leclercq, P., & Azar, S. (2005). A freehand-sketch environment for architectural design supported by a multi-agent system. *Computers & Graphics-UK, 29*(6), 905–915. doi:10.1016/j.cag.2005.09.008

Julian, V., Carrascosa, C., Rebollo, M., Soler, J., & Botti, V. (2002). SIMBA: An approach for real-time multi-agent systems. In *Topics in Artificial Intelligence. Proceedings, 2504*, 282–293.

Licsar, A., & Sziranyi, T. (2004). Hand gesture recognition in camera-projector system. In *Computer Vision in Human-Computer Interaction Proceedings, 3058*, 83–93.

Mackenzie, G., & Alechina, N. (2003). Classifying sketches of animals using an agent-based system. In *Computer Analysis of Images and Patterns Proceedings, 2756*, 521–529.

Palanca, J., Aranda, G., & Garcia-Fornes, A. (2009). Building service-based applications for the iPhone using RDF: A tourism application. In *7th International Conference on Practical Applications of Agents and Multi-Agent Systems: Vol. 55* (pp. 421-429).

Park, C. H., & Park, H. (2005). Fingerprint classification using fast Fourier transform and nonlinear discriminant analysis. *Pattern Recognition, 38*(4), 495–503. doi:10.1016/j.patcog.2004.08.013

Paulson, B., & Hammond, T. (2008). PaleoSketch: Accurate primitive sketch recognition and beautification. In *Proceedings of the 13th International Conference on Intelligent User Interfaces* (pp. 1-10). Gran Canaria, Spain: ACM.

Pereira, J., Jorge, J., Branco, V., & Nunes, F. (2000). *Towards calligraphic interfaces: Sketching 3D scenes with gestures and context icons*. In 8th International Conference in Central Europe on Computer Graphics, Visualization and Interactive Digital Media WSCG. Plzen, Czech Republic: University of West Bohemia.

Perez-Delgado, M. L., & Matos-Franco, J. C. (2009). Artificial intelligence for picking up recycling bins: A practical application. In *7th International Conference on Practical Applications of Agents and Multi-Agent Systems: Vol. 55* (pp. 392-400). Berlin, Germany: Springer-Verlag Berlin.

Plimmer, B., & Apperley, M. (2002). Computer-aided sketching to capture preliminary design. In *Proceedings of the Third Australasian Conference on User Interfaces: Vol. 7* (pp. 9-12). Melbourne, Australia: Australian Computer Society, Inc.

Rogers, T. J., Ross, R., & Subrahmanian, V. S. (2000). IMPACT: A system for building agent applications. *Journal of Intelligent Information Systems, 14*(2-3), 95–113. doi:10.1023/A:1008727601100

Rose, A. T. (2005). Graphical communication using hand-drawn sketches in civil engineering. *Journal of Professional Issues in Engineering Education and Practice, 131*(4), 238–247. doi:10.1061/(ASCE)1052-3928(2005)131:4(238)

Rubine, D. (1991). Specifying gestures by example. In *Siggraph 91 Conference Proceedings: Vol. 25* (pp. 329-337). New York, NY: Association of Computing Machinery.

Saeed, K. (2000). Three-agent system for cursive-scripts recognition. In *Proceedings of the Fifth Joint Conference on Information Science: Vols. 1 and 2* (pp. A244-A247).

Tao, Y., Morrow, C. T., Heinemann, P. H., & Sommer, H. J. (1995). Fourier-based separation technique for shape grading of potatoes using machine vision. *Transactions of the American Society of Agricultural Engineers, 38*(3), 949–957.

Tversky, B. (2002). What do sketches say about thinking? In *AAAI Spring Symposium Series - Sketch Understanding* (pp. 148-152).

Wooldridge, M., & Jennings, N. R. (1995). Intelligent agents: Theory and practice. *The Knowledge Engineering Review, 10*(2), 115–152. doi:10.1017/S0269888900008122

Zeleznik, R. C., Herndon, K. P., & Hughes, J. F. (1996). SKETCH: An interface for sketching 3D scenes. In *Proceedings of the 23rd Annual Conference on Computer Graphics and Interactive Techniques* (pp. 163-170). ACM.

Zhang, D., & Lu, G. (2002). A comparative study of Fourier descriptors for shape representation and retrieval. In *Proceedings of 5th Asian Conference on Computer Vision (ACCV)* (pp. 646-651). Springer.

ADDITIONAL READING

Aleixos, N., Naya, F., Contero, M., Jorge, J., Varley, P., & Company, P. (2007). *Interpreting annotated engineering drawings*. In Invited Workshop on Pen Computing. Brown University.

Allvarado, C., & Davis, R. (2005). Sketchread: A multi-domain sketch recognition engine. In *Proceedings of the 17th Annual ACM Symposium on User Interface Software and Technology: Vol. 29* (pp. 518–532).

Bae, S. H., Balakrishnan, R., & Singh, K. (2008). ILoveSketch: As-natural-as-possible sketching system for creating 3D curve models. In *Proceedings of the 21st Annual ACM Symposium on User Interface Software and Technology* (pp. 151-160). New York, NY: ACM Press.

Company, P., Aleixos, N., Naya, F., Varley, P. A. C., Contero, M., & Fernández-Pacheco, D. G. (2008). A new sketch-based computer aided engineering pre-processor. In *Proceedings of the Sixth International Conference on Engineering Computational Technology* (Paper 149). Stirlingshire, UK: Civil-Comp Press.

Company, P., Contero, M., Conesa, J., & Piquer, A. (2004). An optimisation-based reconstruction engine for 3D modelling by sketching. *Computers & Graphics, 28*(6), 955–979. doi:10.1016/j.cag.2004.08.007

Company, P., Contero, M., Naya, F., & Aleixos, N. (2006). A study of usability of sketching tools aimed at supporting prescriptive sketches. In *Eurographics Workshop on Sketch-Based Interfaces and Modeling* (pp. 139-146). Vienna.

Contero, M., Naya, F., & Company, P. Saorin, J. L., & Conesa, J. (2005). Improving visualization skills in engineering education. *IEEE Computer Graphics and Applications, 25*(5), 24–31. doi:10.1109/MCG.2005.107

Contero, M., Naya, F., Jorge, J., & Conesa, J. (2003). CIGRO: A minimal instruction set calligraphic interface for sketch-based modeling. *Lecture Notes in Computer Science, 2669*, 549–558. doi:10.1007/3-540-44842-X_56

Dimri, J., & Gurumoorthy, B. (2005). Handling sectional views in volumen-based approach to automatically construct 3D solids from 2D views. *Computer Aided Design, 37*(5), 485–495. doi:10.1016/j.cad.2004.10.007

Fernández-Pacheco, D. G., Contero, M., Naya, F., & Aleixos, N. (2008). *Introducing 2D sketches in a CAD environment*. In 20° Congreso Internacional de Ingeniería Gráfica (INGEGRAF 08). Valencia.

Fonseca, M. J., Ferreira, A., & Jorge, J. A. (2009). Sketch-based retrieval of complex drawings using hierarchical topology and geometry. *Computer Aided Design*, *41*(12), 1067–1081. doi:10.1016/j.cad.2009.09.004

Hammond, T., & Davis, R. (2002). Tahuti: A geometrical sketch recognition system for UML class diagrams. In *AAAI Spring Symposium on Sketch Understanding* (pp. 59–68).

Hammond, T., & Davis, R. (2009). Recognizing interspersed sketches quickly. In *Proceedings of Graphics Interface*, *324*, 157–166.

Hong, J., Landay, J., Long, A. C., & Mankoff, J. (2002). Sketch recognisers from the end-user's, the designer's, and the programmer's perspective. In *Sketch Understanding Papers from the 2002 AAAI Spring Symposium* (pp. 73–77). American Association for Artificial Intelligence.

Hse, H., & Newton, A. R. (2004). Sketched symbol recognition using Zernike moments. In *Proceedings of the 17th International Conference on Pattern Recognition, Vol. 1* (pp. 367-370). Washington, DC: IEEE Computer Society.

Hutton, G., Cripps, M., Elliman, D., & Higgins, C. (1997). A strategy for on-line interpretation of sketched engineering drawings. In *Proceedings of the Fourth International Conference on Document Analysis and Recognition: Vol. 2* (pp. 771-775). Ulm, Germany.

Jansen, H., & Krause, F. L. (1984). Interpretation of freehand drawings for mechanical design processes. *Computers & Graphics*, *8*(4), 351–369. doi:10.1016/0097-8493(84)90034-7

Kara, L. B., & Stahovich, T. F. (2005). An image-based, trainable symbol recognizer for hand-drawn sketches. *Computers & Graphics-UK*, *29*(4), 501–517. doi:10.1016/j.cag.2005.05.004

Kim, D., & Kim, M. J. (2006). A curvature estimation for pen input segmentation in sketch-based modelling. *Computer Aided Design*, *38*, 238–248. doi:10.1016/j.cad.2005.10.006

Laviola, J. J. Jr, & Zeleznik, R. C. (2007). A practical approach for writer-dependent symbol recognition using a writer independent symbol recognizer. *IEEE Transactions on Pattern Analysis and Machine Intelligence*, *29*(11), 1917–1926. doi:10.1109/TPAMI.2007.1109

Lee, W., Kara, L. B., & Stahovich, T. F. (2007). An efficient graph-based recognizer for hand-drawn symbols. *Computers & Graphics*, *31*(4), 554–567. doi:10.1016/j.cag.2007.04.007

Li, J., Zhang, X., Ao, X., & Dai, G. (2005). Sketch recognition with continuous feedback based on incremental intention extraction. In *Proceedings of the 10th International Conference on Intelligent User Interfaces* (pp. 145-150). ACM Press.

Lipson, H., & Shpitalni, M. (1996). Optimization-based reconstruction of a 3D object from a single freehand line drawing. *Computer Aided Design*, *28*(8), 651–663. doi:10.1016/0010-4485(95)00081-X

Lopes, R., Cardoso, T., Silva, N., & Fonseca, M. J. (2009). Sketch-based interaction and calligraphic tags to create comics online. In *Proceedings of the 6th Eurographics Symposium on Sketch-Based Interfaces and Modeling (SBIM09)* (pp. 13-20). New York, NY: ACM Press.

Mori, Y., & Igarashi, T. (2007). Plushie: An interactive design system for plush toys. *ACM Transactions on Graphics*, *26*(3), 45. doi:10.1145/1276377.1276433

Mukerjee, A., Agrawal, R. B., Tiwari, N., & Hasan, N. (1997). Qualitative sketch optimization. *Artificial Intelligence for Engineering Design, Analysis and Manufacturing, 11*(4), 311–323. doi:10.1017/S0890060400003243

Murugappan, S., Sellamani, S., & Ramani, K. (2009). Towards beautification of freehand sketches using suggestions. In *Proceedings of the 6th Eurographics Symposium on Sketch-Based Interfaces and Modeling (SBIM09)* (pp. 69-76). ACM Press.

Naya, F., Contero, M., Aleixos, N., & Company, P. (2007). ParSketch: A sketch-based interface for a 2D parametric geometry editor. *Lecture Notes in Computer Science, 4551*, 115–124. doi:10.1007/978-3-540-73107-8_13

Nealen, A., Igarashi, T., Sorkine, O., & Alexa, M. (2007). FiberMesh: Designing freeform surfaces with 3D curves. *ACM Transactions on Graphics, 26*(3), 41. doi:10.1145/1276377.1276429

Olsen, L., Samavati, F. F., Sousa, M. C., & Jorge, J. A. (2009). Sketch-based modeling: A survey. *Computers & Graphics, 33*(1), 85–103. doi:10.1016/j.cag.2008.09.013

KEY TERMS AND DEFINITIONS

Agent-Based Systems: Applications implemented on agents

CAD: Computer Aided Design

CAS: Computer Aided Sketching

Free-Hand Sketch Recognition: Recognition of user free-hand inputs

Hierarchical Architecture: Software distributed in some levels of operation

Natural Interfaces: Interfaces without interaction of menus emulating the use of pen and paper

Sketch-Based Modelling: Applications of three-dimensional models that use sketches as inputs

Chapter 15
Gaussian Process–based Manifold Learning for Human Motion Modeling

Guoliang Fan
Oklahoma State University, USA

Xin Zhang
South China University of Technology, P. R. China

ABSTRACT

This chapter studies the human walking motion that is unique for every individual and could be used for many medical and biometric applications. The authors' goal is to develop a general low-dimensional (LD) model from of a set of high-dimensional (HD) motion capture (MoCap) data acquired from different individuals, where there are two main factors involved, i.e., pose (a specific posture in a walking cycle) and gait (a specific walking style). Many Gaussian process (GP)-based manifold learning methods have been proposed to explore a compact LD manifold embedding for motion representation where only one factor (i.e., pose) is normally revealed explicitly with the other factor (i.e., gait) implicitly or independently treated. The authors recently proposed a new GP-based joint gait-pose manifold (JGPM) that unifies these two variables into one manifold structure to capture the coupling effect between them. As the result, JGPM is able to capture the motion variability both across different poses and among multiple gaits (i.e., individuals) simultaneously. In order to show advantages of joint modeling of combining the two factors in one manifold, they develop a validation technique to compare JGPM with recent GP-based methods in terms of their capability of motion interpolation, extrapolation, denoising, and recognition. The experimental results further demonstrate advantages of the proposed JGPM for human motion modeling.

DOI: 10.4018/978-1-4666-1806-0.ch015

INTRODUCTION

Human motion analysis is becoming a popular research topic due to its wide applications such as human detection, tracking, recognition, and 3D character animation etc. It is also a challenging research topic due to the high-dimensional (HD), non-linear, and multi-factor nature of human motion data from different individuals or activities. In this work, we focus on the walking motion, i.e., the *gait*. Many Gaussian process (GP)-based manifold learning algorithms have been proposed to explore the low-dimensional (LD) latent structures from the HD visual or kinematic data, by which the problems of motion analysis or pose estimation can be well constrained. Specifically, the pose manifold is often used to represent the cyclic nature of a gait and can be learned from either kinematic data (Urtasun, Fleet, & Fua, 2006), (Gupta, Chen, Chen, Kimber, & Daivs, 2008), (Ek, Torr, & Lawrence, 2007) or visual data (Elgammal & Lee, 2004a), and the view manifold was also involved in (Lee & Elgammal, 2007) by which it is possible to interpolate gait observations for new views during pose estimation. Moreover, when multiple motion styles from different subjects or activities are involved, two independent style-related linear variables, "identity" and "gait', (Wang, Fleet, & Hertzmann, 2007) or a discrete "style" variable (Elgammal & Lee, 2004b) or separate motion trajectories (Gupta, et al., 2008) were used.

In our early work (Zhang & Fan, 2010), the idea of *gait manifold* was proposed to capture the motion variability among different individuals, by which we also define a continuous-valued gait variable that can be used to extrapolate new gait motions via nonlinear interpolation along the gait manifold. Specifically, the gait and pose manifolds were treated separately for motion modeling where the pose and gait variables are assumed to be independent. Instead, our studies revealed that the two variables may be coupled and should be jointly considered to specify a particular gait

motion sequence. Therefore, we suggested a joint gait-pose manifold (JGPM) recently (Zhang & Fan, 2011) that is learned via a Gaussian process (GP)-based manifold learning method that has a probabilistic representation for robust motion analysis, unlike the one in (Zhang & Fan, 2010) where both the pose and gait manifolds are learnt as the deterministic structure.

The proposed JGPM was intended not only to reflect the coupling relationship between the pose and gait variables, but also to preserve their own manifold structures. It was assumed in our early work (Zhang & Fan, 2010) that the gait manifold has a closed-loop 1D structure while the pose manifold is characterized by a circle. Inspired by (Elgammal & Lee, 2009) where a torus is used to represent multi-view dynamic gait observations featured with two cyclic variables (i.e., pose and view), we suggested a toroidal structure for JGPM (Zhang & Fan, 2011), as shown in Figure 1. Moreover, three versions of JGPM were developed to examine the validity of the assumption that JGPM may follow a toroidal structure, i.e., *torus-based* (JGPM-I), *torus-constrained* (JGPM-II), and *torus-like* (JGPM-III). The first involves a directly nonlinear radial basis function (RBF)-based mapping like the one in (Elgammal & Lee, 2009) without probabilistic learning that serves as a baseline reference. The second is learned via a method extended from a recent topologically-constrained GP algorithm but still remains an ideal torus that is an idealized JGPM with an optimized latent space. The third is learned via a new two-step GP algorithm that tends to balance the ideal structure assumption with the actual intrinsic data structure. It was shown that torus-like JGPM not only outperforms the recent GP algorithms (N. Lawrence & J. Candela, 2006), (K. Grochow, S. Martin, A. Hertzmann, & Z. Popovic, 2004), (Urtasun, et al., 2006), (Wang, et al., 2008) in terms of synthesizing new gait motions (i.e., extrapolation), but also improve video-based motion estimation compared with (Zhang & Fan, 2010). The major advantage of JGPM-III is its

Figure 1. Three versions of JGPM are shown which are imposed with different topology constraints and where the vertical and horizontal circles represent the pose and gait manifolds, respectively. (From X. Zhang and G. Fan, "Joint Gait-Pose Manifold for Video-based Human Motion Estimation", in Proc. IEEE CVPR Workshop on Machine Learning for Vision-based Motion Analysis (MLvMA), Colorado Springs, Colorado, USA, June 25, 2011. @ 2011 IEEE)

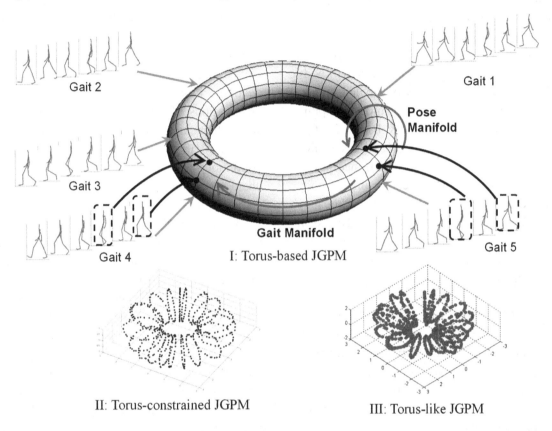

compact, well-organized and smooth latent space that is nicely supported by the torus-like manifold surface, unlike its peers where the latent space is normally relative sparse and less-organized.

In this chapter, we want to revisit the idea of JGPM by comparing them with recent state-of-the-art GP-based approaches in terms of their overall performance and robustness of human motion modeling. Specifically, we will develop a validation technique to evaluate GP-based motion modeling methods with respect to their capability of motion interpolation, extrapolation, denoising and recognition. The detailed comparison will help us further understand the ap-

plicability and suitability of each GP algorithm for different data analysis tasks. Moreover, this study could also provide us some insights to the issue that how the manifold structure in the latent space affects the efficiency and expressiveness of HD data. As the consequence, this study can help us incorporate appropriate prior knowledge in a GP algorithm to encourage an expected or desirable manifold structure.

BACKGROUND

Motion models provide an important kinematic prior for various motion analysis tasks. In this chapter, we review three motion modeling categories, i.e., graphical model-based, physical model-based and dimension reduction (DR)-based approaches. *Graphic model-based approaches* represent the spatial and temporal priors of body parts by learning from a set of labeled images (Lan & Huttenlocher, 2004) or motion capture data (Sigal, et al 2004; Sigal & Black, 2006a). *Physical model-based approaches* (Rosenhahn, et al, 2008), (Vondrak, et al, 2008)) incorporate various kinematic/dynamic constraints of body movements into the inference process. They may not need any training data, but a detailed physical model could be hard to obtain which may also impose some challenges for inference due to the HD nature of the model. For example, the methods in (Brubaker, et al 2007), (Brubaker & Fleet, 2008), (Brubaker, et al, 2010) mainly focus on lower-body motion. *DR-based methods* try to explore the LD intrinsic structure by learning from either kinematic or visual data that can be represented by a few latent variables.

Our research is focused on DR-based motion modeling. DR methods can be roughly grouped into two major categories, i.e., *geometrically-inspired algorithms* and *latent variable model based DR algorithms*. The first group methods seek to preserve the local geometrical or linear proximity among the HD data in the LD manifold, like IsoMap (Tenenbaum, et al, 2000), Local Linear Embedding (LLE) (Roweis & Saul, 2000) and Laplacian Eigenmap (Belkin & Niyogi, 2003). These DR algorithms were used in (Elgammal & Lee, 2004), (Lee & Elgammal, 2007), (Sminchisescu & Jepson, 2004) for human motion modeling and they are normally efficient to discover a LD latent space embedding without initialization or prior constraints. But the mapping function between the LD latent space and HD data space has to be learnt separately. In (Elgammal & Lee, 2009),

an ideal torus-shaped manifold was proposed to represent multi-view dynamic gait observations. The toroidal manifold topology was *designed* based on the cyclic nature of the pose and view factors. Thus the problem of DR becomes a task of finding a non-linear mapping between the torus and corresponding visual observations. In (Lee & Elgammal, 2007), a continue-valued view manifold was learned via non-linear tensor decomposition that is able to interpolate visual observations of unknown views. This method was further extended in our previous work (Zhang & Fan, 2010) to learn a *gait manifold* where a continuous-valued gait variable was proposed to characterize multiple walking styles from different individuals. Unlike (Lee & Elgammal, 2007) where an explicit order is available for the view manifold, a key issue studied in (Zhang & Fan, 2010) is how to determine an appropriate manifold topology for the gait manifold that represents different training gaits in a continuous-way and can be used to synthesize new gait motions.

The second group methods involve a linear or nonlinear mapping to relate the HD data with a LD latent space, such as the Gaussian Process Latent Variable Model (GPLVM) (Lawrence, 2003) and Laplacian Eigenmaps (Lu, et al, 2007). Especially, GPLVM is a generalization of the probabilistic PCA that uses a kernel function to form the HD-LD mapping. Several GPLVM variants were proposed for human motion analysis, such as the Gaussian Process Dynamical Model (GPDM) (Wang, et al., 2008), Scaled GPLVM (S-GPLVM) (Grochow, et al, 2004), Back Constrained-GPLVM (BC-GPLVM) (N. Lawrence & J. Candela, 2006), Balanced GPDM (B-GPDM) (Urtasun et al., 2006) and hierarchical-GPLVM (H-GPLVM) (Lawrence & Moore, 2007). These GP-based methods are often used to deal one continuous variable in the latent space, e.g., pose. On the other hand, multi-style motion analysis may involve multiple latent variables. In (Wang, et al., 2007), a multi-factor GP was proposed to separate "style" and "pose" using two nonlinear

GP kernels. In addition, there were several ways of merging multiple motion-related manifolds in one latent space, such as including an embedding from the observation space to the latent space (OD-GPLVM) (Gupta, et al., 2008), imposing a graphical model (Switch GPDM) (Chen, et al, 2009), encouraging them to conform to a desired topology, for example the topology constrained (LL-GPLVM) (Urtasun et al., 2008). In the following, we will review GPLVM and its variant in more details.

Gaussian Process Latent Variable Model (GPLVM)

Gaussian processes (GPs) are stochastic processes that govern the property of functions and inherit the properties of normal distribution (Rasmussen & Williams, 2006). Just as a Gaussian distribution is fully specified by its mean and covariance matrix, a GP is specified by a mean and a covariance function. GPs are important and useful in statistical modeling because that the normal assumption makes the inference and learning relative easy. For example, if a random process is modeled as a GP, the distributions of various derived quantities can be obtained explicitly. Such quantities include: the average value of the process over a range of times; the error in estimating the average using sample values at a small set of times. GP have been studied in machine learning and statistics field for regression, classification, data modeling etc. GPLVM takes advantages of GP and extends it as a probabilistic manifold learning or DR method. It defines a generative model where given a latent variable $\mathbf{x}_i \in \mathfrak{R}^d$, the observed data point $\mathbf{y}_i \in \mathfrak{R}^D$ can be generated through a noisy process,

$$\mathbf{y}_i = f(\mathbf{x}_i) + \varepsilon, \tag{1}$$

where $\varepsilon : N(0, \beta^{-1}\mathbf{I})$.. The latent variable coordinates and their nonlinear GP mapping to the HD data space are learnt together through GPLVM. Let the HD data be represented as a matrix $\mathbf{Y} = [\mathbf{y}_1, ..., \mathbf{y}_N]$ in which each row is a single training data point, $\mathbf{y}_i \in \mathbb{R}^D$. Let $\mathbf{X} = [\mathbf{x}_1, ..., \mathbf{x}_N]$ be the matrix whose row is the corresponding latent position in the low-dimensional space, $\mathbf{x}_i \in \mathbb{R}^d$. The likelihood of the data given latent positions based on GP is

$$p(\mathbf{Y} \mid \mathbf{X}, \beta) =$$
$$\frac{1}{\sqrt{(2\pi)^{ND} \mid \mathbf{K}_Y \mid}} \exp\left(-\frac{1}{2}tr\left(\mathbf{K}_Y^{-1}\mathbf{Y}\mathbf{Y}^T\right)\right), \tag{2}$$

where $\mathbf{K}_Y$ is a $N \times N$ covariance matrix whose entries are defined by kernel function, $\mathbf{K}_Y(i, j) = k_Y(\mathbf{x}_i, \mathbf{x}_j)$. Here, we use the radial basis function (RBF) defined as

$$k_Y(\mathbf{x}_i, \mathbf{x}_j) =$$
$$\beta_1 \exp\left(-\frac{-\beta_2}{2}\mathbf{d}(\mathbf{x}_i, \mathbf{x}_j)\right) + \beta_3^{-1}\delta_{\mathbf{x}_i, \mathbf{x}_j}, \tag{3}$$

where $\beta = [\beta_1, \beta_2, \beta_3]$ is the kernel hyperparameters, $\mathbf{d}$ is the distance function between $\mathbf{x}_i$ and $\mathbf{x}_j$ and $\delta_{\mathbf{x}_i, \mathbf{x}_j}$ denotes the Kronecker delta. GPLVM maximizes the marginal likelihood (2) with respect to both the latent points $\mathbf{X}$ and the hyper-parameters β, which is equivalent to minimize the negative log of (2), i.e.,

$$\{\hat{\mathbf{X}}, \hat{\beta}\} = \arg\max_{\mathbf{X},\beta} p(\mathbf{Y} \mid \mathbf{X}, \beta)$$
$$= \arg\min_{\mathbf{X},\beta} \left(-\log p(\mathbf{Y} \mid \mathbf{X}), \beta\right), \tag{4}$$

where

$$\mathcal{L}_l = -\log p(\mathbf{Y} \mid \mathbf{X}, \beta)$$
$$= \frac{D}{2} \ln |\mathbf{K_Y}| + \frac{1}{2} tr\left(\mathbf{K_Y^{-1}} \mathbf{Y} \mathbf{Y}^T\right) + \frac{N}{2} \log 2\pi.$$

(5)

There is no closed form solution for (5) and a gradient-based optimization is usually employed. The only pre-defined parameter of GPLVM is the dimensionality of the latent space, i.e., d. Recently proposed Bayesian GPLVM (Titsias & Lawrence, 2010) is able to estimate the dimensionality of latent space by introducing an approximation to the marginal likelihood of the fully marginalized GPLVM. Essentially, GPLVM is a generalization of the probabilistic PCA (PPCA) that estimates the joint density of the data samples and their latent coordinates. Comparing with geometrically-inspired DR algorithms, GPLVM provides a one-way LD-HD mapping function from the latent space to high dimensional data, but there is no HD-LD mapping involved. Also, since GPLVM was original used for non-sequential data analysis, the temporal dynamic property was not considered into the learning and optimization process.

Back-Constrained GPLVM (BC-GPLVM)

In (Lawrence & Candela, 2006), back-constraints were suggested to be incorporated into GPLVM for a smoother and better-behaved model. The smooth covariance function in GPLVM specifies a smooth mapping and ensures that close points in the HD data space remain close in the LD latent space. Unfortunately, the inverse mapping may not be smooth. The BC-GPLVM represents each latent point as a smooth parametric mapping function from its corresponding point in the data space, $\mathbf{x}_i = g(\mathbf{y}_j, \mathbf{Q})$, where $\mathbf{Q}$ is the mapping parameter set. For example, the mapping can be a kernel-based regression model, where regression

on a kernel induced feature space provides the mapping,

$$\mathbf{x}_i = \sum_{q=1}^{N} q_j k(\mathbf{y}_j, \mathbf{y_q}).$$

(6)

Rather than finding the latent position, the learning of BC-GPLVM optimizes the hyper-parameters of the kernel matrix and the mapping parameters by maximizing the likelihood, i.e.,

$$\{\hat{\mathbf{Q}}, \hat{\beta}\} = \arg \max_{\mathbf{Q}, \beta} p(\mathbf{Y} \mid \mathbf{Q}, \beta).$$

(7)

BC-GPLVM encourages points that are close in the data space to be close in the latent space. Also, the mapping from the HD data space to the LD latent space is provided.

Gaussian Process Dynamical Model (GPDM)

GPDM (Wang, et al., 2008) was proposed by augmenting the GPLVM with a GP dynamic prior on the latent positions. In other words, GPDM is a generative latent variable dynamic model, including a LD space, a probabilistic mapping from the latent space to the HD space, and a dynamical model in the latent space. GPDM is derived from a generative model defined as

$$\mathbf{x}_t = \sum_i \mathbf{a}_i \phi_i(\mathbf{x}_{t-1}) + \mathbf{n}_{x,t}$$

(8)

$$\mathbf{y}_t = \sum_i \mathbf{b}_j \psi_j(\mathbf{x}_t) + \mathbf{n}_{y,t}$$

(9)

where $\mathbf{A} = [\mathbf{a}_1, \mathbf{a}_2, \ldots]$ and $\mathbf{B} = [\mathbf{b}_1, \mathbf{b}_2, \ldots]$ are weights, ϕ_i and ψ_j are basis function, and $\mathbf{n}_{x,t}$ and $\mathbf{n}_{y,t}$ are zero-mean white Gaussian noisy. From the Bayesian regression perspective, weights A and B should be marginalized out. With an isotropic Gaussian prior on each $\mathbf{b}_j$, the $\mathbf{B}$ can be marginalized to yield a multivariate Gaussian data likelihood as

$$p(\mathbf{Y} \mid \mathbf{X}, \beta) =$$
$$\frac{1}{\sqrt{(2\pi)^{ND} \mid \mathbf{K}_Y \mid}} \exp\left(-\frac{1}{2} tr\left(\mathbf{K}_\mathbf{Y}^{-1} \mathbf{Y}\mathbf{Y}\right)\right), \quad (10)$$

where $\mathbf{K}_Y$ is a kernel matrix with hyperparameters β that is shared by all observation. The elements of the kernel matrix $\mathbf{K}_Y$ are defined by a kernel function $(\mathbf{K}_Y)_{i,j} = k_t(\mathbf{x}_i, \mathbf{x}_j)$. The latent dynamics follows the similar formulation, i.e., with an isotropic Gaussian prior on $\mathbf{a}_i$, we can marginalize out $\mathbf{A}$ from the joint density over latent positions and weights. The density over latent positions becomes

$$p(\mathbf{X} \mid \alpha) =$$
$$\frac{p(\mathbf{x}_1)}{\sqrt{(2\pi)^{(N-1)d} \mid \mathbf{K}_\mathbf{X} \mid^d}} \exp\left(-\frac{1}{2} tr\left(\mathbf{K}_\mathbf{X}^{-1} \mathbf{X}_{out} \mathbf{X}_{out}^T\right)\right), \quad (11)$$

where $\mathbf{X}_{out} = [\mathbf{x}_2, ..., \mathbf{x}_N]^T$, $\mathbf{K}_\mathbf{X}$ is $(N-1) \times (N-1)$ kernel matrix constructed from $[\mathbf{x}_1, ..., \mathbf{x}_{N-1}]$ and α is the kernel hypermarameters. The learning of GPDM aims at estimating the latent positions and the kernel hyper-parameters. By adopting simple prior distributions of hyper-parameters as in (Wang, et al., 2008), the posterior of GPDM becomes

$$p(\mathbf{X}, \alpha, \beta \mid \mathbf{Y}) \propto p(\mathbf{Y} \mid \mathbf{X}, \beta) p(\mathbf{X} \mid \alpha) p(\alpha) p(\beta). \quad (12)$$

The latent positions and hyper-paremeters are found by maximizing (12),

$$\{\hat{\mathbf{X}}, \hat{\beta}, \hat{\alpha}\} = \arg \max_{X, \beta, \alpha} p(\mathbf{X}, \alpha, \beta \mid \mathbf{Y}). \quad (13)$$

It is equivalent to minimize its negative log defined as

$$\mathcal{L}_d = \frac{d}{2} \ln|\mathbf{K}_\mathbf{X}| + \frac{1}{2} tr\left(\mathbf{K}_\mathbf{X}^{-1} \mathbf{X}_{out} \mathbf{X}_{out}^T\right) \frac{D}{2} \ln|\mathbf{K}_\mathbf{Y}|$$
$$+ \frac{1}{2} tr\left(\mathbf{K}_\mathbf{Y}^{-1} \mathbf{Y}\mathbf{Y}^T\right) + \sum_i \ln \alpha_i + \sum_i \ln \beta_i + \mathrm{C}, \quad (14)$$

where C is a constant. The first two terms associates with the log dynamics density (11), referred as $\mathcal{L}_x$; the following two terms come from the log likelihood $\mathcal{L}_l$ as defined in (5) and the next two terms are the log of prior $\mathcal{L}_p$. GPDM can be naturally extended to multiple motion sequences $\{\mathbf{Y}_i \mid i = 1, ..., P\}$ by concatenating all the input sequences and ignoring the temporal transitions between two sequences.

Scaled-GPLVM (S-GPLVM)

In (Grochow, et al., 2004), a scaled-GPLVM was proposed by including a set of D scale parameter $\mathbf{W} \equiv diag(w_1, ..., w_D)$ to normalize the variation of each dimension in the HD data space. The motivation is straightforward. In many HD data sets, different dimensions do not share the same scale in terms of their variation. The scale parameter is introduced to model the variance in each data dimension. Similar as GPLVM, the likelihood of SGPLVM is

$$p(\mathbf{Y} \mid \mathbf{X}, \beta) =$$
$$\frac{\mid \mathbf{W} \mid^N}{\sqrt{(2\pi)^{ND} \mid \mathbf{K}_Y \mid}} \exp\left(-\frac{1}{2} tr\left(\mathbf{K}_\mathbf{Y}^{-1} \mathbf{Y}\mathbf{W}^2\mathbf{Y}^T\right)\right). \quad (15)$$

Learning of the SGPLVM entails the latent position $\mathbf{X}$, kernel hyperparameters β and scale parameters $\mathbf{W}$. They are estimated by maximizing the above likelihood function as

$$\{\hat{\mathbf{X}}, \hat{\beta}, \hat{\mathbf{W}}\} = \arg \max_{X,\beta,W} p(\mathbf{Y} \mid \mathbf{X}, \beta). \qquad (16)$$

S-GPLVM has D more parameters to estimate but it makes the learning process based on a normalized observation space. The experimental results in (Grochow, et al., 2004a) have demonstrated S-GPLVM's superior performance on the realistic character animation.

Balanced-GPDM (B-GPDM)

GPDM optimizes latent trajectories by incorporating the latent dynamic function. However, the learning of GPDM tends to simultaneously minimize the reconstruction errors in the HD data space and the temporal prediction errors in the LD latent space. When the dataset becomes larger, errors in the data space usually dominate the objective function and latent position estimation. This leads to the un-smoothness even big gaps in the latent space. In (Urtasun, et al., 2006), a balanced-GPDM (B-GPDM) was introduced as a simple yet effective improvement to GPDM that balances the influence of data reconstruction and latent position dynamics by adding a scaling factor, $\lambda = \dfrac{D}{d}$ (the ratio of the HD and LD dimensions) to the dynamic density function. Then the new-log dynamic density function is

$$\mathcal{L}_x = \lambda \left(\frac{d}{2} \ln | \mathbf{K_X} | + \frac{1}{2} tr \left(\mathbf{K_X}^{-1} \mathbf{X}_{out} \mathbf{X}_{out}^T \right) \right). \qquad (17)$$

B-GPDM produces much smoother latent trajectories than GPLVM and GPDM by handling multiple motion sequences. A smoother latent space can better reflect the intrinsic structure in the sequential data and support more effective human motion tracking.

Topologically-Constrained Gaussian Process Dynamic Model (LL-GPDM)

The topological constraints were introduced to the GPLVM and GPDM framework in (Urtasun, et al., 2008) with the objective to handle multiple motion patterns, e.g., walking and running. Specifically, the topological constraints can be obtained from a neighborhood structure learned through a generalized LLE (Saul & Roweis, 2003). In LLE, the neighboring relationship is preserved by finding a LD representation with an optimized set of local weights that can best reconstruct each data point from its neighbors. Hence, these local weights are employed in LL-GPDM as a prior distribution of latent points, defined as

$$p(\mathbf{X} \mid \mathbf{W}) =$$
$$\frac{1}{C} \exp(\frac{1}{\delta^2} \sum_{i=1}^{N} \| \mathbf{x}_i - \sum_{j=1}^{N} \mathbf{w}_{ij} \mathbf{x}_j \|^2), \qquad (18)$$

where $\mathbf{w}_{ij}$ is an element of the weight matrix $\mathbf{W}$ that minimizes LLE-based reconstruction error of the training data, δ^2 is a scaling term and C is a normalization term. Furthermore, certain geometric constraints in the latent space can be explicitly incorporated to compute $\mathbf{w}_{ij}$ for each data point. As the result, LL-GPDM not only preserves the local neighboring relation in the latent space, but also encourages the formation of an expected latent structure, e.g., a cylinder, that can represent multiple cyclic motion patterns, walking and running. Then the latent variable is obtained by maximizing the posterior probability with the prior defined by the LLE-based topology constraint,

$$\{\hat{\mathbf{X}}, \hat{\beta}\} =$$
$$\arg \max_{\mathbf{X},\beta} \left(p(\mathbf{Y} \mid \mathbf{X}, \beta) p(\mathbf{X} \mid \mathbf{W}) p(\beta) \right). \qquad (19)$$

Table 1. Comparison of five GP-based DR algorithms and three versions of JGPM. ($\mathbf{X}$ and $\mathbf{Y}$ indicate the LD latent space and HD space, respectively.)

Features/ GP Methods	Dynamic Prior	Topology Prior	Latent Variable	$\mathbf{X} \rightarrow \mathbf{Y}$ Mapping	$\mathbf{Y} \rightarrow \mathbf{X}$ Mapping
GPLVM	N/A	N/A	pose	GP	N/A
BC-GPLVM	N/A	N/A	pose	GP	kernel function
GPDM	Y	N/A	pose	GP	N/A
SB-GPDM	Y	N/A	pose	GP	N/A
LL-GPDM	Y	cylinder	pose	GP	N/A
JGPM-I	Y	torus	pose and gait	RBF	RBF
JGPM-II	Y	torus	pose and gait	GP	N/A
JGPM-III	Y	torus	pose and gait	GP	N/A

Similarly, the maximization of above equation is equivalent to minimize its negative log. The negative log of $p(\mathbf{Y} \mid \mathbf{X}, \beta)$ is the same as (5) and the negative log of $p(\mathbf{X} \mid \mathbf{w})$ is defined as

$$
\begin{aligned}
\mathcal{L}_w &= -\log(p(\mathbf{X} \mid \mathbf{W})) \\
&= \frac{1}{\delta^2} \sum_{i=1}^{N} \parallel \mathbf{x}_i - \sum_{j=1}^{N} \mathbf{w}_{ij}\mathbf{x}_j \parallel^2 .
\end{aligned} \tag{20}
$$

In the case of LL-GPDM learning, we can introduce the dynamics and locally linear prior together and combine them as the product of posterior. The objective function becomes $\mathcal{L}_d + \mathcal{L}_w$ where $\mathcal{L}_d$ is defined in (14). LL-GPDM formulates the topological constraints as the probabilistic latent variable model and imposes them into the GPLVM/GPDM framework. It provides an effective solution to unify multiple motion trajectories related to different motion styles via a cylinder structure that provides interpretable latent directions enabling with style-content separation and supports a smooth transition between two different motion styles, i.e., walking and running, in the latent space. It is worth mentioning that LL-GPDM is focused on the joint modeling of different motion styles or patterns and it leads to a relative compact manifold structure where all motion trajectories are clustered together.

Summary of Recent GP Algorithms

In this work, we are mainly concerned with multiple gait motions from different individuals. Although abovementioned GP algorithms can handle multiple motions sequences from different individuals or of different activities, they normally involve one latent variable (i.e., pose), and different motion sequences are usually reflected by different trajectories or regions in the latent space. The recently proposed joint gait-pose manifolds (Zhang & Fan, 2011) are featured by a single latent space that integrates two variables (i.e., gait and pose) into one unified manifold structure. The key idea of JGPM is structure-guided manifold learning that seems to be a viable and practical approach for learning a valid manifold from a sparse and unorganized (without an explicit topology) data by incorporating some useful prior knowledge about the manifold structure. All of these GP algorithms are compared in Table 1 with respect to five aspects of the latent space: (1) Is a dynamic prior involved? (2) Is a topology prior used? (3) What kind of latent variables are defined? (4) Is a LD-HD mapping available? (5) Is a HD-LD mapping available?

MAIN FOCUS OF THE CHAPTER

This chapter discusses three issues of human motion modeling using GP-based approaches, mainly those in the GPLVM family. (1) The first issue is *how we can represent the variability of multiple gait motions from different individuals in the latent space*. Traditionally, a GPLVM or GPDM model can be directly learnt from multiple gait motions that leads to multiple trajectories in the latent space, which could be clustered together (Urtasun, et al., 2008) or wide apart (Wang, et al., 2008) (Urtasun, Fleet, & Fua, 2006). However, no explicit variable is used to represent different gait styles. Another approach is to use a discrete variable to characterize multiple gait styles in a multi-factor GP model (Wang, et al, 2007). (2) The second issue is *how to deal with multiple factors in the motion data via a compact and differentiable manifold*. A common practice is to assume that multiple factors are independent, leading to a style-content representation, like those in (Wang, et al, 2007) and (Lee and Elgammal, 2007). Assuming that multiple factors are independent does facilitate the GP-based learning and inference process; however, we may not be able to capture the coupling effect among them for more sophisticated motion analysis. (3) The third issue is *how to evaluate various GP models regarding their performance and applicability of human motion modeling*. A comparative study was presented in (Quirion et al, 2008) where several existing GPLVM-based methods were compared in terms of their performance in character animation.

In the following, we will study these three issues from a different perspective. First, we briefly review the idea of gait manifold to address the first issue. Second, we present the recently proposed joint gait-pose manifolds (JGPM) for gait modeling. Third, we introduce a validation technique by which existing GPLVM-based methods along with three versions of JGPM can be compared in terms their capability of motion interpolation, extrapolation, denoising and recognition. The first two tests are similar to those in (Quirion et al, 2008), while the last two tests are newly added to further examine the recent GPLVM methods in terms of their robustness and accuracy for general motion representation.

Issue 1: Gait Manifold

In our previous research (Zhang & Fan, 2010), we proposed the *gait manifold* to represent the variability of multiple gait motions from different individuals, as shown in Figure 2 where a 1D gait manifold is illustrated to represent five training gaits. Specifically, a continuous-valued gait variable is defined along the gait manifold that allows us to synthesize (or extrapolate) a new gait (Gait A or B) from training gaits. The gait manifold can be learned from a set of training gaits where the intrinsic structure is unclear, unlike other manifolds often used, e.g., the pose or view manifolds that have a well-defined sequential and cyclic structure. The key to learn the gait manifold is to determine an appropriate manifold topology that specifies an optimal (in some sense) adjacency or neighboring relationship among training gaits in the latent space.

Due to the intrinsic similarity among all human gaits, the gait manifold was assumed to have a 1D closed-loop structure, and then the manifold topology becomes a certain ordering relationship among the training gaits. For example in Figure 2, the topology of the 1D gait manifold is Gait 1→ Gait 2→ Gait 3→ Gait 4→ Gait 5→ Gait 1. Specifically, we suggested the shortest-closed-path as the topology of the gait manifold that supports the best local smoothness for interpolation. A kinematic gait generative model (KGGM)

Figure 2. The illustration of a gait manifold used for gait synthesis from five training gaits (From X. Zhang and G. Fan, "Dual Generative Gait Models for Human Motion Estimation from a Single Camera", IEEE Trans. Systems, Man and Cybernetics, Part B, April 2010. @ 2010 IEEE).

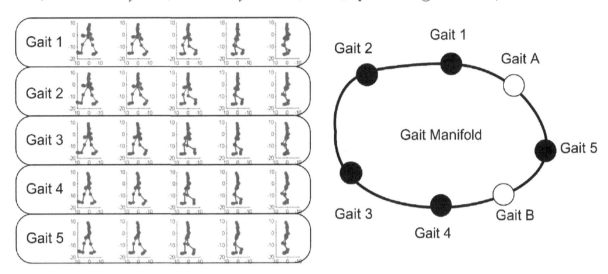

was developed by using a non-linear tensor decomposition in (Zhang & Fan, 2010) where both gait and pose manifolds are involved for motion modeling.

The learning of KGGM involves three steps. First, we apply RBF mapping to map all human gait data to a circular-shaped pose manifold, and we can stack on mapping matrices into a tensor. Then, through tensor decomposition, we can factorize out a set of gait vectors in the tensor coefficient space each of which corresponds to a training gait. Third, we use the spline-fitting method to connect all training gait vectors into a continuous closed-loop gait manifold according to certain manifold topology, where all gait vectors are treated as anchor points. It is worth mentioning that under different distance functions, we may have different manifold topologies, leading to different gait manifolds, as shown in Figure 3. We studied three distance functions. The first is the Euclidean distance in the tensor coefficient space (Zhang & Fan, 2010). The second is the mis-match error between two gaits directly computed from the joint 3D positions and accumulated over all poses (Zhang, et al, 2009). The third one is the

DFT-based gait descriptor (Yam, et al, 2004). It was found that the third one provides the gait manifold with the best interpolation capability. In KGGM, the gait and pose variables that are assumed to be independent are estimated separately and sequentially during inference. However, our observations reveal that these two factors are inter-related in specifying a specific gait sequence. This motivates us to propose the joint gait-pose manifold (JGPM) that unifies the two variables into one manifold structure (Zhang & Fan, 2011).

Issue 2: Joint Gait-Pose Manifolds (JGPMs)

In (Zhang & Fan, 2011), we presented three versions of JGPM, i.e., *torus-based*, *torus-constrained* and *torus-like* with different levels of topology constraints imposed.

Torus-based JGPM (JGPM-I)

The torus-based JGPM (JGPM-I) is parameterized by two angular variables, $g \in [0, 2\pi)$, representing *pose* and *gait* respectively. Given p and g, a latent

Figure 3. Illustration of various gait manifolds with different manifold topologies in the low dimensional gait space, where each of five training gaits is represented by a coefficient vector

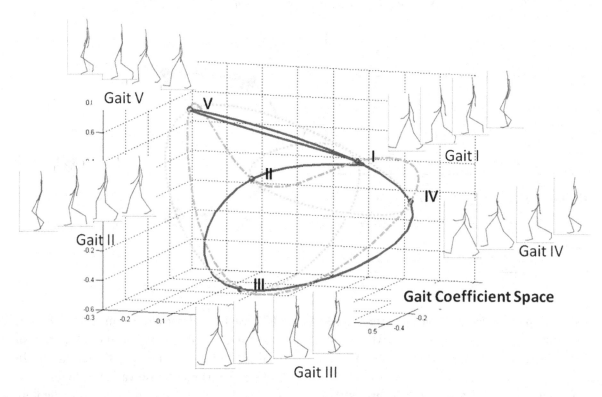

point on JGPM-I can be uniquely defined along the torus by $\mathcal{T}(p,g) = [t_x^{(p,g)}, t_y^{(p,g)}, t_z^{(p,g)}]^T$ as

$$t_x^{(p,g)} = (r_h + r_v \cos(g))\cos(p),$$
$$t_y^{(p,g)} = (r_h + r_v \cos(g))\sin(p), \qquad (21)$$
$$t_z^{(p,g)} = r_v \sin(p),$$

where and r_h and r_v are two radius values of the horizontal and vertical circles along the torus. Given N_g training gaits of N_p poses $\mathbf{Y} = \{\mathbf{y}_{(i,j)} \mid i = 1, ..., N_g, j = 1, ..., N_p\}$, where $\mathbf{y}_{(i,j)}$ denotes a vector of Euler angles of all body joints for pose j of gait i, we can construct JGPM-I according to the given manifold topologies. The pose variable is uniformly distributed between $[0, 2\pi)$ and the gait variable is distributed non-

uniformly between $[0, 2\pi)$ according to the shortest-closed-path across all training gaits given a certain distance metric, such as the one used in our previous work (Zhang & Fan, 2010). Hence, $\mathbf{y}_{(i,j)}$ corresponds to a unique point on JGPM-I defined by (21). Similar to (Elgammal & Lee, 2009), a non-linear mapping function can be learnt via a radial basis function (RBF) as,

$$\mathbf{y}_{(i,j)} = \mathbf{B} \cdot \varphi(\mathbf{x}_{(i,j)})$$
$$= \mathbf{B} \cdot \varphi(\mathcal{T}(c_p \cdot i, c_g \cdot j)), \qquad (22)$$

where $c_p (p = 1, ..., N_p)$ and c_g are $(g = 1, ..., N_g)$ two scaling constants to convert the two index numbers into an angular value between $[0, 2\pi)$, and $\varphi(\cdot)$ is a non-linear kernel function defined as

$$\varphi(\mathbf{x}_{(i,j)}) = [\phi(\mathbf{x}_{(i,j)}, \mathbf{c}^1), ..., \phi(\mathbf{x}_{(i,j)}, \mathbf{c}^L)], \qquad (23)$$

where $\phi(\cdot, \cdot)$ is a radial basis function (here we use Gaussian) and $\{\mathbf{c}^l \mid l = 1, ..., L\}$ are kernel centers uniformly distributed along JGPM. The torus-based JGPM is a rigid conceptual manifold that does not consider any influence of the training data. We use this manifold as the starting point to test our hypothesis and the initialization for the following two JGPMs where the GP-based learning is involved.

Torus-Constrained JGPM (JGPM-II)

In the torus-constrained JGPM (JGPM-II), the ideal torus structure is still retained but the distribution of latent points is optimized via GP-based learning. Rather than directly computing the 3D coordinate of every latent point, we can optimize the values p and g for all training data, $\mathbf{p} = (p_1, ..., p_{N_p})$ and $\mathbf{g} = (g_1, ..., g_{N_g})$, by encouraging the latent structure to resemble an expected manifold topology. JGPM-I provides the desired manifold topology and neighboring relationship for each latent point in JGPM-II. Specifically, we extended the LL-GPDM algorithm proposed in (Urtasun, et al., 2008) by using the topology constraint derived from JGPM-I. Therefore, we firstly identify a set of neighboring points for each latent point $\mathbf{x}(i, j)$ along JGPM-I. We also incorporate the toroidal shape constraint by computing a local covariance matrix for each latent point from its neighbors. By solving a constrained least squares problem (Saul & Roweis, 2001), we can find a weight matrix ω that is composed of weights for each latent point. During the learning process, $p(\mathbf{X} \mid \omega)$ is used as the topology prior that encourages latent points to be distributed in a way like those in JGPM-I. Then the learning of JGPM-II is to maximize the following posterior probability,

$$p(\mathbf{X}, \alpha, \beta \mid \mathbf{Y}, \omega) \propto p(\mathbf{Y} \mid \mathbf{X}, \beta) p(\mathbf{X} \mid \alpha) p(\alpha) p(\beta) p(\mathbf{X} \mid \omega) \qquad (24)$$

where the first four terms are defined according to GPDM, i.e., $p(\mathbf{Y} \mid \mathbf{X}, \beta)$ is the likelihood function, $p(\mathbf{X} \mid \alpha)$ is the dynamic prior, $p(\alpha)$ and $p(\beta)$ are prior models for hyperparameters. $\mathbf{X}$ can be further represented as $\mathbf{X} = \mathcal{T}(\mathbf{p}, \mathbf{g})$, which indicates an ideal torus structure represented by the two sets of radian values corresponding to all training data. Hence by optimizing $\mathbf{p}$ and $\mathbf{g}$ in (24), we can obtain an ideal toroid structure for JGPM-II where latent point positions are learnt through the GP-based optimization.

Torus-like JGPM (JGPM-III)

One may wonder that an ideal toroidal shape may be still too rigid and too ideal for real motion modeling. Thus we further proposed a torus-like JGPM (JGPM-III) that couples the pose and gait manifolds in a structure that only resembles a torus. Unlike JGPM-I and JGPM-II, each pose or gait manifold may not be a perfect circle in JGPM-III. Particularly, we proposed a two-step *local-global GPLVM* (LG-GPLVM) algorithm as shown in Figure 4. We firstly learn a 2D pose manifold for each gait separately via GPDM that are treated as a set of *local* models. Then, these local models are aligned together in a 3D latent space to form a *global* torus-like structure by a GPLVM algorithm that optimizes a set of rigid transforms (including rotation and translation parameters) according to the gait manifold topology (i.e., ordering relationship) among all training gaits.

Given a data set with N_g different gaits of N_p poses, we can denote the data set as $\mathbf{Y} = \{\mathcal{Y}_i\}_{i=1}^{N_g}$, where $\mathcal{Y}_i = \{\mathbf{y}_{(i,j)}, j = 1, ..., N_p\}$ and each $\mathbf{y}_{(i,j)}$ is a D-dimensional data vector for pose j in gait i, i.e., $\mathbf{y}_{(i,j)} \in \mathfrak{R}^D$. For each gait $\mathcal{Y}_i$, we can learn its latent coordinates individually via GPDM,

Figure 4. The learning process of torus-like JGPM (JGPM-III) by the two-step LG-GPLVM. (From X. Zhang and G. Fan, "Joint Gait-Pose Manifold for Video-based Human Motion Estimation", in Proc. IEEE CVPR Workshop on Machine Learning for Vision-based Motion Analysis (MLvMA), Colorado Springs, Colorado, USA, June 25, 2011. @ 2011 IEEE)

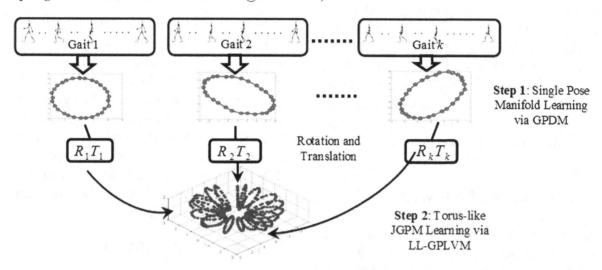

$$\{\mathbf{G}_i, \boldsymbol{\Phi}_i\} =$$
$$\arg \max_{\mathbf{G}_i, \boldsymbol{\Phi}_i} p(\mathcal{Y}_i \mid \mathbf{G}_i, \boldsymbol{\beta}_i) p(\mathbf{G}_i \mid \boldsymbol{\alpha}_i) p(\boldsymbol{\alpha}_i) p(\boldsymbol{\beta}_i), \quad (25)$$

where $\mathbf{G}_i = \{\mathbf{g}_{ij} \mid j = 1, ..., N_p\}$ is a set of 2D latent points learnt from $\mathcal{Y}_i$ and $\boldsymbol{\Phi}_i = \{\alpha_i, \beta_i\}$ denotes the associated hyper-parameters. We use the RBF kernel for the likelihood computation. $p(\mathbf{G}_i \mid \alpha_i)$ is the dynamic model in the latent space for gait i. Hence, we have N_g pose manifolds in their own latent spaces $\{\mathbf{G}_i, \boldsymbol{\Phi}_i\}_{i=1}^{N_g}$. It was shown that for a single gait, GPDM can learn a smooth circular shape pose manifold with a good reconstruction capability. The question now is how to integrate these separated pose manifolds into the same latent space that can globally characterize gait variability and locally preserve their respective structure. We define $\mathbf{x}_{(i,j)} \in \mathfrak{R}^3$ as the latent point in a joint space, corresponding to $\mathbf{y}_{(i,j)}$. To align individual pose manifolds, each latent point $\mathbf{x}_{ij}$ can be defined as,

$$\mathbf{x}_{(i,j)} = \mathbb{F}(\mathbf{g}_{ij}, \theta_i), \quad (26)$$

where $\theta_i = [\mathbf{R}_i, \mathbf{T}_i]$, representing the rotation $\mathbf{R}_i$ and translation $\mathbf{T}_i$ matrix of $\mathbf{G}_i$. $\mathbf{g}_{ij}$ is the j-th point in the $\mathbf{G}_i$ pose manifold. Hence, the latent point in the joint gait-pose space is the function N_g pose manifolds, $\{\mathbf{G}_i, \boldsymbol{\Phi}_i\}_{i=1}^{N_g}$. The learning process of the global JGPM structure can be formulated as a topology constrained GPLVM framework. The JGPM is initialized by placing the individual pose manifold according to the gait manifold learnt in JGPM-II. Our goal is to optimize hyper-parameters $\Theta = \{\theta_i\}_{i=1}^{N_g}$ that maximizes the joint probability function defined as

$$p(\mathbf{Y}, \mathbf{X}, \xi) \propto p\left(\mathbf{Y} \mid \{\mathbb{F}(\mathbf{G}_i, \theta_i)\}_{i=1}^{N_g}, \xi\right) p(\Theta) p(\xi), \quad (27)$$

where $\{\mathbb{F}(\mathbf{G}_i, \theta_i)\}_{i=1}^{N_g}$ denote all latent variables $\mathbf{X}$ in JGPM-III, computed as (27). $p(\Theta)$ is the prior model of the gait topology structure. It encourages the individual pose manifold follows the order and distance relationship of the pre-defined gait manifold topology, and it plays the same role as $p(\mathbf{X} \mid \omega)$ in JGPM-II that encourages the formation of a toroidal structure. $p(\xi)$ is the prior of hyperparameters in the kernel function defined in the likelihood function $p(\mathbf{Y} \mid \{\mathbb{F}(\mathbf{G_i}, \theta_i)\}_{i=1}^{N_g}, \xi)$. The likelihood of $\mathbf{Y}$ is defined on all latent points from N_g gaits, written as

$$p(\mathbf{Y} \mid \mathbf{X}) = p(\mathbf{Y} \mid \{\mathbb{F}(\mathbf{G}_i, \theta_i)\}_{i=1}^{N_g} \xi) =$$
$$\frac{1}{\sqrt{(2\pi)^{(N_g \times N_p)D} \mid \mathbf{K}_{Y|G,\Theta} \mid}} \exp\left(-\frac{1}{2} tr\left(\mathbf{K}_{\mathbf{Y|G},\Theta}^{-1} \mathbf{YY}^T\right)\right),$$

$$(28)$$

where $\mathbf{K}_{\mathbf{Y|G},\Theta}$ is a $(N_g N_p) \times (N_g N_p)$ matrix generated by the RBF kernel, defined as

$$\mathbf{k}_{\mathbf{Y|G},\Theta}\left(\mathbf{x}_{(i,j)}, \mathbf{x}_{(m,n)}\right) =$$
$$\xi_1 \exp\left(-\frac{\xi_2}{2} \parallel \mathbf{x}_{(i,j)} - \mathbf{x}_{(m,n)} \parallel\right) + \xi_3^{-1} \delta_{x_p, x_q},$$

where $\mathbf{x}_{(i,j)}$ and $\mathbf{x}_{(m,n)}$ are two latent points corresponding to pose j in gait i and pose n in gait m, respectively. Then we have $\mathbf{x}_{(i,j)} = \mathbb{F}(\mathbf{g}_{ij}, \theta_i)$ and $\mathbf{x}_{(m,n)} = \mathbb{F}(\mathbf{g}_{mn}, \theta_m)$. $\parallel \mathbf{x}_{(i,j)} - \mathbf{x}_{(m,n)} \parallel$ denotes the Euclidean distance between $\mathbf{x}_{(i,j)}$ and $\mathbf{x}_{(m,n)}$. Due to the two-step learning, the torus-like JGPM (JGPM-III) preserves the closed-loop property of the pose and gait manifolds but could deviate from the ideal torus constraint. The deviation from an ideal torus that makes the torus-like JGPM reflect the actual intrinsic structure of the actual intrinsic structure of the underlying data is necessary. Compared to JGPM-I and JGPM-II, JGPM-III balances the expected topology con-

straints with actual data structure by having a more flexible manifold structure.

Issue 3: Model Validation

To compare the above three JGPMs with existing GPLVM-based methods, we propose a model validation technique in (Fan & Zhang, 2011) by which we can examine and evaluate each model in terms of their robustness and performance of human motion modeling. Since each GP algorithm can learn a latent space along with a LD-HD mapping from a set of training motion data that are almost noise-free, we can use it as a prior model to process (e.g., denoise or interpolate) an input motion sequence that could be noisy or incomplete. A better GP model should provide better denoising or interpolation results.

We used the same validation technique to evaluate the three JGPMs by comparing them with five existing GPLVM-based DR algorithms, including GPLVM, back constrained GPLVM (BC-GPLVM), GPDM, scaled and balanced GPDM (SB-GPDM) and topologically-constrained GPDM (LL-GPDM), via four specific experiments, (1) interpolation, (2) extrapolation, (3) denoising and (4) recognition. These experiments are related but different from (Quirion et al, 2008) that compares recent GP algorithms in the context of character animation regarding the computation time, ease of visualization, interpolation and extrapolation. Interpolation in (Quirion et al, 2008) is concerned with the generalization potential by learning a GP model from down-sampled motion data and applying it to the rest of data for evaluation. While in our work, interpolation is meant to recover full-body motion from partial-body motion. Extrapolation in (Quirion et al, 2008) was only evaluated subjectively without any objective measure, while we want to quantitatively evaluate all GP models in terms of their capability of extrapolating new motion data from unknown subjects. Filtering and recognition are two new experiments studied in this work that were not considered in (Quirion et al, 2008). Specifically, the objective of filtering is to denoise noisy motion data captured from both known and unknown subjects, and that of recognition is to recognize the identity from the underlying noisy motion data. It is worth mentioning that all of these experiments are of great practical interest to make motion analysis possible by using a small number of inertial sensors supported by a strong motion model learned from the Mocap data.

Given an input motion sequence $\{\mathbf{k}_1, ..., \mathbf{k}_T\}$, the goal is to estimate the latent points $\{\mathbf{x}_1, ..., \mathbf{x}_T\}$ and their corresponding kinematics $\{\mathbf{y}_1, ..., \mathbf{y}_T\}$ that maximizes the posterior probability, defined as

$$p(\mathbf{y}_t, \mathbf{x}_t \mid \mathbf{k}_t) \propto p(\mathbf{k}_t \mid \mathbf{y}_t) p(\mathbf{y}_t \mid \mathbf{x}_t, \mathfrak{M}_{GP}) p(\mathbf{x}_t \mid \mathfrak{M}_{GP}), \quad (29)$$

where $\mathfrak{M}_{GP}$ is the learnt GP-based DR model with specific latent space and multi-dimensional Gaussian distribution. The first term $p(\mathbf{k}_t \mid \mathbf{y}_t)$ in (29) is the likelihood that refers to the dissimilarity between testing and estimated kinematics, as

$$p(\mathbf{k}_t \mid \mathbf{y}_t) = \exp -\left(\frac{f(\mathbf{k}_i, \mathbf{y}_i)}{\sigma^2}\right), \quad (30)$$

where σ^2 controls the sensitivity of evaluation and $f(.)$ is a dissimilarity measurement that indicates the degree of mis-match between two sets of motion data. For example, it can be the average 3D joint distance between two motion sequences (where the global motion is not considered.). According to (Lawrence, 2003) and (Wang, et al., 2008), the second term $p(\mathbf{y}_t \mid \mathbf{x}_t, \mathfrak{M}_{GP})$ represents the likelihood of the hypothesized kinematics given a latent position, and it is defined a Gauss-

ian function of $\mathbf{x}_t$, that is, $\mathcal{N}(\mathbf{y}_t \mid \frac{1}{4}_Y(\mathbf{x}_t), \tilde{A}_Y^2(\mathbf{x}_t))$ where,

$$\mu_Y(\mathbf{x}_t) = \mathbf{Y}^T \mathbf{K}_Y^{-1} \mathbf{k}_Y(\mathbf{x}_t), \quad (31)$$

$$\sigma_Y^2(\mathbf{x}_t) = k_Y(\mathbf{x}_t, \mathbf{x}_t) - \mathbf{k}_Y(\mathbf{x}_t)^T \mathbf{K}_Y^{-1} \mathbf{k}_Y(\mathbf{x}_t). \quad (32)$$

The third term $p(\mathbf{x}_t \mid \mathbf{M})$ is the prior probability of latent position $\mathbf{x}_t$ given the learnt latent space. This term can be either the prior knowledge of latent space distribution or the dynamic prior. For example, in the GPDM-based algorithm, $p(\mathbf{x}_t \mid \mathbf{M})$ is defined as a Gaussian to characterize the dynamic model in the latent space. Actually, the model validation is a sequential MAP estimation process that tries to balance "what is *seen*" (the first term in (28)) with "what is *known*" (the 2nd and 3rd terms in (28)), and σ^2 in (27) by adjusting the relative importance of two factors in the MAP estimation.

The validation process is implemented sequentially as shown in Figure 5. Given the first frame of an input motion sequence, we first find the best-matched frame in the training one whose latent point is used as the initialization $\mathbf{x}_1^{(0)}$ in the latent space. Then we use scaled conjugated gradientbased (SCG) hill-climbing to optimize (28). After several SCG iterations, the optimal point $\hat{\mathbf{x}}_1$ is found and its corresponding point in the HD data space is the estimated motion for the first frame. Then $\mathbf{x}_2^{(0)} = \hat{\mathbf{x}}_1$, that is, the estimation of the first frame is used as the initial point for the second frame and so on. Thus a motion trajectory in the latent space along with its corresponding HD motion data can be estimated sequentially. This process is applied to for all GP algorithms in the following experiments. Specifically, in the case of interpolation, since motion data are missing for some body joints, the likelihood function in (2) only involves those joints where motion data are available. Then the esti-

Figure 5. The illustration of the sequential validation process in the latent space where the greyscales indicate the precision with which the manifold was expressed in data-space for that latent point

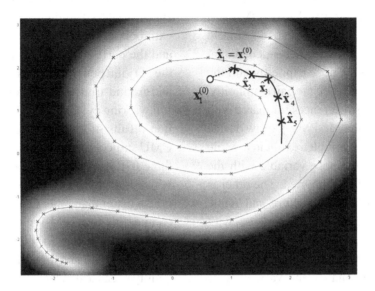

mated motion data are for the full-body with the missing joints recovered. In the case of recognition, we find the optimized latent points for all frames, and then determine the identity for each frame by finding the closest training data point. The recognition accuracy is the percentage of accurately recognized frames over the whole sequence.

EXPERIMENTAL RESULTS AND DISCUSSIONS

We used the same training data set as the one used in (Zhang & Fan, 2010), including 20 training gaits different subjects from CMU Mocap Library[1] each of which is composed of 30 poses in a full walking cycle. Each pose is represented by a set of joint angles. We implemented all five GP-based DR algorithms in Matlab with the reference codes provided by Neil Lawrence[2]. The comparison involves five GPLVM-based algorithms that have been successfully applied on human motion analysis, i.e., (1) GPLVM, (2) BC-GPLVM, (3) GPDM, (4) Scale and Balanced

GPDM (SB-GPDM) and (5) LL-GPDM as well as three JGPMs. Different from their peers, three JGPMs are able to unify two latent variables (pose and gait) into a shared manifold where both dynamic and topology priors are involved. They were tested for video-based human motion estimation in (Zhang & Fan, 2011) that shows the advantages of coupling the two variables together over the one in (Zhang & Fan, 2010) where two variables were independently considered. This section further examines the three JGPMs and other GP algorithms for in terms of their general capability of human motion modeling.

Latent Space Comparison

Ideally speaking, a LD latent space should reflect the intrinsic data structure in an intuitive and meaningful way, and we often prefer a well-organized, smooth and compact manifold structure for human motion modeling. We show the latent spaces learned by the eight GP algorithms in Figure 2. Since the first two were not originally designed for sequential data, their latent spaces were not very organized as expected. Although GPDM and

SB-GPDM show more meaningful motion trajectories, they still cannot to collectively represent multiple gaits in a unified way. LL-GPDM has a relatively well-defined cylinder-shaped manifold structure that specifies two independent latent directions, one along the pose explicitly and the other one along the style (i.e., the gait) implicitly. JGPMs have two main differences compared with LL-GPDM. One is that JGPMs jointly define both the gait and pose variables explicitly, while LL-GPDM involves the pose variable with the other variable implicitly supported. The other is that JGPMs have a closed-structure and while LL-GPDM has an open one. Compared with LL-GPDM, JGPMs, especially JGPMs-II and III, provide a better organized manifold structure to reflect both the commonality and variability of multiple gaits.

Experiment I: Motion Interpolation

We randomly selected five subjects from 20 training ones and picked 2-3 walking cycles for each subject that are not used for training. We studied three interpolation cases, i.e., missing the left arm (3 joints), missing the left leg (3 joints) and missing the left-sided body (6 joints). We used the eight algorithms to recover the full-body motion (18 joints) for each of the 15 partial-body motion data, and computed the averaged 3D joint position errors between the estimated and ground-truth ones[3]. In Figure 7, the errors (mm) of the eight algorithms are presented for three cases. It is shown that JGPM-III provides the best performance. BC-GPLVM, GPDM and SB-GPDM are better than GPLVM due to the back-constraints or dynamic prior involved. LL-GPDM further improves the results, and it is comparable to JGPM-II.

Experiment II: Motion Extrapolation

This experiment examines the synthesis ability of a DR method to represent the motion data from unknown subjects. We selected five new subjects

from the CMU Mocap Library and three subjects from the Brown HumanEva-I dataset (Sigal and Black, 2006b). The eight DR methods were used to extrapolate the eight unknown motion sequences, and the performance is evaluated by computing the 3D joint position errors between the estimated and ground-truth ones averaged over all joints in a full walking cycle. Figure 8 shows the extrapolation results of the eight algorithms for both the CMU subjects and the HumanEva-I subjects. All three JGPMs provide competitive results, among which JGPM-III is again the best one. LL-GPDM is also better than other GP-based algorithms and comparable to JGPM-I and JGPM-II. Generally speaking, the errors for the HumanEva-I dataset are smaller than that for CMU Mocap dataset. It is mainly because that CMU motion data have more joints defined on hands and feet where introduce relative larger errors are usually introduced during motion extrapolation.

Experiment III: Motion Filtering

We used ten CMU Mocap sequences (not in the training data), among which five are from training subjects and used in Experiment I and five are from unknown subjects used in Experiment II. For each motion sequence, we generated three noisy sequences by adding three levels of additive white Gaussian noise (AWGN) to each joint angle. This experiment is especially interesting in the case where low-cost inertial sensors used are for motion capture which may have significant noise due to various disturbances in practice. To simulate the practical motion capture situations, the noise level should be related to the dynamic nature of each joint angle. In other word, we need consider the dynamics of each joint angle to control the noise level in this experiment. We first compute the *dynamic data variance* for each joint angle that is the variance of the frame-wise angle difference in a walking cycle. Three noise levels were considered that are 5%, 10% and 15% of the variance of the frame-to-frame angle varia-

Figure 6. The latent space learnt using different GP-based DR approaches, including (1) GPLVM, (2) BC-GPLVM, (3) GPDM, (4) SB-GPDM, (5) LL-GPDM, (6) JGPM-I, (7) JGPM-II, (8) JGPM-III . IEEE)

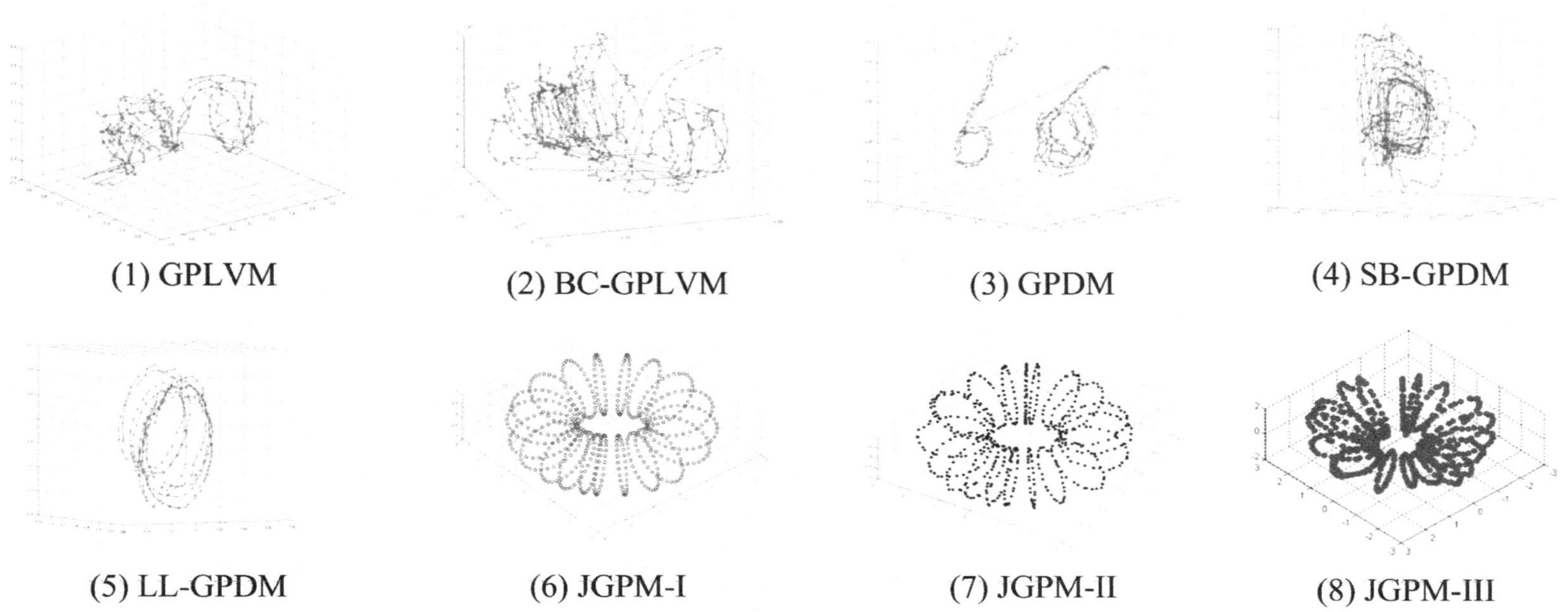

Figure 7. The interpolation results of eight algorithms, i.e., (1) GPLVM, (2) BC-GPLVM, (3) GPDM, (4) SB-GPDM, (5) LL-GPDM, (6) JGPM-I, (7) JGPM-II, (8) JGPM-III. From left to right: the three interpolation cases of missing the left arm, the left leg and the left-sided body.

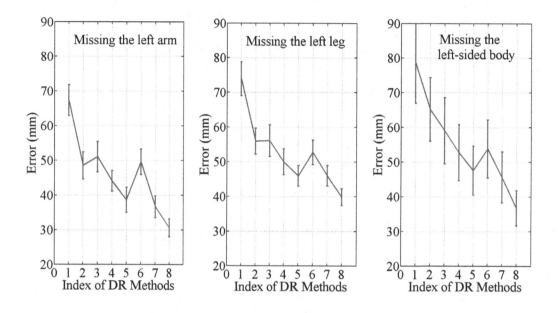

Figure 8. The motion extrapolation results for eight DR methods, i.e., (1)GPLVM, (2) BC-GPLVM, (3) GPDM, (4) SB-GPDM, (5) LL-GPDM, (6) JGPM-I, (7) JGPM-II, (8) JGPM-III. (From X. Zhang and G. Fan, "Joint Gait-Pose Manifold for Video-based Human Motion Estimation", in Proc. IEEE CVPR Workshop on Machine Learning for Vision-based Motion Analysis (MLvMA), Colorado Springs, Colorado, USA, June 25, 2011. @ 2011 IEEE)

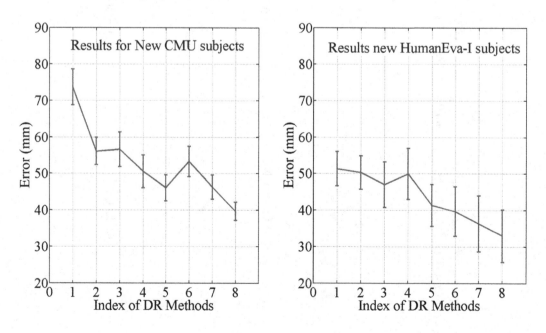

tion for each joint angle. We applied the sequential MAP-based motion estimation process to filter all 30 noisy motion sequences, and computed the averaged 3D joint position errors between the filtered and ground-truth (noise-free) ones. Figure 9 shows the motion filtering results for both training (above) and unknown (below) subjects. As the noise level increases, the advantage of JGPM-III is more and more manifested that is consistently the best in all tests, and LL-GPDM is comparable with JGPM-II both of which show significant improvements over the rest GP algorithms.

Experiment IV: Gait Recognition

From the CMU Mocap dataset, we collected 20 motion sequences that are from the same 20 training subjects but are not used for the modeling learning. Also, we added AWGN noise of 5% and 10% levels on each joint angle in each frame to challenge the recognition task. For each sequence, the recognition accuracy is computed as the percentage of correctly recognized identity for all frames in a sequence, and the averaged accuracies over 20 motion sequences for eight algorithms are shown in Figure 10. Once again, JGPM-III still yields the best results for both noise levels, and all eight algorithms shown comparable recognition performances, ranging from 85% to 92%. This close contest is mainly because that the likelihood function defined in (36) provides a strong evidence for gait recognition. However, if we increase σ^2 in (36) to reduce the sensitivity of (36), the advantages of JGPM-III could be clearer.

Summary

We have tested and compared three JGPMs with existing five GP-based DR algorithms for the human motion modeling. Since our training data contain various walking patterns that cannot be handled very well by the most existing GP algo-

rithms (except for LL-GPDM). The multi-factor nature of the motion data results in a cluttered and unorganized manifold structure in the latent space. LL-GPDM was proposed to model different motion activities (walking and running) as well as the transition between them that is useful for character animation. It can merge multiple gait trajectories onto a cylinder-shaped manifold, where only the pose variable is explicitly defined to capture the common cyclic nature of the periodic motions. On the other hand, JGPMs were proposed to represent one motion activity (e.g., walking), and they are intended to represent the commonality as well as the variability among different gaits by jointly defining the pose and gait variables via a toroidal structure. This kind of models can be used as an effective prior for motion analysis applications where a single activity is of major interest, e.g., gait analysis or tracking. Our experiments reveal that LL-GPDM is comparable with JGPM-II while JGPM-III yields the best performance that provides a compact and smooth latent space for joint modeling of gait and pose variables. The outcome is consistent with our initial motivation of using JGPM for human motion modeling.

FUTURE RESEARCH ISSUES

There are few possible future research directions. (1) The first is *how to improve JGPM learning via a one-step GP optimization where the number of hyper-parameters can be reduced.* Although the current learning algorithm of JGPM-III is effective and relatively straightforward, the two-step approach may not be optimal due to the lack of a joint optimization between the learning of the pose manifold and that of the gait manifold. (2) The second is *how to extend JGPM to video-based motion estimation or other motion analysis applications.* This chapter studies the problem of human motion modeling based on the Mocap data that helps us reveal the intrinsic models of human motion, but in practice, video-based motion

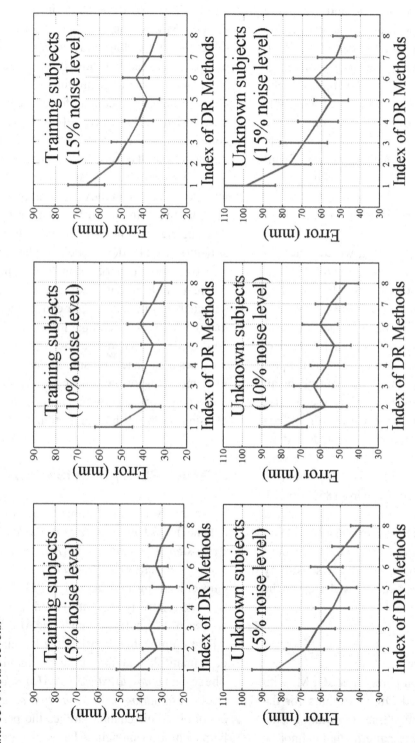

Figure 9. The filtering results of five training subjects (above) and five unknown subjects (below) from eight DR methods, i.e., (1) GPLVM, (2)BC-GPLVM, (3) GPDM, (4) SB-GPDM, (5) LL-GPDM, (6) JGPM-I, (7) JGPM-II, (8) JGPM-III. From left to right: the errors at 5%, 10% and 15% noise levels.

Figure 10. The recognition accuracies under two noise levels 5% (left) and 10% (right), using eight DR methods, i.e., (1) GPLVM, (2)BC-GPLVM, (3) GPDM, (4) SB-GPDM, (5) LLGPDM, (6) JGPM-I, (7) JGPM-II, (8) JGPM-III.

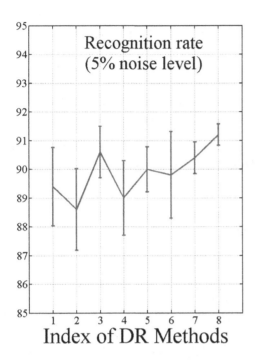 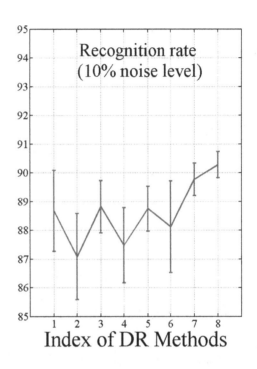

estimation or other motion analysis applications are more practically useful and relevant, where a good motion model plays an important role. (3) The third issue is *how to extend the idea of JGPM to multiple motion patterns other than "walking"*. This could be a challenging problem due to the fact that there could be a lack of smooth transition between different motion patterns.

CONCLUSION

This chapter has studied recent GP-based human motion modeling approaches. We compared our recently proposed JGPMs with the state-of-the-art GPLVM-based models in terms of the performance and robustness of human motion modeling. The proposed JGPM unifies the pose and gait variables into a toroidal manifold structure. Three version of JGPM have been studied,

JGPM -I, JGPM -II, and JGPM –III with different levels of constraints. Especially, a new two-step GP-based learning algorithm is proposed to learn the torus-like JGPM (JGPM-III) that balances the ideal topology constraint and intrinsic data structure. Experimental results show torus-like JGPM (JGPM-III) has the superior performance for motion interpolation, extrapolation, filtering and recognition comparing with existing GP-based manifold learning algorithms. We believe it is mainly because of its compact, well-organized and smooth latent space where the coupling effect between multiple nonlinear factors is explicitly revealed. This structure-guided manifold learning idea could be applied to other DR applications where a shared latent space is preferred to reflect the inter-dependent relationships among multiple factors in an explicit way. Moreover, the progressive improvements from JGPM-I to JGPM-II and JGPM-III show that an appropriate balance is needed between the prior knowledge about the ideal manifold topology and the actual data structure.

ACKNOWLEDGMENT

This work is supported by the National Science Foundation (NSF) under Grant IIS-0347613, and an OHRS award (HR09-030) from the Oklahoma Center for the Advancement of Science and Technology (OCAST).

REFERENCES

Belkin, M., & Niyogi, P. (2003). Laplacian Eigenmaps for dimensionality reduction and data representation. *Neural Computation, 15,* 1373–1396. doi:10.1162/089976603321780317

Brubaker, M., & Fleet, D. (2008). *The kneed walker for human pose tracking.* Paper presented at the IEEE Conference on Computer Vision and Pattern Recognition.

Brubaker, M., Fleet, D., & Hertzmann, A. (2007). *Physics-based person tracking using simplified lower-body dynamics.* Paper presented at the IEEE Conference on Computer Vision and Pattern Recognition.

Brubaker, M. A., Fleet, D. J., & Hertzmann, A. (2010). Physics-based person tracking using the anthropomorphic walker. *International Journal of Computer Vision, 87,* 140–155. doi:10.1007/s11263-009-0274-5

Chen, J., Kim, M., Wang, Y., & Ji, Q. (2009). *Switching Gaussian process dynamic models to simultaneous composite motion tracking and recognition.* Paper presented IEEE Conference on Computer Vision and Pattern Recognition.

Cunado, D., Nixon, M. S., & Carter, J. N. (2003). Automatic extraction and description of human gait models for recognition purposes. *Computer Vision and Image Understanding, 90,* 1–41. doi:10.1016/S1077-3142(03)00008-0

Ek, C. H., Torr, P., & Lawrence, N. (2007). *Gaussian process latent variable models for human pose estimation.* Paper presented at the Conference on Machine Learning and Multimodal Interaction.

Elgammal, A., & Lee, C.-S. (2004a). *Inferring 3D body pose from silhouettes using activity manifold learning.* Paper presented at the IEEE Conference on Computer Vision and Pattern Recognition.

Elgammal, A., & Lee, C.-S. (2004b). *Separating style and content on a nonlinear manifold.* Paper presented at the IEEE Conference on Computer Vision and Pattern Recognition.

Elgammal, A., & Lee, C.-S. (2009). Tracking people on torus. *IEEE Transactions on Pattern Analysis and Machine Intelligence, 31,* 520–538. doi:10.1109/TPAMI.2008.101

Grochow, K., Martin, S., Hertzmann, A., & Popovic, Z. (2004). *Style-based inverse kinematics.* Paper presented at SIGGRAPH.

Gupta, A., Chen, T., Chen, F., Kimber, D., & Daivs, L. (2008). *Context and observation driven latent variable model for human pose estimation.* Paper presented at the IEEE Conference on Computer Vision and Pattern Recognition.

Lan, X., & Huttenlocher, D. (2004). *A unified spatio-temporal articulated model for tracking.* Paper presented at the Computer Vision and Pattern Recognition.

Lawrence, N. (2003). *Gaussian process latent variable models for visualization of high dimensional data.* Paper presented at the Advances in Neural Information Processing.

Lawrence, N., & Candela, J. (2006). *Local distance preservation in the GPLVM through back constraints.* Paper presented at the International Conference on Machine Learning.

Lawrence, N., & Moore, A. (2007). *Hierarchical Gaussian process latent variable models.* Paper presented at the International Conference on Machine Learning.

Lee, C.-S., & Elgammal, A. (2007). *Modeling view and posture manifolds for tracking.* Paper presented at the IEEE International Conference on Computer Vision.

Lu, Z., Carreira-Perpinan, M. A., & Sminchisescu, C. (2007). *People tracking with the Laplacian Eigenmaps latent variable model.* Paper presented at the Advances in Neural Information Processing Systems.

Quirion, S., Duchesne, C., Laurendeau, D., & Marchand, M. (2008). Comparing GPLVM approaches for dimensionality reduction in character animation. *Journal of WSCG, 16*(1-3), 41–48.

Rasmussen, C. E., & Williams, C. K. I. (2006). *Gaussian processes for machine learning.* MIT Press.

Rosenhahn, B., Schmaltz, C., & Brox, T. (2008). *Markerless motion capture of man-machine interaction.* Paper presented at the IEEE Conference on Computer Vision and Pattern Recognition.

Roweis, S., & Saul, L. (2000). Nonlinear dimensionality reduction by locally linear embedding. *Science, 290,* 2323–2326. doi:10.1126/science.290.5500.2323

Saul, L., & Roweis, S. (2001). *An introduction to locally linear embedding.* Technical Report. Retrieved from http://www.cs.toronto.edu/~roweis/lle/publications.html

Saul, L., & Roweis, S. (2003). Think globally, fit locally: unsupervised learning of low dimensional manifolds. *Journal of Machine Learning Research, 4,* 119–155.

Sigal, L., Bhatia, S., Roth, S., Black, M., & Isard, M. (2004). *Tracking loose-limbed people.* Paper presented at IEEE Conference on Computer Vision and Pattern Recognition.

Sigal, L., & Black, M. (2006b). *HumanEva: Synchronized video and motion capture dataset for evaluation of articulated human motion.* Brown University, Tech. Rep. CS-06-08.

Sigal, L., & Black, M. J. (2006a). *Measure locally, reason globally: Occlusion-sensitive articulated pose estimation.* Paper presented at the IEEE Conference on Computer Vision and Pattern Recognition.

Sminchisescu, C., & Jepson, A. (2004). *Generative modeling for continuous non-linearly embedded visual inference.* Paper presented at the International Conference on Machine Learning.

Tenenbaum, J. B., de Silva, V., & Langford, J. C. (2000). A global geometric framework for nonlinear dimensionality reduction. *Science, 290,* 2319–2323. doi:10.1126/science.290.5500.2319

Titsias, M. K., & Lawrence, N. D. (2010). *Bayesian Gaussian process latent variable model.* Paper presented at the Thirteenth International Workshop on Artificial Intelligence and Statistics.

Tresp, V. (2000). *The generalized Bayesian committee machine.* Paper presented at the Knowledge Discovery and Data Mining.

Urtasun, R., Fleet, D. J., & Fua, P. (2006). *3D people tracking with Gaussian process dynamical models.* Paper presented at IEEE Conference on Computer Vision and Pattern Recognition.

Urtasun, R., Fleet, D. J., Geiger, A., Popovic, J., Darrell, T. J., & Lawrence, N. D. (2008). *Topologically-constraint latent variable models.* Paper presented at the International Conference on Machine Learning.

Vondrak, M., Sigal, L., & Jenkins, O. (2008). *Physical simulation for probabilistic motion tracking.* Paper presented at the Proc. IEEE Conference on Computer Vision and Pattern Recognition.

Wang, J., Fleet, D., & Hertzmann, A. (2007). *Multifactor Gaussian process models for style-content separation.* Paper presented at the International Conference on Machine Learning.

Wang, J., Fleet, D., & Hertzmann, A. (2008). Gaussian process dynamical models for human motion. *IEEE Transactions on Pattern Analysis and Machine Intelligence, 30,* 283–298. doi:10.1109/TPAMI.2007.1167

Yam, C., Nixon, M. S., & Carter, J. N. (2004). Automated person recognition by walking and running via model-based approaches. *Pattern Recognition, 37,* 1057–1072. doi:10.1016/j.patcog.2003.09.012

Zhang, X., & Fan, G. (2010). Dual gait generative models for human motion estimation from a single camera. *IEEE Transactions on Systems, Man, and Cybernetics. Part B, Cybernetics, 40,* 1034–1049. doi:10.1109/TSMCB.2010.2044240

Zhang, X., & Fan, G. (2011). *Dual gait generative models for human motion estimation from a single camera.* Paper presented at the IEEE CVPR Workshop on Machine Learning for Vision-based Motion Analysis (MLvMA2011).

Zhang, X., Fan, G., & Chou, L. (2009). *Two-layer gait generative models for estimating unknown human gait kinematics.* Paper presented at the IEEE ICCV Workshop on Machine Learning for Vision-based Motion Analysis (MLvMA2009).

KEY TERMS AND DEFINITIONS

Gait Kinematics: The motion data from a human walking sequence.

Gaussian Process (GP): The generalization of a Gaussian distribution over a finite vector space to a function space of infinite dimension. Just as a Gaussian distribution is fully specified by its mean and covariance matrix, a GP is specified by a mean and a covariance function.

Human Motion Modeling: To develop a low-dimensional dynamic model from high-dimensional Mocap data that can be used for a variety of applications, such as animation, recognition, tracking, etc.

Mocap (Motion) Data: A series joint angles or 3D positions captured from a human motion sequence.

Motion Capture: Motion tracking, or mocap are terms used to describe the process of recording movement and translating that movement on to a digital model.

Non-Linear Dimension Reduction or Manifold Learning: To explore an embedded non-linear manifold within the higher-dimensional space

The Gaussian Process Latent Variable Model (GPLVM): A non-parametric Bayesian method for high dimensional nonlinear data that explicitly models the low dimensional representation of the data's manifold.

ENDNOTES

[1] http://mocap.cs.cmu.edu/

[2] http://staffwww.dcs.shef.ac.uk/people/N.Lawrence/software.html

[3] The angle-based motion data have to be converted to a set of 3D joint positions by using a skeleton model for comparison, the same for the following experiments.

Chapter 16
Probabilistic Graphical Models for Sports Video Mining

Guoliang Fan
Oklahoma State University, USA

Yi Ding
Oklahoma State University, USA

ABSTRACT

Semantic analysis is an active and interesting research topic in the field of sports video mining. In this chapter, the authors present a multi-level video semantic analysis framework that is featured by hybrid generative-discriminative probabilistic graphical models. A three-layer semantic space is proposed, by which the semantic video analysis is cast into two inter-related inference problems defined at different semantic levels. In the first stage, a multi-channel segmental hidden Markov model (MCSHMM) is developed to jointly detect multiple co-existent mid-level keywords from low-level visual features, which can serve as building blocks for high-level semantics. In the second stage, authors propose the auxiliary segmentation conditional random fields (ASCRFs) to discover the game flow from multi-channel key-words, which provides a unified semantic representation for both event and structure analysis. The use of hybrid generative-discriminative approaches in two different stages is proved to be effective and appropriate for multi-level semantic analysis in sports video. The experimental results from a set of American football video data demonstrate that the proposed framework offers superior results compared with other traditional machine learning-based video mining approaches.

DOI: 10.4018/978-1-4666-1806-0.ch016

INTRODUCTION

The goal of video mining is to discover knowledge, patterns, and events in the video data stored either in databases, data warehouses, or other online repositories (Chang, 2002; Mei, Ma, Zhou, Ma, & Zhang, 2005). Its benefits range from efficient video indexing, browsing and summarization to content-based or semantic-based video access and retrieval. Driven by the ever increasing need of numerous multimedia and online database applications, there is a growing need of efficient video search and indexing tools that allow us to quickly find the video data of particular interest from a large amount of video data. In this chapter, we are mainly focused on sports video mining due to its great commercial value and wide popularity among consumers. Current research on sports video analysis signifies two major trends, i.e., event-based analysis that aims at detecting events of special interests, e.g., goals and replays (Shyu, Xie, Chen, & Chen, 2008), and structure-based analysis where the goal to discover the overall semantic evolution of a game (Gupta, Srinivasan, Jianbo, & Davis, 2009). Just like the index and the table of contents (TOC) in a book both of which are useful tools for a reader, event-based analysis and structure-based analysis have complementary nature for semantic video understanding, but they are usually addressed separately in sport video mining research as two different aspects. Our goal is to develop a new video mining paradigm that is able to support both of them. Specifically, we consider the American football video as a case study in our research, where we assume that the video stream has been pre-segmented into a set of consecutive shots each of which corresponds to a specific play in a game.

The semantic evolution of a complete American football game has an interesting multi-level structure as *"game flow → drives → plays "*, as shown in Figure 1, which is also shared by many field-based sports, such as soccer and hockey. The game flow summarizes the overall game progres-

sion by a series of labeled drives and each drive includes a set of annotated plays. It supports both event-based (labeled drives and annotated plays) and structure-based (plays → drives → game flow) video analysis. Specifically, we consider three possible labels for a drive: *scored, non-scored* and *turn-over*, and we also specify three kinds of key-words for each play, *play type* (what happened?), *camera view* (where did it happen?), and *possession* (who was on offense/defense?) Consequentially, we are interested two issues in this research: (1) how to annotate a play by a few mid-level key-words that can be used for high-level game flow analysis; (2) how to group a set of annotated plays into a series of labeled drives each of which has a variable number of plays. For simplicity, these two issues are referred to as keyword detection and game flow analysis in this chapter. Although the two issues are related, they are confronted by different challenges and require different approaches.

Machine learning, especially the probabilistic graphical modeling, is often considered as one of the most effective approaches for video mining (Cheng & Hsu, 2006; Liu, Carbonell, Weigele, & Gopalakarishnany, 2006). However, due to imperfect mid-level keyword detection or limited low-level feature extraction, the missing data problem (i.e., some plays with incomplete keywords) is prevalent in reality for high-level semantic analysis. Unfortunately, this issue is often under-treated in most video mining research. Our work is inspired by three machine learning techniques. One is the segmental hidden Markov models (SHMMs) (Gales & Young, 1993), which can handle short range temporal dependencies from observations that cannot be done in traditional HMMs, another is the Segmentation Condition Random field (SCRF) (Liu, et al., 2006) used in protein fold recognition to capture long range dependencies in both observations and latent states, and the other is the marginalization techniques for missing data handling in (Farhangfar, Kurgan, & Dy, 2008). Particularly, we extend the

Figure 1. A multi-level "game flow → drive → play" representation in a football game that consists a series of labeled drives each of which contains a series of annotated plays

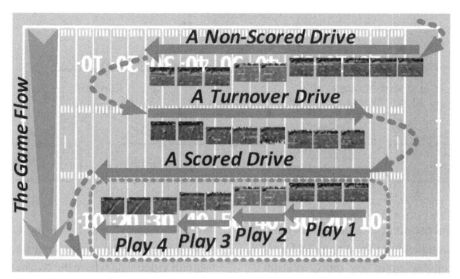

SHMM to a multi-channel SHMM (MCSHMM) that can handle multiple play sequences simultaneously, and then propose a new Auxiliary SCRF (ASCRF) that can capture long-range dependencies between plays and drives with different semantic granularities. As a result, ASCRF can not only perform joint segmentation and recognition to find the game flow from a set of annotated plays, and more importantly, but also handle possible missing keywords in some plays.

The major advantages of our approach are the *explicit semantic modeling* and *direct semantic computing* that are implemented by the game flow representation and hybrid probabilistic graphical modeling framework, which is unique in three aspects:

- First, the three-layer semantic space involving low-level visual features, mid-level keywords, and high-level semantics, provides us a unified video representation of sports video. More importantly, guided by the semantic space, the sports video mining problem is converted into two inter-correlated inference problems that

can be addressed by hybrid probabilistic graphical models.

- Second, mid-level keyword detection is accomplished by a new multi-channel segmentation HMM (MCSHMM). MCSHMM enhances traditional HMMs in terms of two aspects. One is the segmental observation model that can handle variable length of observations for a hidden state. The other is a multi-channel and multi-layer dynamic model that is able to represent complex semantic networks involving multiple inter-correlated co-existing keyword sequences.

- Third, the high-level semantic analysis is addressed by a new auxiliary segmentation CRF (ASCRF). Not only can ASCRF jointly segment and recognize a set of annotated keywords into a series of labeled drives, but also handle the missing data, i.e., incomplete keywords, by adding an auxiliary layer to learn additional contextual information during the model learning stage.

Figure 2. Two perspectives on recent sports video mining research

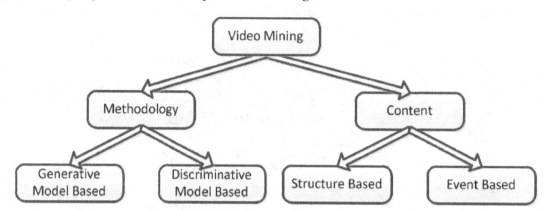

It is worth mentioning that although our current research was conducted on the American football videos, the proposed game flow representation is a quite general paradigm that is applicable to most of field sports video mining applications by integrating certain domain knowledge to re-define the mid-level keywords and drive labels. For example, in a soccer game we can define three types of attacks, i.e., scored attacks, non-scored attacks, and intercepted attacks. Each attack is composed by a few consecutive plays for which we can define some mid-level keywords like play types, e.g., goal kicks, penalty kicks, headers, passes, shoots, and camera views, such as midfield views, end line views, penalty area views, etc.

This chapter is organized as follows. We will first review the related work from two perspectives, semantic video analysis and probabilistic graphical modeling. Second, we present the semantic space for video content representation, by which the problem of sports video mining is converted into three inter-related research issues, low-level feature extraction, mid-level keyword detection, and high-level game flow analysis, among which the latter two are addressed by two different probabilistic graphical models, i.e., HMM-based generative and CRF-based discriminative ones. Then we discuss three research issues in details where we propose MCHSMM for multi-channel keyword detection and ASCRF for

game flow analysis with missing keywords. We report experimental results on a set of American football video data where the two new models are compared with the traditional HMM-based and CRF-based approaches. Finally, we conclude this chapter by providing some discussion for future research.

RELATED WORKS

In this section, we will review recent works on sports video mining from two different perspectives as shown in Figure 2. We first review the recent research on semantic video analysis, and then we briefly present the recent development on probabilistic graphical models.

Semantic Video Analysis Approaches

Recent sports video mining research has two major trends in terms of the semantic video analysis, i.e., the *structure-based* (Kokaram, et al., 2006; Xie, Chang, Divakaran, & Sun, 2003) and *event-based* (Assfalg, Bertini, Colombo, Bimbo, & Nunziati, 2003; T. Wang, et al., 2006) approaches.

Structure-based approaches usually attempt to parse a video sequence in individual segments by detecting scene changes or the boundaries between camera shots in a video stream. It tends to find some commonly shared semantic segments, such as the detection of major play types (Lazarescu & Venkatesh, 2003) or to parse a video stream into different segments (Xie, Chang, Divakaran, & Sun, 2003. They are of limited semantic meaning but can be used to be serving as building blocks for high-level semantic analysis. For example, in (Xie, et al., 2003) a soccer video sequence can be segmented into plays and breaks, and in (Pan, Beek, & Sezan, 2001), the authors classify a video sequence into plays and replays. Both works focused on the detection of general semantic structures in the video data and treated them as the basic semantic components.

Event-based approaches aim to summarize the video data by highlights or specific events of interest. Event detection in sports video can be done at both the object level (Koubaroulis, Matas, & Kittler, 2002; Xu, G. Zhu, Zhang, Huang, & Lu, 2008; Yu, et al., 2003) or the scene level (L. Duan, Xu, Tian, Xu, & Jin, 2005; Li & Sezan, 2002; Naphade & Huang, 2002). Object-level event detection approaches usually associate semantic events with the appearance or behavior of some specific objects. For example, in (Xu, et al., 2008), the author employed object-based features such as the trajectory of a ball or players to detect goals in a soccer game. However, most of semantic events are typically defined on the complex collections of multiple objects. Scene-level event detection algorithms, i.e., (L. Duan, et al., 2005), utilize various visual cues in the video data, including color distribution, specific landmarks, camera motion, and even caption information to detect semantic events. Usually, feature extraction at the scene-level is more robust and efficient compared with the feature extraction at the object-level.

Recently, there are some attempts to integrate these two strategies into one unified framework due to their complementary nature for comprehensive video understanding (Gupta, et al., 2009; Mei, et al., 2005). An interesting video understanding framework was proposed in (Gupta, et al.,

2009) that uses an AND-OR graph to detect the *storyline* from annotated video sequences. This method was mainly designed to handle single-link causal semantic relationships due to the nature of the AND-OR graph. However, we want to consider more complex contextual relationships that may require multi-link undirected dependencies among multiple semantic keywords. In terms of semantics, our goal is to deliver a complete game flow to summarize the whole game that supports both event-based and structure-based video understanding.

Probabilistic Graphical Models

Machine learning approaches, especially probabilistic graphical models, are powerful tools to capture complex variable dependencies, which have been proven effective for semantic video analysis. There are two types of probabilistic graphical models, i.e., generative and discriminative models. Generative models, e.g., DBNs, are usually preferred to handle problems where latent semantic events/structures can be explicitly defined by parametric models based on the features extracted from video (Y. Wang, Sabzmeydani, & Mori, 2007; Xiong, 2005). Discriminative models, e.g., CRFs, are attracting attentions due to its flexibility of capturing long range spatial-temporal correlations (S. B. Wang, Quattoni, Morency, Demirdjian, & Darrell, 2006; T. Wang, et al., 2006). Meanwhile, missing data problems (Roderick J A Little & Rubin, 1986) existing in both cases affect their performance largely if no proper manipulation mechanisms are incorporated, however, they are rarely studied in the context of semantic video analysis.

Dynamic Bayesian networks (DBNs) (Murphy, 2002) provide a unified probabilistic framework to represent various graphical structures. Recently, there have been intensive efforts to enhance DBNs for semantic video analysis in terms of *structuring* and *learning*. The *structuring* refers to how to improve the dynamic model and observation model in generative models. For example, coupled HMMs (CHMMs) (M. Brand, Oliver, & Pentland, 1997) and the factorial HMMs (FHMMs) (P. Wang & Ji, 2005) capture interactions between two parallel Markov, while hierarchical HMMs (HHMMs) (Xie, et al., 2003), with a hierarchical representation accomplish semantic analysis via *primitives* and *structures recognitions*. The segmental HMM (SHMM) was proposed to handle variable-length observations by involving segmental observation models (Gales & Young, 1993), which can capture feature variability both within a segment and across segments. Generally, there are two *learning* issues, one is *structure learning* (Friedman & Koller, 2003) that tries to provide compact and effective model representations by condensing state space and cut state dynamics, the other is *parameter learning* (Ghahramani, 2002) that aims at estimating model parameters given certain model structure. Furthermore, in (Matthew Brand, 1999), concepts of entropic prior and parameter extinction are proposed to optimize model structures and parameter simultaneously.

Compared with DBNs, by relieving the conditional independence assumption, CRFs and their variations are more expressive to capture flexible statistical dependencies on observations and labels. In (T. Wang, et al., 2006), a CRF-based approach is proposed to detect the semantic events, e.g., replay, view, etc., based on a keyword sequence. Different from traditional CRFs where a label is assigned to a single observation, the HCRF (S. B. Wang, et al., 2006) incorporates the sub-sequence of hidden state variables in the CRF to assign a label for an entire observation sequence. Moreover, a Segmentation CRF (SCRF) was proposed in (Liu, et al., 2006) to capture the long range interaction in both observation and semantics for protein segmentation and recognition. Missing data handling was originated from statistics but rarely studied in the context of semantic video analysis. Actually the missing data problem is prevalent in high-level semantic analysis where mid-level keywords may not be always available. There are two major methods for missing data handling, *imputation* and *marginalization* (Roderick J A Little & Rubin, 1986). The imputation attempts to "fill in" the missing data by inferring new values from known values. The marginalization tries to minimize the effect of the missing data from valid observations. In general, the missing data problem could occur both in the learning or inference stage (Rubin, 1976). However, in the case of semantic video analysis, the missing data problem is more prominent in the inference stage when some semantic keywords or labels may not be obtainable due to the limitations of low-level feature extraction or mid-level keyword detection. In this work, we are interested in how to handle missing keywords for high-level semantic analysis, where a new probabilistic graphic model is proposed.

Inspired by these machine learning approaches, we divide our research into two steps. First, we develop a new HMM-based generative model (i.e., MCSHMM) that is able to jointly detect multiple co-existing mid-level keywords. Second, we propose a new CRF-based discriminative model (ASCRF) for game flow analysis that can not only group a set of annotated plays into a series of labeled drives but also is able to handle the plays with missing keywords.

PROBLEM FORMULATION

We believe that explicit semantic modeling and direct semantic computing are effective to bridge the semantic gap and reduce the ambiguity and uncertainty in sports video mining. Therefore, we propose a three-layer semantic space for video representation, which includes *low-level visual features*, a set of *mid-level keywords* and desired *high-level semantics*. This approach supports both general semantic structures and customized events-of-interest, increasing the usability and interactivity of video data.

Figure 3. The three-layer semantic space with the game flow paradigm (top), and two inference problems (bottom) in the football video (the stadium background is from www.nfl.com)

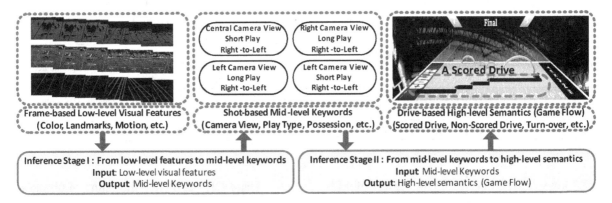

Semantic Space

As shown in Figure 3, we want to advocate the concept of a three-layer semantic space to facilitate the semantic understanding of video content and to support effective user queries. It is our belief that the exploration of high-level semantics from mid-level keywords is more reliable and feasible than from the low-level visual features directly. Our main reasoning is that mid-level semantic structures have relatively stable and repeatable patterns, and they can be more useful and expressive to represent high-level semantics than low-level visual features. Similar video mining paradigms can be found in recent literature (L. Y. Duan, Xu, Chua, Q. Tian, & Xu, 2003; T. Wang, et al., 2006). Correspondingly, we address these research issues as following three aspects:

- *Low-level visual features* are extracted from each frame that can reflect the activity or location in the field, such color distribution, landmarks, and camera motion. These visual features will be used to infer mid-level keywords. Feature extraction is usually computational expensive due to the large data size and it is prone to error and data ambiguity.

- *Mid-level keywords* are recurrent and relatively well-defined shot-based semantics. They can be specified by certain low-level features. Particularly, in an American football video, we select three kinds of keywords. First, *Camera views* that include central, left, right, and end-zone views, i.e., V_c, V_l, V_r, V_e, can be inferred from the color distribution and yard-line angle distribution in a shot. Second, *Play types* that include the long, short, kick, and field-goal plays, i.e., P_l, P_s, P_k, V_e, can be estimated from the pattern of camera motion in a shot. Third, *Possessions* that include right and left possessions, i.e., N_r, N_l, can be determined from the initial camera motion in a shot. These keywords serve as building blocks for high-level semantic analysis.

- *High-level game flow* is a series of labeled drives that can be used to summarize the semantic game evolution and to detect events of interest. In other words, a game flow supports a structure-based and event-based representation. In this work, three kinds of drives are defined, i.e., *scored*, *non drives* and *turn-over drives*. Each drive consists of a variable number of plays each of which is annotated by multi-channel

Table 1. Comparison between two inference stages

	Inference Problem 1	**Inference Problem 2**
Objective	To infer multiple co-existing mid-level keywords from low-level features.	To infer the high-level game flow from multi-channel mid-level keywords.
Inputs (observations)	Low-level visual features; frame-wised; strong temporal dependencies within each shot; conditional independencies with a shot and across shots.	Mid-level keywords; shot-wised; complex temporal and spatial dependencies across multiple keyword channels, possible missing keywords
Outputs (latent states)	Mid-level keywords; well-defined; high recurrence, short range dependencies.	High-level semantics, game flow, labeled drives, long range dependencies.
Approaches	Multi-Channel HMMs (MCSHMMs)	Auxiliary CRFs (ASCRFs)

keywords. By enriching the variety of mid-level keywords, it is possible we can have more detailed labels defined for drives, allowing a more semantic-rich game flow-based video representation framework.

Two Inference Problems

It is our attempt to provide a unified machine learning paradigm where sports video mining is formulated as two related statistical inference problems that are solved by hybrid probabilistic graphical models as shown in Table 1, where two inference problems are compared in different aspects.

Inference Problem 1: Keyword Detection (from Low-Level Features to Mid-Level Keywords)

Mid-level keywords have two main characteristics. One is that they can be represented probabilistically by low-level features, and the other is that their temporal evolutions follow certain dynamics with Markovian properties. Two conditionally-independent assumptions in HMMs are also applicable for keyword detection. Therefore, we consider HMM-based approaches for keyword detection where we still need consider three special issues.

- Issue 1.1: Segmental modeling of observations: Since low-level feature extraction is performed at the frame-level and key-word detection at the shot-level, we need to consider a segmental model that is able to deal with the variable-length observations for shot-level keyword detection.

- Issue 1.2: Multi-channel keyword modeling: Since there are multiple co-existing keywords defined on each shot that may interact with each other, we need a multi-channel and multi-layer dynamic model to capture the temporal dependency both within each channel and across multiple channels, supporting simultaneous multi-channel keyword detection.

- Issue 1.3: Model structure and parameter learning: In order to ensure that multi-channel keyword detection is effective and efficient, we need to develop a more intelligent learning algorithm that is able to optimize the model structure and parameters simultaneously, delivering a compact model structure with a condensed latent space.

Inference Problem 2: Game Flow Analysis (from Mid-Level Keywords to High-Level Game Flow)

Mid-level keywords are used as the building blocks for high-level game flow analysis. However, unlike

Figure 4. Basic visual features: color distribution, yard line angle (left), and camera motion (right)

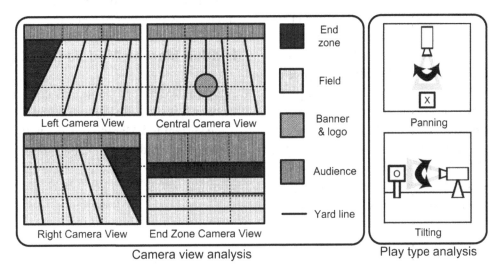

keyword detection, game flow analysis is more challenging due to three main issues.

- Issue 2.1: Joint segmentation and recognition: Since there are a variable number of plays in a drive, we need a joint segmentation and recognition approach that can group a set of annotated plays into a series of labeled drives.
- Issue 2.2: Multiple-to-one semantic mapping: Since each drive label does not have a unique definition and may correspond to many different play combinations, we need to have a flexible model that is able to deal with versatile dependency structure between keywords and drive labels.
- Issue 2.3: Missing keyword handling: Due to error-prone feature extraction process and imperfect keyword detection, it is possible that we may miss a keyword in some plays. For example, the possession that is a very important keyword for game flow analysis cannot be reliably estimated from a play if there is significant motion in the beginning of that shot. We need a model that is capable of missing data handling. This practical issue has been tradition-

ally undertreated in most video mining research.

FEATURE EXTRACTION: VISUAL OBSERVATIONS

At the first layer of the semantic space, relevant low-level visual features are needed to specify the two mid-level semantic structures involved in this work, i.e., play types and camera views. Specifically, there are four play types, i.e., *long play*, *short play*, *field goal*, and *kick off*, four camera views, i.e., *left view*, *central view*, *right view*, and *end-zone view*, and two possessions, i.e., *left-to-right possession*, and *right-to-left possessions*. Correspondingly, we define two sets of visual features in the following.

In Figure 4 (left), we illustrate typical scenes for four different camera views where spatial color distribution and the yard line angle are the two major visual features. Specifically, we employ the robust dominant color region detection algorithm (Ekin, Tekalp, & Mehrotra, 2003) to extract the dominant color region, i.e., the play ground. Then we use Canny edge detection and the Hough transform to detect the yard lines in the region of the playing field. Based on the detected playing field and yard lines, we extract a 6-D feature vector composed by the following (1) the ratio of the dominant color region; (2) the ratio difference of dominant color between the left/right and center parts; (3) the ratio difference of dominant color between the left and right parts; (4) the ratio difference of dominant color between the top and bottom parts; (5) the average angle of all yard lines; (6) the angle difference between the first and last frames in a shot (Ding & Fan, 2006).

Play types and possessions are largely dependent on camera motion. There are mainly two types of camera motion: panning and tilting, as shown in Figure 4. Most play types can be effectively characterized by these two kinds of camera motion. For example, in a long run from right to left, camera motion could be a short right-panning then a long left-panning, which is different from the motion trend of a short run, i.e., a short right-panning followed by a short left-panning. While the possession could be specified by the initial camera motion To estimate camera motion, we can use the optical flow based method (Srinivasan, Venkatesh, & Hosie, 1997) to qualitatively compute motion parameters between two adjacent frames. Also, the frame indices are included as an additional temporal feature to distinguish long plays and short plays. Therefore, a 3-D feature vector is used to represent the play type in each shot.

MID-LEVEL KEYWORDS DETECTION: GENERATIVE MODELS

To detect mid-level keywords, we chose HMM-based generative models. As shown in Figure 5, different keywords can be represented by relevant visual features and multiple mid-level keywords co-exist in in a play, such as possessions, play types and camera views. We first two traditional HMM-based approaches, then we introduce the Multi-channel Segmental HMM (MCSHMM)

that can effectively address the abovementioned three issues in keyword detection.

Hidden Markov Models (HMMs)

A typical HMM for a single channel of mid-level keywords as shown in Figure 6 assumes the underlying system is a Markov process with unknown parameter including a state transition matrix:

$$A = \{a_{k,j} = p(S_t = j \mid S_{t-1} = k) \mid t = 1, ..., T\}, \tag{1}$$

and a probabilistic observation model that we choose Gaussian or Gaussian mixture model

$$p(o_t \mid S_t = k) = N(o_t \mid \mu_k, \Sigma_k), \tag{2}$$

$$p(o_t \mid S_t = k) = \sum_{n=1}^{N} \alpha_n N(o_t \mid \mu_{nk}, \Sigma_{nk}), \tag{3}$$

where k and j are specific mid-level keywords in each channel, which equals to *{1,2,3,4}* for camera views or play types and *{1,2}* for possessions, and the parameter space can be represented by $\Gamma = \{\pi_k, a_{k,j}, \mu_{nk}, \Sigma_{nk}\}$, where π_k is the initial probabilities, $a_{k,j}$ is the transition probabilities, and μ_{nk}, Σ_{nk} are mean and covariance matrix for the Gaussian mixture model. Then, Equation (1) captures the underlying state dynamics, and Equation (2) & (3) characterize observations pertaining to the hidden states either as probability density functions. After EM training (Bilmes, 1997), we can obtain the optimized parameter set,

$$\Gamma^* = \arg\max_{\Gamma} p(o_{1:T} \mid \Gamma), \tag{4}$$

Figure 5. Two representative mid-level keywords: camera views and play types

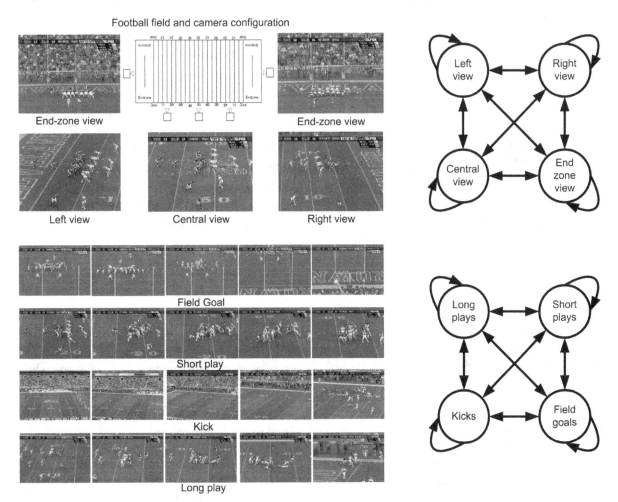

$$p(o_{1:T} \mid \Gamma) = \sum_k \pi_k \prod_{t=1}^{T} p(S_{t+1} \mid S_t) p(o_t \mid S_t = k).$$

$$(5)$$

Then Viterbi algorithm can find the optimized state sequences, i.e., the mid-level keyword sequences as:

$$S_{1:T}^* = \arg\max_{S_{1:T}} P(S_{1:T} \mid o_{1:T}, \Gamma^*).$$

$$(6)$$

The major limitation of the HMM is that each shot is represented by an averaged feature vector that is less representative and informative. This

fact motivates us to improve the observation model in the HMM, i.e., we are expecting to explore the frame-wise features and the temporal dependency across frames in a shot.

Segmental Hidden Markov Models (SHMMs)

To fully utilize frame-wise visual features and temporal dependency across frames in a shot, we invoke a segmental HMM (SHMM) (Gales & Young, 1993) that is able to handle variable-length observations to attack this problem. Instead of generating one observation by each hidden

Figure 6. Generative model based approaches: (a) HMM; (b) SHMM; (c) MCSHMM

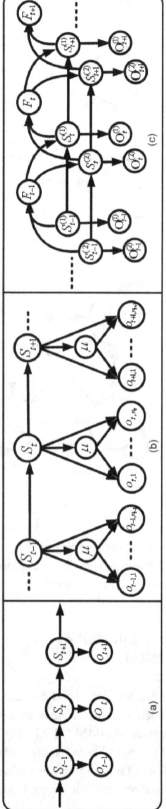

state in the traditional HMM, each hidden state of SHMMs emits a sequence of observations, which is called a segment. In SHMM as shown in Figure 6, observations in a given segment are assumed to be independent to observations of other segments. In addition, all observations in each segment are conditionally independent given the mean of that segment. Thus, the likelihood function is attainable that capture rich statistics of frame-wise features. Here, we can regard segments as mid-level keywords and observations as frame-wise features. A SHMM can be characterized by a set of parameters

$$\Gamma = \{\pi_k, a_{k,j}, \mu_{\mu,k}, \Sigma_{\mu,k}, \Sigma_k\}. \tag{7}$$

π_k is the initial probability, $a_{k,j}$ is the transition probability, $\mu_{\mu,k}$ characterizes the mean of the each segment with variance $\Sigma_{\mu,k}$. Given a shot in time t with n_t observations, i.e., $\mathbf{O}_{1:T} = \{\mathbf{O}_t \mid t = 1, ..., T\}$, the conditional likelihood of $\mathbf{O}_t$ is defined as:

$$p(\mathbf{O}_t \mid S_t = k, \Gamma) =$$
$$\int p(\mu \mid S_t = k, \Gamma) \prod_{i=1}^{n_t} p(o_{t,i} \mid \mu, S_t = k, \Gamma) d\mu, \tag{8}$$

where

$$p(\mu \mid S_t = k, \Gamma) = N(\mu \mid \mu_{\mu,k}, \Sigma_{\mu,k}), \tag{9}$$

$$p(o_{t,r} \mid \mu, S_t = k, \Gamma) = N(o_{t,i} \mid \mu, \Sigma_k), \tag{10}$$

which are both specified by the Gaussian distribution. Then, similar to HMMs, by using a new EM and Viterbi algorithm introduced in (Ding & Fan, 2007a), we can estimate all model parameters as:

$$S_{1:T}^* = \arg\max_{S_{1:T}} P(S_{1:T} \mid o_{1:T}, \Gamma^*). \tag{11}$$

However, SHMM including the HMM based approaches can only detect a single channel mid-level keyword, and model structure, e.g., the state space, is pre-defined, which cannot capture the interaction between different mid-level keywords with a flexible manner.

Multi-Channel Hidden Markov Models (MCSHMMs)

We expect a new model to inherent the merits of the SHMM, and to further explore interactions between mid-level keyword channels. In (Ding & Fan, 2008, 2009), we advance a new multi-channel SHMM model (MCSHMM) that involves multiple *parallel* SHMMs in a two-layer *hierarchical* structure, as shown in Figure 6. We also developed a new learning algorithm that can learn a model with compact structure as well as optimized parameters simultaneously.

Both the dynamic model and the observation model in MCSHMMs have a two-layer structure that greatly enhances its capability of learning and inference. Specifically, at the first layer of the dynamic model,

$$\mathbf{S} = \{S_t^{(h)} \mid t = 1, ..., T; h = 1, 2\}, \tag{12}$$

where $S_t^{(h)}$ denotes the state of shot t in channel h, and at the second-layer of the dynamic model,

$$\mathbf{F} = \{F_t = (S_t^{(1)}, S_t^{(2)}) \mid t = 1, ..., T\}, \tag{13}$$

which represents the state sequence at the second layer where each state consists of two current states at the first layer. At the observation layer,

$$\mathbf{O} = \{o_{t,r}^{(h)} \mid t = 1, ..., T; i = 1, ..., n_i; h = 1, 2\}, \tag{14}$$

in which, $o_{t,r}^{(h)}$ indicates observations of shot t with n_t frames in channel h. Therefore, the MC-SHMM's parameter set $\Gamma = \{\mathbf{A}, \Pi, \Omega\}$ includes following components:

- *Initial probabilities*:

$$\Pi = \{P(S_t^{(1)}), P(S_t^{(2)}), P(F_t \mid S_t^{(1)}, S_t^{(2)})\}. \tag{15}$$

- *Transition probabilities*:

$$\mathbf{A} = \{A_w, w = 1, 2, 3\}, \tag{16}$$

where

$$A_1 = \{P(S_t^{(1)} = m \mid S_{t-1}^{(1)} = n, F_{t-1} = l) \mid m, n = 1, ..., 4, l = 1, ..., 16\},$$
$$A_2 = \{P(S_t^{(2)} = m \mid S_{t-1}^{(2)} = n, F_{t-1} = l) \mid m, n = 1, ..., 4, l = 1, ..., 16\},$$
$$A_3 = \{P(F_t = l \mid S_t^{(1)} = m, S_t^{(2)} = n) \mid m, n = 1, ..., 4, l = 1, ..., 16\}.$$

Observation density functions:

$$p(\mathbf{O}_t^{(h)} \mid S_i^{(h)} = m, \Omega) = \int N(\mu \mid \mu_{\mu,m}^{(h)}, \Sigma_{\mu,m}^{(h)}) \prod_{i=1}^{n_t} N(o_{t,r}^{(h)} \mid \mu, \Sigma_m^{(h)}) d\mu, \tag{17}$$

where
$\Omega = \{\mu_{\mu,m}^{(h)}, \Sigma_{\mu,m}^{(h)}, \Sigma_m^{(h)} \mid h = 1, 2; m = 1, ..., 4\}$
specifies two segmental models, and $o_{t,r}^{(h)}$ denotes

Box 1.

$$p(\mathbf{S}, \mathbf{F}, \mathbf{O} \mid \Gamma) = P(S_1^{(1)}) P(S_1^{(2)}) P(F_1 \mid S_1^{(1)}, S_1^{(2)})$$
$$\prod_{t=1}^{T} P(F_t \mid S_t^{(1)}, S_t^{(2)}) \prod_{t=2}^{T} \prod_{h=1}^{2} P(S_t^{(h)} \mid S_{t-1}^{(h)}, F_{t-1}) \prod_{t=1}^{T} \prod_{h=1}^{2} p(o_{t,r}^{(h)} \mid S_t^{(h)}). \tag{18}$$

the observation from the *r*th frame in shot *t* of channel *h*.

Then, given the dual-channel observations **O** of *T* shots, the joint likelihood is defined as shown in Box 1.

We refer the reader to (Ding & Fan, 2008, 2009) for more details, where a new unsupervised learning algorithm was proposed to learn the model structure and parameters simultaneously. The key idea is to find a compact model structure that has good determinism and minimal ambiguity. We first pre-define a coarse model structure that includes every possible configuration of mid-level keywords, then we use the idea of entropic prior and parameter extinction in (Matthew Brand, 1999) to trim the weakly supported parameters and states, leading to a compact and concise model with good determinism. Then, by using the Viterbi decoding algorithm, we can estimate multiple mid-level keywords at the same time.

HIGH-LEVEL SEMANTICS DISCOVERY: DISCRIMINATIVE MODELS

As aforementioned, mid-level keywords deliver the rudimentary building blocks for high-level semantic discovery because they represent high-level semantics (i.e., events or the game flow) effectively. Particularly, in addition to the play type and camera view, we also introduce another mid-level structure, i.e., *the possession*, which indicates the offense/defense teams and can be easily detected by using the initial camera motion in the beginning of a shot. Thus, given three kinds of mid-level semantic structures of all shots, we aim at detecting the game flow that is composed by a series of labeled drives.

SCRF-based Game Flow Discovery

To discover the game flow, one key issue is how to simultaneously segment and recognize drives

from a series of plays that are annotated with multiple mid-level keywords. Inspired by the protein fold structure analysis in bio-informatics (Liu, et al., 2006), we address this issue by SCRFs, i.e., using segmentation mechanisms for game flow discovery. Compared with the Segmental HMMs (SHMM) (Ding & Fan, 2007a), SCRFs not only discover variable-length segments (i.e., drives) from observation sequences (i.e., labeled plays), but also provide a flexible way to relieve the conditional independence assumption among plays, which further facilitates the following extension for missing data handling.

It is worth mentioning that choosing effective feature functions f_e plays an important role for accurate predictions. In SCRFs, we define the feature set by *drive feature functions* that are described by templates composed of camera views $\{V_c, V_l, V_r, V_e\}$, play types $\{P_l, P_s, P_k, P_f\}$, possessions $\{N_r, N_l\}$. As examples shown in Figure 8, *drive feature functions* mainly control intra or inter dynamics of drives, the length of drive, and the spatial-temporal correlation among keywords, which cover the spatial-temporal relationship between drives and mid-level semantic keywords:

- *Regular structure template*: some regular structures for drives that reflect the domain knowledge of each drive type that have the most common keyword sequences, e.g., $V_c - ... - V_e, P_k - ... - P_f, N_l - ... - N_l$ etc.. We define the feature function $f_{reg-V}(S,D), f_{reg-P}(S,D)$, and $f_{reg-N}(S,D)$, or $f_{reg-VPN}(S,D), f_{reg-VP}(S,D), f_{reg-VN}(S,D), etc.$ on multiple channels, which is equal to 1 if the segment D matches the template, and 0 otherwise.
- *Markovian templates*: the Regular structure template is straightforward and easy to implement. However, it does not consider

the internal dynamics in various drives. Therefore, we build Markovian templates for scored, non-scored, and turnover drives based on temporal relationship of keywords as $f_{Markov-V}(S,D)$, $f_{Markov-P}(S,D)$, and $f_{Markov-N}(S,D)$, which indicate the certain ordering properties of a sequence of keywords in a drive.

- *Special structure templates*: for specific drives, there are some particular expressions, such as the scored drive, it ends at a field goal followed by a kick off $\ldots - P_f - P_k$ or ends by end zone camera view followed by a central camera view $\ldots - V_e - V_c$, therefore we define feature functions for three types of drive, like $f_{spe-V}(S,D)$, $f_{spe-P}(S,D)$, $f_{spe-N}(S,D)$, to reveal some specific expressions of each drive type.

- *Length prediction templates*: there are some trends for the length of a specific type of segment. To consider this property, we employ the Poisson distribution to formulate feature functions of $f_{leng-V}(S,D)$, $f_{leng-P}(S,D)$, and $f_{leng-N}(S,D)$.

As the SCRF shown in Figure 7, the observation sequence $S = \{S_i \mid i = 1, 2, \ldots, I\}$ represents the mid-level keywords sequences including camera views V_c, V_l, V_r, V_e, play types P_l, P_s, P_k, V_e, and possessions N_r, N_l, where I is the total number of plays in a football video; and $D = \{D_u \mid u = 1, 2, \ldots, U\}$ represents the drive label sequence, i.e., the game flow, where U is the total number of drives in the same video. Given the observation sequence S, instead of labeling each observation as $W = \{W_i \mid i = 1, 2, \ldots, I\}$, we label each drive D that contains multiple plays. This SCRF-based formulation not only builds the long-range spatial-temporal dependencies between high-level se-

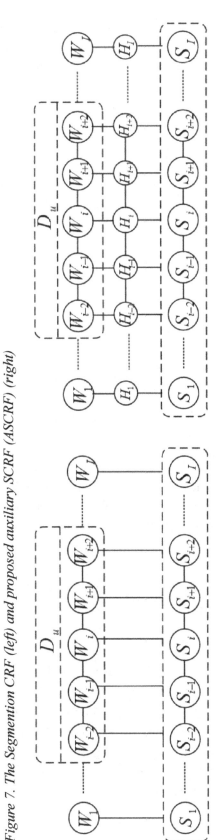

Figure 7. The Segmention CRF (left) and proposed auxiliary SCRF (ASCRF) (right)

Figure 8. Four examples of drive feature functions defined in SCRF that represent different drive types by a few specified keywords (white circle) and unspecified ones (gray circles), including a regular structure template in the camera view channel (a), two regular structure templates involving two channels (b) and (c), and a special structure template involving three channels (d).

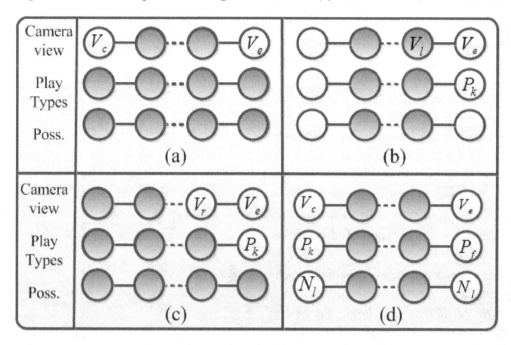

mantics and mid-level keywords, but also provides the mathematical foundations of how to find the optimal segmentations. The SCRF based approach formulates the conditional probabilities as:

$$p(D \mid S) = \frac{1}{Z_0} \exp(\sum_{u=1}^{U} \sum_{e=1}^{E} \lambda_e f_e(S, D_u, D_{u-1})), \qquad (19)$$

where $\{f_e \mid e = 1, \ldots, E\}$ is the set of drive feature functions we select to specify different drives in SCRF, λ_e is the weight of f_e, and E is the number of feature functions, Z_0 is the normalization factor. We can use L-BFGS algorithm (Sha & Pereira, 2003) to optimize λ_e by maximizing the conditional log-likelihood:

$$L_\Lambda = \sum_{u=1}^{U} \sum_{e=1}^{E} \lambda_e f_e(S, D_u, D_{u-1}) - \log Z_0 + \frac{\lambda_e^2}{2\sigma^2}, \qquad (20)$$

where $\frac{\lambda_e^2}{2\sigma^2}$ is the Gaussian prior as a smoothing term to control the parameter space. Specifically, due to its variable-length nature, the ith drive needs to be specified by three parameters, i.e., starting play p_u, ending play q_u, and label D_u, Then after model training, similar to CRFs, we can use Viterbi decoding to search for the optimal segmentation and recognition (along with the number of drives) that maximizes $p(D \mid S)$ at the testing stage. As a result, the game flow is found by determining D_u, p_u, and q_u for all drives.

Handling the Missing Data with ASCRFs

In practice, the missing data problem is possible in high-level semantic analysis due to imperfect keyword detections. In the case of sports video mining, this problem is often under-treated, since it is normally assumed that all keywords can be extracted at a reasonable accuracy. In the field of machine learning, there are two often used schemes to handle missing data, *imputation*, i.e., "filling" the missing data with estimated values, and *marginalization*, i.e., "substituting" the missing data with a distribution estimated from observed ones (Farhangfar, et al., 2008; Roderick J A Little & Rubin, 1986). Due to its generality and robustness, the marginalization-based techniques show better classification performance than the imputation-based ones for handling missing data. Specifically, in this work, we are interested in how to marginalize missing keywords for high-level semantic analysis, and we propose a probabilistic graphical model called Auxiliary SCRF (ASCRF) by adding an auxiliary layer in SCRF, as shown in Figure 7.

The proposed ASCRF is able to learn contextual information in the training stage that is used to mitigate the influence of missing keywords by a marginalization technique in the testing stage. As shown in Figure 7, we introduce an auxiliary layer of $H = \{H_i \mid i = 1, 2, \ldots, I\}$, which indicate whether the current keyword is observable ($H_i = 1$) or not $H_i = 0$. Then, we can formulate the conditional probabilities of all drives as:

$$p(D \mid S) = \sum_H p(D, H \mid S). \tag{21}$$

According to Equation (19), the conditional probability of a drive given a set of keywords can be re-defined as:

$$p(D \mid S) =$$
$$\frac{1}{Z_0} \exp(\sum_H \sum_{u=1}^{U} \sum_{g=1}^{G} \lambda_g f_g(S, H, D_u, D_{u-1})), \tag{22}$$

where two sets of feature functions are involved, i.e., $\{f_g \mid g = 1, \ldots, E\}$ used in (19) and $\{f_g \mid g = E + 1, \ldots, G\}$ introduced to deal with the missing data problem. λ_g is the weight of f_g. Then, the parameters λ_g can be estimated by the LBFGS algorithm as:

$$L_\Lambda =$$
$$\sum_H \sum_{u=1}^{U} \sum_{g=1}^{G} \lambda_g f_g(S, H, D_u, D_{u-1}) - \log Z_0 + \frac{\lambda_g^2}{2\sigma^2}. \tag{23}$$

The core idea of ASCRF is that the auxiliary layer H enables a two-mode learning process. One is the normal learning when all data (i.e., mid-level keywords) are available ($H_t = 1, \lambda_g = 0$ for $g > E$), and the other is a special learning process when a keyword is disabled ($H_t = 0, \lambda_g = 0$ for $g \leq E$) and then some contextual distributions are learned from surrounding and similar keyword sequences to compensate the missing keyword. Two types of correlations are optimized during learning. One is correlations between drives and mid-level keywords; the other is correlations among keywords that can adaptively handle the case involving the missing data. The idea of the auxiliary layer can be applied to CRFs, leading a so-called Auxiliary CRFs (ACRFs) that can also handle the missing data compared with ASCRF.

Compared with feature functions in SCRFs, in ASCRFs, we add (G-E) feature functions in ASCRF that are called *auxiliary feature functions*. Both *auxiliary feature functions* and *drive feature functions* are described by templates that are composed of camera views $\{V_c, V_l, V_r, V_e\}$, play types $\{P_l, P_s, P_k, V_e\}$, possessions

$\{N_r, N_l\}$, as well as the auxiliary layer H. *Auxiliary feature functions* primarily reflect the consistency of keywords in drives, the similarity between drives, and the properties of correlation among missing and existing keywords across drives, which cover the properties of correlation among mid-level keywords within a single drive or between consecutive drives when there are some masks show the mid-level keywords is not available:

Integrity template: when there are some missing mid-level keywords, we need to consider the correlation between reliable keywords and the missing ones, for example, the possession stays consistent and the camera view changes slightly, etc. Therefore, we define the feature function $f_{it}(S, H, D)$ to deliver the pair wise information, which captures intra-drive similarity of keywords that is considered "missed".

Similarity template: To consider similarities between drives with same semantic meaning, but with the missing data, we define an alignment score $f_{sc}(S, H, D)$ to indicate the similarity, which considers the similarities between two drives of the same label with respect to their corresponding keywords, among which one has a missing keyword and the other has complete key-words. In other words, other drives with the same label can be used to learn the distribution for the missing keyword in a given drive.

After ASCRF learning, we can perform game flow analysis for a testing multi-channel keyword sequence S' along with its corresponding auxiliary layer H' via a forward-backward inference process like that of SCRF. We can reformulate the forward probability $\alpha_{m,i}n, l$ as the conditional probability that the drive with label

$$n \in \{1: "scored", 2: "non-scored", 3: "turnover"\}$$

ends at the lth play, given the previous drive with label $m \in \{1, 2, 3\}$ ending at the ith play with

observations $\{S_{i+1}, \ldots, S_l\}$ corresponding to current drive. Then, we define the forward step as:

$$\alpha_{(m,i)}(n, l) =$$
$$\sum_{p,q}\alpha_{(m,i)}(p,q)\alpha_{(p,q)}(n,l)\exp(\sum_{u=1}^{U'}\sum_{g=1}^{G}\lambda_g f_g(S', H', D_u, D_{u-1})),$$
$$(24)$$

where U' is the upper-bound of the number of drives allowed in a game. Then, the backward probabilities $\beta_{n,l}m, i$ is defined as the conditional probability of observations $\{S_{i+1}, \ldots, S_l\}$, given a drive of label m ending at the ith play and a drive of label n ending at the lth play:

$$\beta_{(n,l)}(m, i) =$$
$$\sum_{p,q}\beta_{(n,l)}(p,q)\beta_{(p,q)}(m,i)\exp(\sum_{u=1}^{U'}\sum_{g=1}^{G}\lambda_g f_g(S', H', D_u, D_{u-1})).$$
$$(25)$$

Given a test play sequence annotated with keywords, after the forward-background inference process, we can search for optimal drive segmentation and classification by maximizing the conditional likelihood $p(D | O)$ given the auxiliary layer as:

$$\delta_{(m,i)}(n, l) =$$
$$\sum_{p,q}\delta_{(m,i)}(p,q)\delta_{(p,q)}(n,l)\exp(\sum_{u=1}^{U'}\sum_{g=1}^{G}\lambda_g f_g(S', H', D_u, D_{u-1})).$$
$$(26)$$

Then, the optimal segmentation could be traced back by maximizing $\delta_{m,0}n, T$, which would results in the number of segmented drives and tell us the best patterns of game flow that can match semantic keywords in one complete game, i.e., segmenting the video into drives as well as identifying the semantic meaning of each drive.

EXPERIMENTS AND DISCUSSION

We tested our algorithms on 10 broadcasting NFL games acquired from an online sports video repository. The video data were first automatically segmented into a set of shots, and then by manually removing non-game shots and other breaks like ads, comments and replays. As the result, each game was segmented into 150-200 shots that correspond to a set of consecutive plays. To provide the ground truth data, we also manually annotated plays with three keywords, labeled all drives along with the starting/ending plays. In the following, we first report the results of keyword detection including play types and camera views, where we compare the proposed MCSHMM with several HMM-based approaches. Then, we discuss the experiments of game flow analysis where the keyword of possession is involved with certain missing rates. Especially, two missing data handling techniques are studied and compared, i.e., imputation and marginalization, leading to four models, CRF (with imputation), ACRF(with marginalization), SCRF (with imputation) and ASCRF (with marginalization). In addition, we designed two experimental schemes to examine each four the four models in terms of its robustness of handling the missing data. Scheme I uses the ground-truth information of camera views and play types, and scheme II is based on keyword detection results by using the proposed MCSHMM. In both settings, we control the keyword of possession with 1%-7% missing rates.

Mid-Level Keywords Detection

Seven generative methods and one discriminative model are involved for comparison. Generative models include a supervised GMM (with order 3), the HMM with Gaussian emission (HMM[1]), the HMM with GMM emission (HMM[2]), the embedded GMM-HMM (HMM[3]) (Ding & Fan, 2007b) and the SHMM (Ding & Fan, 2007a), the CHMM with GMM observations (CHMM[1]), the CHMM with segmental observations (CHMM[2]), and the MCSHMM (Ding & Fan, 2008). The first five explore two semantic structures (plays and views) independently and separately, while the last three estimate both jointly. To improve the EM training, we adopted a coarse-to-fine learning strategy that uses the training result of a simpler model to initialize a more complex one. Specifically, we first use K-mean (4-class) to obtain a coarse classification, and this result can be utilized to initialize HMM[1] whose training result can be used to initialize HMM[2], and so on. Training results of SHMM were used to initialize MCSHMM. For the discriminative model, we employ the CRF with shot-wise observations by averaging all frame-wise observations in one shot, which are then quantized as a discrete value in each dimension. Figure 9 shows the experimental results for mid-level semantic structure analysis. It is clearly shown that the MCSHMM outperforms all other algorithms with significant improvements, and the HMM-based generative approaches show clear advantages over the discriminative model, i.e., the CRF-based approach.

As shown in Figure 9, the performance is enhanced from HMMs to the MCSHMM. The reason that SHMM is better than other HMMs is because of the segmental observation model used. The improvement of MCSHMM over other HMMs and SHMM is owing to the hybrid hierarchical-parallel dynamic model involved. The MCSHMM can effectively capture the mutual interaction between two Markov chains by introducing the second-layer dynamics and decision-level fusion that are able to balance the dependency both within each channel and across the two channels. On the contrary, the CRF-based method is less effective than the HMM-based one when they are in same configuration. We expect it is due to the fact that the CRF may not take advantage of rich observation and the available prior knowledge about the distribution of observations and state dynamics during inference.

Figure 9. Classification results of mid-level semantic structures based on 9 different statistical models: (a). Camera view analysis results; (b). Play type analysis results

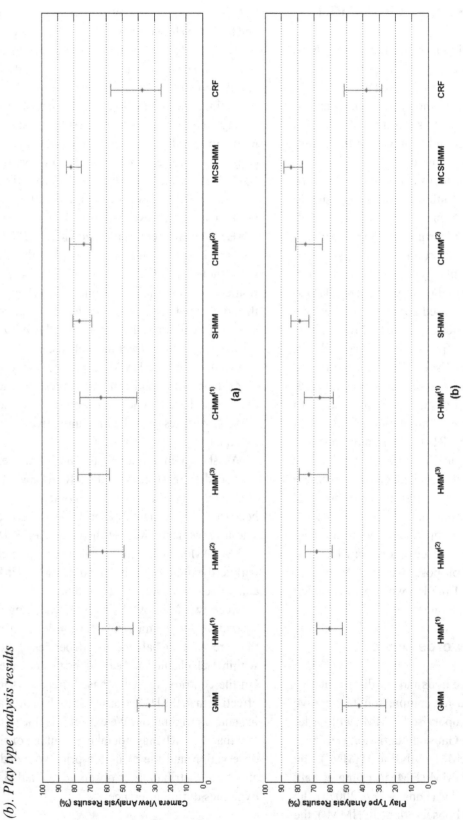

Figure 10. Experimental results for four models in two cases. (a)(b): Results with incomplete possessions and ground-truth views/plays ; (c)(d): Results with views/plays by estimated by MCSHMM.

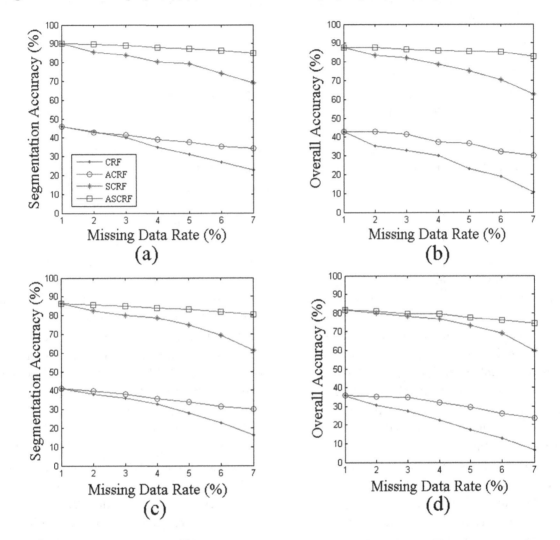

Game Flow Analysis

The experimental results (10-fold cross-validation) of four models, i.e., CRF, SCRF, ACRF, and ASCRF, we tested under two schemes are shown in Figure 10, where we evaluate the performance of game flow analysis by two accuracies. One is for the drive segmentation accuracy, and the other is for overall accuracy including both segmentation and recognition results.

- CRF assigns a drive label for each play. By checking the label consistency of of multiple consecutive plays, we can segment a set of plays into a series of labeled drives. We use the imputation technique to approximate missing keywords by using the nearest neighbors.
- ACRF adds an auxiliary layer in CRF, and it can handle the missing data problem via the marginalization technique to minimize the effect of missing data.

- SCRF supports simultaneous segmentation and recognition that leads a series of labeled drives of variable-length in terms of plays included. The drive label is not defined at the play level. In case of missing data, we impute them by the nearest neighbors.
- ASCRF incorporates an auxiliary layer in SCRF for missing data handling that defines a two-mode learning process to minimize the effect of missing data via the marginalization technique.

When there is no missing keyword, SCRF can reach about 80% and 90% accuracies on both segmentation and recognition under both schemes. On the other hand, CRF fails by either segmenting plays into wrong drives or providing wrong drive labels, leading the poor overall accuracy around 45%. The segmentation model in SCRF makes it possible to segment and recognize drives of variable numbers of plays, and SCRF outperforms CRF by effectively capturing both the long-range and short-range dependencies as well as complex interactions among multi-channel keywords and drive labels.

In the case of missing data handling, we compared the imputation-based CRF and SCRF with the marginalization-based ACRF and ASCRF. We found that, as the missing rate increases, the performance of imputation based methods, i.e., CRF and SCRF, decreases quickly by 20% and 30% respectively, while the performance of ACRF and ASCRF is quite robust compared with their counterparts. Even when the missing rate is around 7%, the proposed ASCRF still produce a similar result as the case without missing data. All of these results demonstrate effectiveness of ASCRF for game flow analysis with the capability missing data handling. However, when the missing data rate is increased to 10%, the ASCRF may not work well. This is mainly because game flow analysis that largely depends on the possession evolution is encumbered when there are more than one or two plays with missing the possession keyword.

CONCLUSION AND FUTURE WORK

In this chapter, we have discussed a new video mining paradigm that is able to support both of structure-based and event-based semantic video analysis via a game flow representation. Our research starts with a three-layer semantic space representation by which the problem of sports video mining is cast as two inter-related inference problems. One to infer mid-level keywords from low-level visual features that are used as the rudimentary semantic units for high-level semantic analysis and the other is to infer the high-level game flow from a set of plays annotated by multi-channel keywords that summarizes the whole game by a series of labeled drives, i.e., events. Specifically, we proposed a new HMM, called the multi-channel segmental HMM (MCSHMM), to explore multiple co-existing mid-level keywords from a set of plays that is superior to existing HMM-based models. We also developed a new CRF, referred to as the auxiliary segmentation CRF (ASCRF), to group a set of annotated plays into a series of label drives that is equipped with two interesting capabilities: joint segmentation-recognition and missing data handling. Compared with other video mining methodologies, it is our attempt to provide a new perspective on the research of sport video mining, where two research issues can be related systematically under one framework and addressed by appropriate probabilistic graphical models. This framework can be extended to other video mining applications by incorporating some domain knowledge, including a problem-oriented semantic space, relevant visual features, informative keywords and meaningful event labels.

In the future, there are two possible research directions along this research. One is to enrich both mid-level keywords and high-level semantics so that this framework can support more informative semantic modeling and more detailed game flow analysis. The other one is to integrate these two issues into one learning and inference process that could provide a joint optimal solution to both mid-level keyword detection and high-level game flow analysis.

ACKNOWLEDGMENT

This work is supported in part by the National Science Foundation (NSF) under Grant IIS-0347613, and an Oklahoma NASA EPSCoR Research Initiation Grant (2009). The authors also thank the reviewers for their valuable comments and suggestions that helped us improve this chapter.

REFERENCES

Assfalg, J., Bertini, M., Colombo, C., Bimbo, A. D., & Nunziati, W. (2003). Semantic annotation of soccer videos: Automatic highlights identification. *Computer Vision and Image Understanding, 92*(2-3), 285–305. doi:10.1016/j.cviu.2003.06.004

Bilmes, J. (1997). *A gentle tutorial on the EM algorithm and its application to parameter estimation for gaussian mixture and hidden Markov models*. ICSI-Report-97-021.

Brand, M. (1999). Structure learning in conditional probability models via an entropic prior and parameter extinction. *Neural Computation, 11*(5), 1155–1182. doi:10.1162/089976699300016395

Brand, M., Oliver, N., & Pentland, A. (1997). *Coupled hidden Markov models for complex action recognition*. Paper presented at the IEEE International Conference on Computer Vision and Pattern Recognition.

Chang, S.-F. (2002). The holy grail of content-based media analysis. *IEEE Multimedia Magazine, 9*(2), 6–10. doi:10.1109/93.998041

Cheng, C.-C., & Hsu, C.-T. (2006). Fusion of audio and motion information on HMM-based highlight extraction for baseball games. *IEEE Transactions on Multimedia, 8*(3), 585–599. doi:10.1109/TMM.2006.870726

Ding, Y., & Fan, G. (2006). *Camera view-based American football video analysis*. Paper presented at the Proc. the Eighth IEEE International Symposium on Multimedia.

Ding, Y., & Fan, G. (2007a). *Segmental hidden Markov models for view-based sport video analysis*. Paper presented at the IEEE International Conference on Computer Vision and Pattern Recognition.

Ding, Y., & Fan, G. (2007b). *Two-layer generative models for sport video mining*. Paper presented at the Proc. IEEE International Conference on Multimedia and Expo.

Ding, Y., & Fan, G. (2008). *Multi-channel segmental hidden Markov models for sports video mining*. Paper presented at the ACM Multimedia Conference.

Ding, Y., & Fan, G. (2009). Sports video mining via multi-channel segmental hidden Markov models. *IEEE Transactions on Multimedia, 11*(7).

Duan, L., Xu, M., Tian, Q., Xu, C., & Jin, S. J. (2005). A unified framework for semantic shot classification in sports video. *IEEE Transactions on Multimedia, 7*(6).

Duan, L. Y., Xu, M., Chua, T. S., Tian, Q., & Xu, C. S. (2003). *A Mid-level Representation Framework for Semantic Sports Video Analysis*. Paper presented at the ACM Multimedia Conference.

Ekin, A., Tekalp, A., & Mehrotra, R. (2003). Automatic soccer video analysis and summarization. *IEEE Transactions on Image Processing, 12*(7), 796–807. doi:10.1109/TIP.2003.812758

Farhangfar, A., Kurgan, L., & Dy, J. (2008). Impact of imputation of missing values on classification error for discrete data. *Pattern Recognition, 41*(12), 3692–3705. doi:10.1016/j.patcog.2008.05.019

Friedman, N., & Koller, D. (2003). Being Bayesian about network structure. A Bayesian approach to structure discovery in Bayesian networks. *Machine Learning, 50*(1), 95–125. doi:10.1023/A:1020249912095

Gales, M., & Young, S. (1993). *The theory of segmental hidden Markov models.* Technical Report CUED/F-INFENG/TR 133, Cambridge University.

Ghahramani, Z. (2002). Graphical models: Parameter learning. In Arbib, M. A. (Ed.), *The handbook of brain theory and neural networks.* MIT Press.

Gupta, A., Srinivasan, P., Jianbo, S., & Davis, L. S. (2009, 20-25 June 2009). *Understanding videos, constructing plots learning a visually grounded storyline model from annotated videos.* Paper presented at the IEEE Conference on Computer Vision and Pattern Recognition, CVPR 2009.

Kokaram, A., Rea, N., Dahyot, R., Tekalp, A. M., Bouthemy, P., & Gros, P. (2006). Browsing sports video: Trends in sports-related indexing and retrieval work. *Signal Processing Magazine, IEEE, 23*(2), 47–58. doi:10.1109/MSP.2006.1621448

Koubaroulis, D., Matas, J., & Kittler, J. (2002). *Colour-based object recognition for video annotation.* Paper presented at the IEEE International Conference on Pattern Recognition.

Lazarescu, M., & Venkatesh, S. (2003, July). *Using camera motion to identify types of American football plays.* Paper presented at the 2003 International Conference on Multimedia and Expo.

Li, B., & Sezan, I. (2002). *Event detection and summarization in American football brocast video.* Paper presented at the SPIE Storage and Retrieval for Media Database.

Little, R. J. A., & Rubin, D. B. (1986). *Statistical analysis with missing data.* John Wiley & Sons, Inc.

Liu, Y., Carbonell, J., Weigele, P., & Gopalakarishnany, V. (2006). Segmentation conditional random fields (SCRFs): A new approach for protein fold recognition. *Journal of Computational Biology, 13*(2), 394–406. doi:10.1089/cmb.2006.13.394

Mei, T., Ma, Y.-F., Zhou, H.-Q., Ma, W.-Y., & Zhang, H.-J. (2005). *Sports video mining with Mosaic.* Paper presented at the 11th International Multimedia Modelling Conference.

Murphy, K. (2002). *Dynamic Bayesian networks: Representation, inference and learning.* UC Berkeley.

Naphade, M., & Huang, T. (2002). *Discovering recurrent events in video using unsupervised methods.* Paper presented at the IEEE International Conference on Image Processing, Rochester, NY.

Pan, H., Beek, P., & Sezan, M. I. (2001). *Detection of slow-motion replay segments in sports video for highlights generation.* Paper presented at the IEEE Int'l Conference on Acoustics Speech and Signal Processing.

Rubin, D. B. (1976). Inference and missing data. *Biometrika, 63*(3). doi:10.1093/biomet/63.3.581

Sha, F., & Pereira, F. (2003). *Shallow parsing with conditional random fields.* Paper presented at the Human Language Technology-NAACL.

Shyu, M.-L., Xie, Z., Chen, M., & Chen, S.-C. (2008). Video semantic event/concept detection using a subspace-based multimedia data mining framework. *IEEE Transactions on Multimedia, 10*(2), 252–259. doi:10.1109/TMM.2007.911830

Srinivasan, M., Venkatesh, S., & Hosie, R. (1997). Qualitative estimation of camera motion parameters from video sequences. *Pattern Recognition, 30*, 593–606. doi:10.1016/S0031-3203(96)00106-9

Wang, P., & Ji, Q. (2005). *Multi-view face tracking with factorial and switching HMM.* Paper presented at the IEEE Workshop on Applications of Computer Vision (WACV/MOTION05).

Wang, S. B., Quattoni, A., Morency, L.-P., Demirdjian, D., & Darrell, T. (2006). *Hidden conditional random fields for gesture recognition.* Paper presented at the IEEE Computer Society Conference on Computer Vision and Pattern Recognition.

Wang, T., Li, J., Diao, Q., Hu, W., Zhang, Y., & Dulong, C. (2006). *Semantic event detection using conditional random fields.* Paper presented at the IEEE Conference on Computer Vision and Pattern Recognition (CVPR).

Wang, Y., Sabzmeydani, P., & Mori, G. (2007). *Semi-latent Dirichlet allocation: A hierarchical model for human action recognition.* Paper presented at the 2nd Workshop on Human Motion Understanding, Modeling, Capture and Animation.

Xie, L., Chang, S., Divakaran, A., & Sun, H. (2003). Unsupervised mining of staistical temporal structures in video. In Rosenfeld, D. D. A. (Ed.), *Video mining.* Kluwer Academi Publishers.

Xiong, Z. (2005). Audio-visual sports highlights extraction using Coupled Hidden Markov Models. *Pattern Analysis & Applications, 8*(1), 62–71. doi:10.1007/s10044-005-0244-7

Xu, C., Zhu, G., Zhang, Y., Huang, Q., & Lu, H. (2008). *Event tactic analysis based on player and ball trajectory in broadcast video.* Paper presented at the International Conference on Content-based Image and Video Retrieval.

Yu, X., Xu, C., Leong, H. W., Tian, Q., Tang, Q., & Wan, K. W. (2003). *Trajectory-based ball detection and tracking with applications to semantic analysis of broadcast soccer video.* Paper presented at the ACM Multimedia.

ADDITIONAL READING

Chen, B. W., Wang, J. C., & Wang, J. F. (2009). A novel video summarization based on mining the story-structure and semantic relations among concept entities. *IEEE Transactions on Multimedia, 11*(2), 295–312. doi:10.1109/TMM.2008.2009703

Demange, S., Cerisara, C., & Haton, J.-P. (2009). Missing data mask estimation with frequency and temporal dependencies. *Computer Speech & Language, 23*(1), 25–41. doi:10.1016/j.csl.2008.02.002

Ding, Y., & Fan, G. (2009). *Event detection in sports video based on generative-discriminative models.* Paper presented at the Workshop on Events in Multimedia (EiMM09) in conjunction with ACM Multimedia.

Fan, J., Elmagarmid, A. K., Zhu, X., Aref, W. G., & Wu, L. (2004). ClassView: Hierarchical video shot classification, indexing, and accessing. *IEEE Transactions on Multimedia, 6*(1). doi:10.1109/TMM.2003.819583

Ghahramani, Z., & Jordan, M. (1996). *Factorial hidden Markov models.* Paper presented at the Conference Advances in Neural Information Processing Systems, NIPS.

Huang, C. L., Shih, H. C., & Chao, C. Y. (2006). Semantic analysis of soccer video using dynamic Bayesian network. *IEEE Transactions on Multimedia, 8*(4), 749–760. doi:10.1109/TMM.2006.876289

Koller, D., & Friedman, N. (2009). *Probabilistic graphical models.* MIT press.

Lavee, G., Rivlin, E., & Rudzsky, M. (2009). Understanding video events: A survey of methods for automatic interpretation of semantic occurrences in video. *IEEE Transactions on Systems, Man and Cybernetics. Part C, Applications and Reviews, 39*(5), 489–504. doi:10.1109/TSMCC.2009.2023380

Li, H., Shi, Y., Chen, M.-Y., Hauptmann, A. G., & Xiong, Z. (2010). *Hybrid active learning for cross-domain video concept detection*. Paper presented at the International Conference on Multimedia, Firenze, Italy.

Marlin, B. M. (2008). *Missing data problems in machine learning*. University of Toronto.

Ngo, C. W., Ma, Y. F., & Zhang, H. J. (2005). Video summarization and scene detection by graph modeling. *IEEE Transactions on Multimedia, 15*(2), 296–305.

Rabiner, L. R. (1989). A tutorial on hidden Markov models and selected applications in speech recognition. *Proceedings of the IEEE, 77*(2), 257–286. doi:10.1109/5.18626

Rui, Y., Huang, T., & Mehrotra, S. (1998). *Constructing table-of-content for video*. Paper presented at the ACM Multimedia.

Shen, J., Tao, D., & Li, X. (2008). Modality mixture projections for semantic video event detection. *IEEE Transactions on Circuits and Systems for Video Technology, 18*(11), 1587–1596. doi:10.1109/TCSVT.2008.2005607

Tu, Z. (2005). *Probabilistic boosting-tree: Learning discriminative models for classification, recognition, and clustering*. Paper presented at the IEEE International Conference on Computer Vision.

Williams, D., Liao, X., Xue, Y., & Carin, L. (2005). *Incomplete-data classification using logistic regression*. Paper presented at the 22nd International Conference on Machine learning.

Worring, M., & Schreiber, G. (2007). Semantic image and video indexing in broad domains. *IEEE Transactions on Multimedia, 9*(5), 909–911. doi:10.1109/TMM.2007.898913

Xie, L., Natsev, A., Smith, J. R., Yan, R., & Tesic, J. (2010). *Probabilistic visual concept trees*. Paper presented at the International Conference on Multimedia, Firenze, Italy.

Xiong, Z. Y., Zhou, X. S., Tian, Q., Rui, Y., & Huang, T. S. (2006). Semantic retrieval of video - Review of research on video retrieval in meetings, movies and broadcast news, and sports. *IEEE Signal Processing Magazine, 23*(2), 18–27. doi:10.1109/MSP.2006.1621445

Xu, C., Wang, J., Lu, H., & Zhang, Y. (2008). A novel framework for semantic annotation and personalized retrieval of sports video. *IEEE Transactions on Multimedia, 10*(3), 421–436. doi:10.1109/TMM.2008.917346

Xu, D., & Chang, S. F. (2008). Video event recognition using kernel methods with multilevel temporal alignment. *IEEE Transactions on Pattern Analysis and Machine Intelligence, 31*(10), 1985–1997.

Yang, J., Yan, R., & Hauptmann, A. G. (2007). *Cross-domain video concept detection using adaptive svms*. Paper presented at the 15th International Conference on Multimedia, Augsburg, Germany.

Zhang, D., Gatica-Perez, D., Bengio, S., & McCowan, I. (2005). *Semi-supervised adapted HMMS for unusual event detection*. Paper presented at the IEEE Conference on Computer Vision and Pattern Recognition.

Zhang, D., Gatica-Perez, D., Bengio, S., & Roy, D. (2005). *Learning influence among interacting Markov chains*. Paper presented at the NIPS.

Zhang, T., Xu, C., Zhu, G., Liu, S., & Lu, H. (2010). *A generic framework for event detection in various video domains*. Paper presented at the International Conference on Multimedia, Firenze, Italy.

Zhu, G., Yang, M., Yu, K., Xu, W., & Gong, Y. (2009). *Detecting video events based on action recognition in complex scenes using spatio-temporal descriptor*. Paper presented at the 17th ACM International Conference on Multimedia, Beijing, China.

KEY TERMS AND DEFINITIONS

Conditional Random Fields: Are undirected graphical models in which the label sequence is defined by log-linear distributions given a particular observation sequence.

Discriminative Models: Are models used for modeling the dependence of unobserved variables on observed variables, which is done by modeling the conditional probability distribution.

Game Flow: Represents the overall semantic evolution of a sports game by a series of events, facts, statements and rules.

Generative Models: Are models for randomly generating observable data given some hidden parameters, which specify a joint probability distribution over observation and label sequences.

Hidden Markov Models: Are directed graphical models in which the system being modeled is assumed to be a Markov process with unknown parameters.

Missing Data Problem: Is the case that no data value is present for the current observation, specifically, it means lacking of mid-level keywords for high-level semantic analysis in sports video mining.

Probabilistic Graphical Models: Are graph-based representations for compactly encoding a complex distribution over a high-dimensional space, in which nodes represent random variables, and arcs represent conditional independence assumptions.

Semantic Space: Represents the content of sports video by a three-layer structure, including low-level features, mid-level keywords, and high-level semantics.

Sports Video Mining: Is the process of discovering knowledge, structures, patterns and events of interests in the sports video data.

Chapter 17
Static and Dynamic Multi-Robot Coverage with Grammatical Evolution Guided by Reinforcement and Semantic Rules

Jack Mario Mingo
Autonomous University of Madrid, Spain

Ricardo Aler
Carlos III University of Madrid, Spain

Darío Maravall
Technical University of Madrid, Spain

Javier de Lope
Technical University of Madrid, Spain

ABSTRACT

In recent years there has been an increasing interest in the application of robot teams to solve some kind of problems. Although there are several environments and tasks where a team of robots can deliver better results than a single robot, one of the most active attention focus is concerned with solving coverage problems, either static or dynamic, mainly in unknown environments. The authors propose a method in this work to solve these problems in simulation by means of grammatical evolution of high-level controllers. Evolutionary algorithms have been successfully applied in many applications, but better results can be achieved when evolution and learning are combined in some way. This work uses one of this hybrid algorithms called Grammatical Evolution guided by Reinforcement but the authors enhance it by adding semantic rules in the grammatical production rules. This way, they can build automatic high-level controllers in fewer generations and the solutions found are more readable as well. Additionally, a study about the influence of the number of members implied in the evolutionary process is addressed.

DOI: 10.4018/978-1-4666-1806-0.ch017

INTRODUCTION

Robot teams are frequently being applied in order to solve certain tasks and we can find examples, mainly related to the behaviour-based robotic at the beginning of the nineties (Mataric, 1992; Parker, 1993; Balch, 1999). However, some studies in other areas were previous or parallel to this approach as (Reynolds, 1987) showed in the simulation with computer graphics of bird flocks or (Tu, 1994) detailed with the simulation of artificial fishes. These works share two distinguishing features: (1) they are behaviour-based, both Arkin's motor schema architecture (Arkin, 1989) or Brooks' subsumption architecture (Brooks, 1986) and architectures that employ simple rules or algorithms based on equations; (2) they try to solve mainly problems about formation of robot teams or simulated animals. Therefore, we can consider these approaches as a simulation of group behaviours in certain animal species like birds, fishes, cattle or insects.

There is another research line close to previous systems in using a robot team but this second approach is more interested in solving classic problems related with autonomous robots than simulating biological systems, even though both approaches take account of biological and natural principles. This alternative approach engages in studying some problems related to spread out, coverage and exploration with group of robots or agents situated in unknown or known environments. Spread, coverage and exploration are terms that Gage introduced with different names (Gage, 1992). Specifically, Gage named them as blanket, barrier and sweep coverage. To him, formation behaviours are an alternative to coverage behaviours with the aim to maintain a spatial relationship among members.

This work is concerned with problems of the second line and it tries to apply a hybrid system based on grammatical evolution and reinforcement learning in order to generate automatically high-level controllers. We hope these controllers will be able to solve static (spread out) and dynamic (exploration) problems in indoor and unknown environments. The system is completely reactive and it does consider neither communication among robots nor a map of the environment in this first stage.

A main aim in this work is to show a new case in that evolutionary methods provide a valuable alternative to manual design of controllers, an inherent problem in many architectures belonging to behaviour-based robotic. To solve this problem, evolutionary robotics (Nolfi, 2000) traditionally has evolved automatic controllers expressed as artificial neural networks although other structures such as programs are also used and we will mention some examples in the next section. Precisely, in this work we use programs to implement the robot controller. Each controller is generated by means of grammatical evolution but we combine this technique with a process that let each controller to learn new programs during its life time. Grammars are a valuable tool in order to create programs or controllers because they let us to specify a hierarchical structure for the behaviours instead of creating a monolithic whole system as artificial neural network evolution generally do. Using grammars we can develop solutions more readable and understandable than monolithic ones.

Besides solving static and dynamic coverage problems we are interested here in analyzing the influence of the number of members in the team during the automatic controller generation process. To check both issues we tested several cases in simulation with groups of 4, 8, 12 and 16 robots. We analyze different simulators but finally we chose the Simbad Robot Simulator (Hugues, 2006) because it offers a 3D environment and it is very simple of managing and integrating with the Java code of the algorithm which this work is based in. Although Simbad is not a very realistic simulator it allows implementing easily a lot of techniques based on artificial intelligence and we are more interested here in analyzing the design of high-level automatic controllers than in studying low level primitives for perception and action.

The rest of the chapter is structured as follow. In section two a background about coverage and exploration is carried out. Section three introduces the algorithm we use here which is known as grammatical evolution guided by reinforcement. In section four we show how this hybrid algorithm can be enhanced in order to include some semantic constraints by means of attributes in the grammar. Section five introduces the problem of static multirobot coverage and section six introduces the problem of dynamic multirobot coverage or exploration. Section seven shows results in both problems. Finally, in section eight some conclusions and future research lines are summarized.

RELATED WORK

Covering an environment is an interesting task to be automated because it might help in cases as building surveillance, environmental monitoring or rescue missions.

We need to define some concepts before analyzing some relevant works. Static coverage stands for spreading the robots in the environment and its main goal is to attain a static equilibrium, i.e., all robots in the team will stop when they are in a target position. Some authors refer to static coverage as spread. On the other hand, dynamic coverage or exploration can be considered a variant of static coverage. The difference between them is simple: exploring robots do not stop when they are in a target position and they usually are endowed with additional behaviours. The aim here is to maximize the coverage area in a complete and optimal way.

Choset carried out a comprehensive study about coverage path planning (Choset, 2001) and he distinguished between offline and online coverage algorithms. The former uses a map of the environment while the latter does not use it. Choset also divided algorithms according to ex-

ploring method. The first approaches were based on heuristic rules but more reliable algorithms were developed subsequently. Most approaches trusted in a decomposition of the environment, mainly in cells and Choset classified them as exact and approximate decompositions. Cell decomposition algorithms are more reliable than heuristic algorithms because the latter cannot assure a complete coverage while the former are better prepared to solve this problem. Some examples of using cell decomposition algorithms are described in (Acar, 2006; Choset, 2000; Latimer, 2002).

We must note here that coverage, as it was defined by Choset, implies that robot or group of robots is moving in the environment with some kind of tool. This way, the robots try to sweep the entire environment. Therefore, the concept would be similar to barrier coverage in terms of Gage's definitions.

Some works about static coverage with multirobot are included in theory control. We can quote here (Cortes, 2004), where adaptive and distributed algorithms to coordinate groups were proposed. These algorithms included limited perception and communication abilities and they needed to know a distribution density function in order to minimize a locational optimization function. This paper showed how optimum coverage is achieved when all the agents converge to a concept known as centroidal Voronoi configuration where each agent is placed in the centre of its Voronoi region. As we comment previously, the algorithms proposed were based on knowing a distribution density function which was its main drawback. This constraint was eliminated in (Schwager, 2006) but a new problem appeared because of each agent needed here to measure the value and gradient of a sense function. The sense function determined the relative importance for each area in the environment. A relaxed version of these constraints was proposed by the same authors in (Schwager, 2007). In this work a new control law was provided and it was not necessary to know the gradient value. There is a remarkable advantage associated with the algorithms based on control theory like (Cortes, 2004; Schwager, 2006; Schwager, 2007) and others in the same line as (Bullo, 2005; Schwager, 2009), namely they provide formal methods to assure the correction of the tasks and they can guarantee optimality in the reactive control laws they provide. Nevertheless, these approaches have some drawback because they work frequently in simulation where it is easier to assure the strong constraints they need.

In a different line to the control theory we can find some examples of coverage which use algorithms based on heuristics in terms of the Choset's categories. For example, in (Howard, 2002a) an incremental dispersion algorithm in order to spread mobile sensor networks was proposed. This algorithm performs by deploying a node each time and it uses some heuristics in order to attain a maximum coverage. Same authors defined a new algorithm in another work. The new algorithm (Howard, 2002b) was based on potential fields. Other robots and obstacles could be avoided thanks to this technique. Within a more behaviour-based robotic line we can find works as (Batalin, 2002) where several algorithms with only local perception and interactions between robots were described with the aim to carry out a spread task.

Regarding the exploration task we can also review remarkable works. A pioneer one was a method based on frontiers that Yamauchi proposed in (Yamauchi, 1998). This work was essentially a multirobot version of his previous idea applied to a single robot. Robots in Yamauchi's method shared perceptual information but they maintained separated global maps and they took independent decisions about exploration. Starting from the frontier concept an alternative method was suggested in (Burgard, 2000). This proposal tried to reduce time in executing the task by coordinating the team so that each individual member could not choice the same frontier.

Some ideas taken of graph theory have been applied in order to solve exploration and coverage

problems as Rekleitis et al. did in (Rekleitis, 2000). A graph was used here to guide the exploration process and to build a map of the environment although this system employed only two robots and one of them had to be static while the other one moved around the world. The first robot acted as a reference for the second one. Another graph-based work was related in (Kong, 2002) where the area was decomposed into cell where each cell width is fixed. The area was represented as an adjacency graph which was incrementally constructed and shared among all the team. Other important graph based alternatives have been implemented to solve barrier coverage but we are reviewing here only works about spreading and exploring tasks. Some works in this line are included in the additional reading section.

Batalin and Sukhatme developed a behaviour based system to explore an environment with a team (Batalin, 2003). Actually, they upgraded a previous system they had implemented in (Batalin, 2002). Evolutionary systems have been developed as well and most works in this area evolve artificial neural networks. However, barrier coverage and formation control are the tasks preferred by these approach. A more detailed review about these topics can be found in (Nolfi, 2006; Mondada, 2004; Trianni, 2008).

We want to finish this review not completely exhaustive with some proposals coming from genetic programming because this line is the nearest this chapter. On the one hand, a system described in (Ito, 2003) showed as genetic programming can supply a control module to explore. This evolved controller exhibited a global behaviour as intelligent and complex as a hand coded controller which was designed to compare with. On the other hand, (Thomason, 2008) and (Rubini, 2009) were more concerned with the composition of heterogeneous teams than with the real exploration task.

GRAMMATICAL EVOLUTION GUIDED BY REINFORCEMENT

Grammatical Evolution guided by Reinforcement (GER) is a hybrid system (Mingo, 2007) which tries to merge evolution and learning in a simple way: individuals of the population can rewrite its own program several times, trying different choices with the same BNF grammar that they used for solving the problem in the respective domain. This process is easy: initially each programmer-individual is evaluated by executing the program created starting from its original chromosome. Then, the individual can create new programs using other grammatical rules. If some learnt program is better than its original genetic program, a replacement Lamarckian mechanism is used. This mechanism substitutes the original genotype by the learnt genotype. Basically the process consists of three stages:

- *Transcription*: In this step the original binary string is transformed into an integer number string.
- *Translation*: The second step uses the integer number string for getting a value that represents the rule to apply for the current non terminal symbol in the grammar.
- *Learning*: The last step uses a reinforcement learning mechanism for generating new programs. New programs are built by considering different rules of the grammar.

Stages 1 and 2 were defined in Grammatical Evolution (GE) (Collins, 1998) while stage 3 was added in GER. Figure 1 shows how the stages of GER work together.

There are several essential items in a standard GER system, excluding the own evolution: *Reinforcement learning, Q-tree, Lamarck hypothesis* and the *exploration-exploitation* trade-off. Evolution in GER performs just as a standard GE or similar evolutionary algorithms do. Next sections describe briefly these items but a more compre-

Figure 1. Stages in grammatical evolution guided by reinforcement

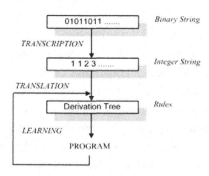

hensive introduction can be found in (Mingo, 2007).

Reinforcement Learning

To apply reinforcement learning in GER the following concepts are needed:

- An programmer-individual represents the agent
- A group of states represent the derivation steps used up to a point in the building of the program. In this case, the program is the controller
- A group of production rules to apply in each of these states

The aim of the programmer-individual is to calculate a policy for the actions appropriate for any state. In GER, an *action* is simple a production rule to be applied. A state is the partial derivation steps sequence applied up to a particular instant. This way, the state 0 would correspond to the start symbol of the grammar; state 1, to the result of substituting the start symbol by one of the production rules appropriate to it; state 2, would result from substituting the left most non terminal symbol by a production rule valid for it; and so on. This process can be conclusive because one of two reasons: 1) the individual generates an analysis tree, that is, a tree whose leaves only contain terminal symbols. In this case, the learnt program is evaluated and its fitness is obtained; 2) the individual does not generate an analysis tree after a determined number of rules selections. In this case, the individual obtains a very poor fitness.

The reinforcement learning process is repeated as many times as it is established by means of a system parameter, and the consequence will be the creation of a group of programs learnt by the individual. Some of these programs could be wrong, and would obtain a very poor fitness; while others would be grammatically right and would obtain a fitness depending of their capacity to solve the problem. Thanks to reinforcement learning each individual of the population can try other production rules on each step while it is building its derivation tree. GER uses a reinforcement learning algorithm based on Q-Learning (Watkins, 1992).

Q Tree

As we have mentioned GER uses a reinforcement learning algorithm based on Q-Learning. However, as the state space can be very big for any domain, instead of using a table for Q values, a tree, called *Q tree* is used.

The Q tree keeps the policy of derivation rules which are more appropriate for each node during the building of a program. For that, in any node of the Q tree, the following information is maintained:

- A numeric value which represents the production rule used to get the state. Root node is the only exception for this rule, since it is labelled with the start symbol of the grammar.
- A group of numeric values which represent the different production rules that can be applied in the state.

Q tree is used by the programmer-individual for creating new programs, i.e. it controls the learning process. Besides, Q tree maintains the whole learning process because it saves all the individual

Table 1. Chromosome of an programmer-individual

0	1	2	0	0

learning processes. In each step, the individual starts with the start symbol of the grammar and it analyzes the Q tree's root. Then, it uses the numeric values in the Q tree and it decides which rule might be used. When it uses the rule, a step is advanced, both in the construction of the derivation tree (start symbol is substituted by the applied rule) and in the construction of the Q tree (a new node is generated which shows the applied rule by means of a numeric value). Now, the leftmost non terminal is analyzed and the Q tree is checked searching Q values available. Obviously, in the exploratory stage, all Q values will be the same because the node is new, but in the exploitation stage there will be different Q values because a previously visited node is being exploited. The maximum Q value will represent the most optimum rule until now and it will be chose. In this way, Q tree is used both explore and exploit the obtained knowledge. The process will continue creating a complete derivation tree and adding new nodes to Q tree (in exploration) or modifying previous Q values (in exploitation). We will review below the exploration-exploitation trade-off.

In order to show how the Q Tree is developed during the process we include an example using the grammar we will describe in the static multi-robot coverage section (see the section for details). Table 1 shows a hypothetical output of a transcription process applied to the initial binary string:

Figure 2 shows the derivation tree for the mapping process corresponding to the chromosome in the example.

Internal nodes in Q tree represent non terminal symbols and leaf nodes are terminal symbols. In this example the chromosome has been used one

Figure 2. Derivation tree for the programmer-individual

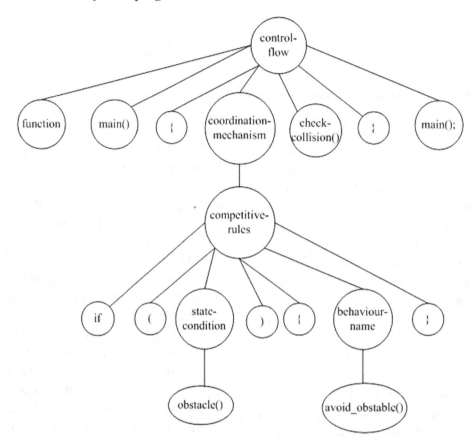

time to generate the tree but we can use it as many times as a system parameter establishes.

While derivation tree is being built a specific process builds the Q tree as well. Initially each Q value is configured with a default value of -1. There are as many slots as maximum number of production rules on each node (in the example there are four Q values because there are four rules associated with the non terminals <state-condition> and <behaviour-name>. When the original genotype program is evaluated, the genotype is crossed and integer values are saved in the Q tree according to the production rule that they select. In this way, in the example, the first node in the Q tree would have as label the start symbol of the grammar <control-flow>. The second node would have as symbol the value 0 (first integer on the string), the third one would save the symbol

1 (second integer on the string) and so on. The nodes of Q tree are linked through pointers from a higher node to lower node. The pointer begins from the rule that will be applied.

Once the original genotype has been evaluated, a learning process is applied. For that, the individual can look for new production rules during a number of learning steps which are defined thanks to a parameter in the system, so the tree grows according to the learning process.

Figure 3 shows the earliest stages in the Q tree as result of a specific execution where *Rw* stands for the *reward* (Mingo, 2007) associated to the individual.

On each node of the Q tree we have represented only rules that correspond to derivation steps tested by the individual. The right branch of the Q tree shows the sequence of derivations

Figure 3. Q tree for the example (original genotype and two learning-steps)

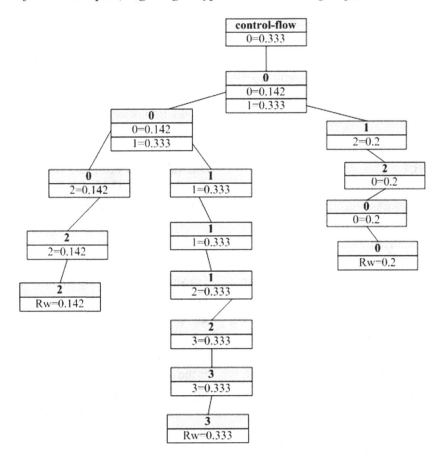

associated to the original genotype (Table 1). Other two sequences of derivations are associated with learnt genotypes and they correspond to the left and middle branches. Reward is propagated from the last derivation (leaf node) to the first one (level one). Reward is measured in inverse proportion to the reached fitness when the program (original or learnt) is executed. In the example, the fitness associated with the right branch was 5 and the reward is 0.2 while the fitness associated with the middle and left branches was 3 and 7. Right branch corresponds to the original genotype in the example and it represents the steps from GER builds the derivation tree which represents the program:

```
function main () { if (obstacle()) {
avoid_obstacle() } check_collision()
}main();
```

While the right branch is derived from the original genotype, the learnt branches (left and middle) are built in the learning process and the rules are selected in a different way. GER chooses the rules applying the reinforcement mechanism and the Q Tree is a key item in this process. As we will see in the next subsection a balance between explore and exploit nodes in the Q Tree is needed. Left and middle branches represent the steps to build two different programs:

```
function main () { if (free_space())
{ spread() } check_collision() }
main();
function main () { if (robot()) {
avoid_robot() } else if (task_end())
{ wait_new_task() } check_collision()
} main();
```

Lamarck Effect

Once the learning process has finished, several programs have been created. If a learnt program gets a fitness value better than the fitness value of the original program, the Lamarck Hypothesis can be applied and learning can revert again over the original genotype. This way, we can replace the original genotype of the individual by one of the learnt genotypes. With the inclusion of Lamarckism in GER this system would be similar to Lamarckian memetic algorithms although some differences exist between both methods, mainly related with the local optimization process.

Exploration-Exploitation Trade-off

A common problem in reinforcement learning is the trade-off between exploring new actions and exploiting previously learnt actions. GER uses an e-greedy strategy for selecting actions (production rules). New production rules are selected between all possible choices for each non terminal and best production rules are selected thanks to the Q values. Random selection is a problem with e-greedy strategies and GER tries to solve it using a non constant factor that varies following the expression:

```
EGreedyFactor=1-(learnStep/learnStep-
sNum)
```

where *learnStep* stands for the current learning step and *learnStepsNum* represents a system parameter which specifies the total number of learning steps. Each learning step means a possibility to learn a new program. This strategy allows the individual approximately explore during the first half in the learning process (it will select new production rules) and exploit the knowledge during the second one (it will select the best known production rules).

SEMANTIC RULES IN GRAMMATICAL EVOLUTION GUIDED BY REINFORCEMENT

Most high-level programming languages are usually described by context-free grammar (CFG). However, this class of grammars are not expressive enough to represent context-sensitive information and domain-dependent knowledge. For this reason, CFG are less powerful than context-sensitive grammars (CSG) but they are easier to use. This is the reason why a remarkable variety of systems have been developed to include semantic aspects in CFG grammars. We do not have space here to review this topic in depth but a detailed introduction can be found in (Shutt, 2003).

GE and GER can assure syntactically correct programs because they use a CFG grammar to build programs but they cannot assure semantic correctness. With the aim to add domain-dependent knowledge a variant of GER with semantic rules has recently been developed (Mingo, 2011).

In GER with semantic rules a translation schema notation (Aho, 1986) is associated with the production rules in the grammar. This way, semantic rules are devoted to incorporate common sense reasoning. In robotic domains we consider common sense reasoning a set of logical rules, i.e. "do not turn left when there is an obstacle in that place" or "does not turn right if the goal is going left". The set of logical rules can be considered as innate knowledge and it is employed when selecting which production rule must be executed. According to Aho et al. a translation scheme as they defined in (Aho, 1986) is a CFG with attributes associated with the non terminal symbols. An attribute has a name and a value. This value is calculated by means of a semantic rule. Semantic rules or actions are included in the right side of the production rules and the order in which an action is executed is determined by its position in the production. When a derivation tree is being built by means of a translation scheme, a node is added when a semantic rule is found in the process. This node does not have children and it is executed when it is visited for the first time. A translation scheme can include inherited and synthesized attributes but GER with semantic rules only use synthesized attributes in order to include common sense reasoning. An attribute is synthesized when its value depends on its children's values. Synthesized attributes present an important advantage because they can be calculated during a single ascendant path of the derivation tree.

From a technical point of view a semantic rule or action will be represented closed in square brackets in the BNF grammar and it can be a conditional or an assignment sentence. In the later case a value will be assigned to the attribute. Conditional sentences will check the attribute's values and will give back a true or false value. A false value means that selected rule makes no sense and a new selection must be done. This way, semantically wrong individuals are avoided. There is an important advantage associated with discarding semantically wrong individuals: we can limit destructive effects frequently produced during the evolutionary process because of bad individuals since they are separated before they execute its code.

STATIC MULTI-ROBOT COVERAGE

In the static coverage or spread problem the goal is to attain a static equilibrium. We consider that robots are in static equilibrium when they are stopped in a place where there is no other robot.

As we comment in the introduction section, a first goal in this paper is to analyze whether GER can builds high-level controllers in an optimum way. An important feature in a high-level controller is its hierarchical structure. We can reach this goal if we define a modular scheme in which a coordination mechanism is used to choose suitable behaviours. A typical coordination mechanism in behaviour-based robotic contains competitive or cooperative rules. Competitive rules are used when the resulting behaviour is produced only by one rule. On the other hand, cooperative rules are useful when the resulting behaviour is the product of applying several rules. In this work we considerer only competitive rules and we use simple *state-action* rules to describe the problem as it is usual in some behaviour-based robotic approaches. We consider a *state* as a primitive behaviour for sensing and an *action* as a primitive behaviour for acting. A primitive behaviour is similar to a high-level function. With this kind of behaviours we can hide the low-level details.

To solve the static coverage task we use a simple grammar which includes logical rules as we mentioned above (see Box 1).

Numbers in the right hand are used to identify the rules and they represent a key factor during the translation and learning processes in GER. As we mentioned above we use high-level functions that represent simple behaviours as *avoid_robot* or *avoid_obstacle* which are self-explanatory but extensions can be easily added if we define rules to create more complex behaviours or new ones. Cooperative rules could be added as well. *Wait_new_task* behaviour simply stops the robot when the state condition *task_end* is true, i.e. when the robot is alone in a place. *Spread* behaviour lets the robot moves following random directions. Besides, *task_end* other behaviours for sensing are included as *robot*, *obstacle* and *free_space*. They only test if a robot, an obstacle or free space is surrounding the robot.

A final consideration must be remarked regarding semantic aspects. They appear in the grammar

Box 1.

```
<control-flow>::= function main(){ <coordination-mechanism>
             check_collision() } main(); [<control-flow>.value='main']
(0)
<coordination-mechanism>::= <competitive-rules>
             [<coordination-mechanism>.value=<competitive-rules>.value]
(0)
<competitive-rules>::= if (<state-condition>)
                          { <behaviour-name> [conditionIfStaCond] }
                          [<competitive-rules>.value='ifCompRules']   (0)
<competitive-rules>::=     if (<state-condition>)
                          { <behaviour-name> [conditionIfStaCond] }
                      else <competitive-rules>
                          [<competitive-rules>.value='ifCompRules']   (1)
<state-condition>::= obstacle()   [<state-condition>.value='obs']       (0)
<state-condition>::= robot()          [<state-condition>.value='rob']       (1)
<state-condition>::= free_space() [<state-condition>.value='fre']       (2)
<state-condition>::= task_end()   [<state-condition>.value='end']       (3)
<behaviour-name>::= avoid_obstacle() [<behaviour-name>.value='avObs']   (0)
<behaviour-name>::= avoid_robot()       [<behaviour-name>.value='avRob']
(1)
<behaviour-name>::= spread()          [<behaviour-name>.value='spre']     (2)
<behaviour-name>::= wait_new_task()   [<behaviour-name>.value='wait']     (3)
```

in square brackets. Basically, semantic aspects assign a value to an attribute. We represent the attribute's value with the *<non terminal>.value* expression. Most semantic aspects are only informative in order to maintain a homogeneous treatment. However, the ***conditionIfStaCond*** label, which is included in both production rules for the non terminal *<competitive-rules>* has a special meaning. This rule lets us to specify common reasoning and it was defined as shown in Box 2.

This semantic constraint stands for the following reasoning. If the robot is in a specific state a specific behaviour should be chosen because a bad choice would produce a semantically wrong individual. When the conditional sentence is true, the consequence is a *'wrong'* value in the corresponding non terminal's attribute. In this case, the non terminal is a competitive rule and a *'wrong'*

value will point the rule out as semantically bad. Of course, this kind of rule is very restrictive and it provides an important bias for learning but we use it because we wanted to accelerate executing time since we did a lot of tests. In any case, we carried out some experiments with a less restrictive semantic rule as well.

In the static coverage problem we define a fitness function in terms of robots that are not static. An optimal value corresponds to a configuration where only two robots are not static. We use this value as a general measure because when we work with 4 or 8 robots, all members in the team will finish in static equilibrium but when we use more robots in a small environment as we use here, there is less room to explore lonely places and in many cases robots do not find its final position because they are continuously moving in circles

Box 2.

```
If ((<state-condition>.value = 'obs') and (<behaviour-name>.value<>'avObs')) or
   ((<state-condition>.value = 'rob') and (<behaviour-name>.value<>'avRob')) or
   ((<state-condition>.value = 'fre') and (<behaviour-name>.value<>'spre')) or
   ((<state-condition>.value = 'end') and (<behaviour-name>.value<>'wait'))
then semantic = wrong
```

Table 2. Evolutionary parameters

Parameter	Value
Population size	15
Maximum Generations	20
Learning steps	7
Crossover probability	0.9
Mutation probability	0.03
Duplication probability	0.05

in order to avoid robots which are already placed on it final positions. We think that in bigger teams as 12 or 16 robots in this environment is not too negative to let a maximum of 2 robots which are not static. In Simbad we only can execute the same controller for all the robots. Some evolutionary parameters are shown in Table 2. Because of the simplicity of the grammar GER only needs a few individuals and generations to find a solution.

In order to check if a robot is alone in a place we divided the environment in 16 virtual circular zones. These zones are not visible at the simulator but they are taken into account for the *task_end()* state and the *wait_new_task()* behaviour. A *task_end* state is achieved when a robot is the only one in a place. If a new robot comes in a busy place it must leave and it has to find a new lonely place. With regard to *free_space()* state and *spread()* behaviour they have a simple meaning: if there is space free the robot can move in a random direction. *Check_collision* behaviour is provided to count the number of collisions and is used to get robots out of a jam.

We finish this section showing in Figure 4 the environment we use in the tests. We ran 10 trials in this experiment for 4 different teams of robots: 4, 8, 12 and 16 members. Summarizing, 40 executions were carried out. Figure 5 shows the environment and the 16 virtual zones.

DYNAMIC MULTI-ROBOT COVERAGE

Dynamic coverage or exploration is similar to spread but in this case, robots do not stop. We use the same environment and we ran 40 executions distributed in the same team compositions that we used in the spreading task.

Fitness function was defined in terms of the number of zones not visited by any robot and we considered an optimum value the case where only one zone was not visited. Evolutionary parameters were maintained as Table 1 showed.

To solve the dynamic coverage task we use the grammar shown in Box 3.

As we can see, the grammar is a bit easier because of only 3 behaviours (avoid robot, avoid obstacle and explore) are needed now instead of 4 behaviours (avoid robot, avoid obstacle, spread and wait task) we used in spreading task. Behaviours are high-level function as well and only 3 states associated with perception are needed. Coordination mechanism is also maintained as competitive rules. In this case, the ***conditionIf-StaCond*** label contains three conditions, one for each state/behaviour pair instead of four conditions as static coverage grammar included.

Figure 4. Simbad test environment

Figure 5. Virtual test environment

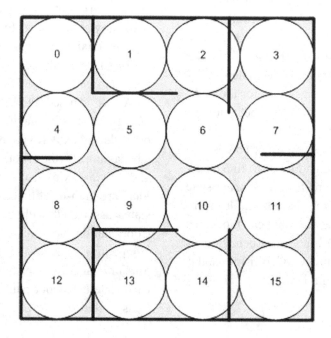

Box 3.

```
<control-flow>::= function main(){ <coordination-mechanism>
            check_collision() } main(); [<control-flow>.value='main']      (0)
<coordination-mechanism>::= <competitive-rules>
            [<coordination-mechanism>.value=<competitive-rules>.value]     (0)
<competitive-rules>::=     if (<state-condition>)
                    { <behaviour-name>     [conditionIfStaCond] }
                    [<competitive-rules>.value='ifCompRules']             (0)
<competitive-rules>::=     if (<state-condition>)
                        { <behaviour-name> [conditionIfStaCond] }
                    else <competitive-rules>
                        [<competitive-rules>.value='ifCompRules']     (1)
<state-condition>::= obstacle()    [<state-condition>.value='obs']       (0)
<state-condition>::= robot()       [<state-condition>.value='rob']       (1)
<state-condition>::= free_space()      [<state-condition>.value='fre']   (2)
<behaviour-name>::= avoid_obstacle() [<behaviour-name>.value='avObs']    (0)
<behaviour-name>::= avoid_robot()      [<behaviour-name>.value='avRob']  (1)
<behaviour-name>::= explore()        [<behaviour-name>.value='expl']     (2)
```

RESULTS

As we comment in the introduction we ran the tests in simulation with a tool called Simbad which was developed in order to provide a simulation environment where machine learning theories could be checked. Simbad does not try to emulate faithfully real situations and it does not reproduce real robots. However, it is a valuable tool in order to test new paradigms in artificial intelligence as evolutionary or other machine learning algorithms. We think this tool is a reasonable choice in a case where we are more interested in showing how high-level automatic controllers can be built by means of a new methodology than in studying how to fit sensors and actuators as it is usual in low-level controller design. What is interesting for us in a first stage is to check whether this methodology can solve problems in multirobot domains and if it is possible to improve the automatic process of building controllers. At the same time, we address a study about how the number of members in the team can influence in this process.

In the test environment, robots are depicted as cylinders and we only add sonar sensors although in Simbad other sensors as cameras, bumpers or light sensors are allowed. With sonar sensors the robots can sense any obstacle and this is all we need according to the previous grammars.

Different tests were realized and we will show results in the next sections. In order to check the effect of the number of robots in the evolutionary process we divided the tests in four groups based on the number of robots working in the environment during the evolutionary process:

- Group I: 4 robots.
- Group II: 8 robots
- Group III: 12 robots
- Group IV: 16 robots

We ran 10 tests on each group and all robots started in the top left corner. To summarize, 40 tests for static coverage and 40 tests for dynamic coverage were executed. Once a valid controller was found on each test, we executed again this

Figure 6. Controller generated by Group I in the spreading task

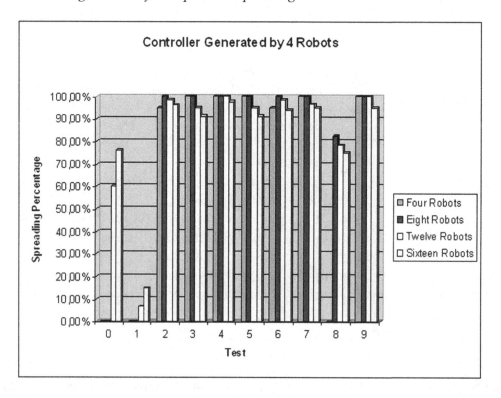

controller for 5 times more but we tested it for all groups, i.e. when a controller developed by group I was found, we executed it for groups I, II, III and IV. We did it in order to check:

- If a controller found with a specific team composition performs also in a different composition. This way, we measure if the number of robots can influence the quality of the solution in the evolutionary process.
- If the solutions found are really good, i.e. if they frequently perform well. This way, we can evaluate possible imperfections in the simulator because of wrong controller is not able to repeat its behaviour subsequently.

Static Coverage

An optimum value of fitness for spreading is defined as a configuration where only two robots

are not static. Figure 6 shows results in group I by test and spreading percentage on each test.

Spreading percentage stands for the number of robots stopped with respect to the total number of robots. Each still robot must be alone in a zone to be considered as a valid value. As we can see in Figure 6 the controllers found in tests 0 and 1 had poor quality and they were not able to reproduce their behaviours subsequently. However, these bad controllers were able to work with 12 and 16 robots in test 0. Smaller groups have fewer possibilities to interact with other robots and behaviours as *avoid_robots* are less probable. However, the fewer robots there are in the environment the more probable they are alone in a place. With 4 and 8 robots evenly situated in the left upper corner, a bad controller can assume they already are well situated when they actually have not started yet. Besides, controllers found in tests 0, 1 and 8 did not include the obstacle (state)/ avoid obstacle (action) pair. It is clear that control-

Figure 7. Controller generated by Group II in the spreading task

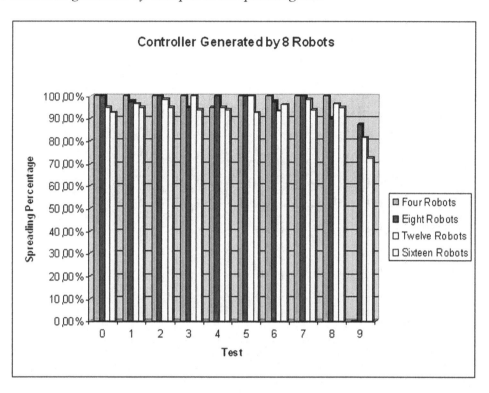

lers without this behaviour do not perform well at all (see tests 0, 1 and 8 in Figure 6). On the other hand, when correct controllers are generated, a group with 4 and 8 robots performs slightly better than a group with 12 and 16 robots. This is reasonable because it is easier to set 4 or 8 robots in a lonely place than to set 12 or 16. Correct controllers all include at least *avoid_obstacle*, *wait_new_task* and *spread* behaviours.

Figure 7 shows results for group II, the group for a controller initially developed with 8 robots.

As we can see in the figure, results are slightly better for group II. Only one controller was created without *avoid_obstacle* behaviour (test 9). When we tested with 12 robots initially in the team we got the results shown in Figure 8.

Results in this case are considerably better than previous ones. All controllers created included *avoid_obst*acle behaviour and we can see an improved performance on each configuration, i.e. a controller created initially with 12 robots in

the team performed equally fine with 4, 8 and 16 robots. Finally, Figure 9 shows results for the last group.

As we can see in Figure 9 if we evolve the system with 16 members the system finds good results in the spreading task too.

All previous figures show the results group by test and they serve to know how the behaviours forming the controller can influence in the results. However, we can show how the system really performed in terms of average spreading percentage. This measure allows us to check if the system is performing well or not. Figure 10 shows results concerning this measure and Table 3 summarises the same results in numeric way.

In Table 3 the columns labelled as 4, 8, 12 and 16 show results achieved for a controller generated by each group when it was executed with a different number of robots. Values are expressed as percentages.

Figure 8. Controller generated by Group III in the spreading task

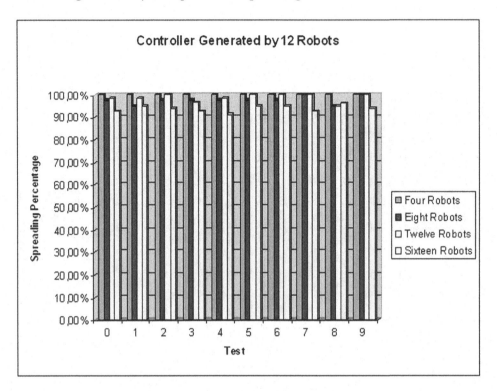

Figure 9. Controller generated by Group IV in the spreading task

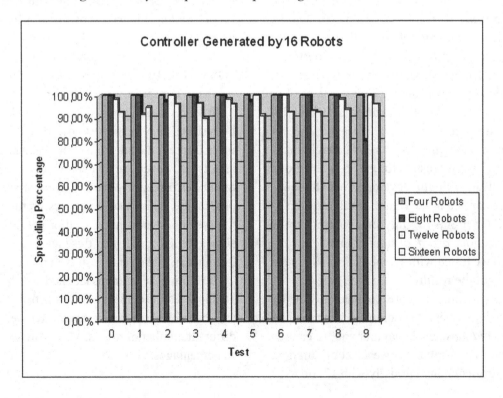

Figure 10. Average spreading percentage for the spreading task

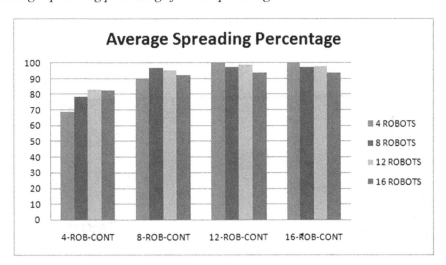

Table 3. Results for spreading task

Group	4	8	12	16
Group I (4 robots)	69.0	78.2	82.8	82.6
Group II (8 robots)	89.5	96.7	96.5	92.0
Group III (12 robots)	100	97.5	98.7	93.7
Group IV (16 robots)	100	97.5	97.7	93.6

An apparent controversy is related with the values 69 and 78.2 corresponding to the controller generated with 4 robots in the environment. When we commented results of Figure 6 we noted that when a correct controller was created a best performance was attained for 4 and 8 robots in the environment. Nevertheless, 69 and 78.2 are lower values than 82.8 and 82.6 which are associated with 12 and 16 robots. Solution to this controversy is the effect of bad controllers in the average value. Remember that three bad controllers (test 0, 1 and 8) were developed when this group was tested.

An important consequence we can infer from Figure 10 and Table 3 is that controllers created with 12 or 16 members performs perfectly in groups with 4 and 8 robots, at least in this task. Another fact, we can infer is that controllers evolved with few members do not perform as well as controllers evolved with more members.

We can argue than a controller created with few members does have fewer opportunities to test all behaviours. Specifically, behaviours like *avoid_robots* are less tested because four members do not interact among them frequently in a large environment. On the other hand, a group of four members attains a static configuration in a few steps because 16 virtual zones are rapidly taken by 4 robots. Generally, in this case all robots finish their task near the starting point and there are fewer opportunities to develop other behaviours apart from *wait_new_task*.

As an example of static coverage we can see in Figure 11 a final configuration that we got in a test with 16 robots.

A typical program generated in a good solution has the following code:

```
function main() { if (obstacle()) {
avoid_obstacle() } else if (task_
end()) { wait_new_task() } else if
(free_space()) { spread() } check_
collision() } main();
```

Figure 11. Example of final configuration with 16 robots

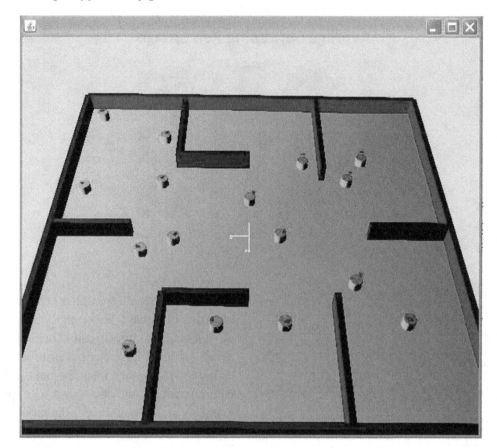

Dynamic Coverage

A correct fitness value was defined in exploration task as the number of places not visited. Optimum fitness corresponds to 0 or 1 value because this value corresponds to the case where only one zone is not visited. Based on this measure we can define exploration percentage as the number of places visited regarding to the total number of places in the environment. In this case, 16 zones were virtually defined.

Figure 12 shows results in group I by test and exploration percentage on each test.

Figure 12 shows specific performance group by test and we can see as four robots do not provide a full exploration in any case. However, the same controller controlling 12 or 16 robots performed well practically in all cases. Exploration

was not full with 8 robots but it exceeded results that 4 robots achieved.

In the group II a controller created with 8 robots in the environment was developed and Figure 13 summarises the results.

As figure above shows a controller initially developed with 8 robots in the environment provide a similar performance as 4 robots provided. Anew, if we put 4 robots in the environment a full exploration is not possible under the same time constraints that other configurations use.

For groups III and IV results are shown in Figures 14 and 15.

Figures show as controllers created with 12 or 16 robots in the environment produce similar results to 4 and 8 cases. So, we can argue that number of robots in the group is not so important when a high-level controller must be evolved

Figure 12. Controller generated by Group I in the exploring task

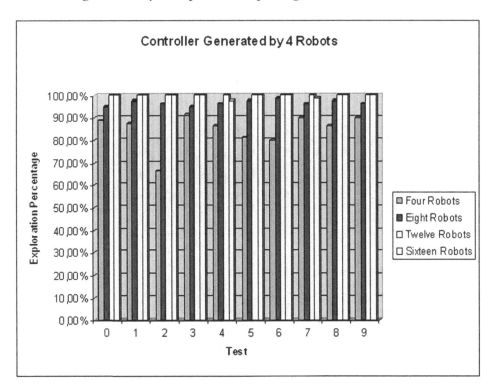

Figure 13. Controller generated by Group II in the exploring task

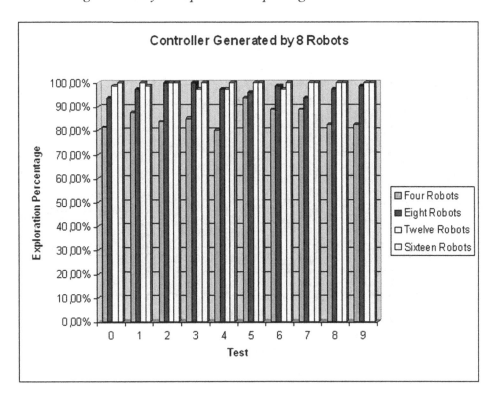

Figure 14. Controller generated by Group III in the exploring task

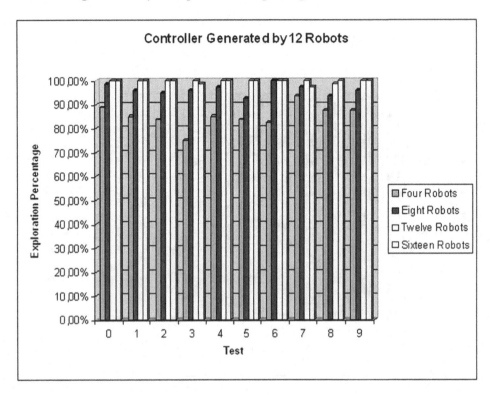

Figure 15. Controller generated by Group IV in the exploring task

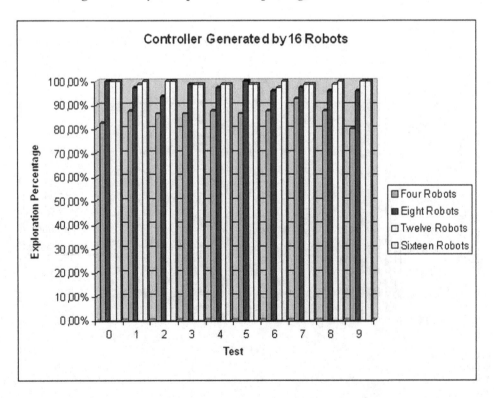

Figure 16. Average spreading percentage for the exploring task

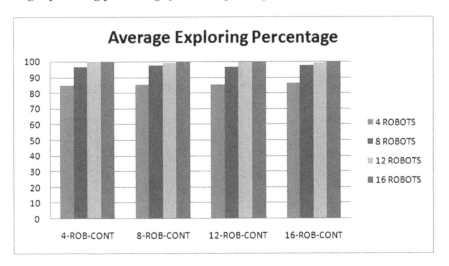

using GER with semantic rules. Number of robots in the group is more influential in exploration percentage. Obviously, the fewer robots we set in the group, the less performance we will get under the same time constraints.

As we did in the spreading task we finish this section showing a figure and a table with the average exploring percentage.

Contrary to what happened in the spreading task where the number of robots in the environment during the process had very influence in the controller design, in the exploring task the team size is not so important and similar results are attained with different compositions. However, the success probability in this task depends on the team size because with 4 or 8 robots the system only can explore around 85% of the environment. With a bigger team the system performed quite well in this task (between 99% and 100%).

Influence of the Semantic Knowledge

In this section we analyze whether there is some advantage when we add semantic rules in the grammar we use to solve problems. This fact has been analyzed in (Mingo, 2011) but we work here

with a team of robots instead of working with only one as that work did.

The Figures 17 and 18 show the results for two different compositions in the team of robots. We used previous results with 8 and 12 robots as representative compositions in the spreading and exploring tasks and we ran each group again without any semantic rules in the grammar. This way, we used a standard GER without semantic to solve spreading and exploring problems in order to compare both approaches.

In Figure 17, SPR-SEM-N (N=8,12) stands for "evolutionary process developed with Semantic GER and N robots initially in the environment" and SPR-STD means "evolutionary process developed with Standard GER and N robots initially in the environment". Similar concepts are also applied to Figure 18 by only swapping SPR (spreading) with EXP (exploring).

Contrary to what we thought the results were apparently comparable to semantic GER in terms of efficiency in solving the task as we can see in Figure 17. However, a detailed analysis carried out in the process of repeating each developed controller for 5 times as we did before revealed important differences in term of efficacy. Table

Figure 17. Success probability with semantic and without semantic rules in the spreading task

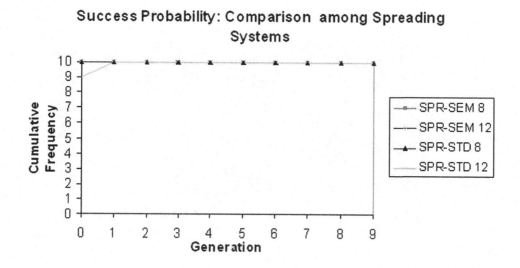

Figure 18. Success probability with semantic and without semantic rules in the exploring task

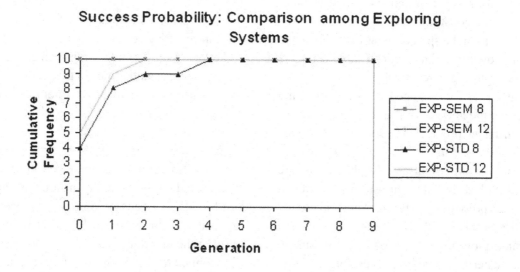

Table 4. Results for exploring task

Group	4	8	12	16
Group I (4 robots)	84.7	96.6	100	99.6
Group II (8 robots)	85.4	97.4	99.1	99.9
Group III (12 robots)	85.2	96.4	99.9	99.6
Group IV (16 robots)	86.4	97.4	99.0	99.5

Table 5. Comparative results in the spreading task for standard and semantic GER

System	4	8	12	16
Spr-Sem-8	89.5	96.7	96.5	92.0
Spr-Sem-12	100	97.5	98.7	93.7
Spr-Std-8	87.0	84.7	73.5	71.0
Spr-Std-12	54.5	86.0	81.0	76.7

5 let us to see how both systems covered the environment with values as percentages.

In Table 5 results for SPR-SEM-8 and SPR-SEM-12 were taken from Table 3. We can appreciate an important degradation in terms of efficacy between standard and semantic GER. Under the same parameters, constraints and fitness definition, a significant descent of spreading percentage is evident. Standard GER got quickly solutions because we defined an optimum fitness value for spreading task when only two robots are not static. We think this is probably a very high value for small groups as 8 or 12. Obviously, semantic GER was executed with this constraint too, but semantic rules can avoid the generation of incorrect individuals. Without the innate knowledge represented by semantic rules the evolved controllers are more exposed to be mistaken as results seem to confirm.

In the second task we can notice in Figure 18 how semantic systems get a bit better performance than standard systems. Semantic GER with 8 and 12 robots is able to find a solution to this problem in the first generation. Essentially, in a simple problem as exploring task is defined here, GER with semantics is able to find solutions in only one generation. This way, there is no evolution and we can argue that the learning step usual in GER systems and the semantic constraints are powerful enough to solve the problem. However, if we use a standard GER we need evolution and learning working altogether.

Table 6 shows differences between standard and semantic GER in the exploring task in terms of average exploration percentage.

In Table 5 results for EXP-SEM-8 and EXP-SEM-12 were taken from Table 4. As we can see in the table, both semantic GER and standard GER shows a good performance when they work with 8, 12 and 16 robots in the team. When only 4 robots are in the team, both systems achieve worse performance because we mentioned before it is more difficult to explore an environment with 4 robots. Despite this constraint, semantic GER

Table 6. Comparative results in the exploring task for standard and semantic GER

System	4	8	12	16
Exp-Sem-8	85.4	97.4	99.1	99.9
Exp-Sem-12	85.2	96.4	99.9	99.6
Exp-Std-8	85.4	97.5	99.0	97.5
Exp-Std-12	77.0	91.7	97.9	98.6

and even standard GER for a controller initially create with 8 robots get valuable results in this case as well. Controllers generated for exploring are reliable with both methods but standard GER needs more generations.

FUTURE RESEARCH DIRECTIONS

Coverage and exploring tasks with a group of agents will be a valuable tool in a future because some human activities would be less dangerous with robots than they are when humans do them. In this sense, we think this topic will be an interesting research line as in fact it is being currently. These problems can be solved with different strategies but we think that a division between high and low level in the design of controllers is needed. The work we propose in this chapter is a contribution to design high-level controllers using evolutionary techniques which we merge with grammars and reinforcement learning to increase the power of the system. On one hand, high-level controllers are hand-designed in the context of the behaviour-based robotic approach. On the other hand, the evolutionary robotic approach usually works with low level controllers and its efforts to develop high level controller are difficult of analyzing because of artificial neural network are the most employed technique and they act as black boxes where the performance is difficult to follow. The work we propose here can be considered as a bridge between both approaches and it allows developing new features in a future. We can think about this word as a base line to broach new problems in the same domain. A couple of issues that it could be solved in a future include:

1. Test semantic GER with more behaviours and more complex too.
2. Add some deliberative techniques such as map building or communication between robots. This way we would include a new step in the high-level controllers automatically design.

CONCLUSION

Multirobot teams are a good solution to solve problems when we have to treat with difficult or dangerous tasks as rescue missions or minesweeping by considering only a few ones. Solutions to these problems have been proposed coming from control theory, behaviour-based robotic or evolutionary robotics. Behaviour-based and evolutionary approaches share similar goals but they generally use different methods and techniques. One of the most important differences between them is related with the structure of the controllers they produce. Behaviour-based systems create modular controllers while evolutionary systems usually build whole controllers. Of course, from a functionality point of view, both paradigms are similar because their controllers produce some kind of behaviour when they are implemented on robots.

Problems in coverage, either static or dynamic have been solved with behaviour-based and evolutionary algorithms and even with hybrid systems. Precisely, we propose in this work a hybrid algorithm to solve problems in static and dynamic coverage. This algorithm is based on Grammatical Evolution, Reinforcement Learning and semantic constraints expressed by means of grammatical rules. We propose a semantic GER system in order to try to fill the gap between behaviour-based and evolutionary methods.

Semantic GER uses evolution to build controllers as evolutionary methods for robotics do but it creates controllers with a modular structure similar to behaviour-based controllers. This way, we can join advantages from both paradigms by building automatically high-level controllers in an evolutionary process which uses behaviour primitives represented as high-level functions. In parallel, we can add innate knowledge about a specific domain by using semantic labels in the production rules of the grammar.

Analyzing results that semantic GER achieved in static and dynamic problems we notice a good performance in terms of execution time and efficacy in the tasks. In a simulated indoor environment which included obstacle as walls, the generated automatic controllers explored around 95%-100% of the environment when each controller was created with 8, 12 and 16 robots in the team. These initial controllers performed equally fine when they were tested again with another composition in the group. A special mention we must do for the controllers created or executed subsequently with 4 robots. These controllers performed a bit worse and they only explored around 84%-87% of the environment (see Figure 16 or Table 4 for details). All results led us to argue that the number of robots is more influential in the fulfilment of the task than in the very evolutionary process.

Regarding static coverage or spreading problem, semantic-GER got really good results with controllers initially generated with 12 and 16 robots (see Figure 10 or Table 3 for details). These controllers spread the robots in similar percentages (93%-100%) in all cases, i.e. with 4, 8, 12 and 16 robots. Controllers created with 8 robots initially in the evolutionary process performed a bit worse and they spread the team around 89%-92% for all configurations (see Figure 10 or Table 3). However, controllers created with 4 robots in the evolutionary process did not perform as well and they only spread the team around 69%-83% (Figure 10 or Table 3). In this case we can suppose a higher influence of the number of members during the evolutionary process. However, reviewing both tasks we can argue that the fewer robots we use during the evolutionary process the less reliable controller we evolved. This is reasonable because the more robots in the team the more possibilities they can interact among them and the more chance for new behaviours can be tested.

Finally, we wanted to analyze how important could be innate knowledge in the evolutionary process and we compared semantic GER with a standard GER executing on the same tasks. If we compare Tables 5 and 6 with Tables 3 and 4 respectively, we can notice how common reasoning incorporated to the rules by means of semantic constraints is profitable both in efficiency and in efficacy. If a task is defined with a less restrictive fitness function, semantic knowledge can help to avoid bad solutions. In any case, semantic rules accelerate the evolutionary process and they can avoid dangerous tests in real environments because of discarding bad individuals.

In order to resume important issues about using semantic-GER to solve problems with multiple robots we can emphasize two aspects:

- *With regard to the algorithm*: A semantic GER system is a promising approach to build automatically high-level controllers with a modular and/or hierarchically structure.
- *With regard to the applicability*: Although semantic GER has been tested only in simulation we think it might be valuable in real environments because semantic rules can avoid useless and harmful individuals. Execution time can be reduced as well and semantic GER usually works with few individuals and generations.

REFERENCES

Acar, E. U., Choset, H., & Lee, J. Y. (2006). Sensor-based coverage with extended range detectors. *IEEE Transactions on Robotics*, 22(1), 189–198. doi:10.1109/TRO.2005.861455

Aho, A. V., Sethi, R., & Ullman, J. D. (1986). *Compilers: Principles, techniques and tools*. Addison-Wesley.

Arkin, R. C. (1989). Motor schema based mobile robot navigation. *The International Journal of Robotics Research*, 8(4), 92–112. doi:10.1177/027836498900800406

Balch, T., & Arkin, R. C. (1999). Behaviour-based formation control for multi-robot teams. *IEEE Transactions on Robotics and Automation*, 20, 1–15.

Batalin, M. A., & Sukhatme, G. S. (2002). Spreading out: A local approach to multi-robot coverage. In *Proceedings of the 6th International Symposium on Distributed Autonomous Robotics Systems*, (pp. 373-382).

Batalin, M. A., & Sukhatme, G. S. (2003). Dynamic coverage via multi-robot cooperation. In *Proceedings on Multi-Robot Systems Workshop at Naval Research Laboratory*, Washington DC, March 17-19, (pp. 295-296).

Brooks, R. A. (1986). Robust layered control system for a mobile robot. *IEEE Journal on Robotics and Automation*, 2, 1–14. doi:10.1109/JRA.1986.1087032

Bullo, F., & Cortes, J. (2005). Adaptive and distributed coordination algorithms for mobile sensing networks. In V. Kumar, N. E. Leonard & A.S. Morse, (Eds.), *Proceedings of the 2003 Block Island Workshop on Cooperative Control, Lecture Notes in Control and Information Sciences*, Vol. 309, (pp. 43-62). New York, NY: Springer Verlag.

Burgard, W., Fox, D., Moors, M., Simmons, R., & Thrun, S. (2000). Collaborative multi-robot exploration. In *Proceedings of the IEEE International Conference on Robotics and Automation (ICRA)*, (pp. 476-481).

Choset, H. (2000). Coverage of known spaces: The boustrophedon cellular decomposition. *Autonomous Robots, 9*, 247–253. doi:10.1023/A:1008958800904

Choset, H. (2001). Coverage for robotics: A survey of recent results. *Annals of Mathematics and Artificial Intelligence, 31*(1-4), 113–126. doi:10.1023/A:1016639210559

Collins, J. J., Ryan, C., & O'Neill, M. (1998). Grammatical evolution: Evolving programs for an arbitrary language. *Proceedings of the First European Workshop on Genetic Programming, Lecture Notes in Computer Science 1391*, (pp. 83-95). Springer-Verlag.

Cortes, J., Martinez, S., Karatas, T., & Bullo, F. (2004). Coverage control for mobile sensing networks. *IEEE Transactions on Robotics and Automation, 20*(2), 243–255. doi:10.1109/TRA.2004.824698

Gage, D. W. (1992). Command control for many-robot systems. *Unmanned Systems Magazine, 10*(4), 28–34.

Howard, A., Mataric, M. J., & Sukhatme, G. S. (2002a). An incremental self-deployment algorithm for mobile sensor networks. *Autonomous Robots, 13*(2), 113–126. doi:10.1023/A:1019625207705

Howard, A., Mataric, M. J., & Sukhatme, G. S. (2002b). Mobile sensor network deployment using potential fields: A distributed, scalable solution to the area coverage problem. In *Proceedings of the 6th International Symposium on Distributed Autonomous Robotics Systems*, (pp. 299-308).

Hugues, L., & Bredeche, N. (2006). Simbad: An autonomous robot simulation package for education and research. In *Proceedings of the International Conference on the Simulation of Adaptive Behaviour*, Rome, Italy, (pp. 831-842).

Ito, K. (2003). Simple robots in a complex world: Collaborative exploration behaviour using genetic programming. In Koza, J. R. (Ed.), *Genetic algorithms and genetic programming* (pp. 91–99). Stanford, CA: Stanford Bookstore.

Kong, C. S., Peng, N. A., & Rekleitis, I. (2006). Distributed coverage with multi-robot system. In *Proceedings of the 2006 IEEE International Conference on Robotics and Automation*, Orlando, Florida, May, (pp. 2423-2429).

Latimer, D., IV, Srinivasa, S., Lee-Shue, V., Sonne, S., Choset, H., & Hurst, A. (2002). Towards sensor based coverage with robot teams. *Proceedings of the 2002 IEEE International Conference on Robotics & Automation*, Washington DC, May, (pp. 961-967).

Mataric, M. (1992). Designing emergent behaviours: From local interactions to collective intelligence. In *Proceedings of the International Conference on Simulation of Adaptive Behaviour: From Animal to Animats, 2*, (pp. 432-441).

Mingo, J. M., & Aler, R. (2007). Grammatical evolution guided by reinforcement. *IEEE Congress on Evolutionary Computation*, Singapore, (pp. 1475-1482).

Mingo, J. M., Aler, R., De Lope, J., & Maravall, D. (2011). *Innate knowledge through semantic rules in grammatical evolution guided by reinforcement applied to robotic problems*. Unpublished.

Mondada, F., Pettinaro, G., Guigrard, A., Kwee, I., Floreano, D., & Denebourg, J.-L. (2004). Swarm-bot: A new distributed robotic concept. *Autonomous Robots, 17*(2-3), 193–221. doi:10.1023/B:AURO.0000033972.50769.1c

Nolfi, S. (2006). Behaviour as a complex adaptive system: On the role of self-organization in the development of individual and collective behaviour. *Complexus, 2*(3-4), 195–203. doi:10.1159/000093690

Nolfi, S., & Floreano, D. (2000). *Evolutionary robotics: The biology, intelligence and technology of self-organizing machines*. Cambridge, MA: The MIT Press.

Parker, L. E. (1993). Designing control laws for cooperative agent teams. In *Proceedings of the IEEE International Conference on Robotics and Automation*, (pp. 582-587).

Rekleitis, I. M., Dudek, G., & Milios, E. E. (2000). Graph-based exploration using multiple robots. In Parker, L. E., Bekey, G. W., & Barhen, J. (Eds.), *Distributed Autonomous Robotics Systems* (*Vol. 4*, pp. 241–250). Springer. doi:10.1007/978-4-431-67919-6_23

Reynolds, C. (1987). Flocks, herds and schools: A distributed behavioural model. *Computer Graphics, 21*(4), 25–34. doi:10.1145/37402.37406

Rubini, J., Heckendorn, R. B., & Soule, T. (2009). Evolution of team composition in multi-agent systems. *Proceedings of the 11ᵗʰ Annual Conference on Genetic and Evolutionary Computation, GECCO'09,* ACM, NY, USA, (pp. 1067-1074).

Schawer, M., Slotine, J. J. E., & Rus, D. (2007). Decentralized, adaptive control for coverage with networked robots. In *Proceedings of the International Conference on Robotics and Automation (ICRA 07)*, (pp. 3289-3294). Rome.

Schwager, M., McLurkin, J., & Rus, D. (2006). Distributed coverage control with sensory feedback for networked robots. In *Proceedings of Robotics*. Philadelphia, PA: Science and Systems.

Schwager, M., Rus, D., & Slotine, J.-J. E. (2009). Decentralized, adaptive coverage control for networked robots. *The International Journal of Robotics Research, 28*(3), 357–375. doi:10.1177/0278364908100177

Shutt, J. N. (2003). *Recursive adaptable grammars*. Master's Thesis, Worcester Polytechnic Institute, Worcester, M. A. August 10, 1993, amended December 16, 2003.

Thomason, R., Heckendorn, R. B., & Soule, T. (2008). Training time and team composition robustness in evolved multi-agent systems. In *Proceedings of the 11ᵗʰ European Conference on Genetic Programming, EuroGP 2008, Lecture Notes in Computer Science vol. 4971*, (pp. 1-12). Springer-Verlag

Trianni, V. (2008). *Evolutionary swarm robotics. Evolving self-organizing behaviours in groups of autonomous robots. Studies in Computational Intelligence* (*Vol. 108*). Berlin, Germany: Springer Verlag.

Tu, X., & Terzopoulos, D. (1994). Artificial fishes: Physics, locomotion, perception, behaviour. In *SIGGRAPH 94 Conference Proceedings*, (pp. 43-50). Orlando, FL: ACM

Watkins, C., & Dayan, P. (1992). Q-learning. *Machine Learning, 8*, 279–292. doi:10.1007/BF00992698

Yamauchi, B. (1998). Frontier-based exploration using multiple robots. In *Proceedings of the Second International Conference on Autonomous Agents*, (pp. 47-53). Minneapolis, Minnesota.

ADDITIONAL READING

Agmon, N., Hazon, N., & Kaminka, G. A. (2006). Constructing spanning trees for efficient multi-robot coverage. *Proceedings of the 2006 IEEE International Conference on Robotics and Automation,* Orlando, Florida, May, (pp. 1698-1703).

Arkin, R. (2000). *Behaviour-based robotics* (2nd ed.). Cambridge, MA: The MIT press.

Balch, T., & Parker, L. E. (Eds.). (2002). *Robot teams: From diversity to polymorphism*. Natick, MA: A K Peters.

Baldassarre, G., Nolfi, S., & Parisi, D. (2003). Evolving mobile robots able to display collective behaviours. *Artificial Life*, *9*(3). doi:10.1162/106454603322392460

Bonabeau, E., Dorigo, M., & Theraulaz, G. (1999). *Swarm intelligence: From natural to artificial systems*. New York, NY: Oxford University Press Studies in the Science of Complexity.

Choset, H. (2005). *Principles of robot motion: Theory, algorithms and implementation*. Cambridge, MA: MIT Press.

Correl, N. (2007). *Coordination schemes for distributed boundary coverage with a swarm of miniature robots: Synthesis, analysis and experimental validation*. Doctoral Thesis, Faculté Informatique et Communications, École Polytechnique Fédérale de Lausanne, 12th October 2007.

Easton, K., & Burdick, J. (2005). A coverage algorithm for multi-robot boundary inspection. In *Proceedings of the 2005 IEEE International Conference on Robotics and Automation,* April 2005, Barcelona, Spain.

Gabriely, Y., & Rimon, E. (1999). Spanning-tree based coverage of continuous areas by a mobile robot. *Annals of Mathematics and Artificial Intelligence*, *31*(1-4), 77–98.

Hazon, N., & Kaminka, G. (2005). Redundancy, efficiency and robustness in multi-robot coverage. In *IEEE International Conference on Robotics and Automation (ICRA)*, Barcelona, Spain, (pp. 735-741).

Hazon, N., Mieli, F., & Kaminka, G. (2006). Towards robust on-line multi-robot coverage. In *IEEE International Conference on Robotics and Automation (ICRA)*, Orlando, FL, USA, (pp. 1710-1715).

Jimenez, P. A., Shirinzadeh, B., Nicholson, A., & Alici, G. (2007). Optimal area covering using genetic algorithms. In *IEEE Advanced Intelligent Mechatronics Conference* (pp. 1-5).

Kapanoglu, M., Ozkan, M., & Yazici, A. (2009). Lecture Notes in Computer Science: *Vol. 5544. Pattern-based genetic algorithm approach to coverage path planning for mobile robots. ICCS 2009* (pp. 33–42). Berlin, Germany: Springer-Verlang.

Martinoli, A. (1999). *Swarm intelligence in autonomous collective robotics: From tools to the analysis and synthesis of distributed control strategies*. Doctoral Thesis, Département D'Informatique, École Polytechnique Fédérale de Lausanne.

Ozcan, M., Yazici, A., & Kapanoglu, M. (2009). Hierarchical oriented genetic algorithms for coverage path planning or multi-robot teams with load balancing. *Proceedings of the first ACM Summit on Genetic and Evolutionary Computing,* Shangai, China, June 12-14.

Parker, G. B. (2002). Learning area coverage using the co-evolution of model parameters. *Proceedings of the Genetic and Evolutionary Computation Conference,* July 2002, (pp. 1286-1293).

Zhang, Y., Antonsson, E. K., & Martinoli, A. (2004). Evolving neural controllers for collective robotic inspection. *Proceedings of the 9th Online World Conference on Soft Computing in Industrial Applications*, September/October.

KEY TERMS AND DEFINITIONS

Dynamic Coverage: Similar to static coverage but robots do not stop when they reach a location but they can move around the environment.

Grammatical Evolution Guided by Reinforcement: A hybrid algorithm which merges grammatical evolution and reinforcement learning.

Grammatical Evolution: An evolutionary algorithm that uses variable length linear genome and a grammar to evolve programs.

Reinforcement Learning: A traditional machine learning approach that tries to find an optimum policy of actions to apply in each specific state.

Semantic Rules: A way of including domain-specific knowledge by means of attributes in a grammar.

Static Coverage: A group of robots are spread in an environment and they stop when they reach a random or specific location.

Chapter 18
Computer–Controlled Graphical Avatars and Reinforcement Learning

Yuesheng He
Hong Kong Baptist University, Hong Kong

Yuan Yan Tang
Hong Kong Baptist University, Hong Kong

ABSTRACT

Controlling Graphical avatars intelligently in real-time applications such as 3D computer simulating environment has become important as the storage and computational power of computers has increased. Such avatars are usually controlled by Finite State Machines (FSM), in which each individual state represents the status of the avatars. The FSMs are usually manually designed, and the number of states and transitions are therefore limited. A more complex approach is needed for the avatar's actions, which are automatically generated to adapt to different situation. The levels of the missions and algorithms for the control are the essential elements to achieve the requirements, respectively. Reinforcement Learning can be used to control the avatar intelligently in the 3D environment. When simulating the interactions between avatars and changeable environments, the problem becomes more difficult than working in a certain unchanged situation. Specific Framework and methods should be created for controlling the behaviors of avatars, such as using hierarchical structure to describe these actions. The approach has many problems to solve such as where the levels of the missions will be defined and how the learning algorithm will be used to control the avatars, et cetera. In this chapter, these problems will be discussed.

DOI: 10.4018/978-1-4666-1806-0.ch018

INTRODUCTION

Designing an intelligent 3D avatar (virtual human) is a challenged work for researchers in the areas of 3D graphics and Machine Learning.

In the 3D graphical animation environment, background 3D objects in computer animation are also usually controlled by the computer. If virtual humans' movements are unrealistic due to their poor intelligence, the animator needs to manually edit them, which will result in a huge amount of extra cost. Traditional techniques such as decision trees and flocking have been used to control such avatars (Norman I. Badler C. B., 1993). However, those techniques can only generate reactive movements, and cannot realize strategic movements that benefit the avatars in the future.

For the applications of virtual human, such as simulating tasks of human's action in the buildings or cities, or accomplish a certain job in a certain environment, the requirement is further amplified by the fact that the user is generally not a skilled engineer and can therefore not be expected to be able or willing to provide constant, detailed instructions (T. Conde, 2006). Any high level plan for the virtual human must be on the base of the low level motion control and can support any optimization approaches which have possibility to be integrated into the motion control mechanism to simulate walking in different environments. Thus, to describe the actions by using hierarchical reinforcement learning and the algorithm of reinforcement learning to solve the Markov Decision Process (MDP) (Prabhu, 2007) problem is one of the key issues.

In this case, a framework of RL has been proposed for bridging the semantic gap effectively and achieving intelligent behaviors of avatars automatically. First, the semantic gap between the low-level computable geometric features and the avatars real physical actions are partitioned into small fragment, and multiple approaches of RL are proposed to bridge these small gaps effectively. Second, Hierarchical Reinforcement algorithms are proposed by incorporating concept ontology and multi-task learning to achieve more complex behaviors such as accomplishing a whole mission.

Thus, a framework for RL based on the average reward optimality criterion will be presented. Formulations of RL based on the average reward MDP model, both for discrete-time and continuous-time will be investigated.

The contents of this chapter will be:

1. The behavioral features of avatars in the 3D graphical environments;
2. Efficient algorithms of Reinforcement learning to achieve intelligent control;
3. A framework of achieving autonomous actions of intelligent avatars;
4. Relationship between the simple actions and complex behaviors of intelligent avatars.

BACKGROUND

Intelligent computer-controlled (Norman I. Badler C. B., 1993) (Anguelov, 2005) avatars (virtual humans) aim to provide virtual characters with realistic behaviors which imply endowing them with autonomy in inhabited virtual environments. Autonomous behavior consists in interacting with users or the environment and reacting to stimulus or events. Reactions are intelligent behaviors which are often been made by virtual humans themselves.

Reinforcement Learning (RL) (Sutton, 1998) (Theodore J. Perkins PERKINS, 2002) is an effective way to control avatars in the 3D graphical environments in real time. Moreover, hierarchical reinforcement learning (HRL) is a general framework for scaling RL to problems with large state and action spaces by using the task (or action) structure to restrict the space of policies.

Meanwhile, avatars are essential in computer animation (Norman I. Badler C. B., 1993) (Norman I. Badler J. A., 2002) (T. Conde, 2006), simulation and games. In many computer games, users can usually control an avatar to interact with other computer-controlled avatars. The intelligence of the computer-controlled avatar is important as it can affect the quality of the animation. In the same time, it provides a strong way to test the effectiveness of the algorithms of RL.

Virtual human, the representation of the geometric and behavioral characters of human in the virtual environment, is one of the new research areas of computer science.

The research work for Virtual human includes many fields such as Computer Graphics, Robotics and Machine Learning. As the developing of the VR technology and its application, the research on virtual human has attracted many researchers. It has wide application areas including industry design, medicine, education, military and entertainment (Molet T, 1996).

In the industry area, virtual human can effectively support the ergonomics (human factor) and training of operation. It can be used in each periods of the digital product management including design, producing, maintaining and training.

In the analysis process of industrial products' prototypes, using virtual human, the human factors of the virtual prototype can be analyzed. It has such important meaning for the human-centered product design, so research on the behavior of virtual human is important for the application of virtual human in the designing phase.

In the entertainment area, virtual human is one the necessary parts of the 3D animations and 3D games.

To achieve the above goals, we should face the challenge from five aspects as Norman Badler described (Norman I. Badler C. B., 1993):

- Create an interactive computer graphics human model.
- Endow it with reasonable biomechanical properties.
- Provide it with "human-like" behaviors.
- Use this simulated figure as an agent to effect changes in its world.

- Describe and guide its tasks through natural language instructions.

MAIN FOCUS OF THE CHAPTER

Issues, Controversies, Problems

Unlike the real world, the graphical environment is simpler. Thus, we can concentrate our research on some basic elements which influence the behavior of virtual humans, such as geometric and physical properties. Thus, methods shall be provided in the following aspects:

- Enabling avatars to take advantage of predictable regularities in their world;
- Allowing them to make maximal use of any supervisory signals, either explicit or implicit, that the graphical world offers;
- Making them easy to be trained by interacting with virtual 3D environments.

Solutions and Recommendations

Methods on the intelligent behaviors of 3D avatar (virtual human) will be discussed in this section.

The Behavioral Features of Avatars

In aspect of avatar's action control, a method of path planning is described to support real-time creation of human walking in virtual environments (T. Conde, 2006). The motion control technique integrates studies from animation, biomechanics, human gait experiments, and psychology, and represents an important initial step toward meeting the locomotion requirements in diverse environments.

First, any high level plan for the virtual human must be on the base of the low level motion control and can support any optimization approaches which have possibility to be integrated into the motion control mechanism to simulate walking in

Figure 1. The finite automaton of elemental actions of virtual humans

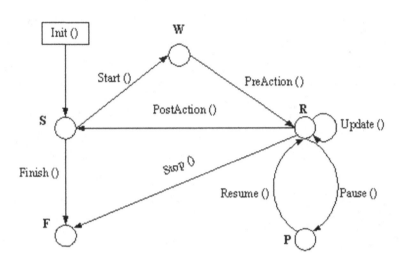

different environments. It is going to be discussed in the following subsection. Second, the method should give virtual human "online" planning ability to adapt different virtual environment. Finally, it is responsive. Since relatively simple inverse kinematics mechanisms and optimal search algorithms are widely used in the computation, interactivity can be easily achieved, which would make the method well suited for virtual environment applications. To achieve the requirement, a reinforcement learning method is presented to control virtual humans' behaviors.

The finite state machine (FSM) is a technique to perform the learning behavior to achieve the foundational requirements which have been presented in the introduction. As the movement and postures should be used by the planning level, the low level is to solve the problem of how to describe the elemental action of a virtual human. So, it is described a basic controlling elements as a finite automaton.

The 5 different States are:

- S -- Stopped: accomplished the initialization

- W--Waiting: ready to start the simulating loop
- R --Running: running the simulating loop
- P --Paused: simulating loop is paused
- F --Finished: the action is finished

We discretized the environmental states according to searching space as Figure 1 shows. A planning based reinforcement learning technique will only learn a sub-optimal policy, the quality of which depends on the search depth limit. To ensure that on the whole an avatar's behavior is optimal, we utilize the Learning approach on dynamic programming.

Therefore the action of avatar in the 3D environment which has been constructed by the computer is a 5-states finite automata. In other words, the interaction between the virtual human and virtual environment is described by a finite automata. With this description, the virtual human will simulate real human's action in the real environment as Figure 2 (Cal3D) (Delta3D) shows. We will easy to make the animation of the virtual human's behaviors in the virtual environment.

Figure 2. Different avatars act their own different actions

Efficient Algorithms of Reinforcement Learning to Achieve Intelligent Control

Machine Learning algorithm is the key method to endow avatars adaptable ability in the different environments. To achieve the effective performance, the elementary behaviors of the whole action of avatars are computed in the Markov process model.

In probability theory and statistics, a Markov process, named after the Russian mathematician Andrey Markov, is a time-varying random phenomenon for which a specific property (the Markov property) holds. In a common description, a stochastic process with the Markov property is one for which conditional on the present state of the system; its future and past are independent (J. Peters, 2003) (Norman I. Badler C. B., 1993).

Markov processes arise in probability and statistics in one of two ways. A stochastic process, defined via a separate argument, may be shown (mathematically) to have the Markov property and

as a consequence to have the properties that can be deduced from this for all Markov processes. Of more practical importance is the use of the assumption that the Markov property holds for a certain random process in order to construct basic scenario, a stochastic model for that process. In modeling terms, assuming that the Markov property holds is one of a limited number of simple ways of introducing statistical dependence into a model for a stochastic process in such a way that allows the strength of dependence at different lags to decline as the lag increases.

Markov Decision Processes (MDPs) (Andrieu, 2003) (J. Peters, 2003) (Sutton, 1998) is used to model the action. The standard approach to solve MDPs is to use dynamic programming, which transforms the problem of finding a good controller into the problem of finding a good value function. However, apart from the other cases which the MDP has been used, the virtual human's 3D graphical environment's elements is easy to be extracted, thus dynamic programming is feasible.

The RL algorithms that we discuss here can be thought of as a way of turning the 3D simulating process into practical algorithms so that they can be applied to avatars' adaptive problems.

There are two key ideas that allow RL algorithms to achieve this goal. The first is to dismantle a complex mission to compactly represent the dynamics of the control problem. This is important for two reasons: First, it allows one to deal with learning scenarios when the dynamics is unknown. Second, even if the dynamics is available, exact reasoning that uses it might be intractable on its own. The second key idea behind RL algorithms is to use powerful function approximation methods to compactly represent value functions in this problem. The significance of this is that it makes dealing with action of avatars as state and action space possible.

What is more, the RL algorithm is based on the assumption of MDPs. We solve this problem by using the Model of Markov chain. The most important part of the model is its transition probabilities.

The transition probabilities[6] of the Markov chain $\{X_n, n \geq 0\}$ are defined by:

$$P_{ij}^{(n)} = P\{X_{m+n=j} \mid X_m = j\}(m \geq 0, n \geq 0)$$

and $P_{ij}^0 = \delta_{ij}$ where δ_{ij} is Kronecker's delta. For n=1 we simplify the notation to P_{ij}. We have for i $i \geq 0$

$$P_{ij}^n \geq 0, \sum_{j=0}^{\infty} P_{ij}^n = 1(n \geq 0).$$

The Chapman-Kolmogorov equations are given by

$$P_{ij}^{m+n} = \sum_{k=0}^{\infty} P_{ik}^m P_{kj}^n (m \geq 0, n \geq 0)$$

In particular

$$P_{ij}^{n+1} = \sum_{k=0}^{\infty} P_{ik} P_{kj}^{(n)}.$$

Markov chain Monte Carlo (MCMC) (Andrieu, 2003) methods (which include random walk Monte Carlo methods) are a class of algorithms for sampling from probability distributions based on constructing a Markov chain that has the desired distribution as its equilibrium distribution.

The idea of Monte Carlo simulation (Andrieu, 2003) (J. Peters, 2003) is to draw an i.i.d. set of samples $\{x^{(i)}\}_{i=1}^{N}$ from a target density p(x) defined on a high-dimensional space χ (e.g. the set of possible configurations of a system, the space on which the posterior is defined, or the combinatorial set of feasible solutions). These N samples can be used to approximate the target density with the following empirical point-mass function

$$p_N(x) = \frac{1}{N} \sum_{i=1}^{N} \delta_{x^{(i)}}(x),$$

Where $\delta_{x^{(i)}}(x)$ denotes the delta-Dirac mass located at $x^{(i)}$. Consequently, one can approximate the integrals (or very large sums) $I(f)$ with tractable sums $I_N(f)$ that converge as follows

$$I_N(f) = \frac{1}{N} \sum_{i=1}^{N} f(x^{(i)}) \xrightarrow[N \to \infty]{a.s.} I(f)$$
$$= \int_{\chi} f(x)p(x)dx.$$

Reinforcement learning (RL) (Sutton, 1998) refers to both a learning problem and a subfield of machine learning. As a learning problem it refers to learning to control a system so as to maximize some numerical value which represents a long-term objective. A typical setting where reinforcement learning operates is shown in system's state and a reward associated with the

Figure 3. The basic reinforcement learning scenario of the avatar

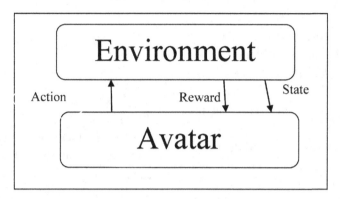

last state transition. It then calculates an action which is sent back to the system. In response, the system makes a transition to a new state and the cycle is repeated. The problem is to learn a way of controlling the system so as to maximize the total reward. The learning problems differ in the details of how the data is collected and how performance is measured.

Based on the MCMC, the avatar's actions between the environments are modeled as following Figure 3.

A discrete Markov decision process (MDP) $M = (S, A, P_{s,s'}^a, R_{s,s'}^a)$ (Prabhu, 2007)is defined by a finite set of discrete states S, a finite set of actions A, a transition Model $P_{s,s'}^a$ specifying the distribution over future states s' when an action a is performed in state s, and a corresponding reward model $R_{s,s'}^a$ specifying a scalar cost or reward.

Any optimal policy π defines the same unique optimal value function V which satisfies the nonlinear constraints [14]:

$$V(s) = \max(R_{s,s'}^a + \gamma \sum_{s' \in S} P_{s,s'}^a V(s'))$$

Where $R_{s,s'}^a = \sum_{s' \in S} P_{s,s'}^a R_{s,s'}^a$ is the expected immediate reward.

The Bellman operator T_π on the space of value function which is used to evaluate the policy π on the space of value faction which is used to evaluate the policy π can be written as:

$$T^\pi(V) = R_{\pi(s)} + \gamma \sum_{s' \in S} P_{s,s'}^{\pi(s)} V^\pi(s')$$

Thus, the value function V_P associated with a deterministic policy P can be defined as:

$$V^\pi(s) = R_{\pi(s)} + \gamma \sum_{s' \in S} P_{s,s'}^{\pi(s)} V^\pi(s').$$

In this chapter we assume that the avatar's action that we wish to control is stochastic. Further, we assume that the measurements available on the system's state are detailed enough so that the controller can avoid reasoning about how to collect information about the state. Problems with these characteristics are best described in the framework of Markov.

Thus, some efficient Reinforcement Learning (e.g. Q-learning and Sarsa) algorithms have been used to control behaviors of virtual human in the 3D graphical environment.

A Framework of Achieving Autonomous Actions of Intelligent Avatars

We have considered the action as a general class of random processes with trajectories in a metric space which are continuous from the right and

Figure 4. Searching space of the reaction with the environment by treating the action is discrete

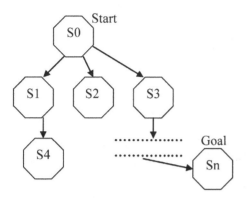

have limits from the left at any point of the half-line. These processes were continuous Markov processes in according to the property of their first exit streams. The structure of these processes of actions is showed in Figure 4 . Thus, it is necessary to develop methods or to modernize traditional methods of investigation, which do not use the simple Markov property.

We can support value functions with to evaluate the actions' policy. Moreover, the above methods suffer from the limitation that the space of available motions is discrete. The parametric space is an abstract space defined by kinematic or physical attributes of motions (Molet T, 1996) (Norman I. Badler C. B., 1993) (T. Conde, 2006). By parameterizing all motion samples in the space, and by blending among multiple motions, motion interpolation can create novel motions that have specific kinematic or physical attributes. We build a continuous parameterized motion space for similar motions that provide efficient control for interpolation.

Motion action context is extensively used in computer animation, because it is able to describe all the subtleties of real human motion. By piecing together with some different type of short motion clips, we can further create novel but realistic motions. Consequently, the way of arranging the clips of motions to achieve specific goals is an important idea which is shown in Figure 5.

A number of algorithms have been developed to represent plausible transitions between motion clips with graph structures. With these techniques, novel motions can be generated simply by building walks on the graph. For off-line applications, where the full motion specification is known in advance, a global sub-optimal or close-to-optimal solution that minimizes an objective function, such as certain energy, can be found. In interactive applications, new input is continuously arriving and the decision for selecting the next clip needs to be made in a very short amount of time.

Therefore, only local search can be performed to generate motions in response to the dynamic 3D environments. The challenge for local search methods is to synthesize motions that require planning. Motion planning is important to achieve realistic results in many scenarios. For example, one may need to prepare well in advance to grasp an object at a particular location. Hence, first of all is to plan a total strategy of the action, then instead of trying to search a point-to-point path on the graph, we are going to face a dynamic changing 3D environment. Thus reinforcement learning techniques is used to train a motion controller off-line, which can make on-line decision quickly in any given situation. Some methods have been proposed in computer animation to utilize reinforcement learning to obtain policies for choosing actions that will increase long term expected rewards.

Thus, the whole motion can be separate into different clips. i.e. if the avatar want to go through a environment with kinds of 3D objects, its motion can be performed as Figure 6 (Cal3D) (Delta3D) shows.

The Simple Actions and Complex Behaviors of Intelligent Avatars

Recognition of the environment and organizing the actions based on it is an elementary portion of 3D avatars complex behaviors.

Figure 5. The framework of the whole procedure of an avatar's actions in the 3D graphical environments

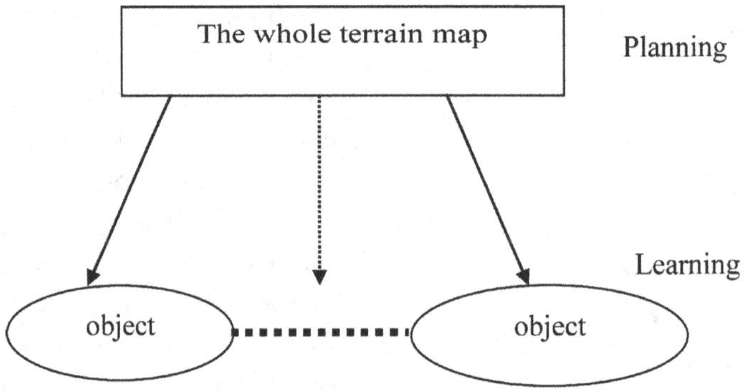

```
        ┌─────────────────────────┐
        │   The whole terrain map  │      Planning
        └─────────────────────────┘
                                            Learning

    ╭──────────╮              ╭──────────╮
    │  object  │•••••••••••••••│  object  │
    ╰──────────╯              ╰──────────╯
```

Figure 6. The avatar interacts with 3D environment – She walks in a 3D graphical environment, gets her object and achieves the mission automatically

We have obtained some achievements on both the reinforcement learning of virtual human's action and automatically recognizing the 3D objects by their shapes methods (Anguelov, 2005) (J. Fehr, 2007) (Robert Osad, 2002) (Ryutarou Ohbuchi, Shape-Similarity Search of 3D Models by using Enhanced Shape Functions, 2005).

In the study of the shape similarity recognition of 3D objects (Ryutarou Ohbuchi, Shape-Similarity Search of 3D Models by using Enhanced, 2005) (Robert Osad, 2002), the first step is to extract robust, concise, yet expressive shape features, and on the development of similarity (or, dissimilarity) comparison methods that conform well to the human notion of shape similarity.

In developing the shape features for 3D models, we first have to decide which class of 3D shape representation we are targeting. A 3D shape may be defined by using any of a number of shape representations, many of which are not mutually compatible. Some of the shape representations are mathematically well founded, allowing for computations of such well-defined properties as volume, surface curvature, or surface (or volume) topology. Unfortunately, since most 3D model formats (VRML, 3D Studio, etc.) have been designed for visualization, they contain only geometric and appearance attributes, and usually lack semantic information to be recognized. A great part of shape representations is not good. For example, a polygon-soup model is a topologically disconnected collection of independent polygons and/or polygonal meshes. Neither volume nor surface curvature can be computed for the model easily. The second step is to classify the features of shapes that have been extracted from the 3D

Figure 7. The different 3D graphical objects with their own feature histograms

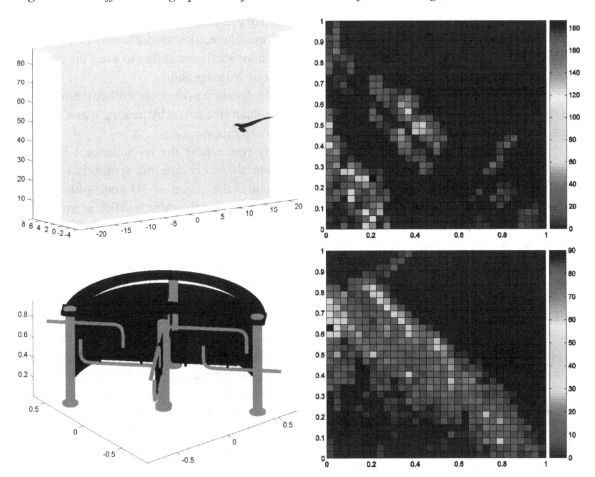

models. Because the shapes seldom have any topology or solid model information; they rarely are manifold; and most are not even self-consistent, it is important to separate them on their features (Robert Osad, 2002).

A method is needed for computing 3D shape signatures and dissimilarity measures for arbitrary objects described by possibly degenerate 3D polygonal models. The object is to represent the signature of a 3D model on measuring global geometric properties of the object. We presented methods to describe the features of models and reduce the dimensionality of them to use them in the 3D animation system.

A specific norm is used to measure the distance between the points of the surface of model and inner product to describe the orientation between them.

Then, the shape histogram is constructed to present the feature of the shapes. The main steps of construction:

1. Get the feature: Randomly choose points from the surface of the 3D models, calculate the distances (and inner product);

2. Dimension reduction: Reducing the hi-dimension feature by projecting it from high dimensional space to low dimensional space;

3. Make Histogram: After reduction, using coefficients to build shape histogram as Figure 7 shows.

The recognition algorithm s, e.g. SVM-based classification strategies can be used to class feature sets to semantically classify regions in graphical 3D models. During training procedure, we compute a large amount of surface Points features with various combinations from parameter space. We apply different kernels to select the most discriminating features. Related parameters are determined by observing the result of the procedure.

Depends on the recognition of models and controlling algorithms for virtual human, we synthesized a 3D animation as Figrue4 shows. Our virtual human can recognize the bug in the 3D environment and go to kick it automatically.

FUTURE RESEARCH DIRECTIONS

Based on the MDP and reinforcement areas, in the next step, we are going to:

- Construct more general framework of state and action space to describe the actions of virtual human based on the hierarchical reinforcement model to instruct wider kinds of their actions.
- Construct basis functions from spectral analysis of diffusion operators where the resulting representations are constructed without explicitly taking rewards into account.

CONCLUSION

Provide discussion of the overall coverage of the chapter and concluding remarks.

This chapter discusses a method for creating virtual human in the 3D graphical environment with learning ability for 3D animation. The example takes different 3D avatars which have different abilities to show different performance

as the environment is dynamically changing. The result of blending actions animation presents that the virtual human has a more human-like behavior and more intelligent ability to adapt the environment by learning ability.

We discuss a work of controlling the motion of 3D human-like avatar by treating it as a Markov Decision Process.

By researching the reinforcement learning, we are able to choose the appropriate method to control the action of 3D human-like avatar. Besides, to treat the value function as a manifold which depends on the states and actions is proved to be an effective way to improve the Q function in the training process.

There are many opportunities to improve the techniques presented here. First, according to the shapes of manifolds, there will be many powerful methods to improve the performance of the learning algorithm. Second, if the virtual human can independently recognizes or classifies the objects and behaves in different way according to them, the system will be much better.

In this case, instead of making the animations frame by frame, the intelligent 3D avatar would be a powerful tool to achieve the work. Moreover, a more effective machine learning algorithm is one of the key parts of this area.

REFERENCES

Andrieu, C. (2003). An introduction to MCMC for machine learning. *Machine Learning*, *50*(1), 5–43. doi:10.1023/A:1020281327116

Anguelov, D. S. (2005). Shape completion and animation of people. *Proceedings of SIGGRAPH*, *05*, 408–416.

Badler, N. I. (1993). *Simulating humans: Computer graphics, animation, and control*. Oxford University Press.

Badler, N. I. (2002). Representing and parameterizing agent behaviors. *Proceedings of Computer Animation, 02*, 133–143.

Cal3D. (n.d.). Retrieved from http://gna.org/projects/cal3d

Chen, D. Y., & Tian, X.-P. (2003). Visual similarity based 3D model retrieval. *EUROGRAPHICS, 2003*, 223–232.

Conde, T. (2006). An integrated perception for autonomous virtual agents: Active and predictive perception. *Computer Animation and Virtual Worlds, 17*(3-4).

Delta3D. (n.d.). Retrieved from http://www.delta3d.org

Fehr, H. B. (2007). *Harmonic shape histograms for 3D shape classification and retrieval*. MVA2007 IAPR Conference on Machine Vision Applications, Tokyo.

Kakade, S. (2002). A natural policy gradient. *Proceedings of Neural Information Processing Systems*.

Molet, T. (1996). A real-time anatomical converter for human motion capture. *Eurographics Workshop on Computer Animation and Simulation*, (pp. 79-94).

Osada, R. (2002). Shape distributions. *ACM Transactions on Graphics, 21*(4), 807–832. doi:10.1145/571647.571648

Perkins, T. J. (2002). Lyapunov design for safe reinforcement learning. *Machine Learning Research, 3*, 803–832.

Peters, J., et al. (2003). Reinforcement learning for humanoid robots. *Proceedings of the Third IEEE-RAS International Conference on Humanoid Robots*.

Prabhu, N. U. (2007). *Stochastic process basic theory and its applications*. World Scientific.

Ryutarou Ohbuchi, T. M. (2005). Shape-similarity search of 3D models by using enhanced shape functions. *International Journal of Computer Applications in Technology, 23*(2-4), 70–85. doi:10.1504/IJCAT.2005.006466

Schneider, J. B. (2003). Covariant policy search. *Proceedings of the International Joint Conference on Artificial Intelligence*, (pp. 1019—1024).

Sutton, R. S. (1998). *Reinforcement learning - An introduction*. MIT Press.

Yuan, Y. T. (2009). *Wavelet theory approach to pattern recognition*. Hong Kong: World Scientific Publishing Company.

Compilation of References

Aberkane, S., Sauter, D., & Ponsart, J. C. (2007). Output feedback stochastic H stabilization of networked fault-tolerant control systems. *Systems and Control Engineering, 221*, 927–935. doi:10.1243/09596518JSCE352

Abonyi, J., Nemeth, S., Vincze, C., & Arva, P. (2003). Process analysis and product quality estimation by self-organizing maps with an application to polyethylene production. *Computers in Industry, 52*(3), 221–234. doi:10.1016/S0166-3615(03)00128-3

Acar, E. U., Choset, H., & Lee, J. Y. (2006). Sensor-based coverage with extended range detectors. *IEEE Transactions on Robotics, 22*(1), 189–198. doi:10.1109/TRO.2005.861455

Achten, H. H., & Jessurun, A. J. (2002). An agent framework for recognition of graphic units in drawings. In *Proceedings of 20th International Conference on Education and Research in Computer Aided Architectural Design in Europe* (pp. 246-253). Warsaw.

Agrawal, R., & Srikant, R. (1994). Fast algorithms for mining association rules in large databases. *20th International Conference on Very Large Data Bases* (pp. 487-499).

Aguilera, P. A., Fernández, A., Reche, F., & Rumí, R. (2010). Hybrid Bayesian network classifiers: Application to species distribution models. *Environmental Modelling & Software, 25*(12), 1630–1639. doi:10.1016/j.envsoft.2010.04.016

Aha, W., & Albert, M. (1991). Instance-based learning algorithms. *Machine Learning, 6*, 37–66. doi:10.1007/BF00153759

Aho, A. V., Sethi, R., & Ullman, J. D. (1986). *Compilers: Principles, techniques and tools*. Addison-Wesley.

Albazzaz, H., & Wang, X. Z. (2006). Historical data analysis based on plots of independent and parallel coordinates and statistical control limits. *Journal of Process Control, 16*(2), 103–114. doi:10.1016/j.jprocont.2005.05.005

Alcalá, R., Alcalá-Fdez, J., Gacto, M. J., & Herrera, F. (2007). Genetic learning of membership functions for mining fuzzy association rules. *16th IEEE International Conference on Fuzzy Systems* (pp. 1-6).

Alexe, A., Gaildrat, V., & Barthe, L. (2004). Interactive modelling from sketches using spherical implicit functions. In *Proceedings of the 3rd International Conference on Computer Graphics, Virtual Reality, Visualisation and Interaction in Africa* (pp. 25-34). Stellenbosch, South Africa: ACM.

Alhajj, R., & Elnagar, A. (2005). Multiagents to separating handwritten connected digits. *IEEE Transactions on Systems, Man, and Cybernetics. Part A, Systems and Humans, 35*(5), 593–602. doi:10.1109/TSMCA.2005.843389

Alhoniemi, E., Hollmén, J., Simula, O., & Vesanto, J. (1999). Process monitoring and modeling using the self-organizing map. *Integrated Computer-Aided Engineering, 6*(1), 3.

Al-Mallahi, A., Kataoka, T., Okamoto, H., & Shibata, Y. (2010). Detection of potato tubers using an ultraviolet imaging-based machine vision system. *Biosystems Engineering, 105*(2), 257–265. doi:10.1016/j.biosystemseng.2009.11.004

Ammar, K., McKee, M., & Kaluarachchi, J. (2011). Bayesian method for groundwater quality monitoring network analysis. *Journal of Water Resources Planning and Management, 137*(1), 51–61. doi:10.1061/(ASCE)WR.1943-5452.0000043

Andersson, L. B., & Whitaker, B. A. (1982). *NASA catalogue of lunar nomenclature* (p. 1097). NASA Reference Publication.

Andrieu, C. (2003). An introduction to MCMC for machine learning. *Machine Learning, 50*(1), 5–43. doi:10.1023/A:1020281327116

Anguelov, D. S. (2005). Shape completion and animation of people. *Proceedings of SIGGRAPH, 05*, 408–416.

Antal, P., Fannes, G., Timmerman, D., Moreau, Y., & De-Moor, B. (2003). Bayesian applications of belief networks and multilayer perceptrons for ovarian tumor classification with rejection. *Artificial Intelligence in Medicine, 29*, 39–60. doi:10.1016/S0933-3657(03)00053-8

Apresjan, J. D. (Ed.). (1988). *Linguistic supporting of the system STAGE-2*. Moscow, Russia: Science. (in Russian)

Apte, A., Vo, V., & Kimura, T. D. (1993). Recognising multistroke geometric shapes: An experimental evaluation. In *Proceedings of the ACM (UIST'93)* (pp. 121-128). Atlanta, Georgia.

Ariana, D., Lu, R., & Guyer, D. (2006). Near-infrared hyperspectral reflectance imaging for detection of bruises on pickling cucumbers. *Computers and Electronics in Agriculture, 53*(1), 60–70. doi:10.1016/j.compag.2006.04.001

Arkin, R. C. (1989). Motor schema based mobile robot navigation. *The International Journal of Robotics Research, 8*(4), 92–112. doi:10.1177/027836498900800406

Armañanzas, R. (2009). *Consensus policies to solve bioinformatic problems through Bayesian network classifiers and estimation of distribution algorithms*. Department of Computer Science and Artificial Intelligence, University of the Basque Country.

Armañanzas, R., Inza, I., & Larrañaga, P. (2008). Detecting reliable gene interactions by a hierarchy of Bayesian network classifiers. *Computer Methods and Programs in Biomedicine, 91*(2), 110–121. doi:10.1016/j.cmpb.2008.02.010

Assfalg, J., Bertini, M., Colombo, C., Bimbo, A. D., & Nunziati, W. (2003). Semantic annotation of soccer videos: Automatic highlights identification. *Computer Vision and Image Understanding, 92*(2-3), 285–305. doi:10.1016/j.cviu.2003.06.004

Asunction, A., & Newman, D. J. (2007). *UCI Machine Learning repository*.

Avilés-Arriaga, H. H., Sucar, L. E., & Mendoza, C. E. (2006). Visual recognition of similar gestures. *Proceedings of the 18th International Conference on Pattern Recognition - ICPR'06*.

Avilés-Arriaga, H. H., & Sucar, L. E. (2002). Dynamic Bayesian networks for visual recognition of dynamic gestures. *Journal of Intelligent and Fuzzy Systems, 12*(3-4), 243–250.

Axelson, D. E., Standal, I. B., Martinez, I., & Aursand, M. (2009). Classification of wild and farmed salmon using Bayesian belief networks and gas chromatography-derived fatty acid distributions. *Journal of Agricultural and Food Chemistry, 57*(17), 7634–7639. doi:10.1021/jf9013235

Azar, S., Couvreur, L., Delfosse, V., Jaspart, B., & Boulanger, C. (2006). An agent-based multimodal interface for sketch interpretation. In *IEEE Workshop on Multimedia Signal Processing* (pp. 488-492). New York, NY: IEEE.

Badler, N. I. (1993). *Simulating humans: Computer graphics, animation, and control*. Oxford University Press.

Badler, N. I. (2002). Representing and parameterizing agent behaviors. *Proceedings of Computer Animation, 02*, 133–143.

Baikov, A. M., Kuzin, E. S., Khakhalin, G. K., & Shamis, A. L. (1980). The context task-oriented analysis of images in terms of semantic network. *Questions of Radio Electronics* [in Russian]. *Topical GT, 1*, 50–58.

Balch, T., & Arkin, R. C. (1999). Behaviour-based formation control for multi-robot teams. *IEEE Transactions on Robotics and Automation, 20*, 1–15.

Baluja, S. (1998). Probabilistic modeling for face orientation discrimination: Learning from labelled and unlabelled data. In *Neural Information Procesing systems (NIPS '98)*, (pp. 854–860).

Baranowski, P., Lipecki, J., Mazurek, W., & Walczak, R. T. (2008). Detection of watercore in 'Gloster' apples using thermography. *Postharvest Biology and Technology, 47*, 358–366. doi:10.1016/j.postharvbio.2007.07.014

Barata, T., Alves, E. I., Saraiva, J., & Pina, P. (2004). Automatic recognition of impact craters on the surface of Mars. *ICIAR*, *2*, 489–496.

Barlow, N. G. (1988). Crater size-distributions and a revised martian relative. *Icarus*, *75*(2), 285–305. doi:10.1016/0019-1035(88)90006-1

Barr, R. E. (2004). The current status of graphical communication in engineering education. In *34th ASEE/IEEE Frontiers in Education Conference: Vol. 3* (pp. S1D8-S1D13). Savannah.

Barreto, G. A. (2007). Time series prediction with the self-organizing map: A review. *Perspectives of Neural-Symbolic Integration*, *77*, 135–158. doi:10.1007/978-3-540-73954-8_6

Bashmakov, A. I., & Bashmakov, I. A. (2006). *Intellectual information technologies*. Moscow, Russia: Published by Moscow State Technical University. (in Russian)

Batalin, M. A., & Sukhatme, G. S. (2002). Spreading out: A local approach to multi-robot coverage. In *Proceedings of the 6th International Symposium on Distributed Autonomous Robotics Systems*, (pp. 373-382).

Batalin, M. A., & Sukhatme, G. S. (2003). Dynamic coverage via multi-robot cooperation. In *Proceedings on Multi-Robot Systems Workshop at Naval Research Laboratory*, Washington DC, March 17-19, (pp. 295-296).

Becker, B., Kohavi, R., & Sommerfield, D. (1997). *Visualizing the simple Bayesian classier.* In KDD Workshop on Issues in the Integration of Data Mining and Data Visualization. Menlo Park, CA: AAAI Press.

Belkin, M., & Niyogi, P. (2003). Laplacian eigenmaps for dimensionality reduction and data representation. *Neural Computation*, *15*(6), 1373–1396. doi:10.1162/089976603321780317

Bellifemine, F., Poggi, A., & Rimassa, G. (2001). Developing multi-agent systems with JADE. In *Intelligent Agents VII Agent Theories Architectures and Languages* (*Vol. 1986*, pp. 42–47). Berlin, Germany: Springer. doi:10.1007/3-540-44631-1_7

Belongie, S., Malik, J., & Puzicha, J. (2002). Shape matching and object recognition using shape contexts. *IEEE Transactions on Pattern Analysis and Machine Intelligence*, *4*(24), 509–522. doi:10.1109/34.993558

Bendaoud, R., & Hacene, M. Rouane, Toussaint, Y., Delecroix, B., & Napoli, A. (2007). *Text-based ontology construction using relational concept analysis*. In International Workshop on Ontology Dynamics. Innsbruck, Austria.

Bennedsen, B. S., & Peterson, D. L. (2005). Performance of a system for apple surface defect identification in near-infrared images. *Biosystems Engineering*, *90*(4), 419–431. doi:10.1016/j.biosystemseng.2004.12.005

Bennedsen, B. S., Peterson, D. L., & Tabb, A. (2005). Identifying defects in images of rotating apples. *Computers and Electronics in Agriculture*, *48*, 92–102. doi:10.1016/j.compag.2005.01.003

Beyer, M., Hahn, R., Peschel, S., Harz, M., & Knoche, M. (2002). Analysing fruit shape in sweet cherry (*Prunus avium* L.). *Scientia Horticulturae*, *96*, 139–150. doi:10.1016/S0304-4238(02)00123-1

Bielza, C., Li, G., & Larrañaga, P. (2011). Multi-dimensional classification with Bayesian networks. *International Journal of Approximate Reasoning*, *52*(6). doi:10.1016/j.ijar.2011.01.007

Bilmes, J. (1997). *A gentle tutorial on the EM algorithm and its application to parameter estimation for gaussian mixture and hidden Markov models*. ICSI-Report-97-021.

Bishop, C. (1995). *Neural networks for pattern recognition*. Oxford University Press.

Blasco, J. (2001). *Concepción de un sistema de visión artificial multiespectral para la detección e identificación de daños en cítricos*. PhD thesis, Valencia.

Blasco, J., Aleixos, N., Cubero, S., Gómez-Sanchis, J., & Moltó, E. (2009b). Automatic sorting of Satsuma (*Citrus unshiu*) segments using computer vision and morphological features. *Computers and Electronics in Agriculture*, *66*, 1–8. doi:10.1016/j.compag.2008.11.006

Blasco, J., Aleixos, N., Gómez-Sanchis, J., Guerrero, J. F., & Moltó, E. (2009d). A survey of Bayesian techniques in computer vision for agricultural and agro-industrial applications. In Soria, E., Martín, J. D., Magdalena, R., Martínez, M., & Serrano, A. J. (Eds.), *Handbook of research on machine learning applications and trends: Algorithms, methods and techniques* (pp. 482–498). Hershey, PA: IGI Global. doi:10.4018/978-1-60566-766-9.ch023

Blasco, J., Aleixos, N., Gómez-Sanchis, J., & Moltó, E. (2009a). Recognition and classification of external skin damage in citrus fruits using multispectral data and morphological features. *Biosystems Engineering, 103*, 137–145. doi:10.1016/j.biosystemseng.2009.03.009

Blasco, J., Aleixos, N., & Moltó, E. (2003). Machine vision system for automatic quality grading of fruit. *Biosystems Engineering, 85*(4), 415–423. doi:10.1016/S1537-5110(03)00088-6

Blasco, J., Aleixos, N., & Moltó, E. (2007a). Computer vision detection of peel defects in citrus by means of a region oriented segmentation algorithm. *Journal of Food Engineering, 81*, 535–543. doi:10.1016/j.jfoodeng.2006.12.007

Blasco, J., Cubero, S., Gómez-Sanchis, J., Mira, P., & Moltó, E. (2009c). Development of a machine for the automatic sorting of pomegranate (*Punica granatum* L) arils based on computer vision. *Journal of Food Engineering, 90*, 27–34. doi:10.1016/j.jfoodeng.2008.05.035

Bloomenthal, M., Zeleznik, R., Cutts, M., Fish, R., Drake, S., Holden, L., & Fuchs, H. (1998). Sketch-n-make: Automated machining of CAD sketches. In *Proceedings of ASME Design Engineering Technical Conferences, Computers in Engineering* (pp. 1-11).

Blum, A., & Mitchell, T. (1998). Combining labeled and unlabeled data with co-training. *Proceedings of 11th COLT Conference* (pp. 92-100).

Borchani, H., Bielza, C., & Larrañaga, P. (2010). Learning CB-decomposable multi-dimensional Bayesian network classifiers. *Proceedings of the 5th European Workshop on Probabilistic Graphical Models (PGM'10)*.

Bosnić, Z., & Kononenko, I. (2007). Estimation of individual prediction reliability using the local sensitivity analysis. *Applied Intelligence, 29*(3), 187–203. doi:10.1007/s10489-007-0084-9

Bosnić, Z., & Kononenko, I. (2008). Comparison of approaches for estimating reliability of individual regression predictions. *Data & Knowledge Engineering, 67*(3), 504–516. doi:10.1016/j.datak.2008.08.001

Bosnić, Z., Kononenko, I., Robnik-Šikonja, M., & Kukar, M. (2003). Evaluation of prediction reliability in regression using the transduction principle. In Zajc, B., & Tkalčič, M. (Eds.), *Proceedings of Eurocon 2003* (pp. 99–103). doi:10.1109/EURCON.2003.1248158

Bousquet, O., & Elisseeff, A. (2000). Algorithmic stability and generalization performance. In *Neural Information Processing Systems*, (pp. 196–202).

Bousquet, O., & Elisseeff, A. (2002). Stability and generalization. *Journal of Machine Learning Research, 2*, 499–526.

Bousquet, O., & Pontil, M. (2003). Leave-one-out error and stability of learning algorithms with applications. In Suykens, J. (Eds.), *Advances in learning theory: Methods, models and applications*. IOS Press.

Boyles, S. F. D., & Waller, S. T. (2007). *A naïve Bayesian classifer for incident duration prediction*. TRB - Transportation Research Board - Annual Meeting, Washington D.C.

Brand, M., Oliver, N., & Pentland, A. (1997). *Coupled hidden Markov models for complex action recognition*. Paper presented at the IEEE International Conference on Computer Vision and Pattern Recognition.

Brand, M. (1999). Structure learning in conditional probability models via an entropic prior and parameter extinction. *Neural Computation, 11*(5), 1155–1182. doi:10.1162/089976699300016395

Brechbuhler, C., Gerig, G., & Kubler, O. (1995). Parametrization of closed surfaces for 3-D shape description. *Computer Vision Graphics and Image Processing, 61*, 154–170. doi:10.1006/cviu.1995.1013

Breierova, L., & Choudhari, M. (1996). *An introduction to sensitivity analysis*. MIT System Dynamics in Education Project.

Breiman, L. (1996). Bagging predictors. *Machine Learning, 24*(2), 123–140. doi:10.1007/BF00058655

Breiman, L. (2001). Random forests. *Machine Learning, 45*(1), 5–32. doi:10.1023/A:1010933404324

Breiman, L., Friedman, J. H., Olshen, R. A., & Stone, C. J. (1984). *Classification and regression trees*. Belmont, CA: Wadsworth International Group.

Bressan, G. M., Oliveira, V. A., Hruschka, E. R. Jr, & Nicoletti, M. C. (2009). Using Bayesian networks with rule extraction to infer the risk of weed infestation in a corncrop. *Engineering Applications of Artificial Intelligence*, *22*(4-5), 579–592. doi:10.1016/j.engappai.2009.03.006

Brooks, R. A. (1986). Robust layered control system for a mobile robot. *IEEE Journal on Robotics and Automation*, *2*, 1–14. doi:10.1109/JRA.1986.1087032

Brubaker, M., & Fleet, D. (2008). *The kneed walker for human pose tracking.* Paper presented at the IEEE Conference on Computer Vision and Pattern Recognition.

Brubaker, M., Fleet, D., & Hertzmann, A. (2007). *Physics-based person tracking using simplified lower-body dynamics.* Paper presented at the IEEE Conference on Computer Vision and Pattern Recognition.

Brubaker, M. A., Fleet, D. J., & Hertzmann, A. (2010). Physics-based person tracking using the anthropomorphic walker. *International Journal of Computer Vision*, *87*, 140–155. doi:10.1007/s11263-009-0274-5

Brucker, F., Benites, F., & Sapozhnikova, E. (2011). Multi-label classification and extracting predicted class hierarchies. *Pattern Recognition*, *44*(3), 724–738. doi:10.1016/j.patcog.2010.09.010

Bryll, R., Rose, R. T., & Quek, F. (2005). Agent-based gesture tracking. *IEEE Transactions on Systems Man and Cybernetics Part a-Systems and Humans, 35*(6), 795-810.

Bullo, F., & Cortes, J. (2005). Adaptive and distributed coordination algorithms for mobile sensing networks. In V. Kumar, N. E. Leonard & A.S. Morse, (Eds.), *Proceedings of the 2003 Block Island Workshop on Cooperative Control, Lecture Notes in Control and Information Sciences*, Vol. 309, (pp. 43-62). New York, NY: Springer Verlag.

Burgard, W., Fox, D., Moors, M., Simmons, R., & Thrun, S. (2000). Collaborative multi-robot exploration. In *Proceedings of the IEEE International Conference on Robotics and Automation (ICRA),* (pp. 476-481).

Burl, M. C., Stough, T., Colwell, W., Bierhaus, E. B., Merline, W. J., & Chapman, C. (2001). Automated detection of craters and other geological features. *International Symposium on Artificial Intelligence, Robotics, and Automations in Space,* Montreal.

Cal3D. (n.d.). Retrieved from http://gna.org/projects/cal3d

Calders, T., Goethals, B., & Mampaey, M. (2007). Mining itemsets in the presence of missing values. *2007 ACM Symposium on Applied Computing* (pp. 404-408).

Cardie, C. (1999). Guest editors' introduction: Machine learning and natural language. *Machine Learning*, *34*, 5–9. doi:10.1023/A:1007580931600

Cardoso-Cachopo, A., & Oliveira, A. (2007). Semi-supervised single-label text categorization using centroid-based classifiers. *ACM Symposium on Applied Computing* (pp. 844-851).

Card, S., Mackinlay, J., & Shneiderman, B. (1999). *Readings in information visualization. Using vision to think.* San Francisco, CA: Morgan Kaufmann Publishers.

Carney, J., & Cunningham, P. (1999). Confidence and prediction intervals for neural network ensembles. In *Proceedings of IJCNN '99, The International Joint Conference on Neural Networks*, Washington, USA, (pp. 1215–1218).

Casella, G., Deufemia, V., Mascardi, V., Gennaro, C., & Martelli, M. (2008). An agent-based framework for sketched symbol interpretation. *Journal of Visual Languages and Computing*, *19*(2), 225–257. doi:10.1016/j.jvlc.2007.04.002

Chang, C., & Lin, C. (2001). *LIBSVM: a library for support vector machines.* Retrieved from http://www.csie.ntu.edu.tw/~cjlin/libsvm/.

Chang, S.-F. (2002). The holy grail of content-based media analysis. *IEEE Multimedia Magazine*, *9*(2), 6–10. doi:10.1109/93.998041

Chen, C.-H., Hong, T.-P., & Tseng, V. S. (2008). A divide-and-conquer genetic-fuzzy mining approach for items with multiple minimum supports. *17th IEEE International Conference on Fuzzy Systems* (pp. 1231-1235).

Chen, J., Kim, M., Wang, Y., & Ji, Q. (2009). *Switching Gaussian process dynamic models to simultaneous composite motion tracking and recognition.* Paper presented IEEE Conference on Computer Vision and Pattern Recognition.

Chen, D. Y., & Tian, X.-P. (2003). Visual similarity based 3D model retrieval. *EUROGRAPHICS, 2003*, 223–232.

Cheng, Y., Johnson, A. E., Matthies, L. H., & Olson, C. F. (2002). Optical landmark detection for spacecraft navigation. *The 13th Annual AAS/AIAA Space Flight Mechanics Meeting*, (pp. 1785-1803). Puerto Rico.

Cheng, C.-C., & Hsu, C.-T. (2006). Fusion of audio and motion information on HMM-based highlight extraction for baseball games. *IEEE Transactions on Multimedia*, *8*(3), 585–599. doi:10.1109/TMM.2006.870726

Chetty, G., & Sharma, D. (2006). Distributed face recognition: A multiagent approach. In. *Proceedings of Knowledge-Based Intelligent Information and Engineering Systems*, *4253*, 1168–1175. doi:10.1007/11893011_148

Chmielewski, M. R., & Jerzy. (1996). Global discretization of continuous attributes as preprocessing for machine learning. *International Journal of Approximate Reasoning*, *15*(4), 319–331. doi:10.1016/S0888-613X(96)00074-6

Choi, N., Song, I. Y., & Han, H. (2006). A survey on ontology mapping. *SIGMOD Record*, *35*(3), 34–41. doi:10.1145/1168092.1168097

Cho, J., Principe, J. C., Erdogmus, D., & Motter, M. A. (2006). Modeling and inverse controller design for an unmanned aerial vehicle based on the self-organizing map. *IEEE Transactions on Neural Networks*, *17*(2), 445–460. doi:10.1109/TNN.2005.863422

Choset, H. (2000). Coverage of known spaces: The boustrophedon cellular decomposition. *Autonomous Robots*, *9*, 247–253. doi:10.1023/A:1008958800904

Choset, H. (2001). Coverage for robotics: A survey of recent results. *Annals of Mathematics and Artificial Intelligence*, *31*(1-4), 113–126. doi:10.1023/A:1016639210559

Chow, C. I., & Liu, C. N. (1968). Approximating discrete probability distributions with dependence trees. *IEEE Transactions on Information Theory*, *14*, 462–467. doi:10.1109/TIT.1968.1054142

Christianini, B., & Shawe-Taylor, J. (2000). *An introduction to support vector machines and other kernel-based learning methods*. Cambridge University Press.

Christiannini, N., & Shawe-Taylor, J. (2000). *Support vector machines and other kernel–based learning methods*. Cambridge University Press.

Cimiano, P. (2006). *Ontology learning and population from text. Algorithms, evaluation and applications*. Springer Science+Busivess Media, LLC.

Cimiano, P., Handschuh, S., & Staab, S. (2004). Towards the self-annotating Web. In S. Feldman, M. Uretski, M. Najork, & C. Wills (Eds.), *Proceedings of the 13th World Wide Web Conference* (pp. 462-471). ACM.

Cimiano, P., Hotho, A., & Staab, S. (2005, August). Learning concept hierarchies from text corpora using formal concept analysis. *Journal of Artificial Intelligence Research*, *24*, 305–339.

Cohen, F., & Sabastiani, F. (2004). An analysis of the relative hardness of reuters-21578 subsets. *Journal of the American Society for Information Science and Technology*, *56*(6), 584–596.

Collins, J. J., Ryan, C., & O'Neill, M. (1998). Grammatical evolution: Evolving programs for an arbitrary language. *Proceedings of the First European Workshop on Genetic Programming, Lecture Notes in Computer Science 1391*, (pp. 83-95). Springer-Verlag.

Conde, T. (2006). An integrated perception for autonomous virtual agents: Active and predictive perception. *Computer Animation and Virtual Worlds*, *17*(3-4).

Cooper, G. F., & Herskovits, E. (1992). A Bayesian method for the induction of probabilistic networks from data. *Machine Learning*, *9*, 309–347. doi:10.1007/BF00994110

Cootes, T., Taylor, C., Cooper, D., & Graham, J. (1995). Active shape models - Their training and application. *Computer Vision and Image Understanding*, *61*(1), 38–59. doi:10.1006/cviu.1995.1004

Cortes, J., Martinez, S., Karatas, T., & Bullo, F. (2004). Coverage control for mobile sensing networks. *IEEE Transactions on Robotics and Automation*, *20*(2), 243–255. doi:10.1109/TRA.2004.824698

Cowell, R. G., Dawid, P. A., Lauritzen, S. L., & Spiegelhalter, D. J. (2003). *Probabilistic networks and expert systems (information science and statistics)*. Springer.

Cubero, S., Aleixos, N., Moltó, E., Gómez-Sanchis, J., & Blasco, J. (2010). Advances in machine vision applications for automatic inspection and quality evaluation of fruits and vegetables. *Food and Bioprocess Technology*, *4*(4), 487–504. doi:10.1007/s11947-010-0411-8

Cunado, D., Nixon, M. S., & Carter, J. N. (2003). Automatic extraction and description of human gait models for recognition purposes. *Computer Vision and Image Understanding, 90*, 1–41. doi:10.1016/S1077-3142(03)00008-0

Dalal, P., Ju, L., McLaughlin, M., Zhou, X., Fujita, H., & Wang, S. (2009). 3D open-surface shape correspondence for statistical shape modeling: Identifying topologically consistent landmarks. In *IEEE International Conference on Computer Vision,* (pp. 1857-1864).

Dalal, P., Munsell, B., Wang, S., Tang, J., Oliver, K., & Ninomiya, H. … Fujita, H. (2007) A fast 3D correspondence method for statistical shape modeling. In *IEEE Conference on Computer Vision and Pattern Recognition,* (pp. 1-8).

Davies, R., Twining, C., Cootes, T., Waterton, J., & Taylor, C. (2002). A minimum description length approach to statistical shape modeling. *IEEE Transactions on Medical Imaging, 21*(5), 525–537. doi:10.1109/TMI.2002.1009388

de Sa, V. (1993). Learning classification with unlabelled data. In J. D. Cowan, G. Tesauro & J. Alspector, (Eds.), *Proceedings of NIPS'93, Neural Information Processing Systems,* (pp. 112–119). San Francisco, CA: Morgan Kaufmann Publishers.

de Waal, P. R., & van der Gaag, L. C. (2007). Inference and learning in multi-dimensional Bayesian network classifiers. *European Conference on Symbolic and Quantitative Approaches to Reasoning with Uncertainty* (Vol. 4724, pp. 501-511).

Deaton, A. (1997). *The analysis of household surveys: A microeconometric approach to development policy. World Bank.* Baltimore, MD: Johns Hopkins University Press.

DeGroot, M. H. (1970). *Optimal statistical decisions.* New York, NY: McGraw-Hill.

DeGroot, M. H. (2004). *Optimal statistical decisions.* Wiley-Interscience. doi:10.1002/0471729000

Delta3D. (n.d.). Retrieved from http://www.delta3d.org

Dempster, A. P., Laird, N. M., & Rubin, D. B. (1977). Maximum likelihood from incomplete data via the EM algorithm. *Journal of the Royal Statistical Society. Series B. Methodological, 39*(1), 1–38.

Department of Statistics at Carnegie Mellon University. (2005). *Statlib – Data, software and news from the statistics community.* Retrieved from http://lib.stat.cmu.edu/

Deutsch, P. (2008). Fault tolerant control system for linear combustion engine. *The 34th Annual Conference on Industrial Electronics* (pp. 198-203). Orlando, FL, USA

Diao, Y., & Passino, K. M. (2001). Stable fault-tolerant adaptive fuzzy/neural control for a turbine engine. *IEEE Transactions on Control Systems Technology, 9*, 494–509. doi:10.1109/87.918902

Díaz Blanco, I., Cuadrado Vega, A. A., Diez González, A. B., Loredo, L. R., Carrera, F. O., & Rodríguez, J. A. (2003). Visual predictive maintenance tool based on SOM projection techniques. *Revue de Metallurgie-Cahiers d Informations Techniques, 103*(3), 307–315.

Díaz Blanco, I., Domínguez González, M., Cuadrado, A. A., & Fuertes Martínez, J. J. (2008). A new approach to exploratory analysis of system dynamics using SOM. Applications to industrial processes. *Expert Systems with Applications, 34*(4), 2953–2965. doi:10.1016/j.eswa.2007.05.031

Díaz, G., Díaz Blanco, I., Arboleya, P., & Gómez-Aleixandre, J. (2006). Zero-sequence-based relaying technique for protecting power transformers and its performance assessment using unsupervised learning ANN. *European Transactions on Electrical Power, 16*(2), 147–160. doi:10.1002/etep.72

Díaz, R., Gil, L., Serrano, C., Blasco, M., Moltó, E., & Blasco, J. (2004). Comparison of three algorithms in the classification of table olives by means of computer vision. *Journal of Food Engineering, 61*, 101–107. doi:10.1016/S0260-8774(03)00191-2

Ding, W. S. (2010). *Automatic detection of craters in planetary images: An embedded framework using feature selection and boosting.* The 19th ACM International Conference on Information and Knowledge Management, Toronto, Canada.

Ding, W., Stepinski, T., Mu, Y., Bandeira, L., Vilalta, R., Wu, Y., et al. (2011). Sub-kilometer crater discovery with boosting and transfer learning. *ACM Transactions on Intelligent Systems and Technology, 2*(4).

Ding, Y., & Fan, G. (2006). *Camera view-based American football video analysis.* Paper presented at the Proc. the Eighth IEEE International Symposium on Multimedia.

Ding, Y., & Fan, G. (2007a). *Segmental hidden Markov models for view-based sport video analysis.* Paper presented at the IEEE International Conference on Computer Vision and Pattern Recognition.

Ding, Y., & Fan, G. (2007b). *Two-layer generative models for sport video mining.* Paper presented at the Proc. IEEE International Conference on Multimedia and Expo.

Ding, Y., & Fan, G. (2008). *Multi-channel segmental hidden Markov models for sports video mining.* Paper presented at the ACM Multimedia Conference.

Ding, Y., & Fan, G. (2009). Sports video mining via multi-channel segmental hidden Markov models. *IEEE Transactions on Multimedia, 11*(7).

Doan, A., Madhavan, J., Domingos, P., & Halevy, A. (2002). Learning to map between ontologies on the semantic web. In *Proceedings of the 11th International Conference on World Wide Web* (pp. 662–673). New York, NY: ACM.

Domingos, P., & Pazzani, M. J. (1996). *Beyond independence: Conditions for the optimality of the simple Bayesian classifier.* International Conference on Machine Learning.

Domínguez González, M., Fuertes Martínez, J. J., Reguera, P., Díaz Blanco, I., & Cuadrado Vega, A. A. (2007). Internet based remote supervision of industrial processes using self organizing maps. *Engineering Applications of Artificial Intelligence, 20*(6), 757–765. doi:10.1016/j.engappai.2006.11.017

Domínguez González, M., Fuertes, J. J., Reguera, P., González, J. J., & Ramón, J. M. (2004). Maqueta industrial para docencia e investigacion. *Revista Iberoamericana de Automática e Informática Industrial, 1*(1), 58–63.

Domínguez González, M., Reguera, P., & Fuertes, J. J. (2005). Laboratorio Remoto para la Enseñanza de la Automática en la Universidad de León (España). *Revista Iberoamericana de Automática e Informática Industrial, 2*(2), 36–45.

Donoho, D. L., & Grimes, C. (2003). Hessian eigenmaps: Locally linear embedding techniques for high-dimensional data. *Proceedings of the National Academy of Sciences of the United States of America, 100*(10), 5591. doi:10.1073/pnas.1031596100

Drucker, H. (1997). Improving regressors using boosting techniques. In *Proceedings of 14th International Conference on Machine Learning,* (pp. 107–115). Morgan Kaufmann.

Duan, L. Y., Xu, M., Chua, T. S., Tian, Q., & Xu, C. S. (2003). *A Mid-level Representation Framework for Semantic Sports Video Analysis.* Paper presented at the ACM Multimedia Conference.

Duan, L., Xu, M., Tian, Q., Xu, C., & Jin, S. J. (2005). A unified framework for semantic shot classification in sports video. *IEEE Transactions on Multimedia, 7*(6).

Duda, R. O., Hart, P. E., & Stork, D. G. (1973). *Pattern classification and scene analysis.* New York, NY: Wiley.

Dutton, J. E., & Ragins, B. R. (2007). Positive relationships at work: An introduction and invitation. In *Exploring positive relationships at work: Building a theoretical and research foundation* (pp. 3–25). Mahwah, NJ: Lawrence Erlbaum Associates Publishers.

Earl, J., Chicarro, A. F., Koeberl, C., Marchetti, P. G., & Milnes, M. (2005). *Automatic recognition of crater-like structures in terrestrial and planetary images.* 36th Annual Lunar and Planetary Science Conference, League City.

Eckert, J., & Eaks, I. (1989). *Postharvest disorders and diseases of citrus. The citrus industry.* University California Press.

Ek, C. H., Torr, P., & Lawrence, N. (2007). *Gaussian process latent variable models for human pose estimation.* Paper presented at the Conference on Machine Learning and Multimodal Interaction.

Ekin, A., Tekalp, A., & Mehrotra, R. (2003). Automatic soccer video analysis and summarization. *IEEE Transactions on Image Processing, 12*(7), 796–807. doi:10.1109/TIP.2003.812758

Elgammal, A., & Lee, C.-S. (2004a). *Inferring 3D body pose from silhouettes using activity manifold learning.* Paper presented at the IEEE Conference on Computer Vision and Pattern Recognition.

Elgammal, A., & Lee, C.-S. (2004b). *Separating style and content on a nonlinear manifold.* Paper presented at the IEEE Conference on Computer Vision and Pattern Recognition.

Elgammal, A., & Lee, C.-S. (2009). Tracking people on torus. *IEEE Transactions on Pattern Analysis and Machine Intelligence, 31,* 520–538. doi:10.1109/TPAMI.2008.101

ElMasry, G., Wang, N., ElSayed, A., & Ngadi, M. (2007). Hyperspectral imaging for nondestructive determination of some quality attributes for strawberry. *Journal of Food Engineering, 81,* 98–107. doi:10.1016/j.jfoodeng.2006.10.016

ElMasry, G., Wang, N., & Vigneault, C. (2009). Detecting chilling injury in Red Delicious apple using hyperspectral imaging and neural networks. *Postharvest Biology and Technology, 52,* 1–8. doi:10.1016/j.postharvbio.2008.11.008

Emelyanov, G. M., & Mikhailov, D. V. (2005). Updating the language knowledge base in the problem of equivalence analysis of semantic images of statements. *Pattern Recognition and Image Analysis, 15*(2), 384–386.

Erives, H., & Fitzgerald, G. (2005). Automated registration of hyperspectral images for precision agriculture. *Computers and Electronics in Agriculture, 47,* 103–119. doi:10.1016/j.compag.2004.11.016

Farhangfar, A., Kurgan, L., & Dy, J. (2008). Impact of imputation of missing values on classification error for discrete data. *Pattern Recognition, 41*(12), 3692–3705. doi:10.1016/j.patcog.2008.05.019

Farrell, J. A., Berger, T., & Appleby, B. D. (1993). Using learning techniques to accommodate unanticipated faults. *IEEE Control Systems Magazine, 13,* 40–49. doi:10.1109/37.214943

Fehr, H. B. (2007). *Harmonic shape histograms for 3D shape classification and retrieval.* MVA 2007 IAPR Conference on Machine Vision Applications, Tokyo.

Fenton, N. E., & Neil, M. (2007). *Managing risk in the modern world: Bayesian networks and the applications.* London, UK: London Mathematical Society, Knowledge Transfer Report.

Ferguson, E. S. (1994). *Engineering and the mind's eye.* The MIT Press.

Fernandes, J. A., Irigoien, X., Goikoetxea, N., Lozano, J. A., Inza, I., & Perez, A. (2010). Fish recruitment prediction, using robust supervised classification methods. *Ecological Modelling, 221*(2), 338–352. doi:10.1016/j.ecolmodel.2009.09.020

Fernández, A., & Salmerón, A. (2008). Extension of Bayesian network classifiers to regression problems. *Proceedings of the 11th Ibero-American conference on AI: Advances in Artificial Intelligence.*

Fernandez, A., & Salmeron, A. (2008). BayesChess: A computer chess program based on Bayesian networks. *Pattern Recognition Letters, 29*(8), 1154–1159. doi:10.1016/j.patrec.2007.06.013

Fernández, L., Castillero, C., & Aguilera, J. M. (2005). An application of image analysis to dehydration of apple discs. *Journal of Food Engineering, 67,* 185–193. doi:10.1016/j.jfoodeng.2004.05.070

Fernandez-Pacheco, D. G. (2010). *Aplicación para reconocimiento de bocetos basada en sistemas multi-agente.* Unpublished Doctoral dissertation, Technical University of Valencia, Valencia.

Fernández-Pacheco, D. G., Albert, F., Aleixos, N., Conesa, J., & Contero, M. (2011). Automated tuning of parameters for the segmentation of freehand sketches. In *Proceedings of the International Conference on Computer Graphics Theory and Applications (GRAP 2011)* (pp. 321-329). Algarve, Portugal.

Fernandez-Pacheco, D. G., Conesa, J., & Aleixos, N. (2010). A new agent-based paradigm for recognition of free-hand sketches. In *Proceedings of International Conference on Computational Science - ICCS 2010: Vol. 1* (pp. 2007-2016).

Fernandez-Pacheco, D. G., Contero, M., Naya, F., & Aleixos, N. (2008). A calligraphic interface in a sketch-based modelling environment. In *20° Congreso Internacional de Ingenieria Grafica INGEGRAF.* Valencia.

Fernandez-Pacheco, D. C., Conesa, J., Aleixos, N., Company, P., & Contero, M. (2009). An agent-based paradigm for free-hand sketch recognition. In *AI*IA 2009 (Vol. 5883*, pp. 345–354). Emergent Perspectives in Artificial Intelligence. doi:10.1007/978-3-642-10291-2_35

Ferreira de Oliveira, M. C., & Levkowitz, H. (2003). From visual data exploration to visual data mining: a survey. *IEEE Transactions on Visualization and Computer Graphics, 9*(3), 378–394. doi:10.1109/TVCG.2003.1207445

FIPA, O. R. G. (2002). *FIPA ACL message structure specification*.

Flanagan, M., & McClure, S. (2002). SYSTRAN and the reinvention of MT. *IDC Bulletin #26459*.

Flasinski, M., Jurek, J., & Myslinski, S. (2009). Multi-agent system for recognition of hand postures. In *Computational Science* (*Vol. 5545*, pp. 815–824). ICCS. doi:10.1007/978-3-642-01973-9_91

Flesch, I., Fernández, A., & Salmerón, A. (2007). Incremental supervised classification for the MTE distribution: A preliminary study. *Actas de Simposio de Inteligencia Computacional, SICO'2007*.

Flores, M. J., Gámez, J. A., Martínez, A. M., & Puerta, J. M. (2009a). *GAODE and HAODE: Two proposals based on AODE to deal with continuous variables*. International Conference on Machine Learning - ICML.

Flores, M. J., Gámez, J. A., Martínez, A. M., & Puerta, J. M. (2009b). *HODE: Hidden one-dependence estimator*. European Conference on Symbolic and Quantitative Approaches to Reasoning with Uncertainty.

Flores, J. L., Inza, I., & Larrañaga, P. (2007). Wrapper discretization by means of estimation of distribution algorithms. *Intelligent Data Analysis, 11*(5), 525–545.

Flores, M. J., Gámez, J. A., Martínez, A. M., & Puerta, J. M. (2011). Handling numeric attributes when comparing Bayesian classifiers: Does the discretization method matter? *Applied Intelligence, 34*(3), 372–385. doi:10.1007/s10489-011-0286-z

Fonseca, M. J., & Jorge, J. (2000). Using fuzzy logic to recognise geometric shapes interactively. In *Proceedings of 9th IEEE Conference on Fuzzy Systems: Vol. 1* (pp. 291-296). San Antonio, Texas.

Freund, Y., & Schapire, R. (1995). A decision-theoretic generalization of on-line learning and an application to boosting. *Computational Learning Theory: Eurocolt*, (pp. 23-37).

Freund, Y., & Schapire, R. (1997). A decision-theoretic generalization of on-line learning and an application to boosting. *Journal of Computer and System Sciences, 55*(1), 119–139. doi:10.1006/jcss.1997.1504

Friedman, N., Geiger, D., & Goldszmidt, M. (1997). Bayesian network classifiers. *Machine Learning, 29*, 131–163. doi:10.1023/A:1007465528199

Friedman, N., & Koller, D. (2003). Being Bayesian about network structure. A Bayesian approach to structure discovery in Bayesian networks. *Machine Learning, 50*(1), 95–125. doi:10.1023/A:1020249912095

Fuertes, J. J., Domínguez, M., Reguera, P., Prada, M. A., Díaz, I., & Cuadrado, A. A. (2010). Visual dynamic model based on self-organizing maps for supervision and fault detection in industrial processes. *Engineering Applications of Artificial Intelligence, 23*(1), 8–17. doi:10.1016/j.engappai.2009.06.001

Gaffney, J. (1973). Reflectance properties of citrus fruit. *Transactions of the ASAE. American Society of Agricultural Engineers, 16*(1), 310–314.

Gage, D. W. (1992). Command control for many-robot systems. *Unmanned Systems Magazine, 10*(4), 28–34.

Gales, M., & Young, S. (1993). *The theory of segmental hidden Markov models*. Technical Report CUED/F-INFENG/TR 133, Cambridge University.

Gámez, J. A., Mateo, J. L., & Puerta, J. M. (2006). Dependency networks based classifiers: Learning models by using independence. *Proceedings of the 3rd European Workshop on Probabilistic Graphical Models*.

Gámez, J. A., Mateo, J. L., & Puerta, J. M. (2007). Learning Bayesian classifiers from dependency network classifiers. *Proceedings of the 8th International Conference on Adaptive and Natural Computing Algorithms (ICANNGA-07)*.

Gámez, J. A., Mateo, J. L., Nielsen, T. D., & Puerta, J. M. (2008). Robust classification using mixtures of dependency networks. *Proceedings of the Fourth European Workshop on Probabilistic Graphical Models (PGM08)*.

Gámez, J. A. (2004). *Abductive inference in Bayesian networks: A review. Advances in Bayesian Networks* (pp. 101–120). Springer Verlag.

Gammerman, A., Vovk, V., & Vapnik, V. (1998). Learning by transduction. In *Proceedings of the 14th Conference on Uncertainty in Artificial Intelligence*, (pp. 148–155). Madison, Wisconsin.

Geiger, D., & Heckerman, D. (1996). Knowledge representation and inference in similarity networks and Bayesian multinets. *Artificial Intelligence, 82*, 45–74. doi:10.1016/0004-3702(95)00014-3

Generalitat Valenciana. (2008). *Aforos estadísticos*. Consellería Agricultura Ganadería i Pesca.

Gerig, G., Styner, M., Jones, D., Weinberger, D., & Lieberman, J. (2001) Shape analysis of brain ventricles using spharm. In *Mathematical Methods in Biomedical Image Analysis*, (pp. 171–178).

Geurts, P. (2001). Dual perturb and combine algorithm. In *Proceedings of the Eighth International Workshop on Artificial Intelligence and Statistics*, (pp. 196–201).

Ghahramani, Z. (2002). Graphical models: Parameter learning. In Arbib, M. A. (Ed.), *The handbook of brain theory and neural networks*. MIT Press.

Ghahramani, Z., & Jordan, M. (1994). Supervised learning from incomplete data via an EM approach. *Advances in Neural Information Processing Systems, 6*, 120–127.

Goetz, A., Vane, G., Solomon, J., & Rock, B. (1985). Imaging spectrometry for Earth remote sensing. *Science, 228*, 1147–1153. doi:10.1126/science.228.4704.1147

Gómez-Sanchis, J., Camps-Valls, G., Moltó, E., Gómez-Chova, L., Aleixos, N., & Blasco, J. (2008b). Lecture Notes in Computer Science: *Vol. 5112. Segmentation of hyperspectral images for the detection of rotten mandarins* (pp. 1071–1080).

Gómez-Sanchis, J., Moltó, E., Camps-Valls, G., Gómez-Chova, L., Aleixos, N., & Blasco, J. (2008a). Automatic correction of the effects of the light source on spherical objects. An application to the analysis of hyperspectral images of citrus fruits. *Journal of Food Engineering, 85*(2), 191–200. doi:10.1016/j.jfoodeng.2007.06.036

Gonzalez, R. C., & Woods, R. E. (2002). *Digital image processing*. Prentice Hall.

Google. (2001). *Inside Google Books*. Retrieved March 15, 2011, from http://booksearch.blogspot.com/2010/10/on-future-of-books.html

Gowen, A. A., Taghizadeh, M., & O'Donnell, C. P. (2009). Identification of mushrooms subjected to freeze damage using hyperspectral imaging. *Journal of Food Engineering, 93*, 7–12. doi:10.1016/j.jfoodeng.2008.12.021

Grishin, V. G., Sula, A. S., & Ulieru, M. (2003). Pictorial analysis: A multi-resolution data visualization approach for monitoring and diagnosis of complex systems. *Information Sciences, 152*, 1–24. doi:10.1016/S0020-0255(03)00044-6

Grochow, K., Martin, S., Hertzmann, A., & Popovic, Z. (2004). *Style-based inverse kinematics*. Paper presented at SIGGRAPH.

Gross, M. D. (1994). Recognising and interpreting diagrams in design. In *Proceedings of ACM (AVI'94)* (pp. 88-94). Bari, Italy.

Guimarães, G., Sousa-Lobo, V., & Moura-Pires, F. (2003). A taxonomy of self-organizing maps for temporal sequence processing. *Intelligent Data Analysis, 4*, 269–290.

Gupta, A., Chen, T., Chen, F., Kimber, D., & Daivs, L. (2008). *Context and observation driven latent variable model for human pose estimation*. Paper presented at the IEEE Conference on Computer Vision and Pattern Recognition.

Gupta, A., Srinivasan, P., Jianbo, S., & Davis, L. S. (2009, 20-25 June 2009). *Understanding videos, constructing plots learning a visually grounded storyline model from annotated videos*. Paper presented at the IEEE Conference on Computer Vision and Pattern Recognition, CVPR 2009.

Hall, M., Frank, E., Holmes, G., Pfahringer, B., Reutemann, P., & Witten, I. H. (2009). The WEKA data mining software: An update. *SIGKDD Explorations, 11*(1), 1–3. doi:10.1145/1656274.1656278

Hamada, Y., Shin, S., & Sebe, N. (1998). A design method for fault-tolerant multivariable control systems—A condition for l-partial integrity. *SICE Transactions, 34*(9), 1184–1190.

Hammond, T., & Davis, R. (2005). LADDER, a sketching language for user interface developers. *Computers & Graphics-UK, 29*(4), 518–532. doi:10.1016/j.cag.2005.05.005

Han, J., Pei, J., & Yin, Y. (2000). Mining frequent patterns without candidate generation. *ACM SIGMOD International Conference on Management of Data* (pp. 1-12).

Harding, P. R. G., & Ellis, T. J. (2004). Recognising hand gesture using Fourier descriptors. In *Proceedings of the 17th International Conference on Pattern Recognition: Vol. 3* (pp. 286-289).

Harris, T. (1993, October). *A Kohonen SOM based, machine health monitoring system which enables diagnosis of faults not seen in the training set.* Paper presented at the Neural Networks, IJCNN '93-Nagoya.

Hartmann, W. K. (1999). Martian cratering VI: Crater count isochrons and evidence for recent volcanism from Mars Global Surveyor. *Meteoritics & Planetary Science, 34*(2), 166–177. doi:10.1111/j.1945-5100.1999.tb01743.x

Hartmann, W. K., & Neukum, G. (2001). *Cratering chronology and evolution of Mars* (pp. 165–194). Chronology and Evolution of Mars.

Hashem, H. (1992). Sensitivity analysis for feedforward artificial neural networks with differentiable activation functions. In *Proceedings of 1992 International Joint Conference on Neural Networks IJCNN92*, Vol. 1, (pp. 419–424).

Hastie, T., & Tibshirani, R. (1990). *Generalized additive models.* London, UK: Chapman and Hall.

Haykin, S. (1999). *Neural networks: A comprehensive foundation.* Prentice-Hall.

He, S.-G., He, Z., Wang, G. A., & Li, L. (2009). *Data mining and knowledge discovery in real life applications: IN-TECH.*

Heckerman, D., Chickering, D. M., Meek, C., Rounthwaite, R., & Kadie, C. (2001). Dependency networks for inference, collaborative filtering, and data visualization. *Journal of Machine Learning Research, 1,* 49–75.

Heimann, T., Wolf, I., Williams, T., & Meinzer, H.-P. (2005). 3D active shape models using gradient descent optimization of description length. In *Information Processing in Medical Imaging, LNCS 3565.*

Heskes, T. (1997). Practical confidence and prediction intervals. In M. C. Mozer, M. I. Jordan, & T. Petsche (Eds.), *Advances in Neural Information Processing Systems, 9,* 176–182. The MIT Press.

Hetchts, E. (1998). *Optics* (3rd ed.). Addison Wesley Longman.

Honda, R., Iijima, Y., & Konishi, O. (2002). *Mining of topographic feature from heterogeneous imagery and its application to lunar craters.* Progress in Discovery Science, Final Report of the Japanese Discovery Science Project.

Hough, V. P. C. (1962). *United States Patent.*

Hovy, E. (2005). Methodologies for the reliable construction of ontological knowledge. In Dau, F., Mugnier, M.-L., & Stumme, G. (Eds.), *Conceptual structures: Common semantics for sharing knowledge* (pp. 91–107). Berlin, Germany: Springer-Verlag. doi:10.1007/11524564_6

Howard, A., Mataric, M. J., & Sukhatme, G. S. (2002b). Mobile sensor network deployment using potential fields: A distributed, scalable solution to the area coverage problem. In *Proceedings of the 6th International Symposium on Distributed Autonomous Robotics Systems,* (pp. 299-308).

Howard, A., Mataric, M. J., & Sukhatme, G. S. (2002a). An incremental self-deployment algorithm for mobile sensor networks. *Autonomous Robots, 13*(2), 113–126. doi:10.1023/A:1019625207705

Hruschka, E. R., Jr., Hruschka, E. R., & Ebecken, N. F. F. (2005). *Applying Bayesian networks for meteorological data mining.* SGAI International Conference on Artificial Intelligence.

Hugues, L., & Bredeche, N. (2006). Simbad: An autonomous robot simulation package for education and research. In *Proceedings of the International Conference on the Simulation of Adaptive Behaviour,* Rome, Italy, (pp. 831-842).

Huxoll, C. C., Bolin, H. R., & Mackey, B. E. (1995). Near infrared analysis potential for grading raisin quality and moisture. *Journal of Food Science, 60*(1), 176–180. doi:10.1111/j.1365-2621.1995.tb05632.x

Igarashi, T., Matsuoka, S., & Tanaka, H. (1999). Teddy: A sketching interface for 3D freeform design. In *Siggraph 99 Conference Proceedings* (pp. 409-416). New York, NY: Association for Computing Machinery.

Ito, K. (2003). Simple robots in a complex world: Collaborative exploration behaviour using genetic programming. In Koza, J. R. (Ed.), *Genetic algorithms and genetic programming* (pp. 91–99). Stanford, CA: Stanford Bookstore.

Jaeger, M. (2004). Probabilistic decision graphs - Combining verification and AI techniques for probabilistic inference. *International Journal of Uncertainty, Fuzziness and Knowledge-Based Systems, 12*(Supplement-1), 19-42.

Jakulin, A., Možina, M., Demšar, J., Bratko, I., & Zupan, B. (2005). Nomograms for visualizing support vector machines. In *KDD '05: ACM SIGKDD* (pp. 108–117). New York, NY: ACM.

Jarrett, R., & Su, P. (2002). *Building tablet PC applications*. Microsoft Press.

Jiang, L., & Zhang, H. (2006). Weightily averaged one-dependence estimators. *Proceedings of the 9th Pacific Rim International Conference on Artificial Intelligence.*

Jiang, E. (2008). Integrating background knowledge into text classification. In Li, H. (Eds.), *Information retrieval technology* (pp. 61–70). Berlin, Germany: Springer. doi:10.1007/978-3-540-68636-1_7

Jiang, L., Zhang, H., Cai, Z., & Su, J. (2005). Learning tree augmented naïve Bayes for ranking. *Database Systems for Advanced Applications, 3453*, 992–992. doi:10.1007/11408079_63

Joachims, T. (1999). Transductive inference for text classification using support vector machines. *Proceedings of 16th ICML Conference* (pp. 200-209).

John, G. H., & Langley, P. (1995). Estimating continuous distributions in Bayesian classifiers. *Conference on Uncertainty in Artificial Intelligence.*

Juchmes, R., Leclercq, P., & Azar, S. (2005). A freehand-sketch environment for architectural design supported by a multi-agent system. *Computers & Graphics-UK, 29*(6), 905–915. doi:10.1016/j.cag.2005.09.008

Julian, V., Carrascosa, C., Rebollo, M., Soler, J., & Botti, V. (2002). SIMBA: An approach for real-time multi-agent systems. In *Topics in Artificial Intelligence. Proceedings, 2504*, 282–293.

Kakade, S. (2002). A natural policy gradient. *Proceedings of Neural Information Processing Systems.*

Kambhampati, C., Perkgoz, C., Patton, R. J., & Ahamed, W. (2007). An interaction predictive approach to fault-tolerant control in network control systems. *Systems and Control Engineering, 221*, 885–894. doi:10.1243/09596518JSCE377

Kammerdiner, A. R., Gupal, A. M., & Pardalos, P. M. (2007). Application of Bayesian networks and data mining to biomedical problems. *AIP Conference Proceedings.*

Karimi, Y., Maftoonazad, N., Ramaswamy, H. S., Prasher, S. O., & Marcotte, M. (2009). Application of hyperspectral technique for color classification avocados subjected to different treatments. *Food and Bioprocess Technology, 5*(1). doi:doi:10.1007/s11947-009-0292-x

Kearns, M. J., & Ron, D. (1997). Algorithmic stability and sanity-check bounds for leave- one-out cross-validation. In *Computational Learning Theory*, (pp. 152–162).

Keim, D. A. (2002). Information visualization and visual data mining. *IEEE Transactions on Visualization and Computer Graphics, 8*(1), 1–8. doi:10.1109/2945.981847

Keogh, E., & Pazzani, M. (1999). Learning augmented Bayesian classifiers: A comparison of distribution-based and classification-based approaches. *Proceedings of the 7th International Workshop on AI and Statistics* (pp. 225-230).

Kerr, M., & Churchill, G. (2000). Bootstrapping cluster analysis: assessing the reliability of conclusions from microarray experiments. *Proceedings of the National Academy of Sciences of the United States of America, 96*, 8961–8965.

Khakhalin, G. K. (2009). Applied ontology in terms of hypergraph. *Proceedings of II All-Russian Conference Knowledge-Ontology-Theory (KONT-09)* (pp. 223-231). Novosibirsk, Russian Federation: Published by Sobolev Institute of Mathematics, Siberian Department of RAN (In Russian).

Khakhalin, G. K., & Voskresenskiy, A. L. (2006). The contextual fragmentation in the linguistic analysis. *Proceedings of 10th National Conference on Artificial Intelligence* (pp. 479-488). Moscow, Russia: Publishing House of Physical-Mathematical Literature (in Russian).

Kim, J., & Muller, J.-P., S., V. G., J., M., & Neukum, G. (2005). Automated crater detection: A new tool for Mars cartography and chronology. *Photogrammetric Engineering and Remote Sensing, 71*, 1205–1217.

Kim, M., Leftcourt, A., Chao, K., & Chen, Y. (2005). Statistical and neural network classifiers for citrus disease detection using machine vision. *Transactions of the ASAE. American Society of Agricultural Engineers, 48*(5), 2007–2014.

Kim, S.-D., Zhang, B.-T., & Kim, Y.-T. (2001). Learning-based intra-sentence segmentation for efficient translation of long sentences. *Machine Translation, 16*, 151–174. doi:10.1023/A:1019896420277

Kjaerulff, U., & van der Gaag, L. C. (2000). Making sensitivity analysis computationally efficient. In *Proceedings of the Sixteenth Conference on Uncertainty in Artificial Intelligence*, (pp. 317-325). San Francisco, CA: Morgan Kaufmann.

Kleijnen, J. (2001). Experimental designs for sensitivity analysis of simulation models. In *Proceedings of EUROSIM 2001.*

Koc, A. B. (2007). Determination of watermelon volume using ellipsoid approximation and image processing. *Postharvest Biology and Technology, 45*(3), 366–371. doi:10.1016/j.postharvbio.2007.03.010

Kohonen, T. (2001). *Self-organizing maps* (*Vol. 30*). Berlin, Germany: Springer.

Kohonen, T., Oja, E., Simula, O., Visa, A., & Kangas, J. (1996). Engineering applications of the self-organizing map. *Proceedings of the IEEE, 84*(10), 1358–1384. doi:10.1109/5.537105

Koh, Y. S., Rountree, N., & O'Keefe, R. (2005). Finding non-coincidental sporadic rules using apriori-inverse. *International Journal of Data Warehousing and Mining, 2*(2), 38–54. doi:10.4018/jdwm.2006040102

Kokaram, A., Rea, N., Dahyot, R., Tekalp, A. M., Bouthemy, P., & Gros, P. (2006). Browsing sports video: Trends in sports-related indexing and retrieval work. *Signal Processing Magazine, IEEE, 23*(2), 47–58. doi:10.1109/MSP.2006.1621448

Kolmogorov, A. (1957). On the representation of continuous functions of several variables by superposition of continuous functions of one variable and addition. *Doklady Akademii Nauk, 114*, 953–956.

Kong, C. S., Peng, N. A., & Rekleitis, I. (2006). Distributed coverage with multi-robot system. In *Proceedings of the 2006 IEEE International Conference on Robotics and Automation,* Orlando, Florida, May, (pp. 2423-2429).

Kononenko, I. (1991). Semi-naive Bayesian classifiers. *EWSL, 1991*, 206–219. doi:10.1007/BFb0017015

Korb, K. E., & Nicholson, A. E. (2010). *Bayesian artificial intelligence,* 2nd ed. Chapman & Hall/CRC Computer Science & Data Analysis.

Koubaroulis, D., Matas, J., & Kittler, J. (2002). *Colour-based object recognition for video annotation.* Paper presented at the IEEE International Conference on Pattern Recognition.

Kozlova, E. A., Michael, G. G., Rodinova, J. F., & Shevchenko, V. V. (2001). *Compilation and preliminary analysis of a catalogue. Lunar and Planetary Science* (p. 1231). XXXII.

Kreuseler, M., & Schumann, H. (2002). A flexible approach for visual data mining. *IEEE Transactions on Visualization and Computer Graphics, 8*(1), 39–51. doi:10.1109/2945.981850

Kukar, M. (2001). *Estimating classifications' reliability and cost-sensitive combination of machine learning methods.* Unpublished doctoral dissertation, University of Ljubljana, 2001.

Kukar, M., & Kononenko, I. (2002). Reliable classifications with machine learning. In Elomaa, T., Manilla, H., & Toivonen, H. (Eds.), *Proceedings of Machine Learning: ECML-2002* (pp. 219–231). Helsinki, Finland: Springer Verlag. doi:10.1007/3-540-36755-1_19

Kurbatov, S. S. (2010). The high-level heuristics for automated formation of knowledge base. *Proceedings of XII National Conference on Artificial Intelligence: Vol. 1* (pp. 231-239). Moscow, Russia: Publishing House of Physical-Mathematical Literature (in Russian).

Kurbatov, S. S. (2011). *A tool of support of knowledge representation language* (in Russian). Retrieved from http://eia--dostup.ru/exp_anal.htm

Kurbatov, S. S., Naidenova, X. A., & Khakhalin, G. K. (2010). On interacting scheme of integrated program complex "Analysis and synthesis of natural language and images". *Proceedings of XII National Conference on Artificial Intelligence: Vol. 1* (pp. 234-242). Moscow, Russia: Publishing House of Physical-Mathematical Literature (in Russian).

Kuzin, E. S., Roitman, A. I., Fominikh, I. B., & Khakhalin, G. K. (1989). *Computer intellectualization*. Moscow: Publishing House of Higher School: Future Considerations of Computation Engineering Series (in Russian).

Laiho, J., Raivio, K., Lehtimäki, P., Hätönen, K., & Simula, O. (2005). Advanced analysis methods for 3G cellular networks. *IEEE Transactions on Wireless Communications, 4*(3), 930–942. doi:10.1109/TWC.2005.847088

Lallich, S., Teytaud, O., & Prudhomme, E. (2007). Association rule interestingness: Measure and statistical validation. In Guillet, F., & Hamilton, H. (Eds.), *Quality measures in data mining* (*Vol. 43*, pp. 251–275). Berlin, Germany: Springer. doi:10.1007/978-3-540-44918-8_11

Lan, X., & Huttenlocher, D. (2004). *A unified spatio-temporal articulated model for tracking*. Paper presented at the Computer Vision and Pattern Recognition.

Langley, P., & Sage, S. (1994). Induction of selective Bayesian classifiers. *Tenth Conference on Uncertainty in Artificial Intelligence*.

Langley, P., Iba, W., & Thompson, K. (1992). An analysis of Bayesian classifiers. *Proceedings of the Tenth Annual Conference on Artificial Intelligence*.

Larrañaga, P. (2010). Multi-label classification. *International Journal of Data Warehousing and Mining, 3*(3), 1–13.

Latimer, D., IV, Srinivasa, S., Lee-Shue, V., Sonne, S., Choset, H., & Hurst, A. (2002). Towards sensor based coverage with robot teams. *Proceedings of the 2002 IEEE International Conference on Robotics & Automation*, Washington DC, May, (pp. 961-967).

Lauritzen, S. L. (1992). Propagation of probabilities, means and variances in mixed graphical association models. *Journal of the American Statistical Association, 87*, 1098–1108.

Lauritzen, S. L., & Jensen, F. (2001). Stable local computation with conditional Gaussian distributions. *Statistics and Computing, 11*(2), 191–203. doi:10.1023/A:1008935617754

Lauritzen, S. L., & Wermuth, N. (1998). Graphical models for associations between variables, some of which are qualitative and some quantitative. *Annals of Statistics, 17*(1), 31–57. doi:10.1214/aos/1176347003

Lawrence, N. (2003). *Gaussian process latent variable models for visualization of high dimensional data*. Paper presented at the Advances in Neural Information Processing.

Lawrence, N., & Candela, J. (2006). *Local distance preservation in the GPLVM through back constraints*. Paper presented at the International Conference on Machine Learning.

Lawrence, N., & Moore, A. (2007). *Hierarchical Gaussian process latent variable models*. Paper presented at the International Conference on Machine Learning.

Lazarescu, M., & Venkatesh, S. (2003, July). *Using camera motion to identify types of American football plays*. Paper presented at the 2003 International Conference on Multimedia and Expo.

Lee, C.-S., & Elgammal, A. (2007). *Modeling view and posture manifolds for tracking*. Paper presented at the IEEE International Conference on Computer Vision.

Lee, D.-J., Schoenberger, R., Archibald, J., & McCollum, S. (2008). Development of a machine vision system for automatic date grading using digital reflective near-infrared imaging. *Journal of Food Engineering, 86*, 388–398. doi:10.1016/j.jfoodeng.2007.10.021

Lefcourt, A. M., & Kim, M. S. (2006). Technique for normalizing intensity histograms of images when the approximate size of the target is known: Detection of feces on apples using fluorescence imaging. *Computers and Electronics in Agriculture, 50*, 135–147. doi:10.1016/j.compag.2005.10.001

Lehtimäki, P., Raivio, K., & Simula, O. (2003). Self-organizing operator maps in complex system analysis. *Lecture Notes in Computer Science, 622–629.* doi:10.1007/3-540-44989-2_74

Lemaire, V., Feraud, V., & Voisine, N. (2008). Contact personalization using a score understanding method. In *International Joint Conference on Neural Networks (IJCNN)* (pp. 649-654). Hong Kong: IEEE Xplore.

León, K., Domingo, M., Pedreschi, F., & León, J. (2006). Color measurement in L*a*b* units from RGB digital images. *Food Research International, 39*, 1084–1091. doi:10.1016/j.foodres.2006.03.006

Leroy, B., Medioni, G., & Matthies, E. J. (2001). Crater detection for autonomous landing on asteroids. *Image and Vision Computing, 19*, 787–792. doi:10.1016/S0262-8856(00)00111-6

Li, B., & Sezan, I. (2002). *Event detection and summarization in American football brocast video.* Paper presented at the SPIE Storage and Retrieval for Media Database.

Licsar, A., & Sziranyi, T. (2004). Hand gesture recognition in camera-projector system. In *Computer Vision in Human-Computer Interaction Proceedings, 3058,* 83–93.

Li, F., & Wechsler, H. (2005). Open set face recognition using transduction. *IEEE Transactions on Pattern Analysis and Machine Intelligence, 27*(11), 1686–1697. doi:10.1109/TPAMI.2005.224

Liming, X., & Yanchao, Z. (2010). Automated strawberry grading system based on image processing. *Computers and Electronics in Agriculture, 71*(S1), S32–S39. doi:10.1016/j.compag.2009.09.013

Lin, C.-T., & Lee, C. S. G. (1996). *Neural fuzzy systems. A neuro-fuzzy synergism to intelligent systems.* Prentice Hall.

Link, W. A., & Barker, R. J. (2010). *Bayesian inference: With ecological applications.* Elsevier.

Little, R. J. A., & Rubin, D. B. (1986). *Statistical analysis with missing data.* John Wiley & Sons, Inc.

Liu, X., Wu, Y., Shi, J., & Zhang, W. (2008). Adaptive fault-tolerant flight control system design using neural networks. *The 2008 IEEE International Conference on Industrial Technology,* (pp. 1-5). Chengdu,China.

Liu, H., Hussain, F., Tan, C. L., & Dash, M. (2002). Discretization: An enabling technique. *Data Mining and Knowledge Discovery, 6*(4), 393–423. doi:10.1023/A:1016304305535

Liu, Y., Carbonell, J., Weigele, P., & Gopalakarishnany, V. (2006). Segmentation conditional random fields (SCRFs): A new approach for protein fold recognition. *Journal of Computational Biology, 13*(2), 394–406. doi:10.1089/cmb.2006.13.394

Lootens, P., Van Waes, J., & Carlier, L. (2007). Description of the morphology of roots of *Chicorium intybus* L. partim by means of image analysis: Comparison of elliptic Fourier descriptors classical parameters. *Computers and Electronics in Agriculture, 58*(2), 164–173. doi:10.1016/j.compag.2007.03.014

Lu, Z., Carreira-Perpinan, M. A., & Sminchisescu, C. (2007). *People tracking with the Laplacian Eigenmaps latent variable model.* Paper presented at the Advances in Neural Information Processing Systems.

Lucas, P. (2004). Restricted Bayesian network structure learning. *Studies in Fuzziness and Soft Computing, 49*, 217–232.

Mackenzie, G., & Alechina, N. (2003). Classifying sketches of animals using an agent-based system. In *Computer Analysis of Images and Patterns Proceedings, 2756,* 521–529.

Maedche, A., & Staab, S. (2000). Discovering conceptual relations from text. In *Proceedings of the 14th European Conference on Artificial Intelligence (ECAI)* (pp. 321–325).

Maedche, A., & Staab, S. (2001, March). Ontology learning for the semantic web. *IEEE Intelligent Systems*, *16*, 72–79. doi:10.1109/5254.920602

Majidian, A., & Martin, T. (2009). Extracting taxonomies from data - A case study using fuzzy formal concept analysis. In *WI-IAT '09: Proceedings of the 2009 IEEE/ WIC/ACM International Joint Conference on Web Intelligence and Intelligent Agent Technology* (pp. 191–194). Washington, DC: IEEE Computer Society.

Mal'kovsky, M. G. (1985). *The dialogue with AI system.* Moscow, Russia: Moscow State University. (in Russian)

Marchant, J. A., & Onyango, C. M. (2003). Comparison of a Bayesian classifier with a multilayer feed-forward neural network using the example of plant/weed/soil discrimination. *Computers and Electronics in Agriculture*, *39*(1), 3–22. doi:10.1016/S0168-1699(02)00223-5

Martin, T., & Shen, Y. (2009, June). Fuzzy association rules in soft conceptual hierarchies. In *Fuzzy Information Processing Society, NAFIPS 2009* (p. 1 - 6).

Martínez, A. M., Webb, G. I., Flores, M. J., & Gámez, J. A. (2011). *Non-disjoint discretization for aggregating one-dependence estimator classifiers.* (Submitted): University of Castilla-La Mancha, Computing Systems Department.

Martínez, M., & Sucar, L. E. (2008). Learning dynamic naïve Bayesian classifiers. *Proceedings of the Twenty-First International Florida Artificial Intelligence Research Society Conference (FLAIRS)* (pp. 655-659).

Martins, R., Pina, P., Marques, J. S., & Silveira, M. (2008). Crater detection by a boosting approach. *IEEE Geoscience and Remote Sensing Letters*, *6*(1), 127–131. doi:10.1109/LGRS.2008.2006004

Martin, T. P., Shen, Y., & Azvine, B. (2008). Granular association rules for multiple taxonomies: A mass assignment approach. In *Uncertainty Reasoning for the Semantic Web I: ISWC International Workshops, URSW 2005-2007, Revised Selected and Invited Papers* (pp. 224–243). Berlin, Germany: Springer-Verlag. doi:10.1007/978-3-540-89765-1_14

Martin, T., Shen, Y., & Azvine, B. (2007). A mass assignment approach to granular association rules for multiple taxonomies. In *Proceedings of the Third ISWC Workshop on Uncertainty Reasoning for the Semantic Web,* Busan. *Korea & World Affairs*, (November): 12.

Mataric, M. (1992). Designing emergent behaviours: From local interactions to collective intelligence. In *Proceedings of the International Conference on Simulation of Adaptive Behaviour: From Animal to Animats,* 2, (pp. 432-441).

Mei, T., Ma, Y.-F., Zhou, H.-Q., Ma, W.-Y., & Zhang, H.-J. (2005). *Sports video mining with Mosaic.* Paper presented at the 11th International Multimedia Modelling Conference.

Melgarejo, P., Martínez, J. J., Hernández, F., Martínez-Font, R., Barrows, P., & Erez, A. (2004). Kaolin treatment to reduce pomegranate sunburn. *Scientia Horticulturae*, *100*(1), 349–353. doi:10.1016/j.scienta.2003.09.006

Mendoza, F., Dejmek, P., & Aguilera, J. M. (2006). Calibrated color measurements of agricultural foods using image analysis. *Postharvest Biology and Technology*, *41*, 285–295. doi:10.1016/j.postharvbio.2006.04.004

Miani, R. G., Yaguinuma, C. A., Santos, M. T. P., & Biajiz, M. (2009). NARFO algorithm: Mining non-redundant and generalized association rules based on fuzzy ontologies. In Aalst, W. (Eds.), *Enterprise information systems* (*Vol. 24*, pp. 415–426). Berlin, Germany: Springer. doi:10.1007/978-3-642-01347-8_35

Mihelčič, M. (2007). Could learning about the structure of relationships lead either to a breakthrough or synthesis in organization theory? In *Proceedings: Beyond Waltz – Dances of Individuals and Organization, 23rd EGOS Colloquium,* Vienna, 4-7 July 2007. London, UK: Sage Publications.

Mihelčič, M. (1992a). Focusing on relationships as a means of accelerating organizational improvement. In Geschka, H., & Huebner, H. (Eds.), *Innovation strategies - Theoretical approaches - Experiences - Improvements - An international perspective* (pp. 141–152). Amsterdam, The Netherlands: Elsevier.

Mihelčič, M. (1992b). Interdependency between perceived quality of companies' organization (organizational excellence) and performance: Some assumptions of correlational study. *Slovenska Ekonomska Revija*, *43*(1), 67–81.

Mingo, J. M., & Aler, R. (2007). Grammatical evolution guided by reinforcement. *IEEE Congress on Evolutionary Computation*, Singapore, (pp. 1475-1482).

Mingo, J. M., Aler, R., De Lope, J., & Maravall, D. (2011). *Innate knowledge through semantic rules in grammatical evolution guided by reinforcement applied to robotic problems*. Unpublished.

Mitchell, T. (1999). The role of unlabelled data in supervised learning. In *Proceedings of the 6th International Colloquium of Cognitive Science*, San Sebastian, Spain.

Molet, T. (1996). A real-time anatomical converter for human motion capture. *Eurographics Workshop on Computer Animation and Simulation*, (pp. 79-94).

Mondada, F., Pettinaro, G., Guigrard, A., Kwee, I., Floreano, D., & Denebourg, J.-L. (2004). Swarm-bot: A new distributed robotic concept. *Autonomous Robots, 17*(2-3), 193–221. doi:10.1023/B:AURO.0000033972.50769.1c

Moral, S., Rumí, R., & Salmerón, A. (2001). *Mixtures of truncated exponentials in hybrid Bayesian networks*. Paper presented at the ECSQARU '01: 6th European Conference on Symbolic and Quantitative Approaches to Reasoning with Uncertainty.

Moral, S., Rumí, R., & Salmerón, A. (2003). *Approximating conditional MTE distributions by means of mixed trees*. Paper presented at the ECSQARU.

Morales, D. A., Bengoetxea, E., & Larrañaga, P. (2008). Selection of human embryos for transfer by Bayesian classifiers. *Computers in Biology and Medicine, 38*, 1177–1186. doi:10.1016/j.compbiomed.2008.09.002

Moretti, S., & Patrone, F. (2008). Transversality of the Shapley value. *Top (Madrid), 16*, 1–41. doi:10.1007/s11750-008-0044-5

Morzy, T., & Zakrzewicz, M. (1998). Group bitmap index: A structure for association rules retrieval. *4th International Conference on Knowledge Discovery and Data Mining* (pp. 284-288).

Moshou, D., Hostens, I., Papaioannou, G., & Ramon, H. (2000). *Wavelets and self-organising maps in electromyogram (EMG) analysis*. Laboratory of Kinesiology, Katholieke Universiteit Leuven.

Možina, M., Demšar, J., Kattan, M., & Zupan, B. (2004). Nomograms for visualization of naive Bayesian classifier. In *PKDD 2004* (pp. 337–348). Berlin, Germany: Springer - Verlag. doi:10.1007/978-3-540-30116-5_32

Murata, T. (1989). Petri nets: properties, analysis, and applications. *Proceedings of the IEEE, 77*(4), 541–580. doi:10.1109/5.24143

Murphy, K. (2002). *Dynamic Bayesian networks: Representation, inference and learning*. UC Berkeley.

MyScript Studio. (2010). Retrieved from http://www.visionobjects.com/en/webstore/myscript-studio/description/

Naidenova, X. A. (2006). *The role of machine learning in mining natural language texts*. Retrieved from http://www.dialog-21.ru/dialog2006/materials/html/Naidenova.htm

Naidenova, X. A., & Shagalov, V. L. (2009). Diagnostic test machine. In M. Auer (Ed.), *Proceedings of the ICL '2009 – Interactive Computer Aided Learning Conference* (pp. 505-507). Kassel, Germany: Kassel University Press. ISBN: 978-3-89958-481-3

Naidenova, X. A., Khakhalin, G. K., & Kurbatov, S. S. (2011). Semantic-syntactic analysis of NL-texts of plane geometry tasks. *System Analysis and Semiotic Modeling: The Materials of the First All-Russian Scientific Conference with the International Participations* (SASM'2011) (pp. 184-191). Kazan, Russia: "Fen" the Academy of Science of Republic Tatarstan (in Russian).

Naidenova, X. A., & Nevzorova, O. A. (2008). Machine learning in tasks of NL-processing: Survey of state-of-the-art investigations. [in Russian]. *News Kazan University, 1*, 3–24.

Naphade, M., & Huang, T. (2002). *Discovering recurrent events in video using unsupervised methods*. Paper presented at the IEEE International Conference on Image Processing, Rochester, NY.

Narin'jany, A. S. (1995). The understanding problem of data-base queries was decided. In R. C. Bukharajev, et al. (Eds.), *DIALOG '95: Computational Linguistics and its Applied Computing, Proceedings of International Seminar* (pp. 206-215). Kazan, Tatarstan: Kazan University Press (in Russian).

Nielsen, J. D., Rumí, R., & Salmerón, A. (2009). Supervised classification using probabilistic decision graphs. *Computational Statistics & Data Analysis*, *53*(4), 1299–1311. doi:10.1016/j.csda.2008.11.003

Nigam, K., McGallum, S., Thurn, S., & Mitchell, T. (2000). Text classification from labeled and unlabeled documents using EM. *Machine Learning*, *39*(2/3), 103–134. doi:10.1023/A:1007692713085

Nolfi, S. (2006). Behaviour as a complex adaptive system: On the role of self-organization in the development of individual and collective behaviour. *Complexus*, *2*(3-4), 195–203. doi:10.1159/000093690

Nolfi, S., & Floreano, D. (2000). *Evolutionary robotics: The biology, intelligence and technology of self-organizing machines*. Cambridge, MA: The MIT Press.

Norris, J. R. (1997). *Markov chains*. Cambridge University Press.

O'Callagnan, J., & Mark, D. (1984). The extraction of drainage networks from digital elevation data. *Computer Vision Graphics and Image Processing*, *28*, 328–344.

Obenland, D., & Neipp, P. (2005). Chlorophyll fluorescence imaging allows early detection and localization of lemon rind injury following hot water treatment. *HortScience*, *40*(6), 1821–1823.

Olesen, K. G. (1993). Causal probabilistic networks with both discrete and continuous variables. *IEEE Transactions on Pattern Analysis and Machine Intelligence*, *15*(3), 275–279. doi:10.1109/34.204909

Omelayenko, B. (2001). Learning of ontologies for the Web: The analysis of existent approaches. In *Proceedings of the International Workshop on Web Dynamics, held in conj. with the 8th International Conference on Database Theory (ICDT'01), London, UK.*

Ordoñez, C., Matias, J. M., Rivas, T., & Bastante, F. G. (2009). Reforestation planning using Bayesian networks. *Environmental Modelling & Software*, *24*(11), 1285–1292. doi:10.1016/j.envsoft.2009.05.009

Ortigosa-Hernandez, J., Rodriguez, J. D., Alzate, L., Lucania, M., Inza, I., & Lozano, J. A. (2011). *Approaching sentiment analysis by using semi-supervised learning of multidimensional classifiers*. Department of Computer Science and Artificial Intelligence. University of the Basque Country.

Osada, R. (2002). Shape distributions. *ACM Transactions on Graphics*, *21*(4), 807–832. doi:10.1145/571647.571648

Osowski, S., & Nghia, D. D. (2002). Fourier wavelet descriptors fro shape recognition using neural networks – A comparative study. *Pattern Recognition*, *35*, 1949–1957. doi:10.1016/S0031-3203(01)00153-4

Othman, L. B., & Yahia, S. B. (2006). Yet another approach for completing missing values. *4th International Conference on Concept Lattices and Their Applications* (pp. 155-169).

Palacios-Alonso, M. A., Brizuela, C. A., & Sucar, L. E. (2010). Evolutionary learning of dynamic naïve Bayesian classifiers. *Journal of Automated Reasoning*, *45*(1), 21–37. doi:10.1007/s10817-009-9130-0

Palanca, J., Aranda, G., & Garcia-Fornes, A. (2009). Building service-based applications for the iPhone using RDF: A tourism application. In *7th International Conference on Practical Applications of Agents and Multi-Agent Systems: Vol. 55* (pp. 421-429).

Palou, L., Smilanick, J., Usall, J., & Viñas, I. (2001). Control postharvest blue and green molds of oranges by hot water, sodium carbonate, and sodium bicarbonate. *Plant Disease*, *85*, 371–376. doi:10.1094/PDIS.2001.85.4.371

Pan, H., Beek, P., & Sezan, M. I. (2001). *Detection of slow-motion replay segments in sports video for highlights generation*. Paper presented at the IEEE Int'l Conference on Acoustics Speech and Signal Processing.

Papageorgiou, C., Oren, M., & Poggio, T. (1998). A general framework for object detection. *Sixth International Conference on Computer Vision*, (pp. 555-562).

Park, B., Lawrence, K., Windhand, W., & Buhr, R. (2002). Hyperspectral imaging for detecting fecal and ingesta contaminants on poultry carcasses. *Transactions of the ASAE. American Society of Agricultural Engineers*, *45*(6), 2017–2026.

Park, C. H., & Park, H. (2005). Fingerprint classification using fast Fourier transform and nonlinear discriminant analysis. *Pattern Recognition*, *38*(4), 495–503. doi:10.1016/j.patcog.2004.08.013

Parker, L. E. (1993). Designing control laws for cooperative agent teams. In *Proceedings of the IEEE International Conference on Robotics and Automation*, (pp. 582-587).

Park, M.-H., & Stenstrom, M. K. (2008). Classifying environmentally significant urban land uses with satellite imagery. *Journal of Environmental Management*, *86*(1), 181–192. doi:10.1016/j.jenvman.2006.12.010

Patton, R., Frank, P., & Clark, R. (1989). *Fault diagnosis in dynamic systems*. Prentice Hall.

Paulson, B., & Hammond, T. (2008). PaleoSketch: Accurate primitive sketch recognition and beautification. In *Proceedings of the 13th International Conference on Intelligent User Interfaces* (pp. 1-10). Gran Canaria, Spain: ACM.

Paulus, I., De Busscher, R., & Schrevens, E. (1997). Use of image analysis to investigate human quality classification of apples. *Journal of Agricultural Engineering Research*, *68*, 341–353. doi:10.1006/jaer.1997.0210

Pavlenko, T., & Chernyak, O. (2010). Credit risk modeling using Bayesian networks. *International Journal of Intelligent Systems*, *25*, 326–344.

Pazzani, M. J. (1996). Searching for dependencies in Bayesian classifiers. *Learning from Data: Artificial Intelligence and Statistics*, *V*, 239–248.

Pereira, J., Jorge, J., Branco, V., & Nunes, F. (2000). *Towards calligraphic interfaces: Sketching 3D scenes with gestures and context icons*. In 8th International Conference in Central Europe on Computer Graphics, Visualization and Interactive Digital Media WSCG. Plzen, Czech Republic: University of West Bohemia.

Pérez, A., Larrañaga, P., & Inza, I. (2006). Supervised classification with conditional Gaussian networks: Increasing the structure complexity from naïve Bayes. *International Journal of Approximate Reasoning*, *43*(1), 1–25. doi:10.1016/j.ijar.2006.01.002

Pérez, A., Larrañaga, P., & Inza, I. (2009). Bayesian classifiers based on kernel density estimation: Flexible classifiers. *International Journal of Approximate Reasoning*, *50*, 341–362. doi:10.1016/j.ijar.2008.08.008

Perez-Delgado, M. L., & Matos-Franco, J. C. (2009). Artificial intelligence for picking up recycling bins: A practical application. In *7th International Conference on Practical Applications of Agents and Multi-Agent Systems: Vol. 55* (pp. 392-400). Berlin, Germany: Springer-Verlag Berlin.

Perkins, T. J. (2002). Lyapunov design for safe reinforcement learning. *Machine Learning Research*, *3*, 803–832.

Peters, J., et al. (2003). Reinforcement learning for humanoid robots. *Proceedings of the Third IEEE-RAS International Conference on Humanoid Robots*.

Plesko, C., Brumby, S., Asphaug, E., Chamberlain, D., & Engel, T. (2005). Automatic crater counts on Mars. *Lunar and Planetary Science*, *XXXV*.

Plimmer, B., & Apperley, M. (2002). Computer-aided sketching to capture preliminary design. In *Proceedings of the Third Australasian Conference on User Interfaces: Vol. 7* (pp. 9-12). Melbourne, Australia: Australian Computer Society, Inc.

Polder, G., van der Heijden, G. W. A. M., Keizer, L. C. P., & Young, I. T. (2003). Calibration and characterization of spectral imaging systems. *Journal of Near Infrared Spectroscopy*, *11*, 193–210. doi:10.1255/jnirs.366

Polycarpou, M. M. (2001). Fault accommodation of a class of multivariable nonlinear dynamical systems using a learning approach. *IEEE Transactions on Automatic Control*, *46*, 736–742. doi:10.1109/9.920792

Polycarpou, M. M., & Helmicki, A. J. (1995). Automated fault detection and accommodation: A learning systems approach. *IEEE Transactions on Systems, Man, and Cybernetics*, *25*, 1447–1458. doi:10.1109/21.467710

Polzer, J., Markworth, M., Jelali, M., Redueles, J. L., Sanfilippo, F., & Lupinelli, M. ... Cuadrado, A. (2009). *Intelligent soft-sensor technology and automatic model-based diagnosis for improved quality, control and maintenance of mill production lines (Softdetect)*. Research Fund for Coal and Steel. European Commission. ISBN: 978-92-79-11980-4

Popov, E. V. (1982). *Communication with computer on natural language*. Moscow, Russia: Nauka. (in Russian)

Porwal, A., Carranza, E. J. M., & Hale, M. (2006). Bayesian network classifiers for mineral potential mapping. *Computers & Geosciences*, *32*, 1–16. doi:10.1016/j.cageo.2005.03.018

Porzio, G. C., & Ragozini, G. (2003). Visually mining off-line data for quality improvement. *Quality and Reliability Engineering International*, *19*(4), 273–283. doi:10.1002/qre.588

Pospelov, D. A. (Ed.). (1990). *Artificial intelligence*. Moscow, Russia: Radio and Communication. (in Russian)

Prabhu, N. U. (2007). *Stochastic process basic theory and its applications*. World Scientific.

Principe, J. C., Wang, L., & Motter, M. A. (1998). Local dynamic modeling with self-organizing maps and applications to nonlinear system identification and control. *Proceedings of the IEEE*, *86*(11), 2240–2258. doi:10.1109/5.726789

Proakis, J. G. (1997). *Tratamiento digital de señaales: Principios, algoritmos y aplicaciones*. Prentice-Hall.

Pydipati, R., Burks, T. F., & Lee, W. S. (2006). Identification of citrus disease using color texture features and discriminant analysis. *Computers and Electronics in Agriculture*, *52*, 49–59. doi:10.1016/j.compag.2006.01.004

Qazi, M., Fung, G., Krishnan, S., Rosales, R., Steck, H., Rao, R. B., et al. (2007). Automated heart wall motion abnormality detection from ultrasound images using Bayesian networks. *Proceedings of the 20th International Joint Conference on Artifical Intelligence*.

Qin, J., Burksa, T., Ritenourb, M., & Bonn, W. (2009). Detection of citrus canker using hyperspectral reflectance imaging with spectral information divergence. *Journal of Food Engineering*, *93*(2), 183–191. doi:10.1016/j.jfoodeng.2009.01.014

Quevedo, R., Mendoza, F., Aguilera, J. M., Chanona, J., & Gutiérrez-López, G. (2008). Determination of senescent spotting in banana (*Musa cavendish*) using fractal texture Fourier image. *Journal of Food Engineering*, *84*, 509–515. doi:10.1016/j.jfoodeng.2007.06.013

Quinlan, J. R. (1986). Induction of decision trees. *Machine Learning*, *1*(1), 81–106. doi:10.1007/BF00116251

Quinlan, J. R. (1993). *C4.5: Programs for machine learning*. San Francisco, CA: Morgan Kaufmann Publishers.

Quirion, S., Duchesne, C., Laurendeau, D., & Marchand, M. (2008). Comparing GPLVM approaches for dimensionality reduction in character animation. *Journal of WSCG*, *16*(1-3), 41–48.

Ragel, A. (1998). Preprocessing of missing values using robust association rules. *2nd European Symposium on Principles of Data Mining and Knowledge Discovery* (pp. 414-422).

Ragel, A., & Crémilleux, B. (1998). Treatment of missing values for association rules. *2nd Pacific-Asia Conference on Research and Development in Knowledge Discovery and Data Mining* (pp. 258-270).

Rajan, S., Punera, K., & Ghosh, J. (2005). A maximum likelihood framework for integrating taxonomies. In *AAAI'05: Proceedings of the 20th National Conference on Artificial Intelligence* (pp. 856–861). AAAI Press.

Rasmussen, C. E., & Williams, C. K. I. (2006). *Gaussian processes for machine learning*. MIT Press.

Rehg, J. M., & Murphy, K. P. (1999). Vision-based speaker detection using Bayesian networks. In Workshop on Perceptual User-Interfaces.

Rekleitis, I. M., Dudek, G., & Milios, E. E. (2000). Graph-based exploration using multiple robots. In Parker, L. E., Bekey, G. W., & Barhen, J. (Eds.), *Distributed Autonomous Robotics Systems* (*Vol. 4*, pp. 241–250). Springer. doi:10.1007/978-4-431-67919-6_23

Rendueles, J., L., González, J. A., Díaz Blanco, I., Diez González, A. B., Seijo, F., & Cuadrado Vega, A. A. (2006). Implementation of a virtual sensor on a hot dip galvanizing line for zinc coating thickness estimation. *Revue de Metallurgie-Cahiers d Informations Techniques*, *103*(5), 226–232.

Reynolds, C. (1987). Flocks, herds and schools: A distributed behavioural model. *Computer Graphics*, *21*(4), 25–34. doi:10.1145/37402.37406

Ridgeway, G., Madigan, D., & Richardson, T. (1999). Boosting methodology for regression problems. In Heckerman, D., & Whittaker, J. (Eds.), *Proceedings of Artificial Intelligence and Statistics* (pp. 152–161).

Robnik-Šikonja, M., & Kononenko, I. (2003). Theoretical and empirical analysis of ReliefF and RReliefF. *Machine Learning Journal*, *53*, 23–69. doi:10.1023/A:1025667309714

Rodionova, F. J., Dekchtyareva, K. I., Khramchikhin, A., Michael, G. G., Ajukov, S. V., & Pugacheva, S. G. (2000). *Morphological catalogue of the craters of Mars*. ESA-ESTEC.

Rodríguez, J. D., & Lozano, J. A. (2008). Multi-objective learning of multi-dimensional Bayesian classifiers. *Proceedings of 8th International Conference on Hybrid Intelligent Systems (HIS 2008)*.

Rogers, T. J., Ross, R., & Subrahmanian, V. S. (2000). IMPACT: A system for building agent applications. *Journal of Intelligent Information Systems*, *14*(2-3), 95–113. doi:10.1023/A:1008727601100

Rose, A. T. (2005). Graphical communication using hand-drawn sketches in civil engineering. *Journal of Professional Issues in Engineering Education and Practice*, *131*(4), 238–247. doi:10.1061/(ASCE)1052-3928(2005)131:4(238)

Rosenhahn, B., Schmaltz, C., & Brox, T. (2008). *Markerless motion capture of man-machine interaction*. Paper presented at the IEEE Conference on Computer Vision and Pattern Recognition.

Rothenhagen, K., & Fuchs, F. W. (2009). Doubly fed induction generator model-based sensor fault detection and control loop reconfiguration. *IEEE Transactions on Industrial Electronics*, *56*(10), 4229–4238. doi:10.1109/TIE.2009.2013683

Roweis, S. T., & Saul, L. K. (2000). Nonlinear dimensionality reduction by locally linear embedding. *Science*, *290*, 2323–2326. doi:10.1126/science.290.5500.2323

Roweis, S., & Saul, L. (2000). Nonlinear dimensionality reduction by locally linear embedding. *Science*, *290*, 2323–2326. doi:10.1126/science.290.5500.2323

Rozental, D. E., Golub, I. B., & Telenkova, M. A. (1995). *Modern Russian*. Moscow, Russia: Foreign Relations. (in Russian)

Rubin, D. B. (1976). Inference and missing data. *Biometrika*, *63*(3). doi:10.1093/biomet/63.3.581

Rubine, D. (1991). Specifying gestures by example. In *Siggraph 91 Conference Proceedings: Vol. 25* (pp. 329-337). New York, NY: Association of Computing Machinery.

Rubini, J., Heckendorn, R. B., & Soule, T. (2009). Evolution of team composition in multi-agent systems. *Proceedings of the 11th Annual Conference on Genetic and Evolutionary Computation, GECCO'09*, ACM, NY, USA, (pp. 1067-1074).

Rumelhart, D., Hinton, G., & Williams, R. (1986). *Learning internal representations by error propagation* (pp. 318–362). Cambridge, MA: MIT Press.

Rumí, R., Salmerón, A., & Moral, S. (2006). Estimating mixtures of truncated exponentials in hybrid Bayesian networks. *TEST: An Official Journal of the Spanish Society of Statistics and Operations Research*, *15*(2), 397–421.

Ryutarou Ohbuchi, T. M. (2005). Shape-similarity search of 3D models by using enhanced shape functions. *International Journal of Computer Applications in Technology*, *23*(2-4), 70–85. doi:10.1504/IJCAT.2005.006466

Saeed, K. (2000). Three-agent system for cursive-scripts recognition. In *Proceedings of the Fifth Joint Conference on Information Science: Vols. 1 and 2* (pp. A244-A247).

Sahami, M. (1996). Learning limited dependence Bayesian classifiers. *Proceedings of the 2nd International Conference on Knowledge Discovery in Databases* (pp. 335-338).

Sahami, M., Dumais, S., Heckerman, D., & Horvitz, E. (1998). A Bayesian approach to filtering junk e-mail. *Proceedings of AAAI Workshop* (pp. 55-62).

Sakai, N., Yonekawa, S., Matsuzaki, A., & Morishima, H. (1996). Two-dimensional image analysis of the shape of rice its application to separating varieties. *Journal of Food Engineering*, *27*(4), 397–407. doi:10.1016/0260-8774(95)00022-4

Sakurai, S., Mori, K., & Orihara, R. (2009). Discovery of association rules from data including missing values. *International Conference on Complex, Intelligent and Software Intensive Systems* (pp. 67-74).

Sakurai, S., & Mori, K. (2010). Discovery of characteristic patterns from tabular structured data including missing values. *International Journal of Business Intelligence and Data Mining, 5*(3), 213–230. doi:10.1504/IJBIDM.2010.033359

Salamaniccar, G., & Loncaric, S. (2010). Method for crater detection from martian digital topography data using gradient value/orientation, morphometry, vote analysis, slip tuning, and calibration. *IEEE Transactions on Geoscience and Remote, 48*(5).

Salamuniccar, G., & Loncaric, S. (2008). GT-57633 catalogue of martian impact craters developed for evaluation of crater detection algorithms. *Planetary and Space Science, 56*(15). doi:10.1016/j.pss.2008.09.010

Salamuniccar, G., & Loncaric, S. (2008). Open framework for objective evaluation of crater detection algorithms with first test-field subsytem based on MOLA data. *Advances in Space Research, 42*, 6–19. doi:10.1016/j.asr.2007.04.028

Saltelli, A., Ratto, M., Tarantola, S., & Campolongo, F. (2005). Sensitivity analysis for chemical models. *Chemical Reviews, 105*(7), 2811–2828. doi:10.1021/cr040659d

Saltelli, A., Tarantola, S., Campolongo, F., & Ratto, M. (2003). *Sensitivity analysis in practice: A guide to assessing scientific models*. London, UK: John Wiley & Sons Ltd.

Sammon, J. W. (1969). A nonlinear mapping for data structure analysis. *IEEE Transactions on Computers, C-18*(5), 401–409. doi:10.1109/T-C.1969.222678

Saul, L., & Roweis, S. (2001). *An introduction to locally linear embedding*. Technical Report. Retrieved from http://www.cs.toronto.edu/~roweis/lle/publications.html

Saul, L., & Roweis, S. (2003). Think globally, fit locally: unsupervised learning of low dimensional manifolds. *Journal of Machine Learning Research, 4*, 119–155.

Saunders, C., Gammerman, A., & Vovk, V. (1999). Transduction with confidence and credibility. In *Proceedings of IJCAI'99*, Vol. 2, (pp. 722–726).

Schapire, R. E. (1999). A brief introduction to boosting. In *International Joint Conferences on Aritifical Intelligence*, (pp. 1401–1406).

Schawer, M., Slotine, J. J. E., & Rus, D. (2007). Decentralized, adaptive control for coverage with networked robots. In *Proceedings of the International Conference on Robotics and Automation (ICRA 07)*, (pp. 3289-3294). Rome.

Schepier, R., & Singer, Y. (2000). BoosTexer: A boosting-based system for text categorization. *Machine Learning, 39*(2/3), 135–168. doi:10.1023/A:1007649029923

Schneider, J. B. (2003). Covariant policy search. *Proceedings of the International Joint Conference on Artificial Intelligence*, (pp. 1019—1024).

Schwager, M., McLurkin, J., & Rus, D. (2006). Distributed coverage control with sensory feedback for networked robots. In *Proceedings of Robotics*. Philadelphia, PA: Science and Systems.

Schwager, M., Rus, D., & Slotine, J.-J. E. (2009). Decentralized, adaptive coverage control for networked robots. *The International Journal of Robotics Research, 28*(3), 357–375. doi:10.1177/0278364908100177

Sebastiani, F. (2002). Machine learning in automated text categorization. *ACM Computing Surveys, 1*, 1–47. doi:10.1145/505282.505283

Seeger, M. (2000). *Learning with labeled and unlabelled data*. Technical report. Retrieved from http://www.dai.ed.ac.uk/~seeger/papers.html

Seeger, M. (2001). *Learning with labeled and unlabeled data. Technical Report*. Edinburgh University.

Serra, J. (1982). *Image analysis and mathematical morphology*. Academic Press.

Sha, F., & Pereira, F. (2003). *Shallow parsing with conditional random fields*. Paper presented at the Human Language Technology-NAACL.

Shachter, R. D., & Kenley, C. R. (1989). Gaussian influence diagrams. *Management Science, 35*(5), 527–550. doi:10.1287/mnsc.35.5.527

Shapley, L. S. (1953). A value for n-person games. In Kuhn, H. W., & Tucker, A. W. (Eds.), *contributions to the theory of games* (*Vol. II*). Princeton, NJ: Princeton University Press.

Shen, J.-J., & Chen, M.-T. (2003). A recycle technique of association rule for missing value completion. *17th International Conference on Advanced Information Networking and Applications*, (pp. 526-529).

Shintani, T. (2006). Mining association rules from data with missing values by database partitioning and merging. *5th IEEE/ACIS International Conference on Computer and Information Science and 1st IEEE/ACIS International Workshop on Component-based Software Engineering, Software Architecture and Reuse* (pp. 193-200).

Shouche, S. P., Rastogi, R., Bhagwat, S. G., & Sainis, J. K. (2001). Shape analysis of grains of Indian wheat varieties. *Computers and Electronics in Agriculture, 33*(1), 55–76. doi:10.1016/S0168-1699(01)00174-0

Shutt, J. N. (2003). *Recursive adaptable grammars*. Master's Thesis, Worcester Polytechnic Institute, Worcester, M. A. August 10, 1993, amended December 16, 2003.

Shyu, M.-L., Xie, Z., Chen, M., & Chen, S.-C. (2008). Video semantic event/concept detection using a subspace-based multimedia data mining framework. *IEEE Transactions on Multimedia, 10*(2), 252–259. doi:10.1109/TMM.2007.911830

Sigal, L., & Black, M. (2006b). *HumanEva: Synchronized video and motion capture dataset for evaluation of articulated human motion*. Brown University, Tech. Rep. CS-06-08.

Sigal, L., & Black, M. J. (2006a). *Measure locally, reason globally: Occlusion-sensitive articulated pose estimation*. Paper presented at the IEEE Conference on Computer Vision and Pattern Recognition.

Sigal, L., Bhatia, S., Roth, S., Black, M., & Isard, M. (2004). *Tracking loose-limbed people.* Paper presented at IEEE Conference on Computer Vision and Pattern Recognition.

Silva, M., & Almeida, L. (1990). Acceleration techniques for the backpropagation algorithm. *Lecture Notes in Computer Science. Neural Networks, 412*, 110–119. doi:10.1007/3-540-52255-7_32

Silverman, B. W. (1986). *Density estimation for statistics and data analysis*. Chapman & Hall/CRC.

Sminchisescu, C., & Jepson, A. (2004). *Generative modeling for continuous non-linearly embedded visual inference.* Paper presented at the International Conference on Machine Learning.

Smola, A. J., & Schölkopf, B. (1998). *A tutorial on support vector regression*. NeuroCOLT2 Technical Report NC2-TR-1998-030.

Song, Q., & Shepperd, M. (2007). Missing data imputation techniques. *International Journal of Business Intelligence and Data Mining, 2*(3), 261–291. doi:10.1504/IJBIDM.2007.015485

Srikant, R., & Agrawal, R. (1995). Mining generalized association rules. In *VLDB '95: Proceedings of the 21th International Conference on Very Large Data Bases* (pp. 407–419). San Francisco, CA: Morgan Kaufmann Publishers Inc.

Srinivasan, M., Venkatesh, S., & Hosie, R. (1997). Qualitative estimation of camera motion parameters from video sequences. *Pattern Recognition, 30*, 593–606. doi:10.1016/S0031-3203(96)00106-9

Stepanova, N., & Emelyanov, G. (2007). Knowledge acquisition process modeling for question answering systems. In V. Soloviev, R. Potapova, & V. Polyakov (Eds.), *Cognitive Modeling in Linguistics*: *Proceedings of IX International Conference* (344-354). Kazan, Tatarstan: Kazan University Press (in Russian).

Stepinski, T. F., & Urbach, E. R. (2009). *The first automatic survey of impact craters on Mars: Global maps of depth/diameter ratio.* 40th Lunar and Planetary Science Conference, (Lunar and Planetary Science XL), The Woodlands.

Stepinski, T. F., Mendenhall, M. P., & Bue, B. D. (2007). Robust automated identification of martian impact craters. *Lunar and Planetary Science*, XXXVIII.

Stepinski, T. F., Mendenhall, M. P., & Bue, B. D. (2009). Machine cataloging of impact craters on Mars. *Icarus, 203*(1), 77–87. doi:10.1016/j.icarus.2009.04.026

Štrumbelj, E., & Kononenko, I. (in press). A general method for visualizing and explaining black-box regression models. *International Conference on Adaptive and Natural Computing Algorithms, ICANNGA2011.*

Štrumbelj, E., & Kononenko, I. (2010). An efficient explanation of individual classifications using game theory. *Journal of Machine Learning Research, 11*, 1–18.

Styner, M., Rajamani, K., Nolte, L.-P., Zsemlye, G., Szekely, G., Taylor, C., & Davies, R. (2003). 3D correspondence methods for model building. In *Proceedings of Information Processing in Medical Imaging* (pp. 63–75). Evaluation of. doi:10.1007/978-3-540-45087-0_6

Su, J., & Zhang, H. (2006). Full Bayesian network classifiers. *Proceedings of the 23rd International Conference on Machine Learning.*

Sun, D.-W. (Ed.). (2007). *Computer vision technology for food quality evaluation*. London, UK: Academic Press, Elsevier Science.

Sun, Z., Wang, J., Howe, D., & Jewell, G. (2008). Analytical prediction of the short-circuit current in fault-tolerant permanent-magnet machines. *IEEE Transactions on Industrial Electronics, 55*(12), 4210–4217. doi:10.1109/TIE.2008.2005019

Surana, A., Kiran, U., & Reddy, P. K. (2010). *Selecting a right interestingness measure for rare association rules.* In 16th International Conference on Management of Data (COMAD).

Sutton, R. S. (1998). *Reinforcement learning - An introduction*. MIT Press.

Szafron, D., Poulin, B., Eisner, R., Lu, P., Greiner, R., & Wishart, D. … Anvik, J. (2006). Visual explanation of evidence in additive classifiers. In *Proceedings of Innovative Applications of Artificial Intelligence – Volume 2*. Menlo Park, CA: AAAI Press.

Takeda, I. R., Hideaki, T., & Shinichi, H. (2001). Rule induction for concept hierarchy alignment. In *Proceedings of the 2nd Workshop on Ontology Learning at the 17th International Joint Conference on Artificial Intelligence (IJCAI)*.

Tanaka, K. L. (1986). The stratigraphy of Mars. *Journal of Geophysical Research, 91*(B13), 139–158. doi:10.1029/JB091iB13p0E139

Tanenbaum, R. A. (2004). *Fundamentals of applied dynamics*. New York, NY: Springer-Verlag.

Tan, P. N., Kumar, V., & Srivastava, J. (2004, June). Selecting the right objective measure for association analysis. *Information Systems, 29*, 293–313. doi:10.1016/S0306-4379(03)00072-3

Tao, Y., Morrow, C. T., Heinemann, P. H., & Sommer, H. J. (1995). Fourier-based separation technique for shape grading of potatoes using machine vision. *Transactions of the ASAE. American Society of Agricultural Engineers, 38*(3), 949–957.

Tenenbaum, J. B., de Silva, V., & Langford, J. C. (2000). A global geometric framework for nonlinear dimensionality reduction. *Science, 290*, 2319–2323. doi:10.1126/science.290.5500.2319

Tenenbaum, J. B., de Silva, V., & Langford, J. C. (2000). A global geometric framework for nonlinear dimensionality reduction. *Science, 290*, 2319–2323. doi:10.1126/science.290.5500.2319

Thomason, R., Heckendorn, R. B., & Soule, T. (2008). Training time and team composition robustness in evolved multi-agent systems. In *Proceedings of the 11th European Conference on Genetic Programming, EuroGP 2008, Lecture Notes in Computer Science vol. 4971*, (pp. 1-12). Springer-Verlag

Throop, J. A., Aneshansley, D. J., Anger, W. C., & Peterson, D. L. (2005). Quality evaluation of apples based on surface defects: Development of an automated inspection system. *Postharvest Biology and Technology, 36*(3), 281–290. doi:10.1016/j.postharvbio.2005.01.004

Throop, J. A., Aneshansley, D. J., & Upchurch, B. L. (1995). An image processing algorithm to find new old bruises. *Applied Engineering in Agriculture, 11*(5), 751–757.

Tibshirani, R., & Knight, K. (1999). Model search and inference by bootstrap bumping. *Journal of Computational and Graphical Statistics, 8*, 671–686.

Titsias, M. K., & Lawrence, N. D. (2010). *Bayesian Gaussian process latent variable model*. Paper presented at the Thirteenth International Workshop on Artificial Intelligence and Statistics.

Tomás, D., & Vicedo, J. L. (2007). Multiple-taxonomy question classification for category search on faceted information. In *TSD'07: Proceedings of the 10th International Conference on Text, Speech and Dialogue* (pp. 653–660). Berlin, Germany: Springer-Verlag.

Tong, S., Wang, T., & Zhang, W. (2008). Fault tolerant control for uncertain fuzzy systems with actuator failures. *International Journal of Innovative Computing and Information Control, 4*(10), 2461–2474.

Torgerson, W. (1958). *Theory and methods of scaling.* Wiley.

Tresp, V. (2000). *The generalized Bayesian committee machine.* Paper presented at the Knowledge Discovery and Data Mining.

Trianni, V. (2008). *Evolutionary swarm robotics. Evolving self-organizing behaviours in groups of autonomous robots. Studies in Computational Intelligence* (*Vol. 108*). Berlin, Germany: Springer Verlag.

Tsoumakas, G., & Katakis, I. (2007). Multi-label classification: An overview. *International Journal of Data Warehousing and Mining, 3*(3), 1–13. doi:10.4018/jdwm.2007070101

Tu, X., & Terzopoulos, D. (1994). Artificial fishes: Physics, locomotion, perception, behaviour. In *SIGGRAPH 94 Conference Proceedings*, (pp. 43-50). Orlando, FL: ACM

Tversky, B. (2002). What do sketches say about thinking? In *AAAI Spring Symposium Series - Sketch Understanding* (pp. 148-152).

Ultsch, A. (2003). *U*-Matrix: A tool to visualize clusters in high dimensional data.* Dept. of Mathematics of Computer Science, University of Marburg.

Unay, D., & Gosselin, B. (2006). Automatic defect segmentation of 'Jonagold' apples on multi-spectral images: A comparative study. *Postharvest Biology and Technology, 42*, 271–279. doi:10.1016/j.postharvbio.2006.06.010

Unay, D., & Gosselin, B. (2007). Stem and calyx recognition on 'Jonagold' apples by pattern recognition. *Journal of Food Engineering, 78*, 597–605. doi:10.1016/j.jfoodeng.2005.10.038

Urbach, E. R., & Stepinski, T. F. (2009). Automatic detection of sub-km craters in high resolution planetary images. *Planetary and Space Science, 57*, 880–887. doi:10.1016/j.pss.2009.03.009

Urtasun, R., Fleet, D. J., & Fua, P. (2006). *3D people tracking with Gaussian process dynamical models.* Paper presented at IEEE Conference on Computer Vision and Pattern Recognition.

Urtasun, R., Fleet, D. J., Geiger, A., Popovic, J., Darrell, T. J., & Lawrence, N. D. (2008). *Topologically-constraint latent variable models.* Paper presented at the International Conference on Machine Learning.

van der Gaag, L. C., & de Waal, P. R. (2006). *Multidimensional Bayesian network classifiers.* Third European Workshop on Probabilistic Graphical Models.

Vapnik, V. (1995). *The nature of statistical learning theory.* Springer.

Vapola, M., Simula, O., Kohonen, T., & Meriläinen, P. (1994, May). *Representation and identification of fault conditions of an anaesthesia system by means of the self organizing map.* Paper presented at the International Conference on Artificial Neural Networks (ICANN'94), Sorrento, Italy.

Vesanto, J. (1997, May). *Using the SOM and local models in time-series prediction.* Paper presented at the Workshop Self-Organizing Maps (WSOM), Helsinki University of Technology, Finland, June 4-6.

Vesanto, J. (1999). SOM-based data visualization methods. *Intelligent Data Analysis, 3*(2), 111–126. doi:10.1016/S1088-467X(99)00013-X

Vesanto, J., & Alhoniemi, E. (2000). Clustering of the self-organizing map. *IEEE Transactions on Neural Networks, 11*(3), 586–600. doi:10.1109/72.846731

Villaverde, J., Persson, A., Godoy, D., & Amandi, A. (2009, September). Supporting the discovery and labeling of non-taxonomic relationships in ontology learning. *Expert Systems with Applications, 36*, 10288–10294. doi:10.1016/j.eswa.2009.01.048

Vinogradova, T., Burl, M., & Mjolsness, E. (2002). Training of a crater detection algorithm for Mars crater imagery. *IEEE Aerospace Conference Proceedings, 7*, (pp. 3201-3211).

Viola, P., & Jones, M. J. (2004). Robust real-time face detection. *International Journal of Computer Vision*, *57*, 147–154. doi:10.1023/B:VISI.0000013087.49260.fb

Visinsky, M. L., Cavallaro, J. R., & Walker, I. D. (1994). Expert system framework for fault detection and fault olerance in robotics. *Computers & Electrical Engineering*, *20*, 421–435. doi:10.1016/0045-7906(94)90035-3

Visinsky, M. L., Cavallaro, J. R., & Walker, I. D. (1995). A dynamic fault tolerance framework for remote robots. *IEEE Transactions on Robotics and Automation*, *11*, 477–490. doi:10.1109/70.406930

Vizing, V. G. (2007). On incidentor colouring in hypergraph. [in Russian]. *Sampling Analysis and Operations Research*, *14*(3), 40–45.

Vlasov, A. V., & Aredova, I. I. (1988). Experimental system of the synthesis of graphic images according to their description in the terms of geometric concepts. *Material of the Conference on Development of Intellectual Possibility of Modern and Perspective Computers* (pp. 123-132). Moscow, Russia: Moscow House of Scientific and Technical Propaganda (MHSTP) (in Russian).

Vondrak, M., Sigal, L., & Jenkins, O. (2008). *Physical simulation for probabilistic motion tracking.* Paper presented at the Proc. IEEE Conference on Computer Vision and Pattern Recognition.

Wang, J., Fleet, D., & Hertzmann, A. (2007). *Multifactor Gaussian process models for style-content separation.* Paper presented at the International Conference on Machine Learning.

Wang, P., & Ji, Q. (2005). *Multi-view face tracking with factorial and switching HMM.* Paper presented at the IEEE Workshop on Applications of Computer Vision (WACV/MOTION05).

Wang, S. B., Quattoni, A., Morency, L.-P., Demirdjian, D., & Darrell, T. (2006). *Hidden conditional random fields for gesture recognition.* Paper presented at the IEEE Computer Society Conference on Computer Vision and Pattern Recognition.

Wang, S., Kubota, T., & Richardson, T. (2004). Shape correspondence through landmark sliding. In *IEEE Conference on Computer Vision and Pattern Recognition*, (pp. 143–150).

Wang, T., Li, J., Diao, Q., Hu, W., Zhang, Y., & Dulong, C. (2006). *Semantic event detection using conditional random fields.* Paper presented at the IEEE Conference on Computer Vision and Pattern Recognition (CVPR).

Wang, T., Tong, S., & Tong, S. C. (2007). Robust fault tolerant fuzzy control for uncertain fuzzy systems with actuator failures. In *Proceedings of the 2nd International Conference on Innovative Computing and Information Control*, Kumamoto, Japan, (p. 44).

Wang, Y., Sabzmeydani, P., & Mori, G. (2007). *Semilatent Dirichlet allocation: A hierarchical model for human action recognition.* Paper presented at the 2nd Workshop on Human Motion Understanding, Modeling, Capture and Animation.

Wang, J., Fleet, D., & Hertzmann, A. (2008). Gaussian process dynamical models for human motion. *IEEE Transactions on Pattern Analysis and Machine Intelligence*, *30*, 283–298. doi:10.1109/TPAMI.2007.1167

Wang, Q., Garrity, G. M., Tiedje, J. M., & Cole, R. J. (2007). Naïve Bayesian classifier for rapid assignment of rRNA sequences into the new bacterial taxonomy. *Applied and Environmental Microbiology*, *73*(16), 5261–5267. doi:10.1128/AEM.00062-07

Watkins, C., & Dayan, P. (1992). Q-learning. *Machine Learning*, *8*, 279–292. doi:10.1007/BF00992698

Webb, G. I., Boughton, J. R., & Wang, Z. (2005). Not so naïve Bayes: Aggregating one-dependence estimators. *Machine Learning*, *58*(1), 5–24. doi:10.1007/s10994-005-4258-6

Wetzler, P., Honda, R., Enke, B., Merline, W., Chapman, C., & Burl, M. (2005). Learning to detect small impact craters. *Seventh IEEE Workshops on Application of Computer Vision*, *1*, 178–184.

Wills, R., Maglasson, W., Graham, D., & Joice, D. (1998). *Postharvest. Introduction to the physiology and hand ling of fruits, vegetables and ornamentals* (4th ed.). CAB International.

Wimalasuriya, D. C., & Dou, D. (2009). Using multiple ontologies in information extraction. In *CIKM '09: Proceeding of the 18th ACM Conference on Information and Knowledge Management* (pp. 235–244). New York, NY: ACM.

Wise, U. D., & Minkowski, G. (1980). *Dating methodology of small, homogeneous crater populations applied to the tempe-utopia trough region on Mars. Goddard Space Flight*. Greenbelt, MD: NASA.

Witten, I. H., & Frank, E. (2005). *Data mining: Practical machine learning tools and techniques* (2nd ed.). San Francisco, CA: Morgan Kaufmann.

Wolpert, D. H. (1992). Stacked generalization. *Neural Networks, 5*, 241–259. doi:10.1016/S0893-6080(05)80023-1

Wood, S. N. (2006). *Generalized additive models: An introduction with R*. Chapman & Hall/CRC.

Wooldridge, M., & Jennings, N. R. (1995). Intelligent agents: Theory and practice. *The Knowledge Engineering Review, 10*(2), 115–152. doi:10.1017/S0269888900008122

Xiao-Bo, Z., Jie-Wen, Z., Yanxiao, L., & Holmes, M. (2010). In-line detection of apple defects using three color cameras system. *Computers and Electronics in Agriculture, 70*, 129–134. doi:10.1016/j.compag.2009.09.014

Xie, L., Chang, S., Divakaran, A., & Sun, H. (2003). Unsupervised mining of staistical temporal structures in video. In Rosenfeld, D. D. A. (Ed.), *Video mining*. Kluwer Academi Publishers.

Xing, J., Jancsók, P., & De Baerdemaeker, J. (2007). Stem-end/calyx identification on apples using contour analysis in multispectral images. *Biosystems Engineering, 96*(2), 231–237. doi:10.1016/j.biosystemseng.2006.10.018

Xiong, Z. (2005). Audio-visual sports highlights extraction using Coupled Hidden Markov Models. *Pattern Analysis & Applications, 8*(1), 62–71. doi:10.1007/s10044-005-0244-7

Xu, C., Zhu, G., Zhang, Y., Huang, Q., & Lu, H. (2008). *Event tactic analysis based on player and ball trajectory in broadcast video*. Paper presented at the International Conference on Content-based Image and Video Retrieval.

Yamauchi, B. (1998). Frontier-based exploration using multiple robots. In *Proceedings of the Second International Conference on Autonomous Agents*, (pp. 47-53). Minneapolis, Minnesota.

Yam, C., Nixon, M. S., & Carter, J. N. (2004). Automated person recognition by walking and running via model-based approaches. *Pattern Recognition, 37*, 1057–1072. doi:10.1016/j.patcog.2003.09.012

Yang, Y., & Pederson, J. O. (1997). A comparative study on feature selection in text classification. *Proceedings of 14th International Conference on Machine Learning* (pp. 412-420).

Yang, Y., & Webb, G. I. (2009). Discretization for naïve-Bayes learning: Managing discretization bias and variance. *Machine Learning, 74*(1), 39–74. doi:10.1007/s10994-008-5083-5

Yan, X., Zhang, C., & Zhang, S. (2005). ARMGA: Identifying interesting association rules with genetic algorithms. *Applied Artificial Intelligence, 19*, 677–689. doi:10.1080/08839510590967316

Yinh, Y. (2003). *Discretization for naïve-Bayes learning*. PhD. Thesis, Monash University.

Yu, X., Xu, C., Leong, H. W., Tian, Q., Tang, Q., & Wan, K. W. (2003). *Trajectory-based ball detection and tracking with applications to semantic analysis of broadcast soccer video*. Paper presented at the ACM Multimedia.

Yuan, Y. T. (2009). *Wavelet theory approach to pattern recognition*. Hong Kong: World Scientific Publishing Company.

Zaffalon, M. (2005). Credible classification for environmental problems. *Environmental Modelling & Software, 20*(8), 1003–1012. doi:10.1016/j.envsoft.2004.10.006

Zaki, M. J., Parthasarathy, S., Ogihara, M., & Li, W. (1997). New algorithms for fast discovery of association rules. *3rd International Conference on Knowledge Discovery and Data Mining* (pp. 283-286).

Zaragoza, J., Sucar, E., & Morales, E. (2011). *A two-step method to learn multidimensional Bayesian network classifiers based on mutual information measures*. Twenty-Fourth International Florida Artificial Intelligence Research Society Conference - FLAIRS24.

Zeleznik, R. C., Herndon, K. P., & Hughes, J. F. (1996). SKETCH: An interface for sketching 3D scenes. In *Proceedings of the 23rd Annual Conference on Computer Graphics and Interactive Techniques* (pp. 163-170). ACM.

Zeng, H., Wang, X., Chen, Z., Lu, H., & Ma, W. (2003). CBC-clustering based text classification requiring minimal labeled data. *Proceedings of 3rd International Conference on Data Mining* (pp. 443-450).

Zhang, D., & Lu, G. (2002). A comparative study of Fourier descriptors for shape representation and retrieval. In *Proceedings of 5th Asian Conference on Computer Vision (ACCV)* (pp. 646-651). Springer.

Zhang, H., & Lu, Y. (2002). Learning Bayesian network classifiers from data with missing values. *TENCON '02 Proceedings, IEEE Region 10 Conference on Computers, Communications, Control and Power Engineering*.

Zhang, H., Jiang, L., & Su, J. (2005). Hidden naïve Bayes. *Proceedings of the 20th National Conference on Artificial intelligence - Volume 2* (pp. 919-924). AAAI Press.

Zhang, X., & Fan, G. (2011). *Dual gait generative models for human motion estimation from a single camera.* Paper presented at the IEEE CVPR Workshop on Machine Learning for Vision-based Motion Analysis (MLvMA2011).

Zhang, X., Fan, G., & Chou, L. (2009). *Two-layer gait generative models for estimating unknown human gait kinematics.* Paper presented at the IEEE ICCV Workshop on Machine Learning for Vision-based Motion Analysis (MLvMA2009).

Zhang, Z., Huo, Z., & Zhang, L. (2008). *Fault-tolerant control research for networked control systems based on quasi T-S fuzzy models.* The 2008 IEEE International Conference on Industrial Technology, (pp. 1-4). Chengdu, China.

Zhang, X., & Fan, G. (2010). Dual gait generative models for human motion estimation from a single camera. *IEEE Transactions on Systems, Man, and Cybernetics. Part B, Cybernetics*, *40*, 1034–1049. doi:10.1109/TSMCB.2010.2044240

Zhang, Z., & Zha, H. (2004). Principal manifolds and nonlinear dimension reduction via local tangent space alignment. *SIAM Journal on Scientific Computing*, *26*(1), 313–338. doi:10.1137/S1064827502419154

Zheng, F., & Webb, G. I. (2005). A comparative study of semi-naïve Bayes methods in classification learning. *Proceedings of 4th Australasian Data Mining Conference (AusDM05.* Zheng, Z., & Webb, G. I. (2000). Lazy learning of Bayesian rules. *Machine Learning*, *41*(1), 53–84. doi:10.1023/A:1007613203719

Zhong, S., Martínez, A. M., Nielsen, T. D., & Langseth, H. (2010). Towards a more expressive model for dynamic classification. *Proceedings of the Twenty-Third International Florida Artificial Intelligence Research Society Conference (FLAIRS)*.

Zien, A., Krämer, N., Sonnenburg, S., & Rätsch, G. (2009). The feature importance ranking measure. In *ECML PKDD 2009: Part II* (pp. 694–709). Berlin, Germany: Springer-Verlag.

Zykov, A. A. (1974). Hypergraphs. *Russian Mathematical Surveys*, *29*(6), 89. doi:10.1070/RM1974v029n06ABEH001303

About the Contributors

Rafael Magdalena-Benedito was born in 1968 in Segovia (Castellón). Between 1986 and 1991, he studied a degree in Physics at the University of Valencia, Computer and Electronic specialty. In 1993 he worked in the company of electro DextroMédica as dictafonía technician in cardiology and medical physics. In 1998 he joined the Group Processing Digital Signal Department, where he currently works on research projects, is an Assistant Professor. His areas of work are data security, multimedia networks, standardization in biomedical engineering, and telemedicine.

Marcelino Martínez-Sober received his B.S. and Ph.D. degrees in Physics in 1992 and 2000, respectively, from the Universitat de Valencia(Spain). Since 1994, he has been with the Digital Signal Processing Group at the Department of Electronics Engineering. He is an Assistant Professor. He has worked on several industrial projects with private companies (in the areas such as industrial control, real-time signal processing, and digital control) and with public funds (in the areas of fetal electrocardiography and ventricular fibrillation). His research interests include real time signal processing, digital control using DSP, and biomedical signal processing, with special interest in developing real time algorithms for non-invasive fetal electrocardiogram extraction.

José M. Martínez-Martínez received the B.Eng. degree in Telecommunication Engineering in 2006, and the M.Eng degree in Electronics Engineering in 2009, both from the University of Valencia, Spain. He is currently working towards the Ph.D. degree in the IDAL research group, University of Valencia. His research interest is machine learning methods, data mining, and data visualization.

Pablo Escandell-Montero received the B.Eng. degree in Telecommunications Engineering in 2006, and the M.Eng degree in Electronics Engineering in 2009, both from the University of Valencia, Spain. Currently, he is working towards the Ph.D. degree in the IDAL research group in the same university. His research interest is machine learning and data mining.

Joan Vila Francés has studied Technical Engineering in Telecommunication and Electronics Engineering, both finished with first class honors, in the University of Valencia (Spain). In 2009 he received a PhD Degree in Electronics Engineering from the same university, where he currently holds a Lecturer position. His teaching is focused on Programmable Digital Systems. He has skills in industrial systems, digital electronics, computing, database management, and Web development.

* * *

Francisco Albert is Associate Professor of Engineering Graphics, CAD, and 3D Animation and Graphic Design with the Engineering Design Department at Universitat Politècnica de València. His fields of interest are focused on graphic pattern analysis, reconstruction and design, and development of spatial abilities using new technologies.

Nuria Aleixos received an MS (1992) and Ph.D (1999) degrees in Computer Science at Universitat Politècnica de València. She worked for private companies since 1990 developing solutions for commercial CAD systems, and worked for two years at the Public Research Institute IVIA developing machine vision systems for automatic fruit inspection. She worked for ten years at Universitat Jaume I de Castelló, and now is Associate Professor of Engineering Graphics and CAD with the Engineering Design Department at Polytechnic University of Valencia. Her fields of interest are focused on modeling methodologies for CAD applications, computer vision systems, image analysis, and calligraphic interfaces.

Ricardo Aler received the MSc in Informatics Engineering from the Universidad Politécnica de Madrid in 1992 and the PhD degree at the same university in 1999. He received the MSc in Decision Support Systems at the Univesity of Sunderland (UK) in 1993. His current research interests include genetic programming, evolutionary computation, machine learning, and brain-computer interface. He has published extensively on these subjects and he has participated in projects both national and international. Currently, he is Associate Professor at the Technical School, Universidad Carlos III de Madrid.

Lobzin Alex was born in Moscow in 1946. In 1969, he graduated from the Moscow State University with the degree in mathematics. Since 1973, he is working at the Research Centre of Electronic Computing Engineering ("NICEVT"), Moscow, in the field of programming and artificial intelligence (computer vision and graphics). He is the author of 5 scientific articles.

Fernando Benites received his M.S. degree in Informatics from the University of Bielefeld, Germany, in 2007. From 2007 to 2009, he worked as a software developer for the document management software company Bitfarm. Since August 2009 he has been employed as a research assistant at the University of Konstanz, Germany, currently working towards a Ph.D. degree on the project, "DAMIART: Data Mining of heterogeneous data with an ART-based neural network." He is also an associated Ph.D. student of the Ph.D. program "Explorative analysis and visualization of large information spaces" at the University of Konstanz founded by the German Research Foundation. Other research interests are Adaptive Resonance Theory, fuzzy neural networks, classification of text and biological data as well as hierarchical multi-label classification.

José Blasco received his MSc (1994) and PhD in Computer Science at Polytechnic University of Valencia (2001). He also received a Master Degree in Computer Aided Design and Manufacturing at Universitat Politècnica de València (1995). He worked during two years at IBM Spain as System Analyst until he joined the Public Research Institute IVIA in 1996, where he is the current manager of the Computer Vision Lab at the Agricultural Engineering Centre. His fields of interest are focused on computer vision, image processing, real-time inspection and hyperspectral imaging for agricultural applications and processes. Has published more than 20 papers in international journals and have participated in the development of several patents.

Zoran Bosnić obtained his Master and Doctor degrees in Computer Science at University of Ljubljana, Slovenia in 2003 and 2007, respectively. Since 2006 he has been employed at Faculty of Computer and Information Science and currently works as an assistant professor in the Laboratory for Cognitive Modeling. He teaches courses on computer networks, communication protocols, and web programming. His research interests include artificial intelligence, machine learning, regression, and reliability estimation for individual predictions, as well as medical and other applications in these areas. He is a (co)author of about 20 research papers and a textbook in international journals and conference proceedings.

Abel A. Cuadrado received the M.S. and Ph.D. degrees in Electronic and Control Engineering from the University of Oviedo in 1998 and 2003, respectively. From April to October 2005, he was a visiting researcher at the Betriebsforschungsinstitut (BFI) in Düsseldorf, Germany. He is currently a Professor in the Department of Electrical, Electronic, Computer and Systems Engineering of the University of Oviedo, in the city of Gijón, Spain. His research interests include supervision of industrial processes, control systems, and digital signal processing.

Sergio Cubero received his MSc in Computer Science at Universitat Jaume I de Castelló (2006) and his Master Degree in Computer Aided Design and Manufacturing at Polytechnic University of Valencia (2009). Currently he is completing his PhD in Design, Manufacturing, and Industrial Project Management at Universitat Politècnica de València. He is working in Public Research Institute IVIA since 2002 in several projects related with the areas of computer vision, image processing, real-time inspection, and machinery design for agricultural applications. Has published 6 papers in international journals and has participated in the development of several patents

Pahal Dalal received the M.E. and Ph.D. degrees in Computer Science and Engineering from the University of South Carolina in 2007 and 2011, respectively. His research interests include computer vision, medical imaging, and machine learning.

Javier de Lope Asiaín received the M.Sc. in Computer Science from the Universidad Politécnica de Madrid in 1994 and the Ph.D. degree at the same university in 1998. Currently, he is Associate Professor in the Department of Applied Intelligent Systems at the Universidad Politécnica de Madrid. His current research interest is centered on the study, design, and construction of modular robots and multi-robot systems, and in the development of control systems based on soft-computing techniques. He is currently leading a three-year R&D project for developing industrial robotics mechanisms which follow the guidelines of multi-robot systems and reconfigurable robotics. In the past he also worked on projects related to the computer-aided automatic driving by means of external cameras and range sensors and the design and control of humanoid and flying robots.

Ignacio Díaz Blanco is Electrical Engineer since 1995, and obtained the PhD degree in Engineering from the University of Oviedo in 2000. In 2001 he spent six months at the Aalto University (formerly Helsinki University of Technology) researching on industrial applications of the self-organizing map. Since 2004 he is Associate Professor at the University of Oviedo, Spain. He has been author or coauthor of more than 30 publications including journals, conferences, and book chapters, most of them about the self-organizing map and its applications. He has participated in projects with public and private financial support about process analysis and monitoring. His main research interests are data analysis, information visualization, control and signal processing, and their applications to process analysis and monitoring.

Alberto Diez González is Electrical Engineer since 1983, and obtained the PhD degree in Engineering from the University of Oviedo in 1988. Since 1989 he has been Associate Professor at the University of Oviedo, Spain, and became full Professor in 2010. He has been author or coauthor of more than 70 publications including journal articles, conferences, and book chapters, most of them about automation, drives, and the self-organizing map and its applications. He has been leader in many projects with public and private financial support about process analysis and monitoring. Dr. Diez was a member of the Executive Committee D2 "Rolling-Flat Products" of the European Commission for six years (1998-2004). His main research interests are automation systems, drives, as well as process analysis and monitoring.

Wei Ding has been an Assistant Professor of Computer Science in the University of Massachusetts Boston since 2008. She received her Ph.D. degree in Computer Science from the University of Houston in 2008. Her main research interests include data mining, machine learning, artificial intelligence, computational semantics, and with applications to astronomy, geosciences, and environmental sciences. She has published more than 50 referred research papers, 1 book, and has 1 patent. She is the recipient of an excellence service award at ACM SIGSPATIAL GIS 2010, a Best Paper Award at IEEE ICCI 2010, a Best Poster Presentation award at ACM SIGSPAITAL GIS 2008, and a Best PhD Work Award between 2007 and 2010 from the University of Houston. Her research projects are currently sponsored by NASA and DOE.

Yi Ding received the B.S. degree in Communication Engineering from Xi'an University of Technology, China, and the M.S. degree in Communication Engineering from Xidian University, China, in 2002 and 2005, respectively. He obtained the Ph.D. degree in Electrical Engineering, Oklahoma State University, 2010. His research interests include multimedia content analysis, pattern recognition, image processing, and computer vision. His current research focuses on machine learning, especially probabilistic, graphical, model based approaches for video mining.

Manuel Domínguez González received the Ph. D. degree in Engineering from University of Oviedo (Spain) in 2003. He is a Professor of Automatic Control and the head of the SUPPRESS research group and the Institute of Automatic Control (AAC-IAF) at the University of León (Spain). His research interests include control engineering, data mining, industrial process monitoring, and virtual/remote laboratories for higher education in engineering

Pablo Escandell-Montero received the B.Eng. degree in Telecommunications Engineering in 2006, and the M.Eng degree in Electronics Engineering in 2009, both from the University of Valencia, Spain. Currently, he is working towards the Ph.D. degree in the IDAL research group in the same university. His research interest is machine learning and data mining.

Guoliang Fan received the B.S. degree in Automation Engineering from Xi'an University of Technology, Xi'an, China, in 1993, the M.S. degree in Computer Engineering from Xidian University, Xi'an, China, in 1996, and the Ph.D. degree in Electrical Engineering from the University of Delaware, Newark,

DE, in 2001. From 1996 to 1998, he was a graduate assistant in the Department of Electronic Engineering at the Chinese University of Hong Kong. Since 2001, Dr. Fan has been an Assistant and Associate Professor in the School of Electrical and Computer Engineering at Oklahoma State University (OSU), Stillwater, OK. His research interests include image processing, computer vision, machine learning, and multimedia. Dr. Fan is a recipient of the 2004 National Science Foundation (NSF) CAREER award. He received the Halliburton Excellent Young Teacher Award in 2004, the Halliburton Outstanding Young Faculty Award in 2006 from the College of Engineering at OSU, and the Outstanding Professor Award from IEEE-OSU in 2008 and 2011. He is an Associate Editor of the *IEEE Trans. Information Technology in Biomedicine, EURASIP Journal on Image and Video Processing*, and *ISRN Machine Vision*. Dr. Fan is a senior member of IEEE.

D.G. Fernández-Pacheco received his BS - Industrial Technical Engineering (2001) and MS - Automation and Industrial Electronics Engineering (2004) degrees at Technical University of Cartagena, Spain, and his Ph.D. degree in Industrial Engineering (2010) at the Technical University of Valencia, Spain. He worked for three years as a researcher at the Technical University of Cartagena developing vision systems for geometric recognition. Now he is an Assistant Professor of Engineering Graphics and CAD with the Graphical Expression Department at the Technical University of Cartagena. His fields of interest are focused on computer vision, multi-agent systems, automation, and control systems. He is member of the CIGR Working Group on Image Analysis for Agricultural Products and Processes.

M. Julia Flores finished her Master Degree in Computer Science in 2000, from the University of Castilla - La Mancha (UCLM). In 2005 she obtained her PhD degree, also by UCLM, having done a six-month research stay during her thesis development at Aalborg University, Denmark. Since 2000 she has worked as Lecturer in UCLM, currently her position corresponds to \emph{contracted} Associate Professor. Dr. Flores is a founder member of the research group Intelligent Systems and Data Mining lab. Her main research lines are probabilistic graphical models (PGMs), inference and reasoning, automatic learning of PGMs, and data mining techniques in general. Evolutionary computation is another field of interest. Lately she has participated in some papers related to applications. She has around 30 publications in these topics. She has participated in the the organization as well as Program Committees of International Conferences, and collaborates with researchers from other Spanish and foreign universities.

Juan José Fuertes received the Ph. D. degree in Engineering from University of Oviedo (Spain) in 2006. He is an Associate Professor of Automatic Control and a member of the Institute of Automatic Control (AAC-IAF) at the University of León (Spain). His current research interests include exploratory data analysis, novelty detection, and dimensionality reduction, especially their applications in process monitoring, and the development of new tools for control education through virtual and remote laboratories.

Jose A. Gamez received his M.S. and Ph.D. degrees in computer science from the University of Granada, Spain, in 1991 and 1998, respectively. He joined the Department of Computer Science, University of Castilla-La Mancha (UCLM) in 1991, where he is currently an Associate Professor. He served as Vice-Dean of the Escuela Polit\'ecnica Superior de Albacete (UCLM) from 1998 to 2004, and he currently serves as Chair of the Department of Computing Systems (UCLM) and is the co-leader of the Intelligent Systems and Data Mining research group. His research interests include probabilistic reasoning, Bayesian networks, evolutionary algorithms, machine learning, and data mining. He has edited five books and published more than 80 papers on these topics. Dr. Gamez has served in the organization of international conferences and workshops as chair, program co-chair and program committee member.

Eric Jiang is Professor of Computer Science and Mathematics at University of San Diego. He received his B.S. in Applied Mathematics from Shanghai Jiao-Tong University, M.A. in Mathematics and M.S. in Computer Science from University of Georgia, and his Ph.D. in Computer Science from University of Tennessee at Knoxville. Professor Jiang's research has been primarily in parallel and distributing computing, data mining, information retrieval, Web mining and machine learning. He co-authored a book "Nonlinear Numerical Analysis and Optimization," and in addition to his journal research publications, he has given a number of presentations at international conferences, workshops, and invited seminars. Professor Jiang is currently serving on the editorial board of *International Journal on Intelligent Data Analysis*, and he has also been a reviewer for ACM/IEEE/SIAM journals and conferences.

Gennady Khakhalin was born at Kirov in 1942. He graduated from the Moscow State University, Physical Department in 1965. In 1965, he started to work as senior researcher at the Research Centre of Electronic Computing Engineering (RCECE) where he was engaged in developing the decision-making system of integral robot (1965–1974) and the system of conceptual goal-directed analysis of images (1975–1979). Under Gennady Khakhalin, the adaptable linguistic translator for analysis and synthesis of NL-sentences (1980–1990) have been developed and used in various applications in a family of systems with NL-text processing (1991–1996). Gennady Khakhalin has developed and delivered the following lecture courses: "Intelligence Systems" and "Development and Building of Intelligence Systems" in Moscow Automobile & Road Institute (1996–2003) and "Artificial Intelligence" for post-graduate students of the Research Centre of Electronic Computing Engineering ("NICEVT") (2005–2011), Moscow. He is also the author of more than 50 scientific articles and a member of the Russia Association for Artificial Intelligence founded in 1989.

Tan Kok Kiong received his B.Eng. in Electrical Engineering with honours in 1992 and PhD in 1995, all from the National University of Singapore. He is currently an Associate Professor with the Department of Electrical and Computer Engineering, National University of Singapore. His current research interests are in the areas of advanced control and auto-tuning, precision instrumentation and control, and general industrial automation.

Igor Kononenko received his PhD in Computer Science in 1990 from University of Ljubljana, Slovenia. He is the Professor at the Faculty of Computer and Information Science in Ljubljana and the head of Laboratory for Cognitive Modeling. His research interests include artificial intelligence, machine learning, and data mining. He is the (co)author of about 200 papers and 13 textbooks (two in English). His papers were cited over 1000 times by other authors. Igor Kononenko was actively involved in research in 20 national and international research projects. He is the member of the editorial board of *Applied Intelligence Journal* and *Informatica Journal*. He was a chair and the proceedings editor of three international scientific conferences.

Tong Heng Lee received the B.A. degree with First Class Honours in the Engineering Tripos from Cambridge University, England, in 1980; and the Ph.D. degree from Yale University in 1987. He is a Professor in the Department of Electrical and Computer Engineering at the National University of Singapore (NUS). He was a Past Vice-President (Research) of NUS. Dr. Lee's research interests are in the areas of adaptive systems, knowledge-based control, intelligent mechatronics, and computational intelligence. He currently holds Associate Editor appointments in the *IEEE Transactions in Systems, Man and Cybernetics; IEEE Transactions in Industrial Electronics; Control Engineering Practice* (an IFAC journal); and the *International Journal of Systems Science* (Taylor and Francis, London). In addition, he is the Deputy Editor-in-Chief of *IFAC Mechatronics* journal. Dr. Lee was a recipient of the Cambridge University Charles Baker Prize in Engineering; the 2004 ASCC (Melbourne) Best Industrial Control Application Paper Prize; the 2009 IEEE ICMA Best Paper in Automation Prize; and the 2009 ASCC Best Application Paper Prize. He has also co-authored five research monographs (books), and holds four patents (two of which are in the technology area of adaptive systems, and the other two are in the area of intelligent mechatronics). He has published more than 300 international journal papers. Dr. Lee was an Invited Panelist at the World Automation Congress, WAC2000 Maui U.S.A.; an Invited Keynote Speaker for IEEE International Symposium on Intelligent Control, IEEE ISIC 2003 Houston U.S.A.; an Invited Keynote Speaker for LSMS 2007, Shanghai China; an Invited Expert Panelist for IEEE AIM2009; an Invited Plenary Speaker for IASTED RTA 2009, Beijing China; an Invited Keynote Speaker for LSMS 2010, Shanghai China; an Invited Keynote Speaker for IASTED CA 2010, Banff Canada; an Invited Keynote Speaker for IFTOMM ICDMA 2010, Changsha China; and an Invited Keynote Speaker for ICUAS 2011, Denver USA.

Delia Lorente received her MSc in Electronics Engineering at Universitat de València (2009) with the award to the best academic expedient. She also received a Master Degree in Electronics Engineering at University of Valencia (2011). She is now a PhD student at the Agro-engineering Centre at the Valencian Institute for Agricultural Research with a predoctoral grant. Her research interests include machine vision, image analysis, automatic inspection, and hyperspectral imaging applied to agriculture.

Darío Maravall received the MSc in Telecommunication Engineering from the Universidad Politécnica de Madrid in 1978 and the PhD degree at the same university in 1980. From 1980 to 1988 he was Associate Professor at the School of Telecommunication Engineering, Universidad Politécnica de Madrid. In 1988 he was promoted to Full Professor at the Faculty of Computer Science, Universidad Politécnica de Madrid. From 2000 to 2004 he was the Director of the Department of Artificial Intelligence of the Faculty of Computer Science at the Universidad Politécnica de Madrid. His current research interests include computer vision, autonomous robots, and computational intelligence. He has published extensively on these subjects and has directed more than 20 funded projects, including a five-year R&D project for the automated inspection of wooden pallets using computer vision techniques and robotic mechanisms, with several operating plants in a number of European countries (Spain, France, Italy, and United Kingdom) and in USA. As a result of this project he holds a patent issued by the European Patent Office at The Hague, The Netherlands.

Ana M. Martínez received the B.E and M.S in information technology from the University of Castilla-La Mancha, Spain, in 2007 and 2008, respectively. She is currently a granted PhD student by the Spanish Ministry of Education, in the Intelligent Systems and Data Mining research group. Her research work currently focuses on (semi-naive) Bayesian classifiers, numeric data processing and domains of competence for these classifiers. She has been a research visitor in Aalborg University (Denmark) and also Monash University, Melbourne (Australia), during a four-month period each one of them.

Miran Mihelčič has been a Professor for several courses such as Business Economics, Theory of Organization, Business Analysis, and Business Functions, especially at the Faculty of Computer and Information Science as well as some other technical faculties of the University of Ljubljana, Slovenia. His research work has become more intense at Cranfield Institute of Technology (now University of Cranfield) in England in 1985, where he worked as a visiting research fellow for nine months. His main research interests are business and organization analysis, management and executive information systems, the relationship between governance and management and distribution of (personal) incomes. He has published over twenty books and participated with papers at more than ten international conferences in Slovenia and abroad. In the past he was active in the editorial boards of magazines in Slovenia; today he is a member of Editorial Advisory Board of *International Journal of Quality and Service Sciences*.

Jack Mario Mingo received the BSc in Informatics Engineering in 1993 and the MSc in Informatics Engineering from the Universidad Politécnica de Madrid in 2002. Currently, he is working in his Ph.D. at the same university. From 1991 he has been working as programmer, analyst, project manager, and databases specialist in several projects related to financial, logistics and telecom services. In parallel with these activities he is a part-time Professor at the Technical School, Universidad Autónoma de Madrid. His current research interests include grammatical evolution, evolutionary computation, and autonomous robots.

Darko Pevec received his Bachelor of Science degree in Computer Science and Mathematics in 2009 from University of Ljubljana, Slovenia. He is currently a PhD student of Computer Science at the Faculty of Computer and Information Science in Ljubljana, employed as a junior researcher in the Laboratory for Cognitive Modeling. His thesis is concerned with reliability estimation of single predictions in supervised learning and his research interests include machine learning, statistical modeling and data visualization. **Miguel A. Prada** received the degree of Dr. in 2009 at the University of León (Spain). He works at the University of León as a postdoctoral researcher. Before joining the University of León, he worked at the Department of Information and Computer Science of the Aalto University (formerly Helsinki University of Technology). His research interests include data analysis, especially their applications in process monitoring and structural health monitoring, and remote laboratories. His work is supported by a grant from the Slovenian Research Agency (P2-0209).

Marko Pregeljc received his PhD in Computer Science in 2011 from the University of Ljubljana, Slovenia. He was an Assistant Professor at the Faculty of Computer and Information Science in Ljubljana. His research interests include exploring the connections between the quality of organization and the economic results of formal social units, based on the use of artificial intelligence, machine learning, and data mining.

Shigeaki Sakurai received a BS degree in Mathematics, an MS degree in Mathematics, and a Ph.D. degree in Engineering from Tokyo University of Science, in 1989, 1991, and 2001, respectively. He became a Professional Engineer of the Information Engineering field in 2004. He is a visiting Professor at the Interdisciplinary Graduate School of Science and Engineering, Tokyo Institute of Technology and is a research scientist at the Advanced IT laboratory, Toshiba Solution Corporation. He is also a director at the Japan Society for Fuzzy Theory and Intelligent Informatics. He took part in the Real World Computing Partnership, which manages one of Japanese national projects in the information technology field, from 1998 to 2000. His research interests include data mining, computational intelligence, and Web technology.

Juan Gómez-Sanchis received a B.Sc. degree in Physics (2000) and a B.Sc. degree in Electronics Engineering from the University of Valencia (2003). He joined at the Public Research Institute IVIA in 2004, developing is Ph.D. in hyperspectral computer vision systems applied to the agriculture. He joined to the Department of Electronics Engineering at University of Valencia in 2008, where he currently works as Assistant Lecturer in Pattern Recognition using Neural Networks

Elena Sapozhnikova received her M.S. degree in Electrical Engineering from the Moscow Power Engineering Institute (Technical University), Moscow, Russia, in 1996 and a Ph.D. degree in Computer Science from the University of Tübingen, Germany, in 2003. Between 2002 and 2006, she was a doctoral as well as a postdoctoral fellow in the Ph.D. program "Chemistry in interphases" of the University of Tübingen. Since April 2008, she has been an Emmy Noether Research Group Leader at the University of Konstanz, Germany, with the project "DAMIART: Data Mining of heterogeneous data with an ART-based neural network" founded by the German Research Foundation. Her research interests include intelligent data analysis and data mining, artificial neural networks, adaptive resonance theory, and hierarchical multi-label classification.

Kurbatov Sergey was born in Moscow in 1946. In 1971, he graduated from Moscow Energy Institute and he got his Diploma in Applied Mathematics. From this institute, he obtained his Doctor's degree (Ph.D.) of Technical Sciences in the programming language LISP in 1979. Since 1980 he works at the Research Center of Computer Technology (official web-site) in the field of artificial intelligence (natural language processing and knowledge representation). Since 1998, he participated in fifteen projects supported by the Russian Foundation for Basic Research (RFBR) and in three of which he took a leading part. The main topics of the projects covered the area of access to the databases on natural language, tools for creating and maintaining knowledge bases. He is the author of more than 25 scientific articles.

Emilio Soria received a M.S. degree in Physics in 1992 and the Ph.D. degree in 1997 in Electronics Engineering from the Universitat de Valencia, Spain. He is an Assistant Professor at the University of Valencia since 1997. His research is centered mainly in the analysis and applications of adaptive and neural systems.

Tomasz Stepinski is the Thomas Jefferson Endowed Chair Professor at the Department of Geography, University of Cincinnati. Previously, he spent 20 years as a staff scientist at the Lunar and Planetary Institute in Houston, Texas. He is a geoscientist with Ph.D. degree in Applied Mathematics from University of Arizona. His present research focus is on intelligent data analysis with applications to terrestrial and planetary data sets. His research is sponsored by NSF and NASA.

Erik Štrumbelj is a Ph.D. student and a young researcher at the University of Ljubljana, Faculty of Computer and Information Science. His research interests include artificial intelligence, machine learning, data mining, and forecasting.

Huang Sunan received his PhD degree from Shanghai Jiao Tong University, Shanghai, China, 1994. Since 1997, he is a Research Fellow in the Department of Electrical and Computer Engineering, National University of Singapore. His research interests include error compensation of high-precision machine, adaptive control, neural network control, and automated vehicle control.

Josep Guimerà Tomàs has a BSc in Industrial Electronics (2008) from the Universitat Politècnica de València (UPV) and a MSc in Biomedical Engineering (2011) from the UPV and the Universitat de València (UV). Currently, he is a PhD student at the IDAL group of the UV. His research interests are focused on machine learning and graphical models.

Ricardo Vilalta is Associate Professor in the Department of Computer Science at the University of Houston. He holds MS and Ph.D. degrees in Computer Science from the University of Illinois at Urbana-Champaign. His research interests are in machine learning, statistical learning theory, data mining, and artificial intelligence. He is recipient of a Fulbright scholarship (1991-97); the Invention Achievement Award from IBM T.J. Watson Research Center (2001); Best Paper Award at the European Conference on Machine Learning (2003); CAREER Award from National Science Foundation (2005); Excellence in Research Award from the Department of Computer Science at the University of Houston (2005); and he is a research member of the National Institute of Researchers in Mexico (2007).

Song Wang received the PhD degree in Electrical and Computer Engineering from the University of Illinois at Urbana-Champaign in 2002. He joined the Department of Computer Science and Engineering at the University of South Carolina, where he is currently an Associate Professor. His research interests include computer vision, medical image processing, and machine learning and have published more than 30 papers in related journals and conference proceedings. He is the Publicity/Web portal Chair of the Technical Committee of Pattern Analysis and Machine Intelligence of the IEEE Computer Society, the Computer Vision Chair of the 7th International Symposium on Visual Computing, the Chair of the 7th IEEE Computer Society Workshop on Perceptual Organization in Computer Vision, and the guest editor of the *Special Issue on Shape Modeling in Medical Image Analysis for Computer Vision and Image Understanding.*

Naidenova Xenia was born at Leningrad (Saint-Petersburg) in 1940. She graduated from Lenin Electro-technical Institute of Leningrad (now Saint-Petersburg Electro-technical University) in 1963 and received the specialty of computer engineering. From this institute, she obtained her doctor's degree (Ph.D.) of Technical Sciences in 1979. In 1995, she started to work as senior researcher at the Scientific Research Centre of Saint-Petersburg Military Medical Academy where she is engaged in developing knowledge discovery and data mining systems to support solving medicine and psychological diagnostic tasks. Under Xenia Naidenova, some advanced knowledge acquisition systems based on machine learning original algorithms have been developed including a tool for adaptive programming applied diagnostic medical systems. She is also the author of more than 170 scientific articles and a member of the Russia Association for Artificial Intelligence founded in 1989.

Xin Zhang received the B.S. degree in Automatic Control from Northwestern Polytechnical University, Xi'an, China, in 2003, and the M.S. and Ph.D. degree in Electrical Engineering from Oklahoma State University, Stillwater, USA in 2005 and 2011. She is now a Lecturer in School of Electronics and Information Engineering, South China University of Technology, P. R. China. Her research interests include computer vision, machine learning, human motion analysis, object tracking and recognition, and medical image processing.

Index